Encyclopedia of Religious Revivals in America

Encyclopedia of Religious Revivals in America

Volume 1, A–Z

Edited by
Michael McClymond

GREENWOOD PRESS
Westport, Connecticut • London

Library of Congress Cataloging-in-Publication Data

Encyclopedia of religious revivals in America / edited by Michael
McClymond.
　　　p. cm.
　　Includes bibliographical references and index.
　　ISBN 0–313–32828–5 ([set] : alk. paper) — ISBN 0–313–32829–3 ([vol.
1] : alk. paper) — ISBN 0–313–32830–7 ([vol. 2] : alk. paper)
　　　1. Revivals—United States—Encyclopedias.　I. McClymond, Michael James,
1958–
BV3773.E53　　2007
269′.240973—dc22　　　　2006006370

British Library Cataloguing in Publication Data is available.

Library of Congress Catalog Card Number: 2006006370
ISBN:　0–313–32828–5 [set]
　　　　0–313–32829–3 [vol. 1]
　　　　0–313–32830–7 [vol. 2]

First published in 2007

Greenwood Press, 88 Post Road West, Westport, CT 06881
An imprint of Greenwood Publishing Group, Inc.
www.greenwood.com

Printed in the United States of America

The paper used in this book complies with the
Permanent Paper Standard issued by the National
Information Standards Organization (Z39.48–1984).

10　9　8　7　6　5　4　3　2　1

Every reasonable effort has been made to trace the owners of copyrighted materials in this book, but in
some instances this has proven impossible. The editor and publisher will be glad to receive information
leading to a more complete acknowledgments in subsequent printings of the book and in the meantime
extend their apologies for any omissions.

#6445346

Contents

List of Entries

Acknowledgments

A large number of people collaborated in the production of this encyclopedia, and it is both my responsibility and my pleasure to acknowledge their hard work and diligent efforts to bring this project to completion. Individuals mentioned here who are not listed in the contributors section of the encyclopedia will have their affiliations noted below.

First and foremost, I wish to acknowledge the indispensable help I received from three Graduate Assistants at Saint Louis University (Farley, Wood, Hawk-Reinhard) and two volunteer Research Assistants (Simpson, White). Michael Farley's name is alongside of mine in the bibliography, since he not only compiled information but also performed multiple searches for new data. He gathered the data for about one-third of all the entries included in the final version of the North American bibliography. John Halsey Wood and David Simpson transcribed the bulk of the primary source entries included in the documentary history. Both Wood and Simpson made judicious comments on the selections that were considered for inclusion. Wood checked the copyright status of many entries in the documentary history and sent out forms for signatures. Dr. Donna Hawk-Reinhard undertook the difficult and laborious task of abridging the entries and then checking the transcribed copies against the originals. She did so with an eye for detail. Jason White checked the bibliographies for all the essays in volume 1 of the encyclopedia against the general bibliography. Though it was the rage of hurricane Katrina that brought White from Loyola University in New Orleans to Saint Louis University, and his time in St. Louis was spent under less than optimal circumstances, his enthusiasm for the work was unflagging. Wayne Sparkman (Covenant Theological Seminary) prepared the list of archival sources published in the encyclopedia, and he deserves full credit for this contribution. Dr. Ron Crown, Reference Librarian at Saint Louis University, made valuable suggestions for additions to the list of archival sources.

The essays in this encyclopedia passed through a "double-blind" review process prior to publication. (That is, the scholarly reviewers of the essays did not know the identity of the essay authors, nor did the essay authors know the identity of the reviewers.) I would like to acknowledge my Board of Review for their labor in reading and commenting on the essays in volume 1. The article reviewers include Professor Randall Balmer (Columbia University), Professor Stanley Burgess (Regent University), Professor John Corrigan (Florida State University), Professor

David D. Daniels III (McCormick Seminary), Professor Gastón Espinosa (Claremont McKenna College), Professor Keith Hardman (Ursinus College), Professor Kathryn Long (Wheaton College), Professor Gary McGee (Assemblies of God Seminary), Professor Russell Richey (Candler School of Theology, Emory University), Professor Stephen Stein (Indiana University), Professor Harry Stout (Yale University), and Professor Ann Taves (University of California–Santa Barbara). Additional commentary and constructive criticism came from the participants in the American Seminar at Saint Louis University for Spring 2005, including my faculty colleagues Professors Belden Lane and Angelyn Dries, and the graduate students Christine Baudin, Daniel Dunivan, Father Oliver Herbel, Laura Llewellyn, and John Halsey Wood. Further commentary on this preface and introduction came from graduate students Lisa-Marie Duffield, Catherine McFarland, and Marcus McArthur.

A number of people either suggested or supplied the texts that were included in the final version of the documentary history published here. These include Professor Randall Balmer, Dr. Stephen Crocco, Professor Angelyn Dries, Professor Gastón Espinosa, Jason Fowler, Professor Thomas Hamm, Donald Haymes, Kenneth Henke, Professor Kathryn Long, Professor Sean Lucas, Professor Gary McGee, Professor Thomas Nettles, Professor Hans Rollmann, Professor Stephen Stein, Wayne Warner, and Professor Douglas Winiarski. I owe them all a debt of thanks for calling my attention to revival texts that were previously unknown to me, and thus broadening the scope of the coverage in the documentary history. I wish also to thank my faculty colleague at Saint Louis University, Professor Elsy Cardona, who translated Nellie Bazan's narrative from Spanish to English. Professor Ana Montero checked the previously translated Spanish texts concerning Olazábal, while the Saint Louis University graduate student, Jenelle Griffin, translated the texts on nineteenth-century Catholic parish missions from French to English. I owe my thanks to David Shocklee, who handled innumerable Interlibrary Loans at the Pius XII Memorial Library of Saint Louis University.

An intrepid band of text transcribers—all affiliated with Covenant Theological Seminary—made it possible to complete in a timely fashion the preliminary work of compiling texts for the documentary history. Without their help, the entire project would have been delayed considerably. These transcribers included Bobby Griffith, Jr., Jonathan D. Mattull, Chad Scruggs, Wayne Sparkman, Stephen and Amy Sterner, T. J. Wolters, and Britton Wood. Dr. Donna Hawk-Reinhard, who abridged and proofread the entries, also transcribed a few of them.

The copyrights to certain texts in the documentary history are held in the names of individuals rather than corporations, and I would like to acknowledge those who gave permission for their printed material to appear in a different format in this encyclopedia. The list includes Professor Robert Coleman, Gerald Derstine, Patricia Fening Gayes, Kenneth Hagin, Jr., Patti Gallagher Mansfield, David Manuel, Oral Roberts, John and Elizabeth Sherrill, Dr. Stephen Sheng (translator of the diaries of John Sung), Kevin Springer, Tom Stipe, Ken Walker, Cathy Wood, and Albert York. Had they not consented to republication, the documentary history would be lacking in a number of areas.

The preparation of the documentary history involved not only the selection of texts but also the preparation of introductions for each entry. A number of people supplied information that went into the introductions, including Professor Candy Gunther Brown, Professor Melvin Dieter, Professor Keith Hardman, Professor Gary McGee, Professor Hans Rollmann, Professor Ann Taves, and Professor Douglas Winiarski. For many of the introductions, I relied on information in written sources, but the just named persons responded promptly and helpfully to my phone and email queries for further data.

The task of illustrating the encyclopedia was much easier because of those who suggested or supplied images. This list includes Professor Fred Beuttler, Dr. Kenneth Brown, Professor Stanley Burgess, David DiSabatino, Professor Gastón Espinosa, Glenn Gohr (Flower Pentecostal Heritage Center, Assemblies of God Seminary), Dr. Stan Ingersol, Professor Jeanne Kilde (Macalester College), Jen Kitchen (Alpha USA), Professor Kathryn Long, Beth Mast and Jim Ruark (Zondervan Corporation), Jeff McAffee (Dixon Pentecostal Research Center, Lee University), Dr. Ken Minkema and Caleb Maskell (The Works of Jonathan Edwards, Yale University), Duane Pedersen (publisher of the *Hollywood Free Paper*), Dr. Mark Roberts (Holy Spirit Research Center, Oral Roberts University), Dr. Douglas Slawson, Wayne Weber (Archivist, Billy Graham Center), Professor Douglas Winiarski, and Cathy Wood (professional photographer, Pensacola, FL). Dr. Randy MacGuire, Assistant Archivist at Saint Louis University, went far beyond the call of duty in providing electronic scans of many pieces of original artwork that I supplied to him.

Complementing the work of Michael Farley and Jason White, a number of students from Saint Louis University transcribed information from various sources for the general bibliography on North American revivals and for the international bibliography. Among them are Christine Keogh, Jonathan Koefoed, Kayla Metz, Abi Ottenberg, and Paul Patterson. All made themselves available for this work on short notice. Dr. David Bundy supplied me with an invaluable list of his own multifarious publications. Also worthy of note are the published bibliographies by that provided a starting point for the preparation of the bibliography in this encyclopedia. The compilers of these previously published bibliographies include David Barrett, Professor Stanley Burgess, Professor Melvin Dieter, Professor Joel Carpenter (Calvin College) and Professor Edith Blumhofer, Professor Norris Magnuson (Bethel Seminary), and Richard Owen Roberts (International Awakening Ministries). The full citations for these previously published bibliographies are given under the editor's names in the bibliography here. Richard Owen Roberts deserves special thanks for hosting me in his home as I was just beginning this project in 2003, and for allowing me to peruse his extensive personal collection of books on religious revivals. Electronic databases made it possible to identify many works that would otherwise have escaped notice. The most helpful electronic databases were WorldCat, ATLA (American Theological Library Association), and America: History and Life.

Last, but not least, I wish to acknowledge Kevin Downing, my editor at Greenwood Press, who showed patience and understanding as the publication schedule for the encyclopedia had to be altered. I hope that he will feel that the final product has justified the time taken to complete the work.

Michael J. McClymond
Clarence Louis and Helen Irene Steber Professor
Department of Theological Studies
Saint Louis University

Preface

Encyclopedia of Religious Revivals in America is the first academic reference work devoted explicitly and wholly to the topic of religious revival in the context of the United States and Canada. Previously published dictionaries and encyclopedias have treated North American religions in general, Fundamentalism, evangelicalism, Pentecostalism, the Charismatic Renewal, African-American religions, and women in American religions. Yet none of these have used the experience and literature of religious revival as their organizing and guiding principle. This work is thus a first of its kind. A total of 227 articles in the first volume of the encyclopedia examine religious revivals from many angles. These articles are the work of 118 scholars, the majority of whom have previously published books or articles on the topics they treated in their essays here. A Board of Review, composed of a dozen nationally recognized research scholars, screened these articles and made suggestions for revisions prior to their appearance here. The members of the Board of Review are listed across from the title page.

The articles in the first volume of the encyclopedia fall into five broad categories. There are essays on *people* (e.g., Billy Graham, Aimee Semple McPherson, Francisco Olazábal), *revival events* (the Great Awakening, Cane Ridge, the Azusa Street Revival), *religious denominations or groups* associated with revivals (Methodists, Pentecostals, Primitive Baptists), *revival practices or phenomena* (the altar call, bodily manifestations, preaching, praying, radio and television, speaking in tongues), and *themes in revivals* (confession of sins, ecstasy, eschatology, foreign missions, material culture, men and masculinity, money and revivals). One hundred fifteen illustrations in the first volume complement the written text, and these include everyday scenes from life of local congregations as well as pictures of well-known revivalists, localities, and events. Many articles in the first volume are related to other articles, and the links between them are indicated by words that appear in bold lettering. Thus, in the article "Cane Ridge Revival," the name "James McGready"—a leader in this revival—appears in bold lettering on its first appearance in the article. This system of internal cross-referencing has been used throughout the first volume. Almost all of the articles contain references to other articles. A researcher might begin with any article in the encyclopedia, and, by following the bold-faced cross-references through a number of steps, link up with all the other articles. There are only two or three degrees of separation between any two articles. Something that becomes clear in the first volume is that religious revival is a well-defined, coherent, and integral field of study.

The second volume includes a wide-ranging documentary history of religious revivals in North America, incorporating 106 entries (with 153 texts), and stretching from the 1527 to 2005. Such a documentary history of North American religious revivals has not been produced before. Only a few collections of revival texts have been published thus far, and these have generally included texts related to a specific time period or theme (e.g., the Great Awakening, early twentieth-century Pentecostalism, etc.). Each entry in the documentary history here is preceded by an introduction, written by the editor, that sets a historical context for the reading and provides background information. The majority of these texts are first-person accounts of revival experiences—either the experiences of an author as part of a larger group of people, or else the experiences that an author witnessed without necessarily sharing in those experiences. Jonathan Edwards's *Faithful Narrative* (1737), for instance, is Edwards's first-hand account of what happened in 1734–35 among the congregants in the church he pastored. Edwards was both an observer and a participant in this revival. In contrast to Edwards's treatise, the anonymous work, *Short Account of the Methodist Camp Meeting* (1808), comes from someone who was an observer and yet not a participant in the revival meeting he described. His power of observation was acute and yet his standpoint regarding what he saw was critical and disapproving. The documentary history is mostly composed of participant-observant accounts, like that of Edwards, and yet it also contains a number of eyewitness accounts from observers who were non-participants. In some cases, the experiences described are individualistic rather than corporate in character (e.g., the selections from Sarah Edwards, Henry Alline, and Charles Finney). Yet in the texts where individuals are recounting their individual experiences, some link exists between the individual experience described and a larger, corporate religious awakening.

Many selections in the documentary history convey a vivid sense of being present at a religious revival. Nathan Cole, for example, describes how he left his farm in Connecticut and traveled by horseback with his wife to hear the revival preaching of George Whitefield:

> And when we came within about half a mile of the road that comes down from Hartford Weathersfield and Stepney to Middletown; on high land I saw before me a Cloud or fogg rising. I first thought it came from the great river [Connecticut River], but as I came nearer the Road, I heard a noise something like a low rumbling thunder and presently found it was the noise of horses feet coming down the road and this Cloud was a Cloud of dust made by the Horses feet. It arose some Rods into the air over the tops of the hills and trees....and as I drew nearer it seemed like a steady stream of horses and their riders, scarcely a horse more than his length behind another, all of a lather and foam with sweat, their breath rolling out of their nostrils in the cloud of dust every jump; every horse seemed to go with all his might to carry his rider to hear news from heaven for the saving of Souls....We went down in the Stream; I heard no man speak a word all the way three miles but every one pressing forward in great haste and when we got to the old meeting house there was a great multitude; it was said to be 3 or 4000 of people assembled together, we got off from our horses and shook off the dust, and the ministers were then coming to the meeting house. I turned and looked towards the great river and saw the ferry boats running swift forward and forward bringing over loads of people....When I saw Mr. Whitefield come upon the Scaffold he looked almost angelical, a young, slim slender youth before some thousands of people with a bold undaunted countenance, and my hearing how God was with him every where as he came along it solemnized my mind, and put me into a trembling fear before he began to preach; for he looked as if he was Cloathed with authority from the Great God, and a sweet solemn solemnity sat upon his brow.

Because of its down-to-earth verbiage and almost novelistic detail, Cole's narrative is more engaging than many other contemporary accounts of the Great Awakening. In addition to such eyewitness accounts, the documentary history includes brief selections from the extensive pastoral, homiletic, controversial, and theological literature on revivals. These works stress the importance of revival, criticize or defend revivals in general, or criticize or defend specific revival preachers, revival events, or revival practices. Enough material has been included in the documentary history to give the reader a feel for some of the major issues and themes that appear in this pastoral literature. On the other hand, the emphasis in selecting texts has been on eyewitness narratives rather than argumentative or evaluative texts.

After the documentary history, the remainder of the second volume consists of three separate bibliographies that together contain references to about 5,600 books, articles, and dissertations on religious revivals. The first bibliography is an unannotated listing of about 3,700 entries on the topic of religious revivals in the United States and Canada. The second bibliography has an international focus and is organized into fourteen sections, according to global regions. This contains about 1,900 entries on revivals outside of North America. The third bibliography lists more than 100 archival collections with materials on religious revivals in North America.

Research on revivals has tended to follow existing denominational and racial boundaries between religious groups. Most people who know something about religious revivals in North America know about one strand in the larger tradition, whether Anglo-Protestant, African American, German American, Scandinavian American, Latino, Congregationalist, Presbyterian, Roman Catholic, Baptist, Methodist, Holiness, Pentecostal, Charismatic, "Third Wave," or Nondenominational. Specialized scholars have scrutinized the North American revival tradition, as it were, through binoculars that enable them to observe small regions in minute detail. *Encyclopedia of Religious Revivals in America* offers both a smaller, intricate view and a larger, panoramic perspective. It allows the reader to see a larger landscape—without binoculars—perhaps for the first time. For this reason, *Encyclopedia of Religious Revivals in America* may help to open up new avenues and approaches for research. As editor, my hope is that the encyclopedia will be both a ready source of information for beginning students and a stimulus for scholars seeking to formulate their research agendas.

Religious Revivals in the American Past and Present

Religious revivals are as American as baseball, blues music, and the stars and stripes. They are, as it were, embedded in the continental soil, whether the stony ground of New England, the red clay of Georgia, the silt of Mississippi, Ohio, or Missouri river towns, the sand of the southwestern deserts, or the paved-over earth of New York City, Boston, Chicago, Dallas, Denver, Los Angeles, and Portland. Moreover, the revival tradition in United States and Canadian history has affected every social class. Men and women, young and old, rich and poor, college-educated and working class, urban and rural, natives and immigrants, and people from many races and ethnicities have all felt the touch of spiritual awakenings during the last three centuries. Despite the lamentable history of racial mistrust, segregation, and violence in American history, religious revivals have been an interracial phenomenon. Like jazz music, religious revivals involved a commingling of black and white influences. Accounts of revivals show that the experiences associated with revivals often transcended social boundaries. People who have little in common with one another in terms of race, ethnicity, vocation, education, or lifestyle have recounted their spiritual experiences in the midst of revivals in remarkably similar ways. The commonalities in the first-person narratives are often more striking than the disparities. The topic of religious revival ramifies into many related topics. A free association test with the word "revival" evokes varied images—gospel music, exuberant worship, altar calls, inner-city rescue missions, televangelism, Pentecostal healing and tongues-speaking, Billy Graham, the religious right, and biblical apocalypticism.

Revivals have been central to religion in North America for two centuries or more. Jerald C. Brauer made the sweeping claim that "revivalism is the most important movement in the history of Protestantism in the United States."[1] William G. McLoughlin found a connection between revivalism and the cultural roots of the North American colonies: "Awakenings have been the shaping power of American culture from its inception. The first settlers came to British North America in the midst of the great Puritan Awakening in England bringing with them the basic beliefs and values that provided the original core of our culture."[2] Furthermore, religious revivals—for all of their importance in the American past—are not merely a thing of the past. Revival in the form of Pentecostalism expanded enormously during the twentieth century and it shows little sign of losing momentum today. A statistical analysis of world Christianity published in the year 2000 revealed that there were 524 million Pentecostal or Charismatic Christians.[3] What is even more impressive is that the movement's growth had occurred in only a century's time. This figure makes Pentecostalism the second most prominent tradition in world Christianity behind Roman Catholicism. Far from disappearing, religious revivals around the globe accelerated during the 1980s and 1990s, and the late twentieth century was a golden age for religious revivals in Africa and Latin America, and in parts of Asia and Oceania. In April 2006, some 45,000 Pentecostal Christians from 113 nations gathered at the Los Angeles Coliseum to celebrate the centennial of the 1906 Azusa Street Revival in Los Angeles, thus honoring the North American origins of their half-billion strong global movement.

Events during the 1990s underscored the continuing importance of revivals in the North American and global contexts. A revival at the Toronto Airport Christian Fellowship drew hundreds of thousands of visitors since its inception on January 20, 1994.[4] Another revival began on June 18, 1995 at the Brownsville Assembly of God Church in Pensacola, Florida, and it drew more than two million visitors in three years.[5] A separate entrance into the church building was set up to accommodate international visitors and the press, and would-be worshippers have waited on the sidewalk as early as 4 A.M. to get a seat for the evening service. Pensacola is hardly a frontier or backwoods setting, while Toronto is among the most culturally diverse cities on earth. Given the ease and affordability of national and international travel, and the instantaneous communication provided by the Internet, the recent revivals in Toronto and Pensacola quickly took on a translocal character and overflowed all national, cultural, and linguistic barriers. Observers from around the world converged on the two cities, and later debated the phenomena they witnessed in email messages and at websites. As a result of such technological advances, contemporary religious revivals may be more widely diffused in their effects than at any previous point in history.

Defining the Terms "Revival" and "Revivalism"

Before it is possible to speak with clarity about "revival," one must define the term. Yet writers use the terms "revival" and "revivalism" in various ways. *Webster's Third New International Dictionary* defines "revival" as "a period of religious awakening: renewed interest in religion" with "meetings often characterized by emotional excitement." "Revivalism," according to the same dictionary, is "the spirit or kind of religion or the methods characteristic of religious revivals." Yet these simple definitions conceal much complexity, arising from competing theologies of revival and a centuries-long debate over the appropriateness of human efforts to promote spiritual awakening. The theological question, in brief, is this: Does the fervor and vitality of a religious revival come directly from God, apart from human efforts on the part of preachers or individual seekers after God? Or is revival fervor something that is channeled through the human efforts of preachers or seekers? The two sides in this debate are generally termed "Calvinist" and "Arminian," even though many participants in the historical controversies were not directly dependent for their ideas on John Calvin (1509–1564) or Jacob Arminius (1560–1609)—the two theologians from whom the schools of thought are named.

Calvinists—who believe that God's purpose and power undergird all human decisions—understand "revival" as an unplanned event that reflects God's initiative, and "revivalism" as a humanly orchestrated effort to stir up religious interest. While most Calvinists use the term "revival" in a positive way, "revivalism" generally has a negative connotation for them, since it may suggest manipulation, theatricality, insincerity, and emotionalism. A Calvinist "revival" is unpredictable and powerful, like a sudden summer storm. By contrast, Arminians assert that revivals occur through divine-human cooperation, including such strenuous exertions as prayer, fasting, and the persuasion of potential converts. The Calvinist author Iain Murray viewed eighteenth- and early-nineteenth-century Calvinistic "revivals" as shifting into late-nineteenth- and twentieth-century Arminian "revivalism," with Charles Finney as key figure in this transition. Murray may be correct that American revivalists beginning in the 1830s or 1840s tended to place more emphasis on strategies to promote revivals. The stress on human exertion is evident in the techniques of mass evangelism used from the mid-1800s onward by Dwight Moody, Billy Sunday, Aimee Semple McPherson, and Billy Graham. On the other hand, it is hard to draw a clear and clean line of division between "revivals" and "revivalism." Calvinists, who wait on God to bring revival, exert themselves to cause it to happen. Arminians, who exert themselves to cause revival, also have to wait on God. These two theologies of revival may be closer in practice than they are in theory.[6]

In the dictionary definition cited above, "revival" is described as a "renewed interest in religion." Yet one person alone with God does not constitute a revival. That might be a transcendent or mystical encounter for the individual in question, but it would not be a revival as such. To have a revival there must be a gathering of people. By definition, a revival is a corporate or collective phenomenon. As a corporate happening, a revival could be analyzed in terms of social psychology, just as one might assess the dynamics of a political street protest or a live sporting event such as the Super Bowl. In such settings, excitement is contagious and spreads rapidly from person to person and from group to group. Revivals should be understood then as *corporate, experiential events*. To call a religious gathering a revival is to suggest that the participants have undergone an *intensification* of experience. The fact that multitudes attend a religious service does not make it a revival as such. An impromptu papal appearance from a balcony at St. Peter's Square might draw a throng of a hundred thousand cheering spectators. Yet that would not in itself make this a Christian or Catholic revival. Contemporary megachurches such as the Willow Creek Community Church in the Chicago suburbs, the Potter's House in Dallas, the Lakewood Church in Houston, and Saddleback Community Church in southern California regularly draw more than 10,000 weekly worshipers and yet this does not mean that they exist in a state of continuous revival. A gathering of a hundred persons might offer a fuller and better picture of revival than a much larger assembly. What distinguishes a revival from the ordinary course of affairs is a pronounced deepening of religious feeling and expression. *Encyclopedia of Religious Revivals in America* is based on a basically qualitative rather than quantitative definition of the term revival.

Because revivals are events, they have beginnings and endings, and it is possible to assign chronological dates to many spiritual awakenings. Such would include the Northampton Awakening of 1734–1735, the Great Awakening of 1740–1741, Cane Ridge Revival of 1801–1802, the Revival of 1857–1858, the Azusa Street Revival of 1906–1909, and many other lesser-known occurrences. In general, the more intense a revival is, the easier it is to specify its starting and ending dates. The chief literary expression of a revival is a narrative or testimony describing the religious experiences of an individual or a community. Jonathan Edwards's *Faithful Narrative* (1737)—which did more than any other text to establish the genre of the revival narrative—spoke of an awareness of God's presence among the inhabitants of Northampton, Massachusetts in 1734–1735 that intensified until "there was scarcely a single person in the town, either old or young, that was left unconcerned about the great things of the eternal world… in the spring and summer following, *anno* 1735, the town seemed to be full of the presence of God."[7] Edwards's account was especially influential because of the insight and intricacy of his descriptions of spiritual experience. One might almost say that *Faithful Narrative* helped to *create* the North American revival tradition, since nothing of its kind had previously been published, and yet subsequently many narratives that were similar to Edwards's began to appear in the 1740s and down to the present day.

Revival as a Christian Tradition

While revivals are corporate, experiential events, the religious experiences that occur in revivals are closely related to intellectual formulations of belief or religious doctrines. The very word "revival" is shot through with explicit Christian associations. The literature of the North American revival tradition makes continual reference to God (in the Christian understanding), God's love, the Trinity, the divinity of Jesus, Jesus' atoning death, eschatology or Jesus' Second Coming, the Holy Spirit, heaven and hell, faith, repentance, holiness or sanctification, and so forth. Revival preaching—whether Presbyterian, Baptist, Methodist, or Pentecostal—involves certain common refrains such as "turn to God," "believe in Jesus," "repent of your sins," and "receive the Holy Ghost [or Holy Spirit]." There is no way to disentangle the descriptions of revival experiences from Christian ideas and teachings. To understand these experiences in historical context requires that we take account of the participants' religious beliefs.

To illustrate the point, one might consider Charles Grandison Finney's description of his conversion experience in his *Memoirs* (1876):

> When I awoke in the morning the sun had risen, and was pouring a clear light into my room. Words cannot express the impression that this sunlight made upon me.…In this state I was taught the doctrine of justification by faith, as a present experience. That doctrine had never taken any such possession of my mind, that I had ever viewed it distinctly as a fundamental doctrine of the Gospel. Indeed, I did not know at all what it meant in the proper sense. But I could now see and understand what was meant by the passage, "Being justified by faith, we have peace with God through our Lord Jesus Christ." I could see that the moment I believed, while up in the woods all sense of condemnation had entirely dropped out of my mind; and that from that moment I could not feel a sense of guilt or condemnation by any effort that I could make. My sense of guilt was gone; my sins were gone; and I do not think I felt any more sense of guilt than if I never had sinned.[8]

For Finney at the time of his conversion, "justification" was not only a doctrine concerning God's acceptance of sinners but a sense, feeling, and experience of God's grace and love. Previously Finney had had an intellectual notion of what was meant by justification, and yet in his time of his spiritual awakening this doctrine became a vital experience for him. This sort of interplay between doctrine and experience, cognitive content and affective response, is common in the narratives within the documentary history.

Because of this intertwining of doctrine and experience, revival experiences of a Christian sort need to be examined against the backdrop of Christian beliefs. To be sure, movements of reform and renewal have often occurred in non-Christian religions and sometimes these have followed paths that parallel Christian revivals.[9] Yet, by and large, religious revivals in North America have occurred within the context of Christian history, belief, and practice, and this context is needed properly to interpret these revivals. For this reason, *Encyclopedia of Religious Revivals in America* is self-consciously limited to groups, movements, individuals, and practices that are either Christian or Christian-based. The absence of non-Christian movements from the encyclopedia reflects the self-defined limits of this reference work. Many worthwhile lines of inquiry had to be omitted to keep a clear a focus on revival as classically understood. The encyclopedia treats the religious group commonly known as the Shakers because its early history is intertwined with that of religious revivalism in Britain, despite the fact that the later development of the movement (e.g., its teaching on Ann Lee as the female manifestation of God) sets it beyond the bounds of Christian orthodoxy. Mormonism receives a brief treatment inasmuch as it emerged against the backdrop of religious revivals in New York State in the early 1800s.

Encyclopedia of Religious Revivals in America is a topical work, and not a general encyclopedia of North American religion or religions. Thus the work thus does not treat religious groups that have no direct or indirect relationship to religious revivals. American Judaism (in its many aspects), Ethical Culture, Christian Science, Religious Science, Theosophy, Native American religions, Vedanta, Hinduism in America, Buddhism in America, American Islam, and Neo-Paganism receive no treatment here at all. Also worth noting is the absence of any substantive discussion of certain Christian groups and denominations. Among the major Christian groups without a specific article devoted to them are the Episcopal Church and the Orthodox Churches. The reason for this is simple. The documentation for an ongoing revival tradition among Baptists, Presbyterians, Methodists, and Pentecostals is abundant, while among Episcopalians it is scant. The emergence of the Charismatic Movement among Episcopalians during the 1960s and 1970s is covered in the essay on the "Charismatic Revival and Renewal," and in several other places. There seems to be virtually no literature on religious revivals within American Orthodoxy— though some Orthodox Christians, such as the "Radstockites," underwent revival experiences that caused them to leave Orthodoxy and join a Protestant group. Unitarianism is not discussed, since there is little if any evidence of a revival tradition within this denomination.

Roman Catholicism—since the mid-1800s the largest Christian communion in North America—might seem to have little connection with religious revival, since this is often understood as a Protestant phenomenon. Catholicism typically stresses participation in the sacraments more than preaching, and when Catholics come forward in a church service it is to receive "the body and blood of Christ" in the Eucharist and not to respond to a visiting evangelist's "altar call." The Protestant preoccupation with assurance of salvation—intensified in the context of a revival service—seems absent from most Catholic parishes, where participants gain a sense of belonging to God through their belonging to the church and sharing in its liturgy and sacraments. Yet a book by an eminent historian of American Catholicism—Jay Dolan's *Catholic Revivalism* (1978)—demonstrated the existence of a revival tradition in U.S. Catholicism centering on "parish missions." These missions brought visiting preachers to stir the faithful to renewed fervor, with special services in the church that continued for up to a month at a time. Sermons at nineteenth-century Catholic parish missions could be just as fiery and flamboyant as those preached by Protestant revivalists. Complementing the work of the parish missions, the "motor missions" of the early to mid twentieth century sent Catholic preachers beyond the walls of the church building—and often into largely non-Catholic regions—to present the Catholic message to people on street corners, in parks, and at other non-church venues. Another point where Roman Catholicism has affinities with the American revival tradition is in the early narratives of Catholic evangelization among Native Americans. Accounts from what were to be Texas and New Mexico in the early 1500s to mid-1600s, and from French Canada in the mid-1600s, report phenomena such as the healing of the sick in response to prayer, revelatory dreams and visions from God, and intense zeal for the new faith on the part of indigenous converts. What one reads is reminiscent of Pentecostalism in the early 1900s. There is an atmosphere of the supernatural in these narratives. Making due allowance for differences between Catholicism and Protestantism, there are sound reasons to include certain aspects of Roman Catholicism in the North American revival tradition.

Seven Characteristics of Revivals

Revival accounts from different eras, geographical regions, and ethnic groups in American history have common themes.[10] Participants in revivals speak of their vivid sense of spiritual things, great joy and faith, deep sorrow over sin, passionate desire to evangelize others, and heightened feelings of love for God and fellow humanity. In times of revival, people often crowd into available buildings for religious services, and fill them beyond capacity. The services may last from morning until midnight or later. News of a revival usually travels rapidly, and sometimes the reports of revival—in person, print, or broadcast media—touch off new revivals in distant localities. During a revival, clergy and other Christian workers may receive many requests for their services, and find themselves harried by inquirers. Sometimes people openly confess their sins in public settings. Another mark of revivals is generosity—individuals willing to give their time, money, or resources to support the work of the revival. Revivals are usually controversial, with opponents and proponents who vehemently criticize one another. Anti-revivalism typically arises in the wake of revivals. Often there are bodily manifestations in revivals, such as falling down, rolling on the ground, involuntary muscle movements, laughing or shouting, and spiritual dancing. Another common feature is an assertion of signs and wonders, such as the healing of the sick, prophecies, visions or dreams revealing secret knowledge, deliverance or exorcism from the power of Satan and the demonic, and speaking in tongues.

As a way of making sense of the many phenomena associated with revivals, let me suggest that revivals in the Christian tradition commonly show *seven characteristics*. In my understanding, only the first of the seven characteristics is essential, since it is part of the very definition of a religious revival. The other six characteristics are common in revivals, and most revivals will manifest both the first characteristic and a number of others. On the other hand, few revivals would clearly manifest all seven characteristics.

A first and defining characteristic of a revival is *intensified experience*. Accounts of revival reflect an intensification of ordinary religious experience. Participants in revivals show a vivid sense of spiritual things, great joy and faith, deep sorrow over sin, a passionate desire to evangelize others, and heightened feelings of love for God and fellow human beings. As noted above, a revival should be understood as a communal event, in which groups of people share this sort of intensified experience. A second characteristic is *bodily manifestations*—such as weeping, shouting, fainting, dancing, and so on. Though some have assumed that these sorts of manifestations have occurred only in Pentecostal revivals, the documentary history shows that a wide range of religious groups have had revivals characterized by bodily manifestations. This includes Calvinists, Quakers, Baptists, Methodists, and adherents of the Holiness Movement, as well as participants in the twentieth-century Pentecostal and Charismatic Movements. The second characteristic is linked to the first. The intensification of experience that occurs in revivals is not confined to the spirit, heart, or mind, but commonly reveals itself in the physical body. Participants in revivals often report sensations of warmth or electricity in their bodies, while others fall to the ground in an unconscious or semi-conscious state. Other bodily manifestations include an urge to dance, shout, or testify to others, speaking in tongues, visions, and reports of divine healing.

A third characteristics of revivals is the report of *extraordinary occurrences*, interpreted by the participants as "signs and wonders" of God's presence. Whether or not these events are properly miracles as such—however one defines that term—they strike the participants as signs of God's working among them. They may involve unlikely coincidences—as when someone prays for financial help and suddenly money turns up from an unexpected source. They may involve supernatural knowledge in the form of dreams, visions, or revelations regarding the secrets of an individual's life or concerning future events. They may involve spiritual or divine healing. A fourth characteristic is the appearance of *issues of spiritual discernment*. Religious revivals almost always raise issues of spiritual discernment for their participants. That is, they force the participants to distinguish between nature and grace, human initiative and divine influence. They may also stimulate a discussion regarding God and Satan, or angelic versus diabolical manifestations. Defenders of a given revival will usually acknowledge that at least some participants in the movement are carried away by their own emotions and thus are not being "led by God." Critics of revivals often charge that manipulation by leaders, mass hysteria, or emotionalism are the best explanations for the phenomena of revivals.

A fifth characteristic is related to the fourth, namely, *issues of lay and clerical authority*. Religious revivals give rise to issues of lay and clerical authority for their participants. That is, revivals raise the question: Who is in charge? People in the midst of an intense spiritual experience often feel that their words and actions carry special authority and may be directly sanctioned by God. Consequently lay participants may believe that they are not bound to follow the directives of their clerical leaders. Thus there arises a familiar clash between "charismatic" and "official" leadership in the midst of and in the aftermath of a revival. Religious revivals are almost always controversial.

A sixth characteristic therefore is *conflict and division in church and community*. Revivals may bring deep disagreements between the participants and the non-participants, and/or among participants themselves. These conflicts usually center on the characteristics already mentioned—intensified experience, bodily manifestations, extraordinary occurrences, and issues of discernment and authority. Since different people assess the revival phenomena in different ways, disagreements arise and often the participants in the revival stigmatize the non-participants as unspiritual, while non-participants regard the participants as fanatical. While these disagreements may occur during the period of the religious revival, they typically take place at a later time. Much of the controversy concerning the Great Awakening, for example, did not take place in the heat of the revival in 1740–41, but rather in 1743–45. Sometimes disagreements over revivals have led to permanent organizational and institutional divisions (e.g., "New Light" vs. "Old Light" Congregationalism, the Methodist Church vs. the Holiness Churches, the Holiness Churches vs. Pentecostalism). A seventh and final characteristic—related to the sixth characteristic—is *the emergence of new associations, organizations, and institutions*. Revivals not only bring conflicts and divisions, but they also engender new forms of association and connection between individuals and groups. The Great Awakening, for example, helped to spawn a new kind of trans-denominational evangelicalism in North America, while the Second Great Awakening encouraged the formation of numerous voluntary associations devoted to various social causes (e.g. abolitionism, temperance, women's rights, etc.). The social and institutional legacy of a given revival may be extremely complex, involving both new divisions and new associations.

These seven characteristics are an indication that religious revivals, for all their influence on the individuals who undergo them, have definite social, historical, and cultural effects. The shared ecstasy that has often occurred in the midst of revivals can leave lasting effects on the participants. The sociologist Émile Durkheim referred to this as "collective effervescence" and he noted that powerful, shared experiences can engender new sense of social identity. It may lead people to view themselves and one another in new ways. It may lead laypersons to challenge those in positions of authority. It may lead people of differing social classes, races, or genders to discover a new affinity with one another. An enduring—and notoriously complex—issue pertains to the social effects of religious revivals. Was the 1740s Great Awakening—in stressing the religious identity, value, and dignity of ordinary people—a kind of inadvertent preparation for the American Revolution in 1776? Some have argued in the affirmative. Was the Second Great Awakening of the early 1800s a key factor in promoting opposition to slavery in the United States prior to the Civil War? Once again, some scholars have said yes. Though the matter is hardly settled, there is at least some evidence linking religious revivals with movements of social change and reform, and this underscores the fact that revivals are corporate events that may affect large groups of people and leave enduring changes in their attitude, sensibility, and outlook.[11]

Introduction

The Academic Study of Religious Revivals
Revival as a Neglected Topic

Academic research on revivals is in a formative stage. On the one hand, there are innumerable works devoted to specific revival movements and revivalists and the bibliographies in the second volume contain about 5,600 entries. On the other hand, relatively little has been done to synthesize and interpret this vast body of literature. Scholars have only just begun to identify the leading trends, themes, issues, and problems for research in the study of religious revivals. One hindrance to progress in this area has been the prevailing university culture, and another has been the ethos of the churches and church-based seminaries.

Few university professors during the twentieth century had much personal connection with or experience of revivals. A measure of detachment from the people or community that one is studying—as any journalist or anthropologist will say—may be needed to give objectivity to one's study and writing. On the other hand, too much detachment can result in lopsided or imbalanced interpretations. Twentieth-century academics who had only read about eighteenth- and nineteenth-century revivals but had never witnessed a revival service often assumed that revivals were a vestige of the past. They were soon to be as scarce as the wooly mammoth. During the 1940s, both the Dean of Harvard Divinity School and William Warren Sweet—a leading historian at the University of Chicago—declared that religious revivals were disappearing. The "best pulpits," said Sweet, no longer mentioned the older "doctrine of conversion."[12] Yet the predictions failed. During the post-World War II era, Billy Graham's revival services thrust him into national and international prominence, Fundamentalist and evangelical congregations added new members as the so-called Mainline Protestant churches declined, and the Pentecostals—the most revivalistic group of all—surprised almost everyone by growing exponentially and then moving upward on the social ladder. The Charismatic Movement of the 1960s and 1970s brought the Pentecostal revival message to mainline Protestants and Roman Catholics, and many of these new "Spirit-filled" Christians were highly educated and affluent. They broke the cultural stereotype of the tongues-speaker as a snake-handler with missing teeth.

A handful of scholars did superb work on North American evangelicalism during the last generation, but religious revivalism was not their primary focus. George Marsden, Mark Noll, Harry Stout, and Nathan Hatch collectively published dozens of first-rate volumes on evangelicalism. They are among the best-published religion scholars, in any sub-discipline, in the United States. Yet, by and large, their works focused on intellectual and cultural aspects of evangelicalism and they paid less attention to experiential issues. The reason may lie in the social and intellectual circumstances of the era. During the 1970s and 1980s, scholars of evangelicalism were striving to demonstrate the intellectual viability of evangelicalism as a field of study—often in the face of skeptical faculty colleagues. Leading evangelical scholars were seeking to discover an American evangelical intellectual tradition. In consequence they directed their attention to areas of intellectual and cultural strength within evangelicalism—the writings of Jonathan Edwards, Calvinistic or Reformed theologies, evangelical engagement in social reform, and Biblical interpretation. To turn from the dialectical subtleties of Jonathan Edwards's writings to the sermons and books of later revivalists could be a bit like leaving a Mozart piano concerto for a professional wrestling bout. Nineteenth- and twentieth-century American revivalists showed vigor and verve, and yet offered little in the way of an intellectual tradition or legacy. Indeed, as Mark Noll argued in *The Scandal of the Evangelical Mind* (1995), and as Richard Hofstadter had earlier argued in *Anti-Intellectualism in American Life* (1963), the revival tradition in North America was not only un-intellectual but anti-intellectual in many of its expressions and effects.

At Protestant church-related seminaries—in distinction from research universities—there has been a general recognition of the importance of revival movements in American religious history. Seminaries often encouraged research into religious revivals that played a role in their respective denominational histories. Seminary professors have done much of the best writing on religious revivals in America. On the other hand, there were limiting factors in the seminaries no less than in the universities. What might be called the denominational mindset hindered a broad-based study of revivals, and it curbed the sympathy and curiosity that might otherwise have flowed beyond institutional boundaries. By and large, Baptists studied Baptists, Presbyterians studied Presbyterians, and so on with all the other religious groups—Methodists, Quakers, Roman Catholics, Pentecostals, and Charismatics. Since most seminaries in North America are maintained by Protestant denominations, the denomination may expect its professor of church history to function as a resident expert on denominational history. The consequence is that Protestant denominational historians have often been more concerned with investigating and celebrating their founders than with understanding religious revivals as such. Similar issues have appeared in the study of African-American history and in women's history. Black scholars have produced the bulk of scholarship on African American revivals. Non black scholars have not generally given much attention to African American religion in general and African American revivals in particular. Women scholars were pioneers in women's history, including the study of women revivalists. The greatest obstacle to the study of religious revival by North American scholars may not have been secular indifference in the universities but Christian factionalism in the churches and seminaries.

Interpreters and Interpretations of Revivals

Two authors of the later twentieth century stand out among others for their efforts to formulate a general interpretation of religious revivals in America. The popular writer and revival preacher, James Edwin Orr, wrote a number of works from the 1950s through the 1970s that amassed factual data on North American and global revivals. Yet despite the abundant information they supplied, Orr's books contained almost nothing in the way of historical, social, or cultural analysis. A revival for Orr was essentially the same whether it happened in Indiana or in India, and consequently Orr did not offer a socially contextual analysis of the revivals he recounted in his numerous books. Orr defined a revival simply as the "outpouring of the Holy Spirit"—a phenomenon not accessible to ordinary academic inquiry. Among university scholars of the last century, William J. McLoughlin of Brown University, was the acknowledged leader in the study of American revivals. He wrote a series of pioneering works, including *Modern Revivalism: Charles Grandison Finney to Billy Graham* (1959) and *Revivals, Awakenings, and Reform: An Essay on Religion and Social Change in America, 1607–1977* (1978). McLoughlin in his 1959 book defined revivalism as "any series of spontaneous or organized meetings which produce religious conversions whether they occur in one church, a dozen churches, or in hundreds of churches under the leadership of a spectacular itinerant evangelist."[13] In the 1978 book he wrote: "Revivalism is the Protestant ritual (at first spontaneous, but, since 1830, routinized) in which charismatic evangelists convey 'the Word' of God to large masses of people, who, under this influence, experience what Protestants call conversion, salvation, regeneration, or spiritual rebirth."[14] Common to both the earlier and later descriptions of revivals by McLoughlin was a stress on the dominating personality of the revivalist and on conversion as the revivalist's goal.

The present author, in his edited volume, *Embodying the Spirit: New Perspectives on North American Revivalism* (2004), expressed both appreciation and criticism of McLoughlin's work on religious revivals. My bibliographic essay took issue with McLoughlin for overemphasizing the influence of revival preachers and for neglecting the role of laypersons in initiating and guiding revivals. The Revival of 1857–58, for example, was a widely diffused and powerful revival and yet not directly associated with any notable preacher or leader. Another problem in McLoughlin is the idea that religious revivals happen among Protestants but not among Roman Catholics. Moreover, McLoughlin's perspective is limited by his assumption that "conversion" is the purpose of revival preaching. Closer analysis indicates that conversion is only one of a number of possible aims of revival preachers and revival meetings. Early Methodist revivals and the later Holiness Movement focused on sanctification as much as conversion, while Pentecostal and Charismatic revivals have stressed the baptism of the Holy Spirit, healing, deliverance, and speaking in tongues. Most problematic of all, McLoughlin separated "revivals" from "awakenings" in his 1978 book, claiming that individual experience needed to be distinguished from large-scale cultural change. Yet separating the individual from the community in this fashion may create more problems than it solves, and my argument in *Embodying the Spirit* was that it is better to conjoin these two aspects in interpreting revivals.

Believers and scholars have generally interpreted revivals in differing ways. Participants in revivals have often asserted that revivals are God's work and that no natural causes can explain them. Genuine revivals are due to a supernatural "outpouring of the Holy Spirit," which, if due to any human factors at all, is a result of concerted prayer. On the other hand, there have been devout authors—including Jonathan Edwards—who invoked natural causes alongside of supernatural or divine factors as causes or reasons for revivals. In the aftermath of the Revival of 1857–58, Christian writers noted that the financial panic of 1857 helped to set the stage for the revival among New York City businessmen, and so they invoked natural alongside of supernatural forms of explanation. Among scholars, there is no consensus as to why revivals occur. Some have noted that the causes of revivals are complex and cannot be reduced to a single causal factor, and that poverty or economic depression alone is not a cause for revivals. If poverty were a major causal factor, then the 1930s would have been a golden age for religious revival—which it was not. Eras of religious revival do not seem to correspond to periods of social strain or turmoil in American history. Scholars have debated whether American revivals have followed a clear pattern of increasing and then declining religious fervor (the cyclic pattern) or rather unfold in a more-or-less continuous development through time (the linear pattern).[15] Another recent debate, initiated by Jon Butler, concerns the colonial spiritual awakenings of the eighteenth-century. Butler argued that revivals during the 1740s were isolated and sporadic, and that the idea of a single, trans-colonial event known as a "Great Awakening" is in fact an "interpretive fiction" originating in the mid-1800s rather than the mid-1700s.[16]

Scholarly explanations for revivals move in multiple directions.[17] McLoughlin's approach, as noted, highlights the personality and influence of the revivalist in causing revivals. Another viewpoint is basing on an idea of communications and networking. According to this view, revivals "happen" when information and fervor flow between otherwise isolated groups and they develop a sense of participation within a larger movement. The star preacher of the Great Awakening, George Whitefield, had a uncanny sense of how to connect evangelical believers scattered in different denominations, how to use the newspapers to gain publicity, and how to use even the opposition against him to advance his cause. Richard Lovelace stressed Whitefield's unifying influence among evangelicals, while Harry S. Stout identified Whitefield's theatricality and media skill as essential to his appeal. Both viewed Whitefield's networking as a key aspect of the Great Awakening.[18] A different approach to explanation is based on so-called primitive psychology. In a century-old book, *Primitive Traits in Religious Revivals* (1905), Frederick Davenport viewed American revivals as an expression of non-rational instincts and emotions that needed to be put under rational control. Davenport implied that religious revivals were destined to disappear in the process of social evolution—an idea challenged by the stunning growth of twentieth-century Pentecostalism. He also aligned his theory of primitive psychology with indefensible racist and chauvinist notions of the superior rationality of white males. Yet Davenport's work highlighted an important theme that deserved fuller consideration, namely, the involuntary or non-rational aspects of revivals, such as the "jerks," falling down, and other bodily manifestations that occurred in the Great Awakening, the Cane Ridge Revival, and Pentecostal revivals. Some explanation is needed as to why people in revivals exhibit such powerful but unintentional bodily symptoms. Ann Taves has recently written on the "fits, trances, and visions" associated with revivals, and so addresses some of the questions posed by Davenport a century ago.[19]

The theory of material or social deprivation—propounded by sociologist Charles Glock, and applied to Pentecostalism by historian Robert Mapes Anderson—holds that revivalist groups offer their members a superior religious status to compensate for their inferior social or economic status.[20] While this theory helps to explain the spread of revivalist movements like Pentecostalism among America's—and later the world's—impoverished masses, it fails to explain to explain why certain revivals (e.g., the Charismatic Renewal) have been influential among people of wealth and influence. The deprivation or compensation theory, argues Grant Wacker, does not account for the initiative, drive, and self-reliance of the leaders and laypersons participating in revivals. The theory portrays them as passive spectators to revival movements, and not as agents in their own individual and social transformation.

Wacker, together with Alan Gilbert, Bernard Semmel, and John Corrigan, offered an interpretation of revivals that might be classified as functionalist. This perspective, indebted to Emil Durkheim, interprets revivalist religion in terms of its function in establishing personal identity and a sense of communal belonging. Wacker comments that early Pentecostalism was "less an effort to escape adversity than a creative resource for dealing with it."[21] Gilbert and Semmel viewed eighteenth-century evangelicalism in Britain as a response to the "anomie and social insecurity" that was caused by urban migration and separation from the life of traditional village communities. Early Methodism offered a "revolutionary message of liberty and equality" to masses of people alienated by the new industrial society.[22] The Revival of 1857–58, for John Corrigan, provided American males an opportunity to show their emotion—even through public weeping—and thus established the display of emotion as a category of collective identity.[23] In her study of gospel hymnody, Sandra Sizer notes that people spoke of the relationship with God or Jesus in terms of emotions "articulated in a communal context." Thus "prayer, testimony, and exhortation were employed to create a community of intense feeling, in which individuals underwent similar experiences … and would thenceforth unite with others in matters of moral decision and social behavior."[24] Shifting from emotion to economics, George Thomas found a close correlation between entrepreneurship and revivalist religion in the nineteenth-century United States, and suggested that revivalism can be seen as an adaptation of Christianity to fit the economic, social, and cultural milieu of entrepreneurial capitalism. Self-determining individuals from the marketplace entered the house of worship on Sunday as self-determining individuals. "The revivalist myth," says Thomas, "was cognitively compelling because it corresponded to their everyday experience as shaped by the dominant cultural myth of individualism."[25]

While it is not clear that any of the proposed theories of revivals is superior to all the rest, the functionalist viewpoint—when combined with insights from the other viewpoints—may go furthest in explaining how those who have participated in religious revivals both responded to the influences of their culture and shaped their culture in intentional ways. Yet after the explanations have been wagered and weighed, one recalls the eighteenth-century words of Jonathan Edwards, who in his *Faithful Narrative* (1737) referred to revivals as a "surprising work." Or as Martin Marty—today's best-known interpreter of American religion—has written: "Why do revivals occur? Answer: 'I don't know.'"[26]

Notes

1. Jerald C. Brauer, Preface to Jonathan M. Butler, *Softly and Tenderly Jesus is Calling: Heaven and Hell in American Revivalism, 1870–1920* (Brooklyn, New York: Carlson Publishing, 1991), xv.

2. William J. McLoughlin, *Revivals, Awakenings, and Reform: An Essay on Religion and Social Change in America, 1607–1977* (Chicago and London: The University of Chicago Press, 1978), 1.

3. David B. Barrett, George T. Kurian, and Todd M. Johnson, eds., *World Christian Encyclopedia*, 2 vols., 2nd ed. (New York: Oxford University Press, 2001), 1:4.

4. Margaret M. Poloma, "The 'Toronto Blessing': Charisma, Institutionalization, and Revival," *Journal for the Scientific Study of Religion* 36 (1997): 257–71.

5. Steve Rabey, "Pensacola Outpouring Keeps Gushing," *Christianity Today*, March 3, 1997, 54–57; Rabey, "Brownsville Revival Rolls Onward," *Christianity Today*, February 9, 1998, 80–81; Leo Sandon, "Pentecost in Pensacola," *Christian Century*, August 27—September 3, 1997, 748–49.

6. This paragraph is not meant to suggest that Calvinists have always supported revivals. Self-described Arminian and Wesleyan Christians have been more consistently positive in their attitude toward revivals than Calvinistic Christians. To a remarkable extent, Calvinistic or Reformed Christians have been historically prominent in arguing for both pro-revival and anti-revival positions. Jonathan Edwards himself was more cautious in defending revivals and more overt in his criticisms of revivals than many later revivalists have realized. On the confessional tradition in Reformed Christianity, and its opposition

to religious revivalism, see the illuminating works by D. G. Hart, *The Lost Soul of American Protestantism* (Lanham, MD: Rowman and Littlefield, 2002), esp. 1–56, and James Bratt, *Antirevivalism in Antebellum America: A Collection of Religious Voices* (New Brunswick, NJ: Rutgers University Press, 2005).

7. Jonathan Edwards, *The Works of Jonathan Edwards, Volume 4: The Great Awakening*, C. C. Goen, ed. (New Haven: Yale U. P., 1972), 149–50.

8. Charles Finney, *Memoirs of Rev. Charles G. Finney*. (New York, 1876), 12–23, excerpted in Hugh T. Kerr and John T. Mulder eds., *Conversions: The Christian Experience* (Grand Rapids: Eerdmans, 1983), 104–12, citing 111.

9. Though nearly a century old, Max Weber's analysis of religious reform in various world religions is still pertinent. See my analysis and critique "Prophet or Loss? Reassessing Max Weber's Theory of Religious Leadership," in David Noel Freedman and Michael J. McClymond, eds., *The Reivers of Paradise: Moses, Buddha, Confucius, Jesus, and Muhammad as Religious Founders* (Grand Rapids, MI: Eerdmans, 2001), 613–58.

10. The paragraph that follows is dependent on Richard M. Riss, *A Survey of 20th Century Revival Movements in North America* (Peabody, MA: Hendrickson Publishers, 1988), 3–7.

11. Further discussion of the possible social effects of revivals is found in Michael J. McClymond, "Issues and Explanations in the Study of North American Revivalism," in Michael J. McClymond, ed., *Embodying the Spirit: New Perspectives on North American Revivalism* (Baltimore: Johns Hopkins University Press, 2004), 1–46, esp. 22–31.

12. William Warren Sweet, *Revivalism in America: Its Origin, Growth, and Decline* (New York: Scribners, 1944), xii–xiv.

13. William G. McLoughlin, *Modern Revivalism: Charles Grandison Finney to Billy Graham* (New York: Ronald Press, 1959), 7.

14. McLoughlin, *Revivals, Awakenings, and Reform*, xiii.

15. On the linear vs. cyclic question, see the "Symposium on Religious Awakenings" published in *Sociological Analysis* 44 (1983): 81–122, comprising R. C. Gordon-McCutchan, "Great Awakenings?" (83–95), Timothy L. Smith, "My Rejection of a Cyclic View of 'Great Awakenings'" (97–102), William G. McLoughlin, "Timepieces and Butterflies: A Note on the Great-Awakening-Construct and Its Critics" (103–10), John L. Hammond, "The Reality of Revivals" (111–15), John Wilson, "Perspectives on the Historiography of Religious Awakenings" (117–20), and Timothy L. Smith's response (121–22).

16. Jon Butler, "Enthusiasm Described and Decried: The Great Awakening as Interpretive Fiction," *Journal of American History* 69 (1982): 305–25, cited and critiqued in McLoughlin, "Timepieces," 107–8.

17. A fuller account of explanatory models for religious revivals is in McClymond, "Issues and Explanations," in McClymond, ed., *Embodying the Spirit*, 31–43.

18. Richard F. Lovelace, *Dynamics of Spiritual Life: An Evangelical Theology of Renewal* (Downers Grove, IL: InterVarsity, 1979), 39; Harry S. Stout, Stout, *The Divine Dramatist: George Whitefield and the Rise of Modern Evangelicalism* (Grand Rapids, MI: Eerdmans, 1991) 60–61.

19. Ann Taves, *Fits, Trances, & Visions: Experiencing Religion and Explaining Experience from Wesley to James* (Princeton, NJ: Princeton University Press, 1999).

20. Charles Glock, "The Role of Deprivation in the Origin and Evolution of Religious Groups," in R. Lee and Martin Marty, eds., *Religion and Social Conflict* (Oxford: Oxford University Press, 1964), 24–36; Robert Mapes Anderson, *Vision of the Disinherited: The Making of American Pentecostalism* (New York: Oxford University Press, 1979), 229.

21. Grant Wacker, *Heaven Below: Early Pentecostals and American Culture* (Cambridge, MA: Harvard University Press, 2001), 10, 200–201.

22. Michael J. Crawford, *Seasons of Grace: Colonial New England's Revival Tradition in Its British Context* (New York: Oxford University Press, 1991), 8; citing Alan D. Gilbert, *Religion and Society in Industrial England: Church, Chapel, and Social Change, 1740–1914* (London: Longman, 1976), 87–93, and Bernard Semmel, *The Methodist Revolution* (New York: Basic Books, 1973), 5, 7–9, 198.

23. John Corrigan, *Business of the Heart: Religion and Emotion in the Nineteenth Century* (Berkeley: University of California Press, 2002), 251–67, citing 251.

24. Sandra S. Sizer, *Gospel Hymns and Social Religion: The Rhetoric of Nineteenth-Century Revivalism* (Philadelphia: Temple University Press, 1978), 52.

25. George M. Thomas, *Revivalism and Cultural Change: Christianity, Nation Building, and the Market in the Nineteenth-Century United States* (Chicago: University of Chicago Press, 1989), 7, 83.

26. Martin E. Marty, "Afterword," in McClymond, ed., *Embodying the Spirit*, 273.

A

ABOLITIONISM AND REVIVALS

The exact relationship between the movement to end slavery and the movement to promote religious revivals has long bedeviled scholars. In the North contemporaries and later scholars noted that the regions most touched by the revivals of the **Second Great Awakening**—the areas of the Yankee migrations into upstate New York, the Western Reserve of Ohio, and portions of Michigan often referred to as the third New England—emerged as centers of abolitionist agitation. Equally important is the British example. In England friends of revival such as William Wilberforce and Thomas Clarkson, with support from the aging father of **Methodist revivals,** John Wesley, emerged as key leaders in the movement to abolish the slave trade and later slavery in the West Indies. At the same time, the evidence connecting revivals with abolitionism is mixed. Because of what has been called the "divided conscience" of northern evangelicals in the United States prior to the **Civil War,** some sectors of northern abolitionists after 1830 began to channel their efforts into the political arena rather than through revivalist religion. After the 1830s, moreover, churches in the **South** maintained a revival tradition that did not engender abolitionist sympathies.

In the aftermath of the American Revolution, many revivalist groups, even in the South and including the Methodists and **Baptists,** opposed slavery. Some scholars have even suggested that these southern Methodists and Baptists were regularly practicing manumission (i.e., freeing their slaves) during this period. In the first three decades of the nineteenth century, as slavery tightened its grip upon the region, many evangelical opponents of slavery migrated to the North. These included evangelically inclined **Quakers** and Methodists such as the legendary Methodist circuit rider **Peter Cartwright,** whose moderate opposition to slavery greatly curtailed his ministry in the South after 1830.

Likewise, the roots of northern abolitionism were distinctly revivalistic. In New England the direct heir of the revivalist Calvinism of **Jonathan Edwards,** Samuel Hopkins, Congregational minister in Newport, Rhode Island (1769–1802), and onetime slave owner, not only **preached** against slavery in a congregation where many profited from the institution but was the organizational genius behind the Providence Abolition Society—one of only two such organizations functioning in the early republic. Hopkins played no small role in the passage of emancipation acts in New England and the Middle Colonies in the years following the American Revolution. While remembered as an activist, Hopkins provided a new theological rational for abolitionism with his doctrine of "disinterested benevolence." In Hopkins's thought sin was selfishness and the essence of Christian duty was disinterested love of God and neighbor, directed especially toward the poor, slaves, and Native Americans. When **Charles Finney** a generation later called for sinners immediately to turn from selfishness to righteousness, it was a short step to conclude that the enslavement of **African Americans** was rooted in selfishness and should immediately be abandoned.

In fact, the entire logic of the "immediate abolitionism" of William Lloyd Garrison was implicitly revivalistic. Raised in a pious Baptist home, Garrison typifies a segment of the abolitionist movement that included such notables as Elizabeth Cady Stanton, Henry B. Stanton, Theodore Weld, early Wesleyan Methodist leader La Roy Sunderlund, and Gerrit Smith. In the course of their struggle against slavery and other evils, they gradually abandoned evangelicalism even as the moral passion of revivalism continued to inspire their reform efforts. As noted by Gilbert Barnes, two-thirds of the delegates to the 1835 Garrisonian New England Antislavery Society were either Baptists or Methodists and many of the others were Congregationalist supporters of revival.

Outside of Garrisonian circles revival converts played an even greater role in the spread of abolitionism. One of the most important was the 1831 Finney convert Theodore Dwight Weld. Enrolling as a student at Lane Theological Seminary in Cincinnati—just across the river from the slave state of Kentucky—Weld gradually converted the entire student body to immediate abolitionism. When the Lane Board of Trustees ordered an end to discussions of slavery, most of the students and the faculty member John Morgan withdrew. In the spring of 1835 the students, Morgan, and a local Cincinnati pastor who had supported them, **Asa Mahan,** relocated to Oberlin College. With the financing of wealthy Evangelical businessman Lewis Tappan, and the leadership of the nation's premier evangelist, Charles Finney, Oberlin College emerged as a key center for abolitionism in the northwestern states of the early 1800s. While Finney did not support national lobbying to end

Woodcut of a supplicant male slave, with the caption "Am I not a man and a brother?" from the broadside publication of John Greenleaf Whittier's antislavery poem, "Our Countrymen in Chains." The design was previously adopted in the 1780s as the seal of the Society for the Abolition of Slavery in England (Broadside, 1837). Courtesy of the Library of Congress.

slavery and never wavered from his belief that all reforms including abolitionism were secondary to evangelical preaching, he insisted that African American students be admitted to Oberlin College and rejected segregated seating on the Oberlin campus. As Finney saw it, the fruits of revivalism—holiness or undivided love of God and neighbor—would lead to the elimination of all sin, including that of slaveholding.

If Finney was the most prominent revivalist to oppose slavery, he was hardly alone. Others included Baptist revivalist **Jacob Knapp, Presbyterians** Albert Barnes and George Duffield, New York Congregationalist pastor George Cheever, and **Lutheran** educator Samuel S. Schmucker. Likewise, immigrant groups that brought distinct revivalist traditions, such as Norwegian "Haugean" Lutherans, strongly opposed slavery, while the growing confessional movements among the **Reformed,** Lutherans, and Anglicans tended to be silent on controversial social issues including slavery.

While Oberlin was the most important abolitionist revivalist center, it was hardly alone. **Free Will Baptists** supported Hillsdale College (Michigan), Wesleyan Methodists supported Adrian College (Michigan), and Wesleyan Methodists founded the Illinois Institute (later renamed as Wheaton College, Illinois) to share in Oberlin's radical passion. In the years after the Civil War as racial egalitarianism waned elsewhere, it continued to be vigorously supported by the Wheaton-based National Christian Association, the **Free Methodist Church,** the Wesleyan Methodist Church, the Oberlin-dominated American Missionary Association, and the Oberlin-inspired Berea College (Kentucky)—all explicitly revivalistic institutions While it goes without saying that not all revivalism inspired social reform or abolitionism, it should not surprise us that two of the most important twentieth-century scholars in the rediscovery of the link between revivalism and abolitionism were raised in Wesleyan Methodist families, Timothy L. Smith and Donald W. Dayton.

Further Reading: Barnes, Gilbert. *The Anti-Slavery Impulse, 1830–1844.* Washington, DC: American Historical Association, 1933; McLoughlin, William G. *Revivals, Awakenings and Reform: An Essay in Religion and Social Change in America, 1607–1977.* Chicago: University of Chicago Press, 1977; Smith, Timothy L. *Revivalism and Social Reform: American Protestantism on the Eve of the Civil War.* Baltimore: Johns Hopkins University Press, 1980; Sweet, William Warren. *Revivalism in America.* New York: Charles Scribner's, 1944.

William Kostlevy

ADVENTISM

see Eschatology and Revivals; Jehovah's Witnesses; Miller, William; Seventh-day Adventists; White, Ellen Gould (Harmon)

AFRICAN AMERICAN REVIVALS

African American revivals have shaped the black church and so the role of the black church in American society. African religious sensibilities and evangelical Protestantism both contributed to these revivals. Within the history of African American revivalism there are five key moments that serve as points of reference within this essay: the "Angolan" revivals (1740–1750), the postcolonial revivals (1780–1810), the Reconstruction-era revivals and **Holiness**-Pentecostal revivals that culminated in the **Azusa Street revival** (1877–1907), the political evangelism of the civil rights movement (1950s–1960s), and the neo-**Pentecostal revivals** (1955–1980).

The first large-scale **conversion** of Africans in North America took place in the Angolan revivals of coastal South Carolina, Georgia, Virginia, and the greater Chesapeake Bay region during 1740–1750. The term *Angolan* refers to actual Angolans as well as other enslaved Africans from the kingdom of Kongo, the Senegambia regions, Iboland, and other areas. Together they forged a new African American identity in colonial North America. Historians Alfloyd Butler and John Thornton noted the influence of enslaved Angolan and Kongolese who brought Roman Catholicism with them from Africa. In 1710 Anglican missionary Francis Le Jau commented on the presence within his South Carolina parish of a few enslaved Angolans who professed to be Roman Catholic and had been baptized by the Portuguese Roman Catholics. A 1742 South Carolina parish transcript recorded that many of the Angolans spoke Portuguese and "many thousands of the Negroes there [in Angola] profess the Roman Catholic religion." Since 8,045 Angolans arrived between 1735 and 1740 in South Carolina, their role in the Christianization of enslaved Africans may have been considerable. Another key to the Angolan revivals was the influence of such white **preachers** as **George Whitefield** and **Gilbert Tennent,** along with many unnamed black exhorters and preachers. This nascent evangelicalism emphasized conversion, the apocalyptic, **deliverance, visions,** and religious enthusiasm. The Angolan revivals of the 1740s occurred in a context where the majority of slaveholders discouraged the evangelization of the enslaved.

Northern mutual-aid societies together with **southern** congregations helped to spawn the postcolonial African American revivals. In 1775 George

Liele established a first major African American congregation in Savannah, Georgia, as the First African Church, followed by a sister congregation in Silver Bluff, South Carolina. In coastal South Carolina and Georgia, the Pray's (Praise) House took shape. The Pray's House was a center for **prayer,** the ring shout, and conversions, often coordinated by volunteer Christian laywomen. Usually located on plantations, the Pray's House developed outside of formal, denominational structures. Liele's successors, Andrew Bryan and Andrew Marshall, extended his ministry, establishing a system with a mother church in Savannah, Georgia, and satellite congregations throughout the region. These congregations offered Sunday schools, youth societies, and Female Education Working Societies.

Mutual-aid societies were Protestant endeavors that sponsored programs with religious, benevolent, and educational purposes, establishing schools, a system of care for the sick and aged, and a political forum. During the 1780s many mutual-aid societies engaged in a vigorous debate about the formation of African American congregations. After having had the experience of self-determination, as well as the indignities of segregation and discrimination in the churches, some mutual-aid societies proceeded to establish themselves as congregations. Newport's African Union Society became the African Union Church by the late 1780s, and the Free African Society founded in 1787 became St. Thomas Episcopal Church and the Bethel **African Methodist Episcopal Church** (AME) in 1794. With the increasing numbers of black Christians during the 1780s and 1790s, new congregations were formed out of black factions within existing white congregations: the Baltimore African Church, from which emerged the African Bethel Church (later Bethel AME Church), and Zion Church in New York City. During the first decade of the 1800s, other congregations also took shape: Joy Street in Boston, Abyssinian **Baptist** in New York City, St. Phillip's Episcopal Church in New York, and African **Presbyterian** Church in Philadelphia.

Four conversion practices dominated the postcolonial revivals: the ring shout, "seeking Jesus," spiritual dying, and the mourners' bench—each with its own set of rituals and sites of activity. In the ring shout, converted believers surrounded the sinner, sang and **danced** in a circular motion, and prayed for the Holy Spirit to descend and usher the sinner into an **ecstatic** experience. Seeking Jesus was a conversion practice in which seekers awaited religious experiences within the woods and then sought guidance from designated tutors in the Pray's House. Religious dying or being "struck" dead by God often occurred in the woods or a cemetery where the sinner passed through an experience of spiritual death and resurrection. The mourners' bench—an early version of the **altar call**—was a designated pew at **camp meeting** sites where sinners experienced godly sorrow for their sins, listened to sermons on judgment and grace, and had songs and prayers offered on their behalf by the converts who encircled them. Camp meetings in the early 1800s featured daylong worship and after-midnight singing and praying. Often these gatherings were biracial. They featured dancing, **shouting,** the singing of slave songs, and sermons by popular black preachers such as Harry Hosier.

During the Reconstruction era, some African American leaders wanted to change the ethos of the camp meeting with its all-day worship, after-midnight praying, and intense emotionalism. They sought to introduce a new revivalism located inside church buildings, schools, and colleges. Daniel Alexander Payne, Henry Jacobs, E. C. Morris, Virginia Broughton, and others campaigned to shift the site of African American revivalism and to revise its form. They rejected the ring shout and its related conversion practices, with the exception of the mourners' bench. They stressed didactic preaching, character building, and **hymn** singing.

Black Holiness meetings, black **restorationism,** and black Pentecostalism emerged during the postbellum era. By the late 1870s the black **Holiness movement** expanded from its beachhead in the black **Methodist** denominations and congregations in North Carolina to New York and Missouri, entering black Baptist, black Presbyterian, and independent religious communities in South Carolina, Michigan, and the mid-South region. This movement rejected the excesses of the camp meetings and

The black church has been a formative factor in African American culture and in American culture generally throughout U.S. history. This photograph, collected by W.E.B. Du Bois, shows worshippers leaving a service in Georgia around 1900. (Daniel Murray Collection) Courtesy of the Library of Congress.

the conversion practices of the ring shout, seeking Jesus, and religious dying. The Holiness movement created a new ethos for the camp meeting. Some within the black Holiness movement challenged the use of the mourners' bench. A pivotal turning point in the African American Holiness movement occurred during the Philadelphia revival (1877–1879). The movement started at Bethel African Methodist Episcopal Church, the historic pulpit of Richard Allen. It occurred during the pastorate of George C. Whitfield, who preached Holiness sermons and scheduled all-day Holiness conferences that were biracial, interdenominational, and affirmative toward female religious leaders. In addition to George C. Whitfield and black Presbyterian pastor Redding B. Johns, the Philadelphia revival launched the ministries of several leading AME Holiness preachers: Bishop Abraham Grant, international evangelist **Amanda Smith,** and author and religious editor Benjamin Tanner. Black

restorationism popularized the teachings of Alexander Campbell among African Americans and challenged the conversion practices of earlier African American revivalism. Its major leader, William Christian, opposed the mourners' bench. He characterized the praying, "godly sorrow," "fits and spasms," and "getting religion" of the "mourners' bench business" as ignorant and unbiblical. The Bible required that the seeker "just accept the word" and be saved. Christian rejected the use of unscriptural church titles, such as Baptist and Methodist, and so spawned antidenominationalism among blacks. By 1900 his fellowship, the Church of the Living God, became the largest non-Baptist and non-Methodist Protestant organization among African Americans, with almost 90 congregations in 11 states of the Midwest and mid-South.

During the early 1900s, the black Holiness movement and black restorationism converged with parallel white groups to play a role in the emergence of

Pentecostalism. The **Azusa Street revival** of 1906–1909 began as a black Holiness revival within a black Holiness mission in Los Angeles, California, and was led by a black Holiness evangelist, **William J. Seymour.** Yet black Pentecostalism fractured the black Holiness movement. Some African American Holiness leaders who embraced Pentecostalism along with all or some of their associated congregations included **Charles Harrison Mason, Mary Magdalena Tate,** and William Fuller. In many cases, entire African American Holiness congregations and institutions embraced Pentecostalism. Black Holiness congregations in Los Angeles, Portland, Memphis, Indianapolis, and New York City were sites for the introduction of Pentecostalism to these cities and places where interracial worship occurred, following the model of the Azusa Street revival. Yet Amanda Smith, **African Methodist Episcopal Zion Church** (AMEZ) bishop Alexander Walters, William Christian, Charles Price Jones, and Virginia Broughton were among the Holiness leaders who opposed Pentecostalism in the black churches. Though some black Holiness leaders severed their relations with the new black Pentecostal leaders, others remained colleagues in ministry with them.

Seymour's Apostolic Faith Mission in Los Angeles became a kind of indoor camp meeting, featuring the same worship style and exuberance as the outdoor services. The altar served as the place to "tarry" for those seeking conversion, **sanctification,** or the **baptism of the Holy Spirit.** Tarrying became a practice associated with black Pentecostalism revivalism in which seekers would come to the altar and continuously repeat such phrases as "Save me, Lord," "Jesus, Jesus, Jesus, Jesus," "Fill me, Lord," and "Thank you, Jesus." Behind these seekers, prayer leaders would stand praying, interceding, and tutoring the seekers in their quest, sometimes continuing day and night. During the Azusa Street revival, participants sang choruses and engaged in the religious dancing, shouting, jumping, and rolling. This revival provided a model for interracialism. From 1906 to 1908, blacks, whites, **Latinos,** Native Americans, and Asians worshipped together at the mission.

Early Pentecostalism struggled with its interracial identity during an era in which most American institutions espoused racial segregation. Frank Bartleman, who witnessed the Azusa Street revival, marveled that "the color line was washed away in the blood [of Jesus Christ]" (Bartleman, *Azusa Street*, 54). In 1908 segregation began to fracture the Pentecostal fellowships. Only a few remained interracial for a decade or more—the **Pentecostal Assemblies of the World** until the 1920s, and the **Church of God in Christ** until the 1930s.

Black Pentecostal revivals elicited a fierce debate over the role of **women** within the ordained ministry. While the majority of black Pentecostal denominations restricted ordination to males, most offered women ministerial positions such as evangelist. Yet a host of new denominations ordained women to the ministry—some giving them access to the pastorate and others a role as either pastor or bishop. Most of the black Pentecostal denominations that embrace full gender equality within the pastorate and bishopric have African American women as founders. Two central leaders of female-led black Pentecostal denominations are Mary Magdalena Tate and Ida Robinson.

The modern civil rights movement legitimated political evangelism or social activism within the black church, according to James Melvin Washington. As itself a form of African American revivalism, the civil rights movement transformed the black church into a protest organization, established its moral integrity, and demonstrated its relevance to society. It used revivalistic methods to mobilize the black community, and made social and political activism—or political evangelism—a vital option among African American Christians. Sociologist Aldon Morris and historian James Melvin Washington note that the black church provided most of the leaders and constituents of the modern civil rights movement as well as the forms of discourse, facilities, networks, and culture that informed the movement. The structure for the mass meetings derived from revival traditions. The tunes and lyrics of spirituals and congregational songs informed the themes and tunes of the freedom songs. Singing was a unifying and empowering event. Testifying allowed blacks to name and demystify injustice and racism. Black sermonic forms underlay the rhetoric of the movement. Calls to conversion were a means to recruit activists and summon segregationists and racially prejudiced persons to repentance. Pray-ins joined with sit-ins, boycotts, and marches as strategies of nonviolent resistance. Political evangelism helped to dismantle segregation and form a society based on racial justice.

Beginning in the 1950s, neo-Pentecostal revivals shifted Pentecostal revivalism from the margins to the center of the black church. The middle-class trend inaugurated in the 1800s by Daniel Alexander Payne—deemphasizing emotion and **bodily manifestations**—was eclipsed by a new Pentecostal revivalism that drew from African American folk religious culture and the political evangelism of the civil rights era. Pentecostalism attracted clergy and members within historic black denominations, especially the AME Church and the Baptist Church. By the 1970s neo-Pentecostal ministers began occupying pastorates in the AME Church. The focal point for the movement during the early 1970s was St. Paul AME Church in Cambridge, Massachusetts, under the pastorate of John Bryant. By the 1980s, neo-Pentecostal AME Church congregations were among the largest in the denomination, including St. Paul in Cambridge, Bethel in Baltimore, Allen Temple in Queens (New York), and Ward in Los Angeles. In the AMEZ Church during the 1980s and 1990s, the neo-Pentecostal movement centered on John A. Cherry and his congregation, the Full Gospel AMEZ Church in Temple Hills, Maryland—a suburb of Washington, DC. Among black Baptists focal points for neo-Pentecostalism were Roy Brown at the Pilgrim Baptist Cathedral in Brooklyn and Paul Morton at St. Stephen Full Gospel Baptist Church in New Orleans. In the 1980s Brown organized a denomination (Pilgrim Assemblies) and Morton spearheaded a neo-Pentecostal Baptist fellowship (the Full Gospel Baptist Fellowship).

During the late twentieth century, African American revivalism has expanded into new congregations and denominations with its new, neo-Pentecostal ethos. Gospel music and praise songs dominate the musical culture with polyrhythmic and percussive sounds. Engaging, exuberant, and celebrative preaching excites and challenges congregations. Conversion centers on accepting Jesus Christ as Lord and Savior as well as discovering the gifts of the Spirit. Exuberance is welcomed as an authentic expression of worship. Political evangelism has also attracted new adherents, initiating social change in some neighborhoods and communities. The old summer revival finds a new home as congregations sponsor January revivals along with women's, **men's**, youth, and children's revivals. From the Angolan revivals, the postcolonial revivals, the Reconstruction-era revivals, and the Holiness-Pentecostal revivals to the political evangelism of the civil rights movement and the neo-Pentecostal revivals of the late twentieth century, African American revivalism has been Africanized, transformed into a cultural and political force, and Pentecostalized. With pivotal leaders, such as unnamed enslaved Angolan and Kongolese Christians, George Liele, Jarena Lee, Daniel Alexander Payne, William Christian, William Seymour, Martin Luther King Jr., Juanita Bynum, and **T. D. Jakes,** African American revivalism holds a distinctive place within the larger revival tradition in North America.

Further Reading: Butler, Alfloyd. *The Africanization of American Christianity.* New York: Carlton Press, 1980; Chappell, David L. "Religious Revivalism in the Civil Rights Movement." *African American Review* 36 (2002): 581–95; Daniels, David Douglas, III. "The Cultural Renewal of Slave Religion: Charles Price Jones and the Emergence of the Holiness Movement in Mississippi." PhD dissertation, Union Theological Seminary, New York City, 1992; Franklin, Robert. *Another Day's Journey: Black Churches Confronting the American Crisis.* Minneapolis: Fortress Press, 1997; Morris, Aldon D. *The Origins of the Civil Rights Movement: Black Communities Organizing for Change.* New York: Free Press, 1984; Pitts, Walter F. "Keep the Fire Burnin': Language and Ritual in the Afro-Baptist Church." In Michael J. McClymond, ed., *Embodying the Spirit: New Perspectives on North American Revivalism,* 196–210. Baltimore: Johns Hopkins University Press, 2004.

David D. Daniels III

AFRICAN METHODIST EPISCOPAL CHURCH

The African Methodist Episcopal Church (AMEC) is one of the earliest and most influential of African American religious denominations in the United States. Its formation was triggered by racial discrimination in the white churches during the late 1700s. In 1786, **Richard Allen** (1760–1831) a former slave from Delaware, organized 42 black Philadelphians for **prayer** meetings and a **Methodist** society, with support from Absalom Jones (1746–1818), William White (1748–1836), and Dorus Ginnings. During 1787, Allen, Jones, and others attended Sunday worship at St. George Methodist Episcopal Church, which, earlier that year, had introduced segregated seating for blacks and whites. During prayer ushers pulled them from their knees, insisting that they move to the proper section of the church building. All of the blacks left St. George Methodist Episcopal Church at this time. For the next few years the group met as the Free African Society.

This society formed a mutual-aid group to meet practical needs and for social interaction among blacks. It also helped to spawn two distinct traditions—Episcopalian and Methodist. Both were revivalistic and taught the importance of both conversion and sanctification. After many meetings and discussions with the white Methodist Episcopal Church leaders, the African Methodist Episcopal Church was chartered in 1794. **Francis Asbury** (1745–1816) named the congregation the Bethel African Methodist Episcopal Church, and it convened in what had been a blacksmith shop. This black group was granted permission by Asbury to conduct worship services, yet with a white pastor.

In 1799 Asbury ordained Allen as a deacon. Conflict continued concerning the ownership of property and the role of whites as leaders over this congregation. Other black congregations in New Jersey, Delaware, Maryland, and other states experienced similar problems. On April 9–11, 1816, black church bodies ruled by whites met at Bethel AMEC in Philadelphia, seeking their independence

Mrs. Juliann Jane Tillman, preacher in the African Methodist Episcopal Church. (Drawn from life by Alfred M. Hoffy; printed by Peter S. Duval; Philadelphia, 1844.) Courtesy of the Library of Congress.

from the Methodist church. The Bethel church sued for independence before the Supreme Court of Pennsylvania, and the court granted its plea. When Daniel Coker (1840–1898) was elected bishop of the Philadelphia church, he declined the offer, and Richard Allen became the first bishop to serve. They followed the teachings of the Methodist Church as established by John Wesley. Today, bishops are the head officers of the church, there are 19 episcopal districts worldwide, and the church organization is managed with annual conferences conducted by the bishops. The AMEC soon became a missionary denomination. In 1827, Scipio Bean went to Haiti as a missionary. Native American Indians were evangelized in the Southwest. Henry McNeil Turner (1834–1915) established most of the AMEC churches in Georgia and other **southern** states. President Abraham Lincoln appointed Turner chaplain of the Negro troops in 1863. He continued his appointment until President Johnson appointed him the first chaplain of the regular U.S. Army. Turner also established AMEC congregations in West and South Africa.

The AMEC is a revivalistic church that believes in **conversion, sanctification,** a life of joy and obedience, and the witness of the Spirit. Some leading AMEC revivalists of the nineteenth century were Jarena Lee, Abraham Grant, and **Amanda Smith,** while in the twentieth century there were Vashti McKenzie and Frank Madison Reid. One AMEC characteristic is a strong emphasis on education. In 1844 the General Convention issued five letters arguing for an educated ministry with an outline of study and the AMEC leadership began their tradition of educational ideals. By 1852, Daniel A. Payne (1811–1893) was elected bishop, and he worked to improve education for all AMEC members. With backing from the white Methodist Episcopal Church, the AMEC founded and ultimately gained full ownership of Wilberforce University in Ohio. It was founded in 1856, and Payne became the first black president of a college in America. The AMEC has the oldest continuous publication for African Americans, the *Christian Recorder,* which first appeared in 1854. From 1797 until his death in 1831, Allen operated a station on the Underground Railroad for escaping slaves, and this work was continued by Bethel AME Church in Philadelphia until Emancipation. The AMEC organization has more religious schools and colleges abroad than any other black denomination in the United States. These include schools in South Africa, England, Haiti, and other countries. The AMEC currently has a membership of 3.6 million, and participates in the National Council of Churches, the World Council of Churches, and such country conferences such as the Caribbean Conference.

Further Reading: African Methodist Episcopal Church Web site. http://www.amecnet.org/; Campbell, James T. *Songs of Zion: The African Methodist Episcopal Church in the United States and South Africa.* New York: Oxford University Press, 1995; Pinn, Anne H., and Anthony B. Pinn. *Fortress Introduction to Black Church History.* Minneapolis: Fortress Press, 2002; Walker, Clarence Earl. *A Rock in a Weary Land: The African Methodist Episcopal Church during the Civil War and Reconstruction.* Baton Rouge: Louisiana State University Press, 1982; Williams, Gilbert Anthony. *The Christian Recorder, Newspaper of the African Methodist Episcopal Church … 1854–1902.* Jefferson, NC: McFarland, 1996.

Sherry Sherrod DuPree

AFRICAN METHODIST EPISCOPAL ZION CHURCH

The African Methodist Episcopal Zion Church (AMEZ) takes its origin from a group led by James Varick, starting in 1796. Together with the **African Methodist Episcopal Church** (AMEC), it is one of two **Methodist** groups that emerged during the 1780s and 1790s to become a black denomination. After many meetings and discussions with Methodist Episcopal Church leaders, a congregation was chartered in 1801 as the African Methodist Episcopal Church of New York City. This black group was granted permission from Bishop **Francis Asbury** to conduct services of worship, but with a white pastor. The AMEC of New York claims to be the first Methodist black church to separate from the Methodist Episcopal Church in the United States. It officially voted itself out of the Methodist Episcopal Church in 1820. Throughout the 1800s, the AMEC of New York was the second-largest independent African American Methodist denomination in the United States. In 1848, the General Conference of the AMEC of New York city voted to add *Zion* to the end of its name in honor of the first congregation and in order to distinguish it from the African Methodist Episcopal Church based in Philadelphia. In 1864, the first AMEZ church to be found in the **South** was the St. Peter AMEZ Church in New Bern, North Carolina. Many new AMEZ congregations were established in the South after the **Civil War.** In 1880 at the AMEZ General Conference assembly meeting in Montgomery, Alabama, the Foreign Mission Board and the Ladies' Mission Society were formed. From its beginning, the AMEZ has followed a policy of nondiscriminatory access to the Communion table.

During the late 1800s the AMEZ expanded outside of the United States. In 1876, Andrew Cartwright organized the first AMEZ churches in Brewerville, Liberia, West Africa. In 1888,

Cartwright organized the first **foreign mission** school with both male and female students. John Bryan Small—who was born and raised in Barbados—came to the United States in 1871, joined the AMEZ Church, and in 1896 became AMEZ bishop to Africa. Small's contribution to the AMEZ Church was to send young Africans to be trained as missionaries in the United States at Livingstone College in North Carolina. Small established the *Zion Missionary Seer Newsletter* to stimulate work in foreign fields. The first two **women** given leadership roles in the AMEZ church were Deacon Julia Foote (ordained 1894) and Elder Mary J. Small (ordained 1895). The AMEZ was second to the **Primitive Methodists** among Methodist bodies in recognizing women as church leaders.

The AMEZ Church has always been a leader in the struggle for freedom, and it numbers among its members **Sojourner Truth,** Frederick Douglass, and Harriet Tubman. During the anti-slavery movement, many AMEZ churches were stations on the Underground Railroad. Martin Luther King Jr. and the civil rights Montgomery bus boycott depended on leaders from the AMEZ church. These included pastors who worked with the Montgomery Improvement Association in Alabama, such as S. S. Seay, E. N. French, and W. J. Powell. King's wife, Coretta Scott King, was a member of the AMEZ church in Marian, Alabama, and her brother is a pastor in the AMEZ Church. The AMEZ Church has joined the Consultation on Church Union (COCU), the Pan Methodist Council, and the World Methodist Council (WMC). It has its headquarters in Lake Junaluska, North Carolina, and has 1.5 million members as of 2004. Twelve active bishops and five retired bishops constitute the governing body of the AMEZ church. The church professes the 25 Articles of Religion that John Wesley extracted from the Church of England's Thirty-nine Articles. It is a revivalistic church that believes in **conversion, sanctification,** a life of joy and obedience, and the witness of the spirit. The New York City AMEZ church, located in Harlem, is known as "the Mother Church." The AMEZ operates four colleges in the United States: Livingstone College in Salisbury, North Carolina; Clinton Junior College in Rock Hill, South Carolina; Lomax-Hannon Bible College in Greenville, Alabama; and Hood Theological Seminary in Salisbury, North Carolina. The AMEZ church has two colleges in West Africa, located in Liberia and Nigeria.

Further Reading: DuPree, Sherry Sherrod. *African-American Holiness Pentecostal Movement: An Annotated Bibliography.* New York: Garland, 1996; Hoggard, James Clinton. *The African Methodist Episcopal Zion Church, 1972–1996: A Bicentennial Commemorative History.* Charlotte, NC: AME Zion, 1998; Hood, J. W. *One Hundred Years of the African Methodist Episcopal Zion Church, or The Centennial of African Methodism.* Chapel Hill: Academic Affairs Library, University of North Carolina, 2001; Johnson, Dorothy Sharpe, and Lula Goolsby Williams. *Pioneering Women of the African Methodist Episcopal Zion Church.* Charlotte, NC: AME Zion, 1996; Pinn, Anne H., and Anthony B. Pinn. *Fortress Introduction to Black Church History.* Minneapolis: Fortress Press, 2002; Walls, William J. *The African American Episcopal Zion Church: Reality of the Black Church.* Charlotte, NC: AME Zion, 1974.

Sherry Sherrod DuPree

AGLOW INTERNATIONAL (WOMEN'S AGLOW)

Aglow International (AI; previously Women's Aglow Fellowship International) is an interdenominational parachurch ministry of Christian **women** ministering to women—"a network of caring women"—with special emphasis on charismatic spirituality and evangelism. It seeks to augment, and not to compete with, activities of local churches and denominations. AI began in Seattle, Washington, in 1967 as the Full Gospel Women's Fellowship (FGWF), a women's counterpart to the charismatic **Full Gospel Business Men's Fellowship International.** By 1972, FGWF had grown to 60 groups meeting throughout the United States, and in 1973, it became international, with fellowships in Canada and New Zealand. In 2004, AI reported operating through more than 3,500 local groups in 155 nations, of which some 1,400 (called "Lighthouses") are in the United States. Today it is the world's largest Christian organization for ministry by women and to women.

Worldwide, these groups—the heart of AI—reportedly reach an estimated 2 million women each month through the "two foundational pillars" of **prayer** and evangelism (including outreach to incarcerated women), friendship, and deeds of practical care. R. Marie Griffith's recent study of AI found that the group offers an experience of deliverance from shame, and especially the shame of victimization by males. The themes of secrecy, and healing through self-disclosure, permeate the spoken messages and printed testimonials. With its stress on women supporting women, AI has more in common with feminist groups, says Griffith, than might at first appear. AI's Trinitarian, evangelical beliefs include the distinctively charismatic belief in the **baptism in the Holy Spirit** evidenced by **speaking in tongues** and in the continuing operation of all of the **charismatic gifts.** Much like the churches of the recent **Apostolic movement,** AI follows the model of "biblical apostolic government," with final authority resting in a self-perpetuating board of directors headed by one president and chief executive officer, currently Jane Hansen, who has led AI since 1980.

Responding to the challenge (of 2003 National Conference guest speaker Barbara Yoder) to "speak the language of the next dimension," in 2004 AI stated its mission anew: "To help restore and mobilize women around the world; to promote gender reconciliation in the Body of Christ as God designed; to amplify awareness of global concerns from a Biblical perspective" ("Mission Statement," www.aglow.org). If this language seems cooler than the charismatic fervency in which AI was born, both leaders and members serving locally continue to report events typical of charismatic renewal—women being **converted,** undergoing **deliverance** from addictions, experiencing **healing,** being baptized in the Holy Spirit, and ministered to through various charismatic gifts. They continue to report such events in fervent charismatic language that evinces influences also from the so-called Third Wave neo-Pentecostal movement and the Apostolic movement. Moreover, recent communications show

that AI is progressing toward its goal of establishing AI in every nation.

From its outset, AI pioneered parachurch charismatic women's ministry. But during its life, ministry opportunities for American charismatic women have multiplied as denominations have revised traditional "ladies' auxiliaries" into "women's ministries" and as newer, independent ministries led by women influence many through well-attended conferences and print, broadcast, and online media. No longer the only large, charismatic women's parachurch ministry, AI has distinguished itself by combining traditional activities and methods (e.g., prayer, evangelism, one-to-one ministry in local groups) with shifts in focus—from marital harmony through submission to the husband's authority to a broader mandate of "gender reconciliation," and from emotional and spiritual wholeness to racial reconciliation, international ministry to Muslims, and support for Israel and Jews. After nearly four decades, AI, an offspring of the **Charismatic Revival and Renewal** of the mid-twentieth century, helps sustain that revival in its contemporary forms.

Further Reading: Aglow International Web site, www.aglow.com; Brasher, Brenda E. *Godly Women: Fundamentalism and Female Power.* New Brunswick, NJ: Rutgers University Press, 1998; Griffith, R. Marie. *God's Daughters: Evangelical Women and the Power of Submission.* Berkeley: University of California Press, 1997.

Mark E. Roberts

ALLEN, RICHARD (1760–1831)

Richard Allen was a pioneering figure in **African American** Christianity in the United States, and is generally regarded as the first national black leader. Born into slavery, Allen taught himself to read and worked to free himself. He went to Philadelphia in 1786 and began efforts with Absalom Jones (1746–1818)—and other African Americans from the St. George's Methodist Church—to **preach** to blacks in the city. His efforts culminated in the founding of the **African Methodist Episcopal Church** (AMEC) in Philadelphia in 1816. Allen's colleague in ministry, Absalom Jones, was the first African American priest of the (Protestant)

Portraits of Rev. Richard Allen (in the center) and other African Methodist Episcopal Church leaders, with scenes that include Wilberforce University, Payne Institute, missionaries in Haiti, and the AME book depository in Philadelphia. Lithoprint. (Boston: J. H. Daniels, ca. 1876.) Courtesy of the Library of Congress.

Episcopal Church, and, like Allen, he had taught himself to read and had labored for his own emancipation.

One Sunday in November 1787, St. George's Methodist Church restricted the movement of the African Americans. They were told by the ushers to move to the balcony, without telling them they could not use the front seats in the balcony. Jones and other black parishioners were pulled from their knees as they were **praying.** These African Americans walked out of St. George's Church, never to return. Several months previously, in April 1787, Allen and Jones and others had organized the Free African Society, a mutual-aid society dedicated to the **abolition** of slavery. It was the first independent African American society in the United States. In 1792, these African Americans decided to erect a church building. Allen and Jones voted to build a **Methodist** church, while most members said they were disappointed with the Methodist Church. They voted instead for an Episcopalian church because of friendly associations

through the mission group Thomas Bray Associates. Therefore the two church groups started constructing buildings for Methodists and Episcopalians at the same time. Jones's church was dedicated in 1794 as the St. Thomas African Episcopal Church. Jones was made the leader as a deacon and licensed as a lay reader. Allen's church was also dedicated in 1794, named the Bethel African Methodist Episcopal Church, and Allen served there as pastor until his death. In 1799, Bishop **Francis Asbury** ordained Allen as the first black deacon in the Methodist church. He was ordained an elder and consecrated as the first bishop among the various African American groups.

Allen's leadership extended far beyond the church. He and Jones helped to found the African Masonic Lodge in 1798. In 1804 Allen organized the Society of Free People of Color for the Promoting the Instruction and School Education of Children of African Descent. In 1809, Allen and Jones founded the Society for the Suppression of Vice and Immorality. Allen opposed plans of the American Colonization Society for resetting free blacks in Africa. In 1876, a statue of Allen was erected in Fairmount Park, Philadelphia—the first such commemoration of a black leader by black people in the United States.

Further Reading: Allen, Richard. *The Life Experience and Gospel Labors of the Rt. Rev. Richard Allen.* Nashville, TN: Abingdon Press, 1983; Mathews, Marcia M. *Richard Allen.* Baltimore: Helicon, 1963; Mwadilifu, Mwalimu I. *Richard Allen: The First Exemplar of African-American Education.* New York: ECA Associates, 1985; Williams, Juan, and Quinton Dixie. *This Far by Faith: Stories from the African American Religious Experience.* New York: Willow Morrow, 2003.

Sherry Sherrod DuPree

ALLINE, HENRY (1748–1784)

Henry Alline led a major religious revival among the New England settlers of Nova Scotia during the years of the American Revolution. He began his public **preaching** in 1776 and continued as an indefatigable and charismatic religious leader until his death from consumption in 1784. His ministry had a significant impact in shaping the response of the New England settlers to the momentous changes taking place in their corner of the Atlantic world.

In 1760, Alline's family, along with many others from New England, moved to lands in Nova Scotia made available by the expulsion of the Acadians during the Seven Years' War. Alline's path to **conversion** followed a typical New England Puritan pattern as he went through several stages of deepening despair at his sinful condition. His wrenching account of a conversion experience on March 26, 1775, begins with a religious awakening at eight years of age, and an intensifying sense of wretchedness as he experienced the sexual urges of his teenage years. He was burdened with guilt because of his "frolicking and carnal mirth" with other young people. Only when he reached a state of hopelessness was he able to experience release through conversion. Alline's sudden rapture was such a classic case that William James cited it in his *Varieties of Religious Experience* (1902).

Alline planned to return to Boston to prepare for a ministerial career, but war and revolution intervened. When American privateers seized the ship he had boarded, he returned to his family in Falmouth. Alline never received any formal training in theology, and this may account for the composite and often confused nature of his doctrinal writings. For him the urgent issue was to reconcile the stern **Calvinist** God who predestined only a few for salvation with a God of love who freely offered salvation to all. Instead of resolving this theological problem, Alline simply lumped together the two images of God. He spoke of a Calvinist God whose unchangeable plan for humans had existed from eternity, while insisting that all **men** and **women** could seek, achieve, and be assured of conversion. Alline's message engendered intense experiences in his mixed male and female audiences. He himself claimed to have been "ravished by the spirit," and testimony from contemporary witnesses suggests that many hearers, especially females, had almost erotic sensations of emotional release during his revival meetings. Some readers judged Alline's writings to be incomprehensible, and John Wesley dismissed them as "miserable jargon" (Bumsted, 19). Even Alline's followers puzzled over them. Once the **ecstasy** of conversion had passed and churches had been established, they ignored his views. Alline himself was impatient with church forms and ceremonies. He avoided committing himself on such basic matters as infant or adult baptism, dismissing all such matters as nonessential.

His early death, and theological crudeness, blocked Alline from having a clear-cut institutional impact. Yet his style gave shape to the **Free Will Baptist** movement, and his followers formed many Baptist congregations. Alline's followers were mostly poor, distrusted by the British, and harried by the Americans. In these threatening circumstances, Alline's confident leadership instilled a sense of community and common destiny among his followers in Nova Scotia. His preaching itineraries crisscrossed the colony, linking isolated pockets of people who had experienced little interaction before this religious outburst shook their lives. In the midst of the upheaval of the Revolutionary

War, the New Englanders in Nova Scotia drew on their Puritan religious traditions, transformed them through the agency of Alline, and created new evangelical Christian communities. Instead of being mere victims of the Atlantic civil war, Alline's followers came to believe that their "lines had fallen in pleasant places" (Psalm 16:6). The religious revival helped Nova Scotians through a time of historical crisis by enabling them to continue living purposefully in the British Empire when most of their relatives back in New England had become part of the new United States.

Further Reading: Bumsted, J. M. "Henry Alline." *Dictionary of Canadian Biography* (1979); Rawlyk, G. A. *Ravished by the Spirit: Religious Revivals, Baptists and Henry Alline.* Kingston, ON: McGill-Queens University Press, 1984; Stewart, Gordon T., ed. *Documents Relating to the Great Awakening in Nova Scotia, 1760–1791.* Toronto: Champlain Society, 1982; Stewart, Gordon T., and G. A. Rawlyk. *A People Highly Favoured of God: The Nova Scotia Yankees and the American Revolution.* Toronto: Macmillan, 1972; Stewart, Gordon T. "Charisma and Integrations: A North American Case." *Comparative Studies in Society and History* 16 (1974): 138–49.

Gordon T. Stewart

ALPHA COURSE

The Alpha Course is an evangelistic parachurch ministry currently being used in 7,300 congregations in North America and some 30,000 congregations around the world, including mainline Protestant, **Roman Catholic,** evangelical, **Charismatic, Pentecostal,** and nondenominational churches. Today approximately 7 million people have completed the Alpha Course. Rev. Charles Marnham (b. 1951) began the Alpha program in 1977 at Holy Trinity Brompton, a large Charismatic Anglican church in central London. He developed Alpha as a way to present the essentials of the Christian faith to new believers. Rev. Nicky Gumbel (b. 1955), another Anglican clergyman at Holy Trinity, took over responsibility for the Alpha Course in 1990 and soon realized that Alpha could be used for evangelizing non-Christians as well as instructing Christians. When spiritual seekers began to register in the course as a part of their journey into faith, Gumbel modified the course to fit their needs. A process of adaptation over 14 years resulted in the Alpha course as it exists today—15 talks given over a 10-week period of time with a retreat weekend to discuss the person and work of the Holy Spirit.

Three factors contributed to the emergence of Alpha: the postmodern spiritual climate of central London, the post-Christian atmosphere pervading Britain today, and the passionate spirituality that is characteristic of Holy Trinity Brompton. Today's non-Christians and post-Christians are seldom ready to make an impromptu faith decision of the sort required in traditional mass evangelism with its **altar call.** Consequently Alpha provides for a gradual process with dialogue between spiritual seekers and church members. Alpha could be described as "dinner, a talk, and some conversation." Alpha is friendship based and involves no hype and no pressure. During an Alpha course, no question is considered out of bounds, too hostile, or too naive. No sincere statement is regarded as too argumentative. No one "chases a seeker down," but participants are free to come and go at their own pace. On the other hand, each Alpha conversation arises out of a presentation of 45–60 minutes with definite theological and intellectual content. This helps to insure that Alpha conversations are not based on mutual ignorance.

Alpha has been employed in a wide variety of churches in the United Kingdom, the United States, and 138 other countries. Currently the program has been translated into 50 languages. The earliest denominations in the United States to adopt the Alpha Course were mainline Protestant churches such the Episcopal Church USA, the United **Methodist** Church, and the **Presbyterian** Church (PCUSA). Research suggests that only 1 percent of mainline Protestant churches in the United States gain even one new member through **conversion** per year, and of those churches in the 1 percent, 75 percent are using the Alpha Course. Alpha continues to spread to new countries, new denominations, and prisons, schools, colleges, universities, and specially targeted urban centers.

Alpha meetings—this one in a prison—bring believers and nonbelievers together to discuss faith issues. The circular seating reflects Alpha's unpressured and nonhierarchical approach to Christian evangelism. Courtesy of Alpha USA.

Further Reading: Alpha Web site. http://alphausa.org/; Gumbel, Nicky. *Alpha Course Manual.* London: Holy Trinity Brompton, 1999; Gumbel, Nicky. *How to Run an Alpha Course: Director Manual.* Elgin, IL: David C. Cook, 1998.

Todd Hunter

ALTAR CALL

In an altar call, a **preacher** or evangelist asks individuals to come forward to the front of a church, building, or other space as a sign of spiritual commitment. The physical acts of arising, standing, and walking forward in public view are outward marks of an inward change. Coming forward signifies faith in God and repentance from sin. Some churches regard the very act of coming forward as equivalent to **conversion.** It may also be an act of testimony whereby a person publicly attests to his or her own newfound faith. Associated with the altar call is the "mourners' bench" or "anxious bench" at the front of the church sanctuary where spiritual seekers go to sit. Terms such as *anxious bench* are often used interchangeably with *altar call* to denote the same set of practices.

From the 1790s onward, the altar call has been one of the most distinctive rituals of American revivalism. Yet scholars debate its origins. No Christian church seems to have used anything like the altar call prior to the 1700s. Some argue that John Wesley and other early **Methodists** used the altar call in their evangelistic ministry in the mid-1700s, yet evidence is lacking to support the claim. In those rare instances where Wesley's *Journal* speaks of someone standing and coming forward during a church service, this seems to have happened without any prompting from the preacher. There is no indication that Wesley self-consciously used the altar call as part of his evangelistic practice. The documents related to **George Whitefield, Gilbert Tennent, Jonathan Edwards,** and other revival preachers of the 1700s are also conspicuously lacking in references to the altar call. David Bennett has examined the evidence related to the origin of the altar call and traces the practice back to the 1790s and possibly the 1780s. British Christians in the early 1800s referred to it as "the American custom," and it seems that the altar call first became a regular practice in the United States rather than Britain. By the early 1800s, the new evangelistic method involved a preacher who called for decision, exhorters on the lookout for anxious souls, and a special place for sitting or kneeling. The Separate Baptists, led by **Shubal Stearns,** may have begun using the altar call in the late 1790s.

In an altar call, the person who comes forward is not necessarily regarded as a convert but possibly as an inquirer or seeker in need of advice and **prayer.** In Methodism during the late 1700s and early 1800s, a mourners' bench was set aside at the front of the sanctuary for people who had unsuccessfully sought to attain a conversion experience. Early Methodist accounts describe "mourners" weeping for their sins, encircled by those praying for them, while others nearby **shouted,** sang, or **laughed** in the joy of a new conversion. The mourners' bench was a study in contrasts. In **African American** tradition, a would-be convert might be surrounded by others who prayed for hours or days for that person to "pass through." Conversion was a lengthy ordeal. Beginning in the 1820s, the mourners' bench became known as the anxious bench, and the change in terms suggests a shift from sadness to anxiety as a dominant emotion. During the twentieth century, the altar call was less associated with emotion. A **Billy Graham** rally does not generally involve weeping or shouting. Decisions for Christ are calm and cool. Yet **Pentecostal revivals** have often preserved the intense emotionalism associated with early Methodist revivals, the **Great Awakening,** and the **Second Great Awakening.** Pentecostal altar calls may be dramatic, cathartic, and emotion-drenched.

An altar call involves people who play differing roles. An evangelist asks for a public display of faith. A congregation prays and waits for people to come forward. Individuals struggle over whether or not to come forward. Already convinced Christians, seated in the congregation, may encourage their friends or family member to come forward. They might even walk the aisle with them as a sign of support. When the individual who comes forward arrives in front, he or she may be asked to consult with a pastor or pastoral assistant or to have church members pray with him or her and for him or her. Over time the altar call has assumed a diversity of forms. Evangelists might ask people to signify their spiritual commitment by raising their hand in the air or standing in place rather than walking to the front. Another custom is for everyone to bow their heads and close their eyes and for those making decisions to raise hands in the air. Only the preacher is supposed to see whose hand has gone up. This is not so much a public declaration of faith but a private transaction between God, the preacher, and the convert. Preachers, moreover, can and do use altar calls to signify something other than a first-time faith decision. An altar call may be used for "rededication" to the Lord (after a period of sin or indifference), for consecration to God (e.g., **sanctification** as taught by the Methodist and **Holiness** traditions), or for a special vocation (e.g., missionary work). In the last case, the altar call is hard to distinguish from ordination. Church leaders or members lay on hands and pray for a special endowment for ministry. Pentecostal altar calls may be wide-ranging in scope. Sinners may come forward for conversion, the sick for **healing,** lapsed believers for spiritual restoration, demon-possessed persons for exorcism, and drunkards and drug users for **deliverance** from addiction. In Pentecostal churches, ordinary Christians seek the **baptism of the Holy Spirit,** the ability to **speak in tongues,** or another new spiritual gift. A fresh impartation of the Holy Spirit may cause someone to fall to the ground in the event known as being "slain in the Spirit." There are a variety of practices and meanings included in the altar call.

Since its first emergence as a regular evangelistic practice, the altar call has been continuously controversial. Books and articles defending or attacking the practice have appeared from the 1820s until the present. The best-known early practitioner was **Charles Grandison Finney,** who was the first revival preacher to offer an explicit defense of the altar call, or anxious bench, as it became known. The anxious bench was part and parcel of Finney's evangelistic summons to immediate decision. Conversion lay in the power of the sinner who resolved to "make himself a new heart." The anxious bench suited Finney's theology of the self-determining individual. Yet it also provoked vehement opposition. **Calvinists** were scandalized by the implication that people could choose to undergo conversion when and where they themselves chose. Conversion, Calvinists believed, came through divine and not human initiative. Furthermore, a hidden and often mysterious process such as conversion could not easily be pinpointed. Finney's critic at Princeton, Albert Dod, argued that decisions made in a time of excitement were often spurious and fleeting. The altar call offered false confidence to the spiritually uncertain. The act of walking to an altar did not save anyone, and yet this was the common impression, reinforced by popular evangelists. The altar call allowed preachers to use emotional manipulation to swell their ranks of supposed converts. John Williamson Nevin's *The Anxious Bench* (1843) lambasted the altar call for diverting attention from a genuine evangelistic concern (do I believe or not?) to a pseudo-issue (will I walk or not?). Nevin held that doctrinal instruction through the catechism, coupled with the sacraments of baptism and the Lord's Supper, were the proper, God-given means of nurturing Christian faith. For Nevin, Finney and his followers mistakenly regarded the altar call as a quasi sacrament conferring grace. C. H. Spurgeon—a Calvinistic Baptist preacher in London—offered a different criticism. He compared the sinner under conviction of sin to a wounded deer, shot with an arrow and seeking seclusion. A soul, awakened to its own unworthiness, wanted privacy with God. The altar call, by impelling seekers to come forward publicly, encouraged self-righteous displays of piety rather than genuine contrition over sin.

During the late nineteenth century and twentieth century, the altar call became a fixture in American revivalism. **Dwight Lyman Moody, Billy Sunday, Aimee Semple McPherson, Billy Graham, Oral Roberts,** and thousands of lesser-known evangelists and ministers conducted altar calls and developed them into distinctive forms. Billy Sunday's converts shook hands with the evangelist. Billy Graham's "inquirers" came forward for spiritual counseling with volunteer workers. Eventually the altar call became a fixture in American culture. "Come to Jesus," in everyday parlance, refers to any critical moment of decision. Critics of the altar call still exist, especially among traditional Protestants, and yet the practice is too entrenched in American revivalism and evangelistic practice to disappear anytime soon. For better or for worse, faith decisions find tangible expression in a walk to the front of the room.

Further Reading: Bennett, David. *The Altar Call: Its Origins and Present Usage.* Lanham, MD: University Press of America, 2000; McLendon, H. R. "The Mourner's Bench." ThD dissertation, Southern Baptist Theological Seminary, 1902; Murray, Iain. *Revival and Revivalism.* Edinburgh: Banner of Truth Trust, 1994; Nevin, John Williamson. *The Anxious Bench.* Chambersburg, PA: 1843; Streett, R. Allen. "The Public Invitation: Its Nature, Biblical Validity, and Practicability." PhD dissertation, California Graduate School of Theology, 1982.

Michael J. McClymond

AMANA COMMUNITY

The Amana Community of central Iowa traces its origin to a radical **Pietist** movement in Germany known as the Inspirationists, or the Communities of the True Inspiration, from 1714. This German group derived from an earlier spiritual movement in France. Believing they were experiencing an endtime outpouring of the Holy Spirit, **ecstatic** prophets and prophetesses in France fled the renewed persecution against Huguenots (i.e., French Protestants) that started after 1685. Their ecstatic messages were accompanied by convulsive and catatonic behavior and apparent manifestations of **speaking in tongues** or glossolalia—presented as the voice of God—and ecstatic **prayer** directed to God. The central message of these French prophets was a call for repentance in the face of an impeding apocalyptic ending to history. As the "church of the desert" (Revelation 12:6), they saw themselves in **eschatological** distress, persecuted by the Christendom of their day.

Some Inspirationists sought refuge in London among Huguenot emigrant communities there, where their radicalism forced them into sectarian exclusion. They took refuge among **Quakers** and Philadelphians, who also manifested an ecstatic and **enthusiastic** spirituality driven by eschatology. Pamphlet warfare ensued with the forces of "Babel" (i.e., the Protestant churches), and this moved the Inspirationists from a solely oral to a written or scribal tradition of **prophetic** transmission. These texts assumed canonical importance in their movement, second only to scripture. Evangelistic forays across the Continent began in 1709, until the community transplanted itself in Berlin and Halle, and from there into Pietist centers in western Germany, where they won converts. Their leaders in the Wetterau district and the principality of Wittgenstein were Eberhard Ludwig Grube and Johann Friedrich Rock. Their goal was to gather the true children of God into end-time eschatological communities. Their fervor led to frequent altercations and arrests at the hands of civil authorities. Although they held love feasts and foot-washing ceremonies, their unity was imperiled by dissension among their leaders, with the more radical factions rejecting all forms of organization. In the midst of that fray, Gruber was elevated to the rank of "Overseer of the Prophet Children." He conducted visitations to the Inspirationist communities, and instituted directors for the communities who collaborated in elders' conferences. Gruber produced a catechism for children and a hymnal, the *Davidisches Psalterspiel*, and the prophets published sensational pronouncements that became influential in the history of German Romantic literature. A decline of the gift of prophecy occurred by 1730 within the communities, and their numbers diminished. Their work had proceeded amid opposition from other Pietist groups, especially at Halle.

By the 1840s, a combination of poor crops in Germany and continuing persecution led the Inspirationists to consider emigration to America. The first Inspirationist community was established in 1843 on a Seneca Indian Reservation in Ebenezer, New York. Within a few years, the proximity of Buffalo (a mere 20 miles away) led the Inspirationists to seek out a more rural setting. A river valley in central Iowa, near Iowa City, became the permanent home for the Inspirationists beginning in 1855. Led by Barbara Heinemann and Christian Metz, they founded seven prosperous villages that

grew until their membership reached 1,800 by 1880. By 1861, the original 3,300 acres owned by the Amana Community had expanded to 26,000. The Amana Society differed from other communal groups in relying on multiple charismatic leaders (known as *Werkzeugen*, or God's "instruments") rather than a single figure. All their goods were held in common. **Men** and **women** sat separately in worship, and celibacy was regarded as preferable to marriage. Inspirationists believed in baptism through the Spirit and not by water. They held daily prayer meetings and two worship services on Sundays. The Great Depression brought economic difficulties to the Amana Community, and a failure to replace the *Werkzeugen* weakened the community's spiritual foundation. Due to dissension, their communal structure was disbanded in 1932, when seven independent congregations were formed and their communal assets were channeled into a joint stock company.

Further Reading: Barthel, Diane L. *Amana: From Pietist Sect to American Community*. Lincoln: University of Nebraska Press, 1984; Shambaugh, Bertha M. H. *Amana, the Community of True Inspiration*. 1908. Reprint, n.p.: Penfield Press, 1988.

J. Steven O'Malley

AMEN CORNER

The term *Amen Corner* traditionally refers to a location in an **African American** church building near the front, usually on the side. Among black **Baptists,** the Amen Corner is the deacons' row or section. Among black **Holiness-Pentecostal** Christians—the special focus of this essay—this section is usually the place where missionaries, the "Mother of the Church," and other **women** and **men pray** before the service begins. These parishioners, sometimes known as "seasoned saints" or "anointed saints," come as David before the Lord. They drive out evil spirits, know God's Word, and know how to pray and get answers from God. They encourage the **preacher** and keep the services lively with "Holy Ghost encounters." They are spiritual cheerleaders, leaders of testimonies as to how the Lord has delivered, altar workers, or missionaries who visit the sick. They may sit with their Bible and a fan or handkerchief in hand, supporting the reading of scripture. On special occasions such as revivals or funerals, they will wear all white garments, including their underclothes and shoes.

In the **South** the saints of the Amen Corner may walk to church singing and praying to encourage others to come to church. If the pastor says, "Give the Lord 47"—a reference to clapping in praise of God in Psalm 47—then the Amen Corner will lead the hand clapping. As the preacher is delivering his sermon, the Amen Corner will respond, reaching a feverish pitch of **shouts** at the climax of the sermon. When the choir sings, "I know the Lord will make a way," the Amen Corner will lead the audience in a response by saying, "Yes he will," or the pastor will say, "What is his name?" and the response will be "Jesus." The people in the Amen Corner moan and echo the leader in words and rhymes. They may say, "Don't hold back, let go and let God," "Have your way, Jesus," "Holy Ghost, come," "Do the work of the Lord," "Go ahead," "Lift him up, Jesus," "Speak through him, Jesus," "That's all right," or "Come, Lord Jesus," or use other short and honored phrases to encourage the preacher and congregation. The saints of the Amen Corner trigger changes in the service, with shouts uttered, bodies swaying, hands clapping, feet stomping, or steps **danced.** With their spiritual discernment, they can see through the disguises of non-Christians. During the service, they may feel detached from their surroundings and pay no attention to the passage of time. The saints of the Amen Corner may be shaking on the benches, **speaking in tongues,** or urging the unsaved to get saved. They may be weak in body but strong in faith—praying with their hands, blessing others, and bringing a rejuvenation of goodwill and health. They act in love and peace to advance God's kingdom.

Many phrases are used in the Amen Corner. Some of the following exclamations may be shouted: "Deliver, Lord," "Make a way," "Power, Lord," "Pray my strength in the Lord," "Holy Ghost, have your way," "Yes, Lord," "My provider," "Hear him," "Work in me, Jesus," "My soul, you are a wonder," "Bless them, Lord," "Help me, Jesus," "Hear my

prayer, oh Lord," "God knows," and "Thank you, Jesus." Other exclamations come when the sermon is coming forth: "So true," "Amen," "Get knowledge," "I'm trusting in you," "The Word, the Word," "Say it now," "Come on now," "Talk, sir," "Yeah," "Walk in the Spirit," "Stand still," and "I will go." Certain phrases pertain to Jesus: "He's worthy of your praise," "Trust in him," "Seek him," "Glory," "Praise the Lord," "Glory to God," "Thank you, Jesus," "Don't be ashamed," "Praise God," and "Pray." Sometimes the clichés are repeated many times in a rhyme or to the tune of music. For example, the song "Yes Lord" from the **Church of God in Christ** may involve one repeated word ("Yes, yes, yes, yes, yes, yes"), two repeated words ("Yes Lord, yes Lord, yes Lord, yes Lord, yes Lord, yes Lord"), or a repeated phrase ("Yes to your will, yes to your way"), and so on.

Today, in opening church services, some African American churches have "praise teams" who initiate worship with songs and praises. The raising of hands, clapping, and hand shaking and hugs with people around them prepare everyone for the sermon. Testimonies are now often omitted. As the sermon reaches its climax, musicians give musical chords to highlight the sermon phrases. An audience caught up in **ecstasy** and enthusiasm and those "happy in the Lord" will shout, "Amen," "Talk to me," or other phrases. This is a modern-day Amen Corner, no longer limited to one part of the sanctuary but instead involving everyone present. In such contemporary services, every person has become an Amen Corner and may shout, "Hallelujah" or "Give the Lord a praise." A literary portrait of the Amen Corner appears in the play *The Amen Corner* (1968) by renowned African American author James Baldwin. He based his description on his formative experiences in a New York City Pentecostal congregation during the 1930s.

Further Reading: DuPree, Sherry Sherrod. *African-American Holiness Pentecostal Movement: An Annotated Bibliography.* New York: Garland, 1996; DuPree, Sherry Sherrod, and Herbert C. DuPree. *African-American Good News (Gospel) Music.* Washington, DC: Middle Atlantic Regional Press, 1993; Hinson, Glenn. *Fire in My Bones: Transcendence and the Holy Spirit in African American Gospel.* Philadelphia: University of

Pennsylvania, 2000. International Gospel Music Hall of Fame and Museum Web site. http://www.gmhf.org/; Smitherman, Geneva. *Black Talk: Words and Phrases from the Hood to the Amen Corner*. Boston: Houghton Mifflin, 1994.

Sherry Sherrod DuPree

ANTI-REVIVALISM, HISTORY AND ARGUMENTS OF

In dealing with this topic, *anti-revivalism* has been taken in a strictly literal sense. While not a concerted movement, anti-revivalism has existed in various forms. Persons designated as anti-revivalist are those who resolutely oppose revivals. The term is not taken to mean anyone who is sympathetic to religious awakenings and criticizes some aspect of it, but rather to mean one who is opposed to both the theory and practice of revivals, and may work to hinder a revival. Criticizing a revival does not, in itself, make someone an anti-revivalist. What is more, opposition to *revivalists* is not the same as opposition to *revivals*. If revivalists are proud, flamboyant, and pretentious, their personalities may evoke negative reactions even among those who support revivals. *Webster's Third New International Dictionary* defines the term *revival* as "a period of religious awakening: renewed interest in religion." When revivals have occurred, there have usually been two thrusts—the revitalization of believers and the **conversion** of nonbelievers—and these two have often been combined. Throughout the history of Christianity there have been some who opposed the revitalization of the church or else endorsed it only on their own terms.

The arguments used by anti-revivalists vary, and at least four distinct lines of opposition to revivals can be distinguished. First, there are *rational critics* (e.g., **Charles Chauncy**), who base their arguments on a certain viewpoint regarding reason and emotion. They regard genuine religion as a calm, cool, rational affair that ought to be practiced without the interference of strong emotions. Since revivals, almost by definition, are highly emotional occasions, the proponents of rational religion may be opposed to revivals. Second, some *traditional Protestants* (including some **Lutherans, Calvinists,** and Anglicans or Episcopalians) have stressed proper order, discipline, and decorum in public worship. They support religious devotion when it is quiet and restrained, but not when loud, raucous, or uninhibited. These traditional Protestants are not anti-revivalists on principle, and yet may be sharply critical of revivals that involve wild and uncontrolled behavior. Third, there are *High Church* or *sacramental Protestants* (e.g., **Horace Bushnell, John Williamson Nevin**) who object to religious individualism and the idea that people receive salvation through an individual, idiosyncratic experience. Such sacramental thinkers stress the individual's organic connection to the community, and the importance of baptism, catechesis, and family for the nurturing of Christian faith. A single emotional experience, on this view, does not transform anyone into a Christian. Fourth, there are *secular critics* of revivals (e.g., Friedrich Engels, H. L. Mencken), who object not only to specific practices of revivalists but to their core message of salvation through Christ. These opponents may disbelieve in God, God's grace, Christ, sin, salvation, heaven, and hell. If they criticize and object or sneer and jeer at revivals, it is because they reject in substance what revivalists **preach** and what converts believe. In practice, these four forms of opposition to revivals overlap with one another, and are not always clearly distinguished.

In the New World, opposition to revival started in Puritan times. William Laud (1573–1645) was made archbishop of Canterbury in 1633 and harried the Puritans out of England in a campaign for strict religious conformity. During the 1620s and 1630s, the great Puritan migration to America took notable scholars, political leaders, and preachers to set up a Christian commonwealth on the bleak shores of New England. The Puritans regarded human nature as sinful, and so believed that the church was in need of periodic periods of renewal. Yet in New England, with each new decade after 1620, revival did not appear. The problem was not overt opposition, but worldliness and concentration on mundane things among laypeople. Increase Mather (1639–1723), pastor of Boston's Second

British artist William Hogarth depicts a reasonable teacher of Christian love (at the lectern) overshadowed by a fanatical preacher dangling images of a devil and a witch. The preacher's falling wig reveals the tonsure of a Catholic monk—a symbol of superstition for eighteenth-century England. Below is an agitated crowd, bystanders reviving an unconscious woman with smelling salts, a couple in the throes of passion, and an emotional gauge that runs from "LUST," "ecstacy," and "madness" to "despair," "madness," and "suicide." "Credulity, Superstition, and Fanaticism" (1762). Joseph Burke and Colin Caldwell, *Hogarth: The Complete Engravings*. New York: Harry N. Abrams, 1968.

THE JERKING EXERCISE. Vol. 1, p. 209

An artist's satire of revivals, called "The Jerking Exercise." Samuel Griswold Goodrich, *Recollections of a Lifetime, or Men and Things I Have Seen*, Vol. 1. New York: Miller, Orton & Co., 1857.

Church, said in 1678 that "the body of the rising Generation is a poor, perishing, unconverted, and (except the Lord pour down his Spirit) an undone Generation" (Hardman, 37 n.6). In 1679 the decline in spirituality was so pronounced that a "Reforming Synod" was called. One pastor, **Solomon Stoddard,** who served in **Northampton,** Massachusetts, from 1669 till his death in 1729, was not content to bemoan the situation, but with powerful preaching had five "harvests" (in 1679, 1683, 1696, 1712, and 1718) in which many people professed conversion.

From 1700 to 1720 there was little specific opposition to revivals, and yet a basis for later anti-revivalism was being laid. The Enlightenment in Britain ushered in Unitarianism, Deism, Arianism,

and other threats to Christian orthodoxy, and in time these tendencies found their way across the Atlantic. Perhaps the first overt opposition arose in connection with **Theodore Frelinghuysen,** a Dutch **Reformed** pastor who arrived from Holland in 1720. Almost immediately he offended the powerful pastors of the Dutch Church in New York, Henricus Boel and Gualtherus DuBois, with his animated preaching and **prayers.** When revival came to the four small churches around Raritan, New Jersey, to which Frelinghuysen was called, these men continued their hostility to him, and it may be said that they were the first recorded anti-revivalists in America. Boel and DuBois were angered with Frelinghuysen's **Pietism,** which

Author and artist, Watson Heston, offers a primitivist or animalist interpretation of revivals in this two-fold image titled, "Prototype of Methodist Revivals." *The Freethinkers' Pictorial Text-Book*, New York: The Truth Seeker Company, 1890, p. 127.

declared that people seeking eternal life must first undergo conviction of their sinful condition, leading to distress and an open **confession of sins.** Frelinghuysen taught that this sort of conversion experience was necessary for salvation. In his churches, he found the Dutch farmers more interested in gambling, drinking, and horse racing than in living a Christian life. While some of Frelinghuysen's sermons are extant, little is known regarding his 28-year ministry. The available evidence suggests that he initiated a spiritual awakening, although statistically its results were small. With his development of private devotional meetings, the transformation of his *voorlesers* (i.e., church officials) into lay preachers, and his insistence on a conversion experience, he anticipated by some 15 to 20 years many of the distinctive ideas and practices of the **Great Awakening.**

In Pennsylvania, a number of Presbyterian ministers were anti-revivalists. This Scotch-Irish Old Side party banded together for several purposes, and remained as a closed group of perhaps 20 members over 30 years. Robert Cross, Samuel Evans, and Francis Alison were its leaders, and their earliest demand was that all ministerial candidates make unconditional subscription to the Westminster Confession. Others in the synod opposed this, saying that creedal subscription was no guarantee of conversion. By 1734 the strife had broadened after William Tennent Sr. opened his school and attracted students who were very pro-revival. It became even more intense in 1738 when a new presbytery, New Brunswick, became a haven for the New Side, that is, those supporting the Great Awakening's beginning. When **George Whitefield** came from England in 1739, the anti-revivalists were infuriated that he joined forces with the New Side to further the revival. They became even more enraged with **Gilbert Tennent**'s sermon "The Danger of an Unconverted Ministry," preached in March 1740 and widely distributed. To the New Side, the Scotch-Irish subscriptionists opposed revivals simply because some of them were not converted, as Tennent claimed in his fiery sermon.

While Whitefield's preaching brought great crowds, it also brought much resistance. In truth, much of this resulted from his youthful brashness and self-promotion. He insisted on publishing his journal, so all could read his criticisms of constituted authority and established ministers, most of whom he considered anti-revivalist. Earlier, in England, he had crossed swords with several Church of England bishops in 1737 and 1738. Then, when he visited Harvard College in 1740, he made it a powerful enemy with comments on its discipline "at low ebb" and its "bad books." Whitefield's clergy baiting and inflammatory accusations against clergy were well planned, and as Harry Stout notes, "his pulpit rhetoric required antagonists" (Stout, 120). The controversies were a public relations dream come true, for they made front-page news, made him look like the underdog, and delighted the crowds who piled out to hear him. Although an Anglican priest, he was happy to debate the Church of England commissaries in Boston, New York, and Savannah, all of whom he considered unconverted and anti-revival, and who in turn denied him pulpits in their dioceses.

When Whitefield toured New England beginning in September 1740, he encountered the leader of the emerging anti-revivalists, Charles Chauncy (1705–1787), co-pastor of Boston's First Church with Thomas Foxcroft. A liberalizing Calvinist during the 1740s, and later a rationalistic Arminian and a Socinian, he distrusted the emotions as befogging the mind. He could have no sympathy with George Whitefield or **Jonathan Edwards,** whose qualified defense of the Great Awakening Chauncy attacked in print. To counter the Awakening, he made an extended trip through New England and gathered information for a massive work, *Seasonable Thoughts on the State of Religion in New England* (1743). In it Chauncy listed many faults he found in the revival. He attacked revival preachers for invading their fellow ministers' parishes without permission. Such behavior, for Chauncy, was prideful and presumptuous. Indeed, the pro-revival party was generally guilty of

"uncharitable judging" with respect to those outside their group. Simultaneously they showed an uncritical attitude toward their own adherents. George Whitefield was surrounded by adulation and a virtual personality cult. Chauncy also opposed public speaking and exhortation from laypersons—a criticism of the 1740s revival at least partially endorsed by Jonathan Edwards. When Chauncy looked at the revival, he saw social disorder and an almost complete breakdown of the proper relationship between ministers and their flocks. Chauncy's *Seasonable Thoughts* is an anti-revivalist classic that anticipates arguments voiced by subsequent critics of revivals. During his later years, Chauncy rejected the traditional Christian teaching on hell. He wrote a manuscript that he kept hidden for a quarter century, in which he rejected the idea of eternal punishment and embraced salvific universalism (i.e., the idea that everyone will eventually go to heaven). He was nearly 80 when he allowed a London publisher in 1784 to print *The Mystery Hid from Ages and Generations … or, The Salvation of All Men.* His closest associates were Jonathan Mayhew and Ebenezer Gay.

Jonathan Mayhew (1720–1766) was originally under Whitefield's influence, but in time he rejected both Christian revivals and Christian orthodoxy. As an Arian, he believed that Christ is inferior to God the Father and yet more than mere man. Hints of heterodoxy on Mayhew's part were detected before his ordination, and only a few Boston pastors were willing to take part in his installation as pastor of the West Church. He corresponded with a number of English anti-Trinitarians, including Richard Price, George Benson, Nathaniel Lardner, and others. In 1755 Mayhew wrote against the doctrine of Christ's divinity. He was expressing, in characteristically blunt fashion, something that his more cautious liberal colleagues only whispered among themselves. Like Chauncy, Gay, Eliot, and other New England liberals, Mayhew was temperamentally anti-revivalist.

In the decades after the Great Awakening, non-religious concerns occupied most Americans. At the ending of the Revolutionary War, there was a period of spiritual deadness in many regions. Yet by the mid-1790s, awakening again flamed, on the western frontier and on college campuses, as the **Second Great Awakening** began. The western revivals in this period are connected with **James McGready** (1760–1817), **Barton W. Stone** (1772–1844), and the Kentucky **camp meetings** beginning at Gasper River in July 1800 and **Cane Ridge** in August 1801. Opponents then and since have dwelt almost exclusively on the emotionalism and excesses of the crowds. The falling, jerking, running, **shouting, dancing,** barking, and other **bodily manifestations** at Cane Ridge provoked vehement criticisms. Many critics at the time, however, were not against revivals as such but rather the wild emotionalism that detracted from revivals. Despite these censures, Sydney Ahlstrom notes that Cane Ridge came at a strategic time and was both a symbol and impetus for a century-long process whereby most of American evangelical Protestantism became "revivalized." The western revivals infused new life into participating churches, and especially the **Methodist** and **Baptist.** Denominational growth was great in the East as well, due to the stimulating effect of the reports of converts made and churches organized in Ohio, Kentucky, Tennessee, and the Carolinas.

In the East, a number of preachers promoted revivals from the late 1790s to the mid-1820s. **Lyman Beecher** (1775–1863) and **Asahel Nettleton** (1783–1844) considered themselves leaders in this endeavor. Both adhered to sane and sober methods in their revivals, bringing little criticism, except from Unitarians. When **Charles G. Finney** (1792–1875) began his evangelistic career, his innovative methods—known as "new measures"—aroused opposition from both Beecher and Nettleton. They upbraided Finney for being judgmental and harsh toward fellow ministers, exhibiting spiritual pride, using crude language in the pulpit, allowing **women** to pray publicly alongside of **men,** and embarrassing people by praying for them by name. In addition many Old School Calvinists became disturbed with Finney's theology, which to them carried the anti-Calvinist implication that human beings have the innate power to bring about their own conversion. Censure of

Finney's methods came especially from John Williamson Nevin (1803–1886), a professor at Mercersburg Seminary who increasingly was emphasizing the churchly and sacramental side of Christianity. His treatise *The Anxious Bench* (1843) summed up his opposition to Finney's ministry and to revival generally. Nevin charged that spiritual decisions made in the context of emotional excitement were likely to be spurious. He proposed that doctrinal instruction and the sacraments of baptism and the Lord's Supper were the proper means of Christian initiation, and not Finney's **altar call.** His pamphlet triggered a flood of replies.

Horace Bushnell (1802–1876), often regarded as the father of American religious liberalism, also was displeased with the effects of revivalism. At Yale Divinity School he studied under **Nathaniel William Taylor.** His first book, *Discourses on Christian Nurture* (1847), gave him immediate notoriety, and was one of the most influential religious books ever published in America. Bushnell said that if a child has been properly instructed, and has seen the Christian faith modeled by parents, then the child may not know a time when he or she was not a Christian. Bushnell was not strictly an anti-revivalist, since he thought that awakenings rendered a good service to those who were deeply enmeshed in sin. The great problem, as he saw it, was that as a result of its "jump and stir," the ordinary operations of God's grace are "swallowed up and lost in the extraordinary" (Bushnell, 143), and people are led to believe that the only entrance into faith is through a convulsive conversion experience in a revival meeting. In the light of New England's tradition of evangelism through awakenings, Bushnell's ideas provoked much reaction. Bushnell was accused of ignoring the Holy Spirit's agency in conversion, and of reducing Christianity to a form of religious naturalism.

The late nineteenth and twentieth centuries brought new arguments against revivals and revivalists. Friedrich Engels—Karl Marx's partner in communism—charged that preacher **Dwight L. Moody** used revivalism to divert the masses from their suffering and call to revolutionary struggle. Liberal Protestants viewed revivalism as politically naive or irrelevant—a movement supporting the status quo rather than social change. The conservative attitudes of **Billy Sunday**—who stated that "America is not a country for a dissenter to live in" (Cohen, 161)—gave support to this view. Eugene Debs asserted that Sunday was a tool of corporate interests and called him a "mountebank" who "prostitutes religion to perpetuate hell on earth" (McLoughlin, 440–43). The writers H. L. Mencken and Sinclair Lewis—author of the anti-revivalist novel *Elmer Gantry* (1927)—lampooned revivalists as bumbling idiots or greed- and lust-driven hucksters. In the 1950s, Reinhold Niebuhr responded to **Billy Graham** with mingled appreciation and censure. For Niebuhr, Graham was sincere and "better than any evangelist of his kind in American history" (quoted in Dullea, 3) and yet his message of individualistic salvation evaded social and political issues. In the post–World War II era, anti-revivalist Protestants concerned themselves with poverty, the cold war, civil rights, Vietnam, the environmental movement, women's right, and gay rights—but not the saving of souls. The very notion of salvation seemed quaint, outmoded, or preposterous to some mainline Protestants.

During these years the **Pentecostal** movement and **Charismatic Renewal** were rapidly spreading, and yet the phenomenon of **speaking in tongues** aroused incredulity and derision among conservative as well as liberal Protestants. Anti-revivalism often took the form of anti-Pentecostalism. The film *Marjoe* (1971) portrayed revivalists as con artists and thus renewed the Elmer Gantry stereotype from the 1920s. Yet the greatest blow to revivalism came from within. A sex-and-money scandal in the 1980s involving **Jim and Tammy Faye Bakker** and **Jimmy Swaggart**—celebrities in Christian media—showed that the private lives of these preachers and revivalists contradicted their public images. The popular perception of revivalists suffered damage, and the 1980s scandals have helped to insure that anti-revivalism in its various forms is alive and well at the commencement of the twenty-first century.

Further Reading: Bratt, James D. *Antirevivalism in Antebellum America: A Collection of Religious Voices.* New Brunswick, NJ: Rutgers University Press, 2005; Bushnell, Horace. "The Spiritual Economy of Revivals of Religions." *Quarterly Christian Spectator* 10 (1838); Cohen, Daniel. *The Spirit of the Lord: Revivalism in America.* New York: Four Winds Press, 1975; Cragg, Gerald R. *The Church and the Age of Reason, 1648–1789.* Baltimore: Penguin, 1970; Cross, Barbara M. *Horace Bushnell: Minister to a Changing America.* Chicago: University of Chicago Press, 1958; Dullea, Charles W. *A Catholic Looks at Billy Graham.* New York: Paulist Press, 1973; Gaustad, Edwin S. *The Great Awakening in New England.* New York: Harper, 1957; Hardman, Keith J. *Seasons of Refreshing: Evangelism and Revivals in America.* Grand Rapids, MI: Baker, 1994; McLoughlin, William G. *Modern Revivalism: Charles Grandison Finney to Billy Graham.* New York: Ronald Press, 1959; Stout, Harry S. *The Divine Dramatist: George Whitefield and the Rise of Modern Evangelicalism.* Grand Rapids, MI: Eerdmans, 1991; Wright, Conrad. *The Beginnings of Unitarianism in America.* Hamden, CT: Shoe String, 1976.

Keith J. Hardman and Michael J. McClymond

ANXIOUS BENCH

see Altar Call

APOSTOLIC MOVEMENT (NEW APOSTOLIC MOVEMENT)

Apostolic movement and *New Apostolic movement* are terms from the 1990s that describe an emerging coalition of local congregations from around the world. Included in the movement are some of the world's largest congregations, in South Korea, sub-Saharan Africa, the Chinese house church movement, Latin American grassroots churches, and independent churches in North America. The movement resists traditional classifications, arising neither from the historic Protestant denominations, nor the older **Roman Catholic,** Orthodox, and Episcopal churches—for whom *apostolic* denotes an unbroken authority of bishops in "apostolic succession" extending to the first-century church. Observers have variously described the churches in this movement as neo-**Pentecostal,** neo-**Charismatic,** independent, and postdenominational. In Latin America, Mike Berg and Paul Prestiz have called them "Fifth Wave" churches, in distinction from the Roman Catholic colonialist immigrants and missions, the mainline Protestant denominations, the churches planted by evangelical faith missions, and the newer denominations.

C. Peter Wagner, who has been instrumental in bringing New Apostolic leaders together in consultations, has settled on the term *New Apostolic Reformation.* This name signifies that the movement is a new thing in church history, a recovery of the New Testament emphasis on the crucial role of apostles and prophets, and perhaps as radical in its implications as the Protestant Reformation of the sixteenth century. New Apostolic churches see themselves as the heirs to a series of restoration movements that preceded them: the Protestant Reformation that brought in the authority of scripture, justification by faith, and the priesthood of all believers; the Wesleyan **Holiness movement** of the eighteenth and nineteenth centuries that restored the idea that Christian holiness is possible; the modern missionary movement that reemphasized Jesus' Great Commission (Matthew 28:18–20) for world evangelization; the Pentecostal movement that highlighted **charismatic gifts** (or the gifts of the Holy Spirit); the **healing** evangelists of the 1940s and 1950s who introduced healing and demonic **deliverance ministries** in the church; the Charismatic Renewal of the 1960s and 1970s that transmitted the gifts of the Spirit to the mainline churches; and the worldwide **prayer** movement, beginning in the 1980s, that underscored the role of intercessory prayer in revivals.

These successive waves of spiritual restoration prepared for the New Apostolic movement in which the "fivefold ministry" (Ephesians 4:11) and the gifts of prophets and apostles became more widely accepted. Wagner asserts—though not all New Apostolic leaders agree—that the governmental gifts of apostles and prophets have existed in the Christian church throughout its history but have not always been recognized. Most New Apostolic churches contrast with denominational churches in the following ways: the pastor has much greater

decision-making authority; church members voluntarily put themselves under the spiritual authority of an "apostle"; leadership is homegrown (raised up from within the ranks of the church); the spiritual style is less heritage driven and more vision driven; pastors often are mid-career changers and not formally educated in residential seminaries; worship style and paradigms are more contemporary, casual, and tolerant of **bodily manifestations** in worship; the practice of prayer takes new forms, such as praise marches, prayer walking, and prayer journeys; tithing is expected and most participants give generously to the congregation; outreach to the nonbelievers and people in need is aggressive and the planting of new churches is assumed to be a normal function of the church; end-time expectations are heightened; and there is great openness to the working of the power of the Holy Spirit in **healing,** deliverance ministry, **spiritual warfare, prophecy,** and prayer.

Further Reading: Cannistraci, David. *Apostles and the Emerging Apostolic Movement.* Ventura, CA: Renew Books, 1996; Eckhardt, John. *Moving in the Apostolic.* Ventura, CA: Renew Books, 1999; Hamon, Bill. *Apostles, Prophets and the Coming Moves of God.* Santa Rosa Beach, FL: Christian International, 1997; Miller, Donald. *Reinventing American Protestantism.* Berkeley: University of California Press, 1997; Thompson, Joseph. *Out of Africa: How the Spiritual Explosion among Nigerians Is Impacting the World.* 2004; Wagner, C. Peter, ed. *The New Apostolic Churches.* Ventura, CA: Regal, 1998; Wagner, C. Peter, and Joseph Thompson, eds. *Out of Africa: How the Spiritual Explosion Among Nigerians Is Impacting the World.* Ventura, CA: Renew Books, 2003; Wagner, C. Peter, and Pablo Deiros, eds. *The Rising Revival: Firsthand Accounts of the Incredible Argentine Revival—and How It Can Spread throughout the World.* Ventura, CA: Renew Books, 1998.

Bayard Taylor

APPALACHIAN REVIVALS

The Appalachian revival, sometimes referred to as the "plain-folk **camp meeting,**" is most often associated with the mountainous regions of the upland **South**—West Virginia, Virginia, Tennessee, Kentucky, North Carolina, Alabama, and Georgia. This passionate, egalitarian, and nonsectarian expression of spiritual life is found in **Baptist, Church of God, Methodist,** Missionary Baptist, **Primitive Baptist, Holiness, Assembly of God,** and **Pentecostal** communities of the Appalachian region. As a social movement initiated at the turn of the nineteenth century, the Appalachian revival quickly spread its multidenominational piety across the rural and urban South to become the most widespread regional religious tradition in the United States. The revival's theological tenets derive from the eighteenth-century Wesleyan doctrine of Christian perfection. Participants affirm their spirituality through a dynamic, intimate relationship with the Holy Spirit. Physical evidence for this relationship commonly comes through **speaking in tongues** or glossolalia, but other **bodily manifestations** such as **shouting, dancing,** and fainting—or practices such as laying hands on the sick for **healing, prophecy,** and **serpent and fire handling**—are outward signifiers of the **baptism in the Holy Spirit.** The unflattering term *Holy Rollers* is a stigma to some practitioners and a badge of persecution to be worn proudly by others. The plain-folk religion involving these practices was much the same whether the worshippers were white or **African American,** despite the fact that the two groups may not have regularly worshipped together.

At the turn of the nineteenth century, a series of camp meetings launched in the South and in the then-western regions of the United States initiated what has been called the Great Revival (also referred to as the **Second Great Awakening**). The South proved fertile ground for the development of this revival because of its strict approach to the Bible and strong devotion to tradition. A new spiritual awakening was noticeable by spring 1799. In July 1800 **James McGready** (1758–1817), a **Presbyterian** minister recognized today as the father of the Great Revival, conducted a four-day meeting for his small Gaspar River congregation in Logan County, Kentucky, where large crowds came from Tennessee, Kentucky, and other neighboring states. The August 7–12, 1801, revival at **Cane Ridge,** Kentucky, was conducted by Presbyterian minister **Barton W. Stone** (1772–1844) and included not only Presbyterians but also Baptists and Methodists. Historians regard it as the frontier phase of the Second Great Awakening, and it represented the largest interdenominational camp meeting held in Appalachia in that era. Many features of the Appalachian revival were grounded in earlier religious movements, including **Pietism,** the sacramental revivalism of the **holy fair,** and a **Calvinist** heritage that emphasized grace and the Holy Spirit.

During the twentieth century, Appalachia experienced the new influence of Pentecostalism. The Pentecostal movement seems to have been unconnected with the earlier revival tradition in Appalachia until Gaston Barnibus Cashwell (1860–1916) returned from visiting the **Azusa Street revival** in Los Angeles. Back in his hometown of Dunn, North Carolina, in December 1906, Cashwell began **preaching** the Pentecostal message in the local Holiness church. While revivalist practices have remained an integral part of Appalachian Pentecostal, Holiness, and Baptist churches, many conservative Presbyterian ministers and congregations eventually rejected the emotionalism of revival services. Cashwell himself changed perspective in 1909, left the Pentecostal Holiness Church (today known as the **International Pentecostal Holiness Church**), distanced himself from Pentecostalism, and rejoined the Methodist Church—though there are no historical records that document his rationale.

Appalachian revivals aim at convincing the unsaved through the preaching of moving sermons and the invitations of the **altar call.** In addition, the congregation is expected to unburden themselves of their difficulties and disappointments. Preachers encourage shouting during worship since it provides emotional release for the worshippers. Weekly celebration of the Lord's Supper and authorization for nonclergy elders to **pray** and preside over Eucharistic services are common in Appalachian congregations. Religious revival, like a family reunion or church homecoming, solidifies a community's shared sense of origin and place, especially in times of individual crisis or social alienation. Revival practices help to shape community life in Appalachia.

Further Reading: Covington, Dennis. *Salvation on Sand Mountain: Snake Handling and Redemption in Southern Appalachia.* Reading, MA: Addison-Wesley, 1995; Jones, Loyal. *Faith and Meaning in the Southern Uplands.* Chicago: University of Illinois Press, 1999; Kimbrough, David. *Reverend Joseph Tarkington: Methodist Circuit Rider from Frontier Evangelism to Refined Religion.* Knoxville: University of Tennessee Press, 1997; Leonard, Bill J., ed. *Christianity in Appalachia: Profiles in Regional Pluralism.* Knoxville: University of Tennessee Press, 1999; McCauley, Deborah Vansau, and Laura E. Porter. *Mountain Holiness: A Photographic Narrative.* Knoxville: University of Tennessee Press, 2003; Tyson, Ruel, Jr., James L. Peacock, and Daniel W. Patterson. *Diversities of Gifts: Field Studies in Southern Religion.* Urbana and Chicago: University of Illinois Press, 1988.

Scott W. Schwartz

ARCHITECTURE AND REVIVALS

Architecture has played an important, if unacknowledged, role in the culture of American revivalism. While **camp and tent meetings** and other temporary installations dominate the popular conception of revival architecture, settings have ranged from these to large, purpose-built facilities. The careful attention given by revivalists to the reception of their message meant that in most cases, **preachers** selected or constructed spaces that best facilitated the delivery of their message. But revivalists also thought about architecture beyond the functional; they imbued their spaces with meanings that in either subtle or explicit ways reinforced the content of their messages. From tents to temples, revivalists have long enlisted architecture to communicate abstract ideas about faith. During the period of the **Great Awakening** (1739–1745), the field preaching of such revivalists as John Wesley in Britain and **George Whitefield** in both Britain and America established a new link between revivalist religion and spaces outside of traditional church buildings. This helped to set the stage for the later development of distinctively revivalistic forms of architecture during the 1800s and 1900s.

Probably the most important tradition in the architecture of revivalism is the camp meeting.

Born in the context of religious democratization in the **Second Great Awakening,** the camp meeting was a counterpoint to early nineteenth-century church life. Often located in wilderness clearings, a simple setting framed folk singing and extemporaneous sermons. **Francis Asbury,** a leading figure in early nineteenth-century American Methodism and a great proponent of camp meetings, would argue that with their rich organs and tall steeples, churches were "contrary to the simplicity of Christ" (quoted in Garber, 34). Without the comportment demanded of refined church spaces, the canvas tents, portable speaking platforms, and outdoor settings of early camp meetings reinforced a sense of spontaneity, heartfelt religion, and immediacy with God.

As camp meetings became institutionalized and began to reoccur in the same location, however, their transient forms became more permanent. The roof eventually covered not just the stage but the seats as well, creating a building type called the tabernacle. Canvas tents were replaced with small cabins, still erected in concentric rows around the stage but increasingly covered in ornamental trim. Even though these gatherings were still "camps," their refined architectural expressions communicated a different message. The mores of Victorian comportment governed these spaces, not the freedom of physical and emotional expression so common in earlier times.

A second long-standing tradition in the architecture of revivalism is the building designed to house the preaching of a particular revivalist. The earliest instance of this in the American context is the purchase and conversion of New York's Chatham Street Theater for **Charles Finney** in 1832. In purchasing this middle-class theater, Finney and his backers established a new tradition of locating the revivalist in a specific space. When revivalists began to travel less frequently and they remained longer in one place, they had the opportunity to think through the formal and aesthetic requirements of their buildings. The theater's comfortable seats and sight lines, open stage, and tiered galleries accommodated large crowds, and this freed Finney from the physical confines of a pulpit. In both the

SISTER AIMEE SEMPLE McPHERSON

618   ANGELUS TEMPLE. LOS ANGELES, CALIF.

This postcard, probably from the late 1930s, portrays Aimee Semple McPherson's Angelus Temple in Los Angeles and includes an inset of the evangelist. Courtesy of Dr. Stanley M. Burgess.

Chatham Street Theatre and his slightly later Broadway Tabernacle, Finney became the actor in an architectural space that depended on spectacle, establishing a lasting relationship between theater design and evangelical architecture. Revivalist **Dwight L. Moody** had commercial buildings converted for use in revivals, such as the Philadelphia Freight Depot in 1875.

This carefully considered emphasis on architecture for specific revivalists would persist through the twentieth century. In the years just before and after World War I, **Billy Sunday** had numerous tabernacles built for his revival services. Yet more impressively, **Aimee Semple McPherson's** 1923 Angelus Temple seated over 5,000 people in a theater-like setting with a large stage to accommodate McPherson's dramatizations. The shockingly original shell of Philip Johnson's 1980 Crystal Cathedral—built for Robert Schuller—houses what was at the time the largest religious auditorium in the country. The transparency of the cathedral's architecture serves to minimize architecture's

traditional function of separating inside from out. The auditorium is so expansive that the majority of Schuller's audience watches him on huge screens, effectively dissolving the distinction between the viewer actually in the space and those watching from the physical—and psychological—comfort of their living rooms through the services of Schuller's broadcast ministry.

Possibly the clearest modern counterpart to early camp meetings are the stadium revivals of speakers like **Billy Graham.** Like the camp meeting, the stadium is a setting distinctly different from that of the church and free from the cultural parameters of traditional religion. Like his revivalist predecessors, Graham uses the setting to suggest that the personal faith he encourages is distinct from "religion." The recent movement of the **Promise Keepers** has capitalized on this even more explicitly. Their revivals are located in the physical space where American **men** are the most comfortable expressing emotion. The associative power of the sports arena allows men in revivals to sing, cry, and hug in ways that

THE BROADWAY TABERNACLE.

Lithograph of the Broadway Tabernacle, which opened for worship in 1836 as a platform for revivalist Charles G. Finney, who had the building designed according to his wishes and drew on the architecture of the theater to create a revivalist-centered sanctuary (ca. 1845). Courtesy of the New York Public Library.

mainstream American masculinity finds unacceptable outside that space.

An important aspect of architecture and religious revival, though not well understood, is the affective psychological power of architecture. In her recent study of the Congregational churches of early nineteenth-century Connecticut, Gretchen Buggeln has demonstrated the ways that expensive and refined neoclassical churches participated in the culture of the Second Great Awakening. She argues that the increasing importance of "feeling" in early nineteenth-century culture meant that elegant church architecture facilitated rather than hampered religious revival. Buggeln explains these church buildings in terms of a new embrace of aesthetics among **Calvinists.** The wilderness context of the camp meeting allowed free emotional and physical expression, while the church buildings used refined spaces to ignite heartfelt religion in the context of an orthodox and orderly setting. Jeanne Kilde's recent study of the architecture of late nineteenth-century American Protestants demonstrates that large auditorium churches with theatrical seats, rich organs, and warm, domestic finishes stirred deep devotional sentiments. Incorporating wood paneling, cushioned seats, stenciling, and decorative stained glass windows meant that evangelical churches were creating a spiritual home for Protestants increasingly devoted to the family. The scholarship of Buggeln, Kilde, and others has

Crowd gathering for revival service at the Scoville Tabernacle in Aurora, Missouri. The tabernacle was a structure more enduring than a tent or brush arbor and yet less sturdy than a standard wood-framed building. It was 124 by 150 feet and could seat 3,600 persons. The protruding chimneys show that the structure was heated. (Photographer R. E. Hinchley, January 24, 1915.) Courtesy of the Library of Congress.

expanded our understanding of revivals and revivalism in the architecture of American religion.

Central to the architecture of the early camp meetings was the belief that physical spaces devoid of Christian signs and symbols manifest a more intense and more personal faith than do traditional church buildings. In the early nineteenth century, revivalists embraced the architecture of the theater, which accommodated large audiences in comfortable seats around an open stage. Nineteenth-century revivalists also came to appreciate that the audience's psychological comfort was just as important as their physical comfort. Architecture has the capacity to affect feelings through association. Both the refined grace of Buggeln's early nineteenth-century churches, the domesticity of Kilde's spiritual homes, and the emotive masculinity of the Promise Keepers' stadiums realize this powerful capacity in architecture.

The success of the late twentieth-century **megachurch** depends to some extent on designs that capitalize on all of these factors. While there is great architectural diversity among megachurches,

the movement builds on principles established in the era of the camp meeting. These self-defined "seeker churches" employ buildings that consciously avoid historic architectural styles, with large, unarticulated spaces that free the visitor from the fear of traditional, historical doctrines or forced participation in an unfamiliar choreographed ritual. Often built to house dynamic personalities, their exteriors approximate sports areas, shopping malls, or office parks—comfortable, everyday spaces of Generation Xers. Their interiors generally contain an auditorium that rivals the best of IMAX theaters. Though contemporary culture has replaced the earlier style of the camp meeting, megachurch revivalists continue the tradition of enlisting architecture in the search for souls.

Further Reading: Brown, Kenneth O. *Holy Ground: A Study of the American Camp Meeting.* New York: Garland, 1992; Buggeln, Gretchen. *Temples of Grace: The Material Transformation of Connecticut's Churches, 1790–1840.* Lebanon, NH: University Press of New England, 2003; Garber, Paul Neff. *The Methodist Meeting House.* New

York: The Methodist Church, 1941; Kilde, Jeanne. *When Church Became Theatre: The Transformation of Evangelical Architecture and Worship in Nineteenth-Century America.* Oxford, UK: Oxford University Press, 2002; Loveland, Anne C., and Otis B. Wheeler. *From Meetinghouse to Megachurch: A Material and Cultural History.* Columbia: University of Missouri Press, 2003; Robins, Roger. "Vernacular American Landscape: Methodists, Camp Meetings, and Social Respectability." *Religion and American Culture* 4 (1994): 165–91; Sargeant, Kimon. *Seeker Churches: Promoting Traditional Religion in a Nontraditional Way.* New Brunswick, NJ: Rutgers University Press, 2000; Weiss, Ellen. *City in the Woods: The Life and Design of an American Camp Meeting on Martha's Vineyard.* New York: Oxford University Press, 1987.

Louis Nelson

ARMINIAN THEOLOGY

see Theology of Revivals

ASBURY, FRANCIS (1745–1816)

Francis Asbury is the acknowledged leader and most influential figure in early American **Methodism.** Asbury was born in 1745 near Birmingham, England, died in 1816 near Fredericksburg, Virginia, and is buried in the Mt. Olivet Cemetery in Baltimore. He had little formal education and was apprenticed for six and a half years to a metal worker. In 1766 he joined John Wesley's Methodist connection and became a local preacher. Five years later, at a meeting in Bristol, he volunteered for service in the Methodist societies in America, and was sent to them with the title "assistant in America." Arriving in Philadelphia in 1771, Asbury found a home among the Methodists and never again returned to England, even for a visit, though he retained his British citizenship. It was he who created the model for itinerant **preaching** and for episcopal practice as it applied to American Methodists. Less than a month after he arrived he noted in his journal, "I judge we are to be shut up in the cities this winter. My brethren seem unwilling to leave the cities, but I think I shall show them the way" (*Journals and Letters*, November 21, 1771).

And show them he did; it was not uncommon for his travels to take him farther in a year than Lewis and Clark traveled on the Voyage of Discovery. He never married nor purchased a home. He was the only preacher sent by Wesley to America who did not leave the country during the American Revolution. His entire life was spent on the road in all sorts of conditions. He, and those whom he led, slept wherever they could find a place or in the out of doors. They ate whatever was available and sometimes they went without. But virtually no place escaped their attention. One of his biographers, Ezra Squier Tipple, describes Asbury as not only having "the genius to lead," but also "the will to govern" (242).

That quality was quickly evident to those with whom he worked, and he rapidly rose to become the acknowledged leader of the rapidly growing Methodist movement in America. In fact, he came in time to exercise a leadership and authority similar to that which John Wesley exercised among Methodists in Great Britain. By 1779, five years before the societies were formally organized into an independent church, Asbury was recognized as the "general assistant in America." By 1784, Wesley was convinced that Methodism in America had been permanently separated from any positive association with the Church of England, of which he considered the Methodists to be a part. Moreover, he knew they were clamoring to be given permission to administer the sacraments in their societies and would take steps on their own to offer them if he did nothing. As a result, in the fall of 1784 Wesley determined to provide the one thing lacking to enable the Americans to become a church—an ordained ministry. Acting on his presumption that as a presbyter he could, under certain extraordinary circumstances, exercise the power of ordination, he laid hands on Richard Whatcoat and Thomas Vasey to ordain them elders and on Thomas Coke to set him aside as a general superintendent. He then sent them to America with instructions to ordain Asbury and elders chosen by the Americans, and to organize the Methodists in America as a separate denomination. Asbury agreed to accept the ordination that Coke offered only if he were elected to the office by the preachers.

Rev. Francis Asbury, Bishop of the Methodist Episcopal Church in the United States. Painted by J. Paradise; engraving by Benjamin Tanner, Philadelphia, 1814. Courtesy of the Library of Congress.

The practical result was to shift the authority in American Methodism from Wesley to the body of preachers, and to Asbury, their leader. A conference of the preachers met in Baltimore in December 1784 in what has become known as the Christmas Conference and organized the Methodist Episcopal Church in America. The newly organized church had almost 15,000 members and just over 80 preachers. On three successive days, Asbury was ordained deacon, elder, and general superintendent. From that time until his death in 1816, he gave oversight to every aspect of the organization and operation of Methodism in America. For the better part of three decades he attended every annual conference and appointed every Methodist preacher to his post. In the process he traveled almost a quarter of a million miles, mostly on horseback, and presided over more than 200 annual conferences. His journal includes striking accounts of religious revivals, some in the form of letters written to him, and centering on the years 1775–1776 and 1784.

Although his authority was challenged from time to time, his preachers never negated it, and his influence enabled the new denomination to withstand challenges that threatened to divide it during the early years. It was this organization that successfully evangelized the western frontier and grew by 1840 to become the largest Protestant denomination in America.

Further Reading: Asbury, Francis. *The Journal and Letters of Francis Asbury.* Ed. J. Manning Potts. 3 vols. London and Nashville, TN: Abingdon Press, 1958; Baker, Frank. *From Wesley to Asbury.* Durham, NC: Duke University Press, 1976; Lee, Jesse. *Short History of the Methodists in the United States of America.* Baltimore: Magill and Clime, 1810; Tipple, Ezra Squire. *The Prophet of the Long Road.* New York: Methodist Book Concern, 1916.

James E. Kirby

ASSEMBLIES OF GOD, GENERAL COUNCIL OF THE

The largest predominately white **Pentecostal** denomination in the United States, the Assemblies of God (AG) currently has 1.6 million adult members and claims 2.8 million adherents of all ages who worship in 12,200 churches. In addition to having congregations in every state, it has established national churches in over 200 countries with a total membership approaching 20 million. Doctrinally, the denomination stands within the evangelical wing of the Protestant tradition. In its **eschatology** it teaches a modified form of dispensationalism, holding to a premillennial, pretribulation rapture of the church. With most other Pentecostal denominations, it teaches that the **baptism in the Holy Spirit** is a second work of divine grace, subsequent to **conversion** or regeneration, and normative for all Christian believers. The denomination teaches that **speaking in tongues** is a necessary evidence of undergoing this experience, which is intended to empower individuals for Christian service. The church practices the baptism of adults (or believer's baptism) by immersion and it holds to a Zwinglian or memorial view of the Lord's Supper.

The AG is part of the Pentecostal movement that traces its origins to a revival that began in a black

A photograph of Iowa and Missouri preachers in the Assemblies of God denomination (early twentieth century). Courtesy of Flower Pentecostal Heritage Center, Springfield, MO.

Holiness mission on **Azusa Street** in Los Angeles in 1906. Within three years the revival had circled the world, taking root in over 100 countries. The central teaching of the revival was that "Jesus is coming soon." Early adherents believed they had been commissioned with a twofold mission: to proclaim the imminent return of Christ to the nations as a witness and to urge the church to put on the "bridal garments" of a holy life in preparation for Jesus' Second Coming as the Bridegroom. Speaking in tongues, the unique feature of the revival, likewise had a twofold function. First, adherents believed this gift would enable them to proclaim their message to the nations in the language of the people. Second, they thought this gift was the seal of the Holy Spirit necessary to membership in the bride of Christ.

The experiences of overseas missionaries soon disproved the idea that speaking in tongues conferred on early Pentecostals an ability to speak at will in the languages of various foreign peoples (a notion known as *xenolalia*). It also soon became clear that most of the existing church leaders would not accept the claim that speaking in tongues was a special seal of the Holy Spirit's presence. Nonetheless the revival swept hundreds of thousands of converts into the new movement. Many of these new adherents came from Wesleyan or Holiness backgrounds. Indeed, several small Holiness denominations accepted the Pentecostal message and entered the movement. In distinction from the Wesleyan and Holiness converts, others were drawn from the **Reformed** tradition, had accepted the Keswick doctrine of the higher Christian life, and understood **sanctification** as a lifelong, gradual process and not as a distinct, momentary experience. These new adherents tended to cluster into independent congregations. The call to organize the General Council of the Assemblies of God in 1914 was directed primarily at these bodies. The organizational effort had a fivefold purpose: to try to achieve better understanding among adherents and teach a common message, to conserve the movement's work at home and abroad, to provide a mechanism to raise and protect funds for mission, to charter local congregations under a legal name, and to establish Bible colleges to train ministers. After a shaky beginning, which included a protest from independent groups who refused to join "a man-made organization" on theological grounds and a doctrinal controversy over the nature of the Trinity that resulted in the loss of over 25 percent of its membership in 1916, the AG nonetheless established itself as a leading Pentecostal denomination.

The AG existed in relative isolation from other Christian groups until 1943, when it accepted an invitation to become a member of the newly formed National Association of Evangelicals. Following World War II it helped to establish the World Pentecostal Fellowship and was instrumental in creating the Pentecostal Fellowship of North American (known previously as the Pentecostal/Charismatic Churches of North America) in 1948. In the wake of the **Charismatic Revival and Renewal** in which the practice of speaking in tongues spread to mainline denominations, the AG leadership has also engaged in cautious informal dialogue with churches holding membership in the National Council of Churches and has had conversations with the Vatican. This period, from 1970 through the mid-1990s, has also witnessed the denomination's greatest sustained growth, averaging a 17 percent gain each year. Yet since the mid-1990s its growth has seemed to reached a plateau. Nonetheless, the AG has achieved peer status with older Protestant denominations before reaching its 100th birthday.

Further Reading: Blumhofer, Edith L. *The Assemblies of God: A Chapter in the Story of American Pentecostalism.* 2 vols. Springfield, MO: Gospel, 1989; Menzies, W. W. *Anointed to Serve: The Story of the Assemblies of God* Springfield, MO: Gospel, 1971.

D. William Faupel

ASSURANCE OF SALVATION

Assurance, in Christian understanding, is the conviction and persuasion that one has received divine salvation. Most historians of theology agree that the debate regarding full assurance of saving faith derives from the sixteenth-century Protestant Reformation. **Roman Catholic** theology, at least prior to the twentieth century, did not have a strong doctrine of assurance, given its emphasis on cooperation in salvation. In Catholic theology salvation is nurtured by the sacramental grace offered by the church, and sin can render this ineffective. In this view assurance was not expected unless one received a special revelation, as taught at the Council of Trent in the mid-1500s. Some contemporary Catholic theologians stress that faith receives its assurance from the Word of God by the work of the Holy Spirit, not from itself.

At the time of the Protestant Reformation assurance became a focus of theological and pastoral discussion. For Luther, Calvin, Bucer, and Zwingli, assurance was a normative component of saving faith. Luther, for example, argued that his evangelical theology could speak to the issue because it pointed away from looking inward at the self. In his view there should be no reliance upon anything we have experienced or presently do through our works. Calvin regarded saving faith as equivalent to assurance (cf. *Institutes* 3.2.7). In time certain Calvinist theologians began to link assurance with **sanctification,** thus relating assurance to one's personal growth in piety. The Westminster Confession of Faith (1648) treated saving faith and assurance in separate chapters, suggesting that the two concepts had begun to diverge from one another.

Though debates regarding assurance have been divisive, all evangelical Protestants agree that assurance is both possible and desirable. The American revival tradition has approached assurance of salvation in two different ways. One side argues that assurance is given directly in the experience of the Holy Spirit, while the other argues that assurance is not directly related to experience but rather to a right understanding of biblical faith. Some have distinguished between an assurance of faith (which is direct) and an assurance of sense (which is reflexive and an act of the soul, and thus indirect). **Methodist revivals** and **Pentecostal revivals** also distinguished between an experience of justification and an assurance of final salvation. Methodists and Pentecostals view assurance as the product of experience rather than doctrinal analysis.

Believing that Christ died for one's sins is something other than being sure that one has so believed. Yet the confusion of these two forms of belief has provoked controversy. On the one hand, there can be a self-conceited assurance that has no solid basis in vital faith. On the other hand, humble, weak, or poorly taught Christians may have serious doubts but still have genuine saving faith. Struggles over assurance have often brought controversies and divisions, and especially in times of revival. Dogmatic theology has wrestled with this problem and asserted a distinction between *certitudo* (an assurance grounded in the promise of the gospel) and *securitas* (a certainty that relies upon visible evidences). One biblical text explicitly links faith with assurance, stating that "faith is the assurance of things hoped for, the evidence of things not seen" (Hebrews 11:1). If faith is tied to hope, then it grasps something not fully possessed, seen, or understood. This suggests that there is always room for growth in faith, which by its very nature stretches out toward the "not yet" of God's unfinished purposes (1 Corinthians 13:12). Debates over assurance have intensified when revival **preachers** called their hearers to make sure of their standing with God. Those who view faith as a present-time experience find assurance of salvation more easily than those who understand faith as a future-oriented hope in God's ultimate goodness.

Further Reading: Beeke, Joel R. *Assurance of Faith: Calvin, English Puritanism, and the Second Dutch Reformation.* New York: Peter Lang, 1991; Bell, M. Charles. *Calvin and Scottish Theology: The Doctrine of Assurance.* Edinburgh: Handsel Press, 1985; Heriot, M. Jean. *Blessed Assurance: Beliefs, Actions, and the Experience of Salvation in a Carolina Baptist Church.* Knoxville: University of Tennessee Press, 1994; Horton, Michael Scott, and J. Matthew Pinson, eds. *Four Views on Eternal Security.* Grand Rapids, MI: Zondervan, 2002.

John Armstrong

AWANA

Awana is a nondenominational youth ministry that assists churches and missions in evangelizing children, from preschool through the teen years, by means of weekly clubs. Awana supplies programs, materials, and training for more than 13,000 churches and is presently a large international ministry working in every state in America and in more than 110 countries.

Awana began in the context of 1920s revivalism. Chicago Gospel Tabernacle pastor Paul Rader, who became America's first nationally known radio evangelist, began a ministry called the Tabernacle Scouts (1922). Rader selected several to lead his effort, including Lance "Doc" Latham, a classically trained pianist. Within months Latham attracted hundreds of boys to Rader's Tabernacle on Sunday afternoons. After a long partnership, Latham became the founding pastor of North Side Gospel Center (1933). From its beginning North Side had youth ministry as a major focus, including clubs for boys and girls. These clubs were the beginning of Awana. In 1950 the name became the Awana Youth Organization, and in 1986 it was changed to Awana Clubs International.

Art Rorheim was the first director of Latham's North Side youth club. With Latham he came up with the name Awana (Approved Workmen Are Not Ashamed), based on the text of 2 Timothy 2:15. Rorheim, like Latham, had little or no formal training for ministry, and had previously been a photographic printer and machinist. After 1933 Awana became outreach oriented and met apart from Sunday school. The clubs were subdivided by age groups. Rorheim developed a strategy centered on games, activities, and talks by a youth evangelist. To foster unity and a sense of belonging, the kids soon had Boy Scout–like uniforms. Though Rorheim had no training in marketing, management, fund-raising, or curriculum development, he soon—with Latham's support—found innovative ways to reach children far beyond their Chicago neighborhood.

All Awana clubs function the same way. Girls were included soon after the original outreach of the 1920s. A 90-minute to two-hour session features three segments: Game Time, Handbook Time, and Council Time. After Game Time is completed, in Handbook Time children work with age-appropriate materials memorizing scripture and engaging in activities related to topics such as patriotism and community service. This segment includes awards given to children for completing their work.

Meetings conclude with singing, puppet shows, Bible stories, and object lessons. Throughout the year, area churches compete in games and Bible quizzes. In the summer, Awana Scholarship Camps occur across America and Canada.

Awana has not been without critics within the evangelical community. Though the movement stresses sin and salvation, it avoids **Calvinistic** theology. Awana teaches that baptism is to be done by immersion, regards the Lord's Supper as a "memorial," and teaches the premillennial return of Christ. Following Latham's original vision, Awana has retained a strong emphasis on accepting Christ as savior, based upon "personal faith in Jesus Christ and His sacrifice for sin," with less stress upon Christ's Lordship and the call to obedience as well as faith.

At one time Awana required churches to receive a charter in order to use its materials and organize a club, but this requirement was dropped in 2001. The ministry now allows each congregation to decide whether or not to register with Awana based upon the church's understanding of the ministry's doctrinal statement and an agreement to use the materials as presented in the curriculum. Awana remains committed to its Fundamentalist doctrinal roots and recently reaffirmed its original statement of faith as drafted at the North Side Gospel Center in Chicago. Awana has an international headquarters located in Streamwood, Illinois (suburban Chicago), with a staff of more than 200 and a budget of over $40 million. Two-thirds of the money given to Awana in 2003 was for the purchase of materials. The remainder came from donations and club registration fees. The ministry benefits from the services of missionary couples who help churches begin clubs in urban areas and small towns. They conduct well over a hundred leadership training events each year.

Further Reading: Awana Clubs International Web site. http://www.awana.org/; *The Story of Awana*. Streamwood, IL: Awana Clubs International, n.d.

John Armstrong

AZUSA STREET REVIVAL

Many **Pentecostal** Christians in North America trace their origins to revival meetings commencing in 1906 at the Apostolic Faith Mission at 312 Azusa Street in Los Angeles, California. This unlikely venue in a dilapidated building in an industrial district of the city achieved such an intensity of revival fervor for a three-year period (1906–1909) that services often merged into a continuous meeting, night and day. Visitors flocked to Azusa Street from just about every region of the United States and from many countries of the world. The meetings functioned as an equipping headquarters, imparting the "Pentecostal blessing" to attendees and sending them out as missionaries. The revival thus had an international impact and helped to establish the "new Pentecostalism" throughout the world.

The Azusa Street meetings surfaced in the context of local revival expectancy, kindled by reports among **Holiness** adherents of revival outpourings in Wales during 1904–1905. Believers yearned for similar manifestations of revival in Los Angeles. One group of enthusiasts opened a storefront mission on Santa Fe Avenue and sought a pastor to lead them. They found an **African American** Holiness **preacher, William J. Seymour,** residing in Houston, Texas, who was willing to accept their invitation. Arriving in February 1906, Seymour's preaching immediately stirred controversy. After only four days of meetings, Seymour found himself locked out of the mission, with no accommodations. They rejected Seymour because he preached a novel doctrine that set him apart from the standard beliefs of the Holiness movement. The Holiness message recognized the **baptism in the Holy Spirit** as a valid Christian experience, but did not associate this blessing with any specific manifestation of the Spirit. Seymour, by contrast, advocated **speaking in tongues** (i.e., an unknown language) as a necessary or evidential sign of the experience of baptism in the Spirit. For the little congregation on Santa Fe Avenue, accepting Seymour's distinctive message implied that their own experience was lacking. Although many in this Holiness group found Seymour's message to be compelling and even attractive, the group as a whole decided to expel Seymour. (Later on, Seymour rejected the "initial evidence" doctrine that within a generation became central in many white Pentecostal denominations, such as the **Assemblies of God.**)

Seymour himself had only recently had adopted the tongues doctrine, and had not yet himself spoken in tongues. While in Houston, Seymour had come into contact with evangelist **Charles Parham,** Holiness preacher and founder of the Apostolic Faith Mission. Seymour was a student in Parham's Bible College, where he first encountered Parham's teaching about Spirit baptism. Because Parham followed the "Jim Crow" customs of racial segregation, he did not allow Seymour to enter his classroom. Instead, Seymour had to sit in the hallway and listen to Parham through an open door. Since 1901, Parham had taught that speaking in unknown tongues is the initial evidence of Spirit baptism. Seymour welcomed this teaching wholeheartedly, making it a hallmark of his early ministry.

Now rejected and without a pastorate, Seymour held to his convictions and dedicated himself to days of **prayer** and **fasting.** People began to seek out this "man of prayer," and soon he was welcomed into the home of the Asberry family. They offered him residence and encouraged him to begin worship services in their home at 214 Bonnie Brae Street. Under Seymour's leadership, a core group formed and attendance escalated. By April, it became obvious that a larger facility was needed for services. The building that formerly housed the Stevens **African Methodist Episcopal Church** at 312 Azusa Street—though in disrepair, and being used at the time as a barn and storage area—was chosen by the group as their new house of worship. Makeshift seating for a sanctuary was arranged downstairs on the dirt floor, and a "Pentecostal upper room" for prayer and living quarters for Seymour were prepared upstairs.

Events converged in mid-April that added to the intense excitement of the first Azusa Street services. A 10-day period of fasting and prayer prior to Easter resulted in dramatic instances of speaking in tongues among members of the group, including Seymour. Members spread the word among area churches, arousing the interest of the media. As meetings began at Azusa Street, the *Los Angeles Times* printed sensational accounts of speaking in tongues, **prophesying,** and **healings** at the mission. Coinciding with of the April 18, 1906 story on Azusa Street were news reports of the devastating 1906 San Francisco earthquake and fire, which took more than 10,000 lives. This shocking occurrence added to the feeling among many that prophetic times were unfolding and that the time of Jesus' return was drawing near.

Exuberance, excitement, and crowds had characterized the services on Bonnie Brae Street, drawing criticism from neighboring residents. Yet the mission on Azusa Street was planted in an industrial zone, where noise and activity could continue day and night without complaint. Situated in the heart of the original black section of Los Angeles—and during some of the worst years of Jim Crow racial segregation—the mission had a skid-row flavor. The unpretentious setting of the mission helped to ensure that blacks and other minority groups of American society felt no sense of exclusion. From the start, the Azusa crowd welcomed everyone, regardless of race or class. A vital factor shaping the success of the Azusa Street revival was its interracial character, encouraged by Seymour. As the son of slaves, Seymour had tasted the bitter fruit of racial prejudice and saw the need to overcome racial divisions with the love of Jesus. He held that it was no coincidence that the multitude gathered in Jerusalem on the Day of Pentecost (Acts 2) was racially diverse. He saw the Pentecostal manifestations at the Azusa mission as a confirmation of God's support for an interracial ministry. Pentecostal power was the proof of Jesus' presence. As Seymour's ministry progressed, he increasingly insisted upon spiritual fruit, and especially Christian love, as the supreme evidence of Spirit baptism. Speaking in tongues, apart from demonstrations of love, did not establish the presence of the Spirit.

Another key to the success of the Azusa Street revival was Seymour's leadership. He maintained supervision of the meetings, without dominating or controlling the proceedings. Because of his flexibility and openness a spontaneous work of the Holy Spirit could take place in the lives of the attendees. Sometimes Seymour would preach, and at other times he prayed privately beneath an empty wooden crate that was also a makeshift pulpit. He could be found at other times making his way through the crowded congregation, exhorting and praying with people according to their needs. Seymour provided firm and decisive leadership when necessary, but his general approach during the revival was to allow the Holy Spirit to move freely, while he positioned himself in the background and kept a prayerful watch upon the proceedings.

Seymour proved an able leader, particularly during the three to four years (1906–1909) when the revival was at its greatest intensity. Crowds were coming and going, both day and night. On Sundays, during peak periods of attendance, approximately 800 were seated inside, with another 500 or more outside. Especially on weekends, as the worship intensified and merged into one continuous service, Seymour found it necessary to retreat to his upstairs living quarters to sleep. Without any prescribed order, the services alternated between singing, testifying, prophesying, and preaching. Throughout the building, people were praying individually for one another. Participants often **shouted** as they experienced spiritual breakthroughs and victories. The Pentecostal upper room on the second floor was a place of quiet, where prayer could continue while the service downstairs entered new phases. On the inside walls of the mission, discarded crutches, canes, braces, and other medical paraphernalia were hung as visible tokens of God's healing power. Finances were never a problem for the mission, even though no offering was taken. People put money in containers near the door, or stuffed bills in Seymour's pockets as he moved through the congregation during services.

Seymour and his staff owned a printing press, and during slack moments, they recorded and produced a newspaper chronicling highlights of the revival. As the mailing list grew, over 50,000 copies of the *Apostolic Faith* newsletter went out, spreading news of the revival throughout the United States and beyond. Holiness groups, located primarily in the **South** of the United States, were the most avid readers of the Azusa newspaper. Revival interest was so high within Holiness denominations that leaders and members alike journeyed to

Azusa Street to witness the meetings firsthand. Visitors often found neutrality impossible in response to the challenge to receive Spirit baptism as evidenced by speaking in tongues. A first hurdle for many white attendees to overcome was racial prejudice. The obvious intermingling and harmony among the races at Azusa Street repulsed some visitors. A willingness to stay at the mission and benefit from the revival required an abandonment of pride and prejudice. Repentance had to precede revival. For those willing to undergo that process, a Pentecostal reformation often followed. Baptism in the Spirit was a total transformation, infusing a missionary impulse to share the message with others.

A prominent example was G. B. Cashwell, a southern white preacher with the Pentecostal Holiness Church (today known as the **International Pentecostal Holiness Church**). Arriving from North Carolina, Cashwell was initially repulsed by what he saw at Azusa Street. Yet he submitted to the process of seeking the Spirit and received Pentecostal Spirit-baptism at the hands of a young African American male. Cashwell returned to North Carolina to introduce others to this experience. Beginning in late 1906, he rented a facility for services and invited leaders from his denomination and from other Holiness groups to attend. Dunn, North Carolina, became the Azusa Street of the Southeast, as hundreds of believers experienced their personal Pentecost in those meetings. Cashwell went on the road, became known as "the Pentecostal prophet to the South," and led in the transformation of his own denomination into a Pentecostal body. Various leaders were exposed to the Azusa revival through Cashwell. One was J. H. King, leader of the Fire Baptized Holiness Church, whose reception of Spirit baptism resulted in the entry of that denomination into Pentecostalism.

One by one, Holiness denominations came under the influence of Azusa Street, and leaders were forced to accept or reject the Pentecostal doctrine and practice. Along with the two groups previously mentioned, the **Church of God (Cleveland, Tennessee)** opted to become Pentecostal. A prominent African American Holiness denomination,

Despite its humble exterior, the building at 312 Azusa Street in Los Angeles became a focal point for the spread of Pentecostalism throughout the United States during 1906–1909 and into dozens of foreign nations. Worship services occurred on the first floor while the second floor provided a retreat for prayer and a residence for Rev. William Seymour. Courtesy of Flower Pentecostal Heritage Center, Springfield, MO.

the **Church of God in Christ,** split down the middle. Their leaders, **Charles Harrison Mason** and C. P. Jones, responded in opposite ways to the Azusa Street proceedings. Mason, with two fellow ministers, traveled to Los Angeles in March 1907 to encounter Azusa Street firsthand. They traveled east again after five weeks, having received Spirit baptism and become convinced Pentecostals. A three-day meeting convened in August 1907 in Jackson, Mississippi to decide whether or not the Church of God in Christ would embrace the new Pentecostalism. Jones, for his part, resisted the influence of Azusa Street and was determined to retain control of the denomination. A sizable minority of the pastors continued with Mason, while the majority followed Jones. The Pentecostal group revised their denominational standards and yet retained the Church of God in Christ name. The Jones group kept their earlier Holiness platform, while adopting a new name, the Church of

Christ (Holiness) USA. The Church of God in Christ grew rapidly, becoming the largest black Pentecostal church in the world. It has some 5.5 million members today.

Among the opponents of the Azusa Street revival, the most surprising may have been Seymour's personal mentor, Charles Parham. Parham journeyed to Azusa Street in October 1906, with Seymour's approval. What Parham saw immediately repulsed him, including unstructured, spontaneous worship and the free intermingling of blacks and whites. In response, Parham seized the pulpit and began castigating the services in harsh language. He declared that God was "sick at his stomach" at the proceedings, and he used crude racial slurs to describe the close association between blacks and whites at Azusa Street. He made unsubstantiated claims that the participants in the revival practiced "free-loveism" and that many spiritualists and occultists had infiltrated the mission. Though Seymour did not

The house at 216 North Bonnie Brae Street (now 214) in Los Angeles, now a historical site, belonged to Richard and Ruth Asberry in April 1906 and was the venue for an emerging group of Pentecostals who there received Spirit baptism. So many crowded inside that the porch collapsed under their weight, and the group moved to a rented facility at 312 Azusa Street. Courtesy of Flower Pentecostal Heritage Center, Springfield, MO.

publicly respond to Parham's denunciations, Seymour's associates at Azusa Street removed Parham from the building and forbade him from returning. Undeterred, Parham held rival meetings nearby, with the express purpose of drawing away people from Azusa Street. After months of unsuccessful effort, Parham left Los Angeles and yet never ceased in his forceful opposition to Azusa Street. After becoming an opponent of the revival, Parham's ministry spiraled into decline and he never regained his former reputation and influence. Shortly after leaving Los Angeles, Parham was charged in a San Antonio, Texas court with committing sodomy (i.e., a homosexual act) with a young male hymn singer. Though the charge was never proven, his reputation was forever tarnished by this episode.

Meanwhile, the influence of the revival continued to escalate, as Azusa Street "alumni" took Pentecostalism beyond the borders of the United States. Missionaries from the peak years of 1906–1909 took the message to over 50 countries, and so many were departing that Seymour and his team was not able to tabulate the full number of missionaries. Among the best known was T. B. Barratt, a Norwegian Methodist pastor. Visiting New York in 1906–1907 on a fund-raising expedition, he encountered a group of Pentecostals that had come from Azusa Street. Through this group, Barratt carried on correspondence with Seymour, until he experienced Spirit baptism in an especially dramatic fashion in New York City. Without ever visiting Azusa Street, Barratt returned to Norway to become a vibrant Pentecostal ambassador. He is credited with initiating the Pentecostal movement in Norway, Sweden, Denmark, Germany, France, and England.

Revival momentum at Azusa Street lessened during 1908. The *Apostolic Faith* newspaper had kept readers in touch with the remarkable happenings at Azusa Street. Many were inspired to visit Los Angeles as a result of reading the newspaper's testimonials. But in 1908, conflict erupted after Seymour's sudden marriage to a younger African American woman, Jennie Moore. The person with primary responsibility for the newspaper, Clara Lum, was deeply offended by Seymour's marriage to Moore, and she accused him of compromising on holiness—a serious charge among early Pentecostals. It is possible that Lum—a white woman—was in love with Seymour and that her anger flowed from romantic disappointment. In any case, Lum abruptly left for Oregon, taking with her the only copy of the newspaper's extensive mailing list of 50,000. With this communication lifeline severed, Azusa's attendance began to decline. The revival continued until 1914, but failed to recapture the glory of the first three years. Seymour continued at the helm of the mission, but racial segregation began increasingly to affect the Pentecostal movement in the aftermath of the 1908 rift with Lum. The unity experienced by those who were present at Azusa Street as believers of all races and classes met together gave way to largely segregated organizations and denominations.

Despite alterations in its original vision, Pentecostalism created for itself a permanent place within the North American and world landscape. Out of Pentecostalism came the tent crusades of the healing movement of the 1940s and 1950s. Seeds were planted that blossomed into the **Charismatic Renewal** movement of the 1960s and beyond, affecting major Christian denominations throughout the world. The Pentecostal and Charismatic movements continue today, and have spawned many of the world's largest Christian congregations. At the root of the mushrooming world revival known as Pentecostalism is a ramshackle building on Azusa Street in Los Angeles, where a revival was kindled whose flames have yet to be extinguished.

Further Reading: Bartleman, Frank. *Azusa Street*. Plainfield, NJ: Logos International, 1980; Nelson, Douglas J. "For Such a Time as This." PhD dissertation, University of Birmingham, UK, 1981; Robeck, Cecil M., Jr. *The Azusa Street Mission and Revival: The Birth of the Global Pentecostal Movement*. Nashville: Nelson Reference and Electronic, 2006; Robeck, C. M., Jr. "William J. Seymour and The Bible Evidence." In Gary B. McGee, ed., *Initial Evidence*, 72–95. Peabody, MA: Hendrickson, 1991; Robeck, C. M., Jr. "Seymour, William Joseph." In Stanley M. Burgess, ed., *The New International Dictionary of Pentecostal and Charismatic Movements*, 1053–58. Grand Rapids, MI: Zondervan, 2002; Synan, Vinson. *The Holiness-Pentecostal Movement in the United States*. Grand Rapids, MI: Eerdmans, 1971.

David Dorries

B

BACKUS, ISAAC (1724–1806)

Born in Norwich, Connecticut, Isaac Backus served as itinerant evangelist, pastor, historian, political activist, and denominational polemicist for **Baptists** in late **colonial** and early national America. He was reared in a "pure" Congregationalist church that rejected the connectional structure of the Saybrook Platform that linked individual congregations to one another. From childhood Backus heard from his mother of the necessity of conviction and **conversion,** and he experienced these in 1741 after months of deep struggle. The **preaching** of Eleazar Wheelock and **James Davenport** prompted his experience of saving faith while "mowing alone in the field." He joined the Congregational Church in Norwich, but was dissatisfied with their reception of persons to Communion who could not testify to a work of gracious conversion. He soon separated along with about 30 other males and a large number of females from the Norwich congregation, becoming a part of the so-called New Light movement.

Backus sensed a call on September 27, 1746, to preach the gospel. The next day, exercising the right of exhortation, he preached from Psalm 53 on the universal corruption of mankind. Soon he began a tour of preaching after the manner of **George Whitefield** for 14 months. In April 1748 a congregation called him as pastor. The dramatic nature of his call to preach thrust him into a controversy of the times concerning the theory that an unconverted man could be useful performing the duties of a minister. Backus wrote *Discourse on the Nature and Necessity of an Internal Call to Preach the Everlasting Gospel* in 1753, and it was published a year later. Not only must a minister be converted, Backus asserted, he must have an internal call from the Holy Spirit. This call would give him such clear views of the condition of immortal souls and the glory of God's love that he would feel constrained by divine power to speak the words of life.

Backus struggled for several years with the issue of baptism. In August 1751 he along with six members of the church were baptized by immersion on profession of faith. After five more years, he became convinced that a tolerance of infant baptism was incompatible with a church composed of saints saved by grace. In 1756 Backus with several other church members constituted a Baptist Church in Middleborough, Massachusetts. At its inception, the church adopted a **Calvinist** confession of faith that affirmed freedom of conscience and a Baptist covenant. According to the church's Baptist principles, the civil government was to defend rich and poor alike, punish moral evil, and encourage virtue, and yet not infringe upon an individual's conscience or dictate any aspect of worship. Communion in the Lord's Supper could only be taken by those who professed their faith and were baptized by immersion in the name of the Father, the Son, and the Holy Spirit. Backus remained as pastor in this congregation until his death in 1806. His marriage to Susannah Mason, begun in 1749, lasted until her death 51 years later.

Backus served as agent for the Baptists of Massachusetts in their struggle for religious liberty in the state. He also served in that capacity for the Warren Association, Rhode Island, on numerous occasions in their active quest for separation of church and state at the national level. His relentless activity in speaking, writing, and debating for religious liberty articulated and advanced the Baptist position on that issue. His *A History of New England with Particular Reference to the Denomination of Christians Called Baptists* (1777) argued for religious liberty and sought to demonstrate that the Baptist view of the church and freedom of conscience provided the most potent protection for Christian orthodoxy. Backus defended Calvinism as strongly as he did religious liberty and maintained an interest in revival throughout his ministry. He believed that the purity of the churches and the freedom of Americans depended on clear, Calvinistic preaching. Among the major influences on Backus were George Whitefield as an itinerant evangelist, **Jonathan Edwards** as a theologian, and John Locke as a philosopher.

Further Reading: Grenz, Stanley. *Isaac Backus: Puritan and Baptist.* Macon, GA: Mercer University Press, 1983; Hovey, Alvah. *A Memoir of the Life and Times of the Rev. Isaac Backus.* Reprint ed. Harrisonburg, VA: Gano Books, 1991.

Thomas J. Nettles

BAKKER, JIM (1939–) AND TAMMY FAYE (BAKKER) MESSNER (1942–)

Jim Bakker and his former wife, Tammy Faye, are televangelists and were founders of the PTL (Praise the Lord) Christian **television** network, which made its greatest impact during the 1980s.

They married in 1961 while students at North Central Bible College. In 1964, Bakker was ordained by the **Assemblies of God.** The following year, the Bakkers were hired by **Pat Robertson** of the Christian Broadcast Network to do a children's TV show, *The Jim and Tammy Show*, and to host *The 700 Club*. In 1973, they helped to found the Trinity Broadcasting Network with Paul and Jan Crouch, inaugurating *The PTL Club* a year later. Beginning as a storefront studio in Charlotte, North Carolina, *The PTL Club* grew to become the flagship program of the Inspirational Television Network, which at its peak aired in more than 14 million homes in the United States and worldwide. By 1987, PTL Enterprises, including state-of-the-art TV production studios and Heritage USA, a four-square-mile Christian retreat center and theme park containing the Grand Hotel, Heritage Tower, a water amusement park, and a home for handicapped children, was valued at $172 million. Heritage USA was intended to be a modern version of the old-time **camp meetings** that shaped America's religious life during the eighteenth and nineteenth centuries.

On March 19, 1987, Jim Bakker resigned as chairman of PTL Enterprises in the wake of the revelation that on December 6, 1980, he had had a sexual encounter with Jessica Hahn, a young church secretary from Long Island. It was then agreed that the organization would be turned over to Jerry Falwell, another televangelist. Although there were media reports that hush money had been paid to Jessica Hahn, Bakker later wrote that this money constituted an out-of-court legal settlement. Through Los Angeles attorney Howard Weitzman, PTL had paid $265,000 for psychological damages arising from the incident. A detailed document had been drawn up and agreed upon in the presence of Superior Court Judge Charles Woodmansee on February 27, 1985, and signed by the judge; Jessica Hahn; her lawyer, Paul Roper; and Scott Furstman, Howard Weitzman's partner (Bakker, 27–28).

After auditors determined that the PTL ministry was in debt by $70 million, its attorneys filed for bankruptcy. An IRS investigation followed, and in

An early photograph of Rev. Jim and Tammy Faye Bakker, engaged in puppet ministry, after being hired in 1965 by Rev. Pat Robertson to host a children's radio and television program, *The Jim and Tammy Show* (ca. 1967). Courtesy of Dr. Stanley M. Burgess.

1989 Jim Bakker was charged with fraud and conspiring to commit fraud for receiving $158 million from 152,903 PTL Lifetime Partners by overselling lifetime partnerships and promising lifetime accommodations at Heritage USA. After a highly publicized trial in 1989, he was convicted and given a 45-year sentence. A federal appeals court reduced the sentence in 1991, and he was paroled in 1994. While he was in prison, Tammy Faye divorced him and married Roe Messner, the developer of Heritage USA and a close family friend.

Shortly after release from prison, Bakker published *I Was Wrong* (1996), in which he repudiated the health-and-wealth or **prosperity** gospel but maintained his innocence of the charges for which he was convicted. The Towers Hotel, he noted, was still in the process of being built at the time of the scandal, and "we were in fact building enough facilities to house the Lifetime Partners" (Bakker, 3). On July 23, 1996, a federal jury ruled in a class action suit that PTL was not selling securities by offering Lifetime Partnerships at Heritage USA, effectively implying Bakker's innocence. Six years later, after reading the lengthy transcripts of the 1989 trial, James A. Albert, a trial attorney and law professor at Drake University, concurred in the book *Jim Bakker: Miscarriage of Justice?* according to which

Bakker was treated unfairly during his trial and was never guilty of fraud in a legal sense.

In 1998, Bakker married Lori Graham of Phoenix and began conducting ministry trips with her to England and Australia. They launched a new television show in January of 2003, *The Jim Bakker Show*, broadcasting from Branson, Missouri, with the help of financing from friends. Tammy Faye, who in her PTL days had been the host of her own show, *Tammy Faye's House Party*, became cohost in 1996 with Jim J. Bullock of the syndicated *Jim J. and Tammy Faye Show*. She has recorded over 25 singing albums, written several books, and appeared on many talk shows. A documentary, *The Eyes of Tammy Faye* (2000), depicted her role as "mother of three religious cable networks" and portrayed the events of the PTL scandal. On March 19, 2004, she announced on CNN's *Larry King Live* that she had inoperable lung cancer.

Further Reading: Albert, James A. *Jim Bakker: Miscarriage of Justice?* Chicago: Open Court Publishing, 2002; Bakker, Jim. *I Was Wrong*. Nashville, TN: Thomas Nelson, 1996; Messner, Tammy Faye. *I Will Survive … and You Can, Too!* New York: Putnam, 2003; "PTL Victims to Receive $6.54 Each." *Christianity Today* 47 (October 2003): 26; Shepard, Charles E. *Forgiven: The Rise and Fall of Jim Bakker and the PTL Ministry*. New York: Atlantic Monthly Press, 1991; White, Cecile Holmes. "Jim and Tammy Bakker." In Charles H. Lippy, ed., *Twentieth-Century Shapers of American Popular Religion*, 14–20. New York: Greenwood Press, 1989.

Richard M. Riss

BAPTISM IN (OF) THE HOLY SPIRIT

Baptism in (or *of*) *the Holy Spirit* is a biblical metaphor that refers to a distinct spiritual experience of receiving God's fullness or power. During the twentieth century, **Pentecostal** and **Charismatic** Christians have used this phrase to describe an experience subsequent to **conversion** that is commonly associated with the exercise of **charismatic gifts** and especially the gift of **speaking in tongues.** In classical Pentecostal theology, speaking in tongues is the outward sign or "initial evidence" of the inward experience of Spirit baptism—a doctrine that came to have a central role in the **Assemblies of God** denomination. The idea is that everyone who undergoes baptism in the Holy Spirit will also speak in tongues. In Charismatic theology, speaking in tongues is an important sign of the Spirit's presence, and yet there is a reluctance to assert that no one is ever baptized in the Spirit without also speaking in tongues. In nineteenth-century American revivalism, some groups used *baptism in the Spirit* to refer to perfection (from sin), empowerment (for service), or preparation (for Jesus' Second Coming). Others equated Spirit baptism with conversion, and not with an experience coming after conversion. Yet an understanding of Christian holiness or **sanctification** as a momentary, identifiable event in personal experience took hold among a wide range of groups in the nineteenth century—including Wesleyans, Oberlin perfectionists, Keswick "deeper life" teachers, and other **Holiness movement** adherents—and this general notion of a "second blessing" following conversion was a part of the theological background to the emergence of the twentieth-century Pentecostal and Charismatic movements.

John Wesley, who championed sanctification or perfection as an experience subsequent to conversion, was perhaps the most influential thinker in introducing a two-stage concept of the Christian life. Yet Wesley himself did not explicitly describe sanctification or perfection as baptism in the Spirit. John Fletcher was among the first **Methodist** thinkers to make this connection. The language of Spirit baptism increased as the nineteenth-century Holiness movement sought to restore the fervor of eighteenth-century Wesleyan revivalism. The Holiness tradition crossed over denominational and theological boundaries, and included **Baptists** and Reformed (i.e., **Calvinistic**) Christians as well as Methodists. In the later 1800s, Holiness advocates began to speak less of "sanctification" and "holiness" and more of "Pentecost," "baptism" (in the Spirit), and "power" or "empowerment." This emerging emphasis prepared the way for the twentieth-century Pentecostal revival. Evangelical revivalists such as **Dwight L. Moody** and **Reuben A. Torrey** both taught and claimed to have undergone Spirit

baptism as an experience of empowerment subsequent to conversion. Unlike the Pentecostals, however, Moody and Torrey did not associate spiritual empowerment with speaking in tongues. Throughout the twentieth century, many American Evangelicals adopted a view of Spirit baptism as equivalent to conversion and so distanced themselves from Pentecostals.

The emergence of Pentecostal **healing** revivalists in the late 1940s and early 1950s brought with it a renewed emphasis on Spirit baptism as empowerment. **Oral Roberts**—a leader in the healing revival—interpreted spiritual empowerment in terms that were more acceptable to mainline Protestants than the classical Pentecostal doctrines. Roberts spoke of "releasing" the Spirit that had already been received by practicing Christians. Such language allowed for continuity between the mainline Protestant traditions and the newer, charismatic experiences. The Christian life was a series of blessings, and could not be reduced to one or two dramatic episodes.

Among contemporary Pentecostal and Charismatic Christians there are differing views on Spirit baptism and speaking in tongues. So-called Wesleyan Pentecostals or Holiness Pentecostals teach three distinct experiences of blessing: conversion, entire sanctification, and Spirit baptism with the accompanying sign of speaking in tongues. Baptistic, Reformed, or "Finished Work" Pentecostals hold to two blessings: conversion and Spirit baptism, with speaking in tongues as initial evidence of Spirit baptism and sanctification as a gradual, lifelong process. Charismatics in **Roman Catholic,** Orthodox, Anglican, and Protestant churches usually interpret Spirit baptism in organic or sacramental terms as an outgrowth of grace already conferred. The new spiritual experience is not a second blessing but an extension of the first blessing given in baptism or confirmation. Recently, some Charismatic thinkers have conceived of Spirit baptism in the perspective of **eschatology.** With Jesus came the final epoch of history. His ministry of baptizing in the Holy Spirit, predicted by John the Baptist, encompassed the entire redemptive process: spiritual regeneration, sanctification, and empowerment as well as social reform and even the cosmic transformation ensuing from Jesus' return to earth.

With the **Toronto Blessing** and **Pensacola revival** of the 1990s, new theological issues emerged. Participants in these revivals described new blessings that transcended their earlier experiences within Pentecostal and Charismatic churches. These revivals offered *more*—a term repeatedly used—for those who already **pray** in tongues and yet are experiencing spiritual barrenness. A theological question arises out of the recent revivals: If Spirit baptism, accompanied by speaking in tongues, proves inadequate in the long run for some Pentecostal or Charismatic Christians, then is there any reason to emphasize only one or two moments of spiritual transition in the Christian life? Would it not be better to conceive the Christian life as a series of blessings, including perhaps three, four, five, or, indeed, an indefinite number of important transitions? Spirit baptism continues to be understood in widely divergent ways among revivalists and renewalists of all stripes in North American Christianity. The striking revivals of the past two centuries have forced Christians continually to reexamine what it means to be baptized in the Holy Spirit.

Further Reading: Keener, Craig S. *Gift and Giver: The Holy Spirit for Today.* Grand Rapids, MI: Baker, 2001; Lederle, H. I. *Treasures Old and New: Interpretations of "Spirit Baptism" in the Charismatic Renewal Movement.* Peabody, MA: Hendrickson, 1988; Synan, Vinson, ed. *Aspects of Pentecostal-Charismatic Origins.* Plainfield, NJ: Logos International, 1975; Synan, Vinson. *The Holiness-Pentecostal Tradition: Charismatic Movements in the Twentieth Century.* Grand Rapids, MI: Eerdmans, 1997.

Larry D. Hart

BAPTIST REVIVALS

Baptist Christians throughout their history have been known for an emphasis on biblical **preaching** and a call to **conversion** or individual faith decision, made by those who are old enough to understand the gospel message and to choose to undergo baptism by immersion. Given these distinctive features, it is not surprising that Baptist churches in North America have a rich tradition of revivals and revivalism. The Baptist stress on local autonomy has allowed each congregation to set its own agenda, often including special meetings for revival preaching and **praying.** The separation of church and state—a Baptist principle that was well established in the aftermath of the **Great Awakening** (1739–1745) and embodied in treatises by Baptist pioneer **Isaac Backus**—fits well with a vision of the church as a community for spiritual revitalization. Baptist churches in America fall into many subcategories, too numerous to mention. There are Baptists of English or British extraction, and others of **German, Scandinavian,** or Continental European background. Among **African Americans,** the Baptist churches, along with the various black Methodist church bodies, are the two largest church traditions, and include such major denominations as the **National Baptist Convention USA and National Baptist Convention of America.** In colonial America, most Baptists were theologically Reformed or **Calvinistic** (also called Regular or Particular). In 1780 the **Free Will Baptist** movement began in northern regions of the United States under the leadership of Benjamin Randall. The moderating of Calvinism among Baptists in the North led to a union of the Randallite movement with the Northern Baptist Church in 1911. By the mid-to-late 1800s many Baptist churches in the North and **South** had softened in their adherence to Calvinism or else embraced an Arminian **theology of revivals** (and were called "general" Baptists). **Primitive Baptists** (also known as Antimission or Hard-Shell Baptists) are opposed in principle to human institutions and organizations, including even missionary societies and Sunday schools. The emphasis in this essay will be on revivals and revival practices among Baptists of English or British background.

The **Great Awakening** of the 1740s affected Baptist life by injecting new zeal, increasing the number of churches and converts, and expanding the movement into new territories. In 1700 only 14 Baptist churches existed in all the colonies, 9 in New England, 4 in the Middle Colonies, and 1 in the South. Individuals converted under the preaching of the Great Awakening had an impact on the stability and growth of Baptists in the colonial period. Among these were Isaac Backus, Benjamin Miller, Oliver Hart, John Gano, **Shubal Stearns,** and Daniel Marshall. Backus in New England; Miller and Gano in the Philadelphia Association and the South; Hart in Charleston, South Carolina; and Stearns and Marshall in the Carolinas were among the itinerant preachers that came out of the Great Awakening. They also planted Baptist churches. Connecticut had no Baptist church until 1705 in Groton, organized by Valentine Weightman. By 1744 there were seven. Due to the New Light and Separate movements beginning in the 1740s, by 1800 more than 60 Baptist churches peppered the state, in spite of consistent opposition from Congregationalist clergy and Yale College.

The Sandy Creek Church in North Carolina, established by Stearns and Marshall, foreshadowed the later exponential growth of Baptists throughout the South. Beginning with 16 people, it became, in the words of Baptist historian Morgan Edwards, "the mother of all the Separate-baptists." In 17 years it spawned 42 churches, from which sprang 125 ministers. Edwards believed in "a preternatural and invisible hand work in the assemblies of the Separate-baptists bearing down the human mind, as was the case in primitive churches" (Edwards, 2:90–97). Largely due to Separate Baptist zeal and revivalistic practice, Baptist churches in the South grew from just 6 in 1740 to 410 by 1790.

Isaac Backus saw an outpouring of revival among the Baptists beginning in 1785, immediately after he had expressed grave concerns about the spread of Universalism (i.e., belief in universal salvation) in the evangelical churches. "Considerable revivals of religion have been granted on our eastern coasts, in New York, in portions of New Jersey, and in some other places" he wrote in 1785, while in other places he observed "profaneness, intemperance, cruel oppression, damnable heresies, and a dead sleep about religion." In later years he reported revivals with hundreds of persons being baptized. In 1792 he remarked that "wonders

In rural regions a river baptism might draw together a congregation or entire village. Baptists generally required a confession of faith or public testimony as a part of this ritual of initiation. (Alan Lomax, photographer; near Mineola, Texas, summer 1935.) Courtesy of the Library of Congress.

of the grace of God have appeared in many places." In 1800 he exclaimed, "The revivals of religion in different parts of our land have been wonderful." He gave lists of Baptist churches in Georgia, South Carolina, and Kentucky that had received large accessions of new members by conversion and baptism. In 1803, he wrote, "In Boston there is the greatest work going on which they have ever known there" and the ripple effect could be observed in many surrounding towns (Hovey, 301–6). Serving as pastor of First Baptist Church in Boston during the 1803–1805 revival was Samuel Stillman, who had been converted under Oliver Hart in Charleston, South Carolina, and ordained as an evangelist in February 1759. He became pastor of First Baptist Church in Boston in 1765 and spent the remainder of his years serving that congregation. During this long ministry several remarkable revivals occurred. The revival Backus reported in 1803 continued through 1804–1805 and received attention in the *Baptist Magazine.*

Backus made mention of a revival that overtook the Baptists of Kentucky in 1800–1803, beginning on the northern border of the state and transpiring for the most part without the emotional excesses seen at **Cane Ridge.** Several counties were affected. John Taylor brought the revival to the Baptist church in Bullitsburg in Boone County. Large increases in church membership occurred in Franklin County, Woodford County, Hardin County, and elsewhere under the preaching of Richard Cave, William Hickman, Joshua Morris, John Gano, Ambrose Dudley, Joseph Redding, and others. In 1800 the Baptists had 7 associations, 106 churches, and 5,119 members. By 1803, there were 10 associations, 219 churches, and 15,495 members. Thus the number of Baptists in the state tripled in just three years. Contemporaries reported that the moral life of Kentucky improved at this time, and that Deism and freethinking declined. Christians stressed spiritual matters and were less inclined to doctrinal squabbling. Among Baptists, divisions between the so-called Regular Baptists and the Separate Baptists were healed and missionary endeavor received a fresh impetus. John Taylor chronicled another revival in Clear Creek church and others in its vicinity in 1822 that greatly affected the black population. Ninety-seven were baptized in eight months, one-third of whom were African American. The sight of master and slave in the same baptismal waters and rejoicing in their common salvation left a lasting impression. Parts of Virginia saw a religious stirring in these years. According to R. B. Semple, "glorious revivals" in many Baptist churches began in 1800 and continued in 1801, and by 1802 many of the revivals were declining. In 1804 a leading minister had been convicted of horse stealing and sent to the penitentiary. By 1805 more revivals were reported with hundreds baptized. By 1807 the churches spoke of "distressing times" and in 1808 the churches

lamented their "languor and lukewarmness" (Semple, 128–34). In Georgia, Daniel Marshall established the first Baptist church in 1772 in Kiokee. Steady growth brought the number to 140 Baptist churches with 11,000 members during the first decade of the nineteenth century.

When William B. Sprague compiled his lectures on revival into a book published in 1832, he appended letters from several leading evangelical thinkers on the subject. Francis Wayland, president of Brown University and a student of the writings of **Jonathan Edwards,** contributed his thoughts on revivals among Baptists. He noted the successful use of a number of means for promoting revivals: active engagement against all known sin, setting apart seasons of prayer and fasting, and more frequent and more faithful preaching of the gospel. Revival preaching needed to stress the extensiveness of human depravity, the exceeding sinfulness of sin, the justice of God in condemning sinners to hell, the total inability of human beings to reconcile themselves to God, the sufficiency of Christ's atonement, the duty of immediate repentance and faith in Jesus Christ, the inexcusableness of delay, the irrationality of excuses used by sinners, the sovereignty of God in the salvation of sinners, the absence of any divine obligation to save sinners, and the necessity of the Spirit's work in each and every conversion. Wayland added that revivals should cultivate deep piety, involve extraordinary effort for the conversion of sinners, and continue as long as possible without causing mental and bodily weariness, preventing people from fulfilling their duties, or provoking an excitement of the passions. Wayland pointed to the errors of using practices without biblical support, relying on human means instead of the Spirit of God, and succumbing to spiritual pride.

Baptists grew along with virtually all other denominations during the **Revival of 1857–1858,** which began in New York City. Across the nation Baptist congregations reported increases in baptisms, membership, and contributions to missionary causes. At the beginning of 1858 Baptists numbered 923,198. During that year the net increase was 70,323, or 7.6 percent of the total membership. By 1860, approximately 18 percent of Baptist membership had been baptized in the past two years. Reports from Alabama, Illinois, Georgia, and other states reported a spiritual awakening during these years. Ironically, this revival preceded the fratricidal carnage of the **Civil War.** During the war, an initial decline in spiritual interest was soon succeeded by a widespread distribution of Bibles and other Christian literature among the soldiers. Colporteurs, Bible Society workers, and camp preachers began to report many converts in both Southern and Northern armies. Baptists were particularly active at this time. In September 1863, John A. Broadus wrote in the *Religious Herald*, "It is impossible to convey any just idea of the wide and effectual door that is now opened for preaching in the Army of Northern Virginia…. In every command that I visit, or hear from, a large proportion of the soldiers will attend preaching and listen well; and in many cases the interest is really wonderful…. Brethren, there is far more religious interest in this army than at home. The Holy Spirit seems everywhere moving among us. These widespread camps are a magnificent collection of camp-meetings…. The rich, ripe harvest stands waiting. Come, brother, thrust in your sickle, and, by God's blessing, you shall reap golden sheaves that shall be your rejoicing in time and eternity."

During the 1830s John Leland had questioned the growing use of the so-called new measures—associated in the northern states with revivalist **Charles G. Finney**—in Baptist revivals. W. T. Brantley by contrast argued for their usefulness in the *Columbian Star and Christian Index*. Basil Manly became suspicious of revivalistic techniques while serving in Charleston, South Carolina, and opposed them more overtly after his experiences in Alabama in the 1840s. Manly warned that professions of faith made in the midst of spiritual excitement are fleeting. The lust for new converts creates carelessness among pastors and allows unbelieving or unconverted persons to crowd into the church. Manly was hesitant about the use of the **altar call** or other forms of physical movement as signs of faith decision. Other Baptists shared his hesitation, and Baptist journals debated the new

measures throughout the nineteenth century. Protracted meetings, the use of the anxious bench, and traveling evangelists such as **B. Fay Mills, Sam Jones,** and **Dwight L. Moody** all received critical evaluation. Moody received more positive comments than negative. Cornelius Tyree complained that the preacher who equated conversion with the act of standing up, coming forward, going to a meeting, or signing a card would deceive more souls than he would help. The theatrics and cupidity of certain revival preachers caused resentment. When a local Methodist pastor in Cincinnati reported that of 1,500 cards placed in the hands of pastors, only 77 indicated seriousness about church connection, the *Christian Index* observed that "the more we see of these 'evangelists' and their work, the less we think of them. Our prayer is that God will deliver his churches from such 'work'" (*Christian Index*, February 16, 1893, 3). Some argued that the scheduling of special revival services (known as "protracted meetings") did not solve the problem of spiritual indifference in the churches. Rather, it made things worse. An article in the *Christian Index* characterized card signing as a "new-fangled piece of machinery for engineering people into the church" (Tucker, 2). Many who signed had no grasp of gospel truth or their own sin. Card signing was thus an "ingenious contrivance of Satan for destroying the churches by filling them with unconverted people." In contrast, George Boardman Taylor had earlier written that "it is highly appropriate to set apart special seasons and use special means for the purpose of ingathering, and that it is perfectly reasonable at such seasons, to expect unusual additions" ("Protracted Meetings"). He noted the possible abuses of revival meetings but thought that churches could take steps to avoid these.

By the close of the nineteenth century, few Baptist authors expressed hesitations about the methods of revival preachers. The *Christian Index*, which had previously been critical, subsequently gave its full endorsement to professional revivalism and its methods. In 1915 it offered a front-page article on "The Secret of Billy Sunday's Power," and concluded that **Billy Sunday**'s success resulted from the preparation for his meetings. Both as a baseball player and as an agent for evangelist **J. Wilbur Chapman,** Sunday had learned the value of preparation. He preceded his Philadelphia meetings with advertisement, a recruited choir, cottage prayer meetings, and the zealous backing of all the evangelical preachers in the city. If Baptist churches did that kind of preparation, the article stated, then they would have more famous preachers and more converts. The earlier note of caution about revival methods was gone by the early twentieth century. The ministry of **Billy Graham,** a Southern Baptist, has received carte blanche acceptance among Baptists from the 1940s up to the present time. Each Graham crusade reports a numbers of "decisions." A four-day mission in San Diego in 2003, for example, reported more than 16,000 spiritual decisions. This emphasis on momentary decisions—rather than the ongoing life of Christian discipleship—makes the discernment of genuine revival more difficult in contemporary Baptist churches than in former generations. Earlier Baptist revivals had effects that were not confined to the signing of decision cards and regular church attendance.

Further Reading: Edwards, Morgan. *Material towards a History of the Baptists.* 2 vols. Danielsville, GA: Heritage Papers, 1984; Fish, Roy J. *When Heaven Touched Earth.* Azle, TX: Needs of the Times, 1996; Hovey, Alvah. *A Memoir of the Life and Times of the Rev. Isaac Backus.* Reprint ed. Harrisonburg, VA: Gano Books, 1991; Murray, Iain. *Revival and Revivalism.* Edinburgh: Banner of Truth Trust, 1994; Orr, J. Edwin. *The Event of the Century.* Ed. Richard Owen Roberts. Wheaton, IL: International Awakening Press, 1989; Semple, Robert B. *History of the Baptists in Virginia.* Reprint ed. Lafayette, TN: Church History Research and Archives, 1976; Spencer, J. H. *History of Kentucky Baptists.* 2 vols. 1895. Reprint, Gallatin, TN: Church History Research and Archives, 1984; Sprague, William B. *Lectures on Revival.* Reprint ed. Edinburgh: Banner of Truth Trust, 1978; Taylor, George Boardman. "Protracted Meetings." *The Religious Herald,* March 28, 1861; Taylor, John. *Baptists on the American Frontier: A History of Ten Churches of Which the Author Has Been Alternately a Member.* Ed. Chester Raymond Young. Macon, GA: Mercer University Press, 1995; Tucker, H. H. "From California."

The Christian Index and Southwestern Baptist, May 11, 1880.

Thomas J. Nettles

BEECHER, LYMAN (1775–1863) AND HENRY WARD (1813–1887)

The Beechers, father and son, were leading voices in the nineteenth-century revivals usually known as the **Second Great Awakening.** Lyman Beecher, who was to become the patriarch of a dynamic and influential family, came under the influence of **Timothy Dwight,** a grandson of **Jonathan Edwards** and president of Yale College when Lyman studied there. In his early ministries in a Presbyterian church in East Hampton, Long Island (1799–1810), and a Congregational church in Litchfield, Connecticut (1810–1826), certain traits appeared that characterized his entire career: interest in revitalizing mainstream Protestantism and determination to improve general culture through moral influence. This led to a pastorate at Hanover Street Congregational Church in Boston, Massachusetts. Despite his liberalizing tendencies, Lyman occupied a conservative position in defending Trinitarianism against burgeoning Unitarians and in sounding a xenophobic alarm over immigration and the consequent increase of **Roman Catholics.** His fiery sermons on the latter subject are thought to have contributed to a mob action that burned an Ursuline convent in 1834.

Lyman was pro-revival from the beginning. He enjoyed a warm, cooperative relationship with **Nathaniel W. Taylor** because both were interested in reformulating traditional doctrines and the **theology of revival** in more individualistic terms. He assured his wide following that "Beecherism" was the equivalent of good, sound **Calvinism.** But he was wary of the "new measures" associated with **Charles G. Finney** and revivals in New York's **Burned-Over District.** For all his positive attitude regarding free will and personal choice in evangelical outreach, Lyman opposed Finney's tactics at first because he thought them too crude. Within a few years, however, he invited Finney to **preach** at his church in Boston. The individual experience of redemption was the starting point for Lyman Beecher, but he always linked that to larger questions of religion in society. For him piety necessarily led to ethical action. So he used his not inconsiderable persuasive powers to enlist support for the American Bible Society, the **temperance movement,** evangelical magazines and newspapers, **foreign missions,** domestic missions, and interdenominational cooperation. While not overt in proclaiming his conviction, Lyman believed that moral reforms helped American life more nearly to approximate the kingdom of God.

Interest in theological education led Lyman to accept the presidency of Lane Seminary (1832–1850) in Cincinnati, Ohio. He also became pastor of the Second Presbyterian Church there. For all his interest in improving culture through ethical influence, he temporized on the antislavery question, preferring gradual emancipation to the radical severity of **abolitionism.** In 1834 a vocal minority of Lane students under the leadership of Theodore D. Weld revolted against such administrative indecision and transferred to a more congenial campus at Oberlin College. This loss did not enhance Lyman's reputation, but he continued to labor for causes in his own way, hoping to insure the survival of his seminary as well. Amid this turmoil of social issues, Lyman was forced to undergo an ordeal of a formal theological nature. A favorable regard for revivals placed Lyman solidly within New School Presbyterianism. Old School proponents had opposed his appointment as Lane's president, and they took steps to try him for heresy in 1834 and 1835. Though Lyman was interested in applying Christian values to human society, his affirmation that people had the ability to repent and respond to God's grace brought strong criticism from rigid Calvinists. He was acquitted, but this local controversy was symptomatic of widespread tensions in the denomination that produced a complete schism in 1837.

In the following generation Henry Ward Beecher added further distinction to the family name. After serving for a decade at two Presbyterian churches in Indiana, he was called in 1847 to the Plymouth Congregational Church in Brooklyn, New York, where he remained pastor for the rest of his life. His

Family portrait of Rev. Lyman Beecher (center), Harriett Beecher Stowe (left), and Rev. Henry Ward Beecher (right). Lyman and Henry were among the best-known ministers in America, while Harriett authored the renowned antislavery novel, *Uncle Tom's Cabin* (1852). (Brady-Handy Photograph Collection, 1855–1865.) Courtesy of the Library of Congress.

dramatic oratory and winning personality nurtured a large, prosperous following there. Never really interested in the theological niceties concerning Christology, miracles, evolution, and future punishment, Henry thought preaching would be effective if it simply created an emotional atmosphere that resonated with the vital experiences of those in the audience. Thus he employed his great expository facility and fertile imagination to convey simple truths about God's love to humanity and God's presence in natural surroundings. A critic claimed that he preached "charity at the price of clarity" (Marsden, 23).

His picturesque, witty sermons also conveyed a sincere earnestness about applying moral principles in the larger world around him. Most of his ideas regarding the culture around him were based on a peculiarly American confidence in freedom, progress, and the possibilities of what human nature might achieve in an open society. Not one to lead the way in social reforms, he was nevertheless quick to adopt popular causes and to assist them with his advocacy. One such issue was abolition, and Henry preached against the Fugitive Slave Law, helped antislavery fighters in Kansas—arming them in 1856 with guns dubbed as "Beecher's Bibles"—and stumped for Republican candidates in elections. During the **Civil War,** he identified the Union cause with God's plan for continued progress. He embodied the hopes and fears of most middle-class citizens in America and articulated popular optimism regarding spiritual growth in a culture undergirded by moral principles.

Henry continued throughout his career to attract national attention as an orator. His addresses were published weekly, and collections of his sermons eventually filled 19 volumes. He was also editor of the *Independent* (1861–1863) and the *Christian Union* (1870–1881). Liberal statements and cautious action made him a star of the lecture circuit as well. Between 1872 and 1876 he was implicated in a complex scandal involving charges of adultery with one of his parishioners, Mrs. Josephine Tilton. Court action ended in a hung jury, and even though the controversy split his church, the majority of its members backed him to the end. This episode tarnished his reputation somewhat, but Henry continued to enjoy a popularity and influence rarely equaled by an American clergyman.

Further Reading: Beecher, Henry Ward. *Yale Lectures on Preaching.* 3 vols. New York: J. B. Ford, 1872–1874; Beecher, Lyman. *Autobiography.* 2 vols. Ed. Barbara Cross. Cambridge, MA: Belknap Press, 1961; Caskey, Marie. *Chariot of Fire.* New Haven, CT: Yale University Press, 1978; Clark, Clifford E., Jr. *Henry Ward Beecher: Spokesman for a Middle-Class America.* Urbana: University of Illinois Press, 1978; Fraser, James W. *Pedagogue for God's Kingdom: Lyman Beecher and the Second Great Awakening.* Lanham, MD: University Press of America, 1985; Harding, Vincent. *A Certain Magnificence.* New York: Carlson, 1991; Marsden, George M. *Fundamentalism and American Culture.* New York: Oxford University Press, 1980; McLoughlin, William G. *The Meaning of Henry Ward Beecher.* New York: Knopf, 1970; Rugoff, Milton. *The Beechers: An American Family in the Nineteenth Century.* New York: Harper and Row, 1981.

Henry Bowden

BIBLE

see Theology of Revivals

BLAIR, SAMUEL (1712–1751)

Samuel Blair was a **Presbyterian** minister, **preacher,** theologian, and outspoken supporter of the **Great Awakening** in the Middle Colonies that his own sermons helped to spread. He subsequently defended the revivals with other New Side ministers, like **Gilbert Tennent,** against the protests of Old Side counterparts in the Presbyterian Synod of Philadelphia. A former student of Gilbert Tennent's father, William Tennent, Blair was also one of the most gifted intellectuals of the time. He founded a classical school near his church in Fagg's Manor, Pennsylvania, that came to rival his teacher's institution in its academic excellence and distinguished graduates, including **Samuel Davies.**

Blair was born in Ireland but immigrated to America in his youth. He was among the first Presbyterians to pursue classical and theological studies under the elder Tennent at the controversial Log College (later Princeton College), originally in Neshaminy, Pennsylvania. Upon graduating Blair came under care of the New Castle or Philadelphia Presbytery, which licensed him to preach in November 1733. He accepted a call to lead the congregation of Shrewsbury, New Jersey, in 1734 at age 22. There Blair remained until the fall of 1739, when he agreed to pastor the New Londonderry church in Fagg's Manor, Pennsylvania. He had also become a founding member of the Presbytery of New Brunswick, part of the wider Synod of Philadelphia, in 1738. This new presbytery encouraged Blair's move in order to give him a wider sphere of opportunity and influence among the predominantly Scotch-Irish immigrant population.

While Blair prepared for his new call, thousands gathered in Philadelphia to hear **George Whitefield,** and young Presbyterian evangelists carried the revival to vacant parishes like that which Blair soon filled. Blair was installed in April 1740 as New Londonderry's first pastor in its

15-year history. Blair had already preached there through the winter to try to educate those who had not yet heard the Christian message of sin and salvation or undergone conversion. In his *Narrative of a Revival of Religion in Several Parts of Pennsylvania* (1744), Blair recounts that during this time some were "brought under deep conviction" (Alexander, 176). In the spring, when Blair had arranged for a neighboring minister to fill his pulpit for two weeks, the guest preacher's sermons caused audible reactions and crying from listeners concerned about the state of their souls. News of the reaction reached Blair while he was still traveling 100 miles away from home. When he returned Blair preached in the same vein twice a week throughout the summer. The attendance increased, as did the vocal and physical manifestations of spiritual concern.

In the meantime, eager evangelists had begun preaching to Presbyterian congregations already supplied with pastors, who resented the intrusion and challenge to their authority. Fearing a possible loss of power, as well as social unrest from the revival, these ministers voted at the Philadelphia Synod's 1739 meeting to review the credentials of graduates from the pro-revival Log College. In 1740 the Synod barred evangelists from preaching without permission. The revival's opponents published *The Querists* (1740), a pamphlet criticizing George Whitefield's sermons and conduct. Blair penned a response, *A Particular Consideration of "The Querists"* (1741), surpassing Whitefield's own point-by-point defense in eloquence and logic, and revealing the intellectual divisions within the synod.

Though defending the prerogatives of evangelists to spread the faith and criticizing ministers of the Old Side for trying to halt the work of God, Blair was moderate in his own approach to revivals. He discouraged disruptive conduct or emotional outbursts in his church, and, unlike Gilbert Tennent in the controversial sermon "The Danger of an Unconverted Ministry" (1740), he avoided judging his colleagues' or congregants' state of salvation. His writing *The Doctrine of Predestination Truly and Fairly Stated* (1742) reveals his thoroughly Calvinistic doctrinal views. At his early death at age 39, Blair was survived by his wife, son (Samuel Blair), sister, and brother, the Reverend John Blair, a professor of divinity at the College of New Jersey, who compiled a volume of Blair's writings published in 1754.

Further Reading: Alexander, Archibald. *Biographical Sketches of the Founder and Principal Alumni of the Log College, Together with an Account of the Revivals of Religion under Their Ministry*. Philadelphia: Presbyterian Board of Education, 1851; Blair, Samuel. *The Works of the Reverend Mr. Samuel Blair*. Philadelphia: W. Bradford, 1754; Heimert, Alan, and Perry Miller, eds. *The Great Awakening: Documents Illustrating the Crisis and Its Consequences*. Indianapolis: Bobbs-Merrill, 1967.

Kaley Carpenter

BLAISDELL, FRANCISCA D. (ca. 1885–1941)

Francisca Blaisdell began her life in Sonora, Mexico, and later became a Mexican American **Assemblies of God** evangelist, missionary, and pastor in the United States and Mexico. She began her lay ministry in 1916 and was ordained by H. C. Ball and Juan L. Lugo as an evangelist in 1923. With her Anglo husband, George Blaisdell, she conducted evangelistic work along the Arizona–Mexico border in Douglas, Arizona, and Nacozari, Sonora, Mexico. In or around 1922 she helped to establish a **women**'s group called Dorcas—a name based on Acts 9:36—in Agua Prieta, Sonora, Mexico, and organized another women's group in Gallina, New Mexico, several years later. She was one of the first **Latinas** to conduct **Pentecostal** ministry along the U.S.–Mexican border, and she pastored congregations in Douglas, Arizona, Agua Prieta, Sonora, Mexico (1932–1933, 1938–1939), and El Paso, Texas (1933–1935). In addition to her ministry in Arizona and Mexico, she conducted annual evangelistic tours through the state of Sonora, Mexico, and the U.S. Southwest from Arizona to El Paso, Texas.

Further Reading: Espinosa, Gastón. "'Your Daughters Shall Prophesy': A History of Women in Ministry in the Latino Pentecostal Movement in the United States." In Margaret L. Bendroth and Virginia L. Brereton, eds.,

Women and Twentieth Century Protestantism, 25–48. Urbana: University of Illinois Press, 2002.

Gastón Espinosa

BODILY MANIFESTATIONS IN REVIVALS

Bodily actions such as falling, **dancing,** and **healing,** as well as vocalizations like **laughing, shouting,** and inarticulate groans and utterances, have been a dramatic feature of religious revivals throughout American history. The Evangelical belief that salvation is gained through a crisis of **conversion,** and a higher spiritual state through a **baptism in the Spirit,** served to create an emotionally charged environment wherein seekers gained **ecstasy** through bodily expressions or vocalizations. Evangelicals developed a repertoire of bodily responses that became part of the ritual of conversion and postconversion spiritual experiences. Such bodily responses highlight the importance of lay interaction, emotional expression, and a longing for the felt presence of God within the revival tradition.

When the **Great Awakening** of the 1740s began in New England, the physical manifestations among those affected by the revival, such as falling and loud crying, raised the specter of enthusiasm such as had appeared a few decades earlier in Europe. For eighteenth-century Christians, enthusiasm was a product of delusion, madness, or even demonic inspiration and created social disorder. **Charles Chauncy,** a Boston minister and formidable opponent of the revival, articulated this view in his sermon "Enthusiasm Describ'd and Cautioned Against" (1742), Viewing enthusiasm as a disease, he noted how it afflicted its victim's "bodies, throwing them into convulsions and distortions, into quaking and tremblings." As a representative of the rationalist strand in eighteenth-century Protestantism, Chauncy believed that the physical disruptions of the revival allowed passion to override reason and so to undermine genuine religion.

Jonathan Edwards, a renowned **Calvinistic** theologian, was the revival's greatest apologist. In contrast to Chauncy, he did not prioritize reason over what he called the affections. He argued that since there is a unity between the soul and the body, it is reasonable to expect that those touched by spiritual truth may exhibit bodily reactions. For example, in *Some Thoughts concerning the Revival* (1743), he recounted his wife's religious experiences and wrote that her body often fell under the weight of "divine discoveries" (332). In making this argument, Edwards sought to undercut the argument that such involuntary acts were unnatural or irrational. He also amassed a number of biblical citations as precedents for bodily manifestations. Yet while he defended certain involuntary acts against those seeking to discredit the revival, he did not wish to promote them, and he made it clear that they cannot be taken as positive signs of the Spirit's work.

Edwards's cautious approach to the body in worship proved too stringent for the Separate **Baptists,** Radical Congregationalists, and, later, **Methodists** who spread the revival fires to the **South.** These groups were known for their enthusiastic worship and accompanying bodily phenomena. Christianity first made significant inroads among the enslaved black population during this phase of the Great Awakening. Blacks were attracted to the prominence given to bodily participation and ecstatic experience in revivalism. As Albert Raboteau shows, these elements of **African American revivals** harkened back to traditional African religious practices like Spirit possession and ritual dancing. As blacks were converted to Christianity and participated in camp meetings, they were given a culturally sanctioned space to continue traditional patterns of religious ritual, although with new theological meanings.

The extent to which black styles of worship influenced white evangelicalism in this period is difficult to determine with precision, although there was opportunity for mutual influence and cross-fertilization at **camp meeting** revivals throughout the nineteenth century. Some contemporary accounts suggest that black shouting was more aggressive than the vocalizations of white evangelicals. Yet the loud shouting that was characteristic of black services became a common element in the conversion experience of many white Methodists. When the Methodist George Watson published a book in 1814 critical of the emotionalism and bodily exercises among fellow Methodists, he derisively pointed to their black origins. According to Ann Taves, the fusion of African performance traditions with revivalist Christianity created an interactive style of worship and placed a greater premium on bodily modes of knowledge than was previously seen in Methodism.

Bodily expressions were prominent among but not unique to Methodists, especially during the revival known as the **Second Great Awakening.** That revival had its beginnings among **Presbyterians** in the famed **Cane Ridge revival** in Kentucky (1801), although other Protestants participated as well. Cane Ridge featured perhaps the most widespread occurrence of diverse bodily phenomena in the history of American revivals. Presbyterian minister and revival promoter **Barton W. Stone** provided a catalogue of the bodily exercises that occurred at Cane Ridge, which he took as signs of God's work. The "falling exercise" was the most common in the early stage of the revival. This trancelike condition would be punctuated by groaning and confession of sin and then ended in joy, sometimes accompanied by laughter, as the penitent experienced salvation. Stone also described "the jerks"—uncontrollable bodily tics that have evoked comparisons with epileptic seizures or Tourette's syndrome. For Stone, involuntary jerking was a witness to God's power against the wicked and a means by which God brought a person to humility in order to receive salvation. The renowned Methodist circuit rider, **Peter Cartwright,** also witnessed and described the bodily manifestations at Cane Ridge, and he interpreted them much as Stone did. Viewed in light of the conversion experience, these bodily paroxysms could be seen as dramatic enactments of the death of sin and rebirth to new life.

Since the Cane Ridge revival took place in the context of a Presbyterian sacramental service, or **holy fair,** Leigh Eric Schmidt argues that participants could also interpret the involuntary motor phenomena they experienced as a form of identification with the afflicted body of Christ. Yet as revivalism developed throughout the nineteenth century, the sacramental idea of mediated grace gave way to a drive toward immediate access to God. For example, as Taves shows, nineteenth-century Methodists applied Old Testament scriptures that spoke of God's manifest presence in the Temple to their camp-meeting experience. And as heirs of the Methodist tradition, **Pentecostals** applied the same scriptures to their bodies. Whereas previous participants in revivals understood their bodies as responding to the Holy Spirit, Pentecostals believed that their bodies had become temples of the Holy Spirit.

The status given to the body in Pentecostalism can be understood in relation to two central practices, **speaking in tongues** and **healing.** Based on the New Testament book of Acts, Pentecostals believe that speaking in tongues is evidence of a postconversion experience known as the **baptism in the Holy Spirit.** Early accounts of initial speaking in tongues reveal that it was often a profoundly embodied experience. Seekers of the experience typically had someone lay hands on them as they **prayed.** If the prayers were effective, the seeker would begin uttering unintelligible syllables, often accompanied by a sense of being physically overwhelmed. Grant Wacker notes that many used the metaphor of electricity flowing through the body to describe the experience, while others used images of heat, fire, or liquid waves. The experience of Spirit baptism convinced Pentecostals that they were both spiritually and physically filled with the Spirit.

Pentecostals had been prepared to view their body as a locus of the Spirit's activity through the divine healing movement. The movement emerged among American evangelicals in the mid-nineteenth century and taught that Christ's atoning death on the cross secures physical healing for those who have faith. Experiences of healing taught the early Pentecostals that God wishes to renew and restore the whole person—body and soul—and that powerful message has been a part of the ministry of most Pentecostal revivalists. While focusing on speaking in tongues and healing, Pentecostalism also renewed the full repertoire of involuntary motor exercises rejected by much of mainstream American Christianity. With the emergence of the **Charismatic Revival** in the early 1960s, Pentecostal practices such as speaking in tongues, divine healing, and falling in the Spirit (or resting in the Spirit) spread to mainline Protestant and **Roman Catholic** churches. Recent participants in the so-called **Toronto Blessing** have experienced bodily phenomena not unlike those seen at Cane Ridge and in early Pentecostalism.

Several theorists find a link between the sorts of bodily behavior discussed above and the social contexts in which they occur. Some argue for a connection between marginal social status and such behavior. In this framework, the extraordinary bodily activity that has occurred in revivals is viewed as an emotional catharsis arising from the frustration caused by deprivation. Thus, these bodily responses are viewed as reactionary and regressive. This theory of religious behavior is vulnerable to criticism when such behavior transcends socioeconomic boundaries. For example, Paul Conkin has challenged its application to the events at Cane Ridge by showing that persons from all levels of society were vulnerable to the bodily exercises.

While deprivation theory may fail as an ultimate explanation for why such phenomena occur, scholars generally discern a relationship between bodily behavior in religion and the social contexts in which it emerges. The anthropologist Mary Douglas proposed an influential theory that sees the body as a symbol of the social order. She argues that conditions are favorable for uninhibited bodily manifestations where there is a weakening of social control and order. This may or may not occur among the socially or economically deprived, but can happen whenever the proper social circumstances exist. Douglas's theory resonates with a commonly held view that the "excesses" of revivalism, including the bodily exercises, were products of the unsettled, backwoods nature of the frontier. As revivalism expanded from the stable environment of New England to the frontier

regions of the South and West, the level of enthusiastic behavior matched and, in the case of Cane Ridge, exceeded that witnessed at the height of the New England revivals. Just as significantly, frontier evangelicalism gave rise to the farmer-**preacher,** who represented a shift away from an educated clerical class toward a more democratic, lay-orientated form of Christianity. Emotional, interactive, and embodied worship flourished in such a setting.

Yet to view the bodily responses in revivals only in reactionary terms ignores the creative dimension of religious expression. This dimension has been emphasized in the work of Victor Turner, especially as it relates to religious ritual. Turner argued that social life contains a dialectic between order or structure and periods of disorder and liminality. This process binds people together in *communitas*. Liminality occurs at the edge or boundary of normal social conditions and makes space for anti-structure and the emergence of new social arrangements. As a medium of social expression, the body comes to play a central role in this creative process. For example, the early Pentecostal acceptance of the spiritual authority of **women,** relatively radical in the social context of conservative Christianity, was often based on a demonstration of spiritual power (e.g., healing) in the liminal setting of a revival service. From the Great Awakening of the 1740s to the more recent Toronto Blessing of the 1990s, bodily expressions have served to bring people together in a spiritual *communitas* wherein people find a source of empowering and creative energy.

Discerning the source of that energy is a major methodological issue. Historians and social scientists are committed to explaining the phenomena discussed above in naturalistic terms. These can range from sociocultural explanations, some of which were described above, to physiological and psychological explanations. Of the latter, a prevalent view is that these behaviors are inducements to dissociative states of consciousness. However, participants in revivals and many theologians have viewed these phenomena as evidence of the supernatural. Between these two strands of interpretation lies a mediating tradition, detailed in Taves's history and emphasized in the work of the nineteenth-century psychologist William James, which views the sorts of experiences detailed above as both religious and natural.

Further Reading: Chauncy, Charles. "Enthusiasm Described and Cautioned Against." In Alan Heimert and Perry Miller, eds., *The Great Awakening: Documents Illustrating the Crises and Its Consequences*, 228–56. Indianapolis and New York: Bobbs-Merrill, 1967; Conkin, Paul K. *Cane Ridge: America's Pentecost*. Madison: University of Wisconsin Press, 1990; Douglas, Mary. *Natural Symbols: Explorations in Cosmology*. 3rd ed. London and New York: Routledge, 1996; Edwards, Jonathan. "The Distinguishing Marks of a Work of the Spirit of God." In *The Works of Jonathan Edwards*, vol. 4, 215–88. Edited by C. C. Goen. New Haven, CT: Yale University Press, 1972; Edwards, Jonathan. *Some Thoughts concerning the Revival*. In *The Works of Jonathan Edwards*, vol. 4, 130–211. Edited by C. C. Goen. New Haven, CT: Yale University Press, 1972; Poloma, Margaret. *Main Street Mystics: The Toronto Blessing and Reviving Pentecostalism*. New York: AltaMira Press, 2003; Schmidt, Leigh Eric. *Holy Fairs: Scotland and the Making of American Revivalism*. 2nd ed. Grand Rapids, MI: Eerdmans, 2001; Taves, Ann. *Fits, Trances, and Visions: Experiencing Religion and Explaining Experience from Wesley to James*. Princeton, NJ: Princeton University Press, 1999; Wacker, Grant. *Heaven Below: Early Pentecostals and American Culture*. Cambridge, MA: Harvard University Press, 2000.

Benjamin Wagner

BORN AGAIN

see Conversion and Revivals

BRAINERD, DAVID (1718–1747)

David Brainerd was an American minister who became famous for his work among the Delaware Indians in New Jersey and Pennsylvania. His diary, published posthumously by **Jonathan Edwards** as *The Life of David Brainerd* (1749), was an inspiration and impetus toward domestic and **foreign missions** among American evangelicals during the late eighteenth and nineteenth centuries. Born in Haddam, Connecticut,

Brainerd was the sixth of nine children. His family possessed comfortable wealth and was well connected politically and personally in the colony. Brainerd's father died when he was nine, his mother five years later. Although he owned land, Brainerd was more inclined to pursue a college degree and enter the ministry. At the age of 21, he began a quest to undergo a true conversion experience. In keeping with the evangelical **Calvinism** of the Connecticut Valley, Brainerd believed conversion to be a process of preparation culminating in a definable moment of true religious awakening. Every true Christian was to have both an intellectual understanding of the gospel and an experiential knowledge of God. According to Brainerd's account, his own spiritual quest culminated on July 12, 1739, a "day forever to be remembered" (Pettit, *Life*, 140).

Not long after his conversion, Brainerd entered Yale to prepare for a career in the ministry. During his time there, Brainerd was identified as one of the more radical students on campus. Not only did he attend unofficial **prayer** meetings, but he regularly challenged fellow students as to their **assurance of salvation.** Brainerd's time at the college coincided with some of the more incendiary events of the **Great Awakening,** and the school added new rules regarding the behavior of its students. Brainerd fell afoul of these restrictions when he criticized the spirituality of one of the faculty. Following his refusal to offer a public apology, he was expelled in November 1741.

Sometime between his expulsion and April 1742, Brainerd began to consider the possibility of serving as a missionary to the Indians. How and why he made this decision is not known. Although his lack of a college degree prohibited him from holding a pastorate in Connecticut, he could have accepted an appointment in Massachusetts, New York, or New Jersey. In July 1742, he was licensed to **preach** by the pro-Awakening Fairfield East Ministerial Association. He spent the next few months as an itinerant preacher, then, in November, he was examined and accepted as a missionary to the Indians by the Society in Scotland for Propagating Christian Knowledge.

Brainerd's initial posting was to Kaunaumeek, on the New York–Massachusetts border. Brainerd worked here for about a year, with limited results, and then relocated to the Forks of the Delaware in eastern Pennsylvania with the intent of moving to the Susquehanna Valley. Despite his best efforts at the Forks and on two trips to the Susquehanna, he failed to see signs of a true revival among the Indians. In June 1745, he visited a small group of Delaware Indians in Crossweeksung, New Jersey, and was immediately struck by their receptivity. For the next several months he divided his time between New Jersey and the Forks of the Delaware as well as making another trip to the Susquehanna. By October 1745, he had decided to focus on the work in New Jersey.

In his ministry to the Indians, Brainerd did his best to re-create the model that had served him so well in his own spiritual pilgrimage. While he made the Indians aware of their sinfulness, he concentrated on imparting to them the forgiveness and love offered by God. He expected and encouraged them to go through a period of preparation, during which time he counseled many of them individually. Once Indians were truly converted, he began to teach them from the Westminster Catechism (1648) with a view to making sure that they truly understood the new life they had embraced. In Brainerd's account of the work among the Indians, he stressed both their acknowledgment of their own sin and a genuine reformation in their lifestyle. Brainerd's accounts of the work contain numerous passages that evoked memories of revivals in the colonial churches during the Great Awakening. The reality of the Indian conversions was attested to in print by local pastors and church leaders.

Brainerd was so struck by the changes in his converts, that he began to use them as co-laborers on subsequent trips to the Forks of the Delaware and the Susquehanna Valley. On several occasions, he was able to record that the Delaware converts had been instrumental in convincing other Indians of their need for conversion. Brainerd continued his labors among the Indians until early in 1747. During this time, the Indians relocated to land near Cranbury, New Jersey. Shortly after this move,

Brainerd's increasingly poor health forced his retirement from the mission field. He died of tuberculosis, in the home of Jonathan Edwards, on October 9, 1747, at the age of 29. The story regarding a romance between Brainerd and Jonathan Edwards's daughter, Jerusha—who also contracted tuberculosis and died—is not supported by reliable sources. Brainerd's brother John continued his work in New Jersey until 1781. Yet Edwards's *The Life of David Brainerd*, through its far-flung readership and influence, may have accomplished more than Brainerd himself achieved during his lifetime in furthering the cause of Christian missions.

Further Reading: Howard, Philip E., Jr. *The Life and Diary of David Brainerd*. Grand Rapids, MI: Baker Books, 1989; Pettit, Norman, ed. *The Life of David Brainerd*. Vol. 7 of *The Works of Jonathan Edwards*. New Haven, CT: Yale University Press, 1985; Pettit, Norman. "Prelude to Mission: Brainerd's Expulsion From Yale." *New England Quarterly* 59 (1986): 28–50; Pointer, Richard W. "'Poor Indians' and the 'Poor in Spirit': The Indian Impact on David Brainerd." *New England Quarterly* 67 (1994): 403–26.

John Grigg

BRANCH DAVIDIANS

The Branch Davidians are an offshoot of the **Seventh-day Adventists.** Their headquarters at Mount Carmel outside Waco, Texas, became the scene of a tragic FBI incident in which, on April 19, 1993, 75 members were killed, including 21 children, after a standoff that began on February 28. One factor contributing to the tragedy may have been a lack of understanding on the part of the FBI regarding millenarian sects and their **eschatological** or apocalyptic understanding of reality.

The Seventh-day Adventists trace their origins to the ministry of **William Miller** (1782–1849), who, based upon his study of scripture, concluded in 1833 that the world would end in or around 1843. After the "Great Disappointment," when Christ did not appear, the Millerite movement splintered. One of the resultant groups developed into the Seventh-day Adventists, who looked to **Ellen G. White** (1827–1915) as a prophet. In 1935, Seventh-day Adventist Victor Houteff (1885–1955) declared himself a prophet, formed the Shepherd's Rod, and established Mount Carmel Center in Waco, Texas. In 1942, they were incorporated as Davidian Seventh-day Adventists. After his death, his wife, Florence, took leadership. When Christ did not return on April 22, 1959, as she predicted, there were several splinter groups. The largest was a group known as the Branch Davidian Seventh-day Adventists, led by Ben Roden. After his death in 1978, his wife, Lois, became the new prophet of the group.

In 1981, when Vernon Howell joined this group, Lois Roden expressed her belief that he would be their next prophet. Howell had grown up in the Seventh-day Adventist Church and had attended an Adventist school until he was drawn to the Branch Davidians. In 1985, he visited Israel and studied the Bible with several rabbis. While there, he said that he had a miraculous meeting with God. After the death of Lois Roden, and after conflict with her son George Roden, Howell became leader of the group. In 1990, Howell legally changed his name to David Koresh and collected many followers, many of whom were African, Hispanic, and Asian. They concurred with him that he was the "Lamb of God" who was destined to unlock the mysteries of the seven seals in Revelation 5. They believed that he must create a "house of David" where his many wives would bear him 24 children who would become the rulers of a new, purer world. They would then rule over the earth. Prior to this, the evil authorities, the "Babylonians," would try to crush them. If they died defending Koresh's prophecies, they would be raised from the dead and return to conquer the Babylonians and rule the world.

Marc Breault, a Branch Davidian from 1984 until 1989, later became a "cult buster" who attempted to discredit Koresh, claiming that he physically abused adults and children for minor infractions and seduced and impregnated young girls. In 1990, Breault convinced a few Branch Davidians in Australia, New Zealand, England, and the United States to join his efforts. He eventually brought his charges to the Australian television producers of *Current Affair*, which aired a program portraying Koresh as a sex-crazed, gun-happy lunatic. Breault then contacted Michigan representative Frederick Upton with his allegations and contacted the U.S. consulate in Melbourne, Australia, which sent warning wires to Washington, DC.

When the Federal Bureau of Alcohol, Tobacco, and Firearms (BATF) raided Mount Carmel on February 28, 1993, there was an exchange of gunfire in which four agents and six Branch Davidians were killed. The FBI then took over the operation, and after a 51-day standoff, there was a second raid in which the compound was burned to the ground, resulting in the death of at least 75 Branch Davidians, including Koresh and 21 children under 15 years of age. During the siege a number of adults and children were released from the compound. According to FBI reports, Koresh had made no threats, set no deadlines, and made no demands. However, the FBI had difficulty deciphering the apocalyptic worldview of the Branch Davidians, who assumed that the raid against them was a sign of the fulfillment of their expectations. The authorities were unable to fathom the recalcitrance of the members of the compound who refused to vacate the premises when ordered to do so. According to the Associated Press, President Bill Clinton told investigators in April of 2000 that he had made a "terrible mistake" in yielding to Justice Department pleas to storm the Branch Davidian compound (Knutsen). In recent years, some remaining Branch Davidians continue to meet at the Mount Carmel site.

Further Reading: Breault, Marc, and Martin King. *Inside the Cult.* New York: Signet Books, 1993; "David Koresh and the FBI's Religious Intolerance." *Harper's,* July 1995, 16–20; Gazerki, William, and Michael McNulty, producers. *Waco: The Rules of Engagement.* VHS. Los Angeles: Somford Entertainment, 1997; Knutsen, Lawrence L. "Clinton: 'Terrible Mistake' on Waco." Associated Press, July 26, 2000; Tabor, James D., and Eugene V. Gallagher. *Why Waco?* Berkeley: University of California Press, 1995.

Richard M. Riss

BRANHAM, WILLIAM (1909–1965)

William Marrion Branham was the leading figure in the **healing** revivals of 1947–1958. Despite

No Pentecostal healing evangelist of the 1950s enjoyed a greater reputation for spiritual power than William Branham. Some of his followers, seeing the unexplained white light above his head in this photograph, interpreted it as a heavenly sign. (Sam Houston Coliseum, Houston, TX; December 24, 1954.) Courtesy of the Library of Congress.

his early impoverishment and lack of formal education, Branham gained a national reputation for dramatic healings, including resurrections from the dead, and particularly accurate **prophetic** knowledge that revealed the nature of diseases and such personal information as unconfessed sins. Branham's healing ministry began in 1946, when he claimed to experience one in a series of supernatural visitations by an angel commissioning him to **pray** for the sick. Ordained in the Missionary **Baptist** Church in 1932, in 1947 Branham held union meetings for Oneness and Trinitarian **Pentecostals**. Gordon Lindsay founded the *Voice of Healing* magazine in 1948 to promote Branham, but after Branham temporarily withdrew from public ministry because of a nervous breakdown later that year, Lindsay began using his magazine to publicize more than a hundred other itinerant evangelists.

Branham typically spent three days of prayer and **fasting** in preparation for each campaign. He refused to begin praying for people until he sensed the presence of an angel standing at his right side. Adopting the common practice of distributing numbered prayer cards that entitled those called to a place in a healing line, Branham made a point of standing to the left of the healing line so that the sick could pass by his angel. Branham claimed to sense the presence of diseases or demons by a physical vibration in his left hand, which was powerful enough to stop his wristwatch. Like many of his contemporaries, Branham prayed over handkerchiefs and ribbons that could be carried to the sick. Although not opposing the work of physicians, as did some healing evangelists, Branham shared a belief common among revivalists that healing was provided for in the atonement of Jesus Christ, and that Satan caused all sickness, sometimes directly through the agency of demons. Branham was willing to pray for non-Christians, but believed that they must become Christians in order to retain their health. Unlike many of his contemporary healing revivalists, Branham was known for his calm demeanor and soft-spoken delivery, which contrasted with his sensational claims, for instance that a photograph taken in 1950 captured a supernatural halo above his head.

By 1955, Branham's ministry had changed dramatically, as he broke with his longtime advocate Gordon Lindsay, faced a tax-evasion lawsuit in 1956, and began to teach doctrines considered heretical by many, including his own identity as the prophet Elijah. Branham died at the age of 56 in an automobile accident. Gordon Lindsay and **Kenneth Hagin Sr.** both claimed that God had warned them of Branham's impending death should he fail to renounce his doctrinal errors. Contemporary followers of Branham, who belong to several independent churches, most significantly the Branham Tabernacle in Indiana and the Tucson Tabernacle in Arizona, continue in the early twenty-first century to publicize Branham's distinctive teachings and revere him as a great prophet and a forerunner of the Second Coming of Jesus Christ.

Further Reading: Chappell, Paul G. "William Branham." In Charles H. Lippy, ed., *Twentieth-Century Shapers of American Popular Religion*, 44–48. New York: Greenwood Press, 1989; Harrell, David Edwin, Jr. *All Things Are Possible: The Healing and Charismatic Revivals of Modern America*. Bloomington: Indiana University Press, 1975; Lindsay, Gordon, in collaboration with William Branham. *William Branham: A Man Sent from God*. Jeffersonville, IN: W. Branham, 1950; William M. Branham official Web site. http://www.williambranham.com/.

Candy Gunther Brown

BROWNSVILLE REVIVAL

see Pensacola (Brownsville) Revival

BURCHARD, JEDIDIAH
(ca. 1790–1864)

Before **Charles Grandison Finney** became a prominent figure in American revivals, Jedidiah Burchard helped to institutionalize many of the so-called new measures during the **Second Great Awakening,** including such practices as the protracted meeting, theatrical **preaching,** public **prayers,** the anxious bench, and inquiry meetings. Indeed, William R. Weeks wrote that Burchard claimed that "the credit of the new measures" belonged to himself (Murray, 240). Burchard was born in Connecticut, but moved to New York state as a young man. After undergoing a **conversion** experience, he went to the town of Adams to study under the direction of George Gale, a **Presbyterian** minister. Burchard was with Gale at Adams when Charles Finney experienced conversion there in 1821. Burchard was licensed by the local Congregational Association in 1822, and went on to receive ordination from the Watertown Presbytery as an evangelist two years later. He became minister of the Cape Vincent Presbyterian Church in 1824, where Charles G. Finney had become a candidate for gospel ministry in June of 1823. Both men labored for the **Oneida** Evangelical Association, conducting revivals throughout upstate New York. Burchard and Finney were acquainted with one another during this period, and it is possible that the more experienced Burchard mentored

Finney in revival practices. Finney wrote a letter in 1829 in which he professed to "love that man" (Murray, 239), but he never publicly acknowledged that Burchard had imparted any of the new measures to him. In fact, Burchard's reputation for creating controversy led Finney to acknowledge Burchard hardly at all.

Burchard appears to have been earnest in his desire to save souls, but his practices frequently brought strife. On at least one occasion he was declared a public nuisance, and many local clergymen wanted to have nothing to do with him. On the other hand, Burchard enjoyed a high degree of popularity among the working classes, which eagerly heard him on the subject of how to "get religion." Burchard excoriated ministers for teaching their flocks that they must pray and wait in hope for God to bring them to salvation. According to Burchard, God had made salvation available by the cross of Christ, and it was up to each individual to make a conscious decision to accept forgiveness and follow after God. When a congregation waited for God to spread revival, they were actually evading their own responsibility and quenching God's Spirit. Burchard told one congregation that his only job was "to glorify God and vindicate the honor and majesty of His name from reproach." He told congregations that "*manner is matter,*" and he demonstrated his belief with so-called theatrical gesticulation, hand clapping, and by modulating his voice from a shout to a soft whisper. He would often strike the pulpit as he preached and punctuate his preaching with shouts of "God Almighty!" (Streeter, 3, 5, 8). To Burchard, the new measures were like a new technological advance, and their worthiness was evidenced by their success in gaining new converts. He made frequent use of the anxious bench or **altar call,** and regarded all who came forward as converts to the faith, and he duly recorded their names in a special notebook.

Burchard used high-pressure tactics in his evangelistic appeals. In Poughkeepsie, New York, a young woman refused to go forward, and he reflected on another young woman who would not go forward at an earlier revival: "God Almighty struck her with consumption, and she is now in her grave." Witnesses criticized Burchard for seeking to gain converts by naming individuals in public and conducting public prayers for them. He told one congregation that they had 15 minutes to respond to the gospel or they would be lost forever. In the inquiry room, as he met privately with spiritual seekers, he was said to have asked for a **confession of sin** and to have pressed for a faith decision. Burchard excited enough interest through his preaching that he was able to spend many years as a revivalist. Yet his following began to diminish in later years, and he left the ministry to improve his financial status and died in Adams, New York, in 1864.

Further Reading: *Burchardism vs. Christianity.* Poughkeepsie, NY: Plott and Ranney, 1837; Cross, Whitney R. *The Burned-Over District: The Social and Intellectual History of Enthusiastic Religion in Western New York, 1800–1850.* Ithaca, NY: Cornell University Press, 1950; McLoughlin, William G., Jr. *Modern Revivalism: Charles Grandison Finney to Billy Graham.* New York: Ronald Press, 1959; Murray, Iain H. *Revival and Revivalism: The Making and Marring of American Evangelicalism, 1750–1858.* Edinburgh: Banner of Truth Trust, 1994; Streeter, Russell. *Mirror of Calvinistic Fanatical Revivals, or Jedidiah Burchard & Company.* Woodstock, VT: C. K. Smith, 1835.

David Simpson

BURNED-OVER DISTRICT

The term *Burned-Over District* refers to an area of New York State lying west of the Catskill and Adirondack Mountains, visited by successive waves of religious excitement from its early settlement until 1860. Its settlers came chiefly from New England, where the **Second Great Awakening** had inspired increased church attendance and concern for public morality. Fervent revivalism was a part of many of the settlers' lives from birth. These transplanted Yankees fell into two general groups—orthodox Protestants, who formed the great majority, and a small but significant minority of heterodox believers who held to unusual metaphysical notions and ideas regarding the perfection of humanity and the attainment of millennial bliss. The area was fertile for fads and extravagances referred to as *ultraism*. Few of the religious eccentricities of this era were without their adherents in this region.

For mainstream Protestants, isolated revivals continued in New England after the **Great Awakening** of the 1740s, and these were especially common in upstate New York. The **Methodists** were especially aggressive, adding 1,512 members in 1808, and similar numbers in other years. In 1815 a **Presbyterian** revival in Utica brought in more than 400 new members, and revivals occurred in 1819 and 1821. Whereas in the Kentucky and Tennessee revivals there was much emotional excess, such sensationalism repulsed the quieter Yankees. Two pro-revival denominations, the Congregationals and the Presbyterians, sent pastors into the region to further awakenings and to found churches. Both stressed an educated clergy and orderly worship, and spurned religious excesses. There was growing cooperation between the two, leading to the adoption of the Plan of Union in 1801, whereby churchgoers could form themselves into one congregation and elect a pastor from either "presbygational" denomination. Another group determined to bring spiritual growth in the region was the American Home Missionary Society (AHMS). By 1827 it was supporting 169 evangelists in seven states, of which 120 were laboring in New York State.

Many settlers from New England were young and indifferent as to which denominational church was available in their area, though seldom were they opposed to Christianity. In rural areas, life was harsh, lonely, and often dangerous, and work was constant and unremitting. The local church offered opportunities for social contacts. The Methodists, with their efficient circuit-rider system and the driving leadership of Bishop **Francis Asbury,** continued their vibrant growth. **Lorenzo Dow,** a powerful Methodist evangelist, after 1808 made the town of Western, New York, his base, holding one three-hour meeting during which 100 people were converted.

The second phase of the awakening came with the **preaching** of **Charles Grandison Finney** (1792–1875). After his 1821 conversion, he became a missionary to the Lake Ontario region, and his reputation as a dynamic speaker grew. In October 1825 he preached in the town of Western, and an awakening began that was to catapult Finney from the backwoods to national notoriety. The Oneida County revivals continued until April 1827, and ushered in six years of spectacular evangelistic activity. After conducting successful revivals in Philadelphia, New York City, and Boston, he held his most powerful revival in Rochester, New York, for six months in 1830–1831, which was accompanied by revivals in other regions during these years. Whitney Cross wrote, "No more impressive revival has occurred in American history…. But the exceptional feature was the phenomenal dignity of this awakening. No agonized souls fell in the aisles, no raptured ones shouted hallelujahs" (Cross, 155–56). Lyman Beecher claimed that 100,000 were converted across the nation within a year, an event "unparalleled in the history of the church" (Cross, 155–56).

While mainstream Protestantism gained converts, ultraisms were also blossoming. Religious emotionalism was setting the stage for heterodoxy. The construction of the Erie Canal, completed in 1823, helped prepare for religious innovation in this region. The demand for laborers and entrepreneurs brought tens of thousands of migrants into this region, and from Utica to Lockport, almost overnight, a wealthy class of bankers, jobbers, merchants, and mill owners appeared. For the Burned-Over District, upheaval and rapid socioeconomic change came to a region that had previously known isolation, settled habits, and unquestioned values. Only a brief mention may be made here of the many **new religious movements** that arose. **Jemima Wilkinson,** the "Publick Universal Friend," in 1794 set up a short-lived community called "Jerusalem" on Seneca Lake. More successful was Ann Lee Stanley, or Mother **Ann Lee,** the founder of the **Shakers** in England. Her trances convinced some that Christ's Second Coming would be in the form of a woman, namely, Lee herself. She emigrated from England with eight followers in 1774, and settled in Albany County, organizing a socialistic, celibate community. By

1794 there were 12 communities. The full blossoming of ultraism in New York State came in the 1820s. In 1828 **William Miller** began to preach that Jesus would return around 1843. Between 1840 and 1843 meetings were held across America, with Miller lecturing over 300 times in one six-month period. He declared that Jesus' return would be between March 21, 1843, and March 21, 1844. When nothing happened, he reset the date at October 22, 1844, leading to disappointment and anger when nothing happened. So widespread was the clamor that churches generally were mocked, including those that had condemned the excitement from the beginning. **Mormonism** also began at about this time in the Burned-Over District. Mormonism's founder, **Joseph Smith,** claimed to have had a vision of God around 1819–1820 in which he learned that all existing Christian churches were mistaken and that there needed to be a **restoration** of the **primitive** church. This restoration, among other things, was to involve the return of the **charismatic gifts** present in the apostolic period. He published *The Book of Mormon* (1830) in Palmyra, New York, translated, as he claimed, from golden plates inscribed in "reformed Egyptian." Soon he and his followers left New York State for an uncertain future. He was murdered in 1844 by a mob in Carthage, Illinois.

Perfectionism, the belief in a capacity for perfect holiness, took several forms. The Shakers sought perfection in celibacy, but John Humphrey Noyes taught that conversion brought complete release from sin, and created a communism that included the marriage relationship—what outsiders condemned as free love. After proselytizing in New York until 1837, he founded the Putney Community in Vermont. Driven out of town, he took his group to New York and began the **Oneida Community** in 1848, where it lasted until 1880. In 1848 another new movement, Spiritualism, shook the nation. At Hydesville, sisters Margaret and Kate Fox reported "rapping" sounds produced by spirit beings that responded to specific questions. Crowds gathered, the sisters became famous everywhere, and the movement grew. Spiritualism made important converts, such as Horace Greeley, editor of the *New York Tribune*, and claimed at its height in the 1850s no less than 67 periodicals, 38,000 mediums, and 2 million adherents nationally. An investigation found that the girls made the rapping sounds with their toes, but this did not bring an end to belief in Spiritualism. The list of ultraisms stemming from New York State could be extended, including Universalism (1820s), antimasonry (1826), the Hicksite schism among the **Quakers** (1827), phrenology, Dr. Sylvester Graham's cracker diet, socialistic communes inspired by Charles Fourier, and a host of minor groups.

Further Reading: Braude, Anne D. *Radical Spirits: Spiritualism and Women's Rights in Nineteenth-Century America.* 2nd ed. Bloomington: Indiana University Press, 2001; Brodie, Fawn M. *No Man Knows My History: The Life of Joseph Smith.* 2nd ed. New York: Vintage, 1995; Cross, Whitney R. *The Burned-Over District: The Social and Intellectual History of Enthusiastic Religion in Western New York, 1800–1850.* Ithaca, NY: Cornell University Press, 1950; Ellis, David M. "Conflicts among Calvinists: Oneida Revivalists in the 1820s." *New York History* 71 (1990): 25–44; Hambrick-Stowe, Charles E. *Charles G. Finney and the Spirit of American Evangelicalism.* Grand Rapids, MI: Eerdmans, 1996; Hardman, Keith J. *Charles Grandison Finney, 1792–1875: Revivalist and Reformer.* Syracuse, NY: Syracuse University Press, 1987. Paperback, Grand Rapids, MI: Baker, 1990; Johnson, Paul E. *A Shopkeeper's Millennium: Society and Revivals in Rochester, New York, 1815–1837.* New York: Hill and Wang, 1978; Morrison, Howard A. "The Finney Takeover of the Second Great Awakening during the Oneida Revivals of 1825–1827." *New York History* 59 (1978): 27–53; Nichols, Robert H. *Presbyterianism in New York State: A History of the Synod and Its Predecessors.* Philadelphia: Westminster, 1963; Rosell, Garth M., and Richard A. G. Dupuis, eds. *The Memoirs of Charles G. Finney: The Complete Restored Text.* Grand Rapids, MI: Zondervan, 1989; Sorin, Gerald. *The New York Abolitionists: A Case Study of Political Radicalism.* Westport, CT: Greenwood, 1970.

Keith J. Hardman

BUSHNELL, HORACE (1802–1876)

Horace Bushnell was a leading pastor-theologian and one of the most famous nineteenth-century Protestant critics of revivalism. His text *Christian Nurture* (1847, revised 1860) became a classic alternative model to revivalist piety. He has also been considered by many to be the father of American religious liberalism. Bushnell was born and spent his formative years in Litchfield County, Connecticut, one of the centers of the revivalistic-centered **Second Great Awakening** in New England, but he seemed never to have warmed to its message. From his parents, he inherited a suspicion of the **theology of revivals** associated with New England in that era. Likewise Bushnell's personal piety never easily fit into the **conversion** model assumed by nineteenth-century revivalism. Since a testimony of conversion was necessary for membership in the Congregational church, Bushnell in his youth and adolescence was not a church member. Even when in early 1821 he did undergo a conversion and became a church member, the conversion was a private experience and not associated with any public religious service.

Later in 1821 Bushnell began his studies at Yale College. There his religious problems continued. Although as a student he was a member of the church at Yale, he began to doubt his earlier conversion. Why he underwent this religious crisis has been variously interpreted but it did impress upon him the fragility of religious commitment, a theme he would emphasize in his later ministry. Upon graduation he first tried his hand at school teaching and then at journalism before deciding to return to Yale and study law. While studying law he was offered a position as tutor at Yale College. As a tutor he experienced the Yale revival of 1831. During this revival he underwent a second conversion. It, too, was atypical, emphasizing the importance of moral service rather than an experience of the transformed heart. He then decided to study for the ministry and graduated from Yale Divinity School in 1832. In 1833 he received a call from North Church (Congregational) in Hartford, Connecticut, where he spent his entire ministry.

At North Church Bushnell experimented with models of piety that differed from the conversion-revival model then common in Connecticut Congregationalism. Fascinated by the organic metaphor, he argued that growth and development were crucial in the Christian life. He expressed his criticisms of revivalism publicly in 1838 in the essay "Spiritual Economies of Revivals of Religion." The true purpose of the church was not the conversion of individuals but the shaping of persons to God's pattern. Conversion and revivals were at best a means to this end. Although they were at times effective, the excitement that revivals evoked was often counterproductive to true religion. By the 1840s Bushnell's pastoral dislike for conversion and revivalism became augmented by the belief that they were fundamentally alien to the New England Puritan tradition. During the 1840s he engaged in a debate with High Church Episcopalians who argued that the Puritan emphasis upon the conversion experience was the source of the fanaticism, heresy, and fractiousness of American Protestantism. Bushnell argued that these attributes flowed not from Puritanism, but from a misunderstanding of Puritanism.

Both the pastoral and historical criticisms came together in his 1847 publication *Discourses on Christian Nurture*, and his 1848 defense of this work, *Views of Christian Nurture*. The thesis of Christian nurture was simply stated: "The child is to grow up a Christian and never know himself to be otherwise." Although this quotation is regularly associated with Bushnell, it only first appeared in this form in the 1861 revision of *Discourses*. Bushnell understood Christianization as a process of development, linked to family life. The influence of the family was organic as well as didactic, and included all sorts of unconscious influences that contributed to religious growth. The family was a vehicle of continuing grace. Bushnell did not hold that one's early environment determined one's character. All growth required personal decision and commitment. Yet he rejected the revival-conversion model because it made the work of saving grace independent and indeed at odds with the normal Christian life. Conversion, Bushnell argued, assumed that the Holy Spirit could only act by conquering or overwhelming the individual. It assumed an atomistic and individualistic vision of the Christian life in which grace could only come after sin.

The logical culmination of this presupposition would be the rejection of infant baptism altogether, and indeed Bushnell labeled the conversion-revival system the "**Baptist** theory of religion." Christian nurture, in contrast, assumed an organic outworking of the spirit in which grace flowed through nature. Bushnell was not unique in attacking revivalism but was distinctive in his elevation of the role of family. Earlier critics such as High Church Episcopalians and the German **Reformed** theologian **John Williamson Nevin** shared in a wide-ranging **Christian nurture debate** that touched on revivals and other ways that churches might initiate new members. Nevin had offered the power of baptism and the catechetical role of the church as alternatives to revivalism. Yet Bushnell, in emphasizing the power of family, said little of baptismal grace or catechetical instruction.

The publication of the *Discourses* by the Massachusetts Sabbath School Society produced a storm of protest. For critics such as the Congregationalist Bennet Tyler, Bushnell weakened or undermined any understanding of human depravity or spiritual regeneration and left the distinction between true believer and nonbeliever hopelessly confused. Bushnell responded to his critics in *Views of Christian Nurture*. There he reprinted his earlier writings on nurture, including his 1844 essay "The Kingdom of Heaven as a Mustard Seed," now retitled "Growth Not Conquest the True Method of Christian Progress." He also included "An Argument for 'Discourses on Christian Nurture,'" which fleshed out his belief that revivalism was alien to true Puritanism. He argued that resting Christian identification on a supernatural conversion (a concept he labeled as an "ictus dei," or a divine blow) was an innovation of the **Great Awakening** and was antithetical to true Puritan piety, which had always been family oriented and communal. The triumph of conversion-oriented piety in the decades after the 1740s undermined the religious heritage of New England and paved the way for the emotionalism and individualism of much popular religion. In contrast, the return of a truly Puritan family-oriented piety could assist in the reunion of Trinitarian

Congregationalists and Unitarians, who had divided over issues flowing from the Great Awakening. Bushnell revised and expanded his work and published it as *Christian Nurture* in 1860. This version removed some of the polemical portions and heightened the emphasis on the mother's role in shaping belief. It is the 1860 edition that has often been reprinted.

For Bushnell, conversion-oriented piety was but one of the issues that needed reconsideration. In 1848 he gave a series of addresses at Yale, Harvard, and Andover Seminary that reexamined the doctrines of the Trinity, Christology (or the doctrine of Christ's nature), and soteriology (or the doctrine of Christ's saving work). These were subsequently published (along with "Preliminary Dissertation on the Nature of Language") as *God in Christ* (1849). *God in Christ* not only questioned individual doctrines but also the usefulness of hard and fast doctrines. The title of his third address—"Dogma and Spirit: Or the True Reviving of Religion"—illustrates his larger goal of emphasizing the spiritual nature of religion over the claims of dogmatic theology. This volume caused a sensation within the Protestant world on both sides of the Atlantic, and Bushnell was brought up on charges of heresy (of which he was never convicted). Bushnell's critique of dogma and defense of organic development has been seen as inaugurating a new era in New England theology, and because of this he has been often deemed the father of American religious liberalism. The accuracy of this claim has been recently challenged, but it is nonetheless true that late nineteenth-century American Protestant liberalism actively adopted Bushnell's ideas of Christian nurture and his criticisms of revivalism and conversion-oriented piety.

Although Bushnell was critical of the conversion-revival tradition, he had a high view of the power of the Holy Spirit. In 1848 he underwent a third conversion through the reading of the French quietist Madame Guyon. In his later writings, beginning with *Nature and the Supernatural* (1858), he began to express an interest in **speaking in tongues** or glossolalia. Furthermore, his criticisms of revivals and revivalism did not prevent him from establishing a friendship with **Charles Grandison Finney.**

Further Reading: Brown, Candy Gunther. "Domestic Nurture versus Clerical Crisis: The Gender Dimension in Horace Bushnell's and Elizabeth Prentiss's Critiques of Revivalism." In Michael J. McClymond, ed., *Embodying the Spirit: New Perspectives on North American Revivalism*, 67–83. Baltimore: Johns Hopkins University Press, 2004; Cheney, Mary B. *Life and Letters of Horace Bushnell.* New York: Harper and Brothers, 1880; Cross, Barbara M. *Horace Bushnell: Minister to a Changing America.* Chicago: University of Chicago Press, 1958; Edwards, Robert L. *Of Singular Genius, Of Singular Grace: A Biography of Horace Bushnell.* Cleveland: Pilgrim Press, 1992; Howe, Daniel Walker. *Making the American Self: Jonathan Edwards to Abraham Lincoln.* Cambridge, MA: Harvard University Press, 1997; Hutchison, William R. *The Modernist Impulse in American Protestantism.* Cambridge, MA: Harvard University Press, 1976; Mullin, Robert Bruce. *The Puritan as Yankee: A Life of Horace Bushnell.* Grand Rapids, MI: Eerdmans, 2002; Munger, Theodore T. *Horace Bushnell: Preacher and Theologian.* Boston: Houghton Mifflin, 1899; Smith, H. Shelton, ed. *Horace Bushnell.* New York: Oxford University Press, 1965.

Robert Bruce Mullin

C

CALVARY CHAPEL

Under the leadership of Chuck Smith (1927–) beginning in 1965, Calvary Chapel quickly became one of the fastest-growing church movements in the United States. Both Chuck Smith and Calvary Chapel played a central role in the growth of the **Jesus People movement** of the late 1960s and early 1970s. Today more than 35,000 people attend Calvary Chapel of Costa Mesa, California, and this congregation has spawned 850 affiliate Calvary Chapels throughout the world, some attended by more than 5,000. Since its origins in the Jesus People movement, Calvary Chapel has given rise to other churches and quasi denominations, including Harvest Christian Fellowship in Riverside, California, now attended by more than 15,000, and the Association of Vineyard Churches, a group with more than 700 congregations.

When Smith began as an associate pastor at Calvary Chapel in 1965, 25 people attended the first Sunday morning meeting. This was preceded by more than 17 years of stagnation on Smith's part, during which he pastored a number of **Foursquare Gospel** churches in Arizona and California. In the early 1960s he founded the Corona Christian Center, which grew rapidly, but he resigned in order to embark upon a more informal ministry style with members of a Bible study class that he was holding in the Newport Beach, California area. Through their three children, Smith and his wife Kay met many young people involved in the countercultural movement of the 1960s. Kay began to **pray** concertedly, organizing prayer-group meetings both late at night and early in the morning. The Smiths then came into contact with Jesus People from the House of Acts in San Francisco's Haight-Ashbury district, and invited some of them to live with them at their home in Newport Beach. They soon began to establish Christian communal houses. Calvary Chapel was therefore attended both by members of the establishment and by young people who were totally disenchanted with the traditional churches. By emphasizing Christian love, Smith was able to hold these groups together. Street **preacher** Lonnie Frisbee was among the most charismatic of the young Christians who ministered alongside of Chuck Smith.

In 1967, Calvary Chapel moved to a rented Lutheran church and then to a run-down school that was purchased and torn down to build a church. By the time the sanctuary of 330 seats was completed in 1969, the church was forced to hold two services, and eventually had to use the outside courtyard for 500 more seats. In 1971, a 10-acre tract of land was purchased on the Costa Mesa–Santa Ana border, where a circus tent was erected

Rev. Chuck Smith, the founder of Calvary Chapel, officiates in an ocean baptism service at Pirates Cove in Corona Del Mar, near Los Angeles, California. (1970s.) Courtesy of David Di Sabatino.

that could seat 1,600. This was soon enlarged to hold 2,000, and construction began on a sanctuary holding 3,300, which, when it celebrated its opening day in 1973, was too small for the 4,000 who attended each of three Sunday morning services. During a two-year period in the mid-1970s, Calvary Chapel of Costa Mesa performed more than 8,000 baptisms, and was instrumental in 20,000 conversions to Christ. *Look, Life, Time,* and *Newsweek* magazines reported on its massive baptisms in the Pacific Ocean at nearby Corona del Mar beach.

In 1982, Smith's desire to take a middle road between Pentecostalism and Fundamentalism led to a falling-out with **John Wimber,** who had been a Calvary Chapel pastor since 1978 and who emphasized **signs and wonders.** Wimber went on to found the Vineyard Christian Fellowship with Ken Gullickson. By 1987, Calvary Chapel's outreach included radio programs and television broadcasts, and its Sunday morning service was widely rebroadcast. The church averaged 200 conversions per week, and its financial commitment to missions exceeded its local budget by over 50 percent. More than a thousand students now attend its Bible College in Twin Peaks, California, which has additional students at 20 extension campuses worldwide. Smith teaches that evangelism is the natural by-product of a healthy church, and that church growth requires sound biblical instruction. His conversational teaching style, simple message, stress on the Holy Spirit, emphasis upon loving rather than judging others, and abhorrence of asking for contributions have all played a part in the movement's impressive growth.

Further Reading: Enroth, Ronald M., Edward E. Ericson Jr., and C. Breckingridge Peters. *The Jesus People.* Grand Rapids, MI: Eerdmans, 1972; Miller, Donald E. *Reinventing American Protestantism.* Berkeley: University of California Press, 1997; Smith, Chuck, and Tal Brooke. *Harvest.* Old Tappan, NJ: Chosen Books, 1987.

Richard M. Riss

CALVINIST THEOLOGY

see Theology of Revivals

CALVINISTIC, PRESBYTERIAN, AND REFORMED REVIVALS SINCE 1730

On the surface, Reformed Protestantism and revivalism would appear to be strange bedfellows. For instance, many popular conceptions reduce Presbyterianism to the twin doctrines of predestination and eternal damnation, thus rendering Presbyterian adherents as "God's frozen chosen." Yet many prominent revival movements and revivalists in the history of the United States have emerged from Presbyterian or Reformed churches. The Dutch Reformed minister **Theodorus Jacobus Frelinghuysen** (1691–1747) is generally regarded as the forerunner of the **Great Awakening** of the 1740s. He pastored in New Jersey's Raritan Valley in the 1720s and became controversial when he judged that some members of his parish were unconverted, and admonished them not to partake of the Lord's Supper unless they repented and underwent **conversion.** Among his protégés was the Presbyterian preacher **Gilbert Tennent,** later to become controversial himself when he publicly declared, not that his congregants, but that his fellow ministers may have been unconverted. **Jonathan Edwards,** who ministered among Congregationalists in Massachusetts, did a brief stint as a Presbyterian minister in New York during his twenties. More important, Edwards, who was the greatest apologist for Calvinism in eighteenth-century **colonial** America, was also a revivalist who devoted profound writings to defending the religious experience that characterized the Great Awakening. The pro-revivalist **Cumberland Presbyterian Church** was born in the fervor of the spiritual awakening that occurred just after 1800 in parts of Kentucky and Tennessee. A key initiator in this "Great Revival" on the frontier was the Presbyterian preacher **James McGready.** The wild exuberance and **bodily manifestations** that occurred in the **Cane Ridge revival** grew out of a traditional Presbyterian communion festival, or **holy fair,** in Kentucky in August 1801.

Charles Grandison Finney, perhaps the most prominent American revivalist of the nineteenth century, began his evangelistic efforts with the backing of the Presbyterian churches in western New York. Just after 1900, **J. Wilbur Chapman** emerged as another nationally known Presbyterian revival **preacher,** from whom the even more celebrated **Billy Sunday** learned how to hold revivals. Sunday, licensed and ordained by the northern Presbyterian Church (the Presbyterian Church in the USA, or PCUSA), paved the way in the early twentieth century for later urban revivalists. **Billy Graham,** arguably the greatest evangelist in American history, was born and reared in the Associate Reformed Presbyterian Church. Beginning in the 1960s and 1970s, the **Charismatic Revival and Renewal** affected Presbyterian pastors and laypersons, and like earlier revival movements, led to strife and controversy within many Presbyterian churches.

Yet if many revivalists and pro-revivalists have been Presbyterian or Calvinistic, the same is true of many **anti-revivalists** as well. The Old Light minister in Boston, **Charles Chauncy,** appealed to Puritan and Calvinist traditions to oppose the Great Awakening of the 1740s. A leading critic of the early 1800s revivals was **John Williamson Nevin**—a professor in a German Reformed seminary and an admirer of John Calvin and especially Calvin's sacramental theology. Calvinistic and Reformed Christians—more perhaps than any other Christian group in American history—have played a double-sided role by both strongly supporting and vehemently denouncing the practices of religious revivalism.

In the eighteenth century, revivals were a new form of Christian devotion that relied upon itinerant preachers, mass meetings, and intense religious experiences. Their appeal was generic among Protestants. As such revivalism was and still is a form of devotion that transcends denominationalism. Because revivalism was nondenominational in origin, its effects baffled denominational leaders as they tried to assess whether revivals were a blessing for church life. For individuals renewed or converted thsrough the preaching of an itinerant evangelist, the value of revivals was obvious. Still, the experience of individual Christians is different from that of a group of churches laboring for a measure of cohesion and uniformity. Where individual Presbyterians may have evaluated revivals simply on the basis of personal experience, church officials used a different standard, namely, whether these religious exercises were harmonious with the existing life and character of the denomination. For the mainstream of American Presbyterianism, revivalism was as much a source of controversy and division as one of renewed zeal and church growth. The history of mainstream American Presbyterian reactions to and involvement with revivalism illustrates Calvinism's ambiguous relationship to revivalism.

Revivalism first made inroads into the colonial Presbyterian Church during the 1730s in the area just to the northeast of Philadelphia, the city that was home to the first presbytery in North America. The leaders of the revivals were a clan of recent Scotch-Irish immigrants to Pennsylvania, the Tennent family. The patriarch of the Tennents was William Sr. (1673–1746), who came to the New World in 1718 as part of the Anglican establishment but soon joined his ancestral fold by taking a call to a Presbyterian church in New York. By 1727 he had moved his family to Bucks County, just outside Philadelphia, to establish a school for ministers known as the Log College (predecessor of Princeton College). Among the students he trained were his sons, William Jr., Gilbert, and John. Of these three, Gilbert (1703–1764) was the most significant for injecting revivalism into Presbyterian circles. He had studied at Yale College while his father pastored in New York and then informally with his father before settling in 1726 in New Brunswick as pastor of a Presbyterian congregation in that New Jersey town.

Having studied at Yale during the same years when Jonathan Edwards was a student there, Gilbert Tennent undoubtedly became acquainted with those features of New England Puritanism that drove Edwards to become one of the prominent revivalists of the Great Awakening. But in New Jersey Tennent encountered the Dutch Reformed pastor Theodore Frelinghuysen, who came to North America with fresh insights from European **Pietism.** Through Frelinghuysen Tennent deepened his interest in the experiential

aspects of faith and gained an appreciation for rigorous church discipline to counter hypocrisy and formalism among church members. Also important for Tennent was the Dutch minister's preaching, which featured itinerancy and demanded that hearers confront the full challenge of God's moral law in order to understand their own inadequacy and need for divine mercy. Tennent emulated Frelinghuysen. He also spearheaded the revivals among Presbyterians in New Jersey and in southeastern Pennsylvania, where his father and brothers ministered.

Although Tennent's revivals were on a much smaller scale than the intercolonial and **transatlantic** ones that would characterize the itinerancy of **George Whitefield,** they still met with opposition within certain quarters of the Presbyterian Church. A chief factor fueling the divisiveness of revivalism was the relative youth of the Presbyterian communion in which Tennent labored. The Presbyterian Church in colonial America began in 1706 with the forming of the Presbytery of Philadelphia. Throughout the first half of the eighteenth century Presbyterianism was a fairly small and unstable church centered in the mid-Atlantic region. Some of the instability owed to the autonomy of the church; it was not sponsored by any Old World communion the way most other denominations in the colonies were. The Presbyterian Church also included a mix of Scotch-Irish Presbyterianism and New England Puritanism, two traditions that although Calvinistic possessed differing estimates of church authority and personal piety. These groups had been able to achieve a measure of cohesion in 1729 when the denomination passed the Adopting Act, an official ruling that established the Westminster Confession and the Westminster Larger and Shorter Catechisms as the doctrinal standard for ordination and instruction. Even so, interpretations differed over what subscribing to the Westminster Standards meant for ministers. Those with strong ties to Scotland and Northern Ireland argued that subscription involved theological uniformity. But those with backgrounds in New England favored a looser arrangement in order to allow for freedom of conscience.

The Tennents and the revivals they nurtured added rancor to these disagreements in two important respects, both having to do with the qualifications for Presbyterian ministers. The first was the education offered at the Log College. Those from Scotland and Northern Ireland believed that those training for the ministry should receive a reputable education from one of the universities in the Old World, or at least at Yale or Harvard. They resisted giving approval to candidates who had trained with William Tennent Sr. The second aspect of this disagreement was the personal devotion that the Log College encouraged in its students. In order to lead revivals, the Tennents argued, ministers themselves needed to have had a conversion experience comparable to that which they were seeking in their hearers. Consequently, the presence of a pro-revival party within the Presbyterian Church revived older disagreements about the nature of creedal subscription. For many of the Scotch-Irish, simply vowing loyalty to the Westminster Standards was sufficient to be a minister, irrespective of a conversion experience. But for the Tennents and those favoring revivals, a candidate for the ministry needed not only to subscribe the Presbyterian doctrinal system but also give evidence of a conversion experience. These tensions became sufficiently uncomfortable to prompt Presbyterian officials in 1738 to form a new jurisdiction, the Presbytery of New Brunswick, which corresponded roughly to the area where the pro-revivalists were established and functioned as a release valve for the disagreements afflicting the church.

This solution to the dilemma posed by revivalism would not last for long. In 1739 George Whitefield (1714–1770) undertook his first tour of the colonies in a much-publicized series of revivals, the likes of which observers had not yet seen, thus launching the Great Awakening. Because he sometimes arrived in towns uninvited by the established clergy, Whitefield stirred up controversy since he was clearly a threat to the authority and influence residential ministers had within their parishes. In the course of these disputes, Gilbert Tennent decided to challenge revivalism's opponents. His famous sermon "The Danger of an Unconverted Ministry," delivered in 1740, accused the revivals' critics of apostasy since their attacks were proof of being unregenerate. This kind of arch-support for the Awakening proved to be decisive in breaking the fragile unity of the young Presbyterian Church. In 1741 the denomination split into two separate churches, the Old Side and the New Side, the former strongest in the vicinity of Philadelphia, the latter residing chiefly in upper New Jersey and New York. These regional differences were not total, and advocates and opponents of revivals could be found in both regions. Because the New Side's congregations were of recent vintage, it would take time for that side of the Presbyterian Church to consolidate and marshal resources.

The Old and New Sides remained separate until 1758. The terms of reunion have seldom attracted the attention that they should because with the 1758 Plan of Union American Presbyterians officially embraced a revivalistic form of Christian devotion. In several respects the resolutions for reunion signaled a victory for the Old Side's commitment to creedal subscription and to the rigors of Presbyterian church polity. But when it came to matters of personal or experiential religion the Plan of Union upheld the views of the pro-revival New Side. Article 6 stated that in addition to accepting the Westminster Standards, candidates for the ministry needed to give evidence of their "experimental acquaintance with religion." This was not the boldest of declarations but it was precisely the point at issue in the disputes of the early 1740s. By so ruling the Presbyterian Church rejected the Old Side's contention that prying into the personal experience of a prospective minister was not necessary if he were already a member in good standing within the church. Article 8 of the plan was decidedly pro-revival. It addressed the controversies about whether the Great Awakening was a genuine work of God or simply a manifestation of religious enthusiasm. The Presbyterian Church formally embraced the former view (New Side) when it declared that revivals, or "religious appearances," were a "blessed work of God's Holy Spirit." To be sure, article 8, the longest of the Plan of Union, went on to qualify exactly the sort of evidence that would count for concluding a revival to be an act of God ("The Plan of Union," cx). But here it is important to observe that the kind of piety fitting for genuine faith was a compendium of the devotion that Jonathan Edwards had elaborated at length in *Religious Affections* (1746). The Plan of Union and the reunion of the Old and New Sides did more than simply heal the division within colonial Presbyterianism. By pronouncing a benediction upon revivalism and the experiential piety central to it, the Presbyterian Church embraced a New World form of devotion that broke with the older churchly and liturgical forms of Scotland and Geneva. This was truly a watershed moment in the history of American Presbyterianism.

The second major division in American Presbyterianism occurred in 1837 and 1838 when the church split again, this time into Old School and New School branches. Although various circumstances had changed the character of the church, several factors bore sufficient similarity to the eighteenth-century division to tempt observers to conclude that the Old School–New School division was basically a repeat of the Old Side–New Side separation. Regional and ethnic differences continued to contribute to differences, with the New England and northern elements in the church constituting New School strongholds and the Scotch-Irish and southern portions of the denomination lining up in the Old School queue. Furthermore, because this division occurred in the aftermath of the **Second Great Awakening,** the temptation to interpret the nineteenth-century debates as repeating the eighteenth-century disputes is even stronger. Still, important reasons exist for distinguishing these two Presbyterian divisions, ones that demonstrate the importance of the 1758 Plan of Union for determining the Presbyterian Church's attitude toward revivalism.

Part of what had set the Old School–New School division into motion was the Plan of Union of 1801 in which Presbyterians and Congregationalists agreed to cooperate in the establishment of churches in the newly expanding nation. This common work

eventually introduced strains of New England theology into the Presbyterian fold that theologians most notably at Princeton Seminary opposed. Specifically, **Nathaniel William Taylor** (1786–1856), who taught at Yale's Divinity School, taught doctrines that directly challenged Presbyterian teaching about original sin and the imputation of Adam's first sin to all humankind. Taylor's ideas received wider circulation in Presbyterian circles through the revivals of Charles Grandison Finney (1792–1875), who also opposed the Calvinistic conception of original sin, and who was ordained as a Presbyterian minister during the 1820s before beginning the revivals for which he would become famous. Albert Barnes (1798–1870), a Presbyterian minister who pastored in Philadelphia, also spread notions similar to Taylor's that questioned whether the guilt of Adam's first sin could legitimately be transferred to all of his offspring. The Presbytery of Philadelphia brought Barnes to trial for his views but he managed to escape conviction. These doctrinal questions, however, along with important differences between Presbyterian and Congregational church polity, as well as competing understandings of the church's responsibility for social reform, led to the division of 1837. At the General Assembly that convened that year, with Old School Presbyterians in the majority, the Presbyterian Church abrogated the 1801 Plan of Union. In so doing it excluded from the denomination all those presbyteries and congregations (600,000 church members in all) from western New York and the upper Midwest.

Although this split was coincidental with the Second Great Awakening and featured prominent revivalists such as Finney, the division between Old School and New School Presbyterians did not follow along pro- and anti-revival lines. To be sure, leading Old School theologians such as Princeton's Charles Hodge (1797–1878) opposed Finney's and Barnes's teaching. Furthermore, the Old School was deeply ambivalent about the sort of social reform that the revivals inspired, particularly abolitionism, which many in the Old School believed was based on an incorrect understanding of what the Bible taught about slavery. Still, despite these specific circumstances of the Second Great

Awakening, Old School Presbyterians, as heirs of the eighteenth-century Presbyterian appropriation of revivalistic piety, were not opposed to revivals per se. Most prominent Old Schoolers, such as Hodge, had undergone a conversion experience during their adolescence and so affirmed the kind of personal piety that the New Side Presbyterians had thought necessary for ordination. Further evidence of Old School Presbyterianism's support for revivalism in principle came with the urban **Revival of 1857–1858,** sometimes called the Prayer Meeting Revival. New York City was one of its centers and Old School Presbyterian ministers there such as Samuel Irenaeus Prime (1812–1885) and James W. Alexander (1804–1859) were important advocates and defenders of that revival.

Presbyterian involvement in the Great Awakening and the Second Great Awakening established a pattern for American Presbyterian attitudes to revivalism. The Reunion of 1758 was crucial, securing a place for revivalism's experiential piety beneath Presbyterianism's seemingly cold and formal exterior. Though Old School Presbyterians in the nineteenth century objected to specific forms of revival, they never took issue with revivalism's underlying zeal and conviction, though John Williamson Nevin did just that in his far-reaching critique *The Anxious Bench* (1843). Into the twentieth century, even after a split between Fundamentalists and Modernists, Presbyterians in the mainline and sideline denominations would not repudiate their history of harmonizing Presbyterian faith and practice with revivalist piety.

During the Charismatic Revival and Renewal of the 1960s and 1970s, new theological issues emerged for Presbyterians with reference to the experience of **baptism in the Holy Spirit,** as evidenced by **speaking in tongues,** and the manifestations of other **charismatic gifts.** Robert Whitaker, a Presbyterian pastor in Chandler, Arizona, underwent Spirit baptism in 1962, and his new Charismatic affiliation led ultimately to his removal from office in 1967. With support from attorney and former minister George "Brick" Bradford, theologian J. Rodman Williams, and a former president of Princeton Seminary, John A. Mackay, the Charismatic Communion of Presbyterian Ministers took shape in 1966 and became a forum for "Spirit-filled" Presbyterians. While the Charismatic movement has maintained a small presence within mainline Presbyterian churches (PCUSA), the more conservative Orthodox Presbyterian Church (OPC) and Presbyterian Church in America (PCA) generally disfavored the practice of the charismatic gifts among their ministers and members throughout the 1970s, 1980s, and 1990s.

The case of Presbyterian engagement with revivalism is exceptional partly because the Continental European expressions of the Reformed tradition, for example, the German and Dutch Reformed, have been historically more critical and wary of awakenings and the piety that underlay them. The primary reason for Reformed opposition to revivalism was summed up well by Nevin, who complained that revivals stressed the subjective experience and life of the individual Christian while the insights of Calvin placed primary importance upon the objective ministry of the church through word and sacrament. Some have argued that the English-speaking branch of Reformed tradition, the Scottish Presbyterians and Puritans, cultivated a kind of piety that made more room for personal experience than the Reformed churches on the Continent. The Westminster Confession of Faith, for instance, includes a chapter on the doctrine of assurance that emphasizes introspection in a manner uncharacteristic of the Continental creeds and catechisms. At the same time, the conditions of church life among seventeenth-century Scottish Presbyterians set into motion practices, such as the communion season (a quarterly gathering of local churches for a week of preparation for and observance of the Lord's Supper), that functioned as a forerunner of the American **camp meeting** that would eventually dominate early nineteenth-century revivalism. Thus American Presbyterian history reveals a set of intricate connections with the cycles of religious awakenings that have periodically punctuated the experience of Protestants in the United States.

Further Reading: Coalter, Milton J., Jr. *Gilbert Tennent, Son of Thunder: A Case Study of Continental Pietism's Impact on the First Great Awakening in the Middle Colonies.* Westport, CT: Greenwood Press, 1986; Hart, D. G. *The Lost Soul of American Protestantism.* Lanham, MD: Rowman and Littlefield, 2002; Long, Kathryn Teresa. *The Revival of 1857–58: Interpreting an American Religious Awakening.* New York: Oxford University Press, 1998. Marsden, George M. *The Evangelical Mind and the New School Presbyterian Experience: A Case Study of Thought and Theology in Nineteenth-Century America.* New Haven, CT: Yale University Press, 1970; Schmidt, Leigh Eric. *Holy Fairs: Scottish Communions and American Revivals in the Early Modern Period.* Princeton, NJ: Princeton University Press, 1989; Trinterud, Leonard J. *The Forming of an American Tradition: A Re-examination of Colonial Presbyterianism.* Philadelphia: Westminster Press, 1949; Westerkamp, Marilyn J. *Triumph of the Laity: Scots-Irish Piety and the Great Awakening, 1625–1760.* New York: Oxford University Press, 1988; Williams, J. Rodman. *Renewal Theology.* Grand Rapids, MI: Zondervan, 1996.

Darryl G. Hart

CAMP MEETINGS AND TENT MEETINGS

During the decades following the American Revolution, a new kind of outdoor sacramental and revival meeting emerged as a powerful religious force in America. It helped ignite the spiritual volcano known in the **South** and in western regions as the Great Revival (or **Second Great Awakening**)—a decades-long exhibition of raw spiritual power that affected large areas of the United States in the early 1800s. A new phase of religious history had arrived. The new practice referred to was the camp meeting, and within 25 years of its beginnings **Methodist** bishop **Francis Asbury** claimed that Methodists held 500 such gatherings on an annual basis. By 1820 that number doubled, and the camp meeting became an American institution and an international phenomenon.

No one knows exactly when and where the first camp meeting was held. Some scholars believe **Presbyterians** founded the institution in southern Kentucky about 1800. The Reverend **James McGready** held sacramental services on his parish

that year, and as the spirit of revival spread, the camp meeting emerged as part of the flood tide of the Great Revival in Kentucky. For over a century this popular thesis has been entrenched in standard historical and reference literature. However, strong new evidence disputes these claims, and points to more than a dozen camp meeting sites in five states that date before 1800. Cattle Creek Camp Meeting is still held near Branchville, South Carolina, and oral tradition dates outdoor services there from 1786. That same year John Bush built a brush arbor camp ground at "Cracker's Neck," in Green County, Georgia, and it became the cradle of Methodism in that area. McWhorter's Camp Meeting, near Mineral Springs, North Carolina, may date from 1787. Documentary evidence indicates a strong camp meeting already existed by 1802. Evidence suggests Effingham County Camp Meeting near Springfield, Georgia, and Zion Camp Meeting in Mecklenburg County, Virginia, date from about 1790. White Oak Camp Meeting in Appling, Georgia, started as a brush arbor encampment, and may date from 1792. Rock Springs Camp Meeting, near Denver, North Carolina, and Cypress Camp Meeting, near Ridgeville, South Carolina, both started in 1794, and Indian Field Camp Meeting, near St. George, South Carolina, may date from 1795. In 1796 Daniel Asbury and Dr. James Hall held the great Union Camp Meeting in Iredell County, North Carolina, and reported at least 500 conversions. That same year John Page conducted a camp meeting on the Greene Methodist circuit in Tennessee. Evidence suggests Camp Chapel United Methodist Church near Baltimore, Maryland, grew out of camp meetings held in that region in the 1790s, and Thomas Smith held a camp meeting on the eastern shore of Maryland in 1800.

The data of these encampments strongly challenges the popular thesis of camp meeting origins, and offers a different interpretation—the camp meeting may have had its beginnings in Georgia or the Carolinas circa 1786. The early roots of the camp meeting lay in many outdoor traditions, including the Scottish **holy fairs;** the British Field Meetings, including the field **preaching** of **George Whitefield** and John Wesley; the West African religious traditions of the **African American** slaves; the outdoor revival services of the Separate **Baptists** in Virginia; early Methodist annual conference revival services; and the Big Meetings of the Pennsylvania Germans. However, the immediate antecedent of the camp meeting was undoubtedly the "outdoor church" on the American frontier.

The pioneers often worshipped out of doors, and they used "stands," "tents," and "brush arbors" as the locus for worship until a meetinghouse could be built. A stand could be just a crude tree-stump pulpit in the woods, but it sometimes included split-log seats for the congregation, who sat in the open grove at hand. A tent was larger, offered protection from the weather for ministers and people, and usually included tables for use in sacramental occasions. William Henry Foote claimed Presbyterians in North Carolina used stands as early 1742, and suggested tents came into common usage by the 1750s. Similar to stands and tents, a brush arbor was a crude but effective structure made from poles and brush, intended to shelter or harbor people from inclement weather. It included a preacher's stand and split-log backless seats for the congregation.

Probably all early frontier ministers preached from a stand, tent, or brush arbor at one time or another. Several prominent North Carolina Presbyterian ministers did, including Dr. James Hall, John Robinson, and the Princeton-trained Robert Archibald. These men preached at Poplar Tent, one of the largest and most showy tents in North Carolina, built about 1764. Methodist circuit riders William Ormund and Daniel Asbury preached from "a stand near the road" in North Carolina; John Heckewelder, missionary to the American Indians, preached from a "stand in the woods" during his travels in Pennsylvania; and Methodist John A. Grenade often preached from a stand during his labors in middle Tennessee. James B. Finley, famed pioneer Methodist circuit rider, reported the use of stands at the legendary **Cane Ridge** meeting of 1801, and one of those was for black slaves.

Up to 25,000 persons attended the Cane Ridge sacramental meeting held near Paris, Kentucky, and it exploded the Great Revival onto the American religious landscape, attracting international attention. Furthermore, it helped make the camp meeting an overnight sensation among Methodists, Presbyterians, Baptists, Christian New Lights, and **Shakers.** Cane Ridge Meeting House still survives, enshrined in a lovely building as a historic Christian landmark.

From this milieu of the outdoor church three architectural forms emerged that established the camp meeting tradition in the American church—the brush arbor, the camp meeting shed, and the canvas tent.

The brush arbor appeared long before the American Revolution, and quickly became the favorite mode for outdoor religious services. It is still used today, and a brush arbor camp meeting has been held for many years at Oatmeal, Texas. So simple a few persons could build one in a single day, so strong it could endure the average summer storm, the brush arbor was so versatile it could be used almost anywhere. These structures looked like an open-sided wilderness picnic pavilion with a thick brush roof. They stood about 10–12 feet high, and varied greatly in size depending on the needs of the local congregation. Trimmed poles set firmly in the ground held up the roof, which consisted of a lattice of smaller poles covered with thick brush (hence the name *brush arbor*). They effectively shielded people from sun and rain, while split logs provided pews for the congregation, and a pulpit for the preacher. Brush arbors were utilitarian structures, and well suited the pioneer preachers as a tool for effective evangelism. It was the tent meeting of its day. A minister would come into an area, build a brush arbor, and hold a camp meeting. Those converted would form the nucleus of a new church. Thousands of brush arbor encampments were held during the nineteenth century, with churches of various denominations founded as a result. Brush arbors also suited the needs of the black slaves. On plantations that encouraged religious services, the "brush house" often served as camp meeting and church. On plantations that refused religious assembly and forced slaves to worship in secret, brush arbors offered natural camouflage in a secluded glade away from prying eyes. For these, and other reasons, blacks often referred to these meeting places as the "hush arbor."

By 1810 a new permanent camp meeting structure began to appear, called a "shed" or "arbor." Fashioned after the old brush arbor, this structure became the locus of worship and ministry on the campground. The genesis of these sheds has been a debated issue, and some scholars assumed no permanent buildings existed before the late 1830s. Then Ellen Weiss discovered the camp shed at Rock Springs Camp Meeting had been built in 1832. Since then two older sheds have been found, one at Mineral Springs, North Carolina (1830), and one at Jonesville, Virginia (1824). A brush arbor preceded each. The present shed at Bell's Camp Ground, near Knoxville, Tennessee, dates from 1880, but the shed it replaced had been built in 1809.

The development of these huge wooden camp meeting sheds helped transform the camp meeting to a national institution, and by the time of the **Civil War** several thousand permanent campgrounds had appeared around the country. Current research shows that at least 80 still survive. Two are Presbyterian: Smyrna Camp, Conyers, Georgia (1827), and Old Lebanon Camp, Ackerman, Mississippi (1850). One is Wesleyan (Wesleyan Methodist), West Chazy Camp, West Chazy, New York (1842); one Advent Christian, Tremont Camp, Marion, Massachusetts (1855); and one German Methodist, Camp Meeting, Santa Claus, Indiana (1849). Seven early black encampments survive, four Methodist, and three **African Methodist Episcopal Zion**: McKenzie's Camp, Catawba County, North Carolina (ca. 1850); Cottonville Camp, Polkton, North Carolina (1860); and Redding Springs Camp, Weddington, North Carolina (1854). The Yellow Creek Tabernacle (1840), located at the living-history museum in Weston, Georgia, is the only early Baptist camp meeting shed extant.

Methodists founded the remaining early surviving encampments, including such ones as Tabernacle Camp, Columbus, Alabama (1828); Ebenezer Camp, Center Point, Arkansas (1822); Shingleroof Camp, McDunnough, Georgia (1821); Empire Grove, East Poland, Maine (1834); Cumberland Grove, Cumberland, Maryland (1830); Wesleyan Grove, Martha's Vineyard, Massachusetts (1835); Felder's Camp, McComb, Mississippi (1810); Sing Sing Camp (Camp Woods), Ossining, New York (1831); Hollow Rock Camp, Toronto, Ohio (1818); Patterson Grove, Huntington Mills, Pennsylvania (1835); and Rockhold Camp, Bluff City, Tennessee (1820).

Although the circus started using canvas tents (or "tops") in 1825, evidence suggests the era of tent meeting revivalism may have begun in 1819 when some Methodists used a cloth tent as an arbor at a camp meeting near Poplar Hill, Tennessee. It is uncertain how rapidly the idea spread, but by 1835 **Charles G. Finney** and other evangelists used huge tents for revivals and camp meetings. Finney's tent at Oberlin, Ohio, would seat 3,000 persons, and the "Great Tent" used by the followers of **William Miller** in the Adventist revival of the 1840s seated over 4,000 people. Edwin Long used a 3,000-seat "Moveable Tent Church" to evangelize eastern Pennsylvania during the 1850s, and Confederate and Union chaplains used "tent chapels" for church and revival services throughout the Civil War.

By the mid-1860s some people claimed the camp meeting was dying out and had passed its point of usefulness. In actuality, leaders had begun to use the camp meeting in exciting new ways, and this brought a major resurgence in the institution. In 1867 Methodist leaders founded the National Camp Meeting Association for the Promotion of Holiness at Vineland, New Jersey, with John S. Inskip as president. Their encampments at Manheim, Pennsylvania (1868), and Round Lake, New York (1869), drew crowds of up to 25,000 people. By 1881 the association had conducted "tabernacle meetings" across the nation and helped transport the camp meeting to India and Australia. Hundreds of encampments and associations sprang up in the United States in the wake of these meetings, and the **Holiness movement** became a worldwide revival.

Other church leaders took the camp meeting idea in completely new directions. In 1872 Lewis Miller decided to use the camp meeting setting as an educational institute for Sunday school teachers.

An early 1800s camp meeting set in the woods, with an excited preacher (in a makeshift stand) raising his arms, young females in agitated movement, and upper-class observers (in hats) aside to the left and right looking on unperturbed. (Hugh Bridport, lithographer; Alexander Rider, artist; Kennedy & Lucas Lithography, 1829.) Courtesy of the Library of Congress.

In 1874 he and John H. Vincent held their first sessions at the Fair Point Camp Meeting on Chautauqua Lake, New York—and **Chautauqua** was born. Sometimes called the Sunday School Camp Meeting, Chautauqua quickly gained national interest, and over 300 such religious assemblies sprang up around the country. Entrepreneurs soon commercialized the Chautauqua idea and took it on the road as a traveling show, and at their peak in 1924 nearly 10,000 such Chautauquas were held, with a total of about 40 million tickets sold. By 1950 these shows disappeared, but religious assemblies were still active in several states. The "mother" Chautauqua has become an institution in itself, and still meets at the original site on Chautauqua Lake, New York.

At this same time, British church leaders adopted their own version of the camp meeting. **Lorenzo Dow** had inspired the first encampment on British soil at Mow Cop in 1807, but opposition hindered the effort from growing. In 1875 leaders held the first Keswick Convention, and also founded the Mildmay Prophetic Conference. These quickly gained international fame, and quickly spread to other countries. They helped influence the formation of the Bible and Prophecy Conference movement in the United States. Many of the U.S. conferences were held at established campgrounds, like Ocean Grove, New Jersey, and Sea Cliff, Long Island, New York. In 1880 **Dwight L. Moody** founded the Northfield Bible Conference at Northfield, Massachusetts, and soon other conference sites appeared, including Niagara on Lake Erie (1883); Winona Lake, Indiana (1895); and Montrose, Pennsylvania (1908), to name a few. Conferences like these helped lay the foundation for modern evangelicalism and the rise of the Fundamentalist movement.

An enormous revival tent belonging to evangelist Oral Roberts, whose "tent cathedrals" have been the world's largest, seating 12,500. (Oral Roberts Evangelistic Association, 1959; New York World-Telegram and the Sun Newspaper Photograph Collection.) Courtesy of the Library of Congress.

Some leaders believed the camp meeting could serve as a forum for certain specialty issues of the day, including the campaign for **temperance** and the growing **healing** movement. In 1874 William H. Boole helped found the National Temperance Camp Meeting Association at Old Orchard Beach Camp Meeting in Maine. The new organization sponsored numerous temperance camp meetings. Leaders at Ocean Grove Camp Meeting in New Jersey combined temperance and **women's** rights, and started the Women's Gospel Temperance Camp Meeting in 1877. In 1873 Dr. Charles Cullis held his first healing convention, and shortly afterward began conducting Healing Camp Meetings at Old Orchard Beach, Maine. These, and the healing encampments held there by **Albert Benjamin Simpson** (founder of the **Christian and Missionary Alliance**), helped establish the divine healing movement in America. These meetings were precursors to the huge healing tent camp meetings of **Maria Woodworth-Etter,** and later the healing tent encampments of **Aimee Semple McPherson, William Branham,** Jack Coe, A. A. Allen, **Oral Roberts,** and others. Healing camp meetings contributed significantly to the **Pentecostal revival** and the modern **Charismatic Renewal.**

Many denominations, missionary organizations, and independent groups adopted the camp meeting after 1870. Numerous ethnic encampments sprang up—African American, Swedish, German, Norwegian, and **Latino**—and several of them still survive. Bloy's Cowboy Camp Meeting at Ft. Stockton, Texas,

A mid-1800s camp meeting, held at Sing Sing, Upper New York State, in August 1859. The upraised arms of the preacher seem more an oratorical gesture than a sign of excitement, and many listeners are looking away from the speaker. (*Harper's Weekly*, September 10, 1859.) Courtesy of Dr. Keith J. Hardman.

was founded in 1890, and today the Ranchmen's Camp Meeting of the Southwest sponsors about 20 encampments in several western states. Most Adventist groups have followed the tradition of the early Millerites (i.e., followers of William Miller), and still hold encampments each year. Some groups not usually associated with the camp meeting tradition also sponsor camp meetings. **Mormons** call their meetings "reunion," and Spiritualists by the thousands still flock to Lilly Dale, New York, and Chesterfield, Indiana.

By its very nature the camp meeting has always been a modified form of intentional community, but with the development of permanent sites some campgrounds became Christian resorts. Wesleyan Grove, at Martha's Vineyard, Massachusetts (1835); Ocean Grove, New Jersey (1869); Lakeside,

Ohio (1872); Petosky, Michigan (1875); and Pacific Palisades, California (1921) are some of the famous examples. During the 1980s, **Jim and Tammy Faye Bakker** took the Christian resort idea to a new level with the development of Heritage Village, North Carolina. At its height this new Christian resort ranked third only behind Disney World and Disneyland in its ability to attract visitors. A large number of camp meetings have actually become Christian summer communities, and permit cottage owners to live on the grounds for up to six months per year. Many examples could be cited.

The twentieth century witnessed continued growth and change in camp meeting and tent meeting revivalism. Dozens of new denominations sprang up, and with them hundreds of official denominational camp meetings. Some later became "district centers" that housed camping facilities for all ages, as well as church headquarters. Some churches developed official "leisure ministries," and the family camping movement became very popular. Other groups adopted the "Christian conference center" and "Christian retreat center" as methods of outreach ministries, and this movement has spread worldwide. The Presbyterian assembly at Montreat, North Carolina (1897), is a superb example. Popular evangelists adopted new methods to reach mass audiences. **Billy Sunday** used huge wooden tabernacles, while **Oral Roberts** used a huge "tent cathedral" that would seat 12,500 people. During the **Jesus People movement,** youth ministers developed the Jesus Festival, sometimes called the youth camp meeting, as a Christian response to the Woodstock Rock Festival of 1969. The first Jesus Festival met in 1970 on the grounds of the Wilmore Holiness Camp Meeting, and "Ichthus" now owns a lovely facility near Wilmore, Kentucky. The largest of these festivals, "Creation," meets at Agape Farm, in central Pennsylvania, and draws thousands of young people every year.

In 1959 Christian camping leaders organized an association to promote the work of Christian camps and conference centers. The new organization soon became international in scope, and in 1968 leaders changed the name to Christian Camping International (CCI). Today the organization literally spans the globe in outreach ministries and membership, and the U.S. CCI alone has over a thousand member organizations.

It may be safely estimated that over 2,000 camp meetings and conferences are held annually around the world. Many of these are small, with a total attendance of less than 3,000 people. Others are simply huge, like the Dahrur Jathra, an independent camp meeting in India, which draws up to 100,000 persons. Founded by Methodist missionary Earl Seamands and patterned after Camp Sychar at Mount Vernon, Ohio, this camp meeting in the tropical forest has become world famous. The Falls Creek Baptist Camp Meeting in Oklahoma has drawn over 10 million visitors in its 80-plus years of history, and the **Church of God (Anderson,**

Indiana) Camp Meeting, founded in 1907, has probably equaled that attendance. Ocean Grove Camp Meeting in Ocean Grove, New Jersey, has likely surpassed both of these encampments in total attendance. Founded in 1869, known as God's Square Mile, Ocean Grove has perhaps drawn up to 15 million visitors through the years.

No one knows how many camp meetings actually exist. From its beginning as a backwoods outdoor revival and sacramental occasion, the camp meeting has grown to become one of the largest and most powerful institutions ever developed by the Christian church. Such successes have caused the camp meeting to grow to enormous proportions, and it can reasonably be estimated that well over 200,000 of these gatherings have been held over the last two centuries. Without a doubt this institution has made a profound impact on the American religious landscape.

Further Reading: Brown, Kenneth O. *Holy Ground, Too: The Camp Meeting Family Tree.* Hazleton, PA: Holiness Archives, 1997; Brown, Kenneth O. *Inskip, McDonald, Fowler: "Wholly and Forever Thine," Early Leadership in the National Camp Meeting Association for the Promotion of Holiness.* Hazleton, PA: Holiness Archives, 1999; Dieter, Melvin E. *The Holiness Revival of the Nineteenth Century.* Metuchen, NJ: Scarecrow Press, 1980; Eslinger, Ellen. *Citizens of Zion: The Social Origins of Camp Meeting Revivalism.* Knoxville: University of Tennessee Press, 1999; Johnson, Charles. *The Frontier Camp Meeting.* Dallas: Southern Methodist University Press, 1955; Weiss, Ellen. *City in the Woods: The Life and Design of an American Camp Meeting on Martha's Vineyard.* New York: Oxford University Press, 1987.

Kenneth O. Brown

CAMPBELL, ALEXANDER (1788–1866)

Alexander Campbell was the leader of the Reformers, or Disciples of Christ, who united in 1832 with the Christians led by **Barton Warren Stone.** Although not a revivalist himself, Campbell's teachings influenced the practice of revivalism in the **Restorationist and Stone-Campbell Movement.** Campbell's father, Thomas Campbell, was a minister

Dr. Alexander Campbell. Though the "Campbellite" movement had roots in the early 1800s revivals, Campbell himself expressed ambivalence regarding the benefits of revivals. (Reproduction of a painting by J. Bogle; c.a. 1857.) Courtesy of the Library of Congress.

of the Anti-Burgher Seceder **Presbyterian** Church in Northern Ireland. Coming to the United States in 1807, he affiliated with the Anti-Burgher Associate Synod of North America. Conflict over his having served Communion to Presbyterians not affiliated with the Associate Synod soon led to his separation from the Associate Synod. In 1809, he organized the Christian Association of Washington County, Pennsylvania, to support the **preaching** of the gospel without regard to human creeds and confessions. Two years later, the Christian Association constituted itself as a church and built a meetinghouse at Brush Run, near the Virginia (now West Virginia)–Pennsylvania border.

In 1812 the Brush Run Church ordained the younger Campbell, who soon became the leading figure in the Brush Run Church. Following his lead, the congregation adopted believer's immersion, which led to ties with the **Baptists.** There were differences, however, between Campbell and most Baptist preachers. One difference was Campbell's teaching that penitent sinners are to be baptized on a simple confession that Jesus is the Christ, the Son of the Living God (Matthew 16:16), rather than on an account of their conversion.

Another difference between Campbell and most Baptist ministers was Campbell's view of the purpose of baptism. Baptism was to give believers an assurance of the forgiveness or remission of their sins. In contrast, most Baptists taught that baptism was merely a seal by which persons who had been converted were set apart as members of the church. Though Campbell believed and taught that baptism was to be administered to penitent believers upon a simple confession of faith and that the purpose of baptism was to assure believers of the forgiveness of their sins, he did not actually apply these beliefs to the practice of revivalism. Yet others did. The first to do so may have been the Christian preacher Benjamin Franklin Hall.

Hall, who was ordained in 1825, reported that he was troubled in the first year of his ministry by observing that some persons who "mourned" their alienation from God did not experience the desired pardon of their sins and transformation of their hearts in **conversion.** The goal of much of the preaching of the Christians to that time (like that of other evangelicals) was to awaken sinners to their situation apart from God and to encourage them to **pray** to Christ for pardon and a new heart. At the close of a sermon, the preachers would often invite the "mourners" to come to the front of the stand or pulpit, where the ministers would kneel among them and pray for them to receive the forgiveness of their sins and a new heart. Hall began to ask himself why some sinners who seemed to be deeply penitent did not receive an assurance of forgiveness and the transformation of their hearts. He claimed that he found the answer to his question in Campbell's view of the purpose of baptism. Penitent believers should not be told to pray to Christ for the forgiveness of their sins and a new heart, but to confess their faith in Christ and be baptized for the remission of their sins. This would result in the assurance of forgiveness desired and the transformation of the penitent sinner's heart in gratitude and joy.

In 1827 Campbell's colleague Walter Scott applied Campbell's teachings to revivalism in his development of a distinctive order of salvation. Scott argued that there were three things for the sinner to do to be saved: believe the gospel of God's love in Jesus Christ, repent of sin, and be baptized. In turn, God would do three things: remit sin, give the Holy Spirit, and grant eternal life. In order to count these items on the fingers of one hand, Scott combined the Holy Spirit and eternal life into the gift of the Holy Spirit. Campbell, himself, was wary of Scott's schematization. Others in the movement, however, readily employed Scott's five-finger exercise with amazing results. By 1860 the Stone-Campbell movement was the fifth-largest religious group in the United States, with a membership of nearly 200,000.

Further Reading: Foster, Douglas A., ed. *Encyclopedia of the Stone-Campbell Movement.* Grand Rapids, MI: Eerdmans, 2004; Richardson, Robert. *Memoirs of Alexander Campbell.* 2 vols. Philadelphia: J. P. Lippincott, 1868, 1870.

D. Newell Williams

CAMPUS AND COLLEGE REVIVALS

Throughout American history, spiritual awakenings on university campuses have resulted in renewed spiritual life among believers and conversions among unbelievers. Higher education began in America with the founding of religious schools to train ministers for the gospel ministry. Harvard College (founded 1636) was closely tied to the Congregational churches of New England and their seventeenth-century **Calvinistic** theology and ethos. Its early presidents were all chosen from the ranks of the clergy. Yale, Princeton, and other American colleges were also founded to train religious leaders for the American colonies. Over time, most of these institutions shifted from their original purpose and severed or at least weakened their ties to organized religion. Religion became something not to be practiced but merely studied as an academic discipline, or even set aside as irrelevant. Skepticism and worldliness became dominant. Some schools could scarcely be recognized as having any Christian belief or heritage. In addition, the founding of secular state colleges meant that those institutions began without any commitment to religious study or practice.

During each season of revival in America, college campuses have shared in the spiritual awakening. Revival movements have often spread to other schools through campus visits by revived students, functioning much like modern-day circuit riders. In American revivals, young people have made an impact on the church as well as the campuses. **Jonathan Edwards,** one of America's greatest theologians and historians of revival, argued that the **Great Awakening** had its greatest impact chiefly among young people. Those of college age tend to be more idealistic than their elders, and that idealism longs for what is genuine and real. Revival also means change, and young persons tend to be open to change. Thus the seeds of awakening often find fertile soil among the young, including students. Yet because student populations are transient, the impact of an awakening on campus tends to be short-lived.

When the Great Awakening hit full stride in 1740, America had only three colleges: Harvard, William and Mary, and Yale. **David Brainerd,** entering Yale in 1739, found what he regarded as an unhealthy spiritual environment on campus, and sensed that his own spiritual vigor was diminishing. In early 1741, Yale College experienced a time of spiritual refreshment. The religious revival not only renewed Brainerd's spiritual life, it also resulted in numerous student **conversions.** The entire student body seemed to be affected. The Great Awakening was an impetus for the creation of many educational institutions. Over the next two decades, schools such as the College of New Jersey (Princeton), Rhode Island College (Brown University), Queen's College (Rutgers University), and Dartmouth were founded to train Christian ministers.

In the wake of the American Revolution, the nation experienced a general lessening of religious zeal. College students mirrored this decline, and some became not merely apathetic but openly antagonistic to Christianity. Observers reported that church attendance among college students decreased, while religious skepticism, profane language, drunkenness, gambling, and sexual licentiousness increased. Bishop Meade of Virginia said that when he met a college graduate during this period of time, he assumed the young person to be a skeptic or avowed unbeliever.

The 1787 revival at Hampden-Sydney College (Virginia) is sometimes regarded as the beginning of the **Second Great Awakening.** Four young men, concerned about the spiritual condition of their school, met on campus to sing and **pray** together. Unsympathetic students found out about this gathering and tried to break up the group, which they regarded as fanatical. When word of the incident reached the college president, John Blair Smith, he invited students to pray with him in his home. More than half the college attended the prayer meeting, and many students were converted. The revival that began there spread throughout the region. Over the next several years, numerous colleges reported times of spiritual awakening. Yale College, under leadership of its president **Timothy Dwight** (the grandson of Jonathan Edwards), saw one-third of its student body converted in 1802. **Lyman Beecher** noted that the revival's impact on campus was so powerful that "infidelity"—that is, skepticism or freethinking—"hid its head" (Beecher, 43). A student described the revived Yale College as a "little temple" where prayer and praise were the delight of the majority of the students (Fisher, 83). Other colleges affected during this season of revival were Amherst, Dartmouth, Princeton, and Williams College. Princeton's president, Ashbel Green, observed that virtually every room on campus became a place of earnest devotion, and that the pressing question was not who had been impacted by the revival, but who had not. A student at Amherst wrote that the revival made every day on campus now seem like a Sabbath.

In 1806, the so-called **Haystack Prayer Meeting** took place at Williams College in Massachusetts. Samuel J. Mills helped lead a group of five students who were praying for revival on the campus. Being forced to seek shelter under the side of a large haystack during a storm, Mills challenged the others to join him in taking the gospel to Asia. "We can do it if we will," he said (Cairns, 262). He led the group in prayer, providing the impetus for the birth of the American **foreign missions** movement. Oberlin College, under the leadership of revivalist **Charles G.**

The evangelical revival of the 1970s appealed to high school and college-age youth, as seen in this postcard from "Rock of Ages '73," held at the Shelby County Fairgrounds in Sidney, Ohio as "a festival of Christian music, art, drama & sharing." Courtesy of Dr. Kenneth O. Brown.

Finney, saw continual periods of revival beginning in 1835, and it became a focal point for revivalism and social reform. **The Revival of 1857–1858,** also know as the Businessman's Revival or Laymen's Revival, was sparked by movements of prayer in cities and towns across America. Several colleges experienced revival during these years, including Oberlin, Dartmouth, Middlebury, Princeton, Williams, Wofford, Amherst, the University of North Carolina, Wake Forest, Wabash, the University of Georgia, Emory, Baylor, and the University of Michigan. Yale had almost one-half of its student body profess faith in Christ. Bowdoin College had 25 percent of the graduating class enter the Christian ministry. Davidson College saw about 80 of its 100 seniors converted. The year of 1858 was perhaps the greatest year ever for college revivals. The revival not only touched existing campuses, but encouraged denominations to begin new schools to train Christian workers.

One of the most far-reaching expressions of campus revival in American history was the **Student Volunteer Movement** (SVM), a student-led initiative in foreign missions, in which student volunteers—who had signed a pledge to become missionaries—sought to recruit their fellow students as missionaries prior to their overseas departure. While foreign missions had been an emphasis on college campuses in North America since the 1806 Haystack Prayer Meeting, mentioned above, the

SVM operated on a larger scale than any previous initiative in Protestant missions. Historian Stephen Neill estimated that the SVM was directly responsible for a greater number of missionary recruits—about 20,000—than any comparable movement in Christian history. The SVM began through the initiative of a brother and sister, Robert and Grace Wilder, whose father had been a missionary to India, and who were studying at Princeton University (then an all-male institution) and Mt. Holyoke College (a **women's** college). Robert and Grace established student missionary societies for **men** and women on their college campuses, and led in prayer sessions for world missions. In the summer of 1886, evangelist **Dwight L. Moody** organized a four-week Bible conference for college students at the Mt. Hermon School in Northfield, Massachusetts, and 251 students from 86 colleges and universities attended. Robert Wilder persuaded Moody to host a missions night at this gathering, and by the end of the conference there were 100 new missionary recruits—the number that students had prayed for.

In the late 1800s and early 1900s, the SVM spread across the United States and Canada, and many British and European campuses were also affected. About 100,000 college students signed a pledge indicating that, if God so willed, they would become foreign missionaries. Though only 20,000 of those who pledged actually left North America, the other 80,000 played a role in fund-raising, prayer, and logistical support for those who went abroad. John R. Mott (1865–1955), and the former Cambridge University cricket player C. T. Studd (1862–1931), were active as students and in later life in recruiting college students to become missionaries. After the First World War, the SVM declined in influence, in part because modernist theology had begun to affect the movement and to challenge traditional ideas of sin and salvation. Some mainline Protestant missionaries began to focus their efforts not on a call to religious **conversion** but on health, education, and programs of social improvement in foreign nations.

During the revivals of 1904–1908, many campuses were affected. Not only Christian institutions such as Taylor University and Asbury College, but also secular colleges and universities such as Cornell, the University of Florida, the University of Michigan, and the University of California at Berkeley experienced outbreaks of revival. A "universal day of prayer for students" was implemented in college after college. Students met together to pray for the spread of the revival, and many if not most of America's colleges saw outbreaks of revival. Numerous students were deeply affected during this season of revival, including E. Stanley Jones, a student at Asbury College. Touched by a campus revival in 1905, Jones committed himself to go to India as a missionary. Jones was not alone—thousands of students headed to the mission field after being touched by campus awakenings during this period of time. Before 1895, less than 1,000 student volunteers were serving as missionaries; in May 1906 alone, more than 3,000 students sailed from America or Europe to foreign mission fields.

Following World War II, there were signs of a resurgence of religious life in America. Revivals began to occur in Christian colleges in 1949 and 1950. Schools impacted include Bethel (Minnesota), Wheaton, North Park, Houghton, Asbury, Seattle Pacific, Multnomah School of the Bible, Westmont, John Brown University, and Northern Baptist Theological Seminary. As students experienced spiritual awakening, many "fellowship groups" sprang up. Some of these postwar student awakenings were triggered by campus visits from **preachers** such as **J. Edwin Orr** and **Billy Graham.** Whereas the **YMCA** had been birthed following the 1857–1858 Prayer Awakening, the campus revivals of the 1940s and 1950s saw the creation of ministries such as **Campus Crusade for Christ.** These Christian organizations would become avenues for maintaining spiritual life on college campuses across the nation in succeeding years. Another growing campus ministry in the 1940s and 1950s was the **Navigators,** which had begun among military personnel, but soon spread to college campuses, emphasizing a disciplined life of Bible memorization, prayer, evangelism, and one-on-one discipleship. **InterVarsity Christian Fellowship** (IVCF), though founded in Great

Yale College has played a pivotal role in American revivals, having experienced awakenings of varied intensity in 1741, 1802, 1831, 1858, 1905, and 1962–1963. The earlier revivals are treated in an 1838 essay by Yale's rhetoric professor, Chauncey Goodrich. (Haines Photo Co.; Conneaut, Ohio; 1909.) Courtesy of the Library of Congress.

Britain as early as 1873, began to expand rapidly in the United States only in the 1940s and 1950s. Since 1948, IVCF has held a triennial missions conference at the University of Illinois at Urbana, and for more than half a century the Urbana Conferences have done much to promote missions awareness on college campuses. Some IVCF chapters participated in the **Charismatic Renewal** of the early 1960s. Under the influence of Harald Bredesen, an ordained Lutheran minister and Charismatic leader, students in the Yale University IVCF spoke in tongues in 1962–1963 and attracted media interest.

On February 3, 1970, a campus revival began at Asbury College in Wilmore, Kentucky. For an entire week classroom study came to a standstill and students sought God and gave spiritual testimony. Asbury students fanned out across the nation to tell of their experience of revival, and by the summer of 1970 the movement spread to more than a hundred colleges, seminaries, and Bible schools. Schools affected included Azusa (Pacific) College, Taylor University, Spring Arbor College, Roberts Wesleyan College, Greenville College, and Southwestern Baptist Theological Seminary, just to name a few. As students from these institutions traveled to spread the news of revival, others were brought into the movement. The students' public testimonies at Asbury College in 1970 often involved an open and specific **confession of sins** before fellow students. This practice arose during

the 1949–1950 awakenings on various campuses, and continued in 1970 and during the campus awakenings of 1995–1996. Young people, in testifying to God, felt a need to acknowledge their secret transgressions and so purge themselves and their campuses of the posturing and insincerity that they detected there.

In the spring of 1995, a campus revival that began at Howard Payne University in Brownwood, Texas, spread to colleges and universities across the nation. Wheaton College was touched by that revival, and Wheaton students became carriers of a "spark" of revival to numerous other institutions, including Trinity Evangelical Divinity School, Greenville, Hope, Taylor, George Fox, Messiah, Cornerstone, Judson, Asbury, Gordon and Eastern Nazarene in Massachusetts, Bethel and Northwestern in Minnesota, and Biola in California. Christian fellowship groups on secular campus such as Louisiana Tech, Murray State in Kentucky, the University of Wisconsin, Yale, Iowa State, and Kansas State University also experienced a movement of revival. Periodic campus awakenings have been a mainstay of American religious history, and the recent campus revivals of the mid-1990s indicate the trend likely will continue in the twenty-first century.

Further Reading: Beecher, Charles. *Autobiography, Correspondence, Etc. of Lyman Beecher.* 1864; Beougher, Timothy K., and Lyle W. Dorsett, eds. *Accounts of a Campus Revival: Wheaton College 1995.* Wheaton, IL: Harold

Shaw, 1995. Reprint, Eugene, OR: Wipf and Stock, 2002; Cairns, Earle. *An Endless Line of Splendor.* Wheaton, IL: Tyndale House, 1986; Fisher, George P. *Life of Benjamin Silliman.* New York: Scribner 1866. Gleason, Michael F. *When God Walked on Campus: A Brief History of Evangelical Awakenings at American Colleges and Universities.* Dundas, ON: Joshua Press, 2002; Green, Ashbel. *A Report to the Trustees of the College of New-Jersey.* New Haven, CT: Hudson and Woodward, 1815; Marsden, George M. *The Soul of the American University: From Protestant Establishment to Established Nonbelief.* New York: Oxford University Press, 1994; Orr, J. Edwin. *Campus Aflame.* Ed. Richard Owen Roberts. Wheaton, IL: International Awakening Press, 1994.

Timothy K. Beougher

CAMPUS CRUSADE FOR CHRIST

Founded by Bill Bright (1921–2003) in 1951 as a local campus ministry, Campus Crusade for Christ has grown to become an international conglomerate of evangelistic ministries and partnerships. An aspiring young businessman from Oklahoma, Bright became a Christian through the influence of the First **Presbyterian** Church of Hollywood. Bright admired the example of several Christian businessmen at the church and sat under the teaching of Hollywood Presbyterian's renowned Christian educator, Henrietta Mears. Along with Mears and several of her other young protégés, Bright in the late 1940s helped lead several sizable revivals at the Forest Home retreat center in the San Bernardino Mountains in southern California. Bright was deeply committed to personal evangelism and led a large witnessing group at his church.

In 1951, Bright founded Campus Crusade on the campus of the University of California at Los Angeles. They formed teams of student leaders—many of whom were star athletes—to present evangelistic talks to campus fraternities and sororities. Bright claimed that over 200 students committed their lives to Jesus Christ during Crusade's first year in ministry. As Bright recruited young **men** and **women** to join his staff, Crusade's ministry spread to campuses across the United States. Since the 1960s, Crusade has mobilized large numbers of its staff and students

to conduct mass evangelistic campaigns at beaches, campuses, and other locations. Crusade organizes spring break trips to Daytona and other popular student destinations at which Crusade students evangelize their peers on the beach. In 1967, Crusade designed a "Berkeley Blitz" to provide a Christian response to student radicalism. Crusade has promoted revivals on campuses by attracting students to evangelistic lectures given by popular speakers such as Jon Braun and Josh McDowell.

Crusade gradually expanded its ministry beyond the college campus to reach churches, executives, high school students, and the military. In the early 1960s, Crusade began conducting Lay Institutes for Evangelism, training sessions at churches that introduced congregations to Crusade's evangelistic methods. In 1958, Crusade launched its first overseas ministry, and international efforts expanded rapidly in the 1970s and 1980s. In 1972, Crusade organized Explo '72, a weeklong training event that attracted 80,000—primarily young people—to Dallas, Texas. A similar event held in Seoul, Korea, two years later attracted upward of 1 million people. Crusade's stated goal in the 1970s was to fulfill the Great Commission—Jesus' call to "make disciples of all nations" in Matthew 28:19–20—in the United States by 1976 and in the world by 1980. In partnership with thousands of local churches, Crusade organized Here's Life, America, a high-profile media and witnessing campaign that utilized the slogan "I Found It!" Although critics doubted the long-term impact of the effort, Bright claimed that the Great Commission had been fulfilled in the United States. Crusade expanded the Here's Life campaigns to cities around the world and also orchestrated programs to reach rural populations around the world. The latter thrust involved use of the "Jesus Film," a movie based on the Gospel of Luke that has served as Crusade's primary overseas evangelistic tool since 1980. The film has been seen by tens of millions of people around the world. In remote locations overseas, Crusade workers have shown the Jesus Film on makeshift screens, using an electrical generator for power, while villagers turn out in droves to watch the first movie they have ever seen.

Crusade has sought to impress upon Christians the necessity of evangelism as central to a fruitful and satisfying Christian life. Crusade teaches that Christians empowered by the Holy Spirit will regularly and effectively share their faith with others. Crusade's most famous evangelistic tool has been a small booklet, *The Four Spiritual Laws.* Bright and his staff wrote the booklet to enable Christians effectively to communicate their beliefs. The booklet encourages prospective converts to **pray** to accept Jesus Christ as their Lord and Savior. Crusade experienced its most rapid staff growth in the late 1960s and early 1970s. In light of the waning of late-1960s idealism, an increased emphasis on overseas ministry, and a proliferation of evangelical campus ministries, Crusade's campus ministry declined in terms of staff and campuses in the late 1970s and 1980s. Rededication to campus evangelism produced renewed growth in the 1990s. In 2001, Stephen Douglass became Crusade's second president, succeeding Bright, who died in 2003.

Further Reading: Campus Crusade for Christ International Web site. http://www.ccci.org/; Quebedeaux, Richard. *I Found It! The Story of Bill Bright and Campus Crusade.* San Francisco: Harper and Row, 1979; Richardson, Michael. *Amazing Faith: The Authorized Biography of Bill Bright.* Colorado Springs, CO: WaterBrook, 2000; Sherer, Joel. "Bill Bright." In Charles H. Lippy, ed., *Twentieth-Century Shapers of American Popular Religion,* 48–56. New York: Greenwood Press, 1989; Zoba, Wendey Murray. "Bill Bright's Wonderful Plan for the World." *Christianity Today,* July 14, 1997, 14–27.

John Turner

CANE RIDGE REVIVAL

The religious gathering at Cane Ridge in Kentucky in early August 1801 is among the most famous religious events in American history. For nearly a week, an estimated 10,000 people converged upon the **Presbyterian** log meetinghouse in rural Bourbon County. The spiritual outpouring, according to several witnesses, was phenomenal. Descriptions of spectacular occurrences at Cane Ridge quickly spread through correspondence and denominational literature. Similar evangelical meetings

appeared in other sections of the country within a matter of months, with equally powerful effect.

What distinguished **camp meeting** revivals from other evangelical events was that the participants came prepared to camp on the grounds. This simple innovation was conducive to a new intensity of religious experience. Camping allowed for a greater number of participants. "For more than half a mile, I could see people on their knees before God in humble prayer," wrote one participant at Cane Ridge. By removing people from the cares of daily life, the camp meeting intensified the effect of evangelical appeals. Individuals, suddenly struck by their spiritual plight, began falling to the ground "as if dead." At times the effect was awesome, with several hundred people "swept down like the trees of the forest under the blast of the wild tornado" (Eslinger, 207). The camp meeting formed a world unto itself as rich and poor, man and woman, black and white, joined to **pray** together. For a few days and nights, participants inhabited a society ruled solely by Christian principles.

Several surviving firsthand accounts provide a vivid picture of the Cane Ridge camp meeting. Members of the congregation had erected a canopied outdoor platform alongside of tables for the sacrament on Sunday. Toward the end of a summer of localized revivals, people braced for an exceptionally large gathering. Wrote one man, "I am on my way to one of the greatest meetings of the kind perhaps ever known....Religion has got to such a height here, that people attend from great distances; on this occasion I doubt not but there will be 10,000 people, and perhaps 500 wagons" (Eslinger, 207). Although attendance estimates varied widely, a crowd of 10,000 people is entirely possible given the population in the region and the advance notice given to the meeting.

Prior to the weekend gathering, by Thursday and Friday the roads to Cane Ridge "were literally crowded with wagons, carriages, horsemen, and footmen, moving to the solemn camp" (Eslinger, 207). Joining Cane Ridge's pastor, **Barton W. Stone,** in presiding over the meeting were 18 Presbyterian ministers, at least four **Methodists,** plus several **Baptist** elders. **Preaching** at the meetinghouse began on Friday night and continued almost without interruption over the next several days. Other preaching was done from improvised pulpits outdoors. The administration of the sacrament on Sunday afternoon provided one of the meeting's central activities, but the passionate evangelical exhortations to sinners rivaled it for dominance. The preaching went on well after sunset and it was by torchlight that the spiritual agony of stricken sinners became most dramatic. On Monday morning, the Cane Ridge crowd began dispersing for home, but people are said to have lingered into Tuesday.

The camp meeting revival was not devised from scratch but rather originated from the traditional Presbyterian sacramental occasion (known in Scotland as the **holy fair**). At the time of Cane Ridge, this heritage was still apparent. But superimposed upon the sacramental occasion were several innovations that together made for a very different kind of religious experience. Although it was customary to hold the sacramental occasion outdoors, the church members from greater distances did not typically camp at the site but rather stayed in the houses and barns of congregants living near the meetinghouse. This simple practical solution had a profound effect. Instead of adjourning at night, proceedings now spilled on toward dawn. The accompanying exhaustion and hunger tended to intensify the manifestations of spiritual crisis. In addition, camping at the meeting grounds immersed participants more completely than had been the case for traditional sacramental occasions. The meeting became a temporary but complete community ruled by Christian principle, an earthly version of heavenly promise. The full immersion over the course of several days intensified evangelical appeals. Thus, while camping began as a practical accommodation by the laity, the clergy realized that it also contributed to the event's evangelical function.

With spiritual awakening a more prominent theme, the sacramental occasion now embraced people of other Protestant denominations in addition to Presbyterians. Interdenominational worship was a new experience for most Kentuckians. Prior to the Great Revival, the infant congregations in the western settlements struggled to reaffiliate old members and gain new adherents. The dearth of congregations during the early years sometimes prompted the pioneer generation to join the nearest organized worship, regardless of denomination. One result was a degree of competition and rivalry. The Presbyterian Church, with its high standards for the admission of new members, found western conditions particularly challenging. Yet some of the church's western ministers had been greatly influenced by earlier revivals in the post-Revolutionary seaboard states, and their concern for evangelical outreach made for a more cooperative atmosphere.

One of these Presbyterian ministers was **James McGready,** the pastor for three congregations in the southern area of Kentucky. Upon assuming his pastoral duties in 1797, McGready made evangelical preaching a prominent part of his ministry but had only modest success until a sacramental occasion held at his Red River congregation in the summer of 1800. Toward the end of the proceedings, in an unusual ecumenical gesture, McGready allowed a Methodist preacher named John McGee, the brother of a Presbyterian colleague, to address the congregation. McGee's heart-stirring exhortation had a dramatic effect upon several members of the congregation. "Suddenly persons began to fall as he passed through the crowd—some as dead." The response stunned McGready and his Presbyterian colleagues. Not knowing how to respond to the **bodily manifestations** they were witnessing, they "acquiesced and stood in astonishment, admiring the wonderful work of God" (Eslinger, 195). Thus, Methodist preaching released a lay response that, while not unprecedented, was unfamiliar to American Presbyterians in the late eighteenth century. Having found a means to reach people, McGready pursued the new, Methodist-influenced style of sacramental occasion at his other two pastoral charges. The phenomenal response soon attracted attention. Some of the newcomers were apparently seeking a spectacle, but their curiosity nonetheless brought them into contact with organized religion.

Traditionally, the Presbyterian sacramental occasions had included evangelical preaching, but seldom had they encompassed a rite of spiritual transformation. Instead Presbyterians believed in a process whereby individuals felt a "conviction" of sin and of their need for God's gift of grace. A period of spiritual seeking, often painful and prolonged, usually followed before the individual experienced release. This second stage—**conversion**—was only known to be authentic after a careful investigation by clergy and elders. Baptism and admission to the church came after a purported convert had been examined and accepted by the church's leaders. At camp meetings, however, this process soon began to be collapsed into a single experience, stemming in large part from the many participants unacquainted with Presbyterian belief and practice. Thus, whereas previously a spiritual awakening had not been a part of the sacramental occasion but rather occurred privately, it now occurred within a group setting. Western Presbyterians did not abandon their procedure for church admission, but their doctrines and practices now suddenly faced challenge from a powerful personal experience.

Conviction of one's sinful nature raised intense feelings of remorse, shame, fright, and helplessness. Convicted people cried, moaned, and sank weakly to their knees. And now they were doing so in each other's presence, impressing sympathetic onlookers. The greater intensity led to what was described as "bodily exercises," physical expressions of spiritual agony seemingly beyond conscious control. The most common form of bodily exercise during this period was to fall suddenly to the ground "as if shot." Persons convicted of their sinfulness and need for God's mercy would fall limply in a manner emulating death. The afflicted sometimes lay in that condition for hours, at varying levels of stupor. Some could pray, some could only moan, and some appeared to be unconscious. According to one witness, "the pulse grows weak, and they draw a hard breath about once in a minute. And in some instances their extremities become cold, and pulse, and breath, and all symptoms of life, forsake them for nearly an hour." Others "shrieked, as if pierced to the breast with a sword on account of their hardness of heart." Most people who succumbed claimed an inability to feel any physical pain. People symbolically fell dead to sin, subordinating themselves

to God in hope that he would send his gift of saving grace and revive them to begin a new spiritual life. Numerous observers insisted that the falling as seen at Cane Ridge was "neither common fainting, nor a nervous affection." These phenomena disturbed orthodox Presbyterians. "The falling down of multitudes, and their crying out … was to us so new a scene, that we thought it prudent not to be over hasty in forming an opinion of it," explained one minister (Eslinger, 219). The public, however, tended to believe that these occurrences were of supernatural origin.

Cane Ridge offered spectators a chaotic scene. When individuals were spiritually stricken and fell, a circle of curious onlookers gathered around them. The huge, unwieldy scale of the event necessitated parallel activities. Several ministers often preached at the same time in different sections of the grounds, and the only event that had been previously scheduled was the sacrament on Sunday afternoon. The meeting grounds were unorganized, so that people ate, slept, and worshipped wherever seemed convenient. The mayhem at Cane Ridge convinced many religious leaders that future events should be organized and structured in order to retain the benefits of camp meeting revivalism but restrain the excesses. Cane Ridge was thus an important turning point in the evolution of early camp meeting revivalism. The emotional excesses and organizational confusion at Cane Ridge produced reservations among more conservative Christians. The extraordinary ability to affect previously nonreligious participants, however, could not be denied. Cane Ridge confirmed the efficacy of the camp meeting format. A strong revival of religion spread throughout the infant congregations of the West, soon named the Great Revival, and considered by some scholars as marking the beginning of the **Second Great Awakening** of the early 1800s.

The huge meeting at Cane Ridge soon attained legendary status, making it subject to several misunderstandings and exaggerations. Cane Ridge has sometimes been mistakenly identified as the first camp meeting, defined as evangelical worship accompanied by participants camping at the meeting grounds. James McGready had himself conducted a number of camp meetings prior to that at Cane Ridge in August 1801, and so the larger event can be seen as the culmination of earlier and smaller gatherings in the region. The interest and curiosity aroused by Cane Ridge led to extensive press reports, some which treated this particular camp meeting as a wholesale innovation—an erroneous idea that continues to be circulated.

Another misunderstanding concerning Cane Ridge did not surface until nearly a century later. Frederick Jackson Turner's "frontier thesis" argued that America's frontier forcefully shaped a unique national culture. As one religious historian, Catherine Cleveland, claimed, the trans-Appalachian pioneers endured lives filled with "hardships and privation, loneliness and solemnity characteristic of sparsely settled regions" (quoted in Eslinger, vii). Distant from established religious communities, people hungered for spiritual solace. The result was the boisterous, chaotic, and emotional camp meeting. The camp meeting was a religion of the heart, not the head, uniquely suited to the conditions of frontier society. Yet the idea of camp meeting revivalism as a product of the frontier environment has received challenge in recent years. John Boles, Leigh Eric Schmidt, and other scholars have traced American Presbyterianism's evangelical heritage not only to the seaboard colonies but also to an earlier wave of revivalism in Scotland. In addition, Ellen Eslinger has shown that the regions of Kentucky where camp meeting revivalism first appeared were those where frontier conditions were already fading into the past. The congregation at Cane Ridge was nearly a decade old by the time of the Great Revival, with an ordained minister. The camp meeting participants already enjoyed good access to formal religious institutions. Moreover, the surrounding region was secure from Indian dangers and had a settled populace. The lush bluegrass soil was developing into a prosperous agricultural region. Kentucky had been admitted as a state in 1792 and government was on a solid foundation. Depicting the Cane Ridge setting as primitive and remote cannot be supported. Indeed, a religious revival on the scale of Cane Ridge would have been impossible under true frontier conditions.

A further misunderstanding concerning Cane Ridge pertains to an extreme form of bodily exercise known as "the jerks." The body of people affected by the jerks would rapidly snap back and forth with great force, but without injury. Other bodily exercises included **dancing,** barking like a dog, and rolling on the ground—all seemingly involuntary physical manifestations of spiritual crisis. Yet some of these reported bodily manifestations alleged to have happened at Cane Ridge seem in fact to have appeared later, after August 1801. At Cane Ridge, observers noted that "the falling exercise was the most noted" (Eslinger, 225). (Some of these bodily manifestations have been well documented in subsequent revivals. Falling to the ground, laughing, and even "animal sounds" were a part of the **Toronto Blessing** revival during the 1990s.)

Although Cane Ridge has been subject to misunderstanding and exaggeration, its importance in American religious history still stands because the meeting in 1801 demonstrated so fully the evangelical power of the camp meeting. It was the descriptions of Cane Ridge more than any of the other early camp meetings that reached the religious press and influenced other sections of the country to adopt camp meeting revivalism as well. In the decades after 1800, camp meeting revivalism would continue to evolve, eventually obscuring its origins in the Presbyterian sacramental occasion. Cane Ridge stands the pivotal event in making camp meeting revivalism a permanent evangelical form in American religion.

Further Reading: Boles, John B. *The Great Revival, 1797–1805: The Origins of the Southern Evangelical Mind.* Lexington: University Press of Kentucky, 1972; Cleveland, Catherine C. *The Great Revival in the West, 1797–1805.* Chicago: University of Chicago Press, 1916; Conkin, Paul K. *Cane Ridge: America's Pentecost.* Madison: University of Wisconsin Press, 1990; Eslinger, Ellen. *Citizens of Zion: The Social Origins of Camp Meeting Revivalism.* Knoxville: University of Tennessee Press, 1999; Rogers, James R. *The Cane Ridge Meetinghouse.* Cincinnati: Standard Publishing, 1910; Schmidt, Leigh Eric. *Holy Fairs: Scotland and the Making of American Revivalism.* 2nd ed. Grand Rapids, MI: Eerdmans, 2001.

Ellen Eslinger

CARTWRIGHT, PETER (1785–1872)

Peter Cartwright was arguably the best-known **Methodist** circuit rider in America. In many ways he came to epitomize the entire group who led the revival on the western frontier. Cartwright was born in Amherst County, Virginia, in 1785, and died at Pleasant Plains, Illinois, in 1872. When he was eight, his family moved to Kentucky, where they eventually settled in Logan County, a place already infamous as a refuge for fugitives, lawbreakers, and renegades and popularly known as Rogues' Harbor. Cartwright recounts in his autobiography (1856) how a group was formed who called themselves Regulators, and fought a pitched battle to regain control of the country. Under the **preaching** of Jacob Lurton, his mother joined a Methodist class and regularly walked four miles to attend. Cartwright described himself in those years as a "wild, wicked boy," but when he was 16 his mother's **prayers** were answered and he fell under conviction, was converted in the Great Revival of 1801, and joined the Methodist Church. His autobiography contains a vivid description of events at the 1801 **Cane Ridge revival.** He was licensed as an exhorter in May of the following year and joined the Western Conference in 1804. During that time he also enrolled briefly in Brown's Academy for the only formal education he ever had.

After joining the conference, his first appointment was to the Salt River and Shelbyville circuits in the Kentucky District. In 1806 he was in Ohio and in 1810 in west Tennessee. He was ordained deacon by **Francis Asbury** and elder by William McKendree. He became a presiding elder in 1812 and held that office in various places until he retired in 1869. In 1823 he moved to Illinois, partly in response to what he perceived to be an increasing tendency on the part of Methodist preachers to defend the institution of slavery. Moreover, he said he did not want his children to marry into families that owned slaves. He was to respond "present" at 46 sessions of that annual conference. In 1828, he ran for the legislature, was elected, and served two terms. He also met, and by his account, debated religion and soundly defeated the **Mormon** leader,

Joseph Smith, whom he called "Uncle Joe." He did not, however, fare so well in 1846 when he ran against Abraham Lincoln, whom he characterized as an "unbeliever," for a seat in Congress.

Cartwright's contribution to the denomination in establishing congregations in Ohio, Illinois, and Indiana can hardly be estimated. By his own account, in just over half a century while traveling in 11 circuits and 12 districts, he had received into the membership of the church 10,000 people. He claimed to have baptized 8,000 children and 4,000 adults and preached at least 200 sermons a year. He was unequaled in his ability to contain and control large revival gatherings, sometimes in the face of those who sought to disrupt them. Although the salary of preachers was set and paid by the conference, he claimed that he had failed to receive the full amount due him by $5,000. But Cartwright was more than a dedicated pioneer preacher. He was also an acknowledged leader of his denomination. Elected by his peers to every General Conference between 1816 and 1852, he exercised considerable influence in their deliberations, and was generally regarded as a thoughtful and fair legislator. Despite his lack of formal education and colorful frontier demeanor, he was shrewd and persuasive in those assemblies. In many ways he was progressive and forward looking. He was steadfast in his opposition to slavery and opposed the division of the denomination in 1844; he saw no need for a formally educated clergy, but was solidly behind the educational outreach of his denomination in establishing colleges and universities.

Further Reading: Cartwright, Peter. *Autobiography of Peter Cartwright.* Ed. W. P. Strickland. New York: Carlton and Porter, 1856; Cartwright, Peter. *Fifty Years as a Presiding Elder.* Ed. W. S. Hooper. Cincinnati: Hitchcock and Walden, 1871.

James E. Kirby

CATHOLIC APOSTOLIC CHURCH

The Catholic Apostolic Church (CAC) was a **restorationist** movement that began in England during the 1830s. This group sought to give a practical demonstration to all Christians of the scriptural mandate to be organized under **apostolic** authority. They sought to restore the functioning of the fourfold offices of church government: apostle, prophet, evangelist, and pastor-teacher. The CAC held that the proper alignment of the Christian church according to this pattern was God's will in preparation for Christ's imminent (i.e., soon to arrive) Second Coming. The CAC was an independent Protestant organization, having no connection with **Roman Catholicism.** The CAC often is called the Irvingite church, but its members disavowed this name. Its roots can be traced to Henry Drummond's annual prophecy conferences (1826–1830) and the 1830 spiritual manifestations in the west of Scotland that were later duplicated in Edward Irving's Regent Square Church in London.

Drummond was the key figure in the founding of the CAC. A wealthy banker and politician, he turned his attention to biblical **eschatology** and church restorationism. His 1826 prophecy conference linked him with other visionaries, such as celebrated London pastor Edward Irving. Drummond led in the organization of the Newman Street Church in London after Irving was ousted from Regent Square for allowing the expression of **charismatic gifts** such as **speaking in tongues** and **prophecy.** A small-scale denomination began to rise up as like-minded pastors and churches began to affiliate with the Newman Street Church. Part of the vision of the new movement included organization under apostolic authority. In 1832, lawyer John Cardale was appointed as the church's first apostle, followed in 1833 by Drummond's appointment. Not aspiring to the office of apostle, Irving remained pastor of Newman Street Church and continued to lead the expanding movement. Illness overtook Irving, leading to his untimely death in 1834 at the age of 42.

With Irving's departure, the apostles were free to govern the movement. The complete number of 12 apostles had been chosen by 1835. Drummond relocated what was now known as the Catholic Apostolic Church to his Albury country estate. In 1840, he built the Apostle's Chapel, which served as the church's international headquarters. Called to witness to the Christian world regarding the imminence of Christ's Second Coming and the necessity of apostolic church government, the CAC apostles traveled to various countries attesting to their vision and learning from their observation of church customs and practices. Sharing their insights, the apostles designed and implemented a new church structure that included a formal **prayer** book, high-church liturgy, and formal vestments for clergy in all their congregations.

A result of the apostles' international exposure was the establishment of local congregations in various countries. Apostle Thomas Carlyle planted numerous CAC churches in Germany. By the 1860s, the German churches were asking for apostles to be appointed locally to keep up with the rapid growth of the movement. Their number depleted by death, the remaining English apostles resisted any additions to the apostleship. They remained convinced that Christ's return was to take place very soon, and so they blocked the initiatives from Germany. The German leaders broke with the English apostles and were excommunicated from the CAC. The "new order" of German apostles, later incorporated as the New Apostolic Church, became a separate apostolic movement in 1863. The NAC decided to discontinue elaborate liturgical practices and uniform vestments in their churches. In addition, they placed no limits as to the number of apostles, and their organization has experienced international growth, particularly in the twentieth century.

As early as 1834, the Catholic Apostolic Church sent emissaries to America to investigate the possibility of making inroads there, both in Canada and the United States. Evangelist William Caird, along with Canadian George Ryerson, a Methodist who later became the CAC pastor in Toronto, undertook the initial voyage. Ryerson and Adam Hope Burwell, convert from the Church of England, were the key CAC leaders in Canada. Burwell pastored for the CAC in Kingston, Ontario. Acceptance of the CAC movement in America came gradually and on a relatively small scale, although apostolic efforts were vigorous. Apostles Francis Woodhouse and Nicholas Armstrong invested effort in planting the CAC in North America. Woodhouse made at least seven trips to the American continent, and seems to have established the first U.S. CAC church in New York City in 1851. Armstrong also crossed the Atlantic several times, and was given charge over U.S. churches in 1860. W. W. Andrews was a respected Congregational minister who led the CAC work in Connecticut. He maintained close ties with Congregationalism, and won many friends to the CAC. His brother, Samuel J. Andrews, also labored in Connecticut, and served both Congregational and CAC churches simultaneously. John S. Davenport, an ordained **Presbyterian** and a Yale graduate, served the CAC during most of his pastoral career. He supervised evangelists for the CAC in the United States. Back on the English home front, the last apostle of the CAC died in 1901, leaving no provision for the ordination of future priests for their congregations. The twentieth century witnessed the dying out of what had been a unique experiment in restored apostleship. The remaining members of the CAC embraced a "time of silence," a state of inactivity and mourning until the return of Christ.

No direct link has been established between the CAC movement in America and the birth of the twentieth-century **Pentecostal** movement. They represented significantly different embodiments of Pentecostal expression. After Irving's death, the apostles of the CAC deemphasized the role of supernatural manifestations, preferring elaborate liturgical ceremony. Although allowing for the continuing impartation of spiritual gifts, CAC services were highly intellectual and liturgical. In contrast, early Pentecostalism placed a premium on the experiential and pragmatic. The spontaneity of the **Azusa Street revival** meetings bore no resemblance to CAC services. The revival at Azusa Street more aptly fit the pattern of the 1830 meetings in the west of Scotland—the early charismatic manifestations that proved to be the spawning ground of the CAC.

Further Reading: Davenport, Rowland A. *Albury Apostles*. Birdlip, Gloucestershire, UK: United Writers, 1970; Dorries, David. "Edward Irving and the 'Standing Sign' of Spirit Baptism." In Gary B. McGee, ed., *Initial Evidence*, 41–56. Peabody, MA: Hendrickson, 1991; Dorries, David. "West of Scotland Revival." In Stanley M. Burgess, ed., *The New International Dictionary of Pentecostal and Charismatic Movements*. 1189–92. Grand Rapids, MI: Zondervan, 2002; Flegg, C. G. *Gathered under Apostles*. Oxford: Oxford University Press, 1992; Shaw, P. E. *The Catholic Apostolic Church*. Morningside Heights, NY: King's Crown Press, 1946.

David Dorries

CHAPMAN, JOHN WILBUR (1859–1918)

J. Wilbur Chapman was a **Presbyterian** evangelist and revivalist. Born in Richmond, Indiana, and trained at Oberlin College, Lake Forest College, and Lane Seminary, Chapman was licensed to **preach** in Northern Presbyterian churches in 1881. After serving increasingly larger Presbyterian and **Reformed** churches in Indiana and New York State, he eventually moved to Bethany Presbyterian Church in Philadelphia in 1890. While there, **Dwight L. Moody** confronted him and challenged him to make his preaching more evangelistic. This challenge led Chapman to greater involvement in evangelistic ministries, assisting **Benjamin F. Mills** and Moody in various revival meetings. In consequence, Chapman in 1893 took a leave of absence of three years from Bethany to go into full-time evangelistic ministry. During this time, he recruited **Billy Sunday** to serve as one of his advance evangelists, and he was also involved in the founding of Winona Lake Bible Conference in northern Indiana. In 1896, Chapman returned to his regular pastorate at Bethany Church and three years later moved to Fourth Presbyterian Church in New York City.

In 1901, Chapman was appointed corresponding secretary of the Presbyterian General Assembly Committee on Evangelism, overseeing more than 50 evangelists serving in over 450 cities throughout the American North. He also developed a friendship with the wealthy John H. Converse, who offered to support Chapman in full-time evangelistic ministry. Chapman accepted this offer and launched back into full-time evangelism in 1903. He would eventually join with Charles H. Alexander as his musician in 1907 to form one of the most important evangelistic teams in the early twentieth century.

Adapting the Progressive Era's emphasis upon specialization and efficiency, Chapman's unique contribution was the "simultaneous campaign." Dividing a city into a number of districts, Chapman would send evangelist-musician teams to conduct meetings at the same time. In addition, these teams would target different constituencies: Social Gospel proponents would be sent to blue-collar neighborhoods, recovering alcoholics to bars, **women** to ladies' meetings, and so forth. By utilizing a simultaneous approach, targeting specialized needs and conditions, the Chapman team was able to maximize efficiencies of scale. This approach was utilized most effectively in Boston in 1909, when the accumulated total attendance neared 800,000.

Chapman was also significant for the way he utilized the era's sentimentality while he concurrently emphasized "muscular Christianity." As North Americans moved from rural areas to the cities, with the concomitant dissolution of extended kin networks, Chapman employed sentimental images of home, family, and "old-time religion" to challenge the new urban middle class to return to Christianity. At the same time, he specifically targeted **men** and measured the success of his campaigns by the number of men who attended and made professions of faith. This attempt to "re-masculinize" the faith was deemed to be vitally important for the future of the church and nation. Though he was not a denominational revivalist, the Northern Presbyterian Church recognized Chapman's contributions by electing him as moderator of the General Assembly in 1917. After he completed his term, he underwent emergency surgery for gallstones and died from complications on Christmas Day 1918.

Further Reading: Bendroth, Margaret Lamberts. "Men, Masculinity, and Urban Revivalism: J. Wilbur Chapman's Boston Crusade." *Journal of Presbyterian History* 75 (1997): 235–46; Crouse, Eric R. "Great Expectations: J. Wilbur Chapman, Presbyterians, and Other Protestants in Early Twentieth-Century Canada." *Journal of Presbyterian History* 78 (2000): 155–67; Soden, Dale E. "Anatomy of a Presbyterian Urban Revival: J. W. Chapman in the Pacific Northwest." *American Presbyterians* 64 (1986): 49–57.

Sean Lucas

CHARISMATIC GIFTS

Charismatic gifts have appeared periodically throughout American revival movements, including such manifestations as **healing, speaking in tongues** (or glossolalia), and revelatory gifts such as **prophecy, visions, dreams,** trances, supernatural knowledge, discernment of spirits, heavenly singing (i.e., reported angelic sounds), and also what are sometimes referred to as "proto-glossolalia"— "groanings too deep for words" (Romans 8:26) and stammerings or ecstatic shouts that could be considered as a rudimentary form of speaking in tongues. Such phenomena occurred in revival movements within various Protestant denominations prior to the **Azusa Street revival** of 1906–1909, as well as in the twentieth-century **Pentecostal** and **Charismatic** movements.

Instances of proto-glossolalia occurred in the **Great Awakening** of the 1740s. Likewise, in the **Cane Ridge revival** of 1801 in Kentucky there were instances of proto-glossolalia, prophecy (from youth as well as adults), visions, dreams, trances, and heavenly singing, speaking in tongues, and supernatural knowledge (such as an ability to specify the name of a person and his or her sin). Also in the early nineteenth century, **camp meeting** revivals near the University of Georgia and around the nation included some instances of glossolalia. The **Cumberland Presbyterian Church,** formed out of the Kentucky-Tennessee revivals, experienced healings, prophecies, miraculous answers to **prayers** regarding weather, groanings, and other gifts. A. J. Gordon, **Baptist** pastor and founder of Gordon College, concluded that all the charismatic gifts were to be restored to the church after observing instantaneous healings at **Dwight Moody's** meetings. In *The Ministry of Healing* (1882), Gordon recounts instances of healing in Delaware, Pennsylvania, New Jersey, and other locations in the eighteenth and nineteenth centuries among early American Baptists. Russell Conwell, Baptist pastor and theologian from Philadelphia, in his biography of the renowned British Baptist Charles Spurgeon devoted an entire chapter to Spurgeon's healing ministry, claiming that thousands were healed through Spurgeon's prayers. This furthered the acceptance of healing in America, especially among Baptists.

Trances, visions, and dreams occurred periodically in early nineteenth-century **Methodist revivals,** as well as other denominations and in the **Holiness movement.** Some claim that glossolalia may have occurred in Methodist lay evangelist **Phoebe Palmer's** meetings. Methodist evangelist **Peter Cartwright** experienced spiritual dreams and supernatural knowledge, including one instance in which he discerned correctly that a **Mormon** man was a thief who had welts on his back from punishment for theft. **Charles Finney** recounted that during a powerful experience with the Holy Spirit he "literally bellowed out the unutterable gushings of my soul" (Finney, 20–21). If not an actual experience of speaking in tongues, it could be considered proto-glossolalia. Though Finney did not actively pray for the sick, reports of healings sometimes surfaced in connection with his revival meetings. Finney occasionally manifested something like a gift of prophecy, predicting to the husband of an unconverted woman who was dying that she would not die from the illness and would not die in her sins. Consequently, the woman was healed and converted. Ethan O. Allen, a descendent of the famed colonial leader and deist, experienced healing in a Methodist class meeting in 1843 and subsequently launched into what was perhaps the first ministry of healing and **deliverance** from evil spirits (or exorcism) in North American history. An **African American** woman from New England, Mrs. Edward Mix, was healed in one of his meetings and also began a healing ministry. A sickly young Episcopalian woman named Carrie Judd (Montgomery) received healing through Mrs. Mix and founded a healing home.

Presbyterian Higher Life leader William Boardman was one of the earliest **Reformed** leaders to teach divine healing. Arising out of the faith homes of Johann Christoph Blumhardt, Dorothea Trudel, Otto Stockmayer, and Elizabeth Baxter in Europe, more than 30 healing homes were established in the United States, including those of New England Episcopalian physician Charles Cullis,

Carrie Judd Montgomery, and several in the **Christian and Missionary Alliance.** Healings, tongues, prophecies, trances, visions, and dreams occurred in the revival meetings of Holiness evangelist **Maria Woodworth-Etter** in the late 1800s. Just before and after 1900, **John Alexander Dowie** initiated a major healing ministry centered on his Christian community in Zion, Illinois. Occasional reports of healing, prophesying, and speaking in tongues surfaced in Moody's meetings. Moody's associate **Reuben A. Torrey** recalled that a man praying for revival had a prophetic vision of crowds of people coming to hear Torrey speak. Street evangelist Jerry McAuley experienced a visionary trance that led to his founding of a rescue mission. Prophecy occurred in the Adventist movement, and in the late 1800s "Gift Adventists" in New England spoke in tongues and interpreted tongues. A revival in 1896 in Cherokee County, North Carolina, included glossolalia and healings. Reports of speaking in tongues also came from Tennessee and Georgia.

In 1877 Presbyterian pastor **Albert Benjamin Simpson,** a friend of A. J. Gordon, experienced a vivid dream about Asians going to hell, which stirred his missionary vision. In 1881 he experienced a dramatic healing at Cullis's camp meeting and subsequently he began to hold healing services. Out of these experiences he founded the Christian and Missionary Alliance (CMA). Simpson and his organization, probably more than any other at the time, emphasized the restoration of all of the different charismatic gifts. For this reason, he is often considered a forerunner of the Pentecostal movement even though he never fully embraced all of its teachings and practices. Prefiguring the later "power evangelism" movement associated with **John Wimber** and **C. Peter Wagner** beginning in the 1980s, Simpson taught that **signs and wonders** would accompany the **preaching** of the gospel, confirming the salvation message that was presented and thus leading many people to **conversion.** CMA writings reported healings, dreams, visions, prophecies, audible voices, and such miracles as raising from the dead, supernatural provision of material needs, protection from harm, and invulnerability to poisoning. At one of Simpson's conventions in 1885 he received a spiritual impression that someone was resisting the Lord. When a woman responded, saying she was the one, Simpson anointed her for healing; she fell unconscious under the power of the Spirit, and then arose healed. Simpson made reference to a black woman who manifested a primal form of tongues in his services prior to 1897. The early CMA anticipated the concept of "missionary tongues" that became associated with Pentecostal pioneer **Charles Parham.** Sometimes called *xenolalia* or *xenoglossa*, this was an interpretation that viewed speaking in tongues as consisting in foreign languages actually spoken in overseas regions, and tongues-speakers as people supernaturally prepared with this gift to become foreign missionaries to those regions.

The American pioneer in deliverance ministry, Ethan O. Allen, helped to introduce the idea of conflict between Christian believers and evil spirits. Methodists, such as George Peck and George D. Watson, along with Christian and Missionary Alliance leaders were early proponents of the concepts of **spiritual warfare,** exorcism, and the spiritual authority of the believer (i.e., the ability of every Christian to thwart evil spirits). Canadian CMA missionary John MacMillan wrote an early book on the authority of the believer in 1932, referring to spiritual-warfare experiences as a basis for his teaching.

The 1904–1905 Welsh Revival initiated a period of seeking and preparing for revival in America. Charismatic gifts such as prophecies and visions that had been features of the Welsh Revival raised American expectations. Los Angeles Baptist pastor Joseph Smale visited the Welsh Revival, and delivered a report on the remarkable events to his congregation in May 1905. As he was speaking, a wave of revival broke out among his congregants that included dreams, visions, and forms of proto-glossolalia such as groaning and inarticulate prayers, setting the stage for the Azusa Street revival in Los Angeles the next year. While scattered incidents of speaking in tongues occurred in the nineteenth century, Charles Parham initiated the first teaching and experiences of speaking in tongues as the "initial

evidence" of the **baptism in the Holy Spirit** in 1901 at Topeka, Kansas. With the Azusa Street revival beginning in April 1906, the teaching of tongues-speaking as the initial evidence of the baptism in the Spirit became commonplace. A variety of charismatic gifts, but especially glossolalia, spread rapidly throughout North America and indeed throughout the world, as Pentecostalism rapidly became a global phenomena in the 10–20 years following the beginning of the Azusa Street revival in 1906. Smale's church experienced Pentecostal revival in June. Smale and groups like the CMA were receptive to charismatic gifts, but they opposed the initial evidence doctrine, later disavowed as well by Azusa Street leader **William Seymour.** During the 1920s, and until his death in 1937, the **Latino** preacher and revivalist **Francisco Olazábal** conducted revivals in Mexico, the United States, and Puerto Rico that made **healing** an integral part of his evangelistic mission.

Free Will Baptists who experienced speaking in tongues organized the Pentecostal Free Will Baptist Church in 1908 in Dunn, North Carolina. Many who experienced tongues-speaking and other charismatic gifts were rejected by their denomination and joined the emerging Pentecostal movement. Some did not believe that speaking in tongues was a necessary evidence of Spirit baptism, and so they chose to align themselves with groups like the CMA. Healing ministries abounded in the early Pentecostal movements, especially those associated with F. F. Bosworth, Charles Price, Maria Woodworth-Etter, and **Aimee Semple McPherson.**

The **Latter Rain movement,** beginning in 1948, emphasized charismatic gifts bestowed through the laying on of hands, especially prophecy and the appointment of apostles and prophets. However, because of certain doctrines associated with the movement, it was deemed heretical by the **Assemblies of God.** Also in the 1940s many healing ministries arose through such people as Gordon Lindsay, **Oral Roberts, William Branham,** and **Kathryn Kuhlman,** the latter two of whom especially manifested a prophetic gift of supernatural knowledge. The Charismatic movement began to arise in the 1950s and 1960s as the **Full Gospel Business Men's Fellowship International** founded by Demos Shakarian reached business and professional people of many mainline denominations. Charismatic gifts appeared in various denominations as leaders experienced glossolalia, revelational gifts, and healing in the Episcopal (Dennis Bennett), Lutheran (Larry Christianson), Methodist (Tommy Tyson), Nazarene (Warren Black), Mennonite (Gerald Derstine), and Presbyterian (James Brown) churches. Healing was an emphasis of the Episcopalians Emily Gardiner Neal, Morton Kelsey, and Agnes Sanford. The **Roman Catholic** Charismatic Renewal began in 1967 in Pittsburgh, Pennsylvania (and almost simultaneously in Latin America, in Bogotá, Columbia). The **Jesus People movement** involved many manifestations of charismatic gifts. Don Basham, in his book *The Miracle of Tongues* (1973), documented more than two dozen cases of xenolalia. Prominent Christian healing ministries since the 1960s have included Charles and Francis Hunter, **Benny Hinn, Francis MacNutt,** and Richard Roberts. Supernatural knowledge has been prominent in the ministries of Benny Hinn, John Wimber, **Pat Robertson,** Richard Roberts, and many others.

In 1962 an evangelical renewal movement at Yale University included glossolalia and healings, which then spread to other **college campuses** as well. The Asbury College (Kentucky) revival of 1970 included an expression of charismatic gifts such as prophecy and tongues, but these were not emphasized. The 1971–1972 Canadian revival in Saskatoon, though like Asbury not a charismatic movement, included a few charismatic elements such as healings, prophecy, dreams, deliverance from demons, and glossolalia. Exorcism became a theme of the Charismatic movement during the 1970s and 1980s, with some leaders like Don Basham and Derek Prince performing mass public sessions for deliverance ministry. John Wimber, Francis MacNutt, Doris Wagner, and many others also practiced deliverance ministry. The spiritual warfare movement of the 1990s and early twenty-first century links the so-called Third Wave and Charismatic movements, emphasizing corporate intercession and confronting territorial

spirits in what is sometimes called strategic-level spiritual warfare. Deliverance movements have increased among noncharismatic evangelicals such as Fred Dickason, Merrill Unger, Ed Murphy, and Neil T. Anderson. In the 1990s, Anderson spoke of a "truth encounter" (John 8:32) with evil spirits, rather than a "power encounter." Though he does not term his procedure *exorcism*, his approach has strong similarities to the early Christian exorcistic rites prior to baptism, involving a renunciation of Satan and all evil influences and practices of one's past, together with a spoken proclamation of the truths of the Christian gospel and the fact of one's new identity in Christ. Many deliverance practitioners in the Pentecostal and Charismatic movements are now using Anderson's principles and procedures as pre-exorcism or as a prophylactic (i.e., protection in advance), thus preventing any need for a direct confrontation with evil spirits.

Throughout American history, controversies have arisen related to alleged spiritual gifts that many evangelical Protestants have regarded as false, counterfeit, or demonic in origin. **Peter Cartwright** warned of counterfeit tongues, prophecy, and healings among the **Mormons** and trances and visions from a Universalist group called the Halcyon Church. Tongues, visions, trances, prophecy, and songs written in unknown tongues occurred among the **Shakers,** which developed concurrently with the **Second Great Awakening,** although their doctrines and practices were considered aberrant by mainstream Christians. Recent unorthodox groups such as The Way and the Children of God exhibit phenomena that resemble the tongues-speaking and prophesying that occur in more orthodox Pentecostal and Charismatic groups. Both noncharismatic evangelical teachers and charismatic deliverance ministers have warned of counterfeit charismatic gifts, including demonic tongues, healing from occult sources, and prophetic revelation or supernatural knowledge resulting from psychic powers.

The Third Wave movement of the 1980s and following—the First Wave being the Pentecost movement and the Second Wave the Charismatic movement—encompassed mainline denominations and other evangelical groups who practice charismatic gifts but do not necessarily believe in a baptism in the Spirit subsequent to conversion, or in tongues-speaking as an essential spiritual experience. Prominent Third Wave teachers have included John Wimber—founder of the Vineyard Church—and C. Peter Wagner. Notable theologians who have experienced and embraced charismatic gifts include Jack Deere (formerly of Dallas Theological Seminary), J. Rodman Williams (Presbyterian), and Wayne Grudem (Baptist). The prophetic movement of the late twentieth century, led by Bill Hamon, Chuck Pierce, Cindy Jacobs, Mike Bickle, Paul Cain, and others of the **Kansas City prophets,** put emphasis on personal prophecies, the establishment of prophetic and apostolic leadership, and training people in how to prophesy. Some have regarded it as a resurgence of the Latter Rain movement. Revivals of the 1990s that featured charismatic manifestations and spread throughout North America included the **Toronto Blessing** and the **Pensacola revival,** and the Smithton (Missouri) revival.

Further Reading: Burgess, Stanley M., and Gary B. McGee, eds. *Dictionary of Pentecostal and Charismatic Movements.* Grand Rapids, MI: Zondervan, 1988; Finney, Charles. *Memoirs.* New York: A.S. Barnes, 1876; Graf, Jonathan L. *Healing: The Three Great Classics on Divine Healing.* Camp Hill, PA: Christian Publications, 1992; Harrell, David Edwin, Jr. *All Things Are Possible: The Healing and Charismatic Revivals in Modern America.* Bloomington: Indiana University Press, 1975; Hyatt, Eddie L. *2000 Years of Charismatic Christianity.* Lake Mary, FL: Charisma House, 2002; Kelsey, Morton T. *Tongue Speaking: An Experiment in Spiritual Experience.* Garden City, NY: Doubleday, 1968.

Paul L. King

CHARISMATIC REVIVAL AND RENEWAL

Most historians of the modern Charismatic Renewal date its beginnings to April 3, 1960, when Rev. Dennis Bennett of St. Mark's Episcopal Church, Van Nuys, California, publicly disclosed that he had experienced the fullness of or **baptism in the Holy Spirit,** including a gift of "unknown tongues." This seminal event marked the beginning of the renewal in historic mainline churches, although Bennett's announcement was preceded by numerous "stirrings" before 1960. It can be argued, for example, that the leading **healing** evangelists of the late 1940s, such as **William Branham, Oral Roberts,** T. L. Osborn, and Gordon Lindsay, were not under Classical **Pentecostal** denominational control, and that their followers who received a baptism in the Holy Spirit during the 1940s and 1950s could not be classified as Pentecostal.

In 1951, Demos Shakarian—a rich California dairy farmer of Armenian descent—founded the **Full Gospel Business Men's Fellowship International.** This organization provided a venue of charismatic fellowship for non-Pentecostal Christians. Meanwhile, David Du Plessis, a Classical Pentecostal (i.e., a member of a church group or denomination that officially endorses the **charismatic gifts**), heeded a 1936 prophecy by Smith Wigglesworth in which he was singled out as one who would express "Pentecostal truths" to those within historic or mainline church traditions. His outreach helped to create an environment for the later acceptance of the Charismatic Renewal in mainline Protestant denominations and in **Roman Catholicism.** In the 1940s and 1950s several American ministers underwent charismatic experiences and chose to stay within their denomination, rather than joining a Pentecostal church or becoming independent, as had been typical in earlier years. Included in this group were Harold Bredesen, a young **Lutheran** minister who experienced Spirit baptism in 1946; Tommy Tyson, a North Carolina United **Methodist** pastor who became a charismatic in 1951; Agnes Sanford, filled with the Spirit in 1953–1954, and a healing evangelist who emphasized healing in Anglican circles; and James Brown, a **Presbyterian** minister who experienced spiritual giftings beginning in 1956.

From this seedbed of renewal came the self-disclosure of Dennis Bennett, followed by articles in *Newsweek* (July 4, 1960) and *Time* (August 15, 1960), that opened a broader consciousness among American Christians that they were witnessing a new movement of the Spirit that combined Pentecostal blessings with historic church affiliation. Soon after a church official called for his resignation from St. Mark's in Van Nuys, Bennett resigned and accepted a call to become vicar of St. Luke's in Seattle, Washington, an Episcopal church mission that the bishop had planned to close. St. Luke's quadrupled in attendance in the next year. Bennett began receiving invitations to speak from a wide spectrum of historic churches, spreading the news that the Spirit's outpouring was without denominational boundary. In 1962 Episcopal bishops issued a positive statement, "New Movements in the Church," that encouraged the spread of the Charismatic Renewal. During the early 1960s individuals in virtually every major Protestant tradition (including Baptist, Lutheran, Mennonite, Methodist, and Presbyterian) were experiencing renewal in the Holy Spirit. One of the most significant leaders was American Lutheran pastor Larry Christenson of San Pedro, California, who received Spirit baptism in August 1961 and made his experience public on Pentecost 1962. Christenson attempted to relate the Pentecostal experience to the Lutheran tradition through his teaching on the subject and his pamphlet "Speaking in Tongues … a Gift for the Body of Christ." The American Lutheran Church (ALC) issued an official statement in 1964, however, rejecting any promotion of glossolalia and restricting its usage to private devotions.

The Lutheran Church–Missouri Synod (LC-MS) took an even more aggressive stance toward the Charismatic outpouring among them. The result was a church trial for Donald Pfotenhauer a pastor in Minneapolis, Minnesota, who was filled with the Spirit late in 1964. The LC-MS objected especially to the gift of **prophecy,** which was seen as detracting from the uniqueness of God's word in scripture. Despite Pfotenhauer's dismissal in 1970, LC-MS pastors, including Rodney Lensch, Don Matzat, Delbert Rossin, and theologian Theodore Jungkuntz, continued to express charismatic teachings. Spirit-filled Presbyterian ministers also faced internal opposition. Robert Whitaker, a pastor in Chandler, Arizona, baptized in the Spirit

in 1962, was removed from office in 1967. These difficulties led Whitaker, James Brown, and others to form the first denominational charismatic body, the Charismatic Communion of Presbyterian Ministers. Its leader was George C. "Brick" Bradford, a former attorney who had been expelled from the ministry and who had helped Whitaker win in an appeal process. Some others among the Presbyterian Charismatics were theologian J. Rodman Williams, who later produced the most complete Charismatic systematic theology to that date, *Renewal Theology* (1996, initially three volumes), and John A. Mackay, a former president of Princeton Theological Seminary, whose reputation added credibility to the Charismatic Renewal. The Charismatic movement affected **African American** denominations as well as largely white churches. Among the denominations influenced were the **African Methodist Episcopal Church** (AMEC), and black **Baptists,** leading to the emergence of the Full Gospel Baptist Church Fellowship, International, which held its first conference in New Orleans, Louisiana, in 1994.

The spread of the renewal to the Roman Catholic Church in 1967 added an entirely new dimension to the Charismatic movement. It began simultaneously at Duquesne University in Pittsburgh, Pennsylvania, and in Bogotá, Columbia. Virtually all of the early leaders in the United States were academics who had been strongly influenced by the debates and decrees of the Second Vatican Council, which had recognized in 1964 the vital importance of charismatic gifts in the life of the church. Pope John XXIII had **prayed** that the council might be a new Pentecost for the church. In mid-February 1967, Ralph Keifer and Patrick Bourgeois, lay instructors in the Department of Theology at Duquesne University, a Catholic institution under the direction of the Holy Ghost Fathers, experienced baptism with the Holy Spirit. The renewal spread to the University of Notre Dame and Michigan State University. Two participants, Ralph Martin and Stephen Clark, accepted a speaking invitation from the Catholic chaplain at the University of Michigan, after which Ann Arbor, Michigan, and South Bend, Indiana, became two foci for the Catholic Charismatic

Renewal in the United States. Early leaders in the renewal in the United States interpreted the outpouring of the Spirit on **college campuses** as the renewal for which Pope John XXIII had prayed at the opening of the Vatican II Conference some years earlier—"as by a new Pentecost," in the Pope's now famous phrase. This movement grew rapidly in both numbers and maturity, with greater emphasis on renewed parishes and much greater Catholic interest in Bible study.

The term *Charismatic Renewal* broadly refers to two groupings. The first are those mainline historic churches, both Protestant and Catholic, that experienced spiritual invigoration during the second half of the twentieth century. The second group, the neo-Charismatics, includes the independent, nondenominational, and postdenominational congregations and groups that cannot be classified as either Pentecostal or Charismatic. They share a common emphasis on the Holy Spirit, spiritual gifts, Pentecostal-like experiences (though not Pentecostal terminology), signs and wonders, and power encounters. They include the so-called Third Wave or neo-Pentecostals—earlier terms that no longer seem adequate to describe nondenominational Charismatics who are part of fourth and later waves of renewal, or those who do not identify with Classical Pentecostals.

The **shepherding movement** or discipleship movement is just such a distinctly nondenominational group. It appeared in 1974 as a reaction to the increasing independence of many charismatic Christians who were leaving their denominational churches and joining independent churches and prayer groups. The shepherding movement taught that every believer, including ministers, needed to submit to a "shepherd" or pastoral leader. This relationship was seen as necessary for developing spiritual maturity. Five popular charismatic Bible teachers—Don Basham, Bob Mumford, Derek Prince, Charles Simpson, and Ern Baxter—led the movement. Through conferences and the *New Wine* magazine, a national network of churches and prayer groups was established, led by those who submitted to the five named above. At its peak, some 100,000 adherents were involved in this association. Opposition arose against the movement, led by **Pat Robertson** of the Christian Broadcasting Network and the Full Gospel Business Men's Fellowship. Attempts to reconcile these differences failed. The movement eventually floundered in the 1980s when the original leaders struggled among themselves and finally dissolved their formal relationship in 1986.

In the United States, perhaps the most fervent neo-Charismatics are included in the **Apostolic (or New Apostolic) movement.** They are distinct from traditional denominationally based Christianity because they focus their trust on spiritual leaders, identified as contemporary apostles and prophets, who often are linked by loosely structured apostolic networks. They argue for the restoration of the "fivefold ministries" mentioned in the New Testament book of Ephesians: "It was [Christ] who gave some to be apostles, some to be prophets, some to be evangelists, and some to be pastors and teachers, to prepare God's people for works of service, so that the body of Christ may be built up until we all reach unity in the faith and in the knowledge of the Son of God and become mature, attaining to the whole measure of the fullness of Christ" (4:11–13, New International Version). Quite naturally, apostles and prophets run counter to existing ecclesiastical structures, and it is not surprising that many Classical Pentecostal and Charismatic groups are struggling with aspiring, and sometimes self-proclaimed, apostles and prophets among them. **C. Peter Wagner** is the most prominent modern American apostle, although other notables include Bill Hybels, Michael Fletcher, David Kim, Billy Joe Daugherty, Roberts Liardon, and William Kumuyi. Among the more prominent prophets are Bill Hamon, Rick Joyner, Mike Bickle, and Paul Cain (the latter two associated with the **Kansas City prophets**). In the 1980s the Charismatic movement also experienced the rise of the **signs and wonders** practice and teaching, with **John Wimber** and his Vineyard Christian Fellowship, based in Yorba Linda, California, leading the way. Signs and wonders were seen as a normal element in evangelism and church growth.

The international Charismatic Renewal, both in denominational churches and among nondenominationals, has experienced extraordinary growth. By 2000, over 523 million Christians were numbered within the larger Spirit-filled renewal, with only 66 million being Classical Pentecostals and the remainder Charismatics (176 million) and neo-Charismatics (295 million). While the Pentecostal-Charismatic Renewal has grown less rapidly in the United States than in some other regions (e.g., Brazil, or parts of Africa), it remains the most powerful contemporary revival movement in North America.

Further Reading: Bittlinger, Arnold, ed. *The Church Is Charismatic*. Geneva: World Council of Churches, 1981; Burgess, Stanley M., and Ed van der Maas, eds. *The New International Dictionary of Pentecostal and Charismatic Movements*. Grand Rapids: MI: Zondervan, 2002; Du Plessis, David J. *The Spirit Bade Me Go*. Plainfield, NJ: Logos, 1970; Hamon, Bill. *Apostles and Prophets and the Coming Moves of God*. Santa Rosa Beach, FL: Christian International, 1997; Harrell, David. *All Things Are Possible: The Healing and Charismatic Revivals in Modern America*. Bloomington: Indiana University Press, 1975; Hocken, Peter. *The Glory and the Shame: Reflections on the Outpouring of the Holy Spirit*. Guildford: Eagle/Inter-Publishing, 1994; Hocken, Peter. *Streams of Renewal*. Exeter, UK: Paternoster Press, 1997; Jones, Charles Edwin. *The Charismatic Movement: A Guide to the Study of Neo-Pentecostalism, with Emphasis on Anglo-American Sources*. 2 vols. ATLA Bibliography Series 30. Metuchen, NJ, and London, UK: American Theological Library Association and Scarecrow Press, 1995; McDonnell, Killian, ed. *Presence, Power, Praise: Documents on the Charismatic Renewal*. 3 vols. Collegeville, MN: Liturgical Press, 1980; Moore, S. David. *The Shepherding Movement: Controversy and Charismatic Ecclesiology*. New York: Continuum, 2003; Quebedeaux, Richard. *The New Charismatics II*. San Francisco: Harper and Row, 1983; Sherrill, John L. *They Speak with Other Tongues*. Grand Rapids, MI: Baker, 1964; Wagner, C. Peter, ed. *The New Apostolic Churches*. Ventura, CA: Regal Books, 1998; Wagner, C. Peter. *The Third Wave of the Holy Spirit: Encountering the Power of Signs and Wonders*. Ann Arbor, MI: Servant Books, 1988; Williams, J. Rodman. *Renewal Theology, Systematic Theology from a Charismatic Perspective*. Grand Rapids, MI: Zondervan, 1990.

Stanley M. Burgess

CHAUNCY, CHARLES (1705–1787)

Charles Chauncy, influential pastor of the Congregational First Church of Boston, was a vocal leader of the Old Light **anti-revivalists** who opposed the mid-eighteenth-century movement known as the **Great Awakening.** He was also a member of the so-called black brigade of New England clergy who agitated against English rule in the period leading up to the American Revolution. Chauncy's widely distributed sermons and tracts chronicled the excesses of the revival and opposed **Jonathan Edwards's** positive assessment of the impact of the Great Awakening on the colonies. The Edwards-Chauncy debate during the Great Awakening was perhaps the most influential public controversy over religious revivals in American history, and echoes of their arguments from the 1740s continued throughout the 1700s, 1800s, and 1900s. Strongly influenced by Enlightenment rationalism, Chauncy's views would eventually facilitate a shift among New England Congregationalists away from **Calvinist** Orthodoxy and toward rational religion and Unitarianism.

From the first, Chauncy reacted cautiously to the burst of enthusiasm during the 1730s and 1740s that surrounded the itinerant ministry of revival leaders such as **George Whitefield** and **Gilbert Tennent.** In 1741, he warned his parishioners against simplistic notions of **conversion.** Though some may experience strong emotions at regeneration, he noted, God worked differently in each individual. Furthermore, not all clergy should be expected to adopt the revival leaders' dramatic **preaching** styles, which were calculated to create a deep sense of conviction. Chauncy especially feared the growing threat that the revival and itinerant preachers posed to the established clerical order. As the revival continued, more and more laypeople claimed divine guidance (sometimes through **prophecy, visions, and dreams**) and began to exhort others despite their lack of training. Others attacked ministers who were opponents of the revival, questioning the genuineness of these ministers' conversions and therefore their spiritual authority. For Chauncy, these attacks, participated in the revival mistook their own passions for supernatural guidance. These "enthusiasts" were caught up in a false spirituality that evidenced itself in bodily convulsions, freakish conduct, an imagined favor with God, and, most importantly, a dismissal of rational thought.

Chauncy's most comprehensive response to the revival, *Seasonable Thoughts on the State of Religion in New-England,* appeared in 1743. In preparation for the book, Chauncy corresponded with hundreds of ministers regarding the excesses of the revival and traveled over 300 miles through New England, New Jersey, and New York to observe its impact for himself. *Seasonable Thoughts* explicitly countered Edwards's defense of the revival entitled *Some Thoughts concerning the Present Revival of Religion* (1743). Though both acknowledged the disorders that accompanied the revivals, Edwards considered them accidental to the true work of God. Chauncy, on the other hand, found them the defining mark of the movement. The constraining power of scripture and reason were desperately needed in order to rein in the growing disorder.

The prioritization of reason (or mind, understanding, or intellect) over emotion (or heart, affections, or passions) in Chauncy's thinking marked a difference between his position and that of Edwards. Both sought to reconcile their Puritan heritage with Enlightenment themes that stressed individualism and rationalism. Each saw value in the affections as well as in the understanding. Continuing a long-standing debate within Puritan circles regarding the relationship between the will and the intellect, Chauncy emphasized an enlightened mind that restrained the lower faculty of the affections when necessary. Edwards, on the other hand, described the will in terms of the affections and elevated them to a prominent position alongside the understanding in religious experience.

Despite the strong conservative impulse in Chauncy's theology and social theory, his focus on rationalism and on the individual's ability to cultivate reason placed him within the liberal tradition, as evidenced by his espousal of Universalism later in life (i.e., the doctrine that all humans will ultimately receive salvation). Though Chauncy

Midlife portrait of Charles Chauncy. Because of his steadfast character, he became known by the nickname "Old Brick," which had been applied to the building of the First Church in Boston, where he was pastor from 1727 to 1787. Courtesy of the Billy Graham Center Archives, Wheaton, IL.

along with the primacy placed on individual experience, emotional outbursts, and **bodily manifestations** in the revivals, undermined New England's traditional emphasis on social order. In opposing the Great Awakening, Chauncy asserted that he was upholding the Puritan practices and values of his seventeenth-century forebears.

By 1742 Chauncy had seen enough. The flamboyant revival leader **James Davenport** came to Boston and sought a meeting to ascertain the status of Chauncy's soul. Chauncy used the opportunity to instead castigate Davenport for his divisive practices as well as his claims to communicate directly with God—claims that Chauncy attributed to an overworked imagination. Shortly thereafter, Chauncy's sermon "Enthusiasm Described and Cautioned Against" (1742) clearly spelled out his opposition to the revival. He argued that many who never fully embraced rational religion, his writings would contribute to a growing discontent with inherited religious views and help to undermine the very Puritan tradition that he valued so highly.

Further Reading: Corrigan, John. *The Hidden Balance: Religion and the Social Theories of Charles Chauncy and Jonathan Mayhew.* Cambridge, UK: Cambridge University Press, 1987; Griffin, Edward M. *Old Brick: Charles Chauncy of Boston, 1705–1787.* Minneapolis: University of Minnesota Press, 1980.

Joseph Williams

CHAUTAUQUA

The founders of Chautauqua, Rev. John Heyl Vincent and Lewis Miller, both **Methodists** from the Midwest, envisioned Chautauqua as an interdenominational center for the training of Sunday school teachers. But Chautauqua's mission quickly expanded beyond its church-based origins. The first Chautauqua assembly was held in 1874 on the shores of Chautauqua Lake in far-western New York State. By the 1880s, Chautauqua was heralded as the nation's leading center for adult education, its burgeoning lecture series and cultural programs supported by a gate fee charged to middle-class Victorian families eager to enjoy a week of rest and relaxation on the lake. As news of the Chautauqua assembly's success spread, hundreds of independent Chautauqua assemblies sprouted in small towns from Maine to California. Vincent's correspondence course, entitled the Chautauqua Literary and Scientific Circle (CLSC), was also successful. By century's end, 264,000 students, over three-quarters of them **women,** had enrolled in the four-year reading program, and some had received official (if mostly symbolic) diplomas to commemorate their efforts. Chautauqua's system of self-culture rarely found an audience beyond its northern, white, Protestant, middle-class base. Nevertheless, Chautauqua should be viewed as one of the three most important social movements of the Social Gospel, as famous in its day as the **Salvation Army** and **Young Men's Christian Association,** and perhaps more effective than both in popularizing the liberal creed of reformers like Jane Addams and Jacob Riis among an audience whose support would prove indispensable to the cause of Progressive reform in the early twentieth century.

Chautauqua's relationship with Protestant revivalism is complex. The original Chautauqua assembly, and scores of the independent assemblies, was founded on a preexisting Methodist campground. These Methodist **camp meetings,** numbering in the hundreds and some dating back to the **Second Great Awakening** of the early 1800s, originated as permanent headquarters for summer revivals and showcases for the Methodists' famously charismatic **preachers** called circuit riders. Their emotional style of revival preaching never abated in the **South.** But in the North, some middle-class Methodists rejected "old-time" revivals as crude and superficial. John Heyl Vincent exemplified this trend. As a young man, he was a circuit rider in Pennsylvania. But as Chautauqua's director in the 1870s, he once stopped an impromptu revival and demanded that the preacher step down, adding, "No meeting of any kind can be held without the order of the authorities."

Chautauqua's priorities, like those of the Social Gospel movement more broadly, focused on middle-class anxieties about social order during a time of labor violence, corporate excess, and urban squalor in the Gilded Age. Far from expressing revivalist impulses, then, Chautauqua positioned itself as the successor to the revivalism of a bygone era, a symbol of the more refined Christian spirit of the modern age. In addition, women dominated the Chautauqua assemblies and circles. Indeed, the women who founded the Woman's Christian **Temperance** Union met first at Chautauqua. Many subscribed to a Protestant feminism that rejected religious arguments for male supremacy and called for an expanded role for godly women in the public sphere. Inspired by Chautauqua's embrace of open debate and democracy, in the 1890s a Philadelphia group created the Jewish Chautauqua Assembly while another group of **Roman Catholics** inaugurated the Catholic Chautauqua Assembly, located in Plattsburgh, New York.

For all of its accomplishments, however, by 1920 the Chautauqua movement was over. Women activists had created new avenues of political expression by that point. The CLSC went into decline, and most of the assemblies fell prey to competition

People socializing at Chautauqua, New York, with Lake Chautauqua in the background. With roots in revivalism, this summer gathering evolved into a cultural festival, with well-heeled attendees here wearing clothing fashionable a century ago. (1908.) Courtesy of the Library of Congress.

from for-profit correspondence courses and traveling Chautauqua tent shows in the 1910s. Chautauquans were not secularized by any means. But while religion still dominated private life, Chautauqua's public discourse, once rife with the language of evangelical Protestantism, now revolved around citizenship training, the importance of the arts and humanities, and other themes that still dominate modern secular liberalism. The last commercial tent Chautauqua folded in the early 1930s. Yet the original Chautauqua locality continues to be a meeting place even today. While the democratic impulses that characterized the great "educational revival" are muted, the growing summer program of lectures, concerts, operas, and dance performances suggests a revival of interest in the arts among an ever-narrowing segment of American society that can afford its skyrocketing housing costs.

Further Reading: Rieser, Andrew C. *The Chautauqua Moment: Protestants, Progressives, and the Culture of Modern Liberalism.* New York: Columbia University Press, 2003.

Andrew C. Rieser

CHRISTIAN AND MISSIONARY ALLIANCE

The Christian and Missionary Alliance is a missionary-sending denomination founded by **Albert Benjamin Simpson,** the origins of which date back to 1887. The movement grew out of a convention ministry Simpson had in North America. In Old Orchard Beach, Maine, the site of Simpson's first convention, the gathered people voted in 1887 to form two organizations, the Christian Alliance and the Evangelical Missionary Alliance. The Christian Alliance was formed to bring together Christians who shared a concern for **foreign missions,** so that they could support and encourage one another. The Evangelical Missionary Alliance was formed to be a missionary-sending society. In 1897, after 10 years, the two groups merged to become the Christian and Missionary Alliance (CMA). The CMA differed from most mission societies of its time in that it did not focus on only one or two specific regions in the world. Instead the CMA had a global thrust. As early as 1898 it had between 250 and 280 missionaries in all continents. The toll exacted on early missionaries was high. Many died because of political violence, or as a result of harsh living conditions. Others suffered from chronic health problems and had to return to North America.

From its inception, the CMA has laid emphasis on Christian education. The first classes of the Missionary Training College were held in 1883 in New York City. In 1897 the school became the Missionary Training Institute and moved to Nyack, New York, just north of New York City. The CMA's idea for the missionary training schools helped to initiate the establishment of Bible schools and Bible institutes across the United States. In the early twentieth century, the CMA established three more schools: Toccoa Falls Bible Institute (Toccoa Falls College) in 1907 in Georgia, founded by R. A. Forrest; the St. Paul Training Home (Crown College) in 1916 in Minnesota, founded by J. D. Williams; and Simpson Bible Institute (Simpson College) in 1921 in California, founded by W. W. Newberry.

The **Pentecostal** movement of 1906–1911 sparked a controversy within the CMA that threatened to divide it. The central issue related to the exercise of **charismatic gifts.** Pentecostalism shared with the CMA a central teaching regarding the **baptism in the Holy Spirit,** and Simpson himself trained many of its early leaders, so the two groups seemed quite similar. But the difference lay in the outward manifestation of the Spirit, or **speaking in tongues.** Simpson did not feel that Christian believers needed to speak in tongues, and he advocated orderly conduct during worship services. Because of Simpson's ambivalence about speaking in tongues, a sizable segment of the CMA membership left the organization to join the burgeoning Pentecostal movement. Simpson never intended his society to become a denomination, although it became increasingly evident over the years that this is what it had become. The CMA had all the trappings of a standard denomination: a constitution, a yearly council meeting, a board of directors, a publishing company, colleges, and graduate schools of ministry. Finally, in 1974, a new constitution was ratified, making the CMA what it in effect already was, a denomination.

Further Reading: Niklaus, Robert, John Sawin, and Samuel Stoesz. *All for Jesus: God at Work in the Christian and Missionary Alliance over One Hundred Years.* Camp Hill, PA: Christian Publications, 1996; Thompson, A. W. *A. B. Simpson: His Life and Work.* Camp Hill, PA: Christian Publications, 2001; Tozier, Alden. *Wingspread: Albert B. Simpson: A Study in Spiritual Attitude.* Camp Hill, PA: Christian Publications, 1988; Tucker, Ruth A. *From Jerusalem to Irian Jaya: A Biographical History of Christian Missions.* Grand Rapids, MI: Zondervan, 1983.

Jeffrey Cook

CHRISTIAN CATHOLIC CHURCH

see Dowie, John Alexander

CHRISTIAN CHURCH(ES)

see Restorationism and the Stone-Campbell Movement

CHRISTIAN NURTURE DEBATE

In the mid-nineteenth century, **Horace Bushnell** offered a major critique of revivalism that broke with popular revivalist approaches to the **conversion** of children and sparked a sharp theological debate about Christian initiation and spiritual formation in children. In 1846, Bushnell, the minister of the North Congregational Church of Hartford, Connecticut, delivered a series of lectures on Christian nurture to his ministerial association. Contrary to the common Puritan and revivalist practice of seeking the conversion of the church's children in late childhood or early adulthood, Bushnell argued that Christian parents ought to raise their children as Christians from their earliest days and expect that such Christian nurture will gradually form Christian faith and character in their children without the need for a distinct conversion experience. Bushnell published his lectures as *Discourses on Christian Nurture* (1847).

Bushnell rejected revivalism's approach to Christian nurture because it imposed the paradigm of an adult conversion experience upon children. Revivalists, following their Puritan predecessors, sought well-defined conversion experiences marked by acute conviction of personal sinfulness and guilt, a conscious act of repentance and trusting in Christ for salvation, followed by a memorable experience of joy and peace. Since young children did not often undergo such a decisive spiritual transition, revivalists tended to treat children born to Christian parents as condemned sinners until they underwent a conversion experience that matched the revivalist paradigm. Bushnell argued that this theology of conversion resulted in an excessive dependence upon revivalist techniques and the neglect of a consistent, daily nurture as a means of spiritual growth. Revivalists failed to recognize the capacity for faith and piety in children, and consequently they neglected the spiritual formation of children during the years when their character is most profoundly shaped. Even when the expected conversions took place, he lamented that the new converts had to overcome ingrained habits of sin that could have been avoided if their spiritual training had begun much earlier.

As an alternative to the revivalist paradigm, Bushnell argued that the "true idea of Christian education" is "that the child is to grow up a Christian. In other words, the aim, effort and expectations should be, not, as is commonly assumed, that the child is to grow up in sin, to be converted after he comes to a mature age; but that he is to open on the world as one that is spiritually renewed, not remembering the time when he went through a technical experience, but seeming rather to have loved what is good from his earliest years" (Bushnell, 4). The root of his alternative paradigm was a theory of the organic connection between parents and children. Bushnell used the term *organic* to describe the gradual emergence of a child's individual identity and character from the corporate life of the family. Just as sap from a tree flows into and nourishes a new branch, so the spiritual life of parents flows into and shapes the malleable soul of the child. This process of formation within the family is the primary means by which God imparts spiritual life and moral character to children. Bushnell focused great attention on the influences that shape children in their very earliest years. Before children can even speak, their spiritual life is profoundly formed by parental

relational warmth, moral example, and model of appropriate feelings of love for God. Bushnell's theory implied a gradualistic view of conversion and regeneration, and evoked confidence in the efficacy of Christian nurture. Whereas revivalists expected that most children in the church would remain unconverted until later in life, Bushnell taught that the divinely established norm for the church's children is that they all grow up as faithful Christians.

Bushnell's challenge to revivalist practices elicited a sharp rebuttal from Bennet Tyler, a staunch **Calvinist,** Congregationalist minister, and president of the East Windsor Theological Institute of Connecticut. Other critical reviews also began to appear in various Congregational periodicals across New England. Under increasingly heavy pressure, the publisher, the conservative Massachusetts Sabbath School Society, stopped selling Bushnell's book. In response to the society's decision, Bushnell defended his views in a pamphlet entitled *An Argument for "Discourses on Christian Nurture."* In October, Bushnell published *Views of Christian Nurture, and of Subjects Thereto* (1848), a book-length treatment of Christian nurture that included earlier articles on revival, the original *Discourses*, his *Argument* rebuttal, and two new chapters on the nature of the family and revival. Not to be outdone, Tyler responded to *Views of Christian Nurture* with a collection of seven letters in 1848 that elaborated his earlier criticisms.

Yet not everyone responded so negatively to Bushnell's work. He received support from fellow Congregationalist and Yale professor Noah Porter as well as several Unitarian journals. Substantive reviews of Bushnell's work came from the pens of the **Presbyterian** theologian and professor Charles Hodge and the German **Reformed** theologian and professor **John Nevin,** and they—together with Bennet Tyler's review—reveal the plurality of perspectives on the conversion and spiritual growth of children that existed among American Calvinists. Bennet Tyler rejected Bushnell's theory of Christian nurture because he believed that children needed to undergo a definite experience of conversion unmediated by the influence of familial or ecclesial relations. Unlike Bushnell, Tyler maintained that regeneration and conversion occur by a supernatural, instantaneous act of the Spirit. Conversion must be instantaneous because it is the point of transition between the two mutually exclusive states of condemnation and spiritual death on the one hand and justification and spiritual life on the other. Furthermore, conversion is a supernatural work of God, and therefore unmediated by natural laws. According to Tyler, the primary goal of Christian nurture was not to instruct children as Christian disciples but rather to convince children of the reality of their sinful, unregenerate state of alienation from God and to lead them into conversion through a profession of faith. Furthermore, Tyler shared the view of many revivalists that this sort of conversion and profession of faith usually does not occur in early childhood. Most children of Christian parents would undergo a distinctly memorable conversion experience in their teenage years following a period of conscious rebellion and alienation from God.

Hodge and Nevin joined Bushnell in rejecting revivalist methods for eliciting conversion experiences and revivalist criteria for identifying a genuine conversion. Unlike Tyler, they did not feel that revivalism offered a proper paradigm for the spiritual life of children. Hodge praised Bushnell for recognizing the profound spiritual connection between parents and children and the spiritual significance of Christian nurture from the beginning of a child's life. Rather than public **preaching** or participation in revivals, Hodge claimed that nurture is the ordinary means by which the children of Christians become the children of God. Hodge expected that conversions would most often occur quietly as a matter of course in the early stages of Christian instruction, and thus faithful Christian parents should expect that their children will grow up as faithful Christians. On the other hand, Hodge took issue with Bushnell's attempt to explain the "mechanics" of child conversion by appealing to a natural law of organic connection between parents and children. Hodge considered Bushnell's theory naturalistic because he attributed spiritual formation exclusively to a natural, organic process of

spiritual development arising from properties inherent in human relationships. According to Hodge, human beings are born in a state of spiritual death that can only be overcome by a supernatural act of regeneration that intervenes in the natural order to infuse new spiritual life. Thus the efficacy of parental influence upon the spiritual life of their children results not from a power inherent in natural human relationships but rather from God's consistent fulfillment of his covenant promise to bring supernatural regeneration to the children of believers.

Nevin agreed with both Hodge's praise and critique of Bushnell's theory, but he rooted his theology of conversion and spiritual formation in a more sacramental view of the church. Like Hodge, Nevin characterized Bushnell's theory of Christian nurture as naturalistic. By attributing the transmission and growth of spiritual life and virtue to the natural, organic relation between parents and children, Bushnell denied the supernatural character of the church as the sacramental bearer of Christ's life, and he wrongly elevated the family as the primary means of grace in place of the church. For Nevin, Christian nurture depends upon an organic union with the supernatural life of Christ initiated in baptism, embodied in the church community, and strengthened by the church's liturgical life and catechesis.

The controversy about Christian nurture died down rather quickly after 1849, when Bushnell became engulfed in fresh debates about other theological issues. Yet he later revisited his work on child nurture after retiring from his pastorate, and produced a significantly revised and expanded work entitled *Christian Nurture* (1860). Three chapters in the work contained the original *Discourses* and a chapter on the organic unity of the family. Many new chapters addressed infant baptism, church membership of children, the cultural ramifications of Christian nurture, and numerous practical questions about child rearing and religious education. Perhaps because of a shift in theological climate during the 1850s, Bushnell's new book elicited little debate. Nonetheless, the long-range impact of the 1860 work was profound. Many have heralded

Christian Nurture as the beginning of the Christian education movement in America.

Further Reading: Bendroth, Margaret. "Horace Bushnell's *Christian Nurture*." In Marcia J. Bunge, ed., *The Child in Christian Thought*, 350–64. Grand Rapids, MI: Eerdmans, 2001; Brown, Candy Gunther. "Domestic Nurture versus Clerical Crisis: The Gender Dimension in Horace Bushnell's and Elizabeth Prentiss's Critiques of Revivalism." In Michael J. McClymond, ed., *Embodying the Spirit: New Perspectives on North American Revivalism*, 67–83. Baltimore: Johns Hopkins University Press, 2004; Bushnell, Horace. *Christian Nurture*. New York: Scribners, 1860; Bushnell, Horace. *Views of Christian Nurture and of Subjects Adjacent Thereto*. Hartford, CT: Edwin Hunt, 1847; Hodge, Charles. "Bushnell on Christian Nurture." *Biblical Repertory and Princeton Review* 19 (1847): 502–39; Nevin, John W. "Educational Religion." *Weekly Messenger*, June 23, 30, 1847; July 7, 14, 1847; Peterson, Edward R. "The Horace Bushnell Controversy: A Study of Heresy in Nineteenth-Century America." PhD dissertation, University of Iowa, 1985; Tyler, Bennet. *Letters to the Rev. Horace Bushnell Containing Strictures on His Book Entitled "Views of Christian Nurture, Subjects Adjacent Thereto."* Hartford, CT: Brown and Parsons, 1848.

Michael A. Farley

CHURCH GROWTH MOVEMENT

The Church Growth movement includes Christian leaders and laypersons who support and implement a number of evangelistic and pastoral principles pioneered by Donald A. McGavran (1897–1990). Church Growth has been defined as "that discipline which investigates the nature, expansion, planting, multiplication, function and health of Christian churches as they relate to the effective implementation of God's commission to 'make disciples of all peoples' (Matthew 28:18–20)" (Towns, 78). *Growth*, for adherents of this school of thought, is a many-sided term that contains multiple aspects. Growth may be biological, as when Christian parents have children who grow up to become Christians. **Conversion** is another avenue for church growth. Internal growth involves a deepening of spiritual life or movement toward Christian maturity. The quantitative expansion of a single church congregation is yet another aspect of growth. Extension involves the planting or establishment of new congregations in a similar cultural context. *Bridging* is a term used to refer to the establishment of new congregations in cultural contexts that are dissimilar from that of the congregation initiating in evangelism or **foreign missions.** The Church Growth movement teaches that God intends for Christian churches to be growing in *all* these areas, and that churches should not settle for stagnant or declining numbers. The Church Growth movement, in pursuing its pastoral, evangelistic, and missionary aims, seeks to integrate biblical principles with insights from the behavioral sciences. Anthropological, sociological, and demographic analysis may provide clues as to how Christian churches can function effectively and flourish within a given cultural setting.

The Church Growth movement draws inspiration from the New Testament Book of Acts; the **Great Awakening** and **Second Great Awakening** in North America; the ministries of John Wesley, **George Whitefield, Charles Finney,** and nineteenth-century British **Baptist preacher** Charles H. Spurgeon; and the Sunday school movement of the 1800s. Yet the birth of the Church Growth movement is usually associated with McGavran's experience as a missionary in India. A fellow missionary, J. Waskom Pickett, had written *Christian Mass Movements in India* (1933), and found out that most of the Christians in India were from the lower castes and had come into churches through mass conversions or "people movements." These movements had occurred with little or no help from Western missionaries. McGavran and Pickett sought to base missionary and evangelistic work on careful statistical analysis and a strategic marshaling of resources toward those groups that were most receptive to the Christian message.

McGavran's controversial book *The Bridges of God* (1955) launched the Church Growth movement and its distinctive themes and terminology. McGavran defined evangelism not just as proclaiming the gospel, but as teaching people the Christian faith until they actually become disciples in churches. He wanted for missionaries to be held accountable for their numerical results, or lack thereof. It was not enough for them to be "doing good" or "sowing seeds." He proposed evangelizing a given population according to "homogenous units" of tribes or castes rather than on the basis of solitary individuals who chose to be converted. He advocated the training or discipling of entire ethnic groups in the Christian faith, rather than the "perfecting" of individual converts. Only after people were fully integrated into churches was it time to focus on perfecting them in their individual spiritual lives.

In 1965 Fuller Theological Seminary invited McGavran to establish Fuller's School of World Mission (now the School of Intercultural Studies). Since then Fuller has been the institutional base for the Church Growth movement, both in its international and North American expressions. Among the School of World Mission's early professors were Ralph D. Winter, who in 1969 founded the William Carey Library, the largest publisher of Church Growth literature, and in 1982 established the U.S. Center for World Mission (also in Pasadena); Win Arn, who in 1973 began the North American Institute for Church Growth; **C. Peter Wagner,** who joined Fuller's faculty in 1971, focusing on North American Church Growth, and who in 1999 left Fuller to establish the World Prayer Center, Global Harvest Ministries, and the Wagner Leadership Institute (all in Colorado Springs); and **John Wimber,** who in 1975 became the founding director of the **Charles E. Fuller** Institute for Evangelism and Church Growth, and then stepped down to become the founding pastor of the Vineyard Christian Fellowship and Vineyard Ministries International.

The Church Growth movement crosses denominational lines. From the 1970s onward, many Christian congregations and denominations, Bible schools, seminaries, and other groups have adopted Church Growth ideas and methodologies. Some examples of the spread of Church Growth teachings include a 15-session extension course, using the text *Perspectives on the World Christian Movement* by Ralph Winter and Steven C. Hawthorne (1981, 1994); David B. Barrett's magisterial *World*

Christian Encyclopedia (first edition, 1982; second edition, 2001); the Lausanne Congress on World Evangelization (Lausanne, Switzerland, 1974), which discussed global missionary strategies; **megachurches** such as David Yonggi Cho's Full Gospel Church in Korea (with some 750,000 current members); the neo-Charismatic or so-called Third Wave movement with its stress on **signs and wonders** as a means of bringing people to faith; and evangelistic efforts in older Protestant denominations, such as the **Alpha Program,** which began in Holy Trinity (Anglican) Church in central London and in the last 20 years has been implemented by about 7,300 congregations in North America and completed by a total of 7 million people in 138 nations. During the last decade or so, the highest rates of church growth in many nations (e.g., South Korea, South Africa, and Nigeria) have been in congregations affiliated with the so-called **Apostolic movement (or New Apostolic movement)** associated with C. Peter Wagner and Church Growth principles. If quantitative measures are an index of spiritual growth, then the Church Growth movement has fulfilled its mandate of promoting growth in Christian churches and denominations around the world.

Further Reading: Rainer, Thom S. *The Book of Church Growth: History, Theology and Principles.* Nashville, TN: Broadman Press, 1993; Towns, Elmer, ed. *Evangelism and Church Growth: A Practical Encyclopedia.* Ventura, CA: Regal, 1995. Wagner, C. Peter, ed. *Out of Africa: How the Spiritual Explosion among Nigerians Is Impacting the World.* Ventura, CA: Regal, 2004.

Bayard Taylor

CHURCH OF CHRIST, CHURCHES OF CHRIST

see Restorationism and the Stone-Campbell Movement

CHURCH OF GOD (ANDERSON, INDIANA)

The Church of God (Anderson, Indiana) was one of the first radical groups to emerge from the nineteenth-century **Holiness movement.** Its principal leader was Daniel Sydney Warner (1842–1895), founder and first editor of the periodical the *Gospel Trumpet*. Many of the group's early leaders and ministers were affiliated with one another through prior connections with the Holiness movement in the Midwest. Thus they were already acquainted with **camp meeting** revivalism, which left an indelible stamp on the ethos of the Church of God.

The Church of God's radicalism involved an opposition to all forms of ecclesiastical organization and institutional structures on the one hand and support for revivalistic conceptions of church and ministry on the other. Eschewing the label denomination and formal rites of church membership, early Church of God people referred to themselves as "the saints" and their group as "the Church of God reformation movement." Its antiorganizational approach led it to favor traveling evangelists over settled pastors, who bore the epithet "hireling ministers." Even big-time revivalists like **Billy Sunday** were targets of criticism. Church of God **preachers** described Sunday's revivals as "handshake religion"—a feeble alternative to true holiness. Daniel Warner, after serving in the **Civil War,** had spent parts of two academic years at Oberlin College, while **Charles Finney** was still president of the college. Yet there is little evidence that Finney had any direct influence on Warner. Instead Warner served as an evangelist and home missionary in John Winebrenner's Churches of God of North America. For Warner and other early leaders in the Church of God movement, revival preaching and itinerant evangelism were normative. In the first decades, meetings gathered around revivalists known as "flying messengers" and few permanent congregations existed. In 1885 Warner created the movement's first "evangelistic company," which, along with himself, included Barney Warren, Frances Miller, Sarah Smith, and Nannie Kigar. The group toured the Midwest and the **South** as well as Ontario in Canada, and it served as a prototype for other Church of God evangelists.

By 1900 meetings were giving way to the first settled congregations. Yet the camp meeting has persisted to the present. In the mid-1880s a "general camp meeting" began to grow in importance over local and regional meetings. Always held in proximity to the location of the Gospel Trumpet Company, from 1907 forward this meeting has occurred at Anderson, Indiana. Recently renamed the North American Convention of the Church of God, it nevertheless continues to be known colloquially as Anderson Camp Meeting. Adherents annually pitch tents and park camping trailers and recreational vehicles at hundreds of sites near a 7,500-seat tabernacle (constructed in 1962) that serves as the focal point of the six-day event.

Further Reading: Smith, John W. V. *The Quest for Holiness and Unity.* Anderson, IN: Warner Press, 1980; Willowby, Richard L. *Family Reunion: A Century of Campmeetings.* Anderson, IN: Warner Press, 1986.

Merle Strege

CHURCH OF GOD (CLEVELAND, TENNESSEE)

The Church of God (Cleveland, Tennessee) is one of the oldest **Pentecostal** denominations in the United States. Beginning with eight members in 1886 in the mountains of eastern Tennessee, it had grown to include almost 7 million members in 169 countries worldwide by 2004. Of these, about 1 million current members are located in the United States. The founding pastor was Richard G. Spurling Sr., a Landmark **Baptist** minister working in the hills of southeastern Tennessee and western North Carolina. Both Spurling and his son (R. G. Spurling Jr.) were interested in revival of their Christian lives by taking the New Testament as their only rule for life and practice and by restoring primitive Christianity to the church. They believed that this would usher in a possibility for a union of all denominations. Consequently the early theological leanings of the Church of God were an intriguing combination of the following movements: **primitivism** or **restorationism, Holiness** teaching, Adventism (focused on biblical **eschatology**), and anti-creedalism. Though the earliest adherents explicitly stated their intention not to start another denomination, the first General

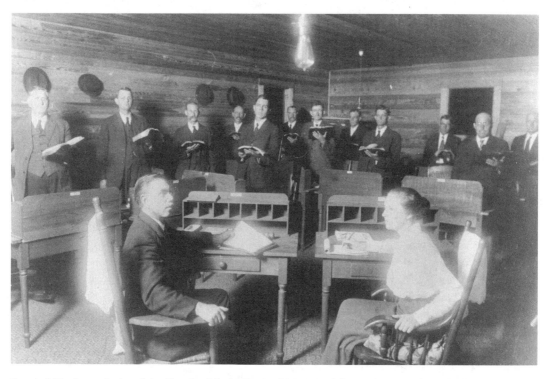

Rev. A. J. Tomlinson, leader of the Church of God (Cleveland, Tennessee) from 1909–1923 (seated left), with secretary Blanche Koon (seated right), and the 12 members of the first Council of Elders standing with open Bibles in hand. Photograph taken in the upper room of the church's headquarters building in 1917. Courtesy of Dixon Pentecostal Research Center, Cleveland, TN.

Assembly in 1906 initiated a series of biennial assemblies that continue to this day. Like several other anti-institutional and nondenominational revival movements in North America from the 1800s and early 1900s—for example, the **Restoration and Stone-Campbell Movement** (in its various branches), the **Church of God (Anderson, Indiana),** the **Christian and Missionary Alliance,** and early Pentecostalism—it began to manifest institutional and denominational characteristics within several decades of its founding.

In Cherokee County, North Carolina, in 1896, about 130 persons of this group experienced what they came to call the **baptism in the Spirit. Men** and **women** experienced **speaking in tongues** at this revival in a schoolhouse. Opposition arose against this unusual phenomenon, but eventually the church began to grow in the face of persecution. As a result of influences emanating from the **Azusa Street revival** in 1906, some members of the Church of

God began to proclaim and experience the baptism of the Spirit on a more regular basis. One individual was highly influential during this period—the first general overseer, **Ambrose J. Tomlinson.** As pastor of a large and influential group in Cleveland, Tennessee, Tomlinson served for almost 15 years as the head bishop of the burgeoning church. With roots in the **Quaker** tradition, Tomlinson was a fiery **preach**er who experienced Spirit baptism himself in 1908. Later, a disagreement over administrative issues caused him to form the **Church of God of Prophecy,** beginning in 1923.

From its inception, the Church of God was indebted to the Holiness movement. It showed Wesleyan or **Methodist** tendencies in its teaching on salvation and especially its view of **sanctification.** Until the latter part of the twentieth century, many of its members believed in the reality of instantaneous sanctification and a complete eradication of sin during a moment of spiritual blessing, usually gained at an altar of **prayer.** Yet many members now view sanctification as a progression in grace rather than as an instantaneous event. Nonetheless, the denomination continues to be classically Pentecostal in its stress on the need for baptism in the Spirit, accompanied initially by speaking in tongues. Some may experience other **bodily manifestations,** such as **dancing** in the Spirit, **shouting** God's praise, "waving" before God, or being "slain in the Spirit" (i.e., falling down). Yet, in accordance with Pentecostal teaching, these manifestations were not as crucial as speaking in tongues.

With their new experience of the Spirit, believers gained a new desire to go throughout the world and preach the Christian gospel. Consequently, evangelism and **foreign missions** have been high priorities as evidenced by the church's growing membership outside of the United States. While the Church of God is predominantly white Caucasian in the United States, it has reached out to people of all races throughout the world. The church teaches that experience in the Spirit helps believers to transcend race, gender, and generational differences. Though previously caught up in the early twentieth-century Fundamentalist movement and its anti-academic attitudes, the Church of God has more recently stressed the need for liberal arts education and seminary training for its pastors. It is still working out its theological positions with greater clarity and thus, like other Pentecostal denominations, it is attempting to think through the theological and practical implications of its experience in the Spirit.
Further Reading: Conn, Charles W. *Like a Mighty Army: A History of the Church of God, Definitive Edition.* Cleveland, TN: Pathway Press, 1996; Spurling, Richard G. *The Lost Link.* Turtletown, TN: Farmer Church of God, 1920. Tomlinson, A. J. *Journal of Happenings.* 5 vols. 1901–1923. Original manuscripts housed in the Dixon Pentecostal Research Center, Cleveland, TN.

Terry L. Cross

CHURCH OF GOD IN CHRIST

The Church of God in Christ (COGIC) is the largest **African American** Holiness **Pentecostal** denomination in North America, with 5.5 million members reported in 2005. The church originated in 1896 through the efforts of **Charles Harrison Mason** (1866–1961) and Charles Price Jones (1865–1949). Both were **Baptist** ministers who met in 1895 in Jackson, Mississippi, and were rejected by their Baptist church in 1899 for insisting that entire **sanctification** was a second work of grace—a basic tenet of the **Holiness movement.** In 1896 Jones conducted a successful Holiness revival in Lexington, Mississippi, and formed the Church of God. In March 1897, Mason was walking the streets of Little Rock, Arkansas, when the Lord revealed to him the name *Church of God in Christ* (based on biblical phrases in 1 Thessalonians 1:1 and 2:14). During 1897 the COGIC was chartered and its headquarters was established in Jackson, Mississippi. The church headquarters was later moved to Memphis, Tennessee, in 1907. The church continued to grow by adding new members in several states of the **South.**

Mason and Jones learned in 1906 of the **Azusa Street revival** in Los Angeles, California, led by **William Joseph Seymour** (1870–1922). In March 1907, Mason, David J. Young, and J. A. Jeter traveled to Los Angeles to learn of and experience the **baptism in the Holy Spirit** at the Azusa Street revival. Mason, Young, and Jeter experienced Spirit baptism, and the three men returned from California. When the three men arrived, their church was already divided over the doctrine of the baptism in the Holy Spirit. After consulting with Jones, Jeter repudiated his own experience of Spirit baptism. In August 1907, the general assembly of the COGIC met in Jackson, Mississippi, for three days and three nights to discuss the future of the church. Following this assembly, "the right hand of fellowship" (i.e., membership) was withdrawn from Mason and all who promulgated the Pentecostal doctrine of **speaking in tongues.** Jones kept with him a majority of the COGIC ministers while the rest went with Mason.

For two years, Mason and Jones were involved in a court battle over the name of the church and control of its properties. In 1909, the courts allowed Mason and his followers to keep the charter and the name COGIC. The year 1907 became the effective new date of founding for the church, and the church's

This Church of God in Christ minister, Elder Kelsey, exemplifies the denomination's tradition of fervent, Spirit-led preaching. (Photographer Gordon Parks; Washington, DC, 1942.) Courtesy of the Library of Congress.

articles were changed to incorporate new teachings on the Holy Spirit. Yet the founding articles of the COGIC did not include any reference to the "initial evidence" doctrine, that is, the idea that speaking in tongues is the necessary outward sign of the baptism in the Holy Spirit. The largely white **Assemblies of God** denomination has maintained the initial evidence teaching as one of its distinctive doctrines. In 1915, Jones and his followers were incorporated as the Church of Christ (Holiness) USA. They continued the Holiness tradition with an episcopal structure of governance by bishops, and their headquarters remained in Jackson, Mississippi.

Mason's third wife, Elsie—whom he married in 1943 after the deaths of two previous wives in 1903 and 1936—became editor-in-chief of the *Whole Truth Newspaper*. The COGIC founded industrial schools in the towns of Pearl and Lexington, in Mississippi, and a health clinic in Holmes County, Mississippi. By 1934, the COGIC had 345 congre-

gations in 21 states, and a membership of more than 25,000. By 1962, membership had increased to 383,000. The membership reached 3.7 million in 1982, and 5.5 million in 2005, with churches established today in 58 countries. Five bishops presently serve the church—I. S. Stafford of Detroit, E. M. Page of Dallas, W. M. Roberts of Chicago, O. T. Jones of Philadelphia, and R. F. Williams of Cleveland. Serving alongside of them are 10 overseers of states. The annual Holy Convocation is held in Memphis each November. The first **women's** leader was Mother Lizzie Woods Roberson (Robinson) (1860–1945), who established the Prayer and Bible Bands and the church's first savings account around 1911. Later female leaders have included Mother Lillian Brooks Coffey (leader from 1945 to 1964); Mother Annie L. Bailey of Detroit (1964–1976); Mother Mattie Carter McGlothen of Richmond, California (1976–1995); Mother Emma Crouch of Dallas (1995–1997); and Mother Willie Mae

Rivers of Goose Creek, South Carolina, a suburb of Charleston (1997–). The women's convention is held in May each year. The COGIC established C. H. Mason Bible Colleges in all jurisdictions to enhance the church's teachings and train pastors. The C. H. Mason Seminary, founded in 1970, is located in Atlanta. On April 3, 1968, Dr. Martin Luther King Jr. delivered his last public address at the Mason Temple, the COGIC headquarters built in 1945. His sermon was entitled "I Have Been to the Mountaintop." Well-known gospel singers had their start in the COGIC, including Samuel Kelsey, Rosetta Tharpe, Andre Crouch, the Winans, the Clarks, the Hawkins Family, the Pace Singers, and Rev. James Moore. The church's best-known publication is the *Whole Truth*, and its hymnal is entitled *Yes Lord!*

Further Reading: Daniels, David Douglas, III. "The Cultural Renewal of Slave Religion: Charles Price Jones and the Emergence of the Holiness Movement in Mississippi." PhD dissertation, Union Theological Seminary, New York City, 1992; DuPree, Sherry Sherrod. *African-American Holiness Pentecostal Movement: An Annotated Bibliography*. New York: Garland, 1996; Mason, Elise Washington. *The Man Charles Harrison Mason*. Memphis, TN: Church of God in Christ, 1997; Pinn, Anne H., and Anthony B. Pinn. *Fortress Introduction to Black Church History*. Minneapolis: Fortress Press, 2002.

Sherry Sherrod DuPree

CHURCH OF GOD OF PROPHECY

The Church of God of Prophecy is a Holiness-Pentecostal denomination (i.e., a **Pentecostal church with roots in the nineteenth-century Holiness movement**), and one of five Church of God groups in Cleveland, Tennessee, that descended from a small group of Christians, led by Richard Spurling and his son, Richard Green Spurling, who in August of 1886 wished to bring spiritual restoration to the Christian Church by freeing themselves from man-made creeds, and by uniting on New Testament principles. Around 1895, the Holiness Movement, together with a Holy Ghost revival under the **preaching** of B. H. Irwin, swept through the region. In 1903 a strong leader, **Ambrose J. Tomlinson,** came as a missionary to **Appalachia,**

and united with Spurling and others in seeking a restoration of the church. In 1907 their churches adopted the name Church of God. The following year, under the preaching of Gaston B. Cashwell, Tomlinson professed a **baptism in the Holy Spirit,** placing the church in the Pentecostal movement. Tomlinson was elected general overseer of the Church of God in 1909.

In 1923, because of a disruption concerning finance and governance, Tomlinson separated from the Church of God. Because of conflicting sources, it is unclear whether he was impeached and forced to resign, or if he initiated the separation. The largest body of this division exists as the **Church of God (Cleveland, Tennessee).** The division under Tomlinson's leadership was quite small, numbering about 8,000 followers. The use of the name Church of God by Tomlinson's group was bitterly opposed by the main Cleveland group. It was only after years of legal dispute that the court upheld Tomlinson's right to use the designation. In 1952, nearly a decade after Tomlinson's death, his group took its current name, the Church of God of Prophecy.

A. J. Tomlinson's son, Milton, became the general overseer. Milton's brother, Homer, refused to submit to this decision of the presbytery and was expelled, and went on to found the Church of God (Huntsville, Alabama). A. J. Tomlinson was convinced that his church was the true and visible church of the scriptures, referred to both in Old Testament prophecies and New Testament references. Historian C. T. Davidson argued for a direct lineage between biblical teachings and Tomlinson's group. The church that Jesus founded lasted until A.D. 325 (the year of the Council of Nicea), when it was layered over with foreign material. Luther removed some of the non-Christian accretions from the apostolic church, and Wesley continued the process. Yet the complete revelation of God's purposes was reserved for June 13, 1903, when Tomlinson restored the Church of God. Tomlinson's teaching is thus an expression of the **primitivist** or **restorationist** notion that true Christianity ceased to exist within a few generations or centuries after the time of Christ, and that a genuine, apostolic church can and should be reinstituted.

The Church of God of Prophecy's doctrinal position is summed up in a list of 29 tenets called Important Bible Truths. The emphasis is on personal holiness—meaning a ban on consumption of liquor, the use of tobacco and narcotics, the wearing of ornamental gold (even a wedding ring), membership in fraternal orders and lodges, and oath taking. Membership is withheld from those living with a second marital partner, unless the first partner is deceased.

Through the experience of **sanctification**—a second work of grace subsequent to **conversion**—the church teaches that the old sinful nature is completely rooted out of the believer's heart. The Church of God of Prophecy teaches that a believer can achieve perfection in this lifetime. Like other Pentecostal groups, the church teaches the necessity of a **baptism in the Holy Spirit,** as evidenced by **speaking in tongues.** The church asserts that no one receives an infilling of the divine Spirit without also speaking in tongues. Tomlinson taught that physical **healing** was included in Christ's atonement, and that going to doctors and taking medicine was contrary to God's Word. Dependence on physicians and medicines brings condemnation to the person involved. In addition, all the **charismatic gifts** of the Spirit and the fruits of the Spirit have been fully restored to the church, as well as the **signs and wonders** accompanying the early apostles. Foot washing is practiced among the saints. The Church of God of Prophecy has congregations and mission stations in over 115 countries, with a membership of over 546,000. It operates an accredited college, homes for children, and youth camps.

Further Reading: Davidson, Charles Theodore. *Upon This Rock.* 3 vols. Cleveland, TN: White Wing Press, 1973–1976; Hunter, Harold D. "Church of God of Prophecy." In Stanley M. Burgess, ed., *New International Dictionary of Pentecostal and Charismatic Movements,* 539–42. Grand Rapids, MI: Zondervan, 2002; Tomlinson, A. J. *Last Great Conflict.* Cleveland, TN: Press of Walter E. Rodgers, 1913. Reprint, New York: Garland, 1985; Tomlinson, Homer A. *The Great Vision of the Church of God.* n.p., n.p., 1939.

Stanley M. Burgess

CHURCH OF THE NAZARENE

The Church of the Nazarene is among the denominations referred to as **camp meeting** churches by historian Melvin E. Dieter. Products of **Methodism's** nineteenth-century **Holiness movement,** they arose in the post–**Civil War** context of the National Camp Meeting Association for the Promotion of Holiness (later National Holiness Association), which from 1867 to 1900 fostered a network of camps, conventions, and state associations across America. Holiness revivalism's original purpose was not the sinner's **conversion**—although it often occurred at such gatherings. Instead the Holiness meetings used the traditional modes of revivalism (such as protracted meetings, camp meetings, **altar calls** or "the mourners' bench," etc.) to lead Christians into the grace of entire **sanctification,** a notion in John Wesley's theology. Three regional denominations—each sprung from this matrix of Holiness revivalism but also imprinted by its own region's unique religious culture—merged in 1907–1908 to create the Pentecostal Church of the Nazarene on a national basis, renamed in 1919 as the Church of the Nazarene. This name change had something to do with the shifting meaning of the term **Pentecostal,** which prior to 1900 was a word generally applied to groups and churches within the Holiness movement, and from 1900 to 1915 came to be used only for those groups that practiced **speaking in tongues.**

Hiram Reynolds, one of the original general superintendents, had been a Methodist pastor, an officer in the Vermont Holiness Association, and later a full-time evangelist. In 1895 Reynolds joined the Association of Pentecostal Churches of America and later served as its home and **foreign missions** secretary. By 1907, this association had congregations extending from Nova Scotia to Iowa. Phineas Bresee, the Nazarenes' key early leader, followed a path much like that of Reynolds. Bresee, promoted the Holiness revival in churches and camps in southern California as a Methodist pastor and district superintendent, and toured the Midwest in 1892, speaking at NHA camp meetings as one of its vice presidents. By 1895, Bresee's prime desire was to create vibrant, up-tempo, family-oriented churches for the urban poor. The first congregation bearing the name Church of the Nazarene began in inner-city Los Angeles in 1895. Bresee's insistence on maintaining a revivalist atmosphere led to the 1898 withdrawal of Dr. J. P. Widney, a prominent Los Angeles physician and college president, and the cofounder who, with Bresee, had given the church its name. By 1907 Bresee's church connections extended from San Diego northward to the Canadian border, and eastward to Illinois.

Nazarene origins in the South were shaped by the "evangelist controversy" in the Methodist Episcopal Church, South, which provided no office of evangelist, prompting **preachers** engaged in that work to withdraw from the appointment system and take local preacher's licenses as their ministerial licenses. This bred conflict between pastors and evangelists, and the 1894 Address of the Southern Methodist bishops deplored "self-styled modern evangelists" modeled after **Dwight L. Moody.** Tightening disciplinary measures forced many evangelists into the independent Holiness movement; many later entered the Church of the Nazarene. Among these were Robert Lee Harris, founder of a Nazarene parent body in Tennessee; C. B. Jernigan, founder of another group in Texas; Reuben "Bud" Robinson, a beloved and well-known evangelist; and R. T. Williams, later a Nazarene general superintendent. The group also included many female evangelists—Mary Lee Cagle of Alabama and Texas, Fannie McDowell Hunter of Kentucky, Emma Irick of Texas, and others— barred from the Methodist ministry by their gender. The Holiness Church of Christ, arising from this milieu, stretched from Georgia to New Mexico at the time of the 1907–1908 merger.

The Church of the Nazarene became a denominational home for hundreds of Methodist evangelists. In the Nazarene imagination, the evangelist became a heroic figure whose entrepreneurial spirit spanned and influenced generations. Revivalism continues today among Nazarenes in district camp meetings and the tendency—although weakening—of congregations to schedule and conduct annual revival services. This revivalist

heritage has influenced the Nazarenes' century-long passion for foreign missions, which has resulted in a 1.5 million-member international denomination in which nearly half the voting delegates to the general meeting are from outside the United States. Indeed, Nazarenes—for better or worse—have been major exporters of American revival methods around the world. Gospel hymnody has also deeply influenced Nazarene life. Nazarenes have shaped that tradition in turn. The Lillenas Music Company, founded in 1925 by Revs. Haldor and Bertha Lillenas, has been a subsidiary of the Nazarene Publishing House since 1930 and a major publisher of religious music. A leading Nazarene family founded and has operated the John T. Benson Music Company of Nashville throughout its history. James D. Vaughn, whose broad influence shaped the Southern gospel music tradition, was an active Nazarene for the latter half of his life.

Further Reading: Bangs, Carl O. *Phineas F. Bresee: His Life in Methodism, the Holiness Movement, and the Church of the Nazarene.* Kansas City, MO: Beacon Hill Press of Kansas City, 1995; Dieter, Melvin E. *The Holiness Revival of the Nineteenth Century.* 2nd ed. Lanham, MD, and London: Scarecrow Press, 1996; Jernigan, C. B. *Pioneer Days of the Holiness Movement in the Southwest.* Kansas City, MO: Nazarene Publishing House, 1919; Jones, Charles Edwin. *Perfectionist Persuasion: The Holiness Movement and American Methodism, 1867–1936.* Metuchen, NJ: Scarecrow Press, 1974; Purkiser, W. T. *Called Unto Holiness.* Vol. 2, *1933–1958.* Kansas City, MO: Nazarene Publishing, 1983; Smith, Timothy L. *Called Unto Holiness: The Story of the Nazarenes; The Formative Years.* Kansas City, MO: Nazarene Publishing House, 1962.

Stan Ingersol

CIVIL WAR REVIVALS

Widespread revivals occurred in both Union and Confederate armies from early 1862 until the end of the Civil War in 1865. Hundreds of thousands of soldiers participated in these religious outpourings as they faced death in battle and from disease. Revivalism peaked after particularly severe battles, but anywhere the armies encamped, soldiers participated in evangelistic religious services. In some ways a continuation of the **Revival of 1857–1858,** the revivals in Civil War armies were largely male events, led by chaplains, missionaries, or lay leaders. They were also ecumenical across the Protestant spectrum, as **Baptists, Methodists, Presbyterians,** Congregationalists, and others joined together in religious meetings. Held around campfires, in chapels and churches constructed by the soldiers, in tents and buildings appropriated for religious use, and in fields and forests, wherever a group of soldiers could assemble, the revivals of the Civil War led to the religious **conversion** of many soldiers.

The best estimates of the number of conversions in wartime revivals range from 100,000 to 200,000 men in the Union armies and as many as 150,000 in the smaller Confederate armies. Thousands more of the already converted and the curious participated in the religious meetings held in army camps across the theaters of war. In no other American war did so many soldiers actively participate in evangelical revivals. For many individual soldiers, military service and especially battles forced them to consider their own mortality. Seeing comrades killed or wounded vividly demonstrated the uncertainty of life. In this context, revivals challenged each soldier to consider his eternal destiny. When soldiers converted, their religious beliefs reassured them that God cared for them and had a purpose for their lives. Their faith also steeled them to endure the hardships of camp life and the peril of combat, while providing a sense of spiritual community with fellow soldiers. Most generals and other officers—whether devout or not—encouraged revivals among the men under their command. They found that Christian soldiers were more disciplined, sober, and reliable in battle and that religious devotion improved the soldiers' morale.

The armies, from the North and the **South,** that marched to war in 1861 contained a significant minority of evangelical Protestants, for whom revivalism was a part of their religious culture. Churches in both sections also sent chaplains, missionaries, and colporteurs (distributors of religious literature) into the ranks to minister to the spiritual needs of the soldiers. The American Bible Society, the Confederate Bible Society, the American Tract Society, and other organizations distributed Bibles, testaments, tracts, and religious newspapers. This Christian literature sustained the religious fervor of the armies between revival services and when the armies were on the march. Aid societies, such as the United States Christian Commission, that arose to meet the spiritual and physical needs of the armies also drew on religious sources of duty. These factors ensured that, under the stresses of a protracted civil war, religion would play a major role in the life of both Northern and Southern armies. The most visible manifestation of religion among Civil War soldiers was the series of revivals in all of the major armies that erupted from 1862 through the end of the war.

Scattered revivals occurred in some encamped Northern armies in the winter and spring of 1862, as the initial enthusiasm for war evaporated and Union successes were few. Revivals arose in the Confederate armies in the aftermath of the retreat from Antietam in September 1862 and continued through the winter and into the spring of 1863. More widespread revivals began in the Union armies in the spring of 1863. The revival spirit also spread to the swelling Union and Confederate army hospitals, filled by the battles of the summer of 1862.

Typical revival meetings began when devout soldiers and a chaplain or missionary began singing **hymns.** The singing drew the faithful, the interested, the curious, and sometimes the mockers to the service, although the number of scoffers declined as the war dragged on and more soldiers were converted. After the singing concluded, a **preacher** delivered a sermon, usually with a strong emphasis on repentance and salvation. In some cases, two or more preachers delivered sermons in the same meeting. Preachers rarely spoke of denominational differences or the finer points of theology. When the sermon ended, the preacher invited those who wanted to repent to come to a specific area to **pray.** There, the preacher or Christian soldiers would pray with the repentant soldiers, and those who

Portrayal of the Atlanta Campaign of the Confederate Army of the Cumberland, featuring the Catholic chaplain Rev. P. P. Cooney in an Easter 1864 service. Both Southerners and Northerners regarded the Civil War as a sacred cause, and this picture combines military and religious images. (American Oleograph, 1877.) Courtesy of the Library of Congress.

were converted might explain to the congregation what had happened to them. The preacher then closed the meeting with a benediction.

Some of the largest revivals in armies on both sides occurred during the winter of 1863–1864. In the Army of the Potomac, Union soldiers constructed churches and chapels for regular preaching services and prayer meetings. In the Department of the South, **African American** soldiers stationed along the Atlantic coast from Virginia to Florida participated in revivals. In the Union armies encamped around Chattanooga, revivalism flourished, and thousands were converted to Christianity. The revivals continued until the armies began moving again in the spring. In the

Army of Northern Virginia, thousands of Confederates participated in the Great Revival of 1863 and 1864. Like their enemies a few miles away, the soldiers constructed chapels—at least 40 in the Army of Northern Virginia—for revival services. During this intensive period of religious activity, approximately 7,000 men, or 10 percent of the army, were converted. In the Army of the Tennessee, in a defensive posture in southeastern Tennessee, revivals began in the winter of 1862–1863 and grew in intensity through the next winter as the army encamped in northwest Georgia. Even within prison camps, such as the one on Johnson's Island in Lake Erie, revivals occurred among Confederate soldiers in 1864. Southern soldiers viewed the

A prayer service in General "Stonewall" Jackson's camp of Confederate soldiers. A few kneel, others lean on their rifles, and yet many seem distracted or disengaged from the religious service. Courtesy of the Library of Congress.

revivals and their attendant conversions as signs of God's favor on the Confederate cause.

The active military campaigns of the summer of 1864 suspended large-scale religious meetings, but when the Army of the Potomac and the Army of the James entered the trenches encircling Richmond, revivals resumed. In General William T. Sherman's army that marched through Georgia and the Carolinas in the last months of the war, soldiers held religious meetings whenever the army halted long enough to do so. As the war turned increasingly against the Confederacy in 1864 and early 1865, revivals provided comfort for those struggling to understand God's purposes in allowing the South to suffer. White Southerners transformed their earlier sense of God's chastisement for specific sins into a belief that God had allowed the overthrow of the Confederacy for some wise though inscrutable purpose. Many

soldiers pointed to the revivals that had occurred in Southern armies as evidence of God's continued favor, and they sought a moral victory in the face of military defeat by proclaiming that Southern armies had been more pious, devout, and spiritual than their Northern counterparts. This belief in the moral superiority of Southern military leaders and Southern soldiers became a cornerstone of the "Lost Cause" myth of the late nineteenth-century South.

After the war, the spiritual fervor of some soldiers who were converted during wartime revivals undoubtedly waned, but many remained faithful to their wartime commitments, filling pews in the North and the South. For most of these soldiers, their service in the Civil War would be the defining event of their lives, and for many, religious faith and wartime revivals played a central role in that experience. The return of Confederate soldiers spurred a postwar revival in southern churches, even as African American members departed to form churches of their own.

Further Reading: Faust, Drew Gilpin. "Christian Soldiers: The Meaning of Revivalism in the Confederate Army." *Journal of Southern History* 53 (1987): 63–90; Miller, Randall M., Harry S. Stout, and Charles Reagan Wilson, eds. *Religion and the American Civil War*. New York: Oxford University Press, 1998; Shattuck, Gardiner H., Jr. *A Shield and Hiding Place: The Religious Life of Civil War Armies*. Macon, GA: Mercer University Press, 1987; Woodworth, Steven E. *While God Is Marching On: The Religious World of Civil War Soldiers*. Lawrence: University Press of Kansas, 2001.

Daniel W. Stowell

COLLEGE REVIVALS

see Campus and College Revivals

COLONIAL AWAKENINGS PRIOR TO 1730

The genealogy of American revivalism prior to 1730 can be traced through three distinct lines: English Puritanism, **German** and Dutch **Pietism,** and Scotch-Irish **Presbyterianism.** Taken as a group, these Protestant traditions shared a family resemblance that included a concern for **preaching** a message of **conversion,** an emphasis on the performance of devotional routines that were designed to facilitate the experience of the new birth, and an exclusivist view of the church that restricted full church membership to converted or regenerate saints. Large stretches of British North America— the old **South,** in particular—were settled by immigrants with ties to one of several state-supported European churches that remained hostile to revivalist innovations well into the eighteenth century. The geographical origins of a distinctive American revival tradition, therefore, lay elsewhere, in the polyglot communities of southeastern Pennsylvania, the disparate rural settlements of central New Jersey, and especially the towns straddling the Connecticut River in New England.

Jonathan Edwards (1703–1758) may have been the first figure in American history to describe religious revivals as discrete events when he noted "a considerable revival of religion" in his famous *Faithful Narrative of the Surprising Work of God* (1737). A full-text search of the online Early American Imprints database for the keyword *revival* in books published in North America between 1639 and 1739 produces only a handful of hits, nearly all of which appeared in the works of New England ministers such as **Cotton Mather** (1663–1728). Most were pleas for a general "revival of religion" that drew upon the Puritan sermon tradition of the jeremiad, in which ministers upbraided the rising generation of congregants for their moral declension and flagging piety. Yet neither the prominent Boston clergyman nor any of his contemporaries used this phrase to refer to a discrete event, and they seldom associated it with mass conversions or the descent of the Holy Spirit. Thus, to speak of colonial "revivals" prior to 1740 is anachronistic and misleading. The century preceding the **Great Awakening** was, instead, the seedtime of American revivalism, a period in which the very concept and definition of "*a revival*" emerged slowly from an inchoate mass of sporadic local events.

Over the first century of European settlement, Protestant leaders nonetheless developed a robust vocabulary to describe the periods of spiritual renewal that occasionally struck individual communities and congregations. In 1716, a youthful Edwards wrote to his sister about a "very remarkable stirring and pouring out of the Spirit of God" in his father's East Windsor, Connecticut, parish (Edwards, *Works of Edwards*, 16:29). Edwards's maverick grandfather and predecessor in the Northampton pulpit, **Solomon Stoddard** (1643–1729), referred to such events as "harvests," while still other ministers spoke in more generalized terms of episodic "awakenings" and "religious commotions" in their parishes. Collectively, these terms encompassed any period of unusual religious concern in which individuals and families pursued the externals of religious practice with greater diligence and scrutinized their souls for signs of divine grace.

It is difficult to quantify the scope and depth of early American religious awakenings owing, in part, to the dearth of statistical and literary evidence—especially for congregations outside of New England. Longitudinal analyses of church-affiliation patterns for individual communities within the Puritan commonwealths, however, conclusively demonstrate that periodic surges in church membership were the norm, beginning with a powerful ingathering of new communicants in Boston in 1634 and continuing sporadically in towns throughout the region over the next century. Still, few of these precursors can be classified as genuine revivals in comparison with the Great Awakening. Large influxes of new church members frequently followed the ordination of a new minister or the adoption of more liberal admission practices. Periods of intensive religious concern occasionally were related to new preaching techniques and renewed interest in conversionist theology. Yet more often than not, they reflected life-course transitions as members of the rising generation came of age and sought access to the sacrament of baptism for their young families. Students of evangelicalism, therefore, should be wary of exporting contemporary definitions of revivalism back into the historical record. The religious stirs and harvests that percolated in early America prior to 1740 seldom conformed to the phenomenon that Edwards would later call "a revival." **William G. McLoughlin,** perhaps the foremost student of American revivalism, has established a useful distinction between the two categories. Drawing upon anthropologist Anthony F. C. Wallace's theory of revitalization movements, McLoughlin argues that revivals "alter the lives of individuals," while awakenings "alter the world view of a whole people or culture." The former, by definition, involves mass conversions; but a general religious stir may manifest itself in a variety of ways including, but not limited to, the experience of spiritual rebirth (xiii).

Among the most dynamic crucibles of early American revivalism was the Connecticut Valley in central New England, where Stoddard worked tirelessly over his five-decade career to promote conversions among his parishioners through powerful preaching and through innovative uses of the sacraments. Few peers accepted Stoddard's radical

position on the Lord's Supper as a "converting ordinance," but colleagues in towns across Connecticut eagerly embraced his notion of charismatic ministry. Stoddard believed that all clergymen had assumed the mantle of the apostle Paul and were sworn to the sacred task of assisting in the conversion of their flocks through fervent preaching. He stressed the need for all ministers to be converted themselves and encouraged his colleagues to preach without notes in order to stir the hearts and affections of their audiences. By the 1720s, Stoddard was thundering from his pulpit on the theme of conversion, and many of these dramatic performances included allusions to the torments of hell that awaited secure and carnal sinners. New Light revivalists would embrace all of these preaching techniques during the Great Awakening two decades later.

Stoddard's innovative and uncompromising evangelism transformed the Connecticut Valley into a hotbed of religious activity. According to Edwards, Northampton experienced five separate harvests between 1679 and 1718. Parishioners downriver in East Windsor frequently cited the formative influence of recent religious stirs in the valley when providing a narrative of their lives prior to admission to the church. Indeed, nearly a dozen Connecticut towns witnessed dramatic surges of religious energy between 1710 and 1733. Then, in 1734–1735, having warmly embraced his grandfather's evangelizing tactics, Edwards through his preaching triggered a **Northampton awakening** that reverberated down the valley. He claimed that 300 of his parishioners experienced conversion in a single year and maintained that nearly three dozen other towns, parishes, and smaller neighborhoods in central New England had also received "a very extraordinary dispensation of Providence" that far exceeded God's "usual and ordinary way." Edwards's *Faithful Narrative* characterized the Northampton awakening as the focal point of a singular "pouring out of the Spirit of God" extending from Connecticut to New Jersey (Edwards, *Works of Edwards,* 4:154, 157). *Faithful Narrative* quickly became the literary standard by which all subsequent revival narratives would be measured.

Churches in eastern New England also experienced unusual periods of dramatic growth, but unlike the Connecticut Valley stirs and harvests, these occasions of intensified religious concern were invariably connected with natural calamities that ministers and laypeople alike associated with the "frowns" of divine providence. One of the most dramatic religious awakenings in early American history erupted in the wake of a series of earthquakes that struck the Merrimack Valley in Massachusetts beginning on the night of October 29, 1727. Although no one was killed, the powerful shocks rattled chimneys and toppled stone fences in a 300-mile radius. The Great Earthquake, as it was subsequently called, quickened the pace of religious life in every town from Boston to down-east Maine, as parishioners assumed greater diligence in the performance of what Puritan ministers called the "practices of piety"—private devotional routines such as Bible study, closet meditation, and family **prayer.** Over the next six months, local clergymen published more than 20 sermons on the providential significance of the event and led their congregations in rituals of public contrition and covenant renewal in a concerted effort to improve the "good impressions" that had been created by the violent tremors.

Near the seismic epicenter, Haverhill, Massachusetts, minister John Brown (1696–1742) penned a unique account of the surging popular piety that followed the earthquakes. In the weeks that followed the initial shocks, he counseled anxious parishioners from morning until night with little rest. More than 200 people joined Brown's church in full communion over the next 12 months—more than 10 times the yearly average—while an additional 148 "owned the covenant" (and so became noncommunicating members who did not share in the Lord's Supper). Baptisms increased dramatically, as well, with numerous adults and entire unchurched households receiving baptism simultaneously. Yet among the scores of church-admission narratives that have survived from the Haverhill awakening, none describes a distinct conversion experience. The Great Earthquake may have accelerated the pace of religious life in town, but there is little evidence to suggest that Brown's parishioners moved beyond the preliminary stages of legal terror (i.e., a fear of God that was not united with any confidence in God's mercy). In the traditional Puritan morphology or sequence of conversion, those frightened by the earthquake might only have arrived at the first step in the process.

An even more striking example of this pattern occurred a decade later, when a virulent outbreak of diphtheria carried off as many as one in five children in northern New England over a brief two-year period. Laymen and laywomen once again elevated their devotional practices, and churches in Essex County, Massachusetts, New Hampshire, and Maine thronged with new communicants. Yet this period of awakening, like the fleeting good impressions that preceded it in 1727, was driven primarily by the laity's desire to placate a wrathful deity. Frightened parishioners hoped that greater diligence in their devotional performances might heal their dying children and protect their families from God's afflictive scourge. Revivalist language of conversion and the outpouring of the Holy Spirit—a theological vocabulary that was gaining currency in the Connecticut Valley during these same years—was noticeably absent from lay accounts of the "Great Earthquake" and "Throat Distemper" awakenings.

Unlike New England, the middle colonies harbored perhaps the most religiously heterogeneous population in the Atlantic world during the period between 1690 and 1740. William Penn's "Holy Experiment" in Pennsylvania received three-quarters of the nearly 250,000 German and Scottish immigrants who arrived over the course of the eighteenth century. Though dominated by English colonists, New York, New Jersey, and Pennsylvania were home to substantial populations of Dutch, Swedish, Finnish, and French settlers, as well. Frequent religious exchange among these groups created an environment conducive to theological innovation, ecclesiastical fluidity, and lay initiative—formative elements of an American revival tradition.

Nearly all of the immigrant groups in the Middle Colonies participated in religious denominations with strong ties to Continental Pietism, though

German-speaking settlers perhaps best represented its diffuse theological impulses. Prominent Pietist theologians in Germany, such as Philip Jacob Spener (1635–1705) and August Hermann Francke (1663–1727), blended **Lutheran** doctrine with Christian ecumenism and an experiential emphasis on "heart religion"—a belief that true piety consists in the movement of the affections rather than the intellect. Pietism developed a broad following among the laity in both the **Reformed** and Lutheran churches but was particularly pronounced among the many German sectarian groups that migrated to Pennsylvania in the wake of the devastating Thirty Years' War. Few German communities experienced unusual seasons of religious awakening prior to 1740, and yet their Pietist inclinations established a fertile field for the revivals launched by the Anglican evangelist **George Whitefield** (1714–1770) during his first American tour.

It was the fluid social and religious structure of the middle colonies, moreover, that provided an opportunity for a young German clergyman named **Theodorus Jacobus Frelinghuysen** (1691–ca. 1747) to minister to the several Dutch congregations that lay along the Raritan River in central New Jersey. Born in Westphalia and deeply committed to evangelical Pietism, Frelinghuysen, like Stoddard, championed charismatic preaching and conversionist theology. Arriving in New Jersey in 1718, he proceeded to alienate local elites by condemning the conservatism of the Dutch *classis* (i.e., church council) in New York City and questioning the spiritual fitness of several members of his own congregation. Frelinghuysen claimed to possess powers of spiritual discernment through which he could ascertain the state of a person's soul. Consequently, he refused to serve the Lord's Supper to parishioners that he considered unregenerate and denied the sacrament of baptism to their children. In 1723, a group of aggrieved congregants drafted a formal complaint in which they charged Frelinghuysen with doctrinal errors, fomenting schism, mental instability, and homosexual transgressions with a local schoolmaster; yet later revivalists including Edwards and Whitefield maintained that the evangelist's unwavering dedication to the

This woodblock print accompanied the second edition of John Cotton's *A Holy Fear of God* (1727). It shows people running during the 1727 New England earthquake, toppling buildings, biblical verses on the world's end, and a declaration that earthquakes are "a Warning to Sinners and Comfort to the Children of God." Courtesy of the New York Public Library.

doctrine of the new birth produced several powerful awakenings in the Raritan Valley during his stormy three-decade pastorate.

Scotch-Irish Presbyterians formed the third, and perhaps most important, strand of mid-Atlantic evangelicalism. Emigrating families from Ulster and the lowland regions in Scotland carried with them a dynamic tradition of seasonal sacramental festivals—colloquially known as **holy fairs**—that provided a template for regular periods of intensified religious worship. Originally organized during the 1620s as a form of political protest against the incursions of the Anglican episcopacy, Scottish sacramental seasons quickly evolved into grand Eucharistic spectacles that lasted for several days. Worshippers traveled for miles and gathered at outdoor sites where they listened to teams of ministers preach powerful sermons on the necessity of the new birth. The climax of the festival occurred on the Sabbath day, when hundreds of pious pilgrims sat down together to receive the Lord's Supper. Witnesses to these events often noted that they were attended with dramatic **bodily manifestations** of the Holy Spirit, as participants wept openly, cried out in distress, fell to the ground under the weight of their sins, embraced others in Christian fellowship, or experienced rapturous **visions** of the risen Christ.

By the early 1720s, Scottish congregations had successfully transplanted their unique communion rituals to colonial America. Among the earliest advocates of this distinctive sacramental practice were William Tennent Sr. (1673–1746) and his sons **Gilbert Tennent** (1703–1764) and William Tennent Jr. (1705–1777). Promoters of the Great Awakening often praised William Tennent Jr. for his role in stimulating a powerful awakening in Freehold, New Jersey, during the 1730s. Ordained at nearby New Brunswick in 1726, his brother Gilbert began his career as a close friend of Frelinghuysen, and, like his mentor, he quickly developed a reputation for confrontational demeanor and a fiery preaching style. Drawing upon his knowledge of Scottish communion seasons, he would later help to introduce the practice of protracted revival meetings to New England Congregationalists during a 1741 preaching tour.

When Whitefield arrived in the American colonies for the first time in 1739, he encountered a fractured religious landscape peopled by a kaleidoscopic array of Protestant immigrant groups, many of whom had brought nascent revivalist traditions with them or had developed them over time. Collectively, the ministers of various ethnic backgrounds and denominational persuasions gradually established a coherent **theology of revivalism** that centered on the notion that God works periodically throughout history by means of supernatural "effusions" of the Holy Spirit.

With the possible exception of the Anglicans, most religious denominations in the northern colonies shared a belief that religion in the New World languished in an acute state of decline. Clerical leaders responded by implementing strategies for engineering stirs and harvests that included public rituals of renewing the church covenant, innovative forms of sacramental worship, fiery preaching techniques, specialized prayer meetings, hymn singing, pastoral counseling, correspondence networks, and printed pamphlets. Most religious communities in the colonies experienced occasional surges in church affiliation—whether the result of generational maturation, affective preaching, liturgical calendars, or providential wonders—and these "seasons of grace," in turn, primed the laity to expect such events in the future.

At the same time, the emerging revival strategies varied from region to region, and there were numerous lines of tension even within individual denominations. Stoddard's preaching style, for example, does not appear to have influenced parishes in eastern New England, where liberal clergymen accented the outward performance of devotional rituals and downplayed the traditional Puritan teaching on conversion. German Pietists sometimes withdrew into inward-looking sectarian movements, rather than project their proselytizing energies outward into communal revivalism or ecumenical initiatives. Nativist impulses in the New Jersey awakenings of the 1730s led Scotch-Irish settlers to set themselves apart from other members of their multiethnic populace. Frelinghuysen's radicalism rankled his Dutch contemporaries in ways that prefigured the actions of the incendiary New Light itinerant **James Davenport.** Frelinghuysen's case suggests that even the Lord's Supper could become a source of contention. A regular calendar of sacramental holy fairs helped connect Scottish immigrants with the traditional sources of Presbyterian spiritual renewal. Yet in New England, an increased emphasis on the duties of participating in the Lord's Supper led to charges of formalism and spiritual deadness during the revivals of the 1740s. Tensions would persist between evangelizing clergymen and their flocks, who often viewed their earthly pilgrimage in practical terms that clashed with their pastors' well-honed conversion theologies.

Puritans, Pietists, and Presbyterians shared a family resemblance and a commitment to the generalized phenomenon that Cotton Mather called the "revival of religion." Yet fractures between and among them created a culture in which efforts to construct a **transatlantic** understanding of the Spirit's work during the Great Awakening of the 1740s would bring acrimonious debate, shifting theological alliances, and schism—as well as intensified piety, mass conversions, and communal reformation.

Further Reading: Balmer, Randall Herbert. *A Perfect Babel of Confusion: Dutch Religion and English Culture in the Middle Colonies.* New York: Oxford University Press, 1989; Crawford, Michael J. *Seasons of Grace: Colonial New England's Revival Tradition in Its British Context.* New York: Oxford University Press, 1991;

McLoughlin, William G. *Revivals, Awakenings, and Reform: An Essay on Religion and Social Change in America, 1607–1977.* Chicago: University of Chicago Press, 1977; Schmidt, Leigh Eric. *Holy Fairs: Scottish Communions and American Revivals in the Early Modern Period.* 2nd ed. Grand Rapids, MI: Eerdmans, 2001; Stoeffler, F. Ernst, ed. *Continental Pietism and Early American Christianity.* Grand Rapids, MI: Eerdmans, 1976; Ward, W. R. *The Protestant Evangelical Awakening.* New York: Cambridge University Press, 1992; Westerkamp, Marilyn J. *Triumph of the Laity: Scots-Irish Piety and the Great Awakening, 1625–1760.* New York: Oxford University Press, 1988.

Douglas Winiarski

CONFESSION OF SINS IN REVIVALS

The confession of sins has often played a role in religious revivals, but in a variety of forms. In the **Northampton revival of 1734–1735** under **Jonathan Edwards,** confessions of sin were not generally by public testimony but through private conversations. It was through conversations with his parishioners that Edwards first discovered changes in the people he described in his *Faithful Narrative of the Surprising Work of God* (1737). After a young woman acknowledged her sexual sin privately to Edwards and expressed her God-given resolve to change, the transformation of her life soon became evident to all, and "God made it … the greatest occasion of awakening to others"(Edwards, *Works,* 4:116–17) in Northampton, Massachusetts. In *Some Thoughts Concerning the Present Religion* (1743), Edwards advocated public confession on the part of those who had opposed the **Great Awakening** or hindered its progress. In the early 1760s, and especially under John Wesley, confession was associated with "conviction of sin" or pangs of conscience, accompanied in some cases by sudden outcries, **shouting,** or various **bodily manifestations.** Confessions of sin were generally brief and nonspecific. Wesley's *Short History of the People Called Methodists* records some examples: "Blessed be the Lord for ever, for He has purified my heart," "Praise the Lord with me; for He has cleansed my heart from sin," and "Blessed be the Lord, for He

hath pardoned all my sins!" (Heitzenrater and Baker, 9:473).

Confession of sin during the **Second Great Awakening** in America usually took a similar form. John Lyle's descriptions of events during sacramental meetings at Point Pleasant and Lexington, Kentucky, in June of 1801 are richly illustrative: "He found himself to be a great sinner. He deeply groaned but talked sensibly"; "many fell and agonized and groaned under the sense of sin, and many I hope were delivered and rejoiced with trembling"; "when she was put in the carriage she was able to converse and expressed her sense of sin and hope of mercy through the Lord Jesus" (Cleveland, 176, 179, 180). In each of these cases, the confession of sin was short and pithy, and was part and parcel of a larger conversion process involving a variety of elements that usually included seeking and finding pardon from God. "What must I do to be saved?"—this was the frequent cry at the revival of July 1839 in Kilsyth, Scotland, under William Chalmers Burns. During the **Revival of 1857–1858** there were more frequent and fuller public confessions of sin than in most previous revivals. In one case, a man confessed to having wandered into the Fulton Street **prayer** meeting in New York City with the intention of murdering a woman and then committing suicide.

In the twentieth century, revivals have been characterized by spontaneous, unpremeditated confessions of sins. The **campus and college revivals** of 1950, 1970, and 1995 are especially illustrative. One of the most widely publicized of these revivals was at Wheaton College in 1950. On February 8, a student asked V. Raymond Edman, Wheaton's president, if he could devote a few minutes in the evening chapel service to explain to the students how God had forgiven his sin and had given him victory in his life. He was permitted to do so, with the result that other students arose and spoke. Before long, 60 people were standing in line waiting to confess their sins publicly. These confessions continued all night long and throughout the following day and night. Finally, at 9 A.M. on February 10, President Edman ended the public meeting and asked those who

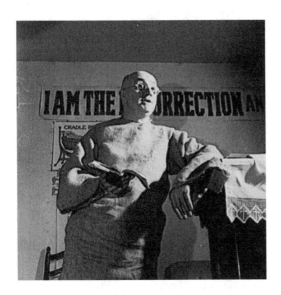

Brother Edwin Foote addressing the First Wesleyan Methodist Church in Washington, DC. He is wearing sackcloth to reprimand the congregation for not attending the revival meeting the preceding week. (Photographer Esther Bubley, March 1943.) Courtesy of the Library of Congress.

still wished to speak to go to another location on campus, where the meeting continued until 2 P.M. that day.

While the revival was in progress, news of it reached John H. Thompson, an editor for the *Chicago Tribune*, who went to the campus to cover it. His initial cynicism gave way to surprise at the emotional intensity and sincerity of the students. News releases then appeared on the front pages of newspapers in Chicago, Miami, Los Angeles, Seattle, and New York. Photographs appeared in *Time* and *Life* magazines on February 20, 1950, with articles entitled "42 Hours of Repentance" and "College Revival Becomes Confession Marathon." Chaplain W. Wyeth Willard, assistant to the president, reported that many hearts were moved, a spirit of forgiveness filled the campus, students and faculty made amends for past sins, and people resolved to lead better Christian lives. Earle E. Cairns wrote that "the debate team also had its period of confession and prayer on the way back to Wheaton between Louisville, Kentucky, and Wheaton. Several churches in Wheaton also experienced revival" (136).

Similar events took place at about that time on campuses throughout the United States, Canada, and even in China. Colleges and seminaries across North America were affected. In the central region, the revival touched the Prairie Bible Institute in Three Hills, Alberta; Bethel College in St. Paul, Minnesota; and Northern Baptist Seminary and North Park College in Chicago. In the Western states, the revival spread to California Baptist Seminary, Whitworth College, Simpson Bible Institute in Seattle, the University of Washington, Seattle Pacific College, and Northwest Bible College. In the **South,** awakenings occurred at John Brown University in Arkansas; Lee College in Cleveland, Tennessee; and Asbury Theological Seminary in Wilmore, Kentucky. Scenes of confession often spread from these campuses to churches of many denominations.

Scenarios of the same type were repeated in 1970, at which time Asbury College was particularly prominent, then again in 1995, although in this case the initial impetus came within the context of a church service. According to the *Chronicle of Higher Education* (May 19, 1995, A39–A40), on January 22, 1995, at Coggin Avenue Baptist Church in Brownwood, Texas, two students from Howard Payne University, a Christian institution, stood up and confessed their sins. As a result, many others started to confess their own sins before the congregation. On January 26, a similar event then took place on the campus of Howard Payne. Word quickly spread to other colleges, and Howard Payne students were soon being invited to other college campuses that experienced similar revivals. From these schools, more students were invited to still other schools, where there were yet further revivals.

The confession of sins that took place during these campus revivals is illustrative of a phenomenon that has occurred in many twentieth-century revivals. These events were noteworthy due to their length and the extensive publicity that some of them received. It is not surprising that younger people—lacking titles or positions of responsibility in campus, church, or society—were generally more forthcoming in publicly acknowledging their faults than their elders with titles and positions and more to lose by admitting to private sins. During the 1995–1996 college awakenings, professors and administrators were sometimes surprised or even scandalized by the students' outspokenness, and some questioned the wisdom of allowing public confessions to take place. On certain campuses, leaders viewed the marathon confessions of sins as bad publicity for their institutions, and sought to bring the confessions to an end. Yet many students, for their part, saw the practice of confessing sins as a way of breaking through the hypocritical posturing that often characterized student life at Christian colleges.

Further Reading: Adney, David H. *China: Christian Students Face the Revolution.* Downers Grove, IL: Inter-Varsity Press, 1973; Beougher, Timothy, and Lyle Dorsett, eds. *Accounts of a Campus Revival: Wheaton College 1995.* Wheaton, IL: Harold Shaw, 1995; Cairns, Earle E. *V. Raymond Edman: In the Presence of the King.* Chicago: Moody Press, 1972; Cleveland, Catharine C. *The Great Revival in the West, 1797–1805.* Chicago: University of Chicago Press, 1916; "College Revival Becomes Confession Marathon." *Life,* February 20, 1950, 40–41; "42 Hours of Repentance." *Time,* February 20, 1950, 56–58; Heitzenrater, Richard P., and Frank Baker, eds. *The Works of John Wesley* 24 vols. Nashville: Abingdon, 1984–2003; James, Henry C., and Paul Rader. *Halls Aflame.* Wilmore, KY: Asbury Theological Seminary, 1966; Kinlaw, Dennis. "A Revival Account: Asbury 1970." Videotape. Cleveland: American Portrait Films, 1988; Orr, J. Edwin. *Campus Aflame.* Glendale, CA: Gospel Light, 1971; Riss, Richard M. "College Revivals." http://www.grmi.org/renewal/Richard_Riss/history/college.html.

Richard M. Riss

CONTEMPORARY CHRISTIAN MUSIC

see Hymns, Hymnody, and Christian Music in Revivals

CONVERSION AND REVIVALS

Religious conversions and spiritual transformations are essential to revivals and revivalism. By the very nature of what a revival is, it is supposed to facilitate religious belief in nonbelievers and move those who are already believers to a point of renewed commitment and a stronger, more complete manifestation of their faith. During a revival, the nonbeliever's spiritual status is supposed to be transformed into faith and the believer's spiritual status is to be reignited and magnified. Powerful psychological forces operate to bring such changes about. Because of this, understanding how revivals occur requires knowledge about the psychological processes involved in conversion and spiritual transformation. Contemporary debates about the nature of conversion were prefigured in nineteenth-century discussions of **Christian nurture** and the searching criticisms of revivalism offered by **Horace Bushnell.** At issue was whether religious change is best understood as a sudden and total event, or as a gradual and partial process.

Both religious conversion and spiritual transformation have *change* as their central element. Conversion may be understood as a subset in the larger category of spiritual transformation. Conversion refers to the change in a person from believing in, adhering to, or following one religion to believing in, adhering to, or following another religion. Spiritual transformation includes conversion but also refers to a broader category of changes including those that are partial rather than total, and those that have some developmental basis. This would include the renewal or strengthening of a preheld belief. It may also include changes along dimensions that are not necessarily religious, such as the adoption of new values, goals, or purposes. Revivalism emphasizes the *religious* manifestations of spiritual transformation. Conversion is widespread though not universal in world religions. Three major religions—Christianity, Islam, and Buddhism—can be considered as missionary religions that encourage their participants to invite others into the faith. Attracting new believers is encouraged in some **new religious movements** and has been documented in ancient times as well. It seems, therefore, that systems of religious meaning—from ancient to contemporary times—have enough motivational power to move people to expend energy, use resources, and perhaps even sacrifice their lives, in order to spread their message.

The process of conversion involves a complex interaction of psychological and social factors. The psychological needs underlying conversion may be primarily emotional in nature (e.g., fear of hell, existential anxiety, feeling of lack of safety, lack of self-esteem), or more cognitive (e.g., lack of a coherent picture of the world, the need for purpose), or a blend of the two. Revivalists have based their appeals to potential converts on one or more of these needs. Earlier, "old-fashioned" revival **preaching** emphasized the danger of hell-fire, whereas more recent evangelists may urge hearers to turn to God to cope with their every-day problems or to resolve conflicts within the family.

Psychologists and sociologists of religion draw a distinction between *active* versus *passive* conversion. If conversion is a passive process—the older of the two views—it is something that happens to someone. Presumably this could occur either in accordance with or against a person's will. The forces acting to produce the conversion might come from within the individual (e.g., unknown psychic needs) or from the outside (manipulation and pressure by a group). A prototype for passive conversion is the case of the apostle Paul (Acts 9)—turned from being a persecutor to an adherent of the Christian community after his reported **vision** of Jesus. If conversion is an active process—a view developed within sociological literature since 1970—then the person in question is a seeker pursuing answers to questions, purpose in life, social contact, a sense of belonging, or the satisfaction of other social-psychological needs. This person's active quest eventually leads to a change in religious affiliation or to an increased commitment to a religion already held.

A psychological understanding of conversion highlights the importance of a public sign or ritual in securing or sealing the newfound religion in a person's mind. The new convert may be expected to be baptized, give testimony before a congregation, or encourage others to join the faith through preaching, teaching, or missionary activities. Going

forward in an **altar call** before an audience as a public confirmation of one's acceptance of the new faith, as done in a **Billy Graham** crusade, has a powerful psychological effect in confirming one's belief to oneself. Hence those who show their acceptance of the faith in a public way are more likely to continue in it, whereas those who do not do so are more likely to fall away. The psychological effect of a public expression of the newfound faith is to reduce any remaining cognitive dissonance resulting from the commitment itself, to minimize doubts, and to help establish a new sense of religious identity.

Psychological ideas about conversion have differed in the degree to which they regard conversion as a single event, or else as a process that occurs to greater or lesser degrees and over varying stretches of time. The view of conversion as a process is the more recent approach. The person's personality and social environment are factors in the conversion process. Research that examines the relationship between religious conversion and personality suggests that some people have a personality or personal needs that make them prone to seek and find a religion. Sometimes this need is for a sense of belonging to a group and to minimize loneliness, although it can also be for answering questions about life meaning, identity, or worldview. There is often a match between a person's particular needs and the religious teaching adopted or the religious group joined.

Psychologists have found little evidence that conversion changes a person's basic traits or temperaments. For example, a person who tends to be assertive and close-minded before conversion is not likely to become submissive and open-minded after conversion. Instead, the person will usually remain close-minded and assertive, but these traits will be expressed within the framework of the newly adopted religion. The apostle Paul might serve as an illustration, since his core traits were the same before and after his conversion but were directed to serve opposite purposes, first in opposition to and then as an evangelist for Christianity. Though a person's traits may not change in conversion, other levels of personality—especially midlevel goals, behaviors, and ideals—may change during or after conversion, as well as more global aspects of personality such as overall life narrative, self-definition, purpose in life, and worldview.

Because religion is about meaning, conversion and spiritual transformation can be understood as a change in a person's meaning system. A meaning system comprises a person's attitudes, beliefs, values, goals, and mental representations of the behaviors related to them, sense of self or self-definition, sense of purpose or meaning in life, and object of ultimate concern. It is an interactive network in which a change in one element can put pressure on the others to change also. Confrontations that press upon one or more of the elements of the meaning system may, if they are sufficiently strong, indirectly act as a force upon the other elements, and press toward a transformation of the whole system. This would be an example of the most radical type of religious conversion, sometimes called a *quantum change*, which, though dramatic and noteworthy, is the exception rather than the rule. It is a stereotype of old-fashioned revivalism that genuine conversion involves an immediate and total spiritual transformation, changing a sinner into a saint. More often than not, conversions and spiritual transformations occur in a partial and gradual fashion, and take place over a stretch of time rather than all at once.

Further Reading: James, William. *Varieties of Religious Experience*. New York: Longmans, 1902; Miller, William R, and Janet C'deBaca. *Quantum Change: When Epiphanies and Sudden Insights Transform Ordinary Lives*. New York: Guilford, 2001; Malony, H. Newton, and Samuel Southard. *Handbook of Religious Conversion*. Birmingham, AL: Religious Education Press, 1992; Nielsen, Michael. "Psychology of Religion Pages." http://psychwww.com/psyrelig/; Paloutzian, Raymond F. *Invitation to the Psychology of Religion* 2nd ed. Boston: Allyn and Bacon, 1996; Paloutzian, Raymond F. "Religious Conversion and Spiritual Transformation: A Meaning System Analysis." In Raymond F. Paloutzian and Crystal L. Park, eds., *Handbook of the Psychology of Religion and Spirituality*. 331–47. New York: Guilford Press, 2005; Paloutzian, Raymond F, James R. Richardson, and Lewis R. Rambo. "Religious Conversion and Personality Change." *Journal of Personality* 67 (1999): 1047–79; Pargament, Kenneth. I. *The Psychology of Religion and Coping*. New York: Guilford, 1997; Rambo, Lewis R. *Understanding Religious Conversion*. New Haven, CT: Yale University Press, 1993; Spilka, Bernard, Ralph R. W. Hood Jr., Bruce Hunsberger, and Richard Gorsuch. *The Psychology of Religion: An Empirical Approach*. 3rd ed. New York: Guilford, 2003.

Raymond F. Paloutzian

COPELAND, KENNETH (1937–)

Kenneth Copeland is an independent neo-**Charismatic** teacher, prominent televangelist, author, and advocate of the "Word of Faith," "Positive Confession," or **prosperity theology** movement often associated with the late **Kenneth Hagin Sr.** of Tulsa, Oklahoma. According to this teaching, what an individual believer chooses to believe inwardly and speak outwardly may be brought into existence in the physical world. This understanding of scripture is based upon the recognition that since God spoke the universe into existence and since humanity was created in the image of God, it follows that people who are in line with God's purposes should also be able to do anything according to God's will through faith. Such works of faith are accomplished through the power of the tongue. The Positive Confession movement also emphasizes the idea that there is great prosperity, or flourishing of spirit, soul, and body, for those who do not love their own lives but lay them down for Jesus Christ.

Originally from Abilene, Texas, Copeland became a young entertainer who in 1957 recorded "Pledge of Love" for Imperial Records, which reached the top 10 and sold 300,000 copies. The day that the song was released he was drafted into the U.S. Army. By the time he was discharged, his song had dropped off the charts and his name had been forgotten. He later said, "I didn't realize it then, but nothing I set my hand to do would succeed until I got my heart right" (Kenneth Copeland Ministries, *The First 30 Years*, [1997] 16). Copeland married Gloria Neece of Center Point, Arkansas, in 1962. Later the same year he gave his life to

God. He reported that the following year the Lord told him to go to Oral Roberts University in Tulsa, Oklahoma, but that it took him until December of 1966 to do so, at which time he realized that he was in the will of God for the first time in his life. He wrote that immediately after enrolling, as he left the registrar's office, the Lord told him to go to the executive offices of the school on the top floor of the same building, which was off-limits for students. Here, he ran into Oral Roberts, who, because of Copeland's prior experience as a commercial pilot, put him to work as a copilot on Roberts's cross-country crusade flights.

While a student at ORU, he attended Kenneth Hagin's Tulsa seminars, but because he was unable to pay for the seminar tapes, he offered the title to his car as payment. Copeland and his wife, Gloria, returned to Fort Worth, Texas, in 1968, where they founded an evangelistic association. Although their meetings only began as Bible studies in local homes, they grew rapidly. The Copelands began publishing a periodical, the *Believers' Voice of Victory*, in 1973. After an extended time of **prayer** two years later, Copeland said that God had told him to **preach** the Christian gospel "on every available voice," or in every available medium. In 1976, therefore, he and his wife began **radio** broadcasts, quickly reaching most parts of North America. Within three years, they launched a successful international **television** ministry. In 1981, they began using special satellite communications, and initiated a global religious broadcast the next year. His ministry has been accompanied by many reports of healing from many diseases, including cancer and AIDS. Copeland's ministry may have had an impact on that of Rodney Howard-Browne—a neo-Charismatic minister, originally from South Africa, who was associated with Randy Clark and others who became leaders in the **Toronto Blessing.** In 1992 or 1993, in the midst of a revival service, Copeland laid his hands upon Howard-Browne, who fell to the floor. Copeland then knelt down, laid his hands upon him again, and declared that God was calling him to greater things in his ministry (Riss).

Copeland's teachings may have been influenced by those of E. W. Kenyon (1867–1948), whose theology has been criticized as scripturally imbalanced, and/or derived from unscriptural metaphysical ideas. These ideas may have had their origin in the nineteenth century at Emerson College of Oratory in Boston, a spawning ground of the New Thought movement. Copeland and others in the Word of Faith movement including Kenneth Hagin, Jerry Sevelle, Charles Capps, and Frederick K. C. Price, have been severely criticized for an imbalanced emphasis upon material prosperity and the idea of positive confession. Among his leading critics is **Hank Hanegraaff** of the Christian Research Institute in Rancho Santa Margarita, California. By the late 1990s, Copeland and his wife had written more than 60 books and had a thriving prison ministry to over 60,000 inmates. Their daily and weekly *Believer's Voice of Victory* television broadcasts were airing on nearly 500 stations worldwide, and their periodicals were reaching a combined circulation of almost 700,000. Their teaching materials have been translated into over 20 languages.

Further Reading: Hanegraaff, Hank, and Erwin M. de Castro. "What's Wrong with the Faith Movement? Part Two: The Teachings of Kenneth Copeland." *Christian Research Journal* 15 (Spring 1993): 1–10; Kenneth Copeland Ministries. "About KCM." http://www.kcm.org/about/index.php; Kenneth Copeland Ministries. *The First 30 Years: A Journey of Faith*. Fort Worth, TX: Kenneth Copeland, 1997; Riss, Richard. "A History of the Revival of 1992–1995." http://www.grmi.org/renewal/Richard_Riss/history/copeland.html; Savelle, Jerry. *If Satan Can't Steal Your Joy, He Can't Have Your Goods*. Tulsa, OK: Harrison House, 1983.

Richard M. Riss

CUMBERLAND PRESBYTERIAN CHURCH

The Cumberland **Presbyterian** Church began out of a dispute between pro- and anti-revival factions of the Cumberland Presbytery of the Presbyterian Church in the United States of America. The controversy arose in the wake of the Great Revival just after 1800, on what was then the western frontier of the United States. Encompassing what was known as "the Cumberland Country" in southwest Kentucky and central Tennessee, Cumberland Presbytery was organized in 1803 out of Transylvania Presbytery by order of the Kentucky Synod. In 1805, the conflict had reached such a state that a commission of the Kentucky Synod, acting on hearsay or unsubstantiated charges, dissolved Cumberland Presbytery and suspended from all exercise of ministry five ordained ministers, six probationers, and 15 licensed exhorters. Those suspended appealed the action, but after more than four years of efforts to have their appeal heard, three of the suspended ministers met on February 4, 1810, and organized an independent Cumberland Presbytery. By the time a General Assembly was formed in 1829, the Cumberland Presbyterian Church had grown rapidly, largely due to the evangelistic and itinerant **preaching** of its ministers.

The revival in the Cumberland Country began under the preaching of **James McGready,** a Presbyterian minister of Scotch-Irish descent. Born in Pennsylvania around 1760 and reared in Guilford County, North Carolina, McGready went to Pennsylvania at 17 to study for the Presbyterian ministry. While there he had a deeply spiritual experience during a sacramental meeting near the Monongahela River. From that time, he was convinced of the need for a datable **conversion** experience in the life of every believer. Licensed to preach by Redstone Presbytery in 1788, McGready returned to North Carolina, stopping to visit John Blair Smith at Hampden-Sydney College in Virginia along the way. McGready may have learned some of the techniques of revival preaching from the **campus revival** that was in progress at the college.

McGready's ministry at Stony Creek Church in North Carolina initiated both revival and strong opposition. After he received a letter written in blood, demanding that he leave the area, and found his pulpit burned, McGready decided to relocate to the western frontier. In 1796 he became pastor of three small churches in Logan County, Kentucky: Gasper River, Muddy River, and Red River. Soon after assuming leadership, he asked his congregations to sign a covenant dedicating themselves to observe the third Saturday of each month for one year as a day of **fasting** and **prayer** for the conversion of sinners in Logan County. Sporadic periods of awakening occurred in each of the three churches over the next three years, but in May of 1800, at a four-day sacramental meeting at the Red River meetinghouse, the revival reached its peak. Assisted by four other Presbyterian ministers, and one **Methodist,** McGready witnessed many conversions and extraordinary responses from his congregation. For the sacramental meeting in July at Gasper River, people came from as far as a hundred miles away for what turned out to be the most sizable and influential of the early **camp meetings,** which had begun sporadically in various locations during the 1780s or 1790s. **Barton Stone,** a young Presbyterian minister at **Cane Ridge** and Concord Presbyterian Churches, visited the meeting at Gasper River, and took news of the revival back to central Kentucky. The next year, he would preside over the largest of the western camp meetings when perhaps as many as 10,000 or more gathered at Cane Ridge in August.

The Cumberland Presbyterian ministers, unlike the **restorationists** or the **Stone-Campbell movement** and the **Shakers** with whom they were often confused, intended to perpetuate a Presbyterian theology and polity amenable to revival preaching. At the organization of the independent Cumberland Presbytery in 1810, the presbytery adopted the Westminster Confession and Westminster Shorter Catechism "except the idea of fatality, that seems to be taught under the mysterious doctrine of predestination" (Barrus, Baughn, and Campbell, 76). The Cumberland Synod adopted an amended version of the Westminster Confession in 1813, which sought to make clear the church's commitment to the "whosoever will" gospel. Accused of ordaining illiterate men, the Cumberland Presbyterian Church upheld the need for an educated ministry, while providing flexibility in how the educational standards were applied so that those of exceptional preaching ability, despite their lack of a classical education, could be admitted to office in the church. A significant portion of the Cumberland Presbyterian Church returned to the Presbyterian Church (USA) in a 1906 merger attempt, though a sizable minority refused to recognize the merger and continued the denomination's existence. Today, the church has over 80,000 members in the United States and six other countries.

Further Reading: Barrus, Ben M., Milton L. Baughn, and Thomas H. Campbell. *A People Called Cumberland Presbyterians.* Memphis, TN: Frontier Press, 1972; Conkin, Paul K. *Cane Ridge: America's Pentecost.* Madison: University of Wisconsin Press, 1990; Schmidt, Leigh Eric. *Holy Fairs: Scottish Communions and American Revivals in the Early Modern Period.* Princeton, NJ: Princeton University Press, 1989; Scott, John Thomas. "James McGready: Son of Thunder, Father of the Great Revival." *American Presbyterians* 72 (1994): 87–95.

Daniel J. Earheart-Brown

D

DANCING IN REVIVALS

Dancing in a revival service is a means of expressing joy in God's presence and illustrates the role that bodily participation plays in the worship and character of revivalism. When practiced by groups, dancing in revivals may produce what the sociologist Emile Durkheim called *collective effervescence*— a sense of energy that transcends the individual. As an individual worship form, revival dancing highlights the spontaneous and lay-centered nature of revival worship. **African Americans** have played an instrumental role in integrating religious dance with revivalism. Dancing, accompanied by steady drumbeats, is integral to African religious ritual. Through such activity, worshippers in African traditional religions hoped to achieve contact or communion with, or possession by, their gods. In this context, dancing facilitates an ecstatic experience. When African slaves came into contact with American revivalism, with its emphasis on an emotional experience of conversion, they found a venue for continuing traditional patterns of religious expression, although these were invested with new theological meanings.

The dance most frequently practiced by slaves was a circular dance known as the ring shout. In this ritual, dancers circled around a singer or musician, shuffling their feet and interacting with one another with **shouting** and singing in call-and-response style. Such dancing is described in accounts of nineteenth-century **camp meetings,** often in a manner meant to discredit the practice as irrational or excessive. Although blacks danced the ring shout in segregated areas of the camp meetings, there were also occasions during camp meetings in which blacks and whites worshipped together. Accounts from the 1800s suggest that the religious dancing of blacks influenced whites to dance as well. The influence of the ring shout on revivalism may go well beyond dancing. Historian Ann Taves suggests that the common practice in revivals of establishing **prayer** circles around a person seeking **conversion** emerged from the ring shout.

While the ring shout was a communal ritual, individualized dancing has also occurred during revivals. An early instance might be the "dancing exercise" at the **Cane Ridge revival** (1801), which some believers engaged in after undergoing a dramatic conversion. More recently, **Pentecostals,** whose worship style was influenced by black spirituality, have practiced "dancing in the Spirit." These spontaneous dances can occur at any point in the service as a worshipper moves up and down the aisles of the churches, often with arms upraised. Though social dancing is frowned upon by Pentecostals, believers dancing in the Spirit see themselves

A woman "dancing in the Spirit" during the General Assembly of the Church of God of Prophecy denomination. A sign above reads "Quiet While Speaker Speaks" showing that the gathering might tend to be boisterous and yet had rules to be followed (ca. 1930.) Courtesy of Dixon Pentecostal Research Center, Cleveland, TN.

as dancing before the Lord, as David did when the ark of the covenant was brought to Jerusalem (2 Samuel 6:14). Today such dancing is more frequent among African American Pentecostals than white Pentecostals, since the worship of the latter group often resembles that of mainstream evangelicalism. **Charismatic** Christians, influenced by Pentecostals, have continued the practice of religious dancing, usually as an accompaniment to contemporary worship music.

In times of religious excitement during a revival service, Pentecostals might engage in a "Jericho march," named after the episode in the Bible when the Israelites marched seven times around the city of Jericho and the walls fell down. The Jericho march begins spontaneously as congregants form a circle around the perimeter of the church. Typically there is singing and shouting during the march, which lasts until the enthusiasm dies down and people begin returning to their seats. As a corporate

dance that generates a sense of collective energy and identity, the Jericho march is reminiscent of the African ring shout.

It is hard to draw a clear line of demarcation between dancing that happens spontaneously in worship or revival services and dancing that is planned and choreographed in advance. Much religious dancing is somewhere in the middle, neither completely spontaneous nor completely planned. Contemporary African American churches may set aside nights for worship that feature performers from the congregation who sing, play musical instruments, act in a skit, and dance. Dancing in this context is premeditated and planned, though some aspects of the bodily movement may be decided on the spur of the moment—"as the Spirit moves." The styles of music one hears may range from traditional gospel to soul, rhythm and blues, rap, or hip-hop, accompanied by bodily movement that runs the gamut from ballet to jazz, mimed gestures, or MTV-influenced dancing styles. Similarly, white Charismatic Christians from mainline Protestant and **Roman Catholic** churches may engage in dancing during worship that is at least partially choreographed and could reflect some formal training in dance. Some contemporary Charismatic services feature groups of dancers that function in a concerted fashion, though without knowing in advance what movements will take place. A dance leader senses what movements are appropriate for the occasion, mood, and music, and leads a group whose movements answer to those of the leader—a sort of choreographic equivalent of the African American call-and-response in worship. Both black and white dancers in worship settings may use special costumes or props, and carry colorful streamers or banners with Bible verses, names of God, or other Christian sayings or images.

Further Reading: Challingsworth, Nell. "Charismatic Joy of Liturgical Dance." In David Martin and Peter Mullen, eds., *Strange Gifts? A Guide to Charismatic Renewal*. 123–26. Oxford: Basil Blackwell, 1984; Raboteau, Albert J. *Slave Religion: The "Invisible Institution" in the Antebellum South*. New York: Oxford University Press, 1978; Spittler, Russell P. "Spirituality, Pentecostal and Charismatic." In Stanley M. Burgess and Eduard M. Van Der Maas, eds., *Dictionary of Pentecostal and Charismatic Movements*, rev. ed., 1096–1102. Grand Rapids, MI: Zondervan, 2002; Taves, Ann. *Fits, Trances and Visions: Experiencing Religion and Explaining Experience from Wesley to James*. Princeton, NJ: Princeton University Press, 1999.

Benjamin Wagner

DAVENPORT, JAMES (1716–1757)

James Davenport was a revivalist and **Presbyterian** minister in Southold, Long Island, who became well known during the **Great Awakening** of the 1740s for his itinerant **preaching** and religious excesses. Davenport came from a long line of distinguished clergymen and was settled as a Presbyterian minister in Southold, Long Island, in 1738. In 1740, Davenport became involved in the revival, working with leaders such as **George Whitefield** and **Gilbert Tennent.** His tendency to go to extremes was evident from the beginning. He once addressed his congregation for 24 hours. He trav-

eled through New York and New Jersey with Whitefield, who noted in his journal that through Davenport "the blessed Jesus has of late done great things" (*George Whitefield's Journals* [1960], 373).

Davenport soon began itinerant preaching tours of his own, preaching first in East Hampton, Connecticut, and then traveling along the Connecticut coast between New Haven and Stonington with Benjamin Pomeroy, a minister from Hebron, Connecticut. His preaching was popular in Connecticut, but his unorthodox behavior turned many against him. He sang in the streets and preached with unusual emotion. He claimed special illumination from God and believed that he could distinguish true believers from the reprobate. Most disruptive of all was his practice of publicly identifying ministers he considered "unconverted" and encouraging their parishioners to worship elsewhere.

In May 1742, due in large part to Davenport, the Connecticut General Assembly passed the Act for Regulating Abuses and Correcting Disorders in Ecclesiastical Affairs, which effectively forbade itinerant preaching. Soon afterward, two laymen from Stratford, Connecticut, lodged a complaint against Davenport and Pomeroy for disturbing the peace. Both ministers were arrested, and the newspapers reported that so many of Davenport's supporters were present during the trial that the governor appointed 30 men to guard the assembly. Pomeroy was discharged, but Davenport was declared "under the influence of enthusiastical impressions and impulses, and thereby disturbed in the rational faculties of his mind," and deported to Southold (*Boston Weekly News Letter*, June 10, 1742, 2).

Undeterred, Davenport arrived in Boston in June 1742 for another preaching tour and was interviewed by the associated ministers of Boston and Charlestown. Although they found Davenport to be "truly pious," they could not condone his propensity to act on sudden impulses and his encouragement of lay preaching, so they closed their pulpits to him. Davenport therefore preached outdoors in Boston and neighboring towns, causing the same unrest he had in Connecticut and dominating the Boston newspapers during the summer months. By mid-August, Davenport was again arrested, declared insane, and deported. He was censured by his Southold congregation for abandoning his church duties, but not dismissed.

After Davenport's preaching tour, religious separatists in New London, Connecticut, invited him to assist them in organizing into a church, and he arrived there on March 2, 1743. On March 6, based on impressions he had received through **dreams,** Davenport ordered his followers to burn their wigs, jewelry, and fine clothing so they would not be tempted by such worldly possessions. Davenport himself threw his plush breeches into the fire. Also included in the bonfire were numerous religious books, many written by highly esteemed men such as Increase Mather, Samuel Sewall, and Benjamin Colman. Heavily reported by the newspapers, this incident caused Davenport to be denounced even by revival supporters. After returning to Southold, Davenport was dismissed by his church and suffered a protracted illness. Earnest appeals from colleagues Solomon Williams and Eleazer Wheelock convinced Davenport of his errors and he eventually recanted, publishing his *Confessions and Retractions* in 1744. In his confession, Davenport noted that he had been suffering from a "long Fever" and "cankry Humour" and had been led by "the false spirit" during his indiscretions.

His intemperate behavior aided the cause of those against the revival, including **Charles Chauncy,** who cited Davenport as an example of everything that was wrong with the revival. After the incidents of 1743–1744, Davenport did not figure prominently in the revival again and eventually became pastor of a Presbyterian church in Freehold, New Jersey. Proceedings for his dismissal had begun there when he died in 1757.

Further Reading: Stout, Harry S., and Peter Onuf. "James Davenport and the Great Awakening in New London." *Journal of American History* 71 (1983): 556–78; Tracy, Joseph. *The Great Awakening: A History of the Revival of Religion in the Time of Edwards and Whitefield.* 1841. Reprint, New York: Arno Press, 1969.

Lisa Herb Smith

DAVIES, SAMUEL (1723–1761)

Samuel Davies, poet and writer of **hymns,** revivalist, and college president, served as a New Light **Presbyterian** evangelist in Anglican Virginia. Davies was born in New Castle, Delaware, in 1723, of Welsh **Baptist** descent. He received his formal training under New Light Presbyterian **Samuel Blair** at Blair's Log College, which was akin to that of the **Tennents** in Neshaminy, Pennsylvania. Blair established Fagg's Manor Presbyterian Church as a home to revivals during the **Great Awakening** and to his own humble log college for the training of ministers. Blair's revival account was published in Thomas Prince's *Christian History* in 1744, serving as a model for Davies, who credited Blair as his singular influence, eulogizing him as his "father, tutor, pastor, friend" (Pilcher, *Samuel Davies*, 11–12).

After his training, Davies was ordained in 1747 by the Synod of New York as an evangelist to Hanover County, Virginia—where Whitefield had preached in 1745. Davies, Blair, and others conducted preaching tours, but the Hanoverian dissenters—so called for their rejection of the established Anglican church—wanted more stable leadership. Just before Davies arrived in 1747, his new bride, Sarah Kirkpatrick, died while pregnant, leaving him "under melancholy," as he wrote (*Memoir of the Rev. Samuel Davies* [1832], 20). He remarried shortly after he arrived in Virginia to Jane Holt, from a prominent Anglican family in Williamsburg. Davies began his career with a strong revival fervor in his preaching, transplanting the Scottish communion season practice of protracted meetings or **holy fairs.** His sermons aimed at the salvation of his auditors, sparking the long 10-year reign of the Hanover County Revival, which not only furthered Presbyterianism but also spawned the Baptist presence in the Anglican colony. Davies spent much time on horseback as his ministry encompassed a five-county region and, by 1752, included seven meetinghouses. He was known for his oratory, hailed by the likes of Patrick Henry, and for his endeavors to bring religious liberty to Virginia, efforts later applauded by Thomas Jefferson.

Not everyone in Virginia was receptive to Davies and his revival messages, and he faced opposition from three Old Light Presbyterian ministers in Virginia and from numerous Anglicans. Davies's itinerant preaching and his popularity raised the ire of the established clergy, an oft-repeated phenomenon in revival history. Opposition to Davies extended beyond matters ecclesiastical. He received **African American** slaves into the membership of his churches and he advocated educating both slaves and Indians, though many regarded such measures as a threat to both the ecclesiastical and civil establishment. Virginia's Anglican clergy appealed to the governor and to the Anglican bishop of London, prompting Davies to write to the latter in his defense. Davies acknowledged that he was perceived as an "uninvited intruder into these parts," yet he assured the bishop that he did not preach sectarianism, but rather "'tis the conversion and salvation of men [that] I aim to promote" (quoted in Pilcher, *Samuel Davies*, 129–130). Davies overcame the opposition, retaining his license to preach and securing freedom for the Presbyterian churches in Virginia, thus making him an early figure in religious disestablishment.

In addition to preaching with a view to **conversion,** Davies sought to educate his parishioners. As his biographer George William Pilcher points out, the sprawling congregations under his care prevented him from establishing a school. Nevertheless, he incorporated his educational mission into his sermons and established a system of book distribution. His church members were reading such Puritan staples as Thomas Boston's *Fourfold State* (1720) and other well-known revival texts, such as **Jonathan Edwards's** works and especially his *Life of David Brainerd* (1749). Davies's own reading expanded beyond these to include works of poetry, leading to a collection he authored, *Miscellaneous Poems* (1752), and hymns, such as "Great God of Wonders." Through these activities, Davies ranks as one of the most significant figures of the Great Awakening in the **South.** From 1753 to 1755, he accompanied Gilbert Tennent to Scotland on a fund-raising tour for the College of New Jersey (late known as Princeton College). Upon his return,

he established the first presbytery in Virginia at Hanover in 1755. His work in Virginia was interrupted by an invitation to succeed Jonathan Edwards as president of the College of New Jersey. Though first turning down the offer, Davies eventually consented and arrived in September 1758. Like **Jonathan Dickinson,** Aaron Burr, and Jonathan Edwards, who preceded him in office, Davies's tenure was quite short, lasting only 18 months until his death on February 4, 1761, at 37 years of age.

Further Reading: Davies, Samuel. *Sermons on Important Subjects.* 3 vols. New York: Robert Carter, 1851; Pilcher, George William. *Samuel Davies: Apostle of Dissent in Colonial Virginia.* Knoxville: University of Tennessee Press, 1971.

Stephen J. Nichols

DECONVERSION AND REVIVALS

A religious revival can have unanticipated consequences when the event in some way alienates or offends participants or potential converts. The experience may be severe enough to cause a rejection of the religion and, in some instances, a crisis of faith. This is called *deconversion* in that it denotes a "turning from" faith rather than the "turning to" faith that is implied in the term **conversion.** In their North American context, revivals and awakenings have been marked by a certain degree of indeterminacy—unintended or unforeseen outcomes brought about by the outbreak of spiritual activity. Historically, the less desirable and ironic outcomes tend to be overlooked by revivalists who judge their success in terms of positive responses, especially in the form of sudden conversions. Evidence for deconversion is more difficult to come by, but a brief survey of anecdotal accounts indicates how varied the experience can be. Intellectual doubt, moral or ethical revulsion, and emotional turmoil associated with a particular belief or practice may all serve as contributing factors.

Both during and after the **Northampton awakening of 1734–1735,** Jonathan Edwards wrote in his influential work *Faithful Narrative* (1737) that some people resisted or rejected what he called "the surprising work of God." The famous **preacher** keenly observed how needless distresses of thought could impede the journey to salvation—distresses due most often to a theological misunderstanding of divine mercy or a psychological predisposition to stubbornness and pride. As far as Edwards was concerned, hard hearts and mental blindness accounted for these responses. But as a new generation of more liberally minded New Englanders came of age, a different interpretation emerged. William Ellery Channing, a Unitarian leader of the early 1800s, understood his own reaction to the New Divinity of Edwards's successors as a clearheaded rejection of a morally repulsive and intellectually appalling theology. Samuel Hopkins—Jonathan Edwards's disciple and, at one time, Channing's pastor—offended Channing by teaching that God uses evil, suffering, and even the eternal damnation of sinners to increase his own glory.

As revivalism underwent a new wave of innovation and intensity in the early nineteenth century, the techniques or "new measures" of evangelists like **Charles Finney** sometimes sparked negative consequences. Theologian and pastor **Horace Bushnell** thought the heightened emotional expectations of the **altar calls** and anxious benches disturbed and, perhaps, thwarted a legitimate faith already established in the home through **Christian nurture.** His own experiences at revivals were unsettling, casting doubt on his prior sense of God's presence. Another theologian and contemporary, **John Williamson Nevin,** recalled the painful experience of feeling like an outcast from the church because he did not undergo a dramatic conversion experience during a college revival. Like Bushnell, he found the emotional intensity of revivals to be disorienting and overly subjective. Revivals were poorly suited to stable middle-class communities that could form Christians through gradual processes of domestic nurture and churchly piety. Even a less stereotypical Victorian like Elizabeth Cady Stanton felt so bombarded by fear and guilt after sitting at an anxious bench that she suffered a nervous breakdown and never again returned to the evangelical fold.

Later in the nineteenth century, disaffection from revivalism was sometimes associated with a growing sense of incongruity between evangelical religion and society. Reflecting the crisis of faith of the late Victorian era, Washington Gladden—an early proponent of the Social Gospel—criticized revivals in part because of his inability as a child to find spiritual **assurance** according to prescribed evangelical methods. His lonely search was so painful in its consequences that he later viewed it as part of a wider ethical problem of self-absorbed individualism. Along with contemporaries like Jane Addams and Lyman Abbott, he never experienced the requisite emotions associated with revivals, but sought redemption instead in the wider realm of social activism and reform.

The rise of **Pentecostalism** at the turn of the twentieth century and a more recent neo-Pentecostal or **Charismatic** resurgence provides yet another perspective on the relationship between revivals and deconversion. A failure to attain a certain religious experience—in this case, the **baptism in the Holy Spirit** as signified by **speaking in tongues** or glossolalia—is a marked feature of some deconversion accounts. This time, however, the language of victimization sometimes expresses the crisis individuals undergo in what one former Pentecostal describes as a "claustrophobic chrysalis" of emotionalism. Even among those who speak in tongues, one finds occasional references to feelings of estrangement whenever an individual fails to maintain commitment and loyalty to particular beliefs, practices, or leaders. Religious disaffection may occur when individuals, acting in good conscience, find that they cannot fully endorse the teachings and practices of their faith community. Groups that are highly authoritarian in style, with leaders who claim to be acting under direct divine guidance, may provoke disillusionment or anger if the group's leader or the group as a whole fails to live up to its ideals. Internet discussion groups with labels like "Post-Pentecostal" or "Post-Charismatic" devote themselves to individuals who are recovering from such ordeals, but the scope of these movements has yet to be determined.

Further Reading: Barbour, John D. *Versions of Deconversion: Autobiography and the Loss of Faith.* Charlottesville: University of Virginia, 1994; Harrold, Philip. "'A Transitional Period in Belief': Deconversion and the Decline of Campus Revivals in the 1870s." In

Michael J. McClymond, ed., *Embodying the Spirit: New Perspectives on North American Revivalism*, 109–24. Baltimore: Johns Hopkins University Press, 2004; Rose, Anne C. *Victorian America and the Civil War.* New York: Cambridge University Press, 1992; Smail, Tom, Andrew Walker, and Nigel Wright. *The Love of Power or the Power of Love: A Careful Assessment of the Problems within the Charismatic and Word-of-Faith Movements.* Minneapolis: Bethany House, 1994.

Phil Harrold

DELIVERANCE AND DELIVERANCE MINISTRY

Deliverance is commonly understood in **Pentecostal** and **Charismatic** churches as the divine act of being set free from demonic influence or demonic possession. Deliverance focuses on exorcism and teaching Christians about their authority in Christ over the demonic realm. It is linked to a biblical concept of **spiritual warfare** (Ephesians 6:10–17; Daniel 10), according to which good and evil spiritual beings—human and nonhuman—are engaged in a battle for supremacy in the visible and invisible realms. Belief in deliverance from demons was a part of the divine **healing** movement in American revivalism. By the 1870s, the healing movement had become a force to contend with in the major evangelical denominations in North America. Belief in the practice waned in evangelical churches before the dawn of the Pentecostal movement at the turn of the twentieth century. As a result, Pentecostalism became the new haven for healing and deliverance practices during the decades after 1900. Since the 1960s, however, as a result of the Charismatic Revival and Renewal in mainline Protestant, evangelical, and **Roman Catholic** churches, healing and deliverance ministries have become increasingly widespread outside of classical Pentecostal contexts.

Early Pentecostal leaders, such as **Charles Parham** and **William Seymour,** were ardent advocates of divine healing and deliverance from demons. Healing became one of the principles of the Pentecostal "fivefold gospel" (Jesus as Savior, Sanctifier, Spirit Baptizer, Healer, and Coming King). Pentecostals underscored exorcism as among

the **signs and wonders** of the **latter rain** of the Spirit (Joel 2:28) that was to restore to the churches the deliverance ministries of Jesus (Matthew 12:28) and the early church (Acts 16:18) in preparation for Christ's speedy **eschatological** return. Such healing was also understood as the effect of Christ's victory on the cross over death and the demonic forces, recalling what theologian Gustaf Aulen called the classical theory of the atonement. Provision for healing and deliverance, having been accomplished, once and for all, through Christ's death, was available to Christians who sought for it with faith and persistence.

Since the 1960s, the Charismatic movement in the mainline churches tended to accent deliverance as a spiritual gift in the church, whereby God has given certain people gifts of discernment, revelation, and spiritual authority to overcome Satan and evil spirits. Itinerant deliverance ministries flourished on the fringes of the Pentecostal and Charismatic movements, and they stirred controversy through their teaching that Christian believers—in addition to non-Christians and unbelievers—were among those who needed to experience deliverance from demons and demonic influences. Derek Prince and Don Basham were on the forefront of this movement. Deliverance ministries became popular among the so-called Third Wave churches that are open to extraordinary or **charismatic gifts** of the Spirit but do not identify themselves as either Pentecostal or Charismatic. The publications and guest appearances of popular authors like Charles Kraft and **C. Peter Wagner** furthered the trend. Defenders of deliverance ministries have noted that a dismissal of exorcisms as mythological or superstitious reflects a Western bias that is untypical throughout much of the non-Western world.

For some observers, the most controversial feature in the theology of the modern deliverance ministries involves the belief that genuine Christians can be "demonized" or possessed of a demon. From early on, most Pentecostals rejected the notion that Christians can exist under an alien lordship. Charles W. Conn of the Pentecostal denomination the **Church of God (Cleveland, Tennessee)** quipped that "Christ will not share a Christian with the devil" (Hollenweger, 379). Some have also detected in deliverance ministries an unhealthy preoccupation with the demonic realm or a one-sidedly supernatural understanding of complex human conditions that may require medical or therapeutic aid rather than a dramatic exorcism. As noted by writers on exorcism in the Roman Catholic Church, an attempted exorcism of a pathological patient could actually intensify the patient's delusions. This is not to say that human evil and sickness do not confront us with a deep mystery that even science has not fully understood. Hollenweger warns, however, that "anyone who uses the devil as a stop-gap to explain the 'inexplicable' makes him a meaningless figure" (Hollenweger, 381). Implied in this statement is the assumption that the demonic is generally more meaningfully detected as implicit within a complex human or social situation that also involves natural processes. Deliverance ministries may function best if they are accountable to discerning pastors and overseers, and coordinate their efforts with other types of healing ministry, including the medical and psychiatric arts.

In part because non-Western cultures typically embrace a supernaturalist worldview that includes the reality of Satan and evil spirits, the books, videos, and Web sites associated with C. Peter Wagner and other deliverance teachers have made an impact around the world since the 1990s. In parts of Africa, such as Nigeria, the recent North American emphasis on "warfare **prayer**" has blended with earlier indigenous African customs of witchcraft eradication to produce a new sort of deliverance ministry, in which people go to special prayer locations to have demonic influences removed from their lives, families, and homes. Entire congregations or villages may gather to perform rituals of exorcism to break the influences of the old gods and spirits, and to pronounce words of Christian blessing and conviction. Deliverance ministries—often inspired by North American precedents and practices—have been globalized in recent decades and are now flourishing in various parts of the world.

Further Reading: Basham, Don *Deliver Us from Evil.* Ventura, CA: Chosen Books, 1972; Dayton, Donald W. "The Rise of the Evangelical Healing Movement in Nineteenth-Century America." *Pneuma* 9 (1982): 49–65; Hollenwegor, Walter J. *The Pentecostals.* Minneapolis: Augsburg, 1972. Kraft, Charles. *Defeating Dark Angels: Breaking Demonic Oppression in the Believer's Life.* Ventura, CA: Vine Books, 1992; Newport, J. P. "Satan and Demons: A Theological Perspective." In J. W. Montgomery, ed., *Demon Possession: A Medical, Historical, Anthropological and Theological Symposium,* 342–56. Minneapolis: Bethany Fellowship, 1976; Prince, Derek. *They Shall Expel Demons: What You Need to Know about Demons—Your Invisible Enemies.* Ventura, CA: Chosen Books, 1998; Scanlan, Michael, and Randall J. Cirner. *Deliver Us from Evil Spirits: A Weapon for Spiritual Warfare.* Ann Arbor, MI: Servant Books, 1980; Wagner, C. Peter. *Engaging the Enemy: How to Fight and Defeat Territorial Spirits.* Ventura, CA: Regal Books, 1991.

Frank Macchia

DEPRIVATION THEORY

see Revivals and Revivalism, Definitions and Theories of

DICKINSON, JONATHAN (1688–1747)

Jonathan Dickinson was a **Presbyterian** theologian, educator, and revivalist. In his day, his reputation as a **Calvinistic** theologian was nearly as high as that of his more famous contemporary, **Jonathan Edwards.** Born in Hatfield, Massachusetts, he graduated from Yale College and took his MA degree immediately thereafter. For almost 40 years, from 1708 to 1747, he was pastor of the Elizabethtown Presbyterian Church in New Jersey. Perry Miller called him "the most powerful mind in his generation of American divines," and C. A. Briggs declared him "the great representative American Presbyterian of the Colonial period, the symbol of all that was noble and generous in the Presbyterian Church" (Briggs, 176–77).

At the end of the seventeenth century, Presbyterianism in England, Scotland, and Ireland was in turmoil over the rise of Arianism (i.e., a denial of Jesus' divinity) and other major theological issues. Those seeking stringent tests of orthodoxy demanded subscription to the Westminster Confession (1648) and Catechisms. In 1698 the

General Synod of Ulster voted for mandatory subscription, and this was followed by church strife that paralleled earlier events in Scotland. In 1718–1719 an anti-creedal trend developed that ultimately carried most of the Presbyterian congregations in England into Unitarianism. American Calvinists watched with grave concern lest such controversies and heresy be repeated in the New World. Scotch-Irish Presbyterians generally wanted to require formal subscription to the Westminster Confession by all members of the Presbyterian clergy. Yet a rift appeared. Presbyterians of English descent and Puritan heritage—firm believers in the message of personal **conversion** soon to be proclaimed by evangelists in the **Great Awakening**—were convinced that mere subscription alone by clergy was no guarantee of their salvation. Dickinson, elected to the powerful office of Synod moderator year after year, became the leader of the more moderate English wing. His convictions, expressed in books and sermons, were that no creed, however authoritative, could be completely adequate, and that a far better way of assuring that ministerial candidates were indeed converted was to propose "strict examination … before they are admitted to the exercise of that sacred function" (Dickinson, *Remarks Upon a Discourse*, 16). In 1729 he authored the Adopting Act, whereby "scruples" against some minor matter in the Standards could be declared by a candidate before ordination. This compromise calmed the two parties for a short period.

With Francis Makemie (1658–1708), Dickinson led in opposing attempts at establishing Anglicanism as a state-supported church in the middle and southern colonies. In numerous pamphlets he stressed that God alone grants human rights, and no government ought to pretend that it confers rights on human beings through its benevolence. Human governments in fact take many rights away, and thus cannot claim to confer rights that are, at best, only partially recognized or restored. Dickinson spoke of humankind's God-given rights in such phrases as "the unalienable rights of mankind" 40 years before the Declaration of Independence used such terms (Dickinson, *The Vanity of Human Institutions*, 3).

The wide circulation of his sermons was influential not only in preventing Anglican establishment, but also in beginning a popular desire for total independence from England.

Beginning in 1739, the Great Awakening brought controversy among various Protestant groups in North America, and in 1741 the Presbyterians underwent an internal division. Dickinson favored the revival but at first kept a mediating position. Seeing that Old Side **anti-revivalists** were bent on a church split or schism, he joined with **George Whitefield** and **Gilbert Tennent**'s New Side in 1741, providing theological works to curb revivalist excesses and to align revivalism with moderate Calvinism. One of the institutional embodiments of the awakening, in which Dickinson played a part, was the College of New Jersey (later Princeton College), for men preparing for the New Side ministry. William Tennent Sr. had been conducting his Log College at Neshaminy, Pennsylvania, for some years, but advancing age forced him to close it in 1744. Many young men had been converted in the 1740s awakening and wished to enter the ministry, and so the need for a pro-revival college was paramount. Dickinson and others wished to continue Tennent's tradition, and asked Governor Lewis Morris of New Jersey for a charter. Their request was rejected. After Morris died in 1746, his successor, John Hamilton, signed a charter. Classes began in Dickinson's Elizabethtown manse in late May 1747, with him as first president until his death only five months later. The college was then moved to Newark, and in 1756 permanently established in Princeton. A prolific and profound theologian, Dickinson was regarded as the finest champion of Calvinism in the American colonies, with the exception of Jonathan Edwards.

Further Reading: Briggs, Charles Augustus. *American Presbyterianism*. Edinburgh: T. & T. Clark, 1885; Cameron, Henry C. *Jonathan Dickinson and the College of New Jersey*. Princeton, NJ: C. S. Robinson, 1880; Dickinson, Jonathan. *Remarks upon a Discourse Entitled an Overture*. 1729; Dickinson, Jonathan. *The Vanity of Human Institutions in the Worship of God*. 1736; Hardman, Keith J. "Jonathan Dickinson and the Course of American Presbyterianism, 1717–1747." PhD dissertation, University of Pennsylvania, 1971; Harlan, David C. "The Travail of Religious Moderation: Jonathan Dickinson and the Great Awakening." *Journal of Presbyterian History* 61 (1983): 411–26.

Keith J. Hardman

DISCIPLES OF CHRIST

see Restorationism and the Stone-Campbell Movement

DOW, LORENZO (1777–1834)

Lorenzo Dow, an eccentric revival **preacher** sometimes known as "Crazy Dow," had a role in the creation of the **Primitive Methodist Church** in England. Dow was born in Coventry, Connecticut, in 1777 and died in Georgetown, District of Columbia, in 1834. Like many in his time, he had no formal education. Claiming to have been under the influence of religion since the age of 4, Dow underwent a dramatic conversion when he was 13 and began to preach when he was 18. Dow applied for membership in the Connecticut Conference in 1796, but was refused. Two years later he was admitted on trial and briefly preached under appointment in New York, Massachusetts, and Vermont, but was dropped from membership because of his erratic behavior and because, without the permission of conference, he left to begin preaching in Ireland. Although he applied unsuccessfully to be readmitted to conference membership, he always considered himself a **Methodist** in principle and continued to preach and to follow Methodist doctrine.

Dow was adamant and outspoken in his opposition to **Roman Catholicism,** which he regarded as a heresy leading to Universalism (i.e., the idea that all persons will be saved) and to Deism. He regarded the Jesuits as both enemies of true religion and a threat to the government of the United States. In 1799 he claimed to have received and followed a divine call to preach to Roman Catholics in Ireland. His appearance and manner of preaching caused the Irish to conclude that he was mentally unstable and he returned home with little to show for his effort of 20 months. Upon his return, he went to the **South** for his health and was among

Lithograph of revivalist Lorenzo Dow. (A. T. Lee; Philadelphia, 1834.) Courtesy of the Library of Congress.

the first Protestants to preach in the territory of Alabama.

Though lacking official sanction, Dow traveled constantly and he reportedly covered several hundred thousand miles and preached thousands of open-air sermons over the course of his lifetime. Audiences came to hear him sometimes as much from curiosity as from religious interest. Dow's behavior was unpredictable. He might simply preach, interrogate a member of the audience, dialogue with hecklers, or—according to one report—smash a chair to pieces as an object lesson. People were intrigued. Dow was known for dashing from place to place, preaching, and departing without saying another word, sometimes by leaping out of an open window. He was also known for declaring he would come again in a year and appearing promptly on time. His dramatic sermons were popular with **African Americans** as well as white audiences.

In 1804 he married Peggy, who became his constant companion, and the following year the two of them traveled for him to preach again in Great Britain. On this trip, he visited both Ireland

Photograph of the interior of Shiloh Tabernacle, John Alexander Dowie's congregation in Zion City, IL, while Dowie was at the peak of his fame and influence. (Photographer George R. Lawrence, July 17, 1904.) Courtesy of the Library of Congress.

and England. In 1806, while visiting in Staffordshire, he met Hugh Bourne and William Clowes, founders of the Primitive Methodist Church, who emerged as leaders in a movement to turn the Methodist Church back to its revivalistic roots and grassroots character. Dow spoke to them of the dramatic revivals going on in North America and especially of the startling harvest of converts from what he deemed to be Pentecostal power present at **camp meetings.** The result was that on May 31, 1807, the first English equivalent of the American camp meeting was held on Mow Cop, a mountain situated on the border between Staffordshire and Cheshire. The meeting lasted a full day, and Dow was one of those who preached.

In addition to his preaching Dow wrote extensively, including a long memoir published as *History of Cosmopolite, or The Writing of Rev. Lorenzo Dow* (1854). Despite his eccentricities, Dow, who described himself as a "Son of Thunder," was known for zeal and dedication throughout a long and fruitful ministry.

Further Reading: Dow, Lorenzo. *History of Cosmopolite, or The Writings of Rev. Lorenzo Dow.* Cincinnati: Applegate, 1854; Dow, Lorenzo. *Life and Travels of Lorenzo Dow.* Hartford, CT: Lincoln and Gleason, 1804; Sellers, Charles Coleman. *Lorenzo Dow the Bearer of the Word.* New York: Minton, Balch, 1928.

James E. Kirby

DOWIE, JOHN ALEXANDER (1847–1907)

Born in Scotland and raised in Australia, John Alexander Dowie emigrated to the United States in 1888 and became one of the most influential leaders in the emergent American divine **healing** movement. Dowie had his first experience with healing prayer in 1874 and had founded the International Divine Healing Association by 1888. He opened a small chapel during the Chicago World's Fair in 1893, but attracted little notice until he reputedly healed Buffalo Bill Cody's niece and Abraham Lincoln's cousin. Dowie publicized his ministry through the *Leaves of Healing* magazine, founded in 1894, claiming a readership of 40,000 by 1901. In 1895, Dowie established the Zion Tabernacle and opened several healing homes in Chicago, and was served with more than a hundred warrants for his arrest for operating a hospital without a license. In order to bypass the Illinois constitution's licensing requirements, he founded the Christian Catholic Church in 1896. The new denomination had gained an estimated membership of 50,000 worldwide by 1900. Dowie claimed to pray for more than a thousand people per week. He preached to crowds numbering as many as 20,000 at a time, attracting more than 100,000 attendees to a series of meetings held in New York City in 1903.

John Alexander Dowie in priestly robes—clothing related to Dowie's controversial claim (beginning in 1901) that he was "the Messenger of the Covenant" or "Elijah the Restorer" predicted in the biblical Book of Malachi. Courtesy of Flower Pentecostal Heritage Center, Springfield, MO.

Dowie was one of the first modern healing revivalists to teach that the atonement provides for healing as well as forgiveness. He is perhaps best remembered for his uncompromising antimedical stance, exemplified by his infamous tract "Doctors, Drugs, and Devils, or The Foes of Christ the Healer" (1896), and for founding the city of Zion, Illinois, in 1900 as a sanctuary of healing and **holiness.** Many of the leading twentieth-century healing evangelists trace their beginnings to Zion, including F. F. and B. B. Bosworth, Dr. Phineas Yoakum, Raymond T. Richey, Gordon Lindsay, and John G. Lake. Dowie is also credited as a precursor of the **Pentecostal revivals. Charles Fox Parham** attempted to take over leadership of Zion on his way to the **Azusa Street revival** in 1906.

In 1901, Dowie began to preach doctrines considered by many heretical, including his own identity as Elijah the Restorer, first apostle of the eschatological or end-times church. He suffered a stroke in 1906 and faced a series of charges concerning his mental health and moral character, including accusations of sexual and financial irregularities, which led to the bankruptcy of Zion City. In 1907, Dowie's onetime followers voted to remove him as head of Zion City and the Christian Catholic Church. He died of a stroke at the age of 59.

Further Reading: Harlan, Rolvix. "John Alexander Dowie and the Christian Catholic Apostolic Church in Zion." PhD dissertation, University of Chicago, 1906; Lindsay, Gordon. *The Life of John Alexander Dowie, Whose Trials, Tragedies, and Triumphs Are the Most Fascinating Object Lesson of Christian History.* Shreveport, LA: Voice of Healing Publishing Company, 1951.

Candy Gunther Brown

DREAMS

see Prophecy, Visions, and Dreams

DUTCH REFORMED CHURCH

see Calvinistic, Presbyterian, and Reformed Revivals since 1730; Frelinghuysen, Theodorus Jacobus

DWIGHT, TIMOTHY (1752–1817)

Timothy Dwight, Congregationalist pastor, theologian, revivalist, poet, **hymn** writer, and president of Yale College from 1795 to 1817, led the college in a major revival during 1802–1803 and published an influential systematic theology that influenced subsequent revivalists. This son of Timothy Dwight and Mary Edwards was born in 1752 in **Northampton,** Massachusetts—the town where his grandfather **Jonathan Edwards** had once **preached** and led a revival in 1734–1735. A child prodigy, Dwight read the Bible at four and mastered basic Latin grammar at six. His mother taught him at home. He entered Yale College at 13, received a BA in 1769, and served as its tutor (1771–1777) while gaining the MA in 1772. He began curricular experiments at Yale emphasizing classics and poetry. He helped to found the Connecticut Wits, a group that developed a distinctive American literature and school of literary criticism. His greatest poetical works included *The Conquest of Canaan* (1785), an attempt to give the New World an epic like Homer's *Iliad*, and *Greenfield Hill* (1794), a portrait of idealized Connecticut village life. His gift of poetry found expression in anthems and 33 hymns, of which the best known is "I Love Thy Kingdom, Lord."

In 1777 Dwight married Mary Woolsey in New Haven and later was ordained as a Congregational pastor in June. Dwight studied theology under his uncle Jonathan Edwards Jr. During the Revolutionary War, Dwight served as a chaplain; and following the war he served as representative to the Massachusetts state legislature (1781–1782) and became pastor of the Greenfield Hill Church, Fairfield, Connecticut (1783–1795), where he established the Greenfield Academy.

When Dwight became president of Yale in 1795, he discovered that many students were attracted to the Enlightenment thought of Voltaire, Rousseau, Thomas Jefferson, and Thomas Paine. To challenge these notions of "infidelity," Dwight developed a two-part strategy. First, he labored to restore confidence in the Bible and based the 1795 debate at Yale on the question "Are the Scriptures of the Old and New Testament the Word of God?" Second, he started a four-year cycle of sermons to provide students with the foundations of Christian doctrine. These were later published as *Theology Explained and Defended* (1818–1819), which was an important textbook of systematic theology until the mid-nineteenth century. **Lyman Beecher,** one of Dwight's students, maintained that Dwight's Christian apologetics and doctrinal preaching to skeptical, freethinking students paved the way for the revivals that came to Yale students in 1802, 1808, and 1815. In 1802 a third of the 225 students were converted, and many of these later worked for revival in New England and New York.

While some have credited Dwight with being the human catalyst for the commencement of the **Second Great Awakening** in New England, more recent research indicates that the Yale revival was part of a larger movement and not the cause of the Second Great Awakening. The Yale revivals paralleled other **college revivals** beginning at Hampden-Sydney College in 1787 and spreading to Washington, Princeton, Andover, and Amherst Colleges. These college revivals began quietly and continued without the turbulent emotionalism of the frontier **camp meeting** revivals. By 1815 the "day of **prayer**" had become a regular feature at Yale and other colleges. As a revival leader Dwight popularized the "experimental" piety of his grandfather Edwards, preached eloquently without the aid of notes, resisted theological dogmatism and precisionism, and stressed the role of the human will and human activity in the **conversion** experience.

Theologically, Dwight followed the broad outlines of his grandfather Edwards's theology. At times Dwight is identified with the New Divinity movement in theology headed by Samuel Hopkins, his uncle Jonathan Edwards Jr., and Joseph Bellamy. Dwight's teachings on the governmental theory of the atonement, original sin, disinterested benevolence, and the halfway covenant linked him with these New Divinity theologians. However, he is called the founder of the "New Haven Theology" that distinguished itself from the former. Dwight preferred Scottish Common Sense philosophy to that of Locke and Berkeley as favored by his grandfather. He founded his theology on the belief that unbounded reason produced distortions. He questioned the dependency of New Divinity thinkers on logic and metaphysical presuppositions. Revivals depended on the commonsense notion of human freedom: people can choose, people do choose, people must choose. Rather than being tangled in a web of **Calvinistic** determinism, Dwight saw that revival was often the outcome of religious practices such as preaching, spiritual counseling, and instruction. Unlike the New Divinity theologians, who placed greater emphasis on divine sovereignty in the process of election to salvation, Dwight emphasized the significance of the human response in conversion. Revivalists such as Lyman Beecher, **Nathaniel William Taylor,** and **Charles Grandison Finney** developed these convictions yet further, and helped to usher in a non-Calvinistic, Arminian, and more human-oriented **theology of revivals** from the 1820s through the 1850s.

Besides his role as a revivalist and theologian, Dwight was an ardent Federalist who attempted to keep the Connecticut Congregationalist churches from being disestablished by law. This earned him the title "Pope of Federalism." Dwight died in 1817 in New Haven, Connecticut.

Further Reading: Berk, Stephen E. *Calvinism versus Democracy: Timothy Dwight and the Origins of Evangelical Orthodoxy.* Hampden, CT: Archon Books, 1974; Cunningham, Charles C. *Timothy Dwight, 1752–1817: A Biography.* New York: Macmillan, 1942; Fitzmier, John R. *New England's Moral Legislator Timothy Dwight, 1752–1817.* Indianapolis: Indiana University Press, 1998; Keller, Charles Roy. *The Second Great Awakening in Connecticut.* New Haven, CT: Yale University Press, 1942,

Arthur Dicken Thomas Jr.

DYER, MARY BARRETT
(ca. 1605–1660)

Mary Barrett Dyer is remembered today as a **Quaker** martyr for religious freedom in Puritan New England. A protégé of Ann Hutchinson, Dyer became a Quaker who gave her life in obedience to what she felt was a divine command to protest against the merciless anti-Quaker laws of **colonial** Massachusetts. Dyer was born Mary Barrett in England, probably between 1605 and 1610, although nothing is known of her life before her marriage in London in 1633 to William Dyer. They are first found in Boston in 1635, when both were admitted to membership in the Boston church. Their admission to full membership bespeaks a firm Puritan commitment. Within a few years, however, the Dyers found themselves embroiled in controversy with Governor John Winthrop and many of the colony's ministers. The Dyers were followers of Ann Hutchinson, who criticized the Puritan churches in Massachusetts as insufficiently reformed and many of their ministers as compromised with a "covenant of works." Hutchinson—who believed herself to be a faithful Puritan, and yet also can be seen as anticipating certain Quaker ideas—asserted that at times she received revelations directly from God. The bitter controversy ended with Hutchinson's banishment to Rhode Island in 1637. The Dyers and other supporters accompanied her. Winthrop made Mary Dyer a particular target by spreading a story that a deformed, stillborn child to which she had given birth while in Boston was a "monster," a sign of divine judgment on her for her heresies.

In 1652, Mary Dyer and her husband returned to England. She remained there for five years, becoming a convert to Quakerism. Quakers were known for their commitment to public **preaching** by **women,** and New England Puritans considered them the most pestilential of all sects. When Dyer landed in Boston on her way home to Rhode Island in 1657, she was immediately arrested and jailed before being banished. By 1658, Massachusetts had made it a capital crime for a Quaker to return to the colony after having been banished. The impact of the law was to draw Quakers to the colony as a protest, and Dyer joined them. In September 1659, she was reprieved while actually on the gallows in Boston. After spending the winter in Rhode Island, she felt impelled to return to Massachusetts again. She was quickly arrested and hanged in Boston Common June 1, 1660.

Further Reading: Rogers, Horatio. *Mary Dyer of Rhode Island.* Providence, RI: Preston and Rounds, 1896; Worrall, Arthur J. *Quakers in the Colonial Northeast.* Hanover, NH: University Press of New England, 1988.

Thomas D. Hamm

E

ECSTASY, THEORIES OF

Psychologists identify ecstasy as a state of intense emotional arousal. Such a state is typically positive and often associated with religion. Early American revivalists such as **Jonathan Edwards** have accepted genuine ecstasy as something coming from God and distinguished it from counterfeit ecstasies produced by purely natural means. During the twentieth century, Fundamentalists and evangelicals, whose approach to their faith is largely cognitive, differed from **Pentecostals,** who stressed the experiential and affective aspects of Christianity. The **baptism in the Holy Spirit** as taught and experienced by Pentecostals is often an ecstatic and intensely emotional or affective experience. Associated with Spirit baptism are such practices as **speaking in tongues,** casting out demons (exorcism or **deliverance**), and **bodily manifestations** such as falling down, **shouting,** and religious **dancing.** Likewise, the **Charismatic Revival and Renewal** since the 1960s in the mainline Protestant and **Roman Catholic** churches has sought to renew religious faith by the cultivation of affective experiences. One of the most distinctive of these experiences is the **holy laughter** associated with the **Toronto Blessing** since the mid-1990s. The insistence on **conversion** experiences in evangelical Protestantism may trigger emotional crises and result in a transformation of belief and behavior—such as that exemplified by the conversion of the apostle Paul (Acts 9).

Ecstatic states have been recognized in all cultures of the world. Anthropologists often interpret them as states of trance in which depersonalization (i.e., loss of self-awareness) occurs. In contexts where the culture supports beliefs in spirits, depersonalization may be interpreted as spirit possession. A possessing spirit may be demonic, benign, or morally ambiguous. Whatever the purported cause, however, possession is associated with ecstatic behavior and is easily identified by its intense emotionality. Anthropologists have speculated that ecstatic states function as an outlet for emotional expression among the exploited in a culture, and hence occur with greater frequency among **women,** members of minority groups, and the lower social classes. Yet the prevalence of ecstatic states among all social groups and classes in modern Western cultures suggests that human beings have a need to experience positive emotional states to which they can attribute meaning and especially transcendent meaning. This need may help to explain the permanent appeal of religion.

Social scientists—including anthropologists, historians, psychologists, and sociologists—have long focused upon the study of ecstasy that occurs in religious contexts or is eventually given a religious interpretation. If one assumes that certain ecstatic experiences can be separated from the interpretation attached to those experiences (a debatable proposition among today's scholars), then it is possible that various bodily states of arousal could lend themselves to a variety of interpretations. Under this assumption a state of intense physiological arousal interpreted in religious terms constitutes the experience of religious ecstasy. Thus physiological arousal alone is not sufficient to constitute the experience of ecstasy. Religious framing is needed for the experience to be identified as possession by the Holy Spirit, as conversion, or as another sort of religious occurrence. For any experience to be identified in a meaningful way a cognitive frame must be applied to bodily arousal. A religious cognitive frame allows for religious ecstasy, while nonreligious frames allow for secular experiences of ecstasy that have no religious significance. A religious framing of ecstatic states serves both to elicit affective experiences as well as to control the range of their expression. Even Pentecostalism restricts the range of ecstatic expression. Most Pentecostal congregations allow speaking in tongues, dancing, or even shouting, but only certain small groups—especially in **Appalachia**—endorse such dangerous practices as the handling of poisonous **serpents or fire** in worship services.

The distinction between experience and interpretation has led social scientists to focus on the tension between religious and scientific interpretations of ecstasy. It has long been noted that religious ecstasy has similarities to sexual ecstasy, and that for some it may be a substitute. Psychoanalysts have long proposed that the expression of repressed sexuality gives rise to an ecstatic state. This has led both social scientists and religious believers to be reluctant to consider intense emotional arousal as a criterion of religious truth. For some critics of religion, what the faithful interpret as an experience of God might be explained as a hypnotic trance based on illusion. Psychologists have produced experiences by means of hypnosis that seem indistinguishable from spontaneous experiences of God,

thus bringing back the problem recognized by Jonathan Edwards that there could be counterfeit ecstasies—produced by purely natural means—that simulate genuine experiences of God.

Even more controversial is the use of chemicals to elicit experiences of ecstasy that are difficult to distinguish from spontaneous religious experiences. In many cultures, chemicals have been used in both religious and secular settings to produce ecstatic states. From the Native American use of peyote and the Brazilian use of ayahuasca to the use in North America of LSD-25 (lysergic acid diethylamide), DMT (N,N-dimethyl-tryptamine), or MDMA, also called Ecstasy (3,4-methylenedioxymethamphetamine), neuropsychologists have documented the physiological processes by which ecstatic states are produced. For those who believe that such chemicals facilitate an otherwise naturally or supernaturally elicited ecstatic experience, the term *entheogen* is now preferred to the older, more secularized term *psychedelic*. Whether ecstatic states produced through chemicals can also be interpreted as God-caused may be debated. Some authors speculate that the origin of religious belief is linked to naturally occurring entheogens, which produce the states of consciousness and affective intensity that theologians have long struggled to understand.

Another controversy—in some ways paralleling the debates over chemically induced ecstasy—relates to the genuineness of conversions occurring in the context of religious revivals. Some charge that these conversions may be artificially produced, perhaps by means of hypnosis. The distinction between genuine and artificial conversions became harder to specify as social scientists have documented the process by which revivalists arouse ecstatic states. Yet even if a proximate cause of an ecstatic state is identified, one cannot rule out an ultimate transcendent origin for that ecstatic state. The psychology of religion cannot resolve the God question. Social scientists restrict their study to proximate causes, all of which are understood in purely naturalistic terms. William James, in *The Varieties of Religious Experience* (1902), set a pattern for later social scientists by focusing on the fruits or consequences of religious experience to identify their legitimacy or value, rather than the proximate causal conditions that elicit the experience and produce the intense affect. The psychological emphasis on the fruits of experience is consistent with anthropological and sociological studies of ecstasy. These studies show that the causes of ecstatic experiences provide little illumination or insight into their psychological, social, and cultural value for participants in, or observers of, these experiences. What is most important is that the ecstatic experience carries spiritual and religious meaning for the participant, regardless of how the experience is proximately caused. All emotional states are correlated with chemical alterations within the body. In this sense, ecstasy is *always* biochemically induced.

When ecstatic states are sought and supported by practices linking someone to a sense of the sacred or transcendent, and supported by social groups that form part of a faith tradition, ecstatic states serve to revitalize and affirm the central tenets and values of the faith tradition. Outside of such supports, experiences of ecstasy can become but isolated "highs" whose pleasure is episodic and without sustained fruits. On the other hand, when religion becomes simply cognitive—a matter of mere belief without emotive or affective experiences—then individuals are likely to seek alternatives where the passion of prophetic fervor can be nourished once again. The Charismatic Revival in both Protestant and Catholic churches is one recent example of the revitalization of established faith traditions by facilitating and supporting ecstatic experiences, interpreted within the framework of established faith traditions.

Further Reading: Burton, Thomas G. *Serpent-Handling Believers*. Knoxville: University of Tennessee Press, 1993; Forte, Robert, ed. *Entheogens and the Future of Religion*. San Francisco: Council on Spiritual Practices, 1997; Gardella, Peter. *Innocent Ecstasy: How Christianity Gave America an Ethic of Sexual Pleasure*. New York: Oxford University Press, 1985; Greeley, Andrew M. *Ecstasy: A Way of Knowing*. Englewood Cliffs, NJ: Prentice Hall, 1974; James, William. *The Varieties of Religious Experience*. 1902. Reprint,

People exhibit different affective and bodily responses in the midst of revivals, as shown in this photograph with some standing and others "overcome by the Spirit" at the Brownsville Assembly of God Church, Pensacola, Florida (ca. 1996–1997). Courtesy of photographer Cathy Wood.

Cambridge, MA: Harvard University Press, 1985; Lewis, I. M. *Ecstatic Religion: An Anthropological Study of Spirit Possession and Shamanism*. Baltimore: Penguin, 1971; Poloma, Margaret M. *Main Street Mystics: The Toronto Blessing and Reviving Pentecostalism*. Walnut Creek, CA: AltaMira Press, 2003; Taves, Ann. *Fits, Trances, and Visions: Experiencing Religion and Explaining Religion from Wesley to James*. Princeton, NJ: Princeton University Press, 1999.

Ralph W. Hood Jr.

EDWARDS, JONATHAN (1703–1758)

During his career as a pastor, **preacher,** revivalist, missionary, **Calvinist** theologian, and college president, Jonathan Edwards oversaw several awakenings within his own church at **Northampton,** Massachusetts, assisted with awakenings in many communities from Maine to Pennsylvania, worked to promote revivalism on an international scale, and published extensively on revival phenomena stemming from the **Great Awakening** of the 1740s. After his lifetime, his legacy for nineteenth-century revivalism and related topics such as **foreign missions** was profound, and he continues to be cited as an authority on **conversion** three centuries since his birth. Dubbed "America's Evangelical," he was arguably this country's most significant and influential practitioner of and commentator on revivalism.

The religious culture, and particularly the familial network, into which Edwards was born placed a strong emphasis on "awakenings," "stirs," or "harvests." As a scion of a powerful extended family within the New England ministerial elite, Edwards was inculcated with a fervent conversionist piety and a penchant to take particular notice of any signs of awakening within individuals or groups. His father, the Reverend Timothy Edwards, though now virtually unknown, was at the time one of the most successful revivalists in Connecticut, having overseen no less than five or six episodes in his church at East Windsor. One of Jonathan's earliest letters describes an awakening in his father's church in 1716. **Solomon Stoddard,** Jonathan's maternal grandfather, enjoyed a reputation as a great evangelist, especially as a preacher of "terror." Fear of hell, Stoddard held, was the first step toward evangelical humiliation and conversion. In his church at Northampton, during the late seventeenth and early eighteenth century, he pastored during five harvests of souls and published significant treatises such as *The Safety of Appearing on the Day of Judgment in the Righteousness of Christ* (1687), *A Guide to Christ* (1714), and *A Treatise on Conversion* (1719). Edwards's extended family also included members of the Williams family, chief among them the Reverend William Williams of Hatfield, who also was renowned as an awakening preacher.

With such a distinguished evangelical pedigree, it is not surprising that when Edwards entered the ministry himself he should seek to encourage the

Jonathan Edwards, portrayed by Joseph Badger, in the only picture done during Edwards's lifetime. The wig, for eighteenth-century males, was a mark of authority (ca. 1750–1755). Courtesy of the Yale University Art Museum.

revival spirit among his hearers. Shortly after becoming the colleague and heir apparent of Stoddard at Northampton, Edwards witnessed a minor revival following the earthquake of 1727 (see **Colonial Awakenings prior to 1730**). Under his grandfather's tutelage in the rhetoric of terror, Edwards warned of God's impending judgment if the people did not repent. This event, which caused concern and increased church membership throughout New England, was an important first step for Edwards, the young awakener.

After Stoddard's death in 1729, Edwards became the full pastor at Northampton and set about to further the revival spirit. Following Stoddard, he cultivated terror preaching on the eternity of hell's torments. He criticized the town's indifference to religion and its preoccupation with business, display, and contention. As an alternative, he preached the reality of "a divine and supernatural light" that renovated the soul and turned one's dispositions to the beauty of holiness. In particular, again following Stoddard's lead in past awakenings, he focused his attention on the young people in his care, exhorting them to reform and to seek true conversion.

Edwards began to see some rewards for his efforts in late 1733, when he noticed some "flexibleness" among the young people (Edwards, *Works*, 4:147). Shortly thereafter, there was "concern" in Northampton's westernmost hamlet of Pascommuck. By the spring of 1734, following the sudden death of a young man, the religious concern had become general. People flocked to Edwards's study to discuss the state of their souls. Religion became "all the talk." Worship services featured marvelous singing in four-part harmony. Doctrinally, Edwards focused on central tenets such as justification by faith alone in order to fight the incursion of what was called Arminianism, a term used somewhat indiscriminately to describe a variety of opinions that were generally non-Calvinist. The euphoria, characterized by a mood of Christian charity, continued through the spring of 1735. Edwards judged that over 300 souls had been converted, and during a two-year period he admitted nearly 250 people into Communion. In one Sabbath alone, 100 people were brought into covenant.

In the spring of 1735, Edwards penned a description of the Northampton awakening for the inquisitive Benjamin Colman, a prestigious Boston minister. Impressed with the account, Colman asked for a fuller rendition and published an abridgment of it in 1736 as an appendix to a sermon by William Williams. Colman sent the abridgment to the famous English dissenting ministers Isaac Watts and John Guyse in London, who asked for the full text and published it in 1737 as *A Faithful Narrative of the Surprising Work of God in the Conversion of Many Hundred Souls in Northampton*. A corrected edition appeared in Boston in 1738, as well as translations into German and Dutch.

A Faithful Narrative brought Edwards and Northampton international attention and made them reference points for the burgeoning **transatlantic** evangelical awakening. The work, written in a clinical style that reflected Edwards's interests in natural science, provided a sociological profile of the town's history and character and an extended

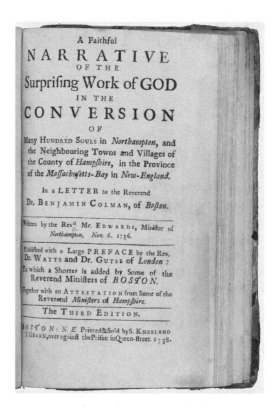

Edward's *Faithful Narrative* (1737) was both the first full-scale revival narrative and the most influential such work ever published. Already in a third edition by 1738, it offered a richly detailed account of the 1734–1735 revival in Northampton, Massachusetts. Courtesy of Dr. Kenneth Minkema.

discussion of "the manner of persons being wrought upon." Though there was a "vast variety," yet Edwards saw "a great analogy in all." Generally, concerned persons began by being convicted of their "miserable condition" and their danger of damnation. Realizing they could do nothing of themselves to change their condition, they experienced humiliation, a dependence on God for mercy and an acknowledgment of divine justice. Following this, persons were "awakened," sometimes suddenly, sometimes gradually, to "gracious discoveries" in their souls. Simultaneously, a "calm of spirit" and a thirsting after God filled them. To provide concrete examples of his conversion type, Edwards recounted the experiences of two individuals in his congregation: Abigail Hutchinson, a young woman who was fatally ill but who was converted before she died; and four-year-old Phebe Bartlett. With its mixture of social anthropology, dispassionate psychological theory, and affecting biography, *A Faithful Narrative* became a key text in the history of revivalism, a manual for other ministers to follow as they sought and guided their own congregations.

But even before *A Faithful Narrative* had been published, the Northampton revival faltered. Edwards's terror preaching had a gruesome effect on some. In early 1735, a Northampton man tried to commit suicide by cutting his throat. A few months later, Edwards's uncle, Joseph Hawley, certain that he was damned, slit his throat and died. The tragedy brought the awakening to an end and dramatically altered Edwards's relationship with his congregation. At no point during the rest of Edwards's time in Northampton would he enjoy the goodwill of his entire congregation. His pastorate would be incessantly contested in one way or another. With talk against the revival in the neighboring towns on the rise, in January 1736 a member of the Northampton congregation was brought to court, fined, and whipped for declaring that Edwards "was as great an instrument as the devil had on this side [of] hell to bring souls to hell" (Judgment against Bernard Bartlett, January 1736, General Session of the Peace, Hampshire County, Connecticut State Library, Hartford).

In response to the withdrawal of the awakening spirit, Edwards resorted to browbeating the congregation, comparing their present worldliness to their piety during the heights of late 1734 and early 1735. In a 1736 sermon on Matthew 5:14, the classic text on the "city on a hill," Edwards even appealed to the town's newfound reputation as a revival center as a means of goading his listeners at least to *behave* like Christians even if they could not *feel* like Christians. There were many critics of the revival who were carefully watching Northampton, and, Edwards warned, "if they see that there ben't answerable fruits, it will exceedingly confirm 'em in their rejecting all such things, as being nothing but mere whimsy and enthusiasm.... They will say, 'There is the

people of Northampton that experienced so much of such sorts of things. See what it comes to'" (Edwards, *Works*, 18:557).

After the Connecticut Valley revival and the backsliding of so many supposed converts, Edwards rethought his position on some important theological issues. Where before the revival an immediate experience of divine light in the soul was sufficient evidence of true conversion, afterward Edwards added persevering Christian practice. Indeed, Edwards now asserted that perseverance was a condition of justification and a means of assurance: "Not only the first act of faith," he wrote in "Miscellanies" no. 729, "but after-acts of faith, and perseverance in faith, do justify the sinner" (Edwards, *Works*, 18:335). In the winter of 1737–1738 Edwards preached a lengthy sermon series on the parable of the wise and foolish virgins to press home the point that a new spiritual sense and Christian practice were both essential signs of grace. Likewise, in manuscript notebooks such as "Sign of Godliness" and "Directions for Judging of Persons' Experiences," entries from the late 1730s and thereafter stressed holiness and practice.

A feature of his parishioners' religious practice that Edwards did not like was their habit of talking about their spiritual experiences in inappropriate ways. In a letter of July 1, 1751, to the Scottish minister Thomas Gillespie, Edwards wrote that when he came among the people of Northampton, he "found it to be too much a custom among them without discretion, or distinction of occasions, places, or companies, to declare and publish their own experiences; and oftentimes to do it in a light manner, without any air of solemnity. This custom has not a little contributed to spiritual pride, and many other evils" (Edwards, *Works*, 16:383). To Edwards, such declarations only led to spiritual pride. Even worse, those who spoke so breezily of their experiences often presumed on their elect state and thought they needed to do no more toward their salvation—they rested on a "supposed day of grace." In sermons beginning in the late 1730s, Edwards warned his hearers repeatedly against placing confidence in relations of religious experiences, against the deceptiveness of "talk of religion," and against making others' experiences their guide.

In the period between revivals Edwards turned to many topics, one of the chief being *A History of the Work of Redemption*, the subject of a sermon series of no less than 30 installments in 1739. Though primarily concerned with critical historical problems regarding the biblical narratives, the original sermon series, which Edwards intended (but did not live long enough) to turn into a major treatise, had its immediate impetus from the religious awakenings. Edwards depicted revivals, with their cyclical nature, as the vehicle that propelled God's providential plan forward.

Despite Edwards's best efforts to promote a new wave of religious attention among his flock, including ambitious sermon series as well as remedial sermons on topics ranging from the importance of Christian knowledge to the dangers of drunkenness, he could generate little interest. But in 1739 he heard of new British evangelists such as the Wesley brothers, and particularly **George Whitefield,** who was preaching to huge crowds and drawing great numbers to conversion. In the hopes that his people would respond, Edwards began the practice of communicating news of revivals elsewhere to his church. He solicited from his growing list of correspondents any reports they had heard of the "advancement of Christ's kingdom." In December 1739, Edwards received a letter from Whitefield, then in New York City, hinting that he could come to Northampton on an upcoming tour of New England. Edwards responded in February 1740 with an invitation to the Grand Itinerant to revive his congregation, though Edwards feared Whitefield might be "disappointed" because they were "more hardened" than most. On a positive note, Edwards did notice that, as with the previous revival, young people were beginning to show "more seriousness" (Edwards, *Works*, 16:80).

Whitefield was not disappointed, nor did he disappoint Edwards and those who gathered to hear him. In October 1740 he preached four times in Northampton and reduced everyone, including Edwards, to tears. Upon his departure, however,

Edwards was left with a congregation that was in a turmoil of excitement and anticipation. Many had been struck by Whitefield's preaching and impressed by his dramatic style. What would happen next? Edwards saw it as his responsibility to make some distinctions about Whitefield and his preaching. In a sermon series on the parable of the sower, he counseled his hearers not to dwell on the eloquence of the speaker or the beauty of his gestures but rather to examine themselves to see if the message he came to deliver—the "new birth"—had any effect. Indeed, as Edwards had conducted Whitefield to East Windsor, to preach at his father's church, he had taken exception to Whitefield's teachings on "impulses" and **assurance of salvation.** After that conversation, Edwards noticed that Whitefield, while cordial, never "made so much an intimate of me, as of some other" (Edwards, *Works*, 16:157). Nonetheless, because Whitefield represented the best hope for widespread revival, Edwards did not criticize him to any great extent in public.

Once again Northampton was experiencing an awakening, and once again the young people led the way. In mid-December "a very considerable work of God appeared among those that were very young," and by spring the "engagedness of spirit" among children and youth was general. Edwards encouraged the youth to meet in separate "conferences" for religious conversation and **prayer,** a revival strategy that complemented exercises involving the entire congregation (Edwards, *Works*, 18:116–17). These meetings continued through the summer of 1741, at which time some were crying out and fainting during worship. Edwards noticed that this revival differed from the previous one in that people were affected "more sensibly and visibly ... by external effects" (Edwards, *Works*, 16:119–20).

Edwards noticed other differences between the earlier and later awakenings in Northampton. There were not nearly as many supposed conversions, and only a small fraction of the number admitted to church membership during 1734–1735. Edwards had learned from the "Little Awakening" not to be so sanguine about persons' professions of their experiences. He was more cautious about claiming converts and admitting new communicants. Also, whereas in 1734–1735 Edwards could claim that people of various ages were touched, in the early 1740s he could find virtually no one from older age groups. Indeed, older church members, many of them brought into the church under Stoddard, were uncertain about or even hostile to the new round of revivals. Edwards's nearly constant focus on the youth contributed to this hostility, but there was doubtless some trepidation about itinerants like Whitefield and the **bodily manifestations** exhibited by some converts. Opposition to the Great Awakening among mature church members seems not to have been restricted to Northampton, and the resulting intergenerational tensions contributed to its divisiveness. Even more, many of the young people in whom Edwards had placed such hopes were implicated in the "Bad Book" episode of 1744, in which young men were caught reading illustrated midwives' manuals and harassing young women.

In the early 1740s, Edwards seems to have had more success as an awakener elsewhere than in his own church. Whitefield had provided the real catalyst, and in early 1742, the young minister Samuel Buel, filling Edwards's pulpit while he was away on a preaching tour, raised the revival spirit to unprecedented heights. Even Sarah Pierpont Edwards, Edwards's wife, experienced her most dramatic religious raptures under Buel's preaching. Meanwhile, during late January and early February, Edwards was preaching to great acclaim in eastern Massachusetts. Several months earlier, in July 1741, a sermon he preached in Enfield set off a dramatic reaction in the congregation. That sermon, "Sinners in the Hands of an Angry God," became a standard for Edwards on his tours, not to mention the one text most associated with him. Though known as an observer of revival phenomena, "Sinners," with its rich use of imagery, shows Edwards's skill as an awakener.

Already established as an expert on revivalism by virtue of A Faithful Narrative, Edwards extended his observations in several treatises during the 1740s. The Distinguishing Marks of a Work of the Spirit of God (1741), Some Thoughts Concerning the Present Revival (1743), and most importantly, A Treatise Concerning Religious Affections (1746) developed a series of "positive" and "negative" signs or marks of true grace in the soul. Distinguishing Marks was first preached at Yale College and was meant to sway the wary rector and faculty to support the revivals. Some Thoughts was a defense of the revivals in response to published condemnations by leading clergy such as **Charles Chauncy** of Boston. Edwards's continuing emphasis on persevering Christian behavior, first seen after the decline of the Connecticut Valley revival, culminated in the 12th and final sign of Religious Affections: "Gracious and holy affections have their exercise and fruit in Christian practice" (Edwards, Works, 2:283). Today, Religious Affections remains one of the most cited texts on revival and conversion psychology.

The 12th sign was as much a lesson learned from Edwards's personal experience as a participant in revivals as it was a response to critics of the revivals who were complaining about the enthusiasm, or irrational behavior, and social disorder that attended them. Converts exhibited all manner of strange bodily manifestations, **women** and **African Americans** were preaching, and those in authority were maligned as unconverted and ungodly if they did not support the New Lights, or pro-revival party. Old Lights, or opposers of the revivals, argued that religion was rational and reasonable, and that a truly Christian society would be calm, orderly, and observant of the proper social hierarchy. The revivals, they feared, were raising the devil more than the Holy Spirit.

If Edwards was not an Old Light, neither was he a thoroughgoing New Light. He, too, feared the disruption of traditional roles and classes. He opposed laymen preaching in public because such a practice challenged the established clergy, and he led a council that condemned the exhorter Bathsheba Kingsley of Westfield. Most significantly, he led the group of ministers that in 1743 convinced **James Davenport,** the controversial preacher operating in the New London, Connecticut, area, to recant. Through the late 1740s, Edwards also inveighed against Separatists, radicals who split off from the standing churches to form churches of their own that would be friendly to New Light sentiments and preaching.

Edwards found other ways to promote revivals that were more palatable to his social conservatism. In conjunction with Scottish evangelicals, he proposed and coordinated quarterly days of prayer for the "pouring out" of God's Spirit. Edwards first broached the idea of a "concert for prayer" in November 1745, and was gratified that it was well received. To further promote the plan, he published *An Humble Attempt* in 1748, prefaced by the original proposal from his Scottish friends. *An Humble Attempt* illustrates the element of **eschatology** or millennialism in Edwards's view on the revival, which peaked in the early 1740s as Northampton and other towns saw renewed conversions. For Edwards, the awakenings were the prelude to the "glorious times," when the church on earth would enjoy a thousand years of peace before the second coming of Christ. In his most optimistic moment, Edwards asserted that the millennium would begin in New England, but this seems to have been a passing fancy for him. Instead his general perspective on revival and the spread of the gospel was global in its scope, and not narrowly focused on North America.

Edwards's participation in the concert of prayer movement highlights his role in the developing international evangelical network. Through correspondence, published journals, educational centers, and charitable organizations, these evangelicals on the Continent, in England, and in America worked to promote, coordinate, and report revivals from a transatlantic perspective. Edwards included among his correspondents Isaac Watts, the famous English dissenting minister and author of **hymns,** and Scottish Presbyterians John Erskine and James Robe, noted for their part in the Cambuslang revival in Scotland in 1742, not to mention a number of provincial leaders, such as Governor Jonathan Belcher and Sir William Pepperrell, who were sympathetic to the evangelical awakening.

Following his dismissal from Northampton in June 1750, Edwards's interest in revivals did not wane, though he never again was personally involved in so large an event as those at Northampton. At his new post as the missionary at Stockbridge, Massachusetts, he could report several new Indian converts, and was greatly interested to learn of awakenings among the students at the newly founded College of New Jersey, where he would serve as president for a few short months before his death in March 1758.

Whatever hard lessons Edwards learned from his experience, his example and writings influenced the history of international revivalism and missions for more than a century after his death. Edwards's works, such as *A History of the Work of Redemption*, were instrumental in the revivals of the 1790s, conducted largely by leaders of the New Divinity, the theological movement spawned by Edwards. In the early nineteenth century, **Lyman Beecher** agreed with the "judicious Edwards" in locating the causes and consequences of the Great Awakening, and **Charles G. Finney** quoted Edwards at length in justifying his revival methods in his preaching in upper New York State. The period was also marked by a tug-of-war between representatives of Andover, Yale, and Princeton seminaries over the currency of Edwards's observations on revivals, among other issues. Through these and later debates, Edwards has become inextricably identified with the Great Awakening and with subsequent revival movements in America and abroad.

Further Reading: Conforti, Joseph A. *Jonathan Edwards, Religious Tradition, and American Culture.* Chapel Hill: University of North Carolina Press, 1995; Crawford, Michael J. *Seasons of Grace: Colonial New England's Revival Tradition in Its British Context.* New York: Oxford University Press, 1991; Curtis, Finbarr. "Locating the Revival: Jonathan Edwards's Northampton as a Site of Social Theory." In Michael J. McClymond, ed., *Embodying the Spirit: New Perspectives on North American Revivalism,* 47–66. Baltimore: Johns Hopkins University Press, 2004; Lambert, Frank. *Inventing the Great Awakening.* Princeton, NJ: Princeton University Press, 1999; Marsden, George M. *Jonathan Edwards: A Life.* New Haven, CT: Yale University Press, 2003; Miller, Perry, et al, eds. *The Works* of *Jonathan Edwards*. 23 vols. New Haven, CT: Yale University Press, 1957–2004; Tracy, Patricia. *Jonathan Edwards, Pastor: Religion and Society in Eighteenth-Century Northampton*. New York: Hill and Wang, 1980.

Kenneth Minkema

ELIOT, JOHN (1604–1690)

John Eliot was a Puritan clergyman and missionary among Native Americans in **colonial** New England for more than four decades in the seventeenth century. Born in 1604, he was the third of seven children whose father was a prosperous landowner in the English shire of Essex. He received an AB degree from Jesus College, Cambridge University, in 1622 and shortly thereafter was ordained a priest in the Anglican Church. Uncomfortable with regular parish work, he taught for a time at a grammar school whose master, Thomas Hooker, had such strong Puritan convictions that Eliot later said his religious life really began only with Hooker's influence. A group of local friends asked Eliot to serve as their minister and to accompany them to the Massachusetts Bay Colony. He agreed to both requests, arriving in Boston aboard the *Lyon* on November 3, 1631.

After a brief stint as teaching elder in the Boston church, Eliot settled as minister to the congregation that his friends had formed in Roxbury. He served as pastor and schoolmaster for more than 57 years, providing spiritual counsel and intellectual guidance for two full generations. Eliot had been good at classical languages and Hebrew at Cambridge, and so he welcomed the chance to learn the local Indian language when an opportunity arose in 1643. Within three years he had acquired a modest proficiency in speaking Massachuset, one of the many dialects of the Algonquian linguistic family. Pastoral duties at the Roxbury church were always his primary responsibility, but Eliot also pioneered in evangelical efforts among Native Americans, and that is where he gained lasting repute.

The message that Eliot conveyed to native listeners was rooted on Puritan theology. He began by emphasizing on the sinfulness of all humankind, and then dwelled on the dreadful wrath of God that

was in store for those who broke the Almighty's commandments. Christ's sacrificial death provided grace sufficient to rescue those whom God chose to redeem from deserved punishment. He promised that this blessing brought the grace of **conversion** to the chosen recipients, and thereafter they had the capacity to reform their moral habits and to enter into covenants with like-minded believers. Eliot **preached** these classic **Calvinist** tenets in his home church and whenever he visited Indian settlements.

Natives in the Western Hemisphere were nonliterate peoples, and it was Eliot's task to reduce the Massachuset tongue to writing. Over the years he compiled a dictionary and a grammar, essential tools for translating Puritan tracts into Algonquian. He imported a printing press for this purpose and produced many pamphlets and a catechism related to conversion experiences and a pious lifestyle. After issuing a translation of the New Testament in 1661, he published *Mamusee Wunneetapanatamwe Up-Biblum God* in 1663, the first complete Bible printed in North America. All this activity stemmed from the Puritan conviction that a proper evangelical spirit derived from a knowledge of sacred scripture and sound theology. These in turn were based on literacy, and Eliot labored to furnish native converts with the instruction that he regarded as essential to Christian identity.

In addition to spreading the gospel among natives, Eliot also brought greater attention to evangelism by publishing accounts of his work for English readers. This mild propaganda increased philanthropic contributions and allowed Eliot to obtain land grants for establishing Christian native communities. Permanent settlement in one place was not a trait among Native Americans, but the Puritan version of Christianity insisted on it, and Eliot urged converts to form new villages where they could regulate their lives according to scriptural standards. Fourteen such self-governing communities were created around Boston, and Eliot, along with a few other Puritan ministers, brought an estimated 10 percent of the Massachuset population under Christian influence. Yet a native uprising in 1675–1676 known as King Philip's War had a disastrous effect on missions and the "Praying

Elliot preaching to the Indians.

Puritan minister John Eliot preaching to the Indians of Massachusetts, presumably in the Massachuset language that he had learned to communicate with them. (Samuel G. Goodrich, *A Pictorial History of America*, New Orleans, 1852.)

Indians." During the conflict the native Christian population dwindled past recovery. Eliot continued his efforts after the war, but subsequent responses to gospel preaching were lukewarm. Natives did not blame him specifically, but they were increasingly wary of the dangers latent in English culture. Eliot's personality was gentle and outgoing. These traits caused many to admire him as an exemplar of Puritan sainthood, an octogenarian who was highly regarded on both sides of the Atlantic.

Further Reading: Eliot, John. *Indian Dialogues*. 1671. Reprint, ed. Henry W. Bowden and James P. Ronda. Westport, CT: Greenwood, 1980; Winslow, Ola E. *John Eliot: Apostle to the Indians*. Boston: Houghton Mifflin, 1968.

Henry Bowden

EMANCIPATION

see Abolitionism and Revivals

END-TIMES

see Eschatology and Revivals; Jehovah's Witnesses; Miller, William; Seventh-day Adventists; White, Ellen Gould (Harmon)

ENTHUSIASM

see Anti-revivalism, History and Arguments of; Ecstasy, Theories of

ESCHATOLOGY AND REVIVALS

The relationship between eschatology and revivals has been complicated. Revivalists have used eschatology to shape their message and method, and leaders with strong eschatological views have used revivals to organize new religious movements. Eschatology is the study of "last things" and includes both individual and cosmic concerns—what happens to people after they die, divine judgment, heaven and hell, and the end of the world. Such notions have always been powerful themes in revival **preaching**, especially the reality of divine judgment and the eternal destiny of individual persons. Accordingly, revivalists have pressed home that "it is appointed unto men once to die, but after this the judgment" (Hebrews 9:27) and "prepare to meet your God" (Amos 4:12). So central are such themes that some have stereotyped revival preaching as essentially a fire-and-brimstone warning of coming judgment for all who reject God's offer of salvation, as illustrated by America's most famous sermon, **Jonathan Edwards**'s "Sinners in the Hands of an Angry God." Even revivalists like **Dwight L. Moody** who emphasized God's abundant love for sinners have also preached the realities of coming judgment and the inevitability of hellfire for the unrepentant. Without these themes, most revival preachers believe, they would lose much of their power to persuade.

At times revivalists have understood spiritual awakenings within a larger, cosmic eschatological framework. Jonathan Edwards viewed the revivals in the mid-1730s as harbingers of the last days and the coming millennium. In *Some Thoughts concerning the Present Revival of Religion in New England* (1743), he argued that the **Great Awakening** in New England could well be "the beginning of the great work of God" (Edwards, *Works* 4:353–58) prophesied in the Bible that would eventually Christianize the world and usher in a millennial age of faith and prosperity. Edwards did not expect the millennium to arrive anytime soon, since the last days for him consisted in a long period of alternating conflict and progress until the final victory of the gospel and the return of Jesus Christ.

In the **Second Great Awakening,** many advocates used such postmillennial views to support and explain the success of revivals and their social reform spin-offs. Yet unlike Edwards, many revivalists believed the millennium was imminent (i.e., coming very soon). In the early 1830s **Charles Finney** and **Lyman Beecher** predicted that if the churches tried a little harder, the millennium might arrive in only three months (or three years). This optimism and confidence that God was Christianizing the world through revivals and other human endeavors remained a mainstream Protestant view throughout the nineteenth century, and it carried over into the Social Gospel movement of the early twentieth century. The term *postmillennialism* denotes the idea—characteristic of American Protestants during the early to mid-1800s—that the church's efforts in Christianizing the world would succeed, and that Christ's return was to come at the end of a golden age in human history.

Some people used the surge in revivals during the early 1800s to build new religious movements based on distinctive eschatological views. The **Shakers** followed the teachings of Mother **Ann Lee,** whom they considered the female incarnation of Christ, and prepared for the coming millennium by establishing communities where the sexes lived mostly apart and remained celibate. John Humphrey Noyes, one of Finney's converts, taught that Jesus had returned to earth in A.D. 70 but decided not to set up his kingdom until his followers demonstrated sufficient levels of authentic love. Accordingly, Noyes established a group in Putney, Vermont, and then the **Oneida Community** in upstate New York, where he encouraged his followers to have sex with each other's spouses under his careful and orderly supervision in a so-called complex marriage that would hasten the coming millennial kingdom.

Other movements used revival "new measures" to promote a premillennial understanding of the last days in which Christ will return to earth *before*

(not after) setting up his millennial kingdom. During the 1830s and early 1840s, the **Mormon** prophet **Joseph Smith** preached an imminent return of Christ and called his followers to gather in Jackson County, Missouri, in anticipation of the New Jerusalem that would be established there. Similarly, **William Miller,** a Baptist preacher from New England, used "millennial arithmetic" to predict Christ's Second Coming by October 22, 1844. Both the Mormons and the Millerites used the imminence of Christ's return to encourage followers to take decisive action and evangelize the lost before it was too late. The Mormons continue to expect a prophet's call to return to Missouri, and many Millerites formed a **Seventh-day Adventist** Church that still uses premillennialism as the centerpiece of its evangelistic efforts.

After the **Civil War,** revivalists increasingly presented a premillennialist outlook to their audiences, thanks to the arrival and spread of dispensationalism from Great Britain. This eschatological perspective predicted, among other things, the restoration of Israel, the coming of the Antichrist, the Great Tribulation, and the Battle of Armageddon before Christ's return. Premillennialism held that things would get worse before they got better. Cataclysm and suffering would come before Christ returned. Dispensationalism presented a complex system of biblical interpretation, centering on prophetic and apocalyptic passages in the Bible, and offering a kind of timetable of future events prior to Jesus' Second Coming. It placed the Jewish people at the center of God's purposes for the world, and insisted that all true believers would be caught up to meet Christ in the air in an event known as the rapture, and so escape the terrible afflictions of the Great Tribulation that awaited those still living on earth. This teaching became known as the doctrine of the pretribulation rapture. Dispensationalism started making inroads among conservative evangelicals in the late 1870s and it became an essential part of Fundamentalism and Pentecostalism by World War I. The annotated Bible edition produced by a Presbyterian layman in St. Louis,

Missouri—C. I. Scofield—and published as *The Scofield Reference Bible* (1909) did much to promote the tenets of dispensationalism. During the twentieth century about 10 million copies of this Bible edition were sold.

Starting with Dwight L. Moody, most of the major professional revivalists have been premillennialists of one kind or another: **Reuben A. Torrey, J. Wilbur Chapman, Billy Sunday, Billy Graham,** and almost all the Christian evangelists of **radio and television.** They have pointed to the imminence of the rapture and the certainty of Christ's return as important incentives to revival work, since so little time remains. Moody said that he looked on the world as a sinking ship and his revival preaching as a lifeboat; God told him to save as many "passengers" as possible before the end (Moody, New Sermons, 535). Dispensationalism also gave revivalists another tool for winning souls. Because the rapture might occur at any moment, sinners had no time to lose. In order to avoid being left behind after the rapture to experience the horrors of the Great Tribulation, sinners needed to decide for Christ now. The power of this left-behind argument has remained strong in and beyond revival circles, as illustrated by the number-one nonfiction bestseller of the 1970s, Hal Lindsey's *The Late Great Planet Earth* (1970); the Billy Graham Evangelistic Association's film *A Thief in the Night*; and Tim LaHaye's *Left Behind* fiction series (1996–present), with more than 60 million copies sold in less than a decade. Revivalists have also used the possible imminence of the rapture to help keep tempted believers on the straight and narrow: Would you want to be doing *that* when Jesus comes?

In short, revival preachers have used various eschatological teachings to promote their work and encourage decisions for Christ; and other religious leaders have used revivals to promote the building of new religious movements based on particular eschatological perspectives.

Further Reading: Edwards, Jonathan. *Works* 23 Vols. New Huron: Yale University Press, 1957–2004. Gaustad, Edwin S., ed. *The Rise of Adventism: Religion and Society in Mid-Nineteenth Century America.* New York: Harper and Row, 1974; Klaw, Spencer. *Without Sin: The Life and Death of the Oneida Community.* New York: Penguin, 1993; Marsden, George M. *Jonathan Edwards: A Life.* New Haven, CT: Yale University Press, 2003; McLoughlin, William G. *Revivals, Awakenings, and Reform.* Chicago: University of Chicago Press, 1978; Moorehead, James H. *World Without End: Mainstream Protestant Visions of the Last Things, 1880–1925.* Bloomington: University of Indiana Press, 1999; Morgan, Douglas. *Adventism and the American Republic: The Public Involvement of a Major Apocalyptic Movement.* Knoxville: University of Tennessee Press, 2001; Stein, Stephen J. *The Shaker Experience in America.* New Haven, CT: Yale University Press, 1992; Underwood, Grant. *The Millenarian World of Early Mormonism.* Urbana: University of Illinois Press, 1999; Weber, Timothy P. *On the Road to Armageddon: How Evangelicals Became Israel's Best Friend.* Grand Rapids, MI: Baker Academic, 2004.

Timothy P. Weber

EVANGELICAL ASSOCIATION

The Evangelical Association was a major expression of **German American** revivalism that arose in the Middle Colonies during the post-Revolutionary era of American history. Its founder, Jacob Albright (1759–1808) was a Pennsylvania-born farmer and Revolutionary War veteran of **Lutheran** parentage. Disturbed by the spiritual and moral decay of his Pennsylvania German society, he experienced conversion through a **United Brethren** preacher and joined a **Methodist** class. Due to the lack of Methodist **preaching** among the Germans, he felt burdened to assume that role, without the benefit of an official appointment. Classes were formed in 1803, and soon his followers ordained him as an "evangelical preacher," which name was adopted as the denominational title in 1816, after Albright's death. A German discipline for the "Newly Formed Methodist Conference," patterned after the Methodist Episcopal discipline, was published by his colleague, George Miller, in 1809, which was followed by the adoption of the title *Die Evangelische Gemeinschaft* (the Evangelical Association).

The mission to reach German Americans with the message of the necessity of the new birth and entire **sanctification** resulted in a shift from its early base in eastern Pennsylvania to the Midwest. Early preachers included, besides George Miller, the **hymn** writers John Walter and John Dreisbach. The election of John Seybert (1791–1860) as the first constitutional bishop in 1839 propelled the denomination on a growth trajectory, paced by Seybert's incessant itinerating throughout the Midwest and Ontario, planting hundreds of congregations among frontier German families. By 1848 he helped found a mission society that launched the first overseas mission, to the German homeland. **Foreign missions** were also founded in Japan (1876), China (1900), and Nigeria (1906), and a domestic mission in the Kentucky **Appalachian** Highlands (1919). The church held to an **abolitionist** position and remained on the forefront of social issues in the nineteenth century.

In 1891 the denomination split over issues related to language and conflicts among leaders, but it was reunited in 1922 to form the Evangelical Church. In the twentieth century, English began to displace German, though German publications, such as the periodical *Die Christliche Botschafter* ("The Christian Ambassador"), continued to be published until 1946. Three colleges and three theological seminaries were maintained, as well as numerous hospitals and benevolent homes in the United States, Germany, and Switzerland. A large order of deaconesses, the Bethesda Deaconess Society, flourished in Germany. The Evangelical Church has also contributed two presidents of the Federal and National Council of Churches in the United States since World War II. In 1946 the Evangelical Church, with over 300,000 members, joined with the Church of the United Brethren in Christ to form the Evangelical United Brethren Church, a body of over 700,000 members in the United States.

Further Reading: Albright, Raymond. *History of the Evangelical Church.* Harrisburg, PA: Evangelical Press, 1942; Behney, J. Bruce, Paul Himmel Eller, and Kenneth W. Krueger. *History of the Evangelical United Brethren Church.* Nashville, TN: Abingdon, 1979; O'Malley,

J. Steven. *Touched by Godliness: Bishop John Seybert and the Evangelical Heritage.* N.p.: Granite Publications, 1984.

J. Steven O'Malley

EVANGELICAL COVENANT CHURCH

The Evangelical Covenant Church is a denomination born of the **Pietist** renewal movement within the **Lutheran** Church of Sweden beginning in the early eighteenth century and reaching its height in the mid-nineteenth century. Founded by Swedish immigrants in Chicago in 1885, the premigration of Pietist believers in Sweden from the Lutheran Church to separate congregations, combined with the experiences in the new world, have defined the church's life and identity. A Covenant Church (*Svenska Missionsförbundet*) had been established in Sweden seven years earlier in 1878. The circumstances that led to its separation from the Church of Sweden had clear connections to the decision of the Covenant Church in North America to distinguish itself from the Lutheran Augustana Synod, founded in 1860. Identifying with a nonsectarian free-church tradition, the Covenant Church distinguished itself from Lutheranism by conceiving of itself as a believers' church (and not a folk or state church) and by seeing the Bible alone as authoritative. While valuing the Lutheran Augsburg Confession (1530) and other ancient and modern creeds and confessions of faith, the Covenant Church does not assign normative, interpretive value to them.

Renewal and revival have been crucial elements of the Covenant Church's beginnings and ongoing life. The background in Sweden was formative to this history. As Pietists, influenced by the classical Halle Pietism of Spener and Francke (brought to Sweden in the 1720s), a primary emphasis was "new life in Christ" and finding a balance of both head and heart. Many were also influenced by the **foreign missions** endeavors of Zinzendorf and the **Moravians,** with expressions of faith (especially in **hymns**) linking conversion as "the one thing needful" to missions at home and abroad.

The Covenanters were known as *läsare* (readers), because of their conventicles (i.e., small gatherings in homes and elsewhere) devoted to the Bible and devotional writings such as Johan Arndt's *True Christianity* (1606). These Swedish Pietists emphasized the role of an awakened laity and clergy that found unprecedented expression in secondary societies devoted to mission, evangelism, **temperance,** and other issues of social justice. From time to time, they faced fierce opposition from the Swedish government and state church, including a ban on conventicles from 1726 to 1858. The most notable leaders were George Scott, an English Methodist pastor in Stockholm from 1830 to 1842, and Carl Olof Rosenius (1816–1868), who organized the Evangelical National Foundation in 1856, to keep the revival within the umbrella of the Church of Sweden. It also provided a means of training and licensing lay colporteurs (i.e., distributors of religious literature), who led much of the evangelistic and mission work. Its spirit was one of ecumenical evangelicalism.

By the 1860s a more defined free-church movement within the Evangelical National Foundation was dividing its mission. The left wing, now known as Mission Friends, was led by Paul Peter Waldenström (1838–1917), who in 1870 precipitated a theological crisis over the State Church's Anselmic confessional interpretation of the doctrine of the Christ's atonement. They argued that God's love and not his wrath was the motive behind the cross, and that humanity rather than God was the one reconciled by the death of Christ. Waldenström based this challenge to legal doctrines of the atonement on an approach to biblical interpretation consistent with a more subjective Pietism, arguing that confessions can be challenged and are not binding. The reaction in Sweden and among Swedish immigrants in America was considerable. It proved to be a catalyst in the emergence of the Covenant Church as a believers' church.

While the earliest Augustana Lutheran congregation in the United States dates to 1848, the Mission Friends began arriving around the close of the Civil War. They formed four congregations in 1868,

separating from the Augustana Synod over perceived clericalism, formalism, and the synod's growing suspicion of the revival movement. The synod disapproved of the strong lay involvement in revivalism and the stress on conversion as a prerequisite for church membership. The Mission Friends attempted to find a Lutheran identity in America during the early 1870s by forming two new synods (the Mission Synod and the Ansgar Synod) to support and connect their newly formed congregations. By the end of the decade, the Mission Friends abandoned the synodical model in favor of the Covenant Church as it had been established in Sweden. By that time, Mission Friends were affected by Anglo American revivalism, particularly the methods of **Dwight L. Moody,** including mass evangelism and prophetic conferences. These influences were also present in Sweden to some extent. They were best represented in a newly arrived immigrant to America in 1876, Erik August Skogsbergh (1850–1939), who became the American Covenant's most notable evangelist. He was known as "the Swedish Moody," and there were many contacts with Moody's work in Chicago and elsewhere.

Prior to the formation of the Covenant Church in the United States in 1885, a conservative minority group emerged from the Mission Friends, with Fredrik Franson and J. G. Princell among its early leaders. They adopted the dispensational ecclesiology and **eschatology** of John Nelson Darby, and eventually took shape as a new denomination, the **Evangelical Free Church.** During the first immigrant generation among the Swedes, a commitment to missions and evangelism held together the two groups of Mission Friends—that is, the emerging Covenant Church and the emerging Evangelical Free Church. Nevertheless, the two groups soon diverged because of their differences in outlook. The Covenant Church has remained committed to its indigenous Lutheran Pietist renewal, while the Free Church has been more profoundly shaped by Fundamentalism and conservative evangelicalism. Throughout its history, the Evangelical Covenant Church has held the work of evangelism, renewal, discipleship, and mission as high priorities, consistent with its origins and its understanding of the church. It has conducted evangelism in a variety of ways over the decades, with the Department of Church Growth and Evangelism providing denominational leadership in this area.

Further Reading: Anderson, Philip J. "The Lively Exchange of Religious Ideals between the United States and Sweden during the Nineteenth Century." In Scott E. Erickson, ed., *American Religious Influences in Sweden*, 31–48. Uppsala, Sweden: Tro och Tanke, 1996; Frisk, Donald C. *The New Life in Christ.* Chicago: Covenant Press, 1969; Olsson, Karl A. *By One Spirit.* Chicago: Covenant Press, 1962.

Philip J. Anderson

EVANGELICAL FREE CHURCH IN AMERICA

The Evangelical Free Church in America (EFCA), headquartered in Minneapolis, Minnesota, is a relatively new Protestant denomination with **Scandinavian** roots, having been formed in 1950 as the result of a merger between the Swedish Evangelical Free Church and the Norwegian-Danish Evangelical Free Church Association. These earlier groups developed out of the immigration of revivalist Swedes, Norwegians, and Danes who came to the United States in the late nineteenth century. This revivalist mentality is illustrated by one of the founding fathers, Fredrik Franson (1852–1908), a Swedish American who worked with the famous American revivalist **Dwight L. Moody.** Franson conducted his own revivals and followed Moody's methodology, including a strong emphasis on **eschatology** and the imminent Second Coming of Christ.

Technically, the EFCA is an association of independent, self-governing churches rather than a denomination governed by a central authority. The church governance is strictly congregational, with 1,300 congregations in the United States and ministries in 45 countries throughout the world. Weekly attendance in these congregations is at 336,000 with only 19,000 non-English-speaking or non-Caucasian attendees. There have been five presidents in the history of the EFCA, which is currently headed by Dr. William J. Hamel, who has also served as the chairman of the National Association of Evangelicals. The distinctive characteristics of the EFCA are included in its name. The term *evangelical* means that it is committed to a conservative doctrinal statement that includes the inerrancy of the Bible and a belief in a premillennial eschatology. The term *free church* imply that the EFCA is not a separatist association, in contrast to many Fundamentalist denominations. This allows members to differ from the denomination's doctrinal statements on what are considered to be minor points of doctrine.

The leading educational institution for the EFCA is Trinity International University, located in Deerfield, Illinois. The school traces its heritage back to a 10-week Bible course held in the basement of one of the Chicago churches of the Swedish Evangelical Free Church in 1897. The old Norwegian-Danish Free Church Association trained its clergy at the Norwegian-Danish Department of Chicago Theological Seminary starting in 1884, which became the Norwegian-Danish Bible Institute and Academy in Rushford, Minnesota, in 1910. The school moved to Chicago under the name Trinity Seminary and Bible Institute in 1946. In 1963 the campus moved to Deerfield, Illinois, and the seminary was named Trinity Evangelical Divinity School (TEDS) and the undergraduate school Trinity College. Under the deanship of Dr. Kenneth Kantzer—formerly of Wheaton College, Illinois—several faculty members came to TEDS from Fuller Theological Seminary, partly as a result of Fuller's decision to adopt a looser definition of biblical inerrancy. TEDS has sought to provide a solid, evangelical education for students who come from a broad range of denominations and seek to serve the worldwide church. Another educational institutional under EFCA sponsorship is Trinity Western University, in Langley, British Columbia, Canada. In 1984, Trinity Western University became the very first "creedal" institution (i.e., governed by a written confession of Christian beliefs) to be accepted as a full member within the Association of Universities and Colleges of Canada (AUCC).

Further Reading: Lindberg, Frank T. *Looking Back Fifty Years over the Rise and Progress of the Swedish Evangelical Free Church of America.* Minneapolis: Evangelical Free Church of America, 1935; McDill, Thomas A. *A Living Legacy: Essays on the Evangelical Free Church Movement—Past, Present and Future.* Minneapolis: Free Church Publications, 1990; Olson, Arnold T. *"The Significance of Silence": The Evangelical Free Church of America.* Minneapolis: Free Church Press, 1981; Olson, Arnold, T. *This We Believe: The Background and Exposition of the Doctrinal Statement of the Evangelical Free Church of America.* Minneapolis: Free Church Publications, 1993.

Martin I. Klauber

F

FALLING

see Bodily Manifestations in Revivals

FALWELL, JERRY (1933–)

Born in Lynchburg, Virginia, Jerry Falwell is the pastor of Thomas Road **Baptist** Church and president of Liberty University, a conservative Christian college and graduate school that he began in 1971 as Liberty Baptist College. He is a second-generation **radio** preacher, with strong connections to American revivalism, having come to faith through the influence of *The Old Fashioned Revival Hour* and the **preaching** of **Charles E. Fuller.**

Converted as an 18-year-old, he attended the fundamentalist Baptist Bible College in Springfield, Missouri, where he graduated in 1956. He returned to his hometown of Lynchburg, Virginia, to found the Thomas Road Baptist Church with 35 people who had left another congregation in the city. He quickly embraced radio ministry and shortly thereafter **television** ministry. This led to his 1968 decision to begin the national television broadcast of the Thomas Road Sunday service called *The Old Fashioned Gospel Hour.* His use of creative means for financing his ministry led to conflict with the Securities and Exchange Commission, which sued him in 1973. A judge ruled in Falwell's favor, but Falwell adopted corporate methods of cost-efficiency, public relations, and fund-raising as a result of this episode. Like most Fundamentalists of his generation, he eschewed political involvement during the 1960s, when some mainline clergypersons were involved in the civil rights struggle and in demonstrations against the Vietnam War. He also confessed later that his early views had been racist. Yet by the 1970s he became overtly political, and separated himself from many of his former Fundamentalist associates. His decision to enter the political sphere did not sit well with them. A leading Baptist Fundamentalist, Bob Jones Jr., called Jerry Falwell "the most dangerous man in America."

Falwell is widely known for his outspoken positions on a number of moral issues, including abortion, pornography, and homosexuality. He is also recognized for his indefatigable support for the nation of Israel and criticism of public education. After efforts in the 1970s to address social and political issues, he founded the Moral Majority (1979) as a political lobby for education and legislation. He stepped down as president of the Moral Majority in 1987 in order to devote more energy to Liberty University. This decision did not, however, remove him from the public arena. He continues to appear on various television programs, answering questions and promoting his views.

The author of several books and numerous articles, Falwell wrote in *Listen, America!* (1980)

that there should be "no doubt that the sin of America is severe" and that the nation is "literally approaching the brink of national disaster." In 2001 he described the September 11 terrorist attacks as divine judgment upon America because of pagans, pro-abortionists, feminists, and homosexuals. He later backed away from these statements when he was severely criticized, even by conservative Christians. In his public statements, Falwell has supported both Christian missions and Jewish nationalism, arguing that "God raised up America in these last days for the cause of world evangelization and for the protection of his people, the Jews." He has defended his public and political public role by saying he is a "private citizen" and remains first and foremost a pastor-evangelist. He has sought, in his dual role, to create a spiritual revolution against negative social trends while also preaching and **praying** for revival. Falwell's theology can be described as Fundamentalist and dispensational. Yet his **conversion** and subsequent intellectual development brought together a pessimistic Fundamentalism with a more optimistic version of American revivalism. On the one hand, he believes that the world will grow worse, morally and spiritually, until Christ's return; on the other hand, he insists that the church has a role to play in promoting public morality.

Historian Nathan Hatch has argued that the American religious scene has regularly produced "popular leaders, persons who derive their authority not from their education or stature within major denominations, but from the democratic art of persuasion." Hatch notes that the ability of such popular leaders to stay "remarkably attuned to popular opinion" allows them "to rise from obscurity to command significant audiences and to organize movements and churches around them" (Hatch, 211). Falwell fits this description as well as any American minister over the last 40 years.

Further Reading: Baranowski, Shelley. "Jerry Falwell." In Charles H. Lippy, ed., *Twentieth-Century Shapers of American Popular Religion*, 133–41. New York: Greenwood Press, 1989; Falwell, Jerry, ed. *The Fundamentalist Phenomenon: The Resurgence of Conservative Christianity*. Garden City, NY: Doubleday, 1981; Falwell, Jerry. *Listen, America!* Garden City, NY: Doubleday, 1980; Falwell, Jerry. *Strength for the Journey: An Autobiography*. New York: Simon and Schuster, 1987; Hatch, Nathan O. *The Democratization of American Christianity*. New Haven, CT: Yale University Press, 1989.

John Armstrong

FASTING AND REVIVALS

Fasting is a voluntary abstinence from food for the purpose of gaining spiritual benefits. It has been a long-standing spiritual discipline in Christianity, and North American Protestants have engaged in this practice in order to promote church-based revival and personal renewal. In the context of revivalism, fasting has been viewed as a way of demonstrating the requisite humility before God that precedes a spiritual blessing and as a means of self-emptying in order to be filled by God. The physical hunger of the person fasting may symbolize a kind of spiritual hunger for God. The fasting believer has an attitude of dependence on God. In Christian contexts, fasting is almost always combined with **prayer.** Someone who practices prayer with fasting is able to pray in an uninterrupted fashion for long periods of time, without having to pause for meals. The discomforts and pains of hunger may be a reminder and an incentive to fervent, night-and-day prayer before God.

Different sorts of fasting exist, because there are different kinds of abstinence from food and drink, and because people determine in different ways the times when they will fast. Some give up all food and drink for a period, while others subsist on water only, consume fluids only (fruit juice, etc.), or abstain from certain kinds of food (e.g., meat, eggs, milk, etc.) but not others. Some fast according to a church calendar, and others fast whenever they perceive a need in their individual lives or in their social context for a concentrated effort in prayer. In **Roman Catholicism** and Eastern Orthodoxy, the most common sort of fasting for most adherents is abstention from meat during the season of Lent, for 40 days prior to Easter Sunday. Lent is a time for penitence and self-examination, and is fittingly accompanied by fasting. Traditionally, Roman Catholics also abstained from eating meat on Fridays. Among revivalistic groups, however, fasting most commonly takes place not according to a church calendar but in a more ad hoc fashion. Individuals set aside their own days for fasting, and, occasionally, churches may call for their entire community to fast and pray at a certain time. Especially since the 1980s, North American evangelicals and **Pentecostals** have increasingly engaged in prolonged water-only fasts for 3, 7, 14, 21, or even 40 days. Such lengthy periods of fasting have precedents in the Bible. The 40-day fast is based on Jesus' 40 days of fasting and temptation in the desert, paralleled by earlier fasts of Moses and Elijah (Luke 4:1–2; Deuteronomy 9:9; 1 Kings 19:8). While an absolute fast—that is, abstaining from all food and drink, including water—is possible for only a few days without endangering health and life itself, a water-only fast can last for weeks at a time.

Fasting was a familiar component of Puritan piety during the American **colonial** period, and it occurred in both public and private settings. Public fasts were frequently called during times of crises, since these were often viewed as God's judgment on sin. Theologian and **Great Awakening** leader **Jonathan Edwards** recommended fasting and prayer as a means to gain the favor of God's presence and usher in a great **eschatological** or end-times revival. Edwards believed that when Christians fasted, God was inclined to respond to their prayers for the advancement of God's kingdom. Fasting held a major place in the spiritual discipline of John Wesley, the founder of **Methodism** and promoter of revivals. In one of his letters, he suggested that the evangelical revivals had occurred in response to the church's prayer and fasting. For Wesley, fasting was a way for Christians to follow the example of ancient Christians, to strip away attachments to material things, to achieve solidarity with the poor, and, finally, to become more fully attuned to God's redemptive purposes.

In the tradition of Edwards and Wesley, contemporary evangelical, **Pentecostal,** and **Charismatic** Christians often draw a link between the widespread revivals of the past and the amount of prayer and fasting that preceded and sustained them. With growing urgency since the 1990s, leaders from these groups have called their constituency to engage in prayer and fasting as a way to promote revival. For instance, at the dawn of the new millennium the late Bill Bright, as president of **Campus Crusade for Christ,** called for 2 million North American Christians to join together in a 40-day fast "to pray for national and worldwide revival."

Some theorists have viewed fasting as a way of inducing an altered state of consciousness. They hold that the states of consciousness sometimes reported in revival meetings are induced by such practices as fasting. There could indeed be a link between fasting and susceptibility to altered states of consciousness. Yet it is obvious that not all revival participants or claimants to religious experience have engaged in fasting and not all revivals have emphasized it. Participants in the **Toronto Blessing** during the 1990s, for example, reportedly did not practice fasting during the early stages of the revival. Perhaps in reaction to consumerism and materialism, fasting and an ascetic, self-denying lifestyle (sometimes called "the fasted life") is gaining ground in certain circles in modern society. Robert Webster estimated in 2003 that there were some 624,000 Web sites dedicated to fasting and its religious or secular benefits. Scholars might consider whether these contemporary approaches to fasting reinforce an individualistic vision of spirituality or else contribute to a more widespread, communal revival.

Further Reading: Berghuis, Kent D. "Christian Fasting: A Theological Approach." PhD dissertation, Trinity International University, Deerfield, IL, 2002; Bright, Bill. *The Coming Revival: America's Call to Fast, Pray, and "Seek God's Face."* Orlando, FL: New Life Publications, 1995; Campus Crusade for Christ. "William R. 'Bill' Bright Memorial Website." http://billbright.ccci.org/; Chatham, R. D. *Fasting: A Biblical Historical Study.* 1987. Reprint, New Brunswick, NJ: Bridge-Logos, 1999; Piper, John. *A Hunger for God: Desiring God through Fasting and Prayer.* Wheaton, IL: Crossway Books, 1997; Prince, Derek. *Shaping History through Prayer and Fasting.* Old Tappan, NJ: Revell, 1973; Rogers, Eric N. *Fasting: The Phenomenon of Self-Denial.* Nashville, TN: Thomas Nelson, 1976; Towns, Elmer L. *Fasting for Spiritual Breakthrough.* Ventura,

CA: Regal Books, 1996; Webster, Robert Joseph, Jr. "The Value of Self-Denial: John Wesley's Multidimensional View of Fasting." *Toronto Journal of Theology* 19 (2003): 25–40.

Benjamin Wagner

FATHER DIVINE, GEORGE BAKER (1877–1965)

Father Divine, George Baker—who was also referred to as Major Jealous—was founder of the Peace Mission Movement (PMM) and one of the most colorful and controversial figures among all **African American** religious leaders. The PMM was founded in Valdosta, Georgia, in 1914; moved to Savannah, Georgia; and then was incorporated in 1919 in Sayville, Long Island, New York. Baker served an apprenticeship as a "latter Messiah" under St. John the Divine, Hickerson, and Samuel Morris—leaders in an elusive, little-known religious group. Divine has stated that he visited **Azusa Street revival** in Los Angeles, California in 1907, though he did not claim to have received the **baptism in the Holy Spirit** there. In general he and his followers said little about Baker's early life and the origins of their group.

Baker was born in 1879 in Rockville, Maryland, and in 1930, he took the name Father Divine. A woman named Eliza Mayfield claimed to be the mother of Father Divine. Yet when Divine was in Harlem his response was "You know God has no mother." As his fame grew, many regarded him as a public nuisance, and in November 1931 Divine with 80 of his followers was arrested and taken to court. After a jury trial of Divine and his followers as a public nuisance, Divine was sentenced to a term in jail and given a $500 fine. The judge, Lewis J. Smith, died of a heart attack on June 7, and Divine's followers later celebrated this date as an annual holiday. Divine's wife, Sister Penny, was known for her free dinners, and these were the forerunner of the lavish banquets that attracted followers. In 1942, Divine moved his PMM headquarters from the Hyde Park, New York, estate—where he was a neighbor of President Franklin D. Roosevelt—to Philadelphia, in order to escape a series of embarrassing lawsuits. Among these was Divine's 1941 trial on charges of lunacy. He traveled to New York City on the weekends to prevent his being arrested there.

Divine said his PMM represented all races, creeds, colors, and nations. He did not use a creed, scripture, or formal pattern in his religious services. Instead his meetings were occasions for songs, impromptu sermons, and banquets. The PMM provided food and lodging for members and visitors. It had an economic impact through its ownership of hotels, restaurants, grocery stores, barbershops, and coal businesses. Divine's "kingdom" stretched to many cities and states. After the death of his first wife, Divine in 1946 married a Canadian woman named Edna Rose Ritching, known as "Sweet Angel." She became the leader of the organization after his death in 1965. Though Divine's followers considered him to be immortal, he died from a heart attack at his mansion in Woodmont, Pennsylvania. The PMM's size and wealth is not public knowledge. The PMM exists outside of North America, in such countries as England, Sweden, Germany, Austria, and Switzerland. It continues with many members who today are senior citizens.

Further Reading: Baer, Hans A. "Peace Mission." In Stephen D. Glazier, ed., *Encyclopedia of African and African-American Religions*, 231–35. New York: Routledge, 2001; Harris, Michael. "Major J. (Father) Divine." In Charles H. Lippy, ed., *Twentieth-Century Shapers of American Popular Religion*, 110–18. New York: Greenwood Press, 1989; Harris, Sara. *Father Divine, Holy Husband.* Garden City, NY: Doubleday, 1953; Hoshor, John. *God in a Rolls Royce: The Rise of Father Divine— Madman, Menace, or Messiah.* New York: Hilman-Curl, 1936; Mother Divine. *The Peace Mission Movement.* Philadelphia: Imperial Press, 1982; Parker, Robert Allerton. *The Incredible Messiah: The Deification of Father Divine.* Boston: Little, Brown, 1937; Watts, Jill. *God, Harlem U.S.A.: The Father Divine Story.* Berkeley: University of California Press, 1992; Weisbrot, Robert. *Father Divine and the Struggle for Racial Equality.* Urbana: University of Illinois Press, 1983.

Sherry Sherrod DuPree

FATHER'S BLESSING

see Toronto Blessing

FIERRO, ROBERTO FELIX (1916–1985)

Dubbed as the "burned-over Irishman," Roberto Fierro was among the leading **Latino** and Mexican American evangelists of the twentieth century. After graduating in 1936 from the Latin American Bible Institute (LABI) of the **Assemblies of God** in San Diego, California, he was ordained an evangelist in 1941. Several years later he established one of the first Spanish-speaking **Pentecostal** radio broadcasts in the United States and became well known for his program *The Cross of Calvary*. His **radio** ministries continued without interruption for some 45 years. In the 1950s he founded the Latin American Evangelistic Association, established a newsletter to raise money and inform people of his crusade schedule, and claimed to have **preached** to more than a million people throughout the United States and Latin America. In 1956 alone he is said to have had more than 750,000 people attend his crusades in the United States, Mexico, and Puerto Rico, and to have won more than 52,000 converts. After a controversy with the Assemblies of God that centered on a personal loan that Fierro received and his unwillingness to submit to the denomination's Anglo leadership, he withdrew from the Assemblies of God in 1961. His later request in 1978 to be reinstated was granted. His fiery personality and preaching in Spanish and English won him support among Latinos and Anglos alike and made him a leading bilingual and bicultural evangelist.

Further Reading: De León, Victor. *The Silent Pentecostals: A Biographical History of the Pentecostal Movement among the Hispanics in the Twentieth Century.* Taylors, SC: Faith Print, 1979.

Gastón Espinosa

FINNEY, CHARLES GRANDISON (1792–1875)

Charles Finney was a renowned American revivalist, reformer, and educator. He was born in 1792 in Warren, Connecticut, the seventh child of Sylvester and Rebecca (Rice) Finney, who traced their ancestry to the origins of New England. His father, a poor farmer, had been a soldier in the Revolutionary War. When Charles was two years old, his parents joined the migration into New York State, settling in Kirkland, **Oneida** County, in the heart of what became known as the **Burned-Over District** (a region later associated with revivals and **new religious movements**). Here he grew up, tilling the soil and cutting trees, developing a strong constitution that served him during his long life. He attended the backwoods schools until he was 14, and then, in 1806, spent two years at the Hamilton Oneida Institute in Clinton.

In 1808 the family moved to Henderson, New York, on Lake Ontario, and Finney was asked to teach in the village school. For four years he did, and then moved to Warren, Connecticut, to live with an uncle, to prepare to enter Yale. His teacher, however, persuaded him that he could master the college curriculum by himself in two years. In the past he had endured backwoods **preaching.** Now for the first time he heard intelligent sermons as he attended the Congregational church. Finney admired the aged pastor, but was distressed that he delivered his sermons in "a monotonous, humdrum way of reading" (Charles G. Finney, *Memoirs* [1876], 6).

Leaving the Warren Academy in 1814, he went to New Jersey to teach in the public schools. Finney was handsome and athletic, six foot two inches tall, and had penetrating blue eyes. As their teacher he would challenge his male teenage students to athletic contests, and he always won, gaining their admiration. He was fond of dancing and of playing the cello. In 1818, the 26-year-old Finney returned to western New York State, tired of the teaching profession and somewhat restless. With a logical mind, and a strong voice, he considered the legal profession, and entered the law office of Benjamin Wright in Adams, New York as an apprentice. In Finney's study of the law, under Wright's tutelage, he found the Bible was often quoted in law books, and this intrigued him. He stated in his memoirs that when he began to study law, he was "almost as ignorant of religion as a heathen" (Rosell and Dupuis, 9). He began attending the **Presbyterian** church, and with his musical abilities he organized the youth into a chorus and trained them. The pastor of the church, a young Rev. George W. Gale, was friendly and a good preacher.

For three years Finney studied law under Wright, and sat under the preaching of George Gale. He became increasingly concerned about his salvation, and believed that if the soul is immortal he needed a great change in his inward state to be prepared for heaven. Still he procrastinated. Finally, on Sunday evening, October 7, 1821, he determined that the question of his salvation must be settled very soon. As he was walking to the law office on Wednesday morning, October 10, he stopped and exclaimed, "I will accept it today, or I will die in the attempt" (Rosell and Dupuis, 18). So he wrote in the celebrated account of his **conversion.** Finney went into the nearby woods, resolving to give his heart to God, or never come out from there. He cried out, "Lord, I take Thee at Thy word" (20). Immediately he found himself in a new state of joy and contentment. He **prayed** for hours. This and subsequent experiences were attended by great emotional excitement, in what he called "a mighty baptism of the Holy Spirit" (Charles G. Finney, *Memoirs* [1876], 20). For several days Finney was so moved by his conversion experience that he wept uncontrollably, spoke of God with everyone he met, and within a short time decided to enter the ministry.

As a law student, Finney had been trained in the use of plain and direct courtroom speech that could sway judges and juries. Despite his friendship with George Gale, he was critical of Gale's preaching style. Tied to his notes in the pulpit and somewhat formal in approach, Gale did not address the congregation directly as "you." Finney could not understand why pastors would not want to be as persuasive in the pulpit as lawyers were in the courtroom. He was also critical of Gale's **Calvinism,** with its doctrine of predestination. To Finney, "gospel salvation … [was] an offer of something to be accepted." All that was necessary to receive it "was to get my own consent to give up my sins, and give myself to Christ" (Rosell and Dupuis, 18).

Rev. Charles G. Finney with his wife Elizabeth. The penetrating gaze, often noted by Finney's hearers, is evident. Elizabeth, whom he married in 1848 after the death of his first wife, organized women's prayer meetings in conjunction with his revival services (1850). Courtesy of Oberlin College Archives, Oberlin, OH.

Despite their theological differences, Gale recognized Finney's exceptional gifts, and put him under the care of the St. Lawrence Presbytery as a ministerial candidate in the spring of 1823. The assembled clergy urged him to go to Princeton Seminary, and were dumbfounded when he replied that he would not put himself under such an influence as they had been under, that he was confident they had been wrongly educated, and they were not ministers that met his idea of what a minister of Christ should be. After that blast, the pastors struggled to regain their composure, but reluctantly agreed to allow Finney to study under Gale's direction. Opposed to Gale's views on the doctrine of Christ's atonement, Finney worked out his own theology on the basis of his study of the Bible. His sessions with Gale, said Finney, were little more than controversy. Gale held to the Old School Presbyterian doctrine of original sin and moral depravity, and when Finney wrote his memoirs in 1868, he claimed that he had denied these doctrines in 1823. But George Gale, writing in 1853, contradicted Finney's claim, saying, "when he [Finney] was licensed and first labored as a missionary, he was very firm and faithful in bringing out this doctrine [of election and original sin]" (Gale, *Autobiography*, 274).

The presbytery met again in December 1823, and among the other items of business was Finney's licensure to preach. When asked if he received the Westminster Confession (1648)—the basis of Presbyterian faith—Finney replied that he had never read it. Nevertheless in March 1824 the Female Missionary Society of the Western District of New York retained Finney as a missionary to Jefferson County, a rural district bordering Lake Ontario. In July 1824, he was ordained a Presbyterian minister, and began pastoral work in the villages of Antwerp and Evans Mills. Finney in this period was resistant to oversight by fellow ministers, and unmindful that he had been given exceptional treatment and sped throughout the process leading to ordination.

In Jefferson County, Finney worked out the evangelistic methods he would use in his ministry. They were based on civilized decorum—directness, relevance to life, and animation, but without sensationalism. He rejected emotionalism and fanaticism. Finney wanted no repetition of the **bodily manifestations** and other excesses of the **Cane Ridge revival.** His methods worked well, and soon Jefferson County was ablaze with revivals.

In October 1824 Finney married Lydia Andrews of Whitestown, Oneida County. A year later, they chanced to meet George Gale in Western, New York, near Lake Oneida. Gale and other church leaders implored Finney to preach there, and again revival broke out. After his stay in Western, in December he was invited to preach at the Congregational church in Rome, New York. There, his personal and extemporaneous pulpit style had great impact, but also his penetrating and hypnotic eyes riveted the congregation. Set under firm brows, his eyes were "large and blue, at times mild as an April sky, and at others, cold and penetrating as polished steel," one clergyman

wrote (William C. Cochran, *Charles G. Finney: Memorial Address* [1908], 16). A fitting companion to the eyes was his majestic voice. Many warned him that being dramatic on the pulpit might woo the lower classes, but would alienate the educated. As Finney suspected, the opposite proved to be the case: "They found that under my preaching judges, and lawyers, and educated men were converted by scores; whereas under their methods such a thing seldom occurred" (Rosell and Dupuis, 84). The Oneida County Revivals of 1825–1827 had begun. Finney left 500 new converts behind in Rome, New York, and then preached in Utica, Troy, Auburn, and other cities of New York State. This touched off seven years of intense revivals, brought in thousands of converts, and catapulted Finney into national prominence.

As Finney's fame grew, his practices came under increasing criticism. **Lyman Beecher** and **Asahel Nettleton** opposed him vigorously, charging that Finney had introduced "new measures"—praying for persons by name, allowing **women** to pray and testify publicly in mixed groups of **men** and women (in apparent contradiction of biblical teaching in 1 Timothy 2:12), encouraging persons to come forward in an **altar call** to the so-called anxious bench, mobilizing groups of workers to visit all homes in the community, and displacing regular church services with "protracted meetings" held for several weeks. Beecher called a meeting of evangelical leaders in July 1827 in New Lebanon, New York. Half the leaders were Finney's supporters, and for three days they debated. Though Beecher and Nettleton had planned to put Finney in his place, none of the resolutions passed by the delegates censured Finney, but instead supported and reinforced him. After much prayer the group adjourned, with Finney's views exonerated.

Lyman Beecher returned to Boston realizing that Finney's influence was growing. He then sought to calm the dissension and align himself with Finney. At the Presbyterian General Assembly in May 1828 there was an agreement between the two sides to halt further disagreement. Finney thus emerged, at age 36, as the leader of the Congregational-Presbyterian campaign for awakening in America, and the recognized head of the **Second Great Awakening.** Demands for his preaching came from cities on the eastern seaboard: Wilmington, Delaware; Philadelphia; and New York City. In the fall of 1830 he began a citywide campaign in Rochester, New York, and this was the first endeavor in American history that deserves to be compared with the urban evangelistic campaigns of the post–**Civil War** era. The entire city and area for miles around banded together in spiritual concern. For six months, from September to March 1831, Finney and a number of other evangelists held forth in multiple pulpits in the metropolitan region. Sectarianism was forgotten and all the churches cooperated. A distinguishing feature was the dignity of the proceedings. There was no falling in the aisles, no shouting of hallelujahs, but Finney, like a lawyer arguing before a jury, with wit and verve, persuaded manufacturers, millers, commercial tycoons, and others to respond to his call to the anxious bench. Taverns closed for good, barrels of liquor were emptied in the sewers, and the theater became a livery stable. Church membership in Rochester, New York, is said to have doubled in six months. This campaign was a watershed in attitudes toward Finney. Prior to Rochester, he was still suspect to many; afterward, he was widely accepted, and his work in this city was the high point of his evangelistic career.

In 1832 Finney, tiring of constant travel, became pastor of the Second Free Presbyterian Church in New York City, for the use of which Arthur and Lewis Tappan, wealthy merchants, had leased the Chatham Street Theater. In time he became dissatisfied with the Presbyterian denomination, and the Broadway Tabernacle was organized for him, its design being constructed according to his own wishes. He withdrew from the Presbyterians in 1836. While in New York he delivered lectures on revivals that were printed weekly in the *New York Evangelist*, and published as *Lectures on Revivals of Religion* (1835). Finney covered topics pertaining to the promotion of revivals and the proper treatment of converts. One of his most famous—and controversial—assertions was that "a revival ... is a purely philosophical result of the right use of the constituted means" (Finney, *Lectures* [1960], 13). With its emphasis on the *human* production of revivals and conversions, this contradicted the prevailing concept—deriving from Calvinistic theology generally and **Jonathan Edwards** more specifically—that revivals were unpredictable acts of God. Yet it was consistent with Finney's self-confident conviction that all that was needed for God to save a sinner was the person's own consent. Finney held that revivals, along with mass conversions, *could* and *should* happen. If Christians used sanctified common sense, by God's grace they *would* happen. The book went through many editions, was widely read abroad, and has had a great impact on many readers. Among those it influenced were the founders of the **Salvation Army,** Catherine and William Booth; George Williams, the founder of the **Young Men's Christian Association;** and **Francisco Olazábal,** the prominent early twentieth-century **Latino** preacher and **healer.**

Much of Finney's importance derives from his work as a reformer, as part of the so-called Benevolent Empire of nineteenth-century American Protestantism. During the first three decades of the nineteenth century, zealous Christians organized thousands of societies seeking to rectify every vice and problem of society. **Abolitionism, temperance,** Sabbath observance, the use of profane language, world peace, education, the rights of women—all these and other issues had societies devoted to them. From the Rochester crusade onward, Finney lent his influence to the entire spectrum of causes, and infused his followers with zeal. He was determined that new converts immediately be put to urgent work in the battle against sin; as he preached, "Every member must work or quit. No honorary members" (Finney, *Lectures* [1960], 404).

Finney began another phase of his long career when he left New York City to become a professor of theology at Oberlin Collegiate Institute in Ohio in 1835. This new school was founded to attract young converts from Finney's revivals, as well as supporters of his new measures and New School views. During the 40 remaining years of his life he was connected with Oberlin College, on which he exerted a powerful influence. From 1851 to 1866 he was president, although relieved of much administrative detail so he could devote some of his energies elsewhere. And from 1835 to 1872 he was also pastor of the First Congregational Church in Oberlin.

Finney carried on his evangelistic work during part of each year, leaving Oberlin and preaching in Boston, Rochester, and other cities. In November 1849 he arrived in England to hold meetings in a number of cities, finally preaching in **Whitefield's** Tabernacle in London until March 1851. He went to England again in 1859–1860, where his preaching had great effect. Finney had always aroused opposition, but as his theology developed at Oberlin, certain aspects of it brought new anger. Previously he had argued with aspects of Calvinism, but now he vexed his friends with evolving views that came close to Arminianism or even Pelagianism (i.e., the teaching that human beings possess an innate ability to obey all of God's commandments). The Oberlin faculty—**Asa Mahan,** John Morgan, Henry Cowles, and Finney—in 1836 began to stress perfectionism, the doctrine that perfect holiness or **sanctification,** or freedom from sin, can be attained in this life. While Finney and Mahan rejected the more radical forms of perfectionism, a widespread reaction to "Oberlin perfectionism" was mounted after 1839, with a number of Finney's longtime friends joining in condemning it.

In advancing his concept of a higher Christian life, Finney advocated a number of causes. He was strong—as was all of Oberlin—on abolitionism. He was an ardent advocate of temperance, and opposed the use of tobacco, and even tea and coffee. For a time Oberlin students experimented with the unusual diet of Dr. Sylvester Graham, and students became so weak that they had to abandon it. Although Finney had been a Mason in his youth, he published a book attacking the order, *The Character, Claims, and Practical Workings of Freemasonry* (1869). His *Lectures on Systematic Theology* were published in two volumes in 1846 and 1847, and after some revision, republished in England in 1851. His other works include *Sermons on Various Subjects* (1834), *Lectures to Professing Christians* (1837), *Skeletons of a Course of Theological Lectures* (1840), *Views of Sanctification* (1840), and *Memoirs of Charles G. Finney* (1876). In the 1840s Finney was an editor of the *Oberlin Quarterly Review* and a frequent contributor to the *Independent* and the *Advance.*

Finney's first wife, Lydia Andrews, died in 1847. He married Elizabeth Ford Atkinson in 1848, after whose death in 1863 he married Rebecca Rayl, the assistant principal of the Ladies' Department at Oberlin. Finney remained vigorous almost to his death, teaching at the college and conducting occasional meetings, until he passed away in 1875. It has been estimated that he was responsible for half a million conversions during his long lifetime.

Further Reading: Barnes, Gilbert H. *The Antislavery Impulse, 1830–1844.* Gloucester, MA: Peter Smith, 1973; Finney, Charles G. *Lectures on Revivals of Religion.* Cambridge, MA: Harvard University Press, Belknap Press, 1960; Finney, Charles G. *Memoirs of Rev. Charles G. Finney.* New York: A.S. Barnes, 1876; Gale, George W. *Autobiography of Rev. George W. Gale.* New York: n.p., 1964; Hambrick-Stowe, Charles E. *Charles G. Finney and the Spirit of American Evangelicalism.* Grand Rapids, MI: Eerdmans, 1996; Hardman, Keith J. *Charles Grandison Finney, 1792–1875: Revivalist and Reformer.* Syracuse, NY: Syracuse University Press, 1987. Paperback, Grand Rapids, MI: Baker Books, 1990; Johnson, Paul E. *A Shopkeeper's Millennium: Society and Revivals in Rochester, New York, 1815–1837.* New York: Hill and Wang, 1978; Lesick, Lawrence T. *The Lane Rebels: Evangelicalism and Antislavery in Antebellum America.* Metuchen, NJ: Scarecrow, 1980; Madden, Edward H., and James E. Hamilton. *Freedom and Grace: The Life of Asa Mahan.* Metuchen, NJ: Scarecrow, 1982; Rosell, Garth M., and Richard A. G. Dupuis, eds. *The Memoirs of Charles G. Finney: The Complete Restored Text.* Grand Rapids, MI: Zondervan, 1989; Smith, Timothy L. *Revivalism and Social Reform in Mid-Nineteenth-Century America.* Nashville, TN: Abingdon, 1957.

Keith J. Hardman

FIRE HANDLING

see Serpent- and Fire-Handling Believers

FOREIGN MISSIONS AND REVIVALS

Revivalism has been a method of recruitment and fund-raising for foreign missions, and an important part of missionary practice, from the **Second Great Awakening** to the present. The heightened spiritual commitments born of revivalism have solidified commitment to foreign missions among young people. Foreign missionaries transported the assumptions and methods of revivalism to the mission fields. Upon returning to the United States, missionaries led missionary meetings and revivals to recruit others for mission support and service.

Although the first American overseas missionaries did not sail until 1812, the **Great Awakening** established the connection between revivalism and mission recruitment. In 1740, New Light **preachers** at Yale College excited many students, including **David Brainerd,** who was then expelled for exhibiting spiritual pride when he criticized one of his instructors. During the 1740s, Brainerd became a missionary to the Native Americans in western Massachusetts and in the Middle Colonies. He led revivals among the Delaware Indians. After Brainerd's untimely death in 1747, his spiritual diaries were published and became devotional classics that inspired missionaries throughout the nineteenth century. Another important early missionary to the Indians who received a missionary calling through revivalism was **African American** John Stewart (1786–1823). Converted in a Methodist **camp meeting** in Ohio, Stewart felt called to preach to Native Americans. He headed northwest in obedience to what he described as a divine voice. Upon reaching the Wyandott Indians, Stewart began to sing and preach. Chiefs and other leaders were converted through Stewart's ministry. Backed by his converts, he sought ordination by the **Methodists.** Stewart's successful ministry inspired the founding of the Methodist Missionary Society in 1820, which began to support Methodists as overseas missionaries.

Since early foreign missionaries tended to be Congregationalists and Presbyterians from the Northeast, they were not usually open to enthusiasm on the mission field. In 1834, missionary Titus Coan (1801–1882) sailed to Hawaii after having been converted in a **Charles Finney** revival and having worked for Finney. In 1836, Coan began an evangelistic tour of the islands that employed Finney's "new measures." His controversial revivalism launched a mass movement in which three-fourths of the native Hawaiians became Protestant Christians. Coan's successes legitimated the use of revivals as a missionary method. The **Revival of 1857–1858** also had an impact on foreign missions by motivating seminary students and young businessmen in major cities to devote themselves to urban and foreign missions.

The power of revivalism for missions was increasingly harnessed as the century wore on, in particular by Methodists, the largest Protestant denomination in America. Methodist **Holiness** missionary William Taylor (1821–1902) held evangelistic campaigns in India, South Africa, and Australia from which grew self-supporting indigenous churches. In Holiness camp meetings and seminary revivals during the 1870s, Taylor's vision for Pauline mission methods (i.e., based on the apostle Paul) sparked the movement of "faith missionaries," who supported themselves on free-will offerings as pioneer "Taylor" missionaries to India, Angola, South America, and other locations. Missionary meetings became a routine feature of Holiness camp meetings and Methodist **women**'s gatherings during the late nineteenth century. Seekers of entire **sanctification** often found that their deepened spiritual experience of "perfect love" manifested itself as a call to missionary service.

In 1886, evangelist **Dwight Moody** held a summer Bible conference for collegiate **Young Men's Christian Association** (YMCA) leaders. During a missionary meeting filled with testimonies and appeals for workers, 100 college **men** volunteered to become foreign missionaries. From this nucleus, the **Student Volunteer Movement** for Foreign Missions (SVM) emerged as a powerful force for sending young men and women to

Minnie Abrams (seated), a Methodist-turned-Pentecostal missionary to India, and Pandita Ramabai (standing), a high-caste Hindu convert to Christianity, educator, and advocate for Indian women. The girls' school Ramabai founded in 1889 (Mukti Mission, Pune, India) underwent revival in 1905 and has continued its work until today. Courtesy of Dr. Stanley M. Burgess.

the mission fields. Student volunteers signed a volunteer pledge indicating their willingness to become missionaries. Quadrennial international student conferences filled with inspirational appeals solidified the missionary call for the thousands who attended. While most student volunteers went out as missionaries under denominational missionary societies, others joined new, nondenominational faith missions that sought to evangelize the unreached interiors of Africa, Asia, and South America. Returned missionaries recruited others at student-led missionary gatherings. For example, in 1888 Hudson Taylor of the China Inland Mission held revival

meetings attended by thousands of YMCA youth in Toronto. Seven YMCA volunteers accompanied him back to China, their initial support paid by pledges gathered during a series of inspirational meetings. Although the SVM declined in the 1920s, the triennial or quadrennial Urbana Conferences, under the sponsorship of **InterVarsity Christian Fellowship,** began in 1946 as a twentieth-century successor to the nineteenth-century legacy of student revival and commitment meetings. With sermons, singing, missionary speeches, **prayer** meetings, information sessions, and the signing of commitment cards, 19,000 young people attended the 20th Urbana Conference in 2003. Participants donated over a million dollars for missions, and thousands of students pledged themselves to mission service. Some 250,000 college students have attended an Urbana Conference during the last 60 years.

During the twentieth century, missionaries and their converts facilitated major revivals that launched movements of indigenous Christianity around the world. As the year 1900 approached, Holiness and **Pentecostal** prayer bands prayed for a great outpouring of the Holy Spirit as a spur to missions before Jesus' **eschatological** Second Coming. Their prayers seemed answered during the first decade of the twentieth century when **speaking in tongues** broke out in multiple locations. In Los Angeles, the **Azusa Street revival** propelled numerous **Pentecostal** missionaries to West Africa, China, and elsewhere, believing that they had received a miraculous gift of foreign tongues (called *xenolalia*) for world evangelization. Pentecostal revival enveloped a girls' school in Pune, India, in 1905. American Holiness missionary Minnie Abrams helped facilitate the Indian revival and then spread news of it to American missionaries in Chile. Missionaries Willis and May Hoover in Chile then launched a Pentecostal revival movement that resulted in the founding of the largest Protestant church in Chile.

In 1907, the Pyongyang revival facilitated by **Presbyterian** and Methodist missionaries launched Korean Christians into widespread domestic and foreign mission activity. Women missionaries in China worked closely with native women evangelists in the Shanghai revival of 1925, a key transition from mission-led to native-led revivals. In Rhodesia (i.e., present-day Zimbabwe), 1918 was known as the "year of the Holy Spirit" because revivals in the Methodist missions resulted in large numbers of converts who carried Christianity across the country. Faith missions like the Oriental Missionary Society used revivalism regularly as a missionary technique that helped bring into being the third-largest denomination in Korea. By the mid-twentieth century, American missionaries had become the conduits for the spread of revivalism, which in turn stimulated the spread of evangelical Christianity throughout the world.

Further Reading: Anderson, Gerald H., ed. *Biographical Dictionary of Christian Missions*. New York: Macmillan Reference USA, 1998; Parker, Michael. *The Kingdom of Character: The Student Volunteer Movement for Foreign Missions (1886–1926)*. Lanham, MD: University Press of America, 1998; Robert, Dana L. *American Women in Mission: A Social History of Their Thought and Practice*. Macon, GA: Mercer University Press, 1997; Robert, Dana L. *"Occupy Until I Come": A. T. Pierson and the Evangelization of the World*. Grand Rapids MI: Eerdmans, 2003; Urbana Conference Web site. http://www.urbana.org/.

Dana L. Robert

FOURSQUARE GOSPEL CHURCH

see International Church of the Foursquare Gospel

FREE METHODIST CHURCH

The Free Methodist Church traces its origins to a mid-nineteenth-century conflict over doctrine and practice within its parent body, the **Methodist** Episcopal Church in the United States. Its emergence shortly after the **Second Great Awakening** exemplifies a tendency for evangelical revival movements to give rise to separate churches or denominations. The Methodist Episcopal Church had been founded in Baltimore in 1784, and during the early 1800s rapidly became the largest organized church body in the nation. Yet

upstate New York's Genesee District—a region that had proved itself fertile ground for religious revivals—was a scene of religious controversy. Beginning in the 1840s, a number of discontented Methodists, led by the charismatic **Benjamin Titus Roberts,** offered a pointed critique of the church's beliefs and practices. Their criticisms were not well received. Roberts and his followers were derisively termed "Nazarites" by the Methodist Episcopal leadership in Buffalo, New York, whom Roberts's followers, in turn, dubbed the "Buffalo Regency."

Roberts's foremost charge against the Regency was its doctrinal liberalization and its repudiation of the **bodily manifestations** associated with revivals. By accommodating itself to a rapidly gentrifying Methodist population, he charged, the church had weakened the classic "landmarks" of Wesleyan doctrine, disempowered its **women,** and was rapidly becoming a "dead and corrupting body" (Roberts, "New School Methodism," 578). Methodism, he argued, must remain true to the original teachings of Wesley and ultimately the primitive church. Moreover, Roberts and his followers opposed the accommodations that were being made by the Methodist Church with institutionalized slavery in the **South,** and the church's growing rejection of **abolitionism.** They reminded the Methodist hierarchy that John Wesley had been a vigorous and lifelong opponent of slavery, and would have condemned any such compromises. They were disturbed by the Methodist clergy's membership in secret societies such as the Freemasons—something they saw as an intolerable diversion for church leaders. They held that Methodism had become too hierarchical, lacked spiritual depth, and had worship services—including hired musicians—that were too formal. The title "Free" Methodist is usually attributed to the reformers' rejection of the common church practice of renting private church pews, priced according to their proximity to the pulpit. Pew rentals often left poorer members without a place to sit during worship. Roberts's supporters tended to be less affluent and more rural than their Methodist opponents.

To the Methodist hierarchy, supported by affluent, progressively minded members in Buffalo and other urban areas, Roberts and his followers were condemned as enthusiasts and fanatics. After a series of church hearings and trials, they were expelled between 1858 and 1860. Their appeals for reconsideration denied, Roberts and the reformers founded the Free Methodist Church at Pekin, Niagara County, New York, August 23, 1860. The new sect was well received in the upper Midwest—another region historically receptive to **camp meetings** and revivalism—and the Western Conference of the Free Methodist Church was organized in June 1861 near St. Charles, Illinois. From this start Free Methodism grew steadily during the remainder of the century, building a presence throughout the United States and Canada, and sponsoring sizable mission efforts in Africa, India, China, and Japan.

In its theology and character, Free Methodism remains similar to the Wesleyan Church and the **Church of the Nazarene.** Its church doctrine holds that Christ's sacrifice is the sole means of satisfaction for sin, that the Holy Spirit works entire **sanctification** in the individual, empowering the believer for service, and restoring believers when they go astray. The denomination claimed some 74,140 members in the United States as of 1999, and continues to support institutions of higher learning including Roberts Wesleyan College, Spring Arbor University, Greenville College, Central Christian College, and Seattle Pacific University.

Further Reading: Free Methodist Church of North America. *The Free Methodist Book of Discipline.* Indianapolis: Free Methodist Publishing House, 1999; Hogue, Wilson T. *History of the Free Methodist Church of North America.* 2 vols. Winona Lake, IN: Free Methodist Publishing House, 1938; M'Geary, John S. *The Free Methodist Church: A Brief Outline History of its Origin and Development.* Chicago: W. B. Rose, 1908; Roberts, B. T. "New School Methodism," in Leslie R. Marson, ed., *From Age to Age a Living Witness: A Historical Interpretation of Free Methodism's First Century.* Winona Lake, IN: Light & Life Press, 1960. Roberts, B. T. *Why Another Sect?: Containing a Review of Articles by Bishop Simpson and Others on the Free*

Methodist Church. Rochester, NY: Earnest Christian Publishing House, 1879.

Daniel C. Palm

FREE WILL BAPTISTS

Free Will Baptists in America trace their history to two separate **Baptist** movements from the eighteenth century. The movements were theologically similar but culturally and geographically distinct. These differences are highlighted by the way each movement responded to the revivals of the eighteenth and nineteenth centuries. The northern Randall movement embraced revivalism, while the older, **southern** Palmer movement generally did not. Though the Randall movement died out with its 1911 merger with the Northern Baptist denomination (subsequently known as the American Baptist Church), the Palmer tradition was slower to embrace revivalism. It was only as individual churches and associations in the southern frontiers of Kentucky, Tennessee, and Arkansas—already touched by the revivalist spirit—joined with the Free Will Baptists of the Palmer tradition that attitudes toward revivalism began to change. The southern movement (or General Conference of Free Will Baptists) moved further toward revivalism through its 1935 merger with the Co-operative General Association of Freewill Baptists—a collection of dissident Randallite churches in Ohio, Missouri, Texas, and Oklahoma. Revivalism has continued to be a strong force in the movement, and what little resistance to revival practices remained in traditionalist regions of North Carolina and Georgia fell away under the influence of the twentieth-century Fundamentalist movement.

The northern movement of Free Will Baptists began with Benjamin Randall (1749–1808). Randall experienced a religious awakening after hearing of the death of **George Whitefield,** whom he had heard **preach** several times. He had brief associations with New Light Congregationalists and **Calvinistic** Baptists before his Arminian tendencies forced him out. He took a pastorate at New Durham, New Hampshire, in 1778, where he began going into the surrounding areas and preaching on the need for repentance. His efforts won many converts and swayed many Calvinistic Baptist ministers to embrace his Arminian positions. Soon quarterly and yearly meetings were set up to provide for better governance and to improve the spiritual tendencies of the regions in which they were held. John Buzzell recounts these revivals and attendant emotional displays in his *Religious Magazine*. The methods and sentiments of revivalism among the northern movement are also demonstrated by Randall's republication in 1804 of Canadian New Light revivalist **Henry Alline**'s *Two Mites* (1781).

Evangelists Ephraim Stinchfield and Clement Phinney brought the movement into Vermont and New York. John Colby held revivals and founded churches in Indiana and Ohio. The movement organized a Home Missions Society in 1834 to plant churches on the western frontier. David Marks (1805–1845), "the boy preacher," held meetings throughout Ohio and gathered large crowds. Known for his enthusiastic nature and evangelistic successes, he was connected with other revivalist leaders, and **Charles Finney** gave his funeral oration. By the middle of the nineteenth century the northern movement embraced social issues such as **abolitionism** and **temperance,** and collaborated with the membership of other denominations to promote these causes. This ecumenical spirit culminated in the merger with the Northern Baptist denomination in 1911.

The southern Free Will Baptists trace their roots to the arrival of Paul Palmer in Carolina in 1719. The growth of the movement was slow but steady. Although they promoted evangelism they also eschewed emotionalism. The movement was decimated in the middle of the century by the arrival of John Gano, a Calvinistic Baptist missionary from Philadelphia who evangelized and reorganized many members of the General Baptist churches who lacked an experience of **conversion** or an **assurance of salvation.** The churches that remained were traditionalist and skeptical of the emotionalism associated with the new revivalist methods. This position softened as the **Second Great Awakening** began to make made inroads into the South in the years after 1800. This change of viewpoint was largely due to the influx of new churches wishing to join in fellowship with the Free Will Baptists. Many of these congregations were composed of Baptists who had already adopted revivalism and become Arminian in theology. This produced a denominational body with mixed attitudes toward revivals. With the rise of Fundamentalism in the twentieth century, and the merger with the western remnants of the Randall movement in 1935, the limited opposition to revivalism waned and the denomination adopted a characteristically affirmative attitude toward revivalism.

Further Reading: Baptist Library Online. http://www.baptistlibraryonline.com/; Buzzell, John. "Religious Intelligence: An Account of Late Reformations and Revivals of Religion." *Religious Magazine* 1 (1811): 23–36: Davidson, William F. *The Free Will Baptists in America: 1727–1984.* Nashville, TN: Randall House, 1985.

Kevin Hester

FRELINGHUYSEN, THEODORUS JACOBUS (1691–1747)

Theodorus Jacobus Frelinghuysen was a Dutch Reformed minister and an important forerunner of the **Great Awakening.** The Frelinghuysen family had supported the Protestant Reformation, and Theodorus's great-grandfather pioneered Lutheranism in the German village of Ergste. His grandfather introduced the family to the **Calvinistic Reformed** tradition in 1669. His father, Johan Henrich, became pastor of a newly established German Reformed church in Hagen, Westphalia, in 1683. He attended *gymnasium* at Hamm for two years, then enrolled at the University of Lingen. At Lingen, Frelinghuysen became committed to the Voetian, rather than Cocceian, school of theology. Frelinghuysen was ordained in 1717 at Loegumer Voorwerk in Oost Friesland, near Emden. After serving as co-regent of the Latin school at Enkhuizen, Noord Holland, Frelinghuysen accepted the call of Classis Amsterdam to serve four small Dutch Reformed congregations in New Jersey's Raritan Valley. Arriving in New Jersey in 1720, Frelinghuysen married Eva Terhune, orphan daughter of a wealthy Long Island farmer. They had five sons and two daughters. All five sons became ministers, and both daughters married ministers.

Those who objected to Frelinghuysen's teachings on regeneration, his intense piety, and his probing **preaching** made his transition to America a difficult one. The preacher objected to some of his members' casual way of living, which included nominal Christianity, irregular church attendance, covetousness, gambling, and dissipation. Frelinghuysen's preaching focused on conviction of sins, **conversion,** and **holiness.** He spoke out forcefully against sin and stressed the Spirit's work of convicting sinners of their sin and the solemn judgment of God against sin. He invited sinners to come to Christ, stressing that only those who have experienced conversion in Christ as needy sinners would be saved. As for holiness, he frequently preached on the Voetian themes of the narrow way of salvation and ways in which internal motives affect external observances.

While some were offended by Frelinghuysen's preaching, most of his congregants rallied behind him. At least 300 people were converted under his ministry. Several small revivals under Frelinghuysen's ministry paved the way for the Great Awakening. His preaching and friendship influenced **Gilbert Tennent,** a **Presbyterian** minister who came to New Brunswick to work among English-speaking colonists. The revival that began under Frelinghuysen in the Dutch community during the 1720s spread to English-speaking settlers under Tennent's ministry, and later blossomed into the Great Awakening of the 1740s under **George Whitefield,** who called Frelinghuysen "the beginner of the great work" (George Whitefield, *A Continuation of the Journal*, no. 5, 2nd ed. [1740], 41).

Frelinghuysen sought to apply the evidences of conversion—repentance, faith, and holiness—as tests for admission to the Lord's Supper. Convinced that many of his members lacked these evidences, Frelinghuysen warned them against partaking of the sacrament. Offended parties complained to Reformed ministers in New York. Some of those pastors—including Gualtherus DuBois (1671–1751) and Henricus Boel (1692–1754)—sided

with them. Other colleagues—Guiliam Bartholf (1656–1726), an itinerant pastor who had been responsible for the original establishment of the four congregations Frelinghuysen served—supported Frelinghuysen.

Matters became very tense when Frelinghuysen openly referred to colleagues who opposed him as "unconverted ministers." On March 12, 1723, several disgruntled members, who became known as the *Klagers* (Complainants), charged Frelinghuysen with preaching false doctrines. The consistories of Frelinghuysen drew up a summons, which they sent to the Klagers, listing the errors of their opponents. Eventually the *Dagers* (Summoners) excommunicated four leading Klagers, sending shock waves throughout the Dutch Reformed community. In 1725 the Klagers responded by sending a 146-page *Klagte* (complaint) to Classis Amsterdam. The *Klagte*, signed by 64 heads of households, presented detailed criticisms of Frelinghuysen and sought his dismissal. Fierce opposition took its toll on Frelinghuysen's health. He underwent several debilitating bouts of mental depression. Between breakdowns, Frelinghuysen continued to spread his teachings through the spoken and printed word.

The controversy between the Dagers and the Klagers raged until, through the prodding of Classis Amsterdam, the factions reached a compromise in 11 "Peace Articles" (adopted November 1733). The articles stated that the consistories would forgive the Klagers and rescind their excommunication, providing the Klagers accepted Frelinghuysen as an orthodox Reformed minister. Though Boel's opposition to Frelinghuysen continued, DuBois inaugurated a movement to join Frelinghuysen's revival party in a bid for independence from Classis Amsterdam. Two parties emerged, the Coetus (Latin, "connection") and the Conferentie. The Coetus included ministers who shared Frelinghuysen's pro-revival, progressive piety. The Conferentie represented those who were anti-revivalist, favored traditional orthodoxy, and wanted to remain "in conference" with Classis Amsterdam. For more than a decade, the two parties engaged in pamphlet warfare. In the end, Frelinghuysen's views and the

Coetus won out shortly after Frelinghuysen's death. Preaching in English was sanctioned, ministers were trained and ordained in America, and the American church was granted autonomy.

In his later years, Frelinghuysen became less judgmental of others. He apologized for calling some of his colleagues unconverted. Reconciliation efforts between Frelinghuysen and DuBois were successful. His untiring work, zeal, and piety triumphed as many of his former enemies came to accept him.

Further Reading: Beeke, Joel R., ed. *Forerunner of the Great Awakening: Sermons by Theodorus Jacobus Frelinghuysen.* Grand Rapids, MI: Eerdmans, 2000; Tanis, James. *Dutch Calvinistic Pietism in the Middle Colonies: A Study in the Life and Theology of Theodorus Jacobus Frelinghuysen.* The Hague: Martinus Nijhoff, 1967.

Joel R. Beeke

FRIENDS

see Quakers (Society of Friends)

FULL GOSPEL BUSINESS MEN'S FELLOWSHIP INTERNATIONAL

The Full Gospel Business Men's Fellowship International (FGBMFI) was founded in 1951 by Demos Shakarian (1913–1993), a wealthy Armenian dairy farmer from California. Intended as a lay fellowship of ordinary businesspeople who could share with one another their experiences of God, it grew to over 3,000 chapters in 87 countries before it split in 1988 and again in 1995. It was one of several major components in the **Charismatic Renewal** of the 1960s and 1970s, and had antecedents in the **Latter Rain movement** of 1948–1949.

Shakarian's family emigrated in 1905 from Kara Kala, Armenia, where they had heard of an outpouring of the Holy Spirit upon hundreds of thousands of Russian Orthodox Christians who **spoke in tongues** and **prophesied** during the late 1800s. The Shakarians were among many from their town who moved to Los Angeles in response to a prophecy of the "boy prophet," Efim Gerasemovitch Klubniken, who warned of coming persecution from the Turks. In 1906, members of this community of Armenians, including Shakarian's grandfather, became participants in the nearby **Azusa Street revival.** Shakarian reported that he, at the age of 13, was healed of deafness after experiencing a sense of God's presence during which he was temporarily unable to get off the floor (see **bodily manifestations in revivals**). Seven years later, in 1933, he married Rose Gabrielian, with whom he began holding summertime evangelistic meetings at Lincoln Park, 10 miles from their home in Downey, California, beginning in 1940.

The following year, at Shakarian's urging, the noted **healing** evangelist Dr. Charles S. Price went to Downey hospital, where he successfully **prayed** for the healing of Shakarian's sister Florence, suffering from multiple hip and pelvis fractures sustained in an automobile accident. From then until his death in 1946, Price shared dinner with Shakarian regularly at a local restaurant. In conversations during the summer of 1944, Shakarian mentioned to Price that he thought it odd that there were far fewer **men** than **women** at **tent meetings.** Price commented that most men regard religion as something for women and children, and they stop attending worship when their business prospers. These conversations became the seedbed for what would later become the FGBMFI. Shakarian began searching for alternatives to tent meetings. In 1945, he and his wife held a dinner gathering for businessmen at Knott's Berry Farm, where he allowed selected participants to give their testimony before the group. He floated the idea of organizing a larger gathering of businesspeople at the Hollywood Bowl at which testimonies could be given, and money was raised for the project. The rally at Hollywood Bowl was attended by over 20,000.

Shakarian arranged for five weeks of successful evangelistic meetings in Fresno, California, in October of 1948 featuring a different evangelist each week, one of whom was **William Branham.** Shakarian later became responsible for arranging **Oral Roberts's** Los Angeles fall 1951 campaign, attended by 200,000 people. During this campaign,

Shakarian communicated privately to Oral Roberts his idea of having businesspeople tell one another about what they have experienced of God. Roberts offered to speak at the first meeting, which took place in October of 1951 at Clifton's Cafeteria in Los Angeles. Although only 18 people attended, Roberts caused a stir when he mentioned in prayer his expectation that there would be a thousand chapters of the new organization. The FGBMFI was incorporated some weeks later, but it met with difficulties during its first year. The size of the meetings remained small and church leaders viewed the group with suspicion. Shakarian spent money on advertising, with little effect. **Pentecostal** statesman David Du Plessis shared his enthusiasm about Shakarian's venture with the World Pentecostal Conference in 1952, but the conference delegates seemed to be concerned that Shakarian was not a clergyman but a dairy farmer.

On December 20, 1952, Miner Arganbright, an FGBMFI board member, recommended that the organization be disbanded due to lack of interest, so Shakarian made preparations to dissolve it at the next weekly meeting. However, on December 26, a friend, the evangelist Tommy Hicks, came to visit, and discussed matters at length with Shakarian and his wife. A powerful prayer experience, and an unexpected donation of $1,000, led Shakarian to persevere with his plans. By summer of 1953 there were nine chapters and a national convention planned for October. During the last night of the convention, the budget for the entire following year was met after one of the speakers, Jack Coe, made an appeal for funds.

By 1989 there were 218 international directors, 3,000 chapters in nearly 100 nations, and over 1 million people regularly attending FGBMFI meetings. Yet the internal politics of the organization was unstable as early as the 1950s. In 1956, **William Branham,** one of the original 17 directors, walked off the platform of the annual convention in Minneapolis just before he was about to speak, and later prophesied that the organization would split twice. This prediction proved accurate, with the formation of the International Fellowship of Christian Businessmen (IFCB) in 1988 and the Business Men's Fellowship (BMF) in 1995.

Further Reading: Shakarian, Demos, John Sherrill, and Elizabeth Sherrill. *The Happiest People on Earth.* Chappaqua, NY: Steward Press, 1975; Sonmore, Clayt. *Who Was William Branham?* Minnetonka, MN: Thy Kingdom Come Ministries, 2004.

Richard M. Riss

FULLER, CHARLES EDWARD (1887–1968)

Charles Fuller was a popular American **radio** evangelist with a national and international audience from the mid-1930s until his death in 1968, and proved influential in the development of twentieth-century evangelicalism at both the popular and intellectual levels. His radio program for years reached a larger audience than any other show, laying the groundwork for the "New Evangelicalism" that would arise around the personality of **Billy Graham,** whom Fuller mentored. Meanwhile, Fuller Theological Seminary would lead the way during the second half of the twentieth century in dealing with major intellectual issues facing evangelicals and grow to become the largest seminary in the Western Hemisphere.

Born in Los Angeles in 1887, Fuller was embedded in the tolerant religious world that marked Southern California before the rise of **Pentecostalism** and the arrival of Fundamentalism. While Fuller flirted with the former and fully embraced the latter, even attending Fundamentalism's flagship institution, the Bible Institute of Los Angeles (now called Biola University), in his early thirties, he retained the irenic spirit of religious cooperation that had marked his region. Fuller's early religious career indicated his interest in evangelism and innovation. Leaving a successful career in orange growing, Fuller helped to found an interdenominational Fundamentalist congregation in Placentia, California, in 1925 that remained in a perpetual state of revival. By hosting guest speakers and employing telephone lines strung from his pulpit to local radio stations, Fuller brought attention to his congregation. Feeling confined by his pastoral role and pondering other opportunities, such as weeklong speaking engagements along the West Coast, Fuller often moved outside his church to evangelize. By 1932 he was broadcasting from several local radio stations in Long Beach.

In 1933 he launched the Gospel Broadcasting Association, an umbrella organization set up to oversee his radio ministry. At the same time, his church asked for his resignation, weary of filling its pulpit with guest **preachers** while Fuller was on the road. This combination of events caused Fuller to throw himself completely into radio work. Over the next four years he experimented with various styles of programming, landing on a formula that combined familiar hymns sung by a chorus; old evangelical standards set to new rhythms and sung by a quartet; letter reading by his wife, Grace Payton Fuller; and revivalist sermons preached in a gentle and affirming fashion. The program, called *The Old Fashioned Revival Hour*, hit all the notes of sentimentality and friendliness that evangelicals of every stripe longed for. The show was picked up by the fledgling Mutual Broadcasting System and grew along with it over the following few years. By 1944, the program was beamed over 600 stations worldwide and provided one-eighth of Mutual's income.

Throughout the 1940s Fuller set the standard in religious broadcasting, boasting some 20 million listeners and acting as a clearinghouse for new ministries springing up in wartime and postwar America. Everyone from Billy Graham to Bill Bright, and organizations from Wycliffe Bible Translators to the **Navigators,** sought Fuller's blessing and time on his program. Even the National Association of Evangelicals used his fame to further its cause, planning their regional and national conferences to coincide with his revival campaigns around the country. Through such a vast and irenic ministry, Fuller helped to lay the foundation for a grassroots movement of neo-Evangelicalism, including those who upheld the fundamentals of conservative Protestantism but were willing to cooperate with those of differing persuasions to further the spread of the gospel.

Fuller's influence extended beyond his radio ministry. In 1947 he cofounded Fuller Theological Seminary in Pasadena, California, with Harold John Ockenga, famed pastor of Park Street Church in Boston. Meant to be the evangelical answer to Princeton Seminary—which had grown too liberal for those clinging to Fundamentalist doctrines—Fuller Seminary brought together a group of top scholars to wrestle with and publish on the major theological and moral issues of the day. While Charles Fuller often disagreed with the faculty and felt their publications hurt his radio ministry by decreasing the audience, he nonetheless allowed a variety of theological opinions to flourish at the seminary. During the 1960s and 1970s, the seminary sat at the center of the storm surrounding the issue of biblical inerrancy.

After ending the live one-hour broadcast of the radio program in 1957, Fuller continued to host a syndicated half-hour version until his death in 1968. It remained immensely popular until the end. To this day, "Heavenly Sunshine," the program's unofficial theme song arranged by Fuller, remains in the memory of millions of Christians worldwide. More importantly, Fuller's efforts at evangelical cooperation and conservative Protestant intellectual influence laid the foundation for the cultural advances of neo-Evangelicalism in the second half of the twentieth century.

Further Reading: Carpenter, Joel. *Revive Us Again: The Reawakening of American Fundamentalism.* New York: Oxford University Press, 1997; Charles E. and Grace Fuller Collection, Du Plessis Archive, Fuller Theological Seminary, Pasadena, California; Fuller, Charles E., and James Elwin Wright. *Manna in the Morning.* Boston: Fellowship Press, 1943; Fuller, Daniel P. *Give the Winds a Mighty Voice: The Story of Charles E. Fuller.* Waco, TX: Word Books, 1972; Goff, Philip. "'We Have Heard the Joyful Sound': Charles E. Fuller's Radio Broadcast and the Rise of Modern Evangelicalism." In Michael J. McClymond, ed., *Embodying the Spirit: New Perspectives on North American Revivalism,* 147–67. Baltimore: Johns Hopkins University Press, 2004; Hangen, Tona. *Redeeming the Dial: Radio, Religion, and Popular Culture in America.* Chapel Hill: University of North Carolina Press, 2002; Lewis, L. David. "Charles E. Fuller." In Charles H. Lippy, ed., *Twentieth-Century Shapers of American Popular Religion,* 148–55. New

York: Greenwood Press, 1989; Marsden, George M. *Reforming Fundamentalism: Fuller Seminary and the New Evangelicalism.* Grand Rapids, MI: Eerdmans, 1987;

Wright, J. Elwin. *The Old Fashioned Revival Hour and the Broadcasters.* Boston: Fellowship Press, 1940.

Philip Goff

G

GARRETTSON, FREEBORN
(1752–1827)

Freeborn Garrettson was one of the first American-born **preachers** in the **Methodist** movement. He was responsible for the planting of its congregations in British North America, Nova Scotia, and the Hudson River Valley. Garrettson was born in 1752 near the mouth of the Susquehanna River in Maryland and died in 1827 in New York City. Because he was the child of a prosperous family, he was tutored by a schoolmaster until he was 18, and for his time had a better than average education. When he was 21 his father died, leaving him the heir to the family fortune. Influenced by the preaching of Robert Strawbridge and Joseph Pilmoor, Garrettson was **converted** and decided at the age of 24 to enter ministry. He is broadly acknowledged, along with his mentor, **Francis Asbury,** to be one of the principal founders of Methodism in America.

A man of strong convictions, he was opposed to war and refused to serve in the Revolution despite his sympathy for the American cause. As a result of this decision, he was threatened and finally imprisoned. Taken before Delaware's governor Caesar Rodney, a friend of the Methodists, he managed to be freed. In 1778 he narrowly escaped being lynched by a mob. He was also opposed to the practice of slavery and, upon entering the ministry, freed the ones he owned. Throughout his life, he held **abolitionist** views and continued actively to oppose slavery. During the American Revolution, Francis Asbury was restricted in his ability to travel and work. For 10 months, Asbury was confined to a refuge in Delaware. During this time Garrettson often acted in Asbury's stead by presiding over quarterly conferences and even, on occasion, appointing the preachers to their stations.

When Methodist leader Thomas Coke and his companions arrived from England in 1784, Garrettson was dispatched to call the preachers to meet in Baltimore for the conference that would result in the organization of the church. He rode 1,200 miles in six weeks, but too often paused to preach along the way and thus failed to notify all of those who were eligible to attend. At the end of the conference, at which he was ordained elder, Garrettson was appointed to begin a missionary effort to English settlers in Nova Scotia. In 1789 it was proposed to make him a general superintendent for the British North American provinces and the West Indies, but the plan was abandoned and Garrettson returned home. He served for a year in the Delmarva Peninsula and then was sent to New England. That plan, too, was shelved, and he began to restore the neglected work in New York and the Hudson River Valley. It was there that he met, and five years later married, Catherine Livingston, the daughter of Judge Robert Livingston. The family was both wealthy and influential, and one of Catherine's brothers helped draft the Declaration of Independence and administered the oath of office to the newly elected George Washington. Catherine's family was dismayed at the prospect of her marriage to Garrettson.

Garrettson's work for the Methodists was highly successful and, in time, he supervised nine districts that included upstate New York and Connecticut. The bulk of his future service to the Methodists was in this area, and the home that he built with Catherine on the banks of the Hudson River was a refuge for them. Asbury named it "Traveler's Rest." In the meantime, the effort in New England had been taken over by **Jesse Lee.** Though there was genuine affection between Asbury and Garrettson, the two had points of disagreement. Garrettson favored the amendment made by Virginian James O'Kelly to limit the bishops' power by allowing preachers to appeal appointments to the annual conference, and he favored the election of presiding elders. Asbury was strongly opposed to both and prevailed. O'Kelly withdrew and formed the Republican Methodist Church. In 1808 Garrettson and the New York delegation supported the creation of a delegated General Conference. In this instance, Asbury joined Garrettson in supporting the resolution and it was done. Garrettson was subsequently elected to every General Conference until he died. At the conference in 1808 Garrettson had the pleasure of joining Asbury in the consecration of the first native-born preacher, William McKendree, as a bishop of the church.

Further Reading: Hughes, J. Theodore. *An Historical Sketch of the Life of Freeborn Garrettson.* Rhinebeck, NY: Rhinebeck United Methodist Parish, 1984; Simpson, Robert Drew, ed. *American Methodist Pioneer: The Life and Journals of the Rev. Freeborn Garrettson.* Rutland, VT: Academy Books, 1984.

James E. Kirby

GERMAN AMERICAN REVIVALS

see Amana Community; Evangelical Association; Lutheran, German American, and Scandinavian American Revivals; Pietism and Revivals

GERMAN REFORMED CHURCH

see Calvinistic, Presbyterian, and Reformed Revivals since 1730; Nevin, John Williamson; Otterbein, Philip William; United Brethren in Christ

GLOSSOLALIA

see Speaking in Tongues (Glossolalia)

GRACE, SWEET DADDY (CHARLES EMMANUEL) (1881–1960)

The man known to both his followers and to outsiders as "Sweet Daddy" Grace—Charles Emmanuel Grace, or Marcelino Manoel da Graca—was the founder of the United House of Prayer for All People (UHPAP) in 1919 in New Bedford, Massachusetts. He was of Portuguese and African ancestry and did not admit to being a Negro. Born in Brava, in the Cape Verde Islands off the coast of West Africa, he died in Los Angeles in 1960. Before Grace founded his own **Pentecostal** church and denomination, he was a part of the **Church of God in Christ** (COGIC) in Newark, New Jersey. He and COGIC founder **Charles Harrison Mason** once disagreed over asking members to give 10 cents for a special rally in order to raise money. Grace left New Jersey for Charlotte, North Carolina, and moved to back to New Bedford in about 1917.

He and his followers built their first church building in 1921, which is still standing. The stated doctrine of the UHPAP is "one Lord, one faith, one baptism and one leader to teach the people." During Grace's lifetime it was the largest predominantly **African American** church denomination in the United States under the direction of a single individual. There was no governing board and Grace alone made all decisions. He demanded total loyalty from his followers. He organized large parades and meetings for his followers, and provided employment and financial benefits to communities through the production of Daddy Grace Products, including hairdressing, toothpaste, coffee, tea, stationery, and cookies. These products were sold in the African American community by salespersons and through advertisements in *Grace Magazine*. Grace instructed people to place the *Grace Magazine* on their bodies wherever they hurt, so that the magazine could transmit its **healing** powers. Female members were taught to remain pure and refrain from worldly lust, while **men** were taught to honor the **women.**

Grace inaugurated peace and goodwill in economically poor communities by erecting church buildings without incurring debt, establishing new businesses, and allowing his church families to live in homes build by the UHPAP. He also bequeathed his personal wealth to the church he founded. Local politicians in several cities and states came to regard Grace and his church as a force to reckon with. He was well known for baptizing his members with a fire hose in public locations to attract media interest and large crowds. Grace organized racially integrated services as early as 1926 in Charlotte, North Carolina, and other cities in the **South.** Worship services in UHPAP congregations centered on Grace. A red-draped chair at the front of each church sanctuary awaited Bishop Grace, in the expectation of his visit to the congregation.

Bishop Walter McCollough, the second leader, instituted a nationwide building program of affordable housing and safe communities with Grace's estate and without the assistance of any federal or state grants. These church communities feature homes, recreation areas, grocery stores, restaurants, and other businesses operated by their members. Bishop Samuel Madison, the third leader, has continued to build and keep the structure that McCollough established. Current UHPAP church programs focus on members' education, scholarships for study, the care of senior citizens, and round-the-clock neighborhood security. Brass bands, shouting, exhortations, and ecstatic worship services are still found in UHPAP churches. Their musical groups include the gospel quartet the Sons of Grace and the Kings of Harmony Jubilee Brass Band—both founded in the mid-1940s. The church

headquarters in Washington, DC, is known as the Little White House and is shaped like the U.S. White House with a gold-domed roof.

Further Reading: Brune, Danielle Elizabeth. "Sweet Daddy Grace: The Life and Times of a Modern Day Prophet." PhD diss. University of Texas at Austin, 2002; Davis, Lenwood G., ed. *Daddy Grace: An Annotated Bibliography.* Westport, CT: Greenwood Press, 1992; DuPree, Sherry Sherrod. *African-American Holiness Pentecostal Movement: An Annotated Bibliography.* New York: Garland, 1996; DuPree, Sherry Sherrod. *Biographical Dictionary of African-American Holiness-Pentecostals, 1880–1990.* Washington, DC: Middle Atlantic Regional Press, 1989; Mjagkij, Nina, ed. *Organizing Black America: An Encyclopedia of African American Associations.* New York: Garland, 2001; Payne, Wardell J., ed. *Directory of African American Religious Bodies.* 2nd ed. Washington, DC: Howard University Press, 1995.

Sherry Sherrod DuPree

GRAHAM, WILLIAM FRANKLIN, JR. (BILLY) (1918–)

His associates claim that Billy Graham has **preached** to more people than anyone else in history. Few would dispute that claim. Himself converted to Christianity during an evangelical revival, Graham went on to become the most influential revivalist of the twentieth century. Throughout his career, Graham's popular appeal lay in his extraordinary charisma, his forceful preaching, and his simple, homespun message: Repent of your sins, accept Christ as savior, and you shall be saved. Behind that simple message, however, stood a sophisticated organization, the Billy Graham Evangelistic Association, which provided extensive advance work and a follow-up program for new converts. Even though he was among the pioneers in the use of television for religious purposes, Graham always shied away from the label "televangelist." During the 1980s, when other television preachers were embroiled in sensational scandals, Graham remained above the fray, and throughout a career that spanned more than half a century, his integrity remained intact, his reputation unblemished.

Born November 7, 1918, near Charlotte, North Carolina, William Franklin Graham Jr. worked on his father's dairy farm, and was raised in a **Presbyterian** congregation. In the fall of 1934, when he was a teenager, Billy Frank, as he was known, accompanied several of his friends to a revival meeting conducted by an itinerant evangelist, Mordecai Ham. The revival had already stirred the passions of many in Charlotte, in large part because of Ham's public speculations about the sexual behavior of students at Central High School and because of his denunciations of the local clergy, many of whom had opposed his revival campaign. Graham recalled later that he had gone to scoff at the preacher, but he was captivated instead. After several meetings, Graham accepted Ham's invitation to come to Jesus, as the choir sang, "Just As I am, Without One plea." Although he worried later that his **conversion** may not have taken hold because he did not evince the emotions that he saw in others, Graham's conversion would shape the direction of his life and would reshape the course of American evangelicalism in the twentieth century.

Prior to enrolling at Bob Jones College, Graham worked the summer of 1936 as a highly successful door-to-door salesman for the Fuller Brush Company. He spent only the fall semester at the fiercely Fundamentalist school, then located in Cleveland, Tennessee, before he transferred to Florida Bible Institute. Jones, the school's founder and president, had tried to bully Graham into staying at Bob Jones College, warning that "if you leave and throw your life away at a little country Bible school, the chances are you'll never be heard of. At best all you could amount to would be a poor country Baptist preacher somewhere out in the sticks" (Pollack, 12).

Graham's decision to leave Tennessee for Tampa may have been motivated less by theological scruples than by the allure of sunshine, but that transition symbolized a larger movement from the starchy Fundamentalism of his childhood, characterized by comprehensive behavioral standards and strict separation from theological liberalism and the perils of "worldliness," toward a more inclusive evangelicalism. Florida Bible Institute was hardly a bastion of liberalism, evangelical or otherwise, but Graham, though he remained theologically conservative throughout his life, ultimately rejected the dour, narrow Fundamentalism of Jones in favor of a less militant evangelicalism, which sought to speak the idiom of the culture in order to communicate the gospel.

While a student in Florida, Graham felt a divine call to preach and began doing so on street corners and, later, as a supply preacher. Several months before completing his studies at Florida Bible Institute, Graham was ordained a Southern **Baptist** minister. Feeling he needed still more education, however, he enrolled at Wheaton College in the western suburbs of Chicago. There he met, and eventually married, Ruth McCue Bell, daughter of missionaries to China, who had initially resisted the advances of the young preacher because he did not aspire to be a missionary. By the time he graduated from Wheaton College in 1943, Graham had developed the simple, earnest preaching style for which he would become famous.

Graham briefly became pastor of a small congregation in Western Springs, Illinois, and, at the invitation of Torrey Johnson, hosted a weekly radio program, *Songs in the Night*. Shortly thereafter, Johnson recruited Graham to preach at Saturday-night rallies in Chicago's Orchestra Hall, part of the outreach for a new organization called **Youth for Christ.** In 1946, Graham joined the staff of Youth for Christ, where he met and befriended Charles Templeton, another itinerant evangelist for Youth for Christ.

Templeton and Graham became known as the Gold-Dust Twins, and many contemporaries regarded Graham as the lesser preacher. Templeton's intellectual restlessness prompted him to apply for admission to Princeton Theological Seminary, where he was admitted, despite the fact that he had never graduated from college. Then, meeting Graham at the Taft Hotel in New York City, Templeton challenged his friend to attend seminary with him in order to deepen his theological understanding. Graham pondered the possibility at length, troubled by Templeton's intimations that elements of the Christian faith were not intellectually

The young Billy Graham preaches energetically under the auspices of Youth for Christ, founded in 1944 with Graham as its first full-time worker. (ca. 1944–1950.) Courtesy of the Billy Graham Center Archives, Wheaton, IL.

defensible. For Graham, a turning point in his life—and in the entire revival enterprise of the twentieth century—occurred shortly thereafter while he was staying at the Forest Home Conference Center in Southern California. While hiking and **praying** there in the San Bernardino Mountains, Graham decided to set aside Templeton's challenge, to banish his own intellectual doubts, and simply to "preach the gospel."

He did just that, descending the mountain to mount his famous Los Angeles revival campaign of 1949. Abetted by prodigious advance work, which would become the hallmark of Graham's evangelistic efforts, Graham, "America's Sensational Young Evangelist," conducted services beneath a circus **tent,** dubbed the Canvas Cathedral, at the corner of Washington and Hill Streets. Graham's enormously successful Los Angeles crusade in 1949 brought him national attention, in no small measure because newspaper magnate William Randolph

Hearst, impressed with the young evangelist's preaching and his anticommunist rhetoric, instructed his papers to "puff Graham" (i.e., give him favorable coverage). From Los Angeles, Graham took his evangelistic crusades around the country and the world, thereby providing him with international renown.

In 1948, following a successful revival campaign in Augusta, Georgia, and a cross-country drive to California, Graham and his associates (whom he always called his "team") met at a motel in Modesto, California. Graham—worried about the caricature of itinerant preachers presented in Sinclair Lewis's *Elmer Gantry* (1927) and widely believed in American society—asked his associates to consider the pitfalls that had discredited earlier revivalists and to propose ways to avoid those perils. After prayer and discussion, they decided on several principles: their salaries would be fixed by the organization, not a portion of the offerings; they would never criticize

Billy Graham Crusade in Seoul, Korea. Over 1 million people attended this crusade in Yoido Plaza, making it Billy Graham's largest meeting held anywhere in the world. (June 1973) Courtesy of the Billy Graham Evangelistic Association.

any religious leader; they would never provide estimates of crowd sizes, lest they be accused of exaggeration; they would take extraordinary precautions to avoid sexual impropriety, or even the appearance of such. Cliff Barrows, Graham's choirmaster and one of the team members present, referred to this set of principles as the Modesto Manifesto, although he insisted there is nothing official about that designation. Graham maintained that he and the team had been abiding by those principles all along, but the codification of the Modesto Manifesto helped to insulate Graham and his associates from any serious accusation of wrongdoing.

During the course of his Portland, Oregon, crusade in 1950, Graham made several decisions that would affect the course of his career and shape the revival enterprise. First, at the urging of several supporters from the world of business, he decided to incorporate his revival organization as the Billy Graham Evangelistic Association, thereby adopting a business model of organization and efficiency. After initial resistance, he also agreed to undertake a **radio** broadcast, *The Hour of Decision*, thereby tapping into the newly expanding universe of electronic media. Later, the Billy Graham Evangelistic Association would **televise** his crusades and would also produce motion pictures under the aegis of World Wide Pictures, a division of the Billy Graham Evangelistic Association.

Above all, however, the association brought corporate efficiency to the world of revivalism. The

organization groomed and then jealously guarded Graham's public image, orchestrated the details surrounding his evangelistic efforts, and provided advance work that would be the envy of a presidential candidate. Once a site had been chosen for one of Graham's crusades, for instance, the planning would take three years, and several staff members would actually relocate to the city in question in order to coordinate the preparations. In addition to Graham, the association also published *Decision* magazine and sponsored a number of "associate evangelists," including Howard Jones, Ralph Bell, and Leighton Ford.

By his own account, Graham has enjoyed close relationships with American presidents, from Dwight Eisenhower to George W. Bush. (Though Graham's first presidential conference was with Harry Truman in the Oval Office, this president was little impressed with the young evangelist.) While purporting to be apolitical, Graham's most notorious political entanglement was with Richard Nixon, whom he befriended when Nixon was Eisenhower's vice president. During the 1960 presidential campaign, Graham met in Montreaux, Switzerland, with Norman Vincent Peale and other Protestant leaders to devise a way to derail the campaign of John F. Kennedy, the Democratic nominee, thereby assisting Nixon's electoral chances. Although Graham later mended relations with Kennedy, Nixon remained his favorite, with Graham all but endorsing Nixon's reelection effort in 1972 against George McGovern.

As the Nixon presidency unraveled amid charges of criminal misconduct, Graham reviewed transcripts of the hitherto secret Watergate-era tape recordings. Although the tapes provided irrefutable evidence of Nixon's various attempts to subvert the Constitution, Graham professed to be physically sickened by his friend's use of foul language. As late as 1992, Graham described Nixon as one of the "great men" he had known (*Crusade*).

Aside from his strident anticommunism in the 1940s and 1950s, Graham's own political leanings have never been well defined—or at least they have never been publicly articulated. He has generally shied away from religiously inspired programs of social reform, insisting that the only way to change society is to "change men's hearts." That statement comports with his **eschatology** of premillennialism, the belief that Jesus will return at any time—before the millennium, 1,000 years of righteousness, predicted in Revelation 20—and that projects of social reform are essentially pointless. The only hope for meaningful change, according to Graham, lies in the aggregate effect of individual conversions rather than in programmatic reforms. Graham has occasionally taken positions on other matters. During the military buildup of the 1980s, the erstwhile cold warrior came out against nuclear proliferation. In 2004, amid various efforts on the part of the Religious Right to post the Decalogue in public places, Graham, nominally a Southern Baptist, told *Newsweek* that he supported such efforts, despite the fact that they violated Baptist principles of liberty of conscience and the separation of church and state.

In 1996, Graham and his wife, Ruth, received the Congressional Gold Medal, the highest honor that Congress can bestow a citizen. Although he consistently enjoyed approbation from the public, and he regularly appeared on lists of most admired people, Graham nevertheless endured criticism from the Right, from Fundamentalists who resented his move toward a more inclusive, irenic evangelicalism. Graham had already earned the enmity of Bob Jones when he left Bob Jones College for Florida Bible Institute after only one semester, and yet the real breach between Graham

and the Fundamentalists came in 1957 during his storied Madison Square Garden crusade in New York City.

Graham had been preaching in Paris in 1955 when word came that the Protestant Council of New York wanted him to conduct a revival campaign in Manhattan. "No other city in America—perhaps in the world," Graham recalled in his autobiography, "presented as great a challenge to evangelism" (298). Sponsors of the crusade secured an option on Madison Square Garden for the summer of 1957, and the revival turned out to be a success, running for 16 weeks and punctuated with massive rallies in Times Square and Yankee Stadium. Fundamentalists like Bob Jones, Carl McIntire, and Jack Wyrtzen were incensed, however, that Graham cooperated with the Protestant Council, whose ranks included theological liberals. They castigated Graham for compromising the faith and renounced him thereafter as a liberal and a turncoat. As late as 1992, for instance, when the executive producer for a PBS documentary on Graham approached McIntire and Bob Jones Jr. for interviews, both refused to comment.

By the twenty-first century, Graham, well into his eighties, had outlived most of his critics and endured as a kind of iconic figure in American revivalism. His evangelistic crusades around the world, his television appearances and radio broadcasts, his friendships with presidents and world leaders, and his unofficial role as spokesman for America's evangelicals made him one of the most recognized religious figures of the twentieth century.

Further Reading: *Crusade: The Life of Billy Graham.* Randall Balmer, executive producer. Arlington, VA: PBS, 1993; Frady, Marshall. *Billy Graham: A Parable of American Righteousness.* Boston: Little, Brown, 1979; Graham, Billy. *Just As I Am: The Autobiography of Billy Graham.* San Francisco: HarperSanFrancisco, 1997; High, Stanley. *Billy Graham: The Personal Story of the Man, His Message, and His Mission.* New York: McGraw-Hill, 1956; Lippy, Charles H. "Billy Graham." In Charles H. Lippy, ed., *Twentieth-Century Shapers of American Popular Religion,* 179–86. New York: Greenwood Press, 1989; Martin, William. *A Prophet with Honor: The Billy Graham Story.* New York: William R. Morrow, 1991; Pollack,

John. *Billy Graham: The Authorized Biography.* New York: McGraw-Hill, 1966.

Randall Balmer

THE GREAT AWAKENING (1739–1745)

The Great Awakening was a powerful renewal of personal and collective Christian devotion in the British North American colonies, lasting from approximately 1739 until 1745. It was Protestant in theological orientation, but manifested itself most strongly outside the relatively confined circles of the established Church of England in the colonies, and flourished in the dissenting sects, especially the Congregationalists of New England, the **Presbyterians** of the Middle Colonies of Pennsylvania and New Jersey, and Presbyterians and **Baptists** in Virginia. It overlapped with similar Protestant revivals in England, Wales, and Scotland, and could trace its lineage to continental **Pietism.** The most ambitious attempt at determining the scope of the Great Awakening was made by Joseph Tracy in 1841, when Tracy estimated that between 25,000 and 50,000 people in New England alone were taken up into the Awakening. Its pressing issues were those of the centrality and nature of personal religious experience. But contests over these issues spilled over into conflicts over the authority of the clergy, ethnic assimilation, institutional control, and, ultimately, the legitimacy of political resistance.

The long-term context of the Great Awakening begins with continental Pietism, which arose among north German Protestants in the 1670s as a movement of protest against the failure of the German princes to achieve a satisfactory solution to the century of Protestant–**Roman Catholic** warfare that had devastated central Europe, and to the theological sterility of the established churches those princes were officially responsible for. Pietism's first great architects were Philip Jakob Spener and August Hermann Francke, who founded Pietism's principal centers of influence at the new university at Halle in 1691 and the **Moravian** community at Herrnhut in 1722. It was a movement that stressed an individual's personal relationship to God more than subscription to an official confession or membership in a state-sponsored church.

Pietism found allies in Europe wherever religious conflict had discredited claims by princes or religious leaders to find a way to religious truth through confessional identity. It found allies in lay societies in the Church of England (and through ecclesiastical mavericks like John and Charles Wesley and **George Whitefield**) and in Britain's English-speaking colonies, where Pietism found both congenial German-speaking hosts in numerous places and a movement with similar historical aspirations in New England Puritanism. Pietist writings clearly had a marked effect on **Cotton Mather,** who was Puritanism's chief figure in a conservative effort to co-opt the impact of Newtonian science.

Mather's extensive network of reading and correspondence was one way of connecting America with Pietist influence. Another was through the movement of immigrant groups or ministers who had attached themselves to Pietism. The Moravians, led by Count Nikolaus L. von Zinzendorf, established major Pietist communities in Pennsylvania and North Carolina; Moravians and Salzburger **Lutherans** built settlements in Georgia; and Palatine Germans became a major presence in Pennsylvania and the Chesapeake. Scotch-Irish Presbyterians, who drank from the wells of both Pietism and English-speaking Puritanism, were a major component in migrations to the middle colonies between 1690 and 1770, and the first theological school (the so-called Log College) devoted to training clergy with the same emphasis as Pietism on personal religious awakening was founded by a Scotch-Irish Presbyterian minister, William Tennent (father of **Gilbert Tennent**), in Neshaminy, Pennsylvania, in 1726. Other immigrant clergy encouraged communal renewals of spirituality within their congregations. Bernardus Freeman, Cornelius van Santvoort, and **Theodore Frelinghuysen** brought the Pietist demand for immediate religious experience into the lives of Dutch-speaking congregations in the Hudson River valley and northern New Jersey.

WHITEFIELD ASSAULTED BY A MOB.

"I thought of Stephen, and was in hopes, like him, to go off in this bloody triumph, to the immediate presence of my Master."

Revival preachers in the mid-1700s encountered opposition and even angry mobs. John Wesley's *Journal* speaks of people throwing stones, as is happening here with George Whitefield. In the quotation, Whitefield states his readiness to suffer martyrdom by stoning, like the biblical Stephen (J. W. Barber). Courtesy of the Billy Graham Center Museum.

Pietist renewal was not greeted with enthusiasm by the established Protestant churches at any point, who regarded the Pietist emphasis on experience as a threat to confessional identity and theological purity, nor did they appreciate Pietism's demand for moral rigorism and its criticism of ministerial laxity. Frelinghuysen was cited in a 146-page complaint by Dutch Reformed pastors to Classis Amsterdam in 1725. In 1728, the Presbyterian synod of Philadelphia imposed a test of loyalty to the Westminster Confession (1648) on all new ordinands that was intended as a rebuke to William Tennent and the Log College's promotion of religious experience, and in 1738, the synod further

required new ordinands to obtain college degrees from approved schools in New England or Europe—in other words, not Neshaminy. New England Puritanism had, from before its founding, been dogged by the problem of what constituted the proper ground of church membership, and although a settlement was reached in 1662 that permitted membership to pass through the line of baptized members, it still withheld full Communion from any who could not give a satisfactory account of personal religious **conversion**. In an effort to bring both parts of this "halfway covenant" into full alignment, many New England ministers implemented a custom of congregational redemption or "owning of the covenant." But in 1672, Northampton's **Solomon Stoddard** threw the halfway covenant to the winds, admitted the entire baptized membership of the town to Communion, and turned all the energies of his **preaching** toward conversion and experience. His reward for this was the hostility of the New England establishment around Boston. But in Northampton, it produced five "harvests" of converts to renewed piety between 1678 and 1717.

Notwithstanding the opposition of the New England establishment, Stoddard made Northampton into an outpost of evangelical piety, and through his vast web of family connections and his dominant personal influence, the Connecticut River valley's Puritan churches followed Stoddard's example. When Stoddard died in 1729, he was succeeded as senior minister of Northampton by his grandson, **Jonathan Edwards,** who presided over yet another harvest—the **Northampton awakening of 1734–1735**—that brought about 300 persons to conversion and a new spiritual life. Similar harvests were gathered by John Rowland (one of William Tennent's pupils) in central New Jersey and by John and William Tennent Jr. in Freehold, New Jersey, in 1733. Up until 1739, communal revivals of religious fervency were largely the result of individual ministers, using conventional ministerial authority to redirect the patterns of piety in their congregations. And they remained comparatively rare. "Never did we hear or read," commented Isaac Watts, in his preface to Edwards's account of

FIELD PREACHING.

"I thought it might be doing the service of my Creator, who had a mountain for his pulpit, and the heavens for a sounding board; and who, when his gospel was refused by the Jews, sent his servants into the highways and hedges."

Open-air preaching was a distinguishing feature in mid-eighteenth-century evangelical revivals, both in Britain and in America, as illustrated in this woodblock print of Rev. George Whitefield. Released from the pulpit, revival preachers could go wherever people might gather to hear them (J. W. Barber). Courtesy of the Billy Graham Center Museum.

the Northampton revival of 1734–1735, "any event of this kind so surprising as the present narrative hath set before us" (Wood, 61).

Both of these conditions changed in 1739, with the arrival in Philadelphia of George Whitefield. As an ordained priest of the Church of England, Whitefield was an unlikely candidate to attract favorable notice from the largely non-Anglican population of the colonies' churches. But Whitefield had come out of the same matrix of awakening in England that produced the Wesleys, and he planned to follow the path of the Moravians to Georgia and found an orphanage there in 1738.

The need to raise money for the orphanage sent Whitefield on a tour of the main port towns of the colonies, where he expected that invitations to preach in the American churches would give him an opportunity to solicit offerings for the orphanage. Whitefield arrived first in Philadelphia, the principal town of British North America, on November 2, 1739, and in short order, his collections for the orphanage were eclipsed by the sensational response to his preaching. Although the product of a conventional Oxford education for the ministry, Whitefield had no scruples about incorporating into his preaching the new appeal to sensibility and the "affections" recommended, at the most philosophical extreme, by the second Earl of Shaftesbury's *Characteristics of Men, Manners, Opinions, Times* (1711), and at the most practical, by the glorification of "sensibility" in popular novels and the Georgian theater. Possessed by a flair for the dramatic, Whitefield turned preaching from a learned exposition of a biblical text to an emotion-laden tragedy whose catharsis lay in the experience of an evangelical "new birth." That this was also the point to which Pietism was aimed only made Whitefield's relations with the dissenting sects warmer, and his connections to the Church of England hierarchy frostier.

Whitefield had already acquired a reputation for sensationalism before venturing to America. But once in the colonies, he became the center of a whirlwind. Benjamin Franklin, hearing him preach in Philadelphia, was amazed both at the sheer power of Whitefield's voice (which Franklin estimated could be heard by 30,000 people out of doors with no trouble) and at his irresistible persuasiveness. Within a week, Whitefield had attracted the notice of William Tennent and publicly endorsed Tennent's struggle with the synod of Philadelphia. He went to New York, returned to Philadelphia, and then went on to Georgia. By the spring of 1740, he was on the move again, returning to Philadelphia and New York, then Charleston, and then finally, on September 14, setting foot for the first time in New England. He entered Boston in triumph, preaching to ever-increasing crowds in the churches and to 23,000 people in Boston Common. He then struck westward to Northampton, where he visited Jonathan Edwards and preached in the Northampton church, and then south into Connecticut and overland back to Philadelphia. In all, Whitefield had preached 175 times.

Whitefield left for England in January 1741, and did not return to America until 1745. In his absence, the enthusiasm his preaching generated erupted in revivals in 34 towns in Massachusetts, 9 towns in the Connecticut River valley, and another 25 in New Jersey and Pennsylvania. A fresh wave of revival swept over Edwards's Northampton, and Edwards himself was soon being called to preach throughout western Massachusetts by ministers who wanted to encourage revivals in their parishes, too. One of these invitations, from the church at Enfield, Connecticut, resulted in Edwards's most famous sermon, and the most famous document of the Awakening, "Sinners in the Hands of an Angry God," preached at Enfield on July 2, 1741. Between 1739 and 1741, American printers turned out 114 publications related to revival interests, almost a quarter of the titles published in British North America. In March 1743, a Boston minister, Thomas Prince, inaugurated a new weekly eight-page magazine, the *Christian History*, modeled after revival magazines in England and Scotland and devoted exclusively to news and accounts of revivals. Whitefield himself proved to be a sophisticated disseminator of his own publications, contracting with Benjamin Franklin (as the colonies' most successful print entrepreneur and the postmaster for the colonial mails) to publish and distribute his sermons and journals through Franklin's affiliates, from Charleston to Boston.

Whitefield's sympathies with the Tennents and with the larger Pietist network prompted suspicion of his preaching and of the revivals even before his first preaching tour of 1739–1740 had ended. His appeal to the passions and his demand for a decisive spiritual rebirth in both ministers and people swiftly alienated the colonies' Church of England clergy, who had no taste for either passion or rebirth. But criticism also began to fester among the Presbyterian and New England clergy. In the

spring of 1740, the Tennents, led by William's son Gilbert, charged the synod of Philadelphia with "unsoundness in some of the principal doctrines of Christianity that relate to experience and practice." The synod wavered over its response, and on March 8, 1740, Gilbert Tennent, borrowing the pulpit of a church in Nottingham, Pennsylvania, delivered "The Danger of an Unconverted Ministry." Not only did Tennent question the spiritual integrity of "unconverted ministers," but he declared it "both lawful and expedient" for awakened parishioners to leave their regularly appointed synod parishes and go "to hear Godly Persons," i.e. pro-revival preachers (Bushman, 93). When the synod of Philadelphia met again in June 1741, the synod replied to Tennent in kind, and the warring factions split, with the revivalists forming an entirely separate synod of New York, and American Presbyterianism divided into Old Side and New Side parties.

Whitefield precipitated a similar face-off in New England by unwisely confiding to his seventh *Journal* a series of observations on the spiritual unfitness of "a great number of ministers" (Murray, 470) in Boston, and when it was printed in London in April 1741, it triggered the first of what would become a cascade of anti-Whitefield letters to the editor and pamphlets. The strife became worse in the fall of 1741, after Thomas Clap, the rector of Yale College, invited Jonathan Edwards as the commencement speaker. Although Edwards had none of Whitefield's showmanship, he was a much better analyst of the psychology of conversion, and his address (which was published in November as *The Distinguishing Marks of a Work of the Spirit of God*) offered a sprightly refutation of the mounting complaints against the Awakening. Instead of silencing the critics, it encouraged Yale students to flout college authority, and in November 1741, Rector Clap decided to make an example of a particularly ardent admirer of Edwards's, **David Brainerd,** by expelling him from Yale. The expulsion only made Brainerd into a martyr, and the uproar grew so great that Clap was forced to suspend classes in April 1742, and send the students home to cool off. Instead of a cool-off, Whitefield's allies in Connecticut opened a rival college in New London, the Shepherd's Tent.

It is easy to sympathize with Whitefield and Tennent as the underdogs. But Whitefield's and Tennent's decision to turn itinerant and preach without permission from the local ministry subverted what little order ministers and magistrates could hope to impose on the wild rim of the British empire. And by offering parishioners their own choice of what preaching to attend, the revivalists were throwing decision making about matters of the spirit into the hands of the laity, who were generally the people least well equipped to judge and the most likely to be duped by religious hucksters.

The proof everyone could point to was **James Davenport.** A Yale graduate, Davenport had been the pastor of a Congregational church on Long Island. But Whitefield cast his shadow over Davenport, and in 1741, Davenport deputized himself as a missionary to Connecticut. When the legislature ordered him arrested and expelled, he took off for Boston. But no matter how bizarre his behavior, Davenport never seemed to lack for disciples, and in March 1743, he returned to Connecticut to organize an illegal "separate" parish in New London, which he inaugurated on March 6 with a bonfire of books, gowns, clothes, and jewelry, including his own "wearing Breeches." Under threat of arrest, Davenport fled to Stanford, suffered a breakdown, and in 1744, issued a *Confession and Retractions* that begged general forgiveness for "misguided Zeal" (Bushman, 54). But for at least three years, Davenport had been the scourge of the unconverted, and when it was over, neither his friends nor his enemies looked the better or wiser.

The New England churches were now as hopelessly split as the Presbyterians in Pennsylvania and New Jersey, dividing into Old Light (anti-Whitefield) and New Light factions. In 1743, the Boston Old Light pastor **Charles Chauncy** published a massive critique of the Awakening, *Seasonable Thoughts on the State of Religion in New England,* and in May 1743, the annual Massachusetts pastors' convention published *Testimony,* an argument against the revivals. Six days later, a meeting of pro-revival ministers was hurriedly called, and in July they replied to the Old Lights with *Testimony and Advice,* signed by 68

ministers (and by Edwards in absentia). But by this point, the Awakening had suffered so many self-inflicted wounds, and had lost so much momentum, that the revivals were on the wane anyway. There would continue to be aftershocks, especially in Virginia in the later 1740s and 1750s, as New Side Presbyterians carried the awakening gospel with them on their next round of migrations. But the principal energies were spent. The volume of revival publications declined to only five by 1746, and even the *Christian History* ceased publication in late 1745.

The splits caused by the Awakening had only one happy ending, and that concerned the Presbyterians, whose rival synods reunited under the surprising aegis of Gilbert Tennent in 1758. In New England, however, the Puritan churches were permanently wrecked, first by Separate congregations who felt they had no choice except to leave the New England establishment completely, legally or not, and then by the Old Lights, who turned increasingly toward Unitarianism and were never reconciled to the New Lights.

Beyond these structural disruptions, there has been little agreement over the long-term results of the Awakening. It has been variously presented as a justification of the truth of evangelical religion (Joseph Tracy), as the last gasp of a hateful religious fanaticism (Vernon Parrington), as the beginning point of a distinctively American culture (Herbert L. Osgood), as the first sign of the political antiauthoritarianism that would produce the Revolution (Alan Heimert, Rhys Isaac), and as a minor and isolated episode in the long-term Christianization of the landscape (Jon Butler). Butler's skepticism about the Awakening contained some legitimate objections—the Awakening was not, after all, a colonies-wide event—but like most skepticisms, it suffered from having originally expected its subject to do too much. Heimert, by contrast, frequently exhibited overreach, and made the Great Awakening a schoolmaster for Revolutionary ideology. And yet, even if the Awakening cannot be claimed as a blueprint for the Revolution, it certainly is symptomatic of the ease with which authority in America could be fragmented. What cannot be dismissed are the institutional effects of the Awakening—not only the sundering of New England Puritanism, but the rush of the competing factions to safeguard their constituencies by founding colleges (Dartmouth, Brown, and Princeton by New Lights, Columbia and Pennsylvania by Old Lights) and, on the revivalists' side, the erection of **foreign missions** agencies (beginning with the American Board of Commissioners for Foreign Missions in 1810).

The most important legacy of the Great Awakening was the formation, not of an American culture or politics, but of a distinctively American evangelical culture, synthesized from the various elements of Pietism, Puritanism, proto-Romantic sensibility, and Edwardsean analysis of the nature of conversion. The long-term influence of that culture stretches beyond the specific question of the Awakening's connections to the Revolution, and attaches it to the **Second Great Awakening,** the **abolitionist** crusade against slavery, the Progressive reformers, and the culture wars of our own time. On those terms, if not the others, the Great Awakening more than deserves its place as an epoch in American history.

Further Reading: Bushman, Richard L., ed. *The Great Awakening: Documents on the Revival of Religion, 1740–1745.* New York: Atheneum, 1970; Gaustad, Edwin Scott. *The Great Awakening in New England.* Chicago: Quadrangle Books, 1968; Heimert, Alan. *Religion and the American Mind: From the Great Awakening to the Revolution.* Cambridge, MA: Harvard University Press, 1966; Isaac, Rhys. *The Transformation of Virginia, 1740–1790.* Chapel Hill: University of North Carolina Press, 1982; Lambert, Frank. *Inventing the "Great Awakening."* Princeton, NJ: Princeton University Press, 1999; Murray, Iain, ed. *George Whitefield's Journals.* Edinburgh: Banner of Truth Trust, 1960; Stout, Harry S. *The Divine Dramatist: George Whitefield and the Rise of Modern Evangelicalism.* Grand Rapids, MI: Eerdmans, 1991; Trinterud, Leonard J. *The Forming of an American Tradition: A Re-examination of Colonial Presbyterianism.* Philadelphia: Westminster Press, 1949; Ward, W. R. *The Protestant Evangelical Awakening.* Cambridge: Cambridge University Press, 1992; Westerkamp, Marilyn. *The Triumph of the Laity: Scots-Irish Piety and the Great Awakening, 1625–1760.* New York: Oxford University Press, 1989; Winslow, Ola Elizabeth. *Jonathan Edwards, 1703–1758.* New York: Macmillan, 1940; Wood, A. Skevington. *The Inextinguishable Blaze: Spiritual Renewal and Advance in the Eighteenth Century.* London: Paternoster Press, 1960.

Allen Guelzo

H

HAGIN, KENNETH E., SR. (1917–2003)

Kenneth Hagin was the leader of the neo-**Charismatic** Word of Faith or Positive Confession movement that has been closely associated with the so-called **prosperity theology.** He was born prematurely in 1917, with a deformed heart. He was not expected to survive, but managed to function for 15 years before becoming an invalid. Hagin was converted to Christ on April 22, 1933, after he claimed to have experienced the horrors of hell on three occasions when, during a 10-minute period, his vital signs failed three times. He reported that, on the way to the hospital in an ambulance, his mind was filled with Mark 11:23–24 (Authorized Version): "What things soever ye desire, when ye pray, believe that ye receive them, and ye shall have them." This faith principle became the guiding dynamic of his life. He began to verbalize or confess his own **healing** daily. Eight months later he claimed that his heart and his incurable blood disease had been cured.

In 1934, Kenneth Hagin began ministry as a lay **preacher** for a small multidenominational country church in Texas, attended primarily by Southern **Baptists.** In 1937 he was **baptized in the Holy Spirit.** Now a **Pentecostal,** he pastored six churches successively between 1937 and 1949. In 1952

Hagin reported that Jesus called him to be a **prophet.** From 1949 to 1963 he served as an itinerant Bible teacher and evangelist, and reported having eight personal visitations from Jesus Christ. Hagin claimed that in the third vision he was granted the gift of discernment of spirits, enabling him to **pray** more effectively for the healing of the sick. He also reported that Jesus gave him a four-step guide to physical, spiritual, and financial health and prosperity: say it, do it, receive it, and tell it.

As a result of his visions, Hagin set up an office in his Garland, Texas, home in 1963, and began distributing his tapes and books. Three years later he moved to Tulsa, Oklahoma. In 1974 he founded Rhema Bible Training Center in Broken Arrow, a suburb of Tulsa. Rhema now has over 23,000 alumni, many of whom have established Word of Faith churches or evangelistic ministries in various countries. There are Rhema extension centers in 13 other nations: Austria, Brazil, Colombia, Germany, India, Italy, Mexico, Peru, Romania, Samoa, Singapore, South Africa, and Thailand. In 1979 he founded the Prayer and Healing Center to provide a place where the sick could come and have an opportunity to build their faith. Healing school continues to be held twice daily on the Rhema campus. Hagin emphasizes the message of uncompromising faith in a God who desires to bless in every area of life those who do not doubt him. Among Hagin's many Positive Confession protégés are

Kenneth Hagin Jr., Kenneth Copeland, Jerry Savelle, Fred Price, Charles Capps, and Robert Tilton.

Hagin and his "health and wealth" faith movement have been attacked ruthlessly by a range of detractors, such as **Hendrik "Hank" Hanegraaff,** John F. MacArthur Jr., and Michael G. Moriarty, who point to Hagin's obvious plagiarism from early faith evangelist E. W. Kenyon (1867–1948), while claiming his ideas came from direct divine inspiration. They also spell out Hagin's "heresies," including his teaching that believers become "little gods." Further, evangelicals have attacked Hagin for his teaching that the atonement was not complete with Jesus' physical death on the cross, but rather with his spiritual death after his descent into hell, where he was tortured by the devil for three days and nights. Above all, Hagin and his supporters are demeaned for their tendency to diminish the traditional doctrines of divine transcendence and divine sovereignty. Kenneth Hagin Sr., died in September 2003, at the age of 86, 10 days after collapsing in his home.

Further Reading: Avanzini, John. "Was Jesus Poor?" *Believer's Voice of Victory,* July/August 1991, 6–7; Capps, Charles. *Authority in Three Worlds.* Tulsa, OK: Harrison House, 1982; Chappell, Paul G. "Kenneth Hagin, Sr." In Charles H. Lippy, ed., *Twentieth-Century Shapers of American Popular Religion,* 186–93. New York: Greenwood Press, 1989; Hagin, Kenneth E. *How to Turn Your Faith Loose.* Tulsa, OK: Faith Library, 1979; Hagin, Kenneth E. *The Key to Spiritual Healing.* Tulsa, OK: Faith Library, 1979; Hagin, Kenneth E. *The Name of Jesus.* Tulsa, OK: Kenneth Hagin Ministries, 1986; Hagin, Kenneth E. *Your Faith in God Will Work.* Tulsa, OK: Kenneth Hagin Ministries, 1995; Hagin, Kenneth E. *Zoe: The God Kind of Life.* Tulsa, OK: Kenneth Hagin Ministries, 1989; MacArthur, John F. *Charismatic Chaos.* Grand Rapids, MI: Zondervan, 1991; McConnell, D. R. *A Different Gospel.* Peabody, MA: Hendrickson, 1988; Moriarty, Michael G. *The New Charismatics.* Grand Rapids, MI: Zondervan, 1992.

Stanley M. Burgess

HANEGRAAFF, HENDRIK (HANK) (1950–)

Hank Hanegraaff is a well-known Christian radio personality and outspoken critic of recent revival movements in North America. He hosts *The Bible Answer Man* program heard daily, as of 2005, on more than 125 radio stations throughout the United States and Canada. He is president of the Christian Research Institute in Rancho Santa Margarita, California; contributes regularly to the *Christian Research Journal;* has written more than 10 books; and has appeared in interviews with Peter Jennings on ABC and on CNN's *Larry King Live.* The Christian Research Institute (CRI), founded in 1960 by Walter Martin (1928–1989) is a Christian apologetics and anticult organization. After Martin's death, Hanegraaff became president. The CRI is one of the largest organizations of its kind in the world. Hanegraaff came to faith in Jesus Christ after examining the scientific evidence for creation and the historical evidence for both the resurrection of Jesus Christ and the inspiration of scripture. Prior to joining the CRI, he spent time with Dr. James Kennedy of Coral Ridge Presbyterian Church in Fort Lauderdale, Florida, in the study of Christian apologetics.

Hanegraaff has been controversial due to his opposition to what he regards as pseudo-Christian cults, including the Word of Faith movement associated with **Kenneth E. Hagin Sr.** and **prosperity theology,** as well as the **Toronto Blessing.** He identified the latter, and similar or related movements such as the **Pensacola (Brownsville) revival,** as parts of a "counterfeit revival" in a book of that title charging that Christianity was undergoing "a shift from faith to feelings, from fact to fantasy, and from reason to esoteric revelation," that proponents of the new "counterfeit" revival used "sociopsychological manipulation and Scripture-twisting tactics," and that they tended to "pepper their appearances with fabrications, fantasies, and frauds" (9, 16, 61). He felt that there were similarities between their methods and the methods of mesmerists and occultists, and that these revivals focused on exotic spiritual and **bodily manifestations** rather than the weightier matters of sin, salvation, and **sanctification.** While the ministry of **Jonathan Edwards** was characterized by dynamic biblical **preaching,** "the message of the counterfeit revival is characterized by delusional experiential pandering.... Rather than testing experience by the objective standard of Scripture, they have subjectively embraced esoteric experiences" (101, 103).

In response to *Counterfeit Revival,* James A. Beverley, professor of theology and ethics at Ontario Theological Seminary in Toronto, wrote a short book, *Revival Wars,* and a book review for *Christianity Today* magazine. Beverley felt that Hanegraaff's book exposed some real excesses and imbalances in current movements, and that he properly criticized an "undue emphasis on strange manifestations," but that "in the end, it is a misleading, simplistic, and harmful book, marred by faulty logic, outdated and limited research, and nasty misrepresentation of key charismatic leaders" ("Counterfeit Critique," 59). On the CRI Web site, Hanegraaff responded that Beverley himself was guilty of many of the same misleading tactics.

Further Reading: Beverley, James A. "Counterfeit Critique." *Christianity Today,* September 1, 1997, 59–60; Beverley, James A. *Revival Wars: A Critique of Counterfeit Revival.* Pickering, ON: Evangelical Research Ministries, 1997; Hanegraaff, Hank. "Counterfeit Critique." Christian Research Institute, January 2005. http://www.equip.org/free/DL210.htm; Hanegraaff, Hank. *Counterfeit Revival.* Dallas: Word, 1997; Riss, Richard M. "Hank Hanegraaff's Criticisms—A Note to Randy Clark." Global Resource Ministries, January 2005. http://www.grmi.org/renewal/Richard_Riss/defense/hank16.html; Spencer, James. *Heresy Hunters.* Lafayette, LA: Huntington House, 1993; Williams, Don. *Revival: The Real Thing: A Response to Hank Hanegraaff's "Counterfeit Revival."* La Jolla, CA: self-published, 1995.

Richard M. Riss

HAYSTACK PRAYER MEETING

The beginnings of interest in **foreign missions** on the part of the nineteenth-century American Protestants may be traced to student influence and specifically to Samuel J. Mills Jr. (1783–1818). Born in Connecticut as the son of a Congregational minister, Mills was brought up in a devout home and in the spring of 1806 enrolled in Williams College, Massachusetts. The **campus** had been deeply affected by the religious awakening of those

years, and students were concerned about spiritual matters. It was Mills's custom to spend Wednesday and Saturday afternoons in **prayer** with other students on the banks of the Hoosack River or in a valley near the college.

One Saturday afternoon in August 1806, Samuel Mills, Harvey Loomis, Byram Green, Francis L. Robbins, and James Richards gathered as usual in the maple grove of Sloan's Meadow. When thunderstorms arose the five students sought refuge from the rain on the leeward side of a large haystack. As they waited out the storm Mills reflected on his recent classroom studies of Asia and the East India Company and spoke to the others of his desire to spread Christianity throughout the world. Mills further focused their discussion and prayer on their own individual missionary obligations. He exhorted his companions with the words that later became their motto: "We can do this, if we will." These first American student volunteers for foreign missions intended to go and serve wherever God might need them. Through their dedication they gave birth to the first student missionary society in America, which helped to spawn the **Student Volunteer Movement,** which resulted in an estimated 20,000 new Protestants missionaries around the world in the late 1800s and early 1900s.

In 1808, Mills and other Williams College students formed the Brethren, a society organized to promote missionary efforts abroad. Following graduation Mills and Richards entered Andover Seminary in 1810, where they recruited Adoniram Judson from Brown, Samuel Newall from Harvard, and Samuel Nott from Union College to join the Brethren. Led by the enthusiasm of Judson, the young seminarians convinced the General Association of Congregational Ministers of Massachusetts to establish the American Board of Commissioners for Foreign Missions in 1810. In February 1812, Rev. and Mrs. Judson, Rev. and Mrs. Newall, Rev. and Mrs. Nott, Rev. Gordon Hall, and Rev. Luther Rice were commissioned as the Board's first missionaries and set sail for Calcutta, India. Adoniram Judson, who later settled in Burma, became one of the best-known missionaries of the nineteenth century. The Haystack movement also led to the formation of societies on other campuses with the explicit purpose of world mission. Princeton College students, for example, formed a group in 1814 and kept close contact with Andover students.

While two of the five Haystack students led the missions movement from Andover Seminary the others pursued missions and service through a variety of avenues. Loomis dedicated his life to domestic missions in the state of Maine. Robbins engaged in missionary work in New Hampshire before returning to pastor a church in his native state of Connecticut. Green **preached** for a short time before serving in New York State government and later in the U.S. Congress. Richards left America in 1815, serving as a missionary in India until his death in 1822. Mills also engaged in missions in the Ohio and Mississippi valleys, in the Southwest United States, and in New Orleans. He influenced the founding of the American Bible Society and the United Foreign Missionary Society before he died in 1818 while returning from a short-term mission trip to Africa with the American Colonization Society. Dedicated in 1867, a 12-foot monument in Williamstown, Massachusetts, marks the spot of the influential 1806 prayer meeting.

Further Reading: Latourette, Kenneth. *These Sought a Country.* New York: Harper, 1950; Omulogoli, Watson. "The Student Volunteer Movement: Its History and Contribution." MA thesis, Wheaton College, IL, 1967; Shedd, Clarence. *Two Centuries of Student Christian Movements.* New York: Association Press, 1934.

Mark W. Cannister

HAYWOOD, GARFIELD THOMAS (1880–1931)

Garfield Thomas Haywood was an **African American** and **Pentecostal** pastor, denominational leader, editor, and composer who played a prominent role in the growth of Oneness Pentecostalism. Oneness Pentecostals reject the doctrine of the Trinity, and, unlike virtually all other Christian groups, they do not baptize their members in the triune name of the Father, Son, and Holy Spirit. Instead they favor a Jesus-centered modalism, and practice rebaptism "in the name of Jesus" for those who were previously baptized in the name of the

Holy Trinity. The Oneness tradition represents a development of impulses that have been prominent in North American revivalism, especially **restorationism** and Jesus-centered devotionalism. In large part due to Haywood's influence, Oneness Pentecostalism found favor with a majority of African American Pentecostals in Indianapolis and spread throughout the Midwest.

Haywood was the third of nine children born to Benjamin and Penny Ann Haywood. When he was three, his parents moved from Greencastle to Indianapolis, Indiana. As a high school student Haywood demonstrated promising artistic ability. At 16 he quit school to help support his family and was hired as a cartoonist for the *Freedman* and the *Recorder*, both Indianapolis-based African American newspapers. In 1902, he married Ida Howard, with whom he had one daughter. In 1908, a defining moment came in Haywood's life when he experienced the **baptism in the Holy Spirit** at a small storefront church of only 13 members. A year later he became the pastor of the small congregation, which suffered persecution because of its interracial character. For the next several years Haywood moved the church to larger buildings throughout Indianapolis as the community experienced steady growth under his leadership. His ministry was characterized by a deep knowledge of the Bible, wide-ranging intellectual curiosity, and dedicated pastoral care.

In 1910 Haywood began publishing the periodical *Voice in the Wilderness.* In 1912 his congregation joined the **Pentecostal Assemblies of the World** (PAW) and began hosting its annual convention. By this time Pentecostals from across the United States and Canada recognized Haywood as an important leader. In 1915 Haywood accepted the emerging Oneness teaching and was rebaptized in the name of Jesus, to the dismay of leaders in the newly formed **Assemblies of God,** which from its inception in 1914 held to Trinitarian theology and Trinitarian baptism. Haywood's congregation, one of the nation's largest African American Pentecostal congregations, followed his embrace of the Oneness message, as did many African American Pentecostal **preachers** in

Indianapolis. The PAW officially adopted Oneness doctrine and elected Haywood its first secretary-treasurer in 1918. Haywood's *Voice in the Wilderness* became the major mouthpiece for the Oneness movement. In this journal Haywood wrote articles that helped define Oneness theology and published hymns that became popular throughout Pentecostalism. Some of the articles provided material for his approximately 13 books and several tracts. A prominent argument in his writings is that the Oneness movement is a divinely appointed, **eschatological** or end-time revival of true **apostolic** belief and practice.

In 1924 Haywood moved his congregation to a new 1,500-seat sanctuary at Fall Creek Boulevard named Christ Temple. That same year many white members of the PAW left to form their own denomination. The PAW reorganized, adopted an Episcopal system, and elected Haywood the first presiding bishop, an office he held until his death in March 1931. As bishop, Haywood was committed to interracial leadership in the PAW, believing that racial unity was fundamental to the Pentecostal revival. Revered in his time, Haywood's legacy continues to influence Oneness Pentecostals today through his writings and the memory of his exemplary leadership.

Further Reading: Bundy, David. "G. T. Haywood: Religion for Urban Realities." In James R. Goff Jr. and Grant Wacker, eds., *Portraits of a Generation: Early Pentecostal Leaders*, 237–53. Fayetteville: University of Arkansas Press, 2002; Golder, Morris E. *The Life and Works of Bishop Garfield Thomas Haywood (1880–1931).* Indianapolis: self-published, 1977; Haywood, Garfield T. *The Life and Writings of Elder G. T. Haywood.* Comp. Paul D. Duga. Portland, OR: Apostolic Book Publishers, 1968.

Benjamin Wagner

HEALING AND REVIVALS

Interest in divine healing has accompanied nearly every American religious revival, especially since the late nineteenth century. Nonetheless, belief in divine healing has often aroused controversy among traditional Protestants. During the Reformation, John Calvin developed a theological position known as *cessationism*. According to this viewpoint, the gifts of the Holy Spirit such as healings and miracles ceased with the canonization of scripture because they were no longer needed to authenticate the ministry of Jesus and the apostles. Many Protestant teachers—both **Lutheran** and **Calvinist**—have interpreted sickness as sent by God for the purpose of **sanctification,** and admonished the sick to endure suffering patiently rather than seek healing. Arguing that Satan rather than God is the author of disease, divine healing advocates emerged from a revivalistic climate that promoted entire sanctification, and maintained that the Holy Spirit could cleanse the body from disease as well as sin, empowering Christians for service. Revivalists drew upon religious **restorationism,** literalist biblical interpretation, and philosophical empiricism to reason from scripture, personal testimony, and medical evidence that modern Christians should expect healings like those recorded in the Bible. In this view, Jesus Christ provided for physical healing as well as spiritual salvation, since in the language of Isaiah 53:5 (Authorized Version), "with his stripes we are healed." Other biblical passages commonly cited include Exodus 15:26, Psalms 103:3, Matthew 8:16–17, Mark 16:18, 1 Corinthians 12:9–10, Hebrews 13:8, James 5:14–16, and 1 Peter 2:24. Because the argument for modern-day divine healing challenged both religious and medical authorities, it has continued to generate considerable controversy.

Prior to the mid-nineteenth century, references to divine healing are relatively rare in the American historical record. Several British and American revivalists reported physical healings that they attributed to supernatural intervention in response to **prayer. Quaker** founder George Fox claimed that during his 1672 missionary journey to America dozens of people received miraculous healings, and that there was one miraculous resurrection from the dead. John Wesley, leader of the eighteenth-century **Methodist revivals,** recorded numerous instances of healing in response to prayer, most famously the healing of his horse. The best-known

John Alexander Dowie's periodical featured this illustration expressing his confidence that Jesus' atoning death provided for healing as well as forgiveness. On the right are biblical verses on healing while below are those influenced by "drugs," "devils," and eating "swine's flesh" (*Leaves of Healing*, Zion, IL, 1901).

evangelist of the **Great Awakening, George Whitefield,** claimed that he himself, after prayer, arose from his deathbed to **preach** the gospel. **Charles Finney,** the foremost revivalist of the **Second Great Awakening,** encouraged his congregations to pray for healing, expecting God to respond to a special form of prayer that he called "the prayer of faith."

The most influential pioneers in the modern divine healing movement were nineteenth-century Europeans who sought a restoration of the gifts of the Holy Spirit experienced by the primitive church. In 1830, Edward Irving of the **Presbyterian** Scottish Church preached to audiences numbering over 10,000 concerning the renewal of the **charismatic gifts,** such as healing and **speaking in tongues.** Irving laid the foundation for the **Catholic Apostolic Church**—a nineteenth-century **charismatic**

group. Johann Blumhardt in Germany and Dorothea Trudel and Otto Stockmayer in Switzerland began in the 1840s and 1850s to oversee healing homes where they prayed for the sick. The American homeopathic physician and Episcopal layman Charles Cullis publicized the European precedents in the 1870s and 1880s through his publishing company, the Willard Tract Repository, which produced a score of major publications and dozens of tracts on faith healing. One of the first full-time itinerant American healing evangelists was Ethan O. Allen, who after his own healing from tuberculosis in 1846, spent the next 50 years traveling around the eastern United States praying for the sick and teaching divine healing. Allen's associate, Elizabeth Mix, was the first **African American** healing evangelist to attract public attention. One of the earliest American theologians to support modern divine healing, **Horace Bushnell,** in *Nature and the Supernatural* (1858), opposed religious revivals but stressed the ongoing activity of the Holy Spirit, adding credibility to the claim that all the charismatic gifts had continued.

Widespread belief in divine healing took root in the religious revivals of the second half of the nineteenth century. The **Revival of 1857–1858** prepared the way by emphasizing the outpouring of the Holy Spirit in power. A significant minority of leaders in the **Holiness movement** and Higher Life revivals of the 1860s–1880s promoted divine healing, including William E. Boardman, **Asa Mahan,** John S. Inskip, Daniel Steele, Thomas C. Upham, A. J. Gordon, and **Hannah Whitall Smith.** Higher Life conferences in Keswick, England, and **camp meetings and tent meetings** like Charles Cullis's and **Albert Benjamin Simpson**'s Old Orchard conventions devoted special services to prayers for healing. The International Conference on Divine Healing and True Holiness that met in London in 1885 attracted nearly 2,000 attendees from at least nine countries. Although **Dwight Moody** disagreed with divine healing teachings, he invited advocates of the doctrine to speak at his Northfield conventions. Proponents during this period included Carrie Judd Montgomery, R. Kelso Carter, and especially **Maria Woodworth-Etter,** who has been called the grandmother of modern **Pentecostalism.** The Holiness, like the later Pentecostal movement, proclaimed a fourfold gospel of Jesus as Savior, Sanctifier, Healer, and Coming Lord. Although prayer for healing occupied a prominent role in many services, salvation from sin always constituted the primary concern of the revivalists, and numerous conversions were reported in all the healing revivals.

The nineteenth-century healing evangelists founded dozens of healing homes, published countless testimonials in widely circulated books and periodicals, and prayed for thousands of the sick at camp meetings, special healing services, and faith conventions held in cities across the United States and Canada. Healing practices included itinerant, tent-meeting revivalism, laying on of hands, anointing with oil, **fasting,** distribution of blessed cloths, prayer over mailed-in requests, use of prayer cards, formation of healing lines, visitation of the sick in homes and hospitals, the Lord's Supper or Communion, and always Bible teaching and personal testimony. In the twentieth century, revivalists added the strategies of **radio and television** evangelism.

The divine healing movement was at its core an ecumenical movement that influenced tens of thousands of individuals in all Christian denominations through revivalistic services. **John Alexander Dowie,** who preached healing to crowds as large as 20,000, founded the city of Zion, Illinois, to promote divine healing and holiness. Out of Zion emerged several of the twentieth-century's leading healing evangelists, including F. F. and B. B. Bosworth, Dr. Phineas Yoakum, Raymond T. Richey, Gordon Lindsay, and John G. Lake. Dowie represented the antimedical wing of the movement, exemplified by his infamous sermon "Doctors, Drugs, and Devils, or The Foes of Christ the Healer" (1896). Despite interdenominational cooperation, several new denominations emerged from the movement, including Dowie's Christian Catholic Church, A. B. Simpson's **Christian and Missionary Alliance,** John G. Lake's Apostolic Church, and **Aimee Semple McPherson's International Church of the Foursquare Gospel.**

By 1903, Pentecostal founder **Charles Fox Parham** attracted overflow crowds to his 2,000-person tent, where he prayed individually for all the sick. The 1906 Pentecostal revivals at **Azusa Street** led by African American **William Seymour** emphasized divine healing. The healing testimonies ranged from relief for minor pains to cures from blindness, deafness, cancers, and paralysis; re-creation of missing body parts; and resurrections from the dead. The large-scale urban healing campaigns that spread from Azusa stalled in the 1930s with the onset of the depression. Radio pioneer Aimee Semple McPherson, who, after several years as a successful itinerant, founded Angelus Temple in 1923 near Hollywood, weathered the difficulties of the Great Depression, regularly filling her 5,000-seat auditorium four times each Sunday.

From 1947 to 1958, the largest healing revival in American history, reported in Gordon Lindsay's *Voice of Healing* magazine, swept across the country. One stimulus for the revival was Franklin Hall's publication of *Atomic Power with God through Prayer and Fasting* (1946). Over a hundred healing evangelists associated with the Voice of Healing network, including **William Branham,** Jack Coe, Louise Nankivell, A. A. Allen, Morris Cerullo, and **A. C. Valdez,** conducted tent crusades with crowds that often numbered in excess of 10,000. T. L. Osborn took the American healing revivals overseas, stimulating a new wave of missionary interest.

Scores of itinerant evangelists operated independently, most notably **Oral Roberts** and **Kathryn Kuhlman,** both of whose ministries flourished into the 1970s. In contrast to Dowie's antagonism toward doctors, Roberts preached the complementarity of medicine and prayer, and Kuhlman insisted on medical verification for every testimonial. The itinerants' success in attracting audiences and finances led to their alienation from established Pentecostal churches, which viewed them as competitors. The Voice of Healing revival transitioned into what has been termed a Testimony Revival as the proliferation of reported conversions and healings created the perception of a new need for teachers, one of the foremost of whom was Derek Prince. Television heightened the public profiles of other healing evangelists, such as Rex Humbard, Ernest Angley, and **Jimmy Swaggart.**

While Pentecostal denominations distanced themselves from divine healing, support grew within mainstream Protestant and post–Vatican II **Roman Catholic** churches, as the **Charismatic Revival and Renewal** mushroomed during the 1960s and 1970s. The Episcopal Church USA endorsed the healing value of the Eucharist, **fasting,** and anointing with oil, and affirmed lay healing ministries like that of Agnes Sanford and Emily Gardiner Neal. The Association of Vineyard Churches, founded by **John Wimber,** promoted charismatic **signs and wonders** in established denominations as well as new styles of worship and Christian music. **Francis MacNutt** brought healing practices into Roman Catholic circles, as well as the wider ecumenical movement, and connected healing with social justice when he stressed the implications of healing for Latin American liberation theologies.

The Word of Faith movement emerged in the 1970s to emphasize the Christians' authority to claim healing and financial **prosperity** based on biblical promises. Leaders included **Kenneth Hagin Sr.,** Paul and Jan Crouch, **Kenneth Copeland,** and the foremost African American in the movement, Frederick Price. Oral Roberts courted a broader audience by joining the Methodists in 1968 and deemphasizing the more controversial of his earlier healing strategies, such as prayer for **deliverance** from demonic oppression, in favor of **conversion,** medical healing, and financial blessings through seed-faith giving. By the 1990s, a new generation had emerged who envisioned themselves as direct descendants of the earlier healing evangelists. Revivalists who belong to the **Apostolic movement,** such as Rodney Howard-Browne, Randy Clark, Todd Bentley, Mahesh Chavda, Heidi Baker, and Bill Johnson were, as of 2005, itinerating across the United States and Canada and hosting international crusades for evangelism and healing. One of the most controversial evangelists, **Benny Hinn,** has consistently attracted record-breaking crowds, including a reported 2 million attendees at his 2004 India crusades.

Belief in divine healing has remained a controversial position even among revivalists. Popular portrayals of faith healers such as the novel *Elmer Gantry* (1927) and the movie *Marjoe* (1972) associate healing with fraudulent practices stemming from the greed of revivalists and the credulity of illiterate audiences. Books written by established religious and medical authorities, including Benjamin Warfield's *Counterfeit Miracles* (1918), William A. Nolen's *Healing: A Doctor in Search of a Miracle* (1974), and **Hank Hanegraaff's** *Counterfeit Revival* (1997), typically dismiss healing claims as resulting from deception, misdiagnosis, hysteria, suggestion, hypnotism, or spontaneous remission. Divine healing revivalists respond by referring to the Bible, personal testimony, and before-and-after medical records.

Further Reading: Baer, Jonathan Richard. "Perfectly Empowered Bodies: Divine Healing in Modernizing America." PhD dissertation, Yale University, 2002; Callahan, Leslie Dawn. "Fleshly Manifestations: Charles Fox Parham's Quest for the Sanctified Body." PhD dissertation, Princeton University, 2002; Chappell, Paul Gale. "The Divine Healing Movement in America." PhD dissertation, Drew University, 1983; Hardesty, Nancy. *Faith Cure: Divine Healing in the Holiness and Pentecostal Movements.* Peabody, MA: Hendrickson, 2003; Harrell, David Edwin, Jr. *All Things Are Possible: The Healing and Charismatic Revivals in Modern America.* Bloomington: Indiana University Press, 1975; Liardon, Roberts. *God's Generals: Why They Succeeded and Why Some Failed.* Tulsa, OK: Albury, 1996; Mullin, Robert Bruce. *Miracles and the Modern Religious Imagination.* New Haven, CT: Yale University Press, 1996; Opp, James William. "Religion, Medicine, and the Body: Protestant Faith Healing in Canada, 1880–1930." PhD dissertation, Carlton University, 2000.

Candy Gunther Brown

HEALTH AND WEALTH GOSPEL

see Prosperity Theology

HINN, BENNY (1952–)

Benny Hinn is a well-known **television** preacher, author, and pastor whose half-hour program *This Is Your Day!* has been seen by television audiences in over 190 nations. Hinn was born Toufik Benedictus Hinn of Greek Orthodox Parents in Jaffa, a mostly Arab community near Tel Aviv, Israel. His mother was half Armenian and half Palestinian. His father, of Greek origin, served in the British Army during World War II and later worked for the Israeli government as secretary for labor exchange, functioning as a liaison to Palestinian Arabs and other internationals seeking employment in Jaffa. As a child, he attended a French **Roman Catholic** school, College des Freres in Jaffa, and was fluent in Arabic, Greek, French, and Hebrew, though afflicted with a severe stuttering problem from an early age. He reported that when he was 11 years old, he had a vision in which Jesus walked into his bedroom. He saw the nail prints in his hands, but nothing was spoken. In 1968, his family moved to Toronto, Canada, where he attended Georges Vanier Secondary School. In February of 1972, while still a student, he had a second vision in which an angel delivered him from chains. About this time, he began to have visions of crowds before him, to which he was **preaching.**

In December 1974, he was asked to preach at Shilo, a fellowship meeting at the Trinity Assembly of God in Oshawa. Hinn has said that the instant he opened his mouth, he felt something touch his tongue. After a few seconds of numbness, he began to preach fluently, and his stuttering problem was gone. After preaching, he invited people to come forward for **prayer,** and they began falling to the ground. As a result of this meeting, in February 1975 a group of ministers asked Hinn to preach in Willowdale, Ontario. Invitations to minister elsewhere began to come to him regularly. At Willowdale, he began using **healing** lines for laying hands on the sick, but in May 1975 he claimed to possess a supernatural "word of knowledge" that allowed him to identify people's ailments before they communicated with him, and publicly declare healings as they occurred. Thus the healing lines became unnecessary. In September 1975, Hinn addressed a **Full Gospel Business Men's Fellowship** meeting in Sault Sainte Marie, Ontario, and he visited the area several more times, with meetings marked by **conversions,** healings, weeping,

and **bodily manifestations.** He spoke at the Tabernacle Church in Melbourne, Florida, giving him more exposure in the United States.

In 1975 the Benny Hinn Evangelistic Association was organized. The following year, the *Toronto Globe and Mail* began reporting on Hinn's meetings, with front-page stories on Hinn's "Miracle Rallies." The *Toronto Star* then ran a story on four healings in Hinn's services. In 1976 and 1977, Hinn spoke at the Conference on the Holy Spirit in Jerusalem sponsored by Logos International, and in 1977 at **Kathryn Kuhlman**'s memorial service in Pittsburgh, Pennsylvania. The Kathryn Kuhlman Foundation then asked him to conduct special miracle services on a continuing basis in Pittsburgh and in other cities throughout Canada and the United States. He contracted with CBS for a time slot on Sunday evenings at 10 P.M. following *60 Minutes,* and entitled the program *It's a Miracle.*

In 1979, Hinn married Suzanne Harthern of Orlando, Florida, and during the following spring, Orlando became the new headquarters for the Benny Hinn Evangelistic Association. About three years later, Hinn started a church in Orlando after his father-in-law, Roy Harthern, resigned as pastor of Calvary Assembly in that city. In 1982, he booked the Tupperware Auditorium near Kissimmee, just outside of Orlando, and in March 1983 the "Miracle Life Center" convened its first service in downtown Orlando. For seven years, the Trinity Broadcast Network (TBN) carried broadcasts of Hinn's services free of charge. In 1990, daily broadcasts, known first as *Miracle Invasion,* then as *This Is Your Day,* began airing on TBN. In the same year, after ministering in Singapore, Hinn began holding healing crusades in large auditoriums and arenas in Phoenix, San Antonio, Charlotte, Long Beach, Manila (Philippines), Buenos Aires (Argentina), Pretoria (South Africa), Bogotá (Columbia), and other places. In 1999, he moved his headquarters to Dallas. In recent years his ministry's international outreach has expanded. Hinn drew a reported 2 million attendees to his 2004 India crusade.

Hinn has received criticism for some of his theological statements. In response to **Hank**

Hanegraaff's charge that he was "twisting Scripture," Hinn wrote, "I do admit there have been times when I have made a statement that was incorrect.... However, I do not believe it is right when a minister corrects his theology ... and the critics continue to bring up that same subject" (176).

Further Reading: Fisher, G. Richard, and M. Kurt Goedelman. *The Confusing World of Benny Hinn.* St. Louis, MO: Personal Freedom Outreach, 1995; Frame, Randall L. "Same Old Benny Hinn, Critics Say." *Christianity Today,* October 5, 1992, 52–54; Hinn, Benny. *He Touched Me.* Nashville, TN: Thomas Nelson Publishers, 1999.

Richard M. Riss

HISPANIC REVIVALS

see Latino(a) Protestant and Pentecostal Revivals; Roman Catholic Revivals

HOLINESS MOVEMENT OF THE NINETEENTH CENTURY

The North American Holiness revival took its rise in the 1820s among **Methodists** who had become concerned about a perceived muting of their church's historic witness to Wesley's doctrine of entire **sanctification** and its critical place in a believer's experience. Its broader vision was to "Christianize Christianity." The revival's supporters always considered the Holiness movement to be the natural extension of the eighteenth-century Wesleyan revival in England and its American colonies. **Francis Asbury** kept the theme of entire sanctification at the center of pioneer American Methodism's remarkable revivalism, but 20 years after his death in 1816, as a steady flow of new **converts,** often ignorant of Wesleyan history and doctrine, filled the pews and pastorates of the church. Many Methodists called for new and specific efforts to advance the cause of Holiness throughout the denomination. The subsequent Holiness revival adopted the "new measures" revivalism of the **Second Great Awakening** to promulgate their Wesleyan Holiness theology. The Wesleyanism of the revival, in turn, was filtered through the biblicism, Puritanism, **Pietism,** millennialism, and commonsense

pragmatism of Protestant evangelicalism in this period. At the same time **Charles G. Finney** and **Asa Mahan** began **preaching** their Oberlin perfectionism, creating a parallel Holiness movement within New School **Calvinism.** These two related renewal movements—sometimes independently, sometimes interactively, and usually cooperatively—altered the face of revivalist Protestantism in calling not only for sinners to be converted but also for Christians to be sanctified wholly and to live under the Lordship of Jesus Christ.

In 1835, laywomen Sarah Lankford and her sister **Phoebe Palmer** relocated the meetings of two Methodist **women's** classes to the common parlor of their shared Manhattan home. These informal conversational gatherings for **prayer,** testimony, and spiritual instruction created the milieu for the birth and growth of the Holiness revival. Known as the Tuesday Meetings for the Promotion of Holiness, they spawned a national network of hundreds of similar meetings that rapidly introduced the incipient renewal movement to widespread and varied Protestant audiences. In 1839, Bowdoin College professor of moral philosophy and Congregationalist Thomas C. Upham received the "second blessing" in the meetings under the leadership of Phoebe Palmer. Thereafter the meetings were opened to **men** as well as women. From its origin, the presence of such a dynamic force within otherwise tightly disciplined Methodism troubled its critics. When Holiness advocate Orange Scott formed the **abolitionist** Wesleyan Methodist Connection in 1843, and when Palmer convert and abolition proponent **Benjamin T. Roberts** organized the **Free Methodist Church** in 1860, the schisms seemed to confirm the separatist tendencies attributed to the revival by its critics. Yet for most of the rest of the century, Methodist leaders of the post–**Civil War** revival kept the mainstream of the Holiness revival within existing denominational structures.

Palmer's "Altar Theology" also aroused opposition. It was a simple syllogism born of her reading of Wesley's understanding of biblical holiness within the complex of issues and practices that characterized contemporary American revivalism.

Phoebe and Walter Palmer, in a pose expressive of their shared life and ministry. (Phoebe Palmer, Walter Palmer, *Four Years in the Old World*, 1866.) Courtesy of Dr. Kathryn Long.

It constituted a "shorter way" to lead seekers to an **assurance** of faith that God had sanctified them wholly. Methodist opponents decried it as poor theology and un-Wesleyan. But the simplicity of its logic and its biblical sacrificial imagery permanently fixed the revivalists' call to "lay all on the altar" in the ethos and practice of large segments of evangelical revivalism.

The 1857 Canadian ministry of Palmer and her physician husband, Walter C. Palmer, marked the first signs of the **Revival of 1857–1858.** The widespread acceptance of Methodist William Arthur's book *The Tongue of Fire* (1856) helped increase the movement's influence within the budding awakening in 1857–1858. Its emphasis on the centrality of the work of the Holy Spirit for effective Christian living popularized themes that were soon to emerge in the revival. In 1859, the Palmers followed the revival as it spread to Great Britain, where they worked with great success until their return to the United States in 1863. Palmer's numerous publications (one in its 50th edition by

midcentury), and her reports on the revival in such contemporary religious journals as the *Guide to Christian Perfection* (beginning in 1839), gave her a wide readership in the evangelical world. With the rise of the women's movement of the twentieth century, Palmer's *The Promise of the Father* (1859)— considered the first full-scale theological defense of women's right to public ministry in Christian history—came again to prominence along with a new recognition of the host of other Holiness women who had followed her example: Catherine Booth, cofounder of the **Salvation Army; African American** evangelist **Amanda Berry Smith;** evangelist and author **Hannah Whitall Smith;** and France Willard, leader of the Woman's Christian **Temperance** Union.

By the beginning of the American Civil War, the once Methodist-centered revival had already crossed denominational lines. Popular **Baptist** evangelist Absalom Backus Earle used "rest of faith" terminology in his sermons and publications to represent the Wesleyan Holiness doctrine and experience to his Baptist audiences. **Presbyterian** William Edwin Boardman's book *The Higher Christian Life* (1858) offered an essentially Wesleyan message clothed in concepts and language less prejudicial to its reception by non-Methodist Christians, and it resulted in a more favorable response to the Holiness message among New School Calvinists. At the same time, the **Quakers** Hannah Whitall Smith and her husband **Robert Pearsall Smith** applied the teachings of the Holiness revival as an instrument of renewal within the troubled Society of Friends. Phoebe Palmer died in 1874, honored by many of the Protestant leaders of the time as the most influential female religious leader of her time. She was known as the mother of the Holiness movement.

The post–Civil War era brought changes to the Holiness revival. By the time of Palmer's death in 1874 followed by Finney's death in 1875, the leadership of the revival had already begun to shift. In July 1867, thousands of people responded to a call by an ad hoc committee of Holiness Methodist ministers for a nine-day national Holiness **camp meeting** to be held in Vineland, New Jersey. At the end of the meeting, numerous testimonies of sanctifications and conversions led the organizing committee to establish the National Camp Meeting Association for the Promotion of Holiness (NCAPH). The members of the new association, under the leadership of its president, New York Methodist pastor John Inskip, agreed henceforth to devote their summer vacation time to Holiness camp meeting evangelism. Inskip became the revival's most dynamic leader, presiding at 47 of the 52 national camp meetings held by the association before his death in 1884, as well as establishing and supervising the publication of the association's journal, the *Christian Standard*, and the plethora of Holiness literature issuing from the NCAPH's publishing house.

The promotional center of the movement had now moved from the intimate forum of the small group Tuesday Meeting to the public setting of camp meetings under the aegis of the National Holiness Association (NHA, the new name for the NCAPH). Its revival activities were supported by hundreds of loosely affiliated interdenominational local, state, and regional Holiness associations. They gave the revival that had been a largely northeastern urban movement a national presence. Over time a growing band of Holiness evangelists became riders on this expansive camp meeting circuit. In their "forest temples" they became shapers of the teachings and emerging worship styles that characterized the Holiness associations and churches of the last quarter of the 1800s. These Holiness churches became known as "camp meeting churches." By the year 2000, Holiness and **Pentecostal** churches and agencies in the United States and Canada were still holding more than 2,000 annual camps, and thousands more took place through their mission agencies around the world.

In the first NHA camp meetings, Robert Pearsall Smith and his wife, Hannah Whitall Smith, testified to their experience of entire sanctification. They became leading figures in the spread of the post–Civil War Holiness–Higher Life revival in British and European Protestant communities that had been largely untouched by the earlier Holiness revivalism of Palmer, Finney, and other Methodist

and Oberlin evangelists. A committee of prominent Anglican evangelicals introduced Robert Smith to receptive audiences in Holiness conventions in England at Oxford, Cambridge, and camp meetings at the Broadlands estate of Lord and Lady Mount-Temple. In the spring of 1875, the revival jumped the Channel to Holland, Belgium, France, and Germany. Smith's simple "Jesus saves me now" message of victorious Christian living swept like a whirlwind through the old Pietist cells in the established churches as well as the constituencies of the newer free churches connected with the Methodists, **United Brethren,** and Evangelical denominations. In May 1875, the Smiths' campaign climaxed in a pan-European convention for the promotion of Christian Holiness at Brighton, England, attended by more than 8,000 evangelical pastors, theologians, and lay leaders.

Reports of the meeting noted the favorable response of this diverse gathering of evangelicals to the biblical teachings of Hannah Smith. She was called "the Angel of the Churches." The Smiths were to be the speakers at a subsequent convention to be held in Keswick, England, in July. Yet rumors of Robert Smith's purported doctrinal deviations and moral turpitude caused his committee to withdraw its support for his ministry. He had been seen in the company of a younger woman, though it is not clear that anything inappropriate had taken place between them. Much later, when the facts of the case became known, many observers thought the judgment against Smith had been too hasty and too harsh. The Smiths returned to the United States, and eventually gave up their public revival ministries.

In spite of Robert's "fall," the European Holiness–Higher Life revival continued to expand. It revived the old Pietist fellowship movements in the **Lutheran** and **Reformed** churches. The free churches were strengthened and new interdenominational Holiness associations were organized. Later, some of these provided leaders and constituents for the European Pentecostal movement. The social services of the German Inner Mission movement were reinforced and expanded. None of these, however, matched the influence of the rise of the

Keswick Convention for the Promotion of Christian Holiness, which kept the Holiness–Higher Life message alive within British and European evangelicalism as it spread the teaching to mission stations worldwide, influenced Christian student movements, and spawned Higher Life movements in the United States and elsewhere as it moved back to America through **Dwight L. Moody's** Northfield (Massachusetts) Conferences.

By the closing decades of the nineteenth century the expanding movement's appeal to members of non-Methodist traditions, including Baptists, Presbyterians (especially **Cumberland Presbyterians**), Mennonites, Quakers, and Adventists, created a mix of issues that heightened tensions between the established churches and interdenominational networks. Methodist critics pressed for increased denominational control over the aggressive and sometimes radical Holiness associations. A growing rift also developed between those Holiness associations that were largely Methodist and the hundreds of others that derived from non-Methodist traditions and yet were equally dedicated to the Holiness revival. The Methodist-controlled NHA's ban on **preaching,** in its camp meetings, on issues such as divine **healing** or the **eschatology** of Jesus' Second Coming added to these intramovement tensions. Holiness leader **Albert B. Simpson's** fourfold gospel—of Christ as Savior, Sanctifier, Healer, and Coming King—was becoming a popular summary of conservative Holiness teaching. Two of these four items—Healer and Coming King—were thus not welcomed at the NHA camp meetings. After 1901, the fourfold idea found its way into Pentecostalism, and even into the name of the Pentecostal denomination founded by **Aimee Semple McPherson,** namely, the **International Church of the Foursquare Gospel.** Some Pentecostals revised the notion of Christ as Sanctifier to that of Baptizer, in reflection of the new emphasis in the early twentieth century on the **baptism in the Holy Spirit** as marked by **speaking in tongues.** Yet for both Holiness adherents and Pentecostals the fourfold idea was a way of stressing the comprehensiveness of Christ's salvation and its application to all aspects of human life and human need.

Out of the mix of external and internal pressures, in the 1880s, the first wave of Holiness "come outers," as they were characterized both by opponents and denominational loyalists in the movement, began to organize new church homes and denominations sympathetic to the revival's **primitivism** and **restorationism,** its Wesleyan doctrines, and the free worship styles of its associations and camp meetings. In 1881, out of his vision of a unified sect-free church gathered together out of all sects by the Holy Spirit, Daniel S. Warner founded what became the **Church of God (Anderson, Indiana).** Several other pioneer Holiness churches were organized in the same period. By the end of the nineteenth century, Holiness adherents seemed to be prevailing in a prolonged debate over the Wesleyan and Methodist authenticity of the Holiness teaching. Yet, at this point, the opponents shifted their ground. Methodist theologians, educated in the new German theologies of the 1800s, forged a new theological agenda for the church. Wesley's legacy and the Holiness question were effectively removed from the church's theological forum. Moreover, the tight strictures of Methodist governance allowed the opponents of the Holiness revival to exert control over the church. A gradual process ensued in which thousands of the Holiness movement's ministers and laypersons were forced to seek new church homes. The two dozen new Holiness denominations that were organized during that period represented the largest formation of new denominations in so short a time up to that point in American religious history. Thousands of other Holiness adherents chose to remain within the Methodist Church even though it was becoming increasingly unfriendly to the Holiness teaching.

In the decade following 1895, the **Church of the Nazarene,** the Pilgrim Holiness Church, the Wesleyan Methodist Church, the **Free Methodist Church,** the Church of God (Anderson, Indiana), and the American corps of the Salvation Army joined other newly formed smaller Holiness churches to become known in world Protestantism as the Holiness Churches. In 1968, the Pilgrim Holiness Church united with the Wesleyan Methodist Church to form the Wesleyan Church.

The interdenominational Christian Holiness Partnership (the direct successor of the original NHA) continues to serve as a coordinating agency for these churches. At the beginning of the twenty-first century, their worldwide constituencies numbered about 10 million. Most of them are members of the National Association of Evangelicals and some of the larger churches are members of the World Methodist Council. After World War II, some small conservative groups who separated from the movement's larger churches came together under the aegis of the Independent Holiness Churches. If one considers not only these Holiness denominations but also the non-Methodist offshoots of the movement—the **Christian and Missionary Alliance,** evangelical ministries born of the Keswick–Higher Life movement, and especially world Pentecostalism in its far-flung expressions—one can sense the enduring impact of the nineteenth-century Holiness revival on the development of evangelical Protestantism.

Further Reading: Dayton, Donald W. *Discovering an Evangelical Heritage.* New York: Harper and Row, 1976; Dieter, Melvin E. *The Holiness Revival of the Nineteenth Century.* 2nd ed. Lanham, MD, and London: Scarecrow Press, 1996; Jones, Charles E. *Black Holiness: Black Participation in Wesleyan Perfectionist and Glossolalic Pentecostal Movements.* Metuchen, NJ, and London: American Theological Library Association and Scarecrow Press, 1987; Jones, Charles E. *A Guide to the Study of the Holiness Movement.* Metuchen, NJ, and London: Scarecrow Press and the American Theological Library Association, 1974; Kostlevy, William. *Holiness Manuscripts: A Guide to Documenting the Wesleyan Holiness Movement in the United States and Canada.* Metuchen, NJ, and London: American Theological Library Association and Scarecrow Press, 1994; Peters, John L. *Christian Perfection and American Methodism.* Nashville, TN: Abingdon Press, 1956; Smith, Timothy L. *Revivalism and Social Reform: American Protestantism on the Eve of the Civil War.* Nashville TN: Abingdon Press, 1957.

Melvin E. Dieter

HOLY FAIRS

Holy fairs were popular religious festivals celebrating the Lord's Supper that arose in sixteenth- and seventeenth-century Scottish **Presbyterianism.** Robert Burns may have coined the term *holy fair* in his 1785 poem of the same name, which portrayed these sacramental occasions in boisterous and irreligious terms. The phenomenon received detailed scrutiny in Leigh Eric Schmidt's *Holy Fairs* (1989; 2nd ed., 2001), whose scholarship is summarized in this essay.

Annual Communion festivals were already established in **Roman Catholic** Scotland during the early sixteenth century. When John Knox, Protestant revolutionary and native Scot, returned to Scotland in the 1550s after sojourns in England and on the Continent, he established Protestantism as the state religion of Scotland with the help of Queen Elizabeth of England. Knox and other Scottish Protestants largely succeeded in replacing the Roman Catholic sacramental festivals with simpler Protestant Communion practices. Protestants viewed the sacramental elements of consecrated bread and wine as parts of a communal meal, and not as objects of special veneration or adoration. In the 1620s Presbyterian pastor and opponent of episcopacy (i.e., church rule by bishops) John Livingston was forced to itinerate around Scotland due to political opposition. Traveling **preachers** like Livingston frequently administered the Lord's Supper at their meetings, and on one occasion a revival occurred under his preaching at a Communion service. This kind of itineration, arising from a peculiar political situation, led to a new form of sacramental piety, the holy fair. Schmidt explains the difference between the Protestant Communion seasons and the previous Roman Catholic observances: "What separated the festal communion from earlier sacraments were such characteristics as outdoor preaching, great concourses of people from an extensive region, long vigils of prayer, powerful experiences of conversion and confirmation, a number of popular ministers cooperating for extended services over three days or more, a seasonal focus on summer, and unusually large numbers of communicants at successive tables" (Schmidt, 24).

In the seventeenth century a division arose between Scottish Presbyterians who supported Oliver Cromwell and those who supported the restoration of the monarchy under Charles II. With the restoration of Charles II in 1660, "Protestors," who earlier opposed Charles and were now suppressed by him, were forced to hold clandestine Communion meetings. Sacramental seasons became symbols of both religious and political dissent. They had a dual purpose for both the unconverted and the converted, as rituals of initiation for the former and rituals of renewal for the latter. By the time Presbyterians began immigrating to America in the early 1700s the Communion seasons were a regular part of Presbyterian spiritual life. **David Brainerd,** a missionary to Native Americans, used holy fairs as a way of replacing aboriginal Indian rituals with Christian services.

Presbyterians settled most heavily in the Middle Colonies, including Pennsylvania and New Jersey, but after the revolutionary war Kentucky and Tennessee became a center of evangelical awakening, often featuring the Lord's Supper as a central ritual. The most famous of the American Presbyterian Communion festivals was the 1801 revival at **Cane Ridge,** Kentucky, under **James McGready,** which was set up with Communion tables in the fashion of the Scottish holy fair. As the revival tradition developed in the early 1800s, participants camped outdoors during these multiday events, and thus the holy fair evolved into the **camp meeting.** Though the Lord's Supper diminished in importance in later camp meetings, the tradition of the camp meeting is indebted to the precedent and the sacramental practices of the Scottish holy fair.

Further Reading: Conkin, Paul. *Cane Ridge: America's Pentecost.* Madison: University of Wisconsin Press, 1990; Schmidt, Leigh Eric. *Holy Fairs: Scotland and the Making of American Revivalism.* 2nd ed. Grand Rapids, MI: Eerdmans, 2001; Westerkamp, Marilyn J. *Triumph of the Laity: Scots-Irish Piety and the Great Awakening, 1625–1760.* New York: Oxford University Press, 1988.

John Halsey Wood Jr.

HOLY LAUGHTER

see Laughing and Shouting in Revivals

HOLY ROLLERS

see Bodily Manifestations in Revivals

HOLY SPIRIT

see Theology of Revivals

HUTCHINSON, ANN

see Women and Revivals

HYMNS, HYMNODY, AND CHRISTIAN MUSIC IN REVIVALS

Music has been a companion to revival **preaching** since the eighteenth century, and its importance seems to have increased during the nineteenth and twentieth centuries. Each major period of awakening introduced new types of hymnody, which incorporated a wide variety of poetic and musical styles. The **Great Awakening** (1739–1745) brought about a transition from **Calvinistic** psalmody (i.e., the singing of biblical psalms) to the freer expressions of the English poet and theologian Isaac Watts (1674–1748). America's **Second Great Awakening** (1795–1835) introduced the hymns of the Wesleys and other English evangelical writers, **camp meeting** songs, the **spirituals** of **African Americans,** and indigenous folk music. The mass revivals of later awakenings (1875–ca. 1915) and **Billy Graham** crusades continued the gospel song tradition and subsequently included styles derived from popular music of the twentieth and twenty-first centuries.

Metrical psalms, rhymed and metered paraphrases of the Psalms and other parts of the Bible, were the first congregational songs in **colonial** churches. John Calvin's theology of worship permitted only unison, unaccompanied singing of strict biblical paraphrases, and colonists sang from English and Dutch psalters. The *Bay Psalm Book* (1640), a collection produced for the Massachusetts Bay Colony, was the first printed volume produced in colonial North America. By the turn of the eighteenth century, the practice of congregational singing had declined to a low state, as a result of the musical illiteracy of most parishioners and the

Larry Norman (1947–) was a key figure in the early "Jesus rock" movement of the late 1960s and early 1970s. Photo taken at Explo '72 in Dallas, Texas. Courtesy of David Di Sabatino.

THE RINES BROTHERS
SINGING EVANGELISTS

Postcard invitation to hear "The Rines Brothers, Singing Evangelists," appearing in or near Wyalusing, Pennsylvania. Sent on November 9, 1908. Courtesy of Dr. Kenneth O. Brown.

practice of "lining out." Prior to the advent of printed words and music, each line of a psalm was sung by the leader (or precentor) and repeated in turn by the congregation. This slow unfolding of each psalm led to improvisation and embellishment by the more talented singers and to the breakdown of true unison singing into discord or heterophony (i.e., two or more versions of the same tune sounding at once).

Isaac Watts had produced the first volume of freely composed hymns in English by one author, *Hymns and Spiritual Songs* (1707), and later *The Psalms of David Imitated in the Language of the New Testament* (1719), in which he freely paraphrased scripture and inserted references to Christ. A new body of material was, therefore, available to match the enthusiastic preaching of revival preachers such as **Gilbert Tennent,**

Jonathan Edwards, and **George Whitefield.** After the Revolution, the adoption of American editions of Watts's psalms and hymns accelerated among New Light or pro-revival Congregationalists and **Presbyterians.** Churches tended to abandon the practice of lining out as they adopted Watts's psalms and hymns in printed form. Singing schools, which began as early as 1720 to improve congregational music by teaching singing by note, were crucial in disseminating the texts of Watts and later English evangelical writers well into the nineteenth century.

A large Congregationalist collection of hymns designed for use in revivals appeared in 1799 as the *Hartford Selection of Hymns*, compiled by Nathan Strong, Abel Flint, and Joseph Steward. This collection contained hymns by English

Just As I Am

CHARLOTTE ELLIOTT

WILLIAM B. BRADBURY

1. Just as I am, with-out one plea, But that Thy blood was shed for me,
2. Just as I am, and wait-ing not To rid my soul of one dark blot,
3. Just as I am, tho' tossed a-bout With many a con-flict, many a doubt,
4. Just as I am—poor, wretched, blind; Sight, riches, heal-ing of the mind,
5. Just as I am—Thou wilt re-ceive, Wilt welcome, pardon, cleanse relieve;

And that Thou bidd'st me come to Thee, O Lamb of God, I come! I come!
To Thee whose blood can cleanse each spot, O Lamb of God, I come! I come!
Fight-ings and fears with-in, with-out, O Lamb of God, I come! I come!
Yea, all I need in Thee to find, O Lamb of God, I come! I come!
Be-cause Thy prom-ise I be-lieve, O Lamb of God, I come! I come!

The hymn "Just As I Am" (lyrics 1835; music 1849) has long been associated with revivalist Billy Graham, who uses it during the altar call at the end of his evangelistic services. From Harold Hart Todd, ed., *The Cokesbury Hymnal* (Nashville: The Cokesbury Press, 1923).

writers John Newton, William Cowper, and Philip Doddridge, and from John Rippon's *A Selection of Hymns* (1787). While revivalistic in nature, this hymnal represented the transition away from strict Calvinistic theology that was occurring during the late eighteenth century. A text-only hymnal, it was accompanied by Jonathan Benjamin's *Harmonia Coelestis* (1799), the first musical collection intended for revivals. Separatists incorporated into their worship hymns from Watts and the Wesleys, Whitefield's *Hymns* (1768), *The Olney Hymns* (1779) of John Newton and William Cowper, and Rippon's *Selection*. In addition to these sources, folk hymns notated from oral tradition also appeared in such **Baptist** collections as Joshua Smith's *Divine Hymns, or Spiritual Songs* (1784).

The Second Great Awakening was a general religious quickening that took place shortly after the formation of the American Republic. It began as early as 1797 and included two developments

important to hymnody—and the rural camp meeting and urban revivalism. **Asahel Nettleton** (1783–1844), a conservative Calvinistic evangelist and opponent of the revival methods of **Charles G. Finney** (1792–1875), borrowed from *The Hartford Selection* to produce *Village Hymns for Social Worship* (1828) as a supplement to Watts's psalms and hymns. *Village Hymns* was important for its introduction of American writers such as Abby B. Hyde, William B. Tappan, and Phoebe Brown and for its inclusion of missionary hymns. Like *The Hartford Selection*, this hymnal was accompanied by a tune source, *Zion's Harp* (1824), by Nathaniel and S. S. Jocelyn.

The most notable revival preacher in this period was Charles G. Finney, who developed the methods of modern revivalism ("new measures") that are still employed by evangelists today. Finney taught that revivals resulted from the use of specific techniques and that individuals had freedom of choice as to their eternal destiny. Music played a minor role in his revivals because of his belief that music was counterproductive to the agonizing spirit of **prayer** required for sinners to come to salvation. Yet an important revival collection was produced as a result of the enthusiasm generated by his revivals. Joshua Leavitt (1794–1873) sought to provide Finney's revivals with immediately appealing music in *The Christian Lyre* (1831). This collection was unique in that it contained both texts and two-part tunes. The music included parodies of popular songs and camp meeting **spirituals** along with hymns that have become standard, such as "O Sacred Head, Now Wounded" (translated by J. W. Alexander), "The God of Abraham Praise (translated by Thomas Olivers), "From Every Stormy Wind That Blows" (Hugh Stowell), and Lowell Mason's tune "Missionary Hymn" to the Reginald Heber text "From Greenland's Icy Mountains." Finney, however, refused to adopt Leavitt's collection for his revivals.

Finney became associated in his pastorate at New York's Broadway Tabernacle with Thomas Hastings (1784–1872), a musical reformer and partner of Lowell Mason (1792–1872). Together Hastings and Mason compiled *Spiritual Songs for Social Worship* (1833), a significant collection that sought to counteract the "vulgar melodies" of Leavitt's book. It was important for its original hymns, such as "My Faith Looks Up to Thee" (Ray Palmer), "The Morning Light Is Breaking" (Samuel F. Smith), and "Hail to the Brightness of Zion's Glad Morning" (Thomas Hastings), and for the direction it charted for urban evangelical church music. The compilers advocated European classical modes for church music, and their views helped shape nineteenth-century choral and congregational music.

The rural phase of the Second Great Awakening found expression in the interracial phenomenon of the camp meeting. Religious fervor, **bodily manifestations** of the Spirit, intense preaching, and the presence of both blacks and whites created a setting in which white camp meeting spirituals and African American spirituals influenced one another. Camp meeting spirituals featured

choruses, whose repetition encouraged wide participation; "wandering refrains," which were attached to any number of hymns; improvisation; and call and response performance (i.e., a leader answered by the worshippers). Each of these characteristics appears in the music of both races. Small "songsters" were compiled to propagate the texts of popular camp meeting spirituals. The first publication to notate folk hymns from oral tradition was Jeremiah Ingalls's *The Christian Harmony* (1805), published in Vermont. By 1868, Joseph Hillman's large collection *The Revivalist* contained both camp meeting songs and the newer gospel songs. Two shape-note tune books, which contained both words and music, also included revival hymnody: John Wyeth's *Repository of Sacred Music, Part Second* (1813) and Ananias Davisson's *Supplement to the Kentucky Harmony* (1820). Among the choruses and hymns that have endured from this tradition are "Amazing Grace, How Sweet the Sound," "Come, Thou Fount of Every Blessing," "Come, Ye Sinners, Poor and Needy," and "On Jordan's Stormy Banks I Stand."

Camp meetings were a crucible for the development of the African American spiritual. Other influences included the formal worship services attended by slaves, worship in separate black congregations, and secret meetings on plantations. Wandering refrains appear in the first hymn collection for a black congregation, Richard Allen's *A Collection of Spiritual Songs and Hymns* (1801). Spirituals combined musical practices brought from Africa, call and response singing, hymn texts of Watts and other evangelical writers, extensive improvisation, and the slave experience reflected in "sorrow songs" (e.g., "Go Down, Moses" and "Steal Away") to form the unique musical expression of the black spiritual. *Slave Songs of the United States* (1867), edited by William Allen, Charles Ware, and Lucy McKim Garrison, was the first published collection of this repertoire. The **Young Men's Christian Association** had previously published "Let My People Go" in 1861 in support of the **abolitionist** cause. Concert tours by the Fisk Jubilee Singers beginning in 1871 and recordings by the

Fisk male quartet helped to disseminate this music throughout the United States and Europe. *A Collection of Revival Hymns and Plantation Melodies* (1883) by Marshall W. Taylor was an influential compilation of revival and gospel songs and spirituals.

A third major period of religious awakening in the late 1800s and early 1900s was characterized by urban mass evangelism, teams of preachers and soloists, and the gospel song. Beginning with **Dwight L. Moody** and Ira D. Sankey (1840–1908) and concluding with **Billy Sunday** (1862–1935) and Homer Rodeheaver (1880–1955), this style of revivalism owed its philosophical and practical underpinnings to Finney but relied on methods of organization and promotion that Moody had borrowed from the business world. At the same time, Moody's services involved a strong appeal to sentiment and emotion. "Song services" became the musical complement to evangelistic preaching as music was employed to persuade sinners to accept the salvation offered through free grace.

The gospel song grew out of earlier folk hymnody, Sunday school songs, and popular secular idioms. Typically a gospel song featured lyrics that could be immediately comprehended, tunes in major mode supported by uncomplicated harmony, simple meters, frequent use of dotted-note rhythms, choruses that often featured a call and response pattern among voice parts, and later influences from ragtime rhythms and chromatic barbershop harmony. Subsequent to the publication of *Gospel Songs* (1874) by the revival singer, Philip Paul Bliss (1838–1876), Sankey and Bliss jointly issued *Gospel Hymns and Sacred Songs* (1875), followed by five additional best-selling volumes, culminating in *Gospel Hymns 1 to 6 Complete* (1894). Among the best-known gospel songwriters were William Bradbury (1816–1868), Fanny J. Crosby (1820–1915), Robert Lowry (1826–1899), James McGranahan (1840–1907), and George C. Stebbins (1846–1945). Charles Alexander (1867–1920) and Homer Rodeheaver (1880–1955) produced recordings that were widely disseminated, in addition to composing some music of their own.

Popular music styles continued to influence revival hymnody throughout the twentieth and into the early years of the twenty-first century. Evangelical composers published numerous hymns in the gospel song idiom, and that style remained the staple of many congregations. The music of the Billy Graham crusades featured the solo singing of George Beverly Shea and massed choirs conducted by Cliff Barrows. Among the composers in this period were John W. Peterson (b. 1921), who wrote "Surely Goodness and Mercy" and "Heaven Came Down and Glory Filled My Soul," and William J. (b. 1936) and Gloria (b. 1942) Gaither, noted for "Because He Lives" and "There's Something About That Name."

African American gospel hymnody, which combined elements of spirituals, rhythm and blues, and the gospel song, became a musical force through revivals spawned by the **Azusa Street revival** in Los Angeles. An early **Holiness** hymn writer and cofounder with **Charles H. Mason** of the **Church of God in Christ,** Charles Price Jones (1865–1949), produced over 1,000 hymns, the most famous being "Jesus Only" (1897). Charles A. Tindley (1851–1933), a renowned **Methodist** preacher, wrote over 45 gospel hymns, among them "Nothing Between," "Leave It There," and "When the Morning Comes." His work influenced Thomas Andrew Dorsey (1899–1993), called the father of gospel music and regarded as the initiator of the **women**'s quartet and the gospel chorus. After a successful career as a blues composer and pianist—having played for blues singer Ma Rainey and composed more than 400 blues and jazz songs—he wrote his first gospel song in 1921 and focused entirely on gospel music from the early 1930s until his death. His most famous works are "Precious Lord, Take My Hand," "Peace in the Valley," and "When I've Done My Best." Lucie E. Campbell Williams (1885–1963) composed the perennial favorite "He Understands; He'll Say, 'Well Done.'" Later exponents of the gospel style included Kenneth Morris (1917–1988), who wrote "Yes, God Is Real"; Roberta Martin (1907–1969); Kenneth Morris (1917–1988); James

Cleveland (1932–1991); and Andrae Crouch (b. 1950).

During the **Jesus People movement,** evangelical music began to borrow extensively from African American soul and rhythm and blues styles, as well as rock and roll, and the new musical forms evolved by the late 1980s and 1990s into a commercial genre known as contemporary Christian music (CCM). The "Jesus rock" movement is generally traced to Larry Norman (b. 1947), whose early record albums, *Upon This Rock* (1970) and *Only Visiting This Planet* (1972), showed that music could have both the energy of rock and roll and a hard-hitting, uncompromising Christian message. Norman's songs dealt with topics as diverse as drugs, sex, money, social injustice, and the Second Coming of Jesus (e.g., the song, "I Wish We'd All Been Ready"), and they sounded a call for **conversion.** Keith Green (1953–1982), a Christian convert of Jewish descent, wrote his first songs at age 8, and at 11 years of age became the youngest member of ASCAP (the American Society of Composers, Authors, and Performers). Green, who founded Last Days Ministries and associated with Lorne Cunningham of **Youth with a Mission,** was as much a revival preacher as a musical performer. Such songs as "Asleep in the Light" and "Altar Call" were a call for evangelical Christians to repent of complacency and worldliness.

Since the pioneering efforts of Larry Norman and Keith Green in the 1970s, CCM has diversified and emerged as a multibillion-dollar business that in 2004 accounted for about eight percent of total sales of recorded music in the United States and exceeded both classical and jazz music in revenues. **Pentecostals** have written new worship songs (e.g., Rev. Jack Hayford's song "Majesty"), as have members of the neo-Charismatic or so-called Third Wave movement spearheaded by **John Wimber**—the founder of the Association of Vineyard Churches and himself a musician and songwriter. As of 2005, some of the most popular Christian songwriters, performers, and bands include Michael W. Smith, Steven Curtis Chapman, Rebecca St. James, Jaci Velasquez, DC Talk, Third Day, Delirious, Jars of Clay, and Amy Grant—this last a crossover musician who records in both sacred and secular styles. Among the prominent African American Christian performers today are Shirley Caesar, Kirk Franklin, Fred Hammond, and Cece Winans. Many of these artists not only perform for large audiences but also write songs that quickly find their way into contemporary worship services in evangelical, mainline Protestant, **Charismatic,** and **Roman Catholic** churches. The boundaries between Christian traditions and denominations have become blurrier than ever when it comes to worship music. In the wake of the Roman Catholic Vatican II conference in the early 1960s, a group of Catholic seminarians at Saint Louis University known as the St. Louis Jesuits—Bob Dufford, John Foley, Tim Manion, Roc O'Connor, and Dan Schutte—wrote many popular Christian songs that have been performed in Protestant churches and parachurch groups as well as Catholic parishes.

While some congregations today feature traditional Christian choral music, Bach cantatas, or revival hymns from the 1700s or 1800s, others host performances of Christian music in styles as diverse as folk, blues, bluegrass, country, jazz, soul, rap, rock, surf, heavy metal, and punk. How much of this new music falls into the category of entertainment, and how much is conducive to worship or to revival preaching, is not always clear. Yet the energy and diversity of today's Christian music scene bodes well for a continuing strong connection between American religious revivalism and the singing of hymns and songs.

Further Reading: Adams, Jere, ed. *Handbook to the Baptist Hymnal.* Nashville, TN: Church Street Press, 1992; Benson, Louis F. *The English Hymn: Its Development and Use.* Richmond, VA: John Knox Press, 1962; Cyber Hymnal. http://www.cyberhymnal.org/; Downey, James C. "The Music of American Revivalism." PhD dissertation, Tulane University, 1969; Echols, Paul C. "Hymnody." In *The New Grove Dictionary of American Music,* 2:446–55. London: Macmillan, 1986; Eskew, Harry, James C. Downey, and Horace Clarence Boyer. "Gospel Music." In *The New Grove Dictionary of American Music,* 2:249–61. London: Macmillan, 1986; Hammond, Paul

Garnett. "Music in Urban Revivalism in the Northern United States, 1800–1835." DMA dissertation, Southern Baptist Theological Seminary, 1974; Lorenz, Ellen Jane. *Glory, Hallelujah! The Story of the Campmeeting Spiritual.* Nashville, TN: Abingdon, 1978; Powell, Mark Allan. *The Encyclopedia of Contemporary Christian Music.* Peabody, MA: Hendrickson, 2002; Reynolds, William J., and Milburn Price. *A Survey of Christian Hymnody.* 3rd ed. Carol Stream, IL: Hope, 1987; Southern, Eileen. *The Music of Black Americans: A History.* 2nd ed. New York: Norton, 1983.

Paul Garnett Hammond

I

INSPIRATIONISTS

see Amana Community

INTERNATIONAL CHURCH OF THE FOURSQUARE GOSPEL

The International Church of the Foursquare Gospel (ICFG) is a **Pentecostal** denomination founded by evangelist **Aimee Semple McPherson** in 1923 in conjunction with the dedication of Angelus Temple at Echo Park in Glendale, California. The IFCP is a missions-oriented church movement rooted in the **Azusa Street revival** of 1906. The name came from a vision seen by McPherson based on Ezekiel 1:4–10—the fourfold ministry of Christ as Savior, Baptizer, Healer, and Coming King. This foundational concept is central to the denomination's evangelical and classical Pentecostal theology. In 2004 the ICFG had more than 4 million members in 38,000 congregations throughout 141 countries, making it one of the largest Pentecostal denominations and one of the fastest growing of all Christian denominations in the world.

The church's founder, Aimee Semple McPherson, was a colorful and popular personality in the first half of the twentieth century. A professed atheist as a child, she was converted by young evangelist Robert Semple, and soon joined him in marriage

and in ministry. Ordained by William H. Durham in 1909, the couple served a short time at Full Gospel Assembly Mission in Chicago. Called to be missionaries to China in 1908, the couple served until Robert died unexpectedly in 1910. Aimee (or "Sister," as she came to be called) returned to the United States with her infant daughter, Roberta. She married Harold Stewart McPherson in 1911. Following the birth of her son Rolph, the couple embarked on an evangelistic ministry. Traveling from Maine to Miami, and eventually coast to coast, she soon established a reputation for drawing crowds through her compelling sermons and creative use of drama. She also had considerable success in **foreign mission** campaigns held in various countries. During these years she drew financial support from many mainline denominational Christians and organizations that came to believe in her ministry.

The McPhersons organized their ministry in Los Angeles, establishing the Echo Park Evangelistic Association and the famous Angelus Temple, which soon gained a membership of over 25,000. They published the *Bridal Call Magazine*, built a **prayer** tower, provided ongoing benevolence for thousands of needy persons, and established the Lighthouse for International Foursquare Evangelism (LIFE) Bible Institute. In 1924 they acquired a powerful radio station, KFSG, that broadcasted throughout

Southern California and syndicated nationally. The remarkable success of Aimee McPherson's ministry in the early 1920s gave ample opportunity for the ICFG to train ministers and establish new churches. She served as president of the denomination until her death in 1944. McPherson's later ministry was overshadowed by events in her personal life—her mysterious disappearance from a beach in Santa Monica in 1926, followed by her reappearance in Arizona some weeks later, and an ill-fated third marriage (ending in divorce) to singer David Hutton in 1933, after her divorce from Harold McPherson. In consequence, McPherson's ministry and the ICFG received less support from mainline Protestant churches beginning in the late 1920s and early 1930s.

Headquartered in Los Angeles, the denomination is currently led by a national board, president, and general supervisor. The organization is administered across the United States in 70 districts, each managed by a supervisor. These supervisors appoint superintendents over local areas who help oversee churches and pastors in a modified episcopal government (i.e., with rule by bishops). Churches elect councils to serve as governing boards. The national corporation owns all church property. ICFG operates separate organizations to support missions and education. A primary division of the national corporation is Foursquare Missions International, which oversees cross-cultural missions operations in 141 countries. Each country operates a Foursquare ministry organization under a separate corporation. Life Pacific College (formerly LIFE Bible Institute), founded at Angelus Temple in 1926 and established in San Dimas, California, in 1992, is the denomination's primary educational institution. The ICFG also operates several college-level Bible institutes and more than 300 local ministry training institutes located throughout the world.

Further Reading: Epstein, Daniel Mark. *Sister Aimee: The Life of Aimee Semple McPherson.* New York: Harcourt Brace Jovanovich, 1993; International Church of the Foursquare Gospel Web site. http://www.foursquare.org/; Van Cleave, Nathaniel M. *The Vine and the Branches: A History of the International Church of the Foursquare*

Gospel. Los Angeles: International Church of the Foursquare Gospel, 1992.

Daniel Hedges

INTERNATIONAL PENTECOSTAL HOLINESS CHURCH

Birthed in the late nineteenth-century **Holiness movement** and the early twentieth-century **Azusa Street revival,** the International Pentecostal Holiness Church (IPHC) was formed in the 1911 merger of the Pentecostal Holiness Church of North Carolina (PHCNC) and the Fire Baptized Holiness Church (FBHC) in Falcon, North Carolina. Both of these predecessor groups had been organized in 1898. The FBHC had its roots in Iowa, and subsequently spread toward the southeastern United States. Its founder was B. H. Irwin and its major leaders included J. H. King (Georgia), S. D. Page (North Carolina), and Daniel Awrey (Tennessee). The PHCNC took shape in Goldsboro, North Carolina, under the leadership of A. B. Crumpler. Its other leaders included J. A. Culbreth, A. H. Butler, Gaston B. Cashwell, and G. F. Taylor—who wrote one of the first book-length defenses of **speaking in tongues** as the initial evidence of the **baptism in the Holy Spirit,** *The Spirit and the Bride* (1907). Leaders in both of the parent bodies of the IPHC had roots in the **Methodist** Episcopal Church, South. They developed relationships through contacts in Holiness **camp meetings.** From Holiness revival magazines, they learned of the April 1906 Azusa Street revival in Los Angeles and the practice of speaking in tongues. In late 1906, Cashwell went to investigate the Azusa revival, and, after undergoing his own experience of Spirit baptism, he went back to **preach** the **Pentecostal** message in North Carolina and across the **South.** Over a three-year period, both the PHCNC and the FBHC accepted the Azusa experience as part of their theology, which helped to facilitate the 1911 merger.

The IPHC has 13 articles of faith that derive from the Apostles' Creed, the Nicene Creed, the Lutheran Augsburg Confession, and the Thirty-Nine Articles of the Church of England. The church holds to the Bible as the inspired and authoritative Word of God, the call to **sanctification** as taught by John Wesley, divine **healing** as provided in the atonement (though medical care is acceptable), the premillennial return of Jesus Christ, and the baptism of the Holy Spirit with speaking in tongues as the initial evidence. Since the 1990s, the IPHC has acknowledged that the gifts named in Ephesians 4:11 (including that of apostle and prophet) continue to operate in the church universal and should be appropriately recognized. The Methodist heritage is still recognized in the organization of the church into conferences with superintendents. The church is headquartered in Oklahoma City, Oklahoma. Every four years a General Conference elects the general superintendent along with other denominational leaders. The IPHC ordains **women** to the ministry and has women as pastors. Persons divorced and remarried may be ordained under certain conditions. Ordination occurs on the conference level and not in the local church.

Through its first 70 years, the IPHC maintained a strong Holiness ethic focusing on outward dress and behavior. The past 30 years has seen a shift from what was perceived as legalism to a more accommodating position with an emphasis on inner transformation through Christ, the Bible, the Holy Spirit, and the community of faith. Since the 1980s, the IPHC has focused on world evangelism and church planting, the intercessory **prayer** renewal movement, youth ministry, and adult discipleship. The church publishes a monthly magazine, *IPHC Experience*. As of 2004, the IPHC had more than 2,000 congregations in the United States with nearly 230,000 members, and nearly 20,000 overseas churches with over 3.7 million members (including affiliates). As noted, the ratio of foreign to domestic congregations in the church is about 10 to 1—a clear testimony to the church's focus on **foreign missions.**

Further Reading: Beacham, Doug. *Rediscovering the Role of Apostles and Prophets.* Franklin Springs, GA: LifeSprings Resources, 2003; Campbell, Joseph E. *The Pentecostal Holiness Church, 1898–1948: Its Background and History.* Franklin Springs, GA: Publishing House of the Pentecostal Holiness Church, 1951; International Pentecostal Holiness Church Web site. http://www.iphc.org/; King, J. H. *From Passover to Pentecost.* 1914. Reprint, Franklin Springs, GA: LifeSprings Resources, 2004; Synan, Vinson. *The Old Time Power: A Centennial History of the International Pentecostal Holiness Church.* Franklin Springs, GA: LifeSprings Resources, 1998.

Douglas Beacham

INTERNET AND REVIVALS

Revivalists throughout American history have used communications media in innovative ways. The **preaching** of **George Whitefield** first put religion into **colonial**-era newspapers that had previously been devoted solely to political and economic affairs. Revival preachers, such as **Aimee Semple McPherson** and **Charles Fuller,** turned to **radio** in the 1920s and 1930s, and **Oral Roberts** and **Billy Graham** expanded into **television** ministry during the 1950s and 1960s. While Internet technology is relatively new, there is nothing new about the use of emergent media by revivalists and in revivals.

The novelty of the Internet's role in revivals arises from its instantaneous, translocal, globe-encircling character. Almost immediately after the emergence of the **Toronto Blessing** in 1994 and the **Pensacola revival** in 1995, e-mail and Internet communication brought the news of the awakening to the world, and both cities for several years became pilgrimage centers for charismatic Christians from all nations who were seeking spiritual recharging and renewal. Participants and observers debated controversial phenomena such as Toronto's "holy laughter" at numerous Web sites. Streaming media and MPEG downloads allowed those who were not present to share in events as they happened in the form of sermons, music, still images, and videos. The World Wide Web became at once the conduit for believers to exchange information about revivals, a channel for books, cassettes, and videotapes to be ordered, a means for fund-raising, and a forum for believers and skeptics alike to share experiences, doubts, questions, affirmations, and criticisms of the revivals.

The Global Day of Prayer—originating in one city and spreading to 160 countries in less than five years—illustrates the potential of Internet technology in the service of religious revivals. A middle-aged businessman in South Africa, Graham Power, reported having a vision of a stadium full of people in united **prayer,** and later organized a prayer service for 45,000 people at a rugby stadium in Cape Town in 2001. By 2004, more than 20 million African Christians joined in the annual day of prayer. By 2005, more than 100 million Christians throughout the world shared in prayer services held on the day of Pentecost in May. A combination of African grassroots involvement and North American promotional skill facilitated an exponential growth in participation. It is hard to imagine such a development in the absence of globally accessible Internet technology.

Revivalism is the sort of religion that would seem to have a natural affinity with the Internet. Pro-revival Christians in the mid-1700s became known as New Lights, and proponents of revival have often been associated with newness, novelty, and innovation not only in the sphere of religion but also in politics, social life, and the media. Revivalist Christianity has little to fear from religious innovation as such. Through Internet technology, revivalists can bring their message into nations—like Saudi Arabia or North Korea—that might otherwise be impregnable to outside influence. Known since the 1700s for criticizing the established religious order, revivalists can use e-mail, Web sites, Web logs (or blogs), and other Internet devices to express their point of view while remaining anonymous if they so choose. The Internet allows anyone to attack, lampoon, and subvert authorities. Online religion—exhibited in more than a million Web sites today—is a booming, buzzing marketplace of ideas where the venerable traditions of historic, mainline Christianity bump up against newfangled and self-made faiths and every sort of religious innovation. Brenda Brasher speaks of cyberspace as "a fiction of public etiquette that orients people in a virtual environment" (Brasher, 5). Cyberspace is nowhere and everywhere. Religion, once situated in cyberspace, is no longer tied to a locality. While this frees Internet religion from the control and constraint of nation-states and local communities, it could also weaken or eliminate human fellowship and interpersonal interaction—traditionally a major factor in revivals.

Yet a study of online interactions among Anglican Charismatics (Campbell, 2005) challenges the idea that Internet use hinders face-to-face, embodied relationships. For the Community of Prophecy (CP) group, online communication was a "supplement" and not a "substitute" for offline interaction (Campbell, 161). Some people were so committed to online religious community that participation in it became part of their daily routine (Campbell, 135). Moreover, this Internet group communicated in some novel ways, such as an online request for spiritual guidance, followed by a "prophecy" given by another person online who knew only the name, and perhaps the age or marital status, of the individual seeking guidance. "A 'prophecy' shared and proved accurate online receives a unique credibility" (Campbell, 85). Another online innovation was the "emoticon" symbolizing spiritual experience. The emailed sign \0/ represented someone worshiping with arms upraised, while ~~~\0/~~~ denotes a Charismatic believer who is immersed "in the river of God" and divine blessing (Campbell, 116).

Participants in online discussion were themselves aware of the limitations of the Internet, as one wrote: "It would be difficult to email you a plate of chocolate chip cookies" (Campbell, 147). Intimate, emotional disclosure, of the sort required in psychological counseling, would not seem to be viable by means of the Internet. Because of its disembodied character, the Internet allows such negative forms of communication as spamming (unwanted or irrelevant messages), flaming (verbal taunts and insults), and stalking (surveillance of one person by another). In Campbell's study, one individual sent out a "public confession of sins in the format of a prayer request." Because of this violation of protocol, the cyber-community exercised discipline by naming the offender, highlighting his email address and tagline, and telling people on the listserv to have nothing to do with him. In another case, an estranged husband went online to discover the whereabouts of his ex-wife (Campbell, 120–21). Yet many have reported positive benefits from participation in an online religious community. A single lawyer in rural Michigan, named Louise, described the Internet as her "altar of remembrance" and noted that her online interaction encouraged her to devote herself more fully to offline relationships in her local church.

In conclusion, then, Internet communication—while not substituting for embodied relationships—has shown a capacity for enhancing the spiritual life of believers in far-flung locations and for promoting religious revival through the transmission of information, advice, encouragement, testimonials, and prayer requests.

Further Reading: Brasher, Brenda E. *Give Me That Online Religion.* San Francisco: Jossey-Bass, 2001; Campbell, Heidi. *Exploring Religious Community Online: We Are One in the Network.* New York: Peter Lang, 2005; Dawson, Lorne L., and Douglas E. Cowan, eds. *Religion Online: Finding Faith on the Internet.* New York: Routledge, 2004; Zaleski, Jeff. *The Soul of Cyberspace: How New Technology Is Changing Our Spiritual Lives.* San Francisco: HarperSanFrancisco, 1997.

Michael J. McClymond

INTERVARSITY CHRISTIAN FELLOWSHIP

As the United States and Canadian branch of the International Fellowship of Evangelical Students, InterVarsity Christian Fellowship (IVCF) is an evangelical Christian organization committed to evangelism and discipleship among **college** students. The movement began in 1873 as a union of university Christian groups in Great Britain. A Canadian ministry emerged in 1928, and in 1939 C. Stacey Woods organized an InterVarsity chapter at the University of Michigan. Filling a niche created by the decline of the **Young Men's Christian Association** (YMCA) and the affiliated **Student Volunteer Movement** for **Foreign Missions,** InterVarsity staff workers created a network of over 50 U.S. campus ministries within several years. InterVarsity participated in the evangelical revivals of the late 1940s and 1950s. Student chapters grew rapidly with the expanding postwar campus population. IVCF proclaimed a "Year of Evangelism"

in 1950 and sent evangelists, including **Billy Graham,** to numerous campuses. Christian students followed up those who expressed an interest in Jesus Christ and organized campus Bible studies. Given the importance of the Greek system to campus social life, IVCF students organized evangelistic teams to present the Christian message in sororities and fraternities. In keeping with the organization's emphasis on foreign missions, IVCF also developed a campus outreach to international students.

After a merger with the Student Foreign Mission Fellowship, IVCF held its first student missionary convention in Toronto in 1946. Since 1948, IVCF has held a triennial foreign missions convention at the University of Illinois at Urbana. Although the conventions began to address pressing social and intercultural issues in the late 1960s, IVCF has maintained its focus on motivating students to consider overseas missions. A few InterVarsity chapters participated in the **Charismatic movement** of the 1960s. In 1962, a number of students in the Yale IVCF chapter spoke in tongues. Within the next few months, the phenomena spread to several other campuses. The organization neither encouraged nor forbade speaking in tongues. IVCF leadership sought to avoid division within chapters and prevent the loss of IVCF's traditional emphases. The number of IVCF chapters peaked at nearly 900 in the early 1970s. During the 1980s, rapid turnover in top leadership sapped the movement's momentum, reflected in smaller attendance at Urbana and a reduced number of campus chapters. Steadier leadership produced renewed growth in the 1990s and early years of the twenty-first century.

Further Reading: Hunt, Keith, and Gladys Hunt. *For Christ and the University: The Story of InterVarsity Christian Fellowship of the U.S.A., 1940–1990.* Downers Grove, IL: InterVarsity Press, 1991; InterVarsity Christian Fellowship Web site. http://www.ivcf.org/; Shelley, Bruce. "The Rise of Evangelical Youth Movements." *Fides et Historia* 18 (January 1986): 47–63.

John Turner

J

JAKES, THOMAS DEXTER (T. D.), SR. (1957–)

Thomas Dexter (T. D.) Jakes Sr. is a **Pentecostal** pastor, **television** evangelist, **African American** Christian leader, prolific author, recording artist, and movie producer. He was born in 1957 to Odith and Ernest Jakes Sr. in South Charleston, West Virginia, the youngest of three children. Raised in Vandalia, West Virginia, he grew up in a **Baptist** church and was **baptized in the Holy Spirit** in a storefront **Apostolic** Church. He attended West Virginia State University and graduated from Center Business College. In 1976, Jakes **preached** his first sermon. In 1980, Jakes became a part-time pastor with 10 members of the Greater Emmanuel Temple of Faith Church in Montgomery. In 1982, he assumed the full-time pastorate of this church and began a local radio ministry entitled *The Master's Plan*. Jakes moved his church from the town of Montgomery to Smithers, and ran revivals every year at the Greater Mt. Zion Pentecostal Church in Bluefield, West Virginia. In these services, Jakes was the preacher, **prayer** leader, piano player, and singer. Jakes married Serita Ann Jamison in 1981, and in 1983 he held his first Bible conference.

In 1987, in a service held at the Charleston Civic Center, Jakes was ordained into the bishopric by Bishop Quander L. Wilson Sr., presiding bishop of the Greater Emmanuel Apostolic Faith Churches. Jakes completed his BA and MA degrees by correspondence courses from Friends University in 1990, and received his DMin degree in 1995. In 1990 he moved his ministry from Smithers to South Charleston, West Virginia, where his congregation grew from 100 members to over 300. In 1990, Jakes began a Sunday school class for abandoned and abused **women** with the title "Woman, Thou Art Loosed." He, with his wife and his prayer warriors, encouraged women to use their past pain as a foundation for new growth and a closer walk with God. In 1992 he preached his most popular sermon, "Woman, Thou Art Loosed," an address to hurting women. Later he established a similar class for hurting **men,** which he called "Manpower." Soon thereafter, Jakes published his first book, *Woman, Thou Art Loosed* (1993), and began a weekly television broadcast, *Get Ready with T. D. Jakes*, on the Trinity Broadcasting Network (TBN) and Black Entertainment Television (BET). Each year Jakes holds a Bible conference at the Charleston Civic Center, and his ministry addresses the needs of the homeless, prisoners, victims of abuse, and other hurting people.

The T. D. Jakes Ministries is affiliated with the Higher Ground Apostolic Church—a Oneness **Holiness** Pentecostal organization of 200 churches, founded in 1988 (on Oneness Pentecostalism, see **Haywood, Garfield Thomas**). Jakes is first vice president and Bishop Andrew Merritt from Detroit is second vice president of Higher Ground. In 1994, Jakes held his first conference for ministers and their spouses, "When Shepherds Bleed." In 1995–1996 he hosted the nationally syndicated radio program *Get Ready*, and purchased the building for the Eagle Nest Church in Dallas that formerly belonged to evangelist W. T. Grant. In May 1996, he moved his own family and 50 other families from West Virginia to Dallas, Texas, to a new location on 34 acres, where he established a congregation known as the Potter's House.

In January 1999, the *New York Times* named Jakes as one of the five evangelists who might become an international evangelist to succeed **Billy Graham.** At the Georgia Dome in Atlanta in 1999, Jakes's meeting broke the national indoor attendance record held by Billy Graham with 87,500 attendees and an additional 20,000 in overflow. The T. D. Jakes Television Ministries has expanded its broadcasting to Europe and South Africa. His Dallas church is known for its state-by-state Adopt-a-Prison campaign to provide state prison systems with satellite broadcast reception equipment for rehabilitative and religious programming. In September 2001, *Time* magazine featured him on the cover and named him America's Best Preacher. He has won Grammy and Dove Award nominations for his musical recording of "Woman, Thou Art Loosed." As of 2005, Jakes has two Sunday services at his church seating 16,000 people and has 30,000 members on his church roll. His church is multiracial and one of the nation's best-known **megachurches.** Jakes's sermons address the problems of racism and social ostracism, and he is called a "Shepherd to the Shattered." He is the author of 29 books, several of which have been on the *New York Times* best-seller list.

Further Reading: Lee, Shayne. *T. D. Jakes: America's New Preacher*. New York: New York University Press, 2005; Van Biema, David. "Bishop Unbound." *Time*, December 11, 2000, 86; Wellman, Sam. *T. D. Jakes*. New York: Chelsea House Publications, 2000.

Sherry Sherrod DuPree

JARRATT, DEVEREUX (1733–1801)

Devereux Jarratt—an Anglican, and later, Episcopal evangelist—led revivals with **Methodists** during the **Great Awakening** in Virginia. In 1781 the early Methodist leader **Francis Asbury** claimed that Jarratt had won more converts than any other **preacher** in Virginia. Devereux Jarratt, the son of Robert Jarratt, a middling farmer, and Sarah (Bradley) Jarratt, was born in New Kent County, Virginia, on January 17, 1733. Reared in a nominal Anglican family, Jarratt underwent evangelical conversion under New Light **Presbyterians** while serving as tutor in the household of Albermarle County planter John Cannon. Jarratt studied under Alexander Martin, a Princeton graduate. Preferring the catholicity of Anglicanism and the benefits of an established church to that of Presbyterian dissenters, Jarratt traveled to London, where he was ordained an Anglican priest in 1763 and met **George Whitefield** and John Wesley. Returning to Virginia in 1763, he became rector of Bath Parish, Dinwiddie County, where he remained until his death. Moving up in society, Jarratt married Martha, the daughter of prominent planter Burnell Claiborne.

Preferring revivalistic sermons to the moralistic homilies of his fellow Anglicans, Jarratt preached on justification by faith alone, the new birth, and hellfire to crowded congregations who responded with emotional outbursts despite his disapproval of emotionalism. He led in a revival among Anglicans from 1764 to 1772 in Virginia and North Carolina. When the Methodist preacher Robert Williams came to Virginia in 1773, Jarratt encouraged and assisted him. Assured that the Methodists were not planning to separate from the Church of England, Jarratt saw them as agents of revival in that body. His cooperation with Methodists resulted in the revival of 1775–1776, the Methodist phase of the Great Awakening. Anglican clergyman Archibald McRoberts and Methodist lay preachers joined Jarratt in conducting revivals. In 1776 Jarratt wrote *A Brief Narrative of the Revival of Religion*, which was delivered to John Wesley and published in London. This work along with *The Life of the*

Reverend Devereux Jarratt, Written by Himself (1806) and *Sermons on Various and Important Subjects* (three volumes, 1793–1794) are important primary sources of the history and preaching of the Methodist revival.

Methodism in those areas of Virginia and North Carolina where Jarratt preached grew from 291 in 1774 to 4,379 in 1777. By 1777 two-thirds of all Methodists in the colonies were located near Jarratt's parish and areas of preaching, so that this region is called the cradle of American Methodism. Since John Wesley used lay preachers in the colonies, Methodists looked to Jarratt, an ordained priest, to perform the sacraments for them on his travels to 29 counties. The Methodist Conference of 1782 thanked Jarratt for his service to Methodists and counseled their **southern** preachers to consult with him. Jarratt refused to leave the Church of England when Methodists separated to form the Methodist Episcopal Church in 1784. He chastised them for their departure. Following this, his audiences dwindled. The Methodists, who had come out strongly for **abolitionism** and the emancipation of slaves, snubbed him, and some said that he would go to hell for holding slaves. Jarratt chose to stand by the Protestant Episcopal Church, newly formed from the Church of England, whose clergy had ridiculed him as an enthusiast, rather than join the Methodists who had previously revered his revival preaching. Despite the spiritual and numerical decline of his denomination after it had been disestablished by law, Jarratt stated the Episcopal Church would "yet arise, and shake herself from the dust and become a praise in the western world" (Jarratt, 129). He determined to spend his remaining days **praying** for the resurrection of the Episcopal Diocese of Virginia but died in 1801 before his expectation had been realized. Methodist bishop Francis Asbury preached at his funeral.

During the **Second Great Awakening,** Episcopalians under their first two evangelical bishops, Richard Channing Moore and William Meade, held up Jarratt as a role model during the revival of the Diocese of Virginia. In 1818 Moore urged priests to imitate Jarratt's example. Meade published a life of Jarratt in 1840 and willed Jarratt's chair to Virginia Theological Seminary in Alexandria to insure that Jarratt would be remembered by the nineteenth-century evangelical Episcopalians who had witnessed the fulfillment of Jarratt's vision.

Further Reading: Gewehr, Wesley M. *The Great Awakening in Virginia, 1740–1790.* Gloucester, MA: Peter Smith, 1965; Jarratt, Devereux. *The Life of the Reverend Devereux Jarratt.* Baltimore: Warner and Hanna, 1806; Thomas, Arthur Dicken, Jr. "The Second Great Awakening in Virginia and Slavery Reform, 1785–1837." PhD dissertation, Union Theological Seminary, Virginia, 1981.

Arthur Dicken Thomas Jr.

JEHOVAH'S WITNESSES

The religious group now known as Jehovah's Witnesses began in 1879 under the leadership of Charles Taze Russell (1852–1916). Russell was a former Congregationalist who, as a young man, had drifted into agnosticism. Russell experienced a renewal of his faith as a result of his contact with the Second Adventists, a church related to the modern **Seventh-day Adventists.** Russell borrowed many Adventist doctrines and developed his core teachings around **eschatology** and the imminent (i.e., soon to come) return of Jesus Christ. Witnesses today still stress the need to proclaim to the world the impending battle of Armageddon (Revelation 16:16), which will destroy all wicked persons. Persons who survive Armageddon will live forever on a paradise earth where no pain, sorrow, or sin will exist, and a select 144,000 will spend eternity in heaven to rule those on earth. Witnesses deviate from mainline Christianity in several ways. Based on their interpretation of the Bible, they reject the doctrine of the Trinity, teach that the Son of God was and is a created being, and that the Holy Spirit is a term that describes God's active force. They also reject the concept of hell as a place of eternal torment, but teach instead that hell is the grave from which people can be resurrected.

The Watchtower Bible Society—the legal organization of the Jehovah's Witnesses—has grown from a handful of members in 1879 to over 6.5 million active members worldwide in 2005.

Over 16 million attended their most important religious celebration, the memorial of Christ's death. This is something like a Eucharistic service with bread and wine, except that only those from the 144,000 chosen persons may participate in the ritual, and most members of the Jehovah's Witnesses do not qualify. Witnesses today are often found in areas where conservative American Protestantism thrives. For the past 30 years, growth has been disproportionately large in small towns and in rural America. Growth in the past decade has also been rapid in Africa and other parts of the developing world, and in former communist nations such as Russia. Most converts to the Jehovah's Witnesses were raised in a Christian denomination, and Witnesses have had only limited success **converting** Hindus, Muslims, or Buddhists to their faith.

The early composition of the Witnesses was largely white and of European descent, but recently the minority members, and especially **African Americans,** have increased considerably. One reason is that the Witnesses teach that all races are literal descendants of Adam and Eve, and consequently all are equal before God. In the United States, more than 52 percent of Witnesses are African American or **Latino.** The Witnesses endeavor to present their message to a non-Western, nonwhite audience, with publications that feature illustrations of black and Asian members. They offer their committed members a highly supportive social group, providing help with personal problems and the mundane tasks of life. Their high moral ideals, including the prohibition of illicit sex, smoking, and excessive drinking, are appealing to many converts. Divorce is allowed only in cases of adultery. Because of the Witnesses' strict stand against nonmarital sex, illegitimacy is lower than among non-Witnesses.

Although nominal followers exist in all religious traditions, most Witnesses exhibit a high level of commitment to their faith and their community. In 2004 Witnesses worldwide spent over 1.2 billion hours proselytizing. They meet five times a week in buildings called Kingdom Halls to study Watchtower publications and hone their proselytizing skills. Witnesses are internationally known for distributing millions of books from door to door and on the street corners of most larger cities. They operate one of the largest printeries in the world, and many of their publications have print runs in the tens of millions of copies and in several hundred languages. Witnesses claim that their primary commitment is to the Old and New Testaments, but they are required to accept Watchtower biblical interpretations and church policies. Disagreement can be grounds for *disfellowshipping*—meaning that the offender will be permanently prevented from associating with other Witnesses. Each year thousands of Witnesses are disfellowshipped, many on charges of immorality, but also for challenging relatively minor points in the Watchtower's interpretation of scripture. Serious problems may arise when members of a family are disfellowshipped while others continue to be Witnesses.

Jehovah's Witnesses have been involved in many legal skirmishes in nations around the world. Most of the problems hinged on conflicts over military duty, the flag salute, and the Watchtower prohibition on blood transfusion. The first well-known blood refusal case occurred in 1951, yet participation in blood transfusion was not a disfellowshipping offense until after 1961, and concessions have been made in this policy in recent years. Generally people who leave the fellowship depart over interpersonal conflicts, or because their own Bible study and theological reflection has caused them to believe that the Witnesses' interpretation is incorrect. The number of college graduates among the Witnesses is less than five percent—below the national average—in part because the Witnesses have, until recently, strongly discouraged education beyond the high school level. Yet with recent changes in attitude, there may be a rise in educational levels in the future.

Further Reading: Bergman, Jerry. *Jehovah's Witnesses: A Comprehensive and Selectively Annotated Bibliography.* Westport, CT: Greenwood Press, 1999; Franz, Raymond. *Crisis of Conscience.* Atlanta: Commentary Press, 1983; Franz, Raymond. *In Search of Christian Freedom.* Atlanta: Commentary Press, 1991; Harrison, Barbara Grizzuti. *Visions of Glory: A History and Memoir of Jehovah's Witnesses.* New York: Simon and Schuster, 1978; Penton,

M. James. *Apocalypse Delayed: The Story of Jehovah's Witnesses.* Toronto: University of Toronto Press, 1997; Reed, David L. *Blood on the Altar: Confessions of the Jehovah's Witness Ministry.* Amherst, NY: Prometheus Books, 1996; Rogerson, Alan. *Millions Now Living Will Never Die: A Study of Jehovah's Witnesses.* London: Constable, 1969.

Gerald Bergman

JERKS

see Bodily Manifestations in Revivals

JESUS PEOPLE MOVEMENT

Many observers in the early 1960s predicted an ongoing and accelerating trend toward secularism in the United States. These same observers were taken by surprise at a Christian resurgence in the late 1960s and early 1970s that affected a range of Christian denominations. The outbreak of experiential Christianity among the young garnered considerable media attention—sometimes in stereotypical ways—through the portrayal of former potheads and free-loving hippies transformed into Bible-quoting "Jesus freaks." The emergence of the Jesus People from a peculiar marriage of Christianity with the counterculture may have been the most unexpected social development of the era.

San Francisco, California, emerged as an early center of the Jesus People in 1967. Four couples there underwent **conversion,** and their experiences culminated in a communal living arrangement, patterned after the early Christians and what they read in the Book of Acts. Led by Ted and Liz Wise, the group opened up a coffeehouse in San Francisco's Haight-Ashbury district and spent the next 18 months attempting to build relationships within the hippie culture through street evangelism, a soup kitchen for transients, and the use of their home as a crash pad for drug users and for the homeless. In this incipient phase, these evangelistic hippies were dubbed "psychedelic evangelists" or "street Christians." A leader among them was Lonnie Frisbee, a hippie turned itinerant evangelist who was pursuing an evangelistic hitchhiking mission along the Southern California coast when he came into contact with Chuck Smith, the pastor of a small church named **Calvary Chapel.** After meeting Lonnie, Chuck and his wife, Kay, asked Frisbee to bring his wife and to begin a ministry attached to his church. Within six months of Frisbee's arrival, Calvary Chapel had grown from 50 members to 2,000.

The Children of God, led by self-proclaimed prophet Moses David Berg, began as a coffeehouse ministry in the Los Angeles suburb of Huntington Beach. Within a few years, however, they had morphed into a band of doomsday-proclaiming radicals spouting antagonistic rhetoric against other church groups. Fleeing North America in the early 1970s, the Children of God took up refuge in various locations throughout the world, adopting a mode of recruitment called "flirty fishing"—amounting to little more than prostitution of its female members. Other California-based personalities and ministries emerged including Arthur Blessitt, the "Minister of the Sunset Strip," who chained himself to a large wooden cross when authorities threatened to evict him from his coffeehouse location in Hollywood. Evangelist Duane Pederson started publishing and distributing the *Hollywood Free Paper* in downtown Los Angeles. John Higgins moved from the communal house outreach under Calvary Chapel and began the Shiloh Youth Revival Centers throughout the Pacific Northwest basin. On the University of California campus at Berkeley, former statistics professor Jack Sparks began a counterculture ministry to intellectuals called the Christian World Liberation Front. Hal Lindsey's *The Late Great Planet Earth*—the best-selling nonfiction book of the 1970s in the United States—capitalized upon the apocalyptic tone of the times. The book was born during Lindsey's short tenure at the Gospel Power and Light House ministry.

Yet the movement was not limited to the California coast. Other Jesus People outposts sprang up across the continent and throughout the world. Evangelist Linda Meissner—who had worked on the streets of New York with David Wilkerson's fledgling Teen Challenge ministry—began the Jesus People Army, which spread to a number of localities before

The Explo '72 conference in Dallas, Texas attracted 80,000 participants, including many youth from the Jesus People Movement (1972). Courtesy of David Di Sabatino.

Meissner affiliated with the Children of God. One of Meissner's lieutenants, an artistic visionary named Jim Palosaari, was sent as an emissary to the Midwest in the early 1970s and launched the Milwaukee Jesus People. This group eventually divided into four separate groups, one of which eventually settled in downtown Chicago as the Jesus People USA.

In 1971 the "Jesus movement" attracted media attention as stories in *Time* and *Look* magazines in the United States, and *Bunte* in Germany, took notice of the groundswell of faith among countercultural youth. *Time* announced, "Jesus is alive and well and living in the radical spiritual fervor of a growing number of Americans who have proclaimed an extraordinary religious revolution in his name" ("The New Rebel Cry"). As the revival gained momentum it spawned experimental communities. Christian communes with names like the House of Acts and the House of Miracles sprang up across the continent. Some participants in these communal

experiments claimed that their experiences paralleled those of the early Christians. Another prominent development was the translation of this newfound spiritual exuberance into music and song. Artists with names such as Agape and the All Saved Freak Band started to use music to draw crowds in order to evangelize. Music festivals and record companies soon entered the picture—the incipient stages of what has grown into the contemporary Christian music (CCM) industry.

Despite the doctrinal wrangling that is a staple of every revival, the common denominator for participants was a spiritual experience that usually began with the hippie quest for truth and ended with Christian conversion. The Jesus People were Christian experientialists, whose version of the gospel was a volatile mixture of countercultural suspicion of authority, **Pentecostal** practice, literal interpretations of the Bible, and aggressive Fundamentalist-style evangelism. By 1974 the Jesus People movement was not as readily identifiable as it

This image from Explo '72 exhibits the joy and confidence of the Jesus People, who proclaimed Christ as the "one way" to salvation (1972). Courtesy of David Di Sabatino.

had been only three years previously. The once highly visible ocean-side baptismal services attended by hordes of **enthusiastic** youngsters had been replaced by more down-to-earth activities. Long-haired street **preachers** focused on teaching Sunday school, preparing for overseas missionary work, or perhaps even attending a Bible college or seminary. Those formerly classifying themselves as Jesus People entered a wide spectrum of Protestant and **Roman Catholic** denominations and found that the established church was not as narrow-minded or spiritually bereft as they once imagined. The idealism of an earlier period gave way to a more complex and holistic view of the church that tempered the movement's countercultural impulses. As the **Charismatic** moment of the revival came to an end, the institutionalization and formalization that the Jesus People had once feared became a part of their journey toward Christian maturity.

The influence of the Jesus People movement is still felt though much of its countercultural appearance is gone. It has had an enduring effect in spiritual renewal. At least four new church denominations—Calvary Chapel, Gospel Outreach, Hope Chapel, and the Vineyard Association—trace their lineage to the Jesus People. The CCM industry now commands over eight percent of all sales of recorded music in North America, outselling both classical and jazz music. Thousands of individual churches were founded or experienced

renewal due to the influx of members. Parachurch **campus and college** organizations, such as **Campus Crusade for Christ,** the **Navigators, Youth for Christ,** and **Youth with a Mission,** to name only a few, benefited from the large number of spiritual converts that were channeled into their programs. The revival also spawned its own parachurch organizations such as Last Days Ministries, Christ Is the Answer Ministries, and the Holy Ghost Repair Shop. In the late 1970s a number of house church leaders who were linked to the Jesus People movement were at the forefront of a migration of evangelicals into Eastern Orthodox Churches. Many of the revival's former adherents, some of whom are just now ascending into positions of authority within church organizations, cite their spiritual experiences among the Jesus People as formative for their later ministry. The contemporary worship styles that have entered increasing numbers of Charismatic, Pentecostal, evangelical, mainline Protestant, and Roman Catholic congregations since the 1990s—and have been marketed by such music companies as Maranatha! Music, Vineyard Music Group, and Integrity Hosanna—trace their origins to the Jesus People movement. Spiritual ripples from this 1970s revival are still visible in North American churches today.

Further Reading: Di Sabatino, David. *The Jesus People Movement: An Annotated Bibliography and General Resource.* Westport, CT: Greenwood Press, 1999; Ellwood, Robert S., Jr. *One Way: The Jesus Movement and Its Meaning.* Englewood Cliffs, NJ: Prentice Hall, 1973; Enroth, Ronald M., Edward E. Ericson Jr., and C. Breckenridge Peters. *The Jesus People: Old Time Religion in the Age of Aquarius.* Grand Rapids, MI: Eerdmans, 1972; Graham, Billy. *The Jesus Generation.* Grand Rapids, MI: Zondervan, 1971; Kittler, Glenn D. *The Jesus Kids and their Leaders.* New York: Warner Paperback Library, 1972; "The New Rebel Cry: Jesus Is Coming!" *Time,* June 21, 1971, 36–47; Pederson, Duane, with Bob Owen. *Jesus People.* Pasadena, CA: Compass Press, 1971; Plowman, Edward E. *The Underground Church: Accounts of Christian Revolutionaries in America.* Elgin, IL: David C. Cook, 1971; Vachon, Brian. "The Jesus Movement Is Upon Us." *Look,* February 9, 1971, 15–21; Ward, Hiley H. *The Far-Out Saints of the Jesus Communes: A First-Hand Report and Interpretation of the*

Jesus People Movement. New York: Association Press, 1972.

David Di Sabatino

JONES, SAMUEL PORTER (1847–1906)

Samuel Porter Jones was a colorful revival **preacher,** active in the late 1800s and just after 1900, primarily in the **South** of the United States. He was born in 1847, in Chambers County, Alabama, to John J. and Nancy Porter Jones. Jones's mother died when he was nine, whereupon his father remarried and moved the family to Cartersville, Georgia. Jones's father was a successful lawyer and businessman, and young Sam tried to pursue his father's footsteps into the field of law. Yet a nervous disorder—diagnosed as "dyspepsia" but possibly a form of bipolar disorder—forced him out of school, and so he studied law at home. Jones was a quick study and was admitted to the Georgia bar in just one year. During this period, Jones began drinking and became an alcoholic in short order. In 1872, he made a solemn deathbed promise to his father that he would quit drinking. He kept his promise and remained sober for the rest of his life. One week after his father's death, in an agonizing struggle to remain sober, Jones had a **conversion** experience. Only two weeks later, Jones gave his first sermon at his grandfather's **Methodist** church.

The nature of Jones's conversion led him to preach a different gospel than the traditional "heart religion" with which people were familiar. Jones believed that his own salvation was a process that began when he quit drinking. He told audiences to stop sinning, or "quit your meanness," and thus "get religion." In his eyes, right actions led to a right relationship with God. Commenting on the evangelist he was most often compared to, Jones quipped, "Mr. Moody lingers about Calvary more than I do. I linger more about Sinai." Moses' giving of the law to Israel mattered to him as much as Jesus' death for sinners. Jones acknowledged the necessity of Christ's atoning death for salvation, but he believed that preaching should start with moral principles of right and wrong. He once commented that he was as likely to talk about Socrates with a sinner as about Jesus, for a lost sinner "has about equal need of them both" (Minnix, 82).

Jones was ordained in November 1872 as a traveling preacher by the North Georgia Conference of the Methodist Episcopal Church, South. In the ensuing eight years, Jones was assigned to four different circuits and saw 2,000 members added to the churches under his charge. In 1884, Jones conducted his first large-scale revival in Memphis, where 13 pastors from five denominations sponsored him to come preach. The revival was so successful that invitations began pouring in from other cities. In 1885, Jones held a revival in Nashville where an estimated 10,000 people were converted, and the meeting marked his emergence as a nationally known revivalist. For the next 21 years, Jones worked tirelessly to conduct revivals throughout the country, primarily in the South. Jones played down denominational differences at his meetings, explaining, "I despise theology and botany, but I love religion and flowers" (Minnix, 10). Jones catered to his crowds by serving up large doses of down-home humor mixed with maudlin appeals to the heart and angry barrages at Christian hypocrites. He was vitriolic in his denunciation of dancing, gambling, and especially drinking: "A man can't drink whiskey and be a Christian, and don't you forget it!" (Jones, 280). He spurned the modernist theology spreading through the country, commenting that "half the literary preachers ... are A.B.'s, Ph.D.'s, D.D.'s, L.L.D.'s, and A.S.S.'s" (Minnix, 119). His biting humor and folksy stories won over rural folk wary of urban life and the urban elite.

Jones saw himself as a warrior fighting against sin and worldliness. Most often, his fight was against liquor, and Jones was an outspoken advocate for **temperance** and Prohibition, viewing alcohol as the cause of numerous social ills. He defended the white southern way of life, including the racial attitudes and racial segregation that characterized his era. Jones died on a train bound for his home in Cartersville, Georgia, in 1906, one day short of his 59th birthday. At the time of his death he was known as "the Moody of the South," yet his legacy was quickly forgotten. It seems that he was too much of an entertainer to be remembered by the church, and too much of a preacher to be remembered by the entertainment world. Jones summed up his own life's work by saying, "The object of all my preaching … has been simply … to make sin hideous and righteousness attractive" (Jones, 16).

Further Reading: Jones, Sam. *Sam Jones' Own Book: A Series of Sermons with an Autobiographical Sketch*. St. Louis: Cranston and Stowe, 1886; Lutzweiler, James. *The Unexamined Revival of Rev. Sam Jones in Charlotte, North Carolina, 25 April 1880–2 May 1890*. Jamestown, NC: Schnappsburg University Press, 1995; McLoughlin, William G., Jr. *Modern Revivalism: Charles Grandison Finney to Billy Graham*. New York: Ronald Press, 1959; Minnix, Kathleen. *Laughter in the Amen Corner: The Life of Evangelist Same Jones*. Athens: University of Georgia Press, 1993.

David Simpson

K

KANSAS CITY PROPHETS

In 1988 **John Wimber,** leader of the Association of Vineyard Churches, developed a close association with Bob Jones, John Paul Jackson, and Paul Cain—a group that soon became known as the Kansas City **prophets.** The three visionaries were connected with Mike Bickle, then senior pastor of the Kansas City Fellowship (KCF), in Kansas City, Missouri—a growing neo-**Charismatic** church. Wimber's fame launched Bickle and the KCF prophets into international prominence and controversy.

In April 1990 some Australian Christian leaders targeted Wimber, Cain, and Jack Deere—a leading Charismatic apologist. The accusations ranged from undermining the authority of the Bible to neglecting the doctrine of Christ's atonement on the cross. The Vineyard strongly denied the accusations. In May of the same year Ernie Gruen, a leading **Pentecostal** pastor in Kansas, issued a 200-page critique of the KCF. He accused the prophets, particularly Bob Jones, of wild speculation, false predictions, and bizarre **visions.** Gruen's report also argued that Bickle's fellowship had an elitist element, arising out of its teaching regarding a new breed of superior Christians.

The KCF became a part of the Association of Vineyard Churches in 1990, and this created a more disciplined environment for the congregation. John Wimber's involvement with Bickle and the Kansas City prophets received a glowing report in David Pytches's *Some Said It Thundered* (1991). In late 1991 Bob Jones was disciplined for sexual misconduct and withdrew from ministry for several years. In 1992 Wimber became less focused on the sort of prophetic ministry characteristic of the KCF, though he continued to schedule speaking engagements in various locations with Bickle and Cain. Yet Bickle broke away from the Vineyard in 1996, in large part because of Wimber's negative reaction to John Arnott and the **Toronto Blessing** revival.

Paul Cain, a native of Texas, emerged as the most famous of the Kansas City prophets. Born in 1929 in Texas, he was raised a **Baptist** and was a figure in the healing revivals through the 1950s. Earlier in life, he had been associated with **William Branham,** one of the most famous of the **healing** evangelists of the 1950s. After 1959 Cain withdrew almost completely from public ministry until he joined with Mike Bickle in the KCF in the mid-1980s. Cain maintained a worldwide itinerary from 1988 to 2004, often in association with Bickle, Jack Deere, and Rick Joyner. In late 2004 these three exercised church discipline against Cain with charges centering on alcohol abuse and homosexual activity.

Rev. Mike Bickle (1955–), with his wife, Diane. Bickle was pastor of the Metro Vineyard Fellowship (later Metro Christian Fellowship) in Kansas City, Missouri. Previously associated with the Kansas City Prophets, he established the International House of Prayer during the 1990s and has sponsored prophetic conferences (Rome, 1991). Courtesy of photographer Dr. Stanley M. Burgess.

Bickle now leads the International House of Prayer and the Friends of the Bridegroom ministry in Kansas City. John Paul Jackson founded Streams Ministries International in 1993, after working in Kansas City and then the Anaheim Vineyard. He is now based in New Hampshire. Bob Jones, a native of Arkansas, has regained his status as a major figure in prophetic circles. He claims that a supernatural spirit being appeared to him on August 12, 2004; identified himself as the "Watcher"; and prophesied a "new day" for the Church. Interest in the Kansas City prophets as a group decreased dramatically after the start of the Toronto Blessing in 1994 and the **Pensacola (Brownsville) revival** in 1995. By then, however, each of these prophets had established an independent status and following. More important, the prophetic focus had become a staple among neo-Charismatics worldwide, due in large part to the endorsements of Mike Bickle and John Wimber.

Further Reading: Beverley, James A. *Holy Laughter and the Toronto Blessing.* Grand Rapids, MI: Zondervan, 1995; Bickle, Mike. *Growing in the Prophetic.* Lake Mary, FL: Creation House, 1996; Deere, Jack. *Surprised by the Power of the Holy Spirit.* Grand Rapids, MI: Zondervan, 1996; Hanegraaff, Hank. *Counterfeit Revival.* Dallas: Word, 1997; MacArthur, John. *Charismatic Chaos.*

Grand Rapids, MI: Zondervan, 1992; Pytches, David. *Some Said It Thundered.* Nashville, TN: Thomas Nelson, 1991; Wimber, Carol. *John Wimber: The Way It Was.* London: Hodder and Stoughton, 1999.

James Beverley

KNAPP, JACOB (1799–1874)

Jacob Knapp was a widely traveled and highly controversial revivalist, active from the 1830s to the 1870s. He was born in Otsego County, New York, in 1799. Knapp's first **preaching** opportunities came during his time in school at Gilbertsville, New York. The **Baptist** church asked him to take charge of worship services, and Knapp did so with the result that nearly all the young people experienced **conversion.** He graduated from Hamilton Literary and Theological Institution (currently Colgate University) in 1825, and had two brief pastorates in Springfield and Watertown, New York. Under Knapp's care, both churches saw a significant increase in membership. Yet as the influence of **Charles G. Finney's** "new measures" revivalism grew, Knapp said that he looked on the past eight years of his ministry as "comparatively wasted." In 1833, Knapp left his pastorate to devote his full energies to itinerant evangelism.

The **Presbyterian** Church of New York was in the middle of a revolution wrought by a group of preachers who taught that individuals were wrong to wait on God to grant them salvation. Instead, God was waiting on people to make a decision to accept the message of salvation. Knapp took both the message and the methods that Presbyterian preachers had been using to produce decisions for Christ and began using them within the Baptist church. In his first 18 months as a revivalist, Knapp stated that "not less than two thousand souls were converted" (Knapp 30). Yet his evangelistic success did not prevent him from encountering resistance. Above all, there was resistance from Baptists who were **Calvinists** and so held to an opposing **theology of revivals.** Knapp's preaching of salvation as a matter of human will was anathema to most Baptist ministers, and they opposed his teaching as heresy. Yet Knapp received an enthusiastic reception from most Baptist congregations, and helped to trigger a backlash against scholarly preaching in some Baptist circles.

A common complaint against Knapp concerned the "distasteful expression" in which he preached against dancing, gambling, Universalism, slavery, and alcohol, and in favor of **abolitionism** and **temperance.** Knapp offered no apologies for his crude language. In his defense, he stated that "God had cast me in a different mould [and] … I felt constrained to call things by their right names, to use most simple language, the most direct arguments, and most matter-of-fact illustrations" (Knapp, 35). From 1835 to 1842, Knapp's reputation as a revivalist grew quickly. The size of his venues increased accordingly, from Utica up to Boston. Knapp enjoyed both the size of his crowds and the size of his income—over $2,000 per year, an exorbitant sum for a preacher of that time.

Knapp's practices earned him the dubious distinction of being among the very first revivalists to be accused of earning excessive profits from his ministry. In the Boston meeting of 1842, while making a heartfelt appeal for the special offering that was to constitute his payment, Knapp wore an outfit of shabby clothes. Among other charges, he was accused of misrepresenting his true financial status to the audience, and his reputation was in jeopardy. Desiring to clear his name, he convened a committee of friends to examine the charges against him. The committee would not declare him innocent, and his appeal to a committee in his home church backfired when they found him guilty. In a desperate attempt to save his reputation, Knapp took his case before the congregation, and was able to obtain a vote of confidence for himself.

Knapp continued on as a revivalist for another 30 years, but he never regained the prominence that he held in his first 10 years of work. He rarely returned to New England after his problems there, spending the majority of his time in the western and mid-Atlantic states. Knapp died in 1874. In his lifetime, it was estimated that he had conducted 150 revival meetings and preached over 16,000 sermons. Knapp himself said he stopped counting converts after the number had reached 100,000. His revivalism influenced not only his generation of Baptists, but the larger Baptist tradition in the United States.

Further Reading: Brackney, William H. *Historical Dictionary of the Baptists.* Lanham, MD: Scarecrow Press 1999; Knapp, Jacob. *Autobiography of Elder Jacob Knapp.* New York: Sheldon, 1868; McLoughlin, William G., Jr. *Modern Revivalism: Charles Grandison Finney to Billy Graham.* New York: Ronald Press, 1959; Murray, Iain H. *Revival and Revivalism: The Making and Marring of American Evangelicalism, 1750–1858.* Edinburgh: Banner of Truth Trust, 1994

David Simpson

KORESH, DAVID

see Branch Davidians

KRAMAR, MARILYNN (1939–), AND CHARISMA IN MISSIONS

Marilynn Kramar is cofounder of Charisma in Missions and a major figure in the **Charismatic Renewal** among **Latinos** in the **Roman Catholic** Church in the United States and Latin America. She was born into a fifth-generation **Pentecostal** home and was the daughter of an **Assemblies of God** minister in Los Angeles. After attending the Central Bible Institute of the Assemblies of God, Marilynn, with her husband, Glenn, left for Colombia in 1967 to serve as Assemblies of God missionaries. Marilynn was licensed in 1968 as a missionary-evangelist in the denomination and Glenn served as the superintendent (1967–1970) of the missions work in Colombia. The Kramars began ecumenical dialogue with Roman Catholics in Colombia, and through this experience they developed a growing interest in Roman Catholicism. This interest continued after their return to Los Angeles in 1972. Influenced by Vatican II, liberation theology, and the deep spirituality of many Catholic priests and nuns they had met in Colombia and Los Angeles, the Kramars left the Assemblies of God to join the Roman Catholic Church. Soon after this, the Kramars applied their earlier evangelistic training for the benefit of Roman Catholicism by founding Charisma in Missions in the fall of 1972 as an international society for Catholic evangelization. With support from Cardinal Timothy Manning of the Archdiocese of Los Angeles, Charisma in Missions began holding evangelistic and renewal services in the Spanish-speaking community throughout California and Latin America. After a difficult divorce, Marilynn became the de facto leader of Charisma in Missions.

Two primary goals of Charisma in Missions are to bring alienated Latino Catholics back into the Roman Catholic Church and to train evangelizers for work among Spanish-speaking Roman Catholics. In 1975, the organization began holding the International Latin Encounter for Renewal and Evangelization, better known as the Latin Encounter (Encuentro Latino). The annual Latin Encounter has grown in attendance from 600 in 1975 to more than 17,000 in 1997. In addition to the Latin Encounter, Charisma in Missions also sponsors the Latin Youth Encounter, an annual family convention, the Catholic Campaigns of Faith, one-day faith rallies, a Missionary Institute of Proclaimers (school of evangelism), spiritual growth seminars, a children's ministry, and a drama ministry. They also sponsor CharisBooks, CharisTapes, CharisMedia, and CharisPublications, and a television program called ¡Alabaré! From 1972 to 1997, Charisma in Missions touched the lives of more than 1 million Latino Catholics in the United States alone. By 1997 there were more than 70,000 U.S. Latinos on the Charisma in Missions mailing list and 220 Spanish-speaking **prayer** assemblies (averaging between 70 and 120 people each) within the Archdiocese of Los Angeles. Charisma in Missions is located in the heart of east Los Angeles and it continues to have the blessing of the Roman Catholic Archdiocese of Los Angeles. Marilynn Kramar may be considered the mother of the Latino Charismatic movement in the United States Roman Catholic Church.

Further Reading: Kramar, Marilynn. *Charisma in Missions: Catholic Missionary Evangelization Society.* N.p., n.d.; Kramar, Marilynn, with Robert C. Larson. *The*

Marilynn Kramar Story: Joy Comes in the Morning. Ann Arbor, MI: Servant Publications, 1990.

Gastón Espinosa

KUHLMAN, KATHRYN (1907–1976)

The daughter of **Baptist** and **Methodist** parents, Kathryn Kuhlman brought faith for divine **healing** and other **charismatic gifts** of the Holy Spirit into mainstream Protestant and **Roman Catholic** churches during the **Charismatic Revival and Renewal** of the 1960s and 1970s. She was among the leading American **women** in healing ministry in the twentieth century. Kuhlman began her career as an itinerant evangelist in 1923 at the age of 16. Her marriage in 1938 to Burroughs A. Waltrip, an evangelist who left his wife and children to marry Kuhlman, nearly ended her career. Kuhlman left Waltrip in 1944 and headed to Franklin, Pennsylvania, where she **preached** to small congregations until one day in 1947 when a woman in the audience announced that she had been healed of a tumor while Kuhlman had been preaching on the Holy Spirit the night before. As other people began to report healings, Kuhlman began to attract overflow crowds of thousands. Kuhlman moved to Pittsburgh, where she held weekly miracle services at the historic Carnegie Hall until 1966, after which she moved to the prestigious First **Presbyterian** Church. Beginning in 1965, Kuhlman added monthly miracle services at the Shrine Auditorium in Los Angeles and occasional services in cities across the United States and in Canada.

Although she shared a belief common among healing evangelists that the atonement provided for healing as well as forgiveness, Kuhlman intentionally distanced herself from the techniques of contemporary Voice of Healing revivalists, whom she faulted for showmanship and for blaming the sick when they were not cured. Kuhlman avoided the practices of distributing **prayer** cards or forming healing lines, although she encouraged people to combine their praying with **fasting** and to express their faith by action. She rarely prayed for individuals at all, instead creating an atmosphere of worship and faith in which people claimed to receive healings through the power

Kathryn Kuhlman was perhaps the world's best-known female Christian evangelist during the 1950s and 1960s (1950s). Courtesy of Flower Pentecostal Heritage Center, Springfield, MO.

Kuhlman gained nationwide publicity through the media of print, radio, and television. Her reputation was enhanced by favorable coverage in the national press, including *Redbook, Time, People, Christianity Today,* and *U.S. Catholic* magazines, and television talk show appearances with Johnny Carson, Mike Douglas, Merv Griffin, and Dinah Shore. One of Kuhlman's most vocal critics was William A. Nolen, MD, whose book *Healing: A Doctor in Search of a Miracle* (1974) was rebutted by another medical doctor who supported Kuhlman, H. Richard Casdorph, MD, PhD, in *The Miracles* (1976); Nolen and Casdorph publicly debated on *The Mike Douglas Show.* With the assistance of two ghostwriters, Emily Gardiner Neal and Jamie Buckingham, Kuhlman published six testimonial booklets and three best-selling collections of healing narratives: *I Believe in Miracles* (1962), *God Can Do It Again* (1969), and *Nothing Is Impossible with God* (1974). Kuhlman also produced a total of 4,000 radio and 500 television broadcasts. Her weekly telecast *I Believe in Miracles,* produced by Dick Ross between 1966 and 1976, was the longest-running 30-minute program filmed in CBS studios. Kuhlman died at the age of 68 from a heart condition, having reportedly refused the prayers of **Oral Roberts** and his wife, Evelyn, for healing.

Further Reading: Buckingham, Jamie. *Daughter of Destiny: Kathryn Kuhlman, Her Story.* Plainfield, NJ: Logos International, 1976; Kathryn Kuhlman Foundation Web site. http://kathrynkuhlman.com/; McCauley, Deborah Vansau. "Kathryn Kuhlman." In Charles H. Lippy, ed., *Twentieth-Century Shapers of American Popular Religion,* 225–33. New York: Greenwood Press, 1989; Warner, Wayne. *Kathryn Kuhlman: The Woman Behind the Miracles.* Ann Arbor, MI: Servant, 1993.

Candy Gunther Brown

of the Holy Spirit. Kuhlman encouraged people to claim their healings as she declared people's medical conditions through the charismatic gift of "the word of knowledge." Unlike certain antimedical proponents of divine healing, Kuhlman insisted that people testifying to healings produce medical verification. She prohibited public **speaking in tongues, prophecy,** and emotional outbursts from members of the audience. She also refrained from preaching on **Pentecostal** taboos such as smoking and drinking. Kuhlman did allow and even encourage such **bodily manifestations** as "resting under the power" or being "slain in the Spirit."

L

LATINO(A) PROTESTANT AND PENTECOSTAL REVIVALS

The origin of Protestantism among Mexican Americans in the United States is uncertain. Though a few Protestants visited Mexico during the colonial period, the first major Protestant evangelistic and revival works began in the then-Mexican territory of Tejas (Texas) around 1820 through the initiative of Joseph Bays, a **Baptist** minister. Three years later, Bays was arrested for **preaching** Protestant doctrine, which was in clear violation of article 3 of the Mexican Constitution of 1824, which stated, "The religion of the Mexican Nation is, and will be perpetually, the Roman Catholic Apostolic. The nation will protect it by wise and just laws, and prohibits the exercise of any other." Despite this prohibition, a growing number of Anglo Americans entering Tejas brought their Protestant traditions with them along with their black slaves. While a number of Protestant churches opened up in Tejas in the 1830s and 1840s, most of their work aimed at reaching the 20,000 Anglos living in the state. Bays and others like him sought to convert those who were not Christian and to revive those that were. Most early Mexican American Protestants were of a Fundamentalist type and held to a strict code of ethics that forbade premarital sex, drinking alcohol,

smoking, gambling, ostentatious dressing, and other worldly activities. Despite their conservative theology and ethics, Latino **Presbyterians, Methodists,** and Baptists founded evangelistic social programs aimed at relieving the suffering in the Mexican community. They operated settlement houses, community centers, health clinics, girls' and boys' clubs, and schools. One study suggests that 60–80 percent of Mexican American conversions to historic Protestant denominations in the early twentieth century were the direct result of evangelistic and revivalist-oriented relief work in the Mexican American community. Most Mexican American Protestants also showed a willingness to cooperate among themselves and believed that Protestant denominations needed to unite in their effort simultaneously to convert and Americanize Mexicans.

The growth of Mexican American Protestantism created a new religious marketplace. This trend toward religious pluralism was strongest in cities like Los Angeles, Chicago, San Antonio, and El Paso, although it was evident in rural areas as well. By 1929, there were at least 10 Mexican American Protestant churches and three settlement houses and community centers in Chicago, each sponsoring its own evangelistic and revival events and meetings. In 1932, Los Angeles had an estimated 28 Mexican American Protestant churches ministering to

Latino revivals have often brought conflicts between Catholics and non-Catholics when Protestant preachers urged hearers to discard their Catholic rosaries, medallions, and saints' images, like those being carved here. (Photographer Edwin Rosskam; Puerto Rico, ca. 1944–1946.) Courtesy of the Library of Congress.

approximately 10,000 adherents. Studies indicate that Protestants made up approximately 10–15 percent of Mexican Americans living in the United States by 1945. One reason the percentage of Latino Protestants has not risen higher in recent decades is the constant influx of new **Roman Catholic** immigrants from Mexico.

Protestantism was able to enter into the Mexican American community because Protestant rituals and traditions replaced similar elements in Mexican Catholicism. Feast days, festivals, annual **camp meetings,** and revival and crusade meetings replaced the drama of popular Catholicism. A passionate evangelist or revivalist preaching the parables of Jesus or hellfire and damnation injected drama into Sunday morning services. In place of colorful home altars there were family and private devotions and wall decorations with scenes from the Bible, evangelistic and revival slogans, and photographs of tent meetings. Mexican Protestants generally rejected popular Catholic traditions as superstitious or diabolical. In place of Catholic tradition, mainstream Protestants emphasized reason and knowledge while

Pentecostals emphasized the work of the Holy Spirit. Popular devotions to traditional saints gave way to a new admiration for living saints—Protestant evangelistic missionaries and martyrs in foreign countries. The charismatic, evangelistic, and revivalist pastor supplanted the figure of the Catholic priest. The emphasis on community in Mexican Catholicism was replaced by a community of small-group Bible studies and by **women's** organizations in the 1930s. Many Mexican Americans found this religious combination appealing because it reminded them of the small villagelike atmosphere they left behind in Mexico.

Mexican Americans during the 1930s and 1940s converted to historic Protestant denominations such as the Methodists, Baptists, and Presbyterians. Yet, as early as the 1930s, Roman Catholics and mainline Protestant leaders lamented that the Pentecostals (referred to as the *Alleluias*) were "stealing sheep" and attracting a growing number of their parishioners into their folds every year. Perhaps the most influential and dynamic of all twentieth-century Latino evangelists was **Francisco Olazábal,** who left the Methodist Episcopal Church to serve in the burgeoning Pentecostal movement. The opposition to Catholic clericalism prevalent in the Mexican American community of the United States prompted many to seek out alternative religious expressions. **Conversion** to Protestantism was fraught with difficulties, however. The strong emphasis on evangelism, a born-again relationship with Jesus Christ, and the belief that Protestants alone possessed and preached religious truth caused strife among Mexican Americans. Sometimes the strife manifested itself in name-calling, loss of jobs or community support in times of personal or family crises, or even physical violence. While this sense of being an outsider in the Mexican American community was too much for some converts, who eventually returned to Roman Catholicism, it only deepened the resolve of others. Much of the conflict between Mexican American Catholics and Protestants pivoted on the converts' critical attitude toward popular Catholic traditions such as the veneration of the Virgin Mary, **praying** to saints, consulting *curandera* folk healers, lighting

CAMPAÑA EVANGELISTICA DE LA CALLE Por el Rev. September, 120 Y LENOX AVE., NEW YORK, N.Y. Francisco Olazábal 1931

A photograph from Francisco Olazábal's Spanish Harlem revival, at 120 Lenox Avenue, New York City (September 1931). Courtesy of Gastón Espinosa.

candles, and praying at home altars. Protestant criticism of Roman Catholicism prompted some priests to lash out against Mexican American Protestants by calling them heretics, wolves, and sons of the devil.

Like their Catholic counterparts, Mexican American Protestants emphasized Americanization. The slogan "Americanization through evangelization" could be heard in almost every Anglo-sponsored Mexican American Protestant work in the United States in the early twentieth century. Reflecting the influence of Anglo American Protestants, new converts were strongly encouraged to learn how to read so that they could study the Bible and learn time-honored American traditions. A tremendous stress on literacy became a distinguishing characteristic of Mexican American Protestantism in the early twentieth century. Consequently, the Protestant community produced a disproportionate percentage of Mexican American community leaders in places such as Los Angeles, California, and El Paso, Texas.

The first Latino Pentecostal revivalists came out of the **Azusa Street revival** of 1906. Mexicans such as Abundio and Rosa López; Jose, Susie, and **A. C. Valdez;** Juan Navarro; Brigido Perez; and many others took the Pentecostal message of revival and spiritual renewal into the migrant farm labor camps and *colonias* throughout Los Angeles, San Diego, and San Bernardino and Riverside counties (all in California) between 1906 and 1909. A separate Mexican Pentecostal movement arose out of a conflict between **William Seymour** and a Mexican contingent that led to the de facto expulsion of Mexicans from the Azusa Street Mission. In 1913

the Latino Pentecostal movement was torn asunder by the Oneness or "Jesus Only" controversy near Los Angeles. This controversy split the Pentecostal world into Trinitarian and Oneness camps, the latter of which denied the doctrine of the Trinity and instead posited that Jesus was himself God the Father, God the Son, and God the Holy Spirit (see **United Pentecostal Church, International**). The Trinitarian and Oneness Pentecostal traditions, despite their theological differences, both placed great emphasis on revivalism.

Latino Pentecostal revivalism originated in the multiethnic context of Azusa Street, and yet after 1914 the movement crystallized into ethnic enclaves and organizations. In 1915, Henry Cleophas (H. C.) Ball, Rodolfo Orozco, and Alice Luce organized a number of independent Mexican Pentecostal churches in Texas to form what is now the Hispanic Districts of the Assemblies of God. Similarly, in 1916, Juan Navarro, Francisco Llorente, and Antonio Casteñeda Nava formally organized a number of loosely affiliated Mexican Oneness churches with the **Pentecostal Assemblies of the World** (PAW). In 1931, they severed their loose connection to the PAW to form what is today known as the Apostolic Assembly of the Faith in Christ Jesus Inc. The Latino Trinitarian Pentecostal movement took a decisive turn away from Anglo American control in 1923 after Francisco Olazábal formed what is now called the Latin American Council of Christian Churches (CLADIC). Almost every indigenous Latino Pentecostal denomination in the United States founded prior to 1960 traces its genealogy back to one of these three movements. Olazábal was perhaps the first Latino evangelist to conduct revival services in all three places where he visited—the United States, Mexico, and Puerto Rico. His far-flung ministry in the 1920s and 1930s laid the foundation for the later expansion of Latino Pentecostalism in the United States, Mexico, and Puerto Rico.

Further Reading: Brackenridge, Douglas, and Francisco García-Treto. *Iglesia Presbiteriana: A History of Presbyterianism and Mexican-Americans in the Southwest.* 2nd ed. San Antonio, TX: Trinity University Press, 1987; Espinosa, Gastón. "El Azteca: Francisco Olazábal and Latino Pentecostal Charisma, Power, and Faith Healing in the Borderlands." *Journal of the American Academy of Religion* 67 (1999): 597–616; Espinosa, Gastón. "'Your Daughters Shall Prophesy': A History of Women in Ministry in the Latino Pentecostal Movement in the United States." In Margaret Lamberts Bendroth and Virginia Lieson Brereton, eds., *Women and Twentieth-Century Protestantism.* 25–48. Urbana: University of Illinois Press, 2002; Espinosa, Gastón, Virgilio Elizondo, and Jesse Miranda. *Latino Religions and Civic Activism in the United States.* New York: Oxford University Press, 2005; González, Justo L., ed. *Each in Our Own Tongue: A History of Hispanic United Methodism.* Nashville, TN: Abingdon Press, 1991; León, Luis D. *La Llorona's Children: Religion, Life and Death in the U.S.-Mexican Borderlands.* Berkeley: University of California Press, 2004; Maldonado, David, Jr., ed. *Protestantes/Protestants: Hispanic Christianity Within Mainline Traditions.* Nashville, TN: Abingdon, 1999; Villafañe, Eldin. *The Liberating Spirit: Towards an Hispanic American Pentecostal Social Ethic.* Grand Rapids, MI: Eerdmans, 1993.

Gastón Espinosa

LATTER RAIN MOVEMENT

The Latter Rain movement was a revival of the mid-twentieth century that, along with the parallel **healing** movement of the same era, was an important component of the post–World War II evangelical awakening. Dubbed by its opponents the "New Order of the Latter Rain," it shared many characteristics in common with the 1906 **Azusa Street revival.** The Latter Rain movement had its origins at Sharon Orphanage and Schools in North Battleford, Saskatchewan, Canada. The revival began on February 14, 1948, after students and faculty had gathered together for a number of days for **prayer** and Bible study. Some of those involved at that time included Herrick Holt (of the North Battleford, Saskatchewan, Church of the **Foursquare Gospel**), P. G. Hunt, George Hawtin (a former pastor of the **Pentecostal** Assemblies of Canada), his brother Ern Hawtin, and Milford Kirkpatrick. After the initial outpouring, people began to travel from all over the world to **camp meeting** conventions in North Battleford publicized by the *Sharon Star.* The Hawtin brothers and their associates began to receive invitations, and the revival spread to many other places, including Glad Tidings Temple in Vancouver, British Columbia, Canada (pastored by Reg Layzell); Bethesda Missionary Temple in Detroit, Michigan (pastored by Myrtle D. Beall); Elim Bible Institute, at that time in Hornell, New York (founded by Ivan Q. Spencer); and Wings of Healing Temple in Portland, Oregon (pastored by Dr. Thomas Wyatt). By 1949, new leaders for the movement began to emerge in these places and elsewhere, while the North Battleford leaders became less central to the movement.

Worldwide in its effects, the Latter Rain movement was one of several catalysts for the **Charismatic Renewal** of the 1960s and 1970s. Sometimes known as the 1948 Revival, it was immediately preceded by an earlier period of 15 or 20 years that many people described as a time of spiritual dryness and lack of the presence of God. The name *Latter Rain* is derived from Joel 2:28, which describes both the "former rain" and the "latter rain" as outpourings of the Spirit of God. The movement interpreted Joel's latter rain as a dual prophecy referring both to the day of Pentecost as described in the second chapter of Acts and to a final outpouring of the Holy Spirit associated with the **eschatological** coming of Christ at the end of the present age. Forty-two years earlier, during the Azusa Street revival, very similar if not identical interpretations of Joel 2:28 were offered with the result that, coincidentally, both movements at their outset were known as the Latter Rain movement, and both soon gave birth to separate periodicals of the same name, the *Latter Rain Evangel.*

Both the original Pentecostal movement (1901–1909) and the Latter Rain movement emphasized the **charismatic gifts,** especially **speaking in tongues** and **prophecy,** which were to be received by the laying on of hands. During the period from 1930 to 1948, the general practice among Pentecostals was to "tarry" for the Holy Spirit, praying and waiting on God for a length of time before receiving the **baptism in the Holy Spirit,** with outward manifestations and signs following. With the onset of the 1948 revival, the practice of the laying on of hands accompanied by prophecy became controversial, due partly to its interference with the custom of "tarrying" for the Spirit, and partly because some people were said to have uncritically accepted whatever had been spoken to them as a God-given prophecy.

Another characteristic common to the 1906 Azusa Street revival and the 1948 Latter Rain movement was the allusion to God's doing a "new thing" in accordance with Isaiah 43:19. Both movements expended a considerable degree of energy in their attempts to obtain a better understanding of God's purposes in this new thing and in their emphasis upon fresh revelation from God. At their outset, both movements recognized the existence of present-day apostles, prophets, evangelists, pastors, and teachers, and both emphasized immediate repentance as necessary in preparation for the coming of Christ. Both movements were severely criticized by the denominations of which they were originally a part. During the Azusa Street revival, such criticisms came from the **Holiness** denominations out of which the Pentecostals arose, whereas in 1948, the criticisms arose from the very denominations that traced their roots to the Azusa Street revival. The 1948 Latter Rain revival was an important influence upon the Charismatic Renewal of the 1960s and 1970s. There was a continuity of many of the institutions of the Latter Rain with those of the Charismatic movement. For example, *Logos Journal,* the latter's most important periodical in its earliest stages, grew out of *Herald of Faith/Harvest Time,* edited by Joseph Mattsson-Boze, an important figure in the Latter Rain movement, and Gerald Derstine, who was associated for several years with J. Preston Eby, another Latter Rain figure.

Further Reading: Riss, Richard M. *Latter Rain.* Mississauga, ON: Honeycomb Visual Productions, 1987; Riss, Richard M. *A Survey of Twentieth Century Revival Movements in North America.* Peabody, MA: Hendrickson, 1988.

Richard M. Riss

LAUGHING AND SHOUTING IN REVIVALS

Laughing and shouting have appeared in many American revivals and serve to highlight the emotional and congregation-led dynamics of the revival tradition. Participants may view shouting as a sign of God's presence in the midst of a gathering, as an encouragement to those seeking **conversion,** or as an expression of spiritual victory or a feeling of release. Laughter may reflect an overwhelming joy in the experience of God's love and acceptance. The crisis of conversion experienced by evangelical Christians, and the further quest—in **Holiness** and **Pentecostal** circles—for additional spiritual experiences such as **sanctification** or **baptism in the Spirit** has created a context for the occurrences of these types of vocalizations. In 1859, the Holiness author George W. Henry published a book-length defense of the practice of shouting in worship, and the work was reprinted at the dawn of the Pentecostal era in 1903.

During the **Great Awakening,** contemporaries like **Jonathan Edwards** noted that "loud cries" were commonly heard. These cries of repentance were responses to sermons that spoke of the gulf between God and humanity created by sin. Yet a more aggressive form of vocalization became prominent in eighteenth-century **African American revivals.** Scholars believe that revival shouting derives in part from traditional African religious ritual. During the slave era, African Americans engaged in the "ring shout," in which dancers would shuffle in a circle around a singer as others were singing, shouting, and stomping their feet. The shout was thus a collective act that allowed for individual expression. During the Great Awakening in Virginia, blacks and whites (especially **Baptists** and **Methodists**), participated in interracial camp meetings that featured shouting among both groups. Shouting continued among blacks throughout the nineteenth and twentieth centuries, often as encouragement to conversion or in response to testimonies.

Some early nineteenth-century Methodists were referred to as "shouting Methodists." Shouting occurred especially in the context of quarterly meetings—extended gatherings of Methodists and itinerant ministers who belonged to the same circuit. Typically shouting began after the sermon was **preached** and consisted in praise to God for grace experienced. The shouter might turn his or her zeal toward others, exhorting them to repent and experience God's forgiveness. Drawing on Old Testament scripture, Methodists used the phrase "the shout of God in the midst of the camp" (1 Samuel 4:6) to refer to their sense of God's presence in their midst. The practice of shouting, while decried by some Methodists as a mark of enthusiasm, had a democratizing tendency. It allowed laypersons, and socially disenfranchised individuals such as **women,** blacks, and children, to participate more fully in worship.

Whereas shouting was central in some strands of the revival tradition, laughter in worship contexts has generally been viewed with suspicion. In his journal, John Wesley mentioned laughter occurring in his meetings, but he condemned it as the "buffeting of Satan" (May 9 and 21, 1740). Yet during the Great Awakening, laughter occurred among those claiming to have visions of Heaven. Laughter also occurred at the famed **Cane Ridge revival,** along with a host of other **bodily manifestations.** The North American revival where laughter has played the most distinctive role is the recent and controversial **Toronto Blessing,** beginning in 1994. This revival had a significant impact on Charismatic and Pentecostal churches in North America, and some other parts of the world. Over a period of several years, hundreds of thousands flocked to the Toronto Vineyard Airport Church to experience the "the Father's blessing" and then return home to promote it in their local churches. The blessing was frequently accompanied by uncontrollable "holy laughter," the sensation of which has been likened to intoxication, thus giving rise to the description of being "drunk in the Spirit." Critics charge that the Toronto Blessing departs from previous revivals by promoting an individualistic, therapeutic-type spiritual experience, instead of the traditional emphasis on repentance and Christ-centered conversion. Defenders of this revival acknowledge that some excesses may have occurred, but claim that holy laughter is a legitimate and biblically defensible response to God's Spirit. According to them, holy laughter is dramatic sign of God's presence and has had a positive impact. Many participants in this revival say that it led them into a new experience of God's love, with lasting effects in their individual lives.

Further Reading: Henry, George W. *Shouting: Genuine and Spurious in All Ages of the Church.* Chicago: Metropolitan Church Association, 1903; Poloma, Margaret. *Main Street Mystics: The Toronto Blessing and Reviving Pentecostalism.* New York: AltaMira Press, 2003; Simpson, Robert. "The Shout and Shouting in Slave Religion of the United States." In Paul Finkelman, ed., *Religion and Slavery,* 34–47. New York and London: Garland, 1989; Taves, Ann. *Fits, Trances and Visions: Experiencing Religion and Explaining Experience from Wesley to James.* Princeton, NJ: Princeton University Press, 1999;

Benjamin Wagner

LEE, ANN (1736–1784)

Ann Lee was a visionary and mystic who led the **Shakers** from England to America in the 1770s. Born in Manchester, England, Lee enjoyed little formal education and remained functionally illiterate throughout her life. She spent her youth working in the oppressive Manchester textile mills. Her marriage to Abraham Standerin was plagued with difficulty, most notably the death of her four children in infancy. In the late 1750s Lee became associated with a boisterous Manchester sect known for its eagerness to disrupt religious services in the city and its enthusiastic modes of worship. Lee quickly gained prominence within the group and she reported remarkable spiritual experiences, including a **vision** of Christ that she received while in prison for causing a religious disturbance. Among other things, Christ informed Lee to embrace celibacy and to take any followers she could to

America. The original Manchester movement soon dissolved, but Lee's sense of charismatic leadership and calling did not.

Lee arrived in America in 1774 with seven followers. Almost immediately her visionary stance and British background raised the ire of both ecclesiastical and government authorities. During this period, Lee apparently referred to herself as the "Queen of Heaven" and the bride of Christ. More than once Lee was accused of witchcraft, and the charge of treason was leveled against the group as the Revolutionary War raged on. Lee and her followers were repeatedly harassed and physically assaulted by angry mobs and imprisoned in 1780 on charges of being British sympathizers. Lee continued her ministry undeterred, however, and continued to receive visions and revelations that guided her community, and rankled religious traditionalists, until her death in 1784—the result of injuries sustained in a mob attack. During this period many followers were attracted to Lee's aggressive proselytizing and her charismatic visions, **prophecies,** and **healings.** After her death, Lee continued to play a major role in the Shaker movement. Subsequent Shaker leaders came to view Lee as the incarnation of Christ in female form while continuing her legacy of communal living and the charismatic, enthusiastic, and visionary worldview that she introduced.

Further Reading: Sasson, Diane. "The Shakers: The Adaptation of Prophecy." In Timothy Miller, ed., *When Prophets Die*, 13–28. Albany: State University of New York Press, 1991; Stein, Stephen J. *The Shaker Experience in America: A History of the United Society of Believers.* New Haven, CT: Yale University Press, 1992.

Stephen C. Taysom

LEE, JESSE (1758–1816)

Jesse Lee was the first historian of American **Methodism,** the founder of the denomination in New England. He was author of the important early work *Short History of the Methodists* (1810), which contains accounts of early Methodist revivals in 1774–1775 and 1783–1784. Lee was born in Prince George County, Virginia, in 1758 and died in 1816. His family members—descendants of early settlers in Virginia—were farmers, and Lee's first education was based on the **prayer** book from which he also learned the catechism. Except for a brief time in a singing school, he had no formal education. His powerful singing voice would serve him well in his ministry. The family lived in proximity to the parish of the Reverend **Devereux Jarratt,** and Jarratt may have played a role in the **conversion** of Lee's father. In 1772 the family fell under the influence of Robert Williams, the first Methodist minister to visit in the vicinity of Petersburg, and two years later gave in their names to join a Methodist society. Lee was converted in this period, then moved to North Carolina, where he farmed, became an exhorter in 1778, and in November 1779 **preached** his first sermon. His routine was interrupted in 1780 when he was drafted into the Continental Army. Because he refused to bear arms, but was willing to serve, he was put under guard and finally assigned to drive a baggage wagon and given an honorable discharge after three months.

By then Lee had become persuaded that he should preach. In April 1782 he attended the meeting of the Virginia Conference at Ellis's meetinghouse. At the close of the conference, **Francis Asbury** asked him to accept an appointment. After putting his affairs in order he joined Edward Drumgoole in North Carolina to form the Caswell Circuit. He joined the conference the following year but refused to be ordained until 1790. In 1784 he was assigned to the Salisbury Circuit, North Carolina. At the annual conference the following year, Lee met the other general superintendent appointed by Wesley, Thomas Coke. Coke held strong antislavery or **abolitionist** sentiments and was looking for any means to divorce the Methodists from association with it. Lee, who was also against slavery, differed from the doctor and urged a more measured approach that he deemed to be better suited to the region. Even before he was ordained, Lee and his work were highly regarded by Asbury, who appointed him in 1789 to membership in the council that was designed to function as an executive committee for the annual conferences. When the council experiment proved to be a failure,

Lee—joined by Thomas Coke and James O'Kelly—in 1792 suggested the creation of a delegated General Conference to govern the connection. This was finally accomplished in 1808 and is in existence today in the United Methodist Church. After serving appointments in Maryland, in 1789 he was assigned for the first time to Connecticut and from there began extensive preaching in Boston, Rhode Island, Vermont, and New Hampshire. He built the first Methodist church in Boston and for many years served as the presiding elder in New England. In 1797 Asbury, who was in poor health, called once again on Lee's services. Traveling with him through the conferences, Lee exercised all the authority of a bishop except for ordinations. In 1800 Lee was a leading candidate for election as bishop, but after two ballots in which the vote was tied, Richard Whatcoat was elected by a narrow margin on the third. If he had been elected, Lee would have been the first American-born preacher to serve in the office.

In 1801 Lee returned to Virginia to serve in the South District and remained there for the remaining 14 years of his ministry. For some time he had been collecting material for what would become the *Short History of Methodists,* and when he went to Baltimore to oversee the final stages of that project, he offered himself and was elected chaplain of the House of Representatives of the U.S. Congress. He served in that capacity until 1813 and then for a year held a similar post in the U.S. Senate. The *Short History* was printed in 1810 with the aid of private contributions. The list of subscribers is included in the book. Early Methodism had few preachers who were more forthright and visionary than Lee.

Further Reading: Lee, Jesse. *Memoir of the Rev. Jesse Lee.* Ed. Milton Thrift. New York: N. Bangs and T. Mason, 1823; Lee, Jesse. *Short History of the Methodists.* Baltimore: Magill and Clime, 1810. Reprint, Nashville, TN: Publishing House, Methodist Episcopal Church, South, 1928; Lee, Leroy. *The Life and Times of the Rev. Jesse Lee.* Richmond, VA: Southern Methodist Publishing House, 1848.

James E. Kirby

LUTHERAN, GERMAN AMERICAN, AND SCANDINAVIAN AMERICAN REVIVALS

German and Scandinavian immigrants began arriving in the North American colonies in the late seventeenth and eighteenth centuries. The former were concentrated in the Middle Colonies (especially Pennsylvania, Maryland, and western New York and Virginia) and the latter, especially Swedes, in New Jersey and Delaware. The major streams of both groups arrived in the nineteenth century, when Germans became the largest ethnic group in the United States, and significant numbers of Scandinavian Lutherans arrived in the upper Midwest.

Revivalism, earlier known as "experimental religion," focused upon an experience of regeneration, or **conversion,** and affective worship as the basis for Christian identity. During the periods of the **Great Awakening** and the **Second Great Awakening** (ca. 1739–1745 and ca. 1795–1835), revivalism in the context of American religious freedom showed an ability to transcend church and denominational barriers and create new spiritual communities. This process occurred both within and without the transplanted immigrant church bodies. Helping to define Anglo American religion in the early national era, revivalism was also significantly represented among Continental immigrant communities and among their descendants. A formative influence on the spirituality of these communities was the literature of Continental Evangelical **Pietism,** a proto-revivalistic movement in European Protestantism beginning in the 1600s.

The earliest communities of German immigrants consisted of Pietist-influenced Mennonites and Dunkers. A party of Mennonites from Krefeld founded Germantown, near Philadelphia, in 1683. Radical Pietism was the earliest religious influence underlying German immigration. Operating with general disdain for existing state church bodies, they drew from Jacob Boehme's theosophical writings, and were influenced by revival **preachers** like Ernst Hochmann von Hochenau, who envisioned an **eschatological** end-time community of the reborn living under the immediate inspiration of the Spirit. Alexander Mack (1679–1735), who withdrew from the **Reformed** Church in Germany to form the Dunkers, known officially as the Church of the Brethren, combined radical Pietist and Anabaptist elements in the congregation that formed in Schwarzenau (Wittgenstein) in 1708. It relocated to Pennsylvania in 1719 under the leadership of Peter Becker. Yet Conrad Beissel (1691–1768), a more radical ascetic, seceded from Becker's community to form a quasi-monastic, Sabbatarian "Order of the Solitary," known as the Ephrata Cloister, which became a center of religious art and music for Pennsylvania Germans and upheld the ideal of an eremitic (i.e., hermit's) life. Prior to the American Revolution, the most prominent Dunker in America was the printer Christoph Sauer (1693–1758), whose press published an edition of Luther's Bible, the first Bible in a Western language printed in North America. Sauer defended the prerogatives of the Pennsylvania Germans against what he regarded as the Anglo American encroachments of Benjamin Franklin's printing house. Adding further to the diversity, the Schwenkfelders, followers of a sixteenth-century reformer from Silesia in Germany, arrived in Georgia in 1734 and soon relocated in Pennsylvania. Radical Pietists formed other eschatological communities that were governed by an ideal of brotherly love or *philadelphia*—a Greek New Testament term that was to become the name of Pennsylvania's leading city. Among the philadelphian communities was that founded by George Rapp (1757–1847) at Harmony, Pennsylvania (1804), and later at New Harmony, Indiana (1815), as well as the **Amana Society** (or Community of True Inspiration) in New York (1842), subsequently removed to Iowa in the 1850s.

An attempt to bring together the numerous sectarian groups in Pennsylvania was initiated in 1742 by Count Nicholas von Zinzendorf (1700–1760) of the *Unitas Fratrem*, or **Moravian** Brethren. From his home base at Herrnhut in Germany, he had organized the heirs of the Bohemian brethren or Hussites into an apostolic order that had a tenuous relationship with the Lutheran state church in Saxony. Trained at the Pietist center of Halle, under

A. H. Francke, Zinzendorf turned away from Francke's orthodox Lutheran theology of salvation in preference for an affective experience of loving relationship with the Lamb of God, leading to liturgical creativity and new **hymn** writing in the community of Herrnhut. Zinzendorf's pursuit of global evangelization resulted in the sending of his missionaries to distant lands, including North America. He envisioned them as a divine diaspora—seed to be planted for sake of the Lamb. Existing church bodies were "tropes" to be renewed and reconciled in Zinzendorf's vision of an emerging philadelphian church where love would prevail. This outlook informed his experiment to unite the sects there into a Congregation of God in the Spirit, which failed in part due to the participants' suspicions of the count's intentions, as well as the determined opposition of Lutheran leader **Henry Melchior Muhlenberg** (1711–1787). Though this early ecumenical effort by Zinzendorf was unsuccessful, the Moravians maintained semicommunal settlements at Nazareth and Bethlehem in Pennsylvania, as well as at Salem in North Carolina.

Radical Pietists, sectarians, and Moravians were soon outnumbered in the Middle Colonies by German Reformed and Lutheran immigrants, nominally aligned with the official state church bodies in Continental Europe. Following the initial efforts of a schoolteacher, Johann Philip Boehm (d. 1749), in organizing the work among the Reformed, that task fell to a Swiss Pietist immigrant, Michael Schlatter (1716–1790), who organized the parish life of the German Reformed in Pennsylvania and Maryland. About the time that Schlatter discontinued his ministry, under pressure from adversaries for his involvement in an English-based charity-school program that was suspected of being anti-German, the growing Pietist and revivalist wing of the German Reformed in America received a new leader. **Philip William Otterbein** (1726–1813) was part of a class of missionary recruits from the Pietist-oriented Herborn Academy (Nassau), commissioned by the Dutch authorities in Amsterdam to train ministers for service in America. In the aftermath of the Revolutionary War, the German Reformed severed their relationship with the Dutch authorities and became an autonomous German Reformed Church in the United States. Its leading theologians during the nineteenth century included the church historian Philip Schaff and **John Williamson Nevin** of the Mercersburg Seminary, who wrote *The Anxious Bench* (1843), a critique of revivalist practices of the mid-nineteenth century and an appeal for a renewal of the church's sacramental life.

The first Lutheran immigrants were the founders of New Sweden, set up on the Delaware in 1638 under the initiative of King Gustavus Adolphus. Early missionaries included John Campanius, known as the Swedish apostle to the Indians. With the decline of immigration, the Swedish community came under the care of the German Lutheran Ministerium of Pennsylvania by the end of the **colonial** era. German Lutherans who were part of the large influx from the Rhineland-Palatinate were being directed toward Penn's colony by the 1730s. It was then that Halle, the educational center for Lutheran Pietism in Germany, became involved in responding to American missionary needs, through the intervention of the court chaplain in London, Friedrich Ziegenhagen. The premier missionary from Halle was Henry Melchior Muhlenberg, who arrived in Charleston in 1742 and proceeded to Pennsylvania, following a visit with the Salzburger immigrants in Georgia. He was largely responsible for instituting the parish system of the Lutheran Church in the Middle Colonies, where he traveled and journaled in a manner not unlike the future **Methodist** circuit preachers.

In the second half of the eighteenth century, the radical Pietist vision to amend the aberrations of the existing branches of German Protestantism in a unified Christian community received new life through the work of Otterbein. During his long tenure in America (1752–1813), he served five Reformed parishes in Pennsylvania and Maryland, culminating in the Evangelical Reformed Church of Baltimore (1774–1813). From the latter base he remained a pastor of the Reformed Church while also laying the groundwork for the work of the fledgling **United Brethren in Christ** (organized in 1800). This work brought together New Light Reformed and Mennonite preachers into an "unpar-

tisan" fellowship in Christ, based on their common experience of the new birth and the disciplines of the holy life. They were motivated by an eschatology that predicted a "more glorious age of the church" emerging from an anticipated harvest of reborn believers that would usher in a new day of Pentecost. Their movement was traced to a "great meeting" (an anticipation of later **camp meetings**) in Pennsylvania, on Pentecost 1767. Otterbein served as a spiritual mentor to the founding bishop of Methodism in America, **Francis Asbury,** sharing in Asbury's consecration as bishop during the Methodist Christmas Conference of 1784. By 1789, Otterbein had prepared a confession of faith that integrated themes from Reformed Pietism and Anabaptism, having also a strong focus on **foreign missions.**

In parallel fashion, a second revivalist group developed among the Pennsylvania Germans through the ministry of a Lutheran lay evangelist, Jacob Albright (1759–1808), who was converted under United Brethren influence and who aspired to pattern his work among German Americans after the doctrine and polity of Anglo American Methodism. Beginning in the 1790s, this newly called farmer-preacher launched an evangelistic ministry among his "unconverted" neighbors, without official denominational sanction. By 1803 classes were organized. His followers consecrated him to the ministry, declaring him to be a "truly evangelical" preacher. They adopted as their name the **Evangelical Association** (*Die Evangelische Gemeinschaft*) in 1816, after Albright's death. In the 1830s they opened a German printing house and published a periodical, *Die Christliche Botschafter* ("The Christian Ambassador"), which appeared until 1946.

Both the United Brethren and Evangelicals were known as "bush meeting" Germans, due to their preference for outdoor revival services. Spreading through the Midwest and beyond, they attracted large numbers of German Americans to their ranks. Leading nineteenth-century missionaries among the United Brethren included Bishop Christian Newcomer and, among the Evangelicals, John Seybert. The Methodist Episcopal Church opened revivalist work among Midwestern Germans in the nineteenth century, led by a Tübingen-educated immigrant and convert to Methodism, Wilhelm Nast, who edited a journal for the German conferences of the Methodist Episcopal Church called the *Die Christliche Apologete* ("The Christian Apologist").

Among Lutherans, the Pennsylvania Ministerium was formed in 1748 under Muhlenberg's leadership at the consecration of St. Michael's Church in Philadelphia, which included German and Swedish pastors and lay delegates. They were about to experience a major influx of Germans, which would result in the formation of scores of new parishes by the 1770s. By 1800, a pan-German tendency led to the formation of union churches, consisting of Lutherans and German Reformed, whose spokesman was the theologian Samuel Schmucker (1799–1873) of Gettysburg Seminary. This unionist outlook declined in the face of massive new German immigration in the nineteenth century, resulting in the forming of new territorial, confessional synods in the frontier states of the Midwest, particularly the Lutheran Church Missouri Synod, organized in 1847, with Carl F. W. Walther (1811–1887) as its leading theologian. Unionist sentiment resurfaced among nineteenth-century Prussian German immigrants in the Midwest, leading to the formation of the Evangelical Synod of North America after the **Civil War.**

The first synod of Norwegian Lutherans was formed in Wisconsin (1846) under the Pietist influence of the Norwegian awakening leader Hans Nielsen Hauge. Disparate groups finally coalesced in 1900 to form the United Norwegian Church. Tensions between traditionalists and those of Pietist inclination also fractured the ranks of Danish and Finnish Lutheran immigrants in the nineteenth century, whose centers were also in the upper Midwest. The period after World War I began an era of reunion among these diverse Lutheran bodies.

In the post–Civil War era, revivalism among Scandinavians led to new denominations. Between 1873 to 1884, the Swedish Augustana Lutheran Church experienced the secession of a Pietist-oriented contingent, who organized the Evangelical Mission Covenant Church in 1884 (now the

Evangelical Covenant Church). It grew in revivalist fashion, extending into the American Swedish community the revivalist, transformative message of Swedish Pietism. Known as Covenanters, its members were recruited in Scandinavia as well as in North America. Revivalism among Scandinavians also included the work of Swedish Baptists and Methodists in North America. The former began with the ministry of an immigrant named Frederick Olaus Nilsson, who organized the first known Swedish Baptist Church in his homeland in 1848, leading to his banishment from Sweden and relocation to America. The Swedish Baptist General Conference was formed in Iowa in 1879. Among Methodists, the Swedish mission began with a ship in New York harbor, operated by Olof Hedstrom, a missionary to visiting seamen who was appointed by the New York Conference in 1845. This successful work spread to the upper Midwest by 1846, where 1.3 million Swedish immigrants arrived in the century after 1830. The Northwest Swedish Conference was the first to be formed, in 1877. Methodist work among Norwegian immigrants began with Ole Petersen in Iowa (1850), leading to the organization of a Northwest Norwegian and Danish Conference (1880). Like German revivalists, Scandinavian Methodists unsuccessfully sought to retain their ethnic identity, especially by founding schools and operating periodicals, although their ultimate assimilation into Anglo culture would be inevitable.

A final expression of revivalism to influence these North American ethnic groups was **Pentecostalism.** With its earliest strongholds in Los Angeles and Chicago, economically deprived immigrants were among the first to taste its fruit, including Germans and Scandinavians. An outreach to the latter group began with William H. Durham's North Avenue Mission, located on Chicago's north side. Studies have shown that Scandinavian Pentecostals strengthened their ethnic social identity through their affiliation with Pentecostalism. In summary, one could say that revivalism has been instrumental in defining the identity and outlook of German Americans and Scandinavian Americans.

Further Reading: Ahlstrom, Sidney A. *A Religious History of the American People.* New Haven, CT: Yale University Press, 1973; Colletti, Joseph. "Ethnic Pentecostalism in Chicago: 1890–1950." PhD dissertation, Birmingham University, UK, 1990; Norwood, Frederick A. *The Story of American Methodism.* Nashville, TN: Abingdon, 1974; O'Malley, J. Steven. *Early German-American Evangelicalism: Pietist Sources in Discipleship and Sanctification.* Metuchen, NJ: Scarecrow, 1995.

J. Steven O'Malley

M

MACNUTT, FRANCIS (1925–)

A former Dominican priest, Francis MacNutt is best known for his role in renewing interest in the **Roman Catholic** Church in divine **healing** and other **charismatic gifts** of the Holy Spirit. Educated at Harvard University, Catholic University of America, and Dominican Seminary in St. Louis, where he received a PhD in theology, MacNutt's healing ministry began in 1967, when he reportedly experienced **baptism of the Holy Spirit** at a charismatic Christian conference in Tennessee. MacNutt asserts that Protestants Tommy Tyson, Agnes Sanford, and **Kathryn Kuhlman** influenced his Christian development. MacNutt established Merton House in St. Louis and helped found the Association of Christian Therapists in 1976. After leaving the priesthood in 1980 in order to marry, MacNutt founded the ecumenical Christian Healing Ministries in Clearwater, Florida, which relocated to Jacksonville in 1987 at the invitation of the Episcopal Diocese of Florida.

MacNutt's ministry is characterized by sacramental approaches to healing, such as celebration of the Eucharist. He has also popularized the practice of "soaking **prayer**," in which MacNutt spends several hours at a time praying for the physical, emotional, and spiritual healing of his congregants. He is known for singing in unknown languages in front of large audiences, and claiming that people are healed as they listen. MacNutt and his staff pray for several hundred people in person every month and avowedly pray for more than 6,000 mailed-in requests monthly. No one is charged for prayer. His organization also refers people requesting information and help to healing resources near their own homes. Like many other healing evangelists, MacNutt teaches that healing is normally God's will and that Satan is the source of disease. He emphasizes the importance of cultivating an atmosphere of love, where the Holy Spirit is welcome. MacNutt seeks to integrate healing through prayer with traditional medical and psychological approaches to healing. He claims that about three-fourths of the people who receive prayer through his ministry—the rates are somewhat higher for emotional needs and lower for physical problems—experience either complete healing or a noticeable improvement.

In the early twenty-first century, MacNutt continues to host conferences that attract those needing healing or wishing to learn how to pray for healing, including church leaders, medical doctors, and psychological counselors from around the country. With his wife and colleague in ministry, Judith, he has travelled to more than 30 countries, and he influences many through books, courses, and tapes, including *The Power to Heal* (1977) and *Deliverance from Evil Spirits* (1995). Many of his publications, such as *Healing* (1974), which sold a million copies in the United States, have also been translated into other languages, including German, Japanese, Spanish, Portuguese, and Chinese.

Further Reading: Chappell, Paul Gale. "The Divine Healing Movement in America." PhD dissertation, Drew University, 1983; Christian Healing Ministries Web site. http://www.christianhealingmin.org/; Hardesty, Nancy A. *Faith Cure: Divine Healing in the Holiness and Pentecostal Movements.* Peabody, MA: Hendrickson, 2003; Villiers, Pieter G. R., ed. *Healing in the Name of God.* Pretoria, South Africa: University of South Africa, C. B. Powell Bible Center, 1986.

Candy Gunther Brown

MAHAN, ASA (1799–1889)

Asa Mahan—evangelist, philosopher, educator, author, editor—devoted most of his long and distinguished life to the promotion of a revival movement that became known as Oberlin perfectionism. Along with his more widely known colleague at Oberlin College, **Charles G. Finney,** he attempted to meld a Wesleyan **Holiness** theology into the **Calvinist** New School theology prevalent in the Congregational churches of their day. Although Finney tended to subordinate his affinities with **Methodism** or Wesleyanism to his New School thought, Mahan became more explicitly Wesleyan in his theology and professional associations.

Born in Vernon, New York, Mahan graduated from Hamilton College in 1824 and from Andover Theological Seminary in 1827. Two years after his ordination in 1829 he became pastor of the Sixth **Presbyterian** Church in Cincinnati, Ohio. There he took up the **abolitionist** cause as the only member of the Lane Theological Seminary's board of trustees and the Cincinnati Colonization Society to support the 1835 Lane Rebellion—an uprising of Lane students in support of immediate abolition of slavery. Opposition to their radical views within the Lane community led Mahan and the dissident students to accept the invitation of John Jay Shipherd to join his newly formed (1833) Oberlin

College in Ohio. Mahan was installed as Oberlin's first president (1835). Both he and Finney began to testify to an experience of entire **sanctification** soon thereafter, and Mahan's *Scripture Doctrine of Christian Perfection* (1839) placed before the general public the Oberlin perfectionists' response to the many questions regarding Christian holiness raised within the college and the community. Mahan's ability to reconcile elements of his New School Calvinism with Scottish Common Sense philosophy, Wesley's doctrine of Christian perfection, and the "new measures" revivalism of Finney established him as a distinctive and influential voice within the nineteenth-century Holiness movement. His teaching went forth in summer revival tents on Oberlin's campus, under banners that carried the words "Holiness Unto the Lord."

Mahan's outspoken nature and his persistent calls for personal commitment to Christian perfection, combined with his bold agenda of social reforms—including abolitionism, the rights of **women, temperance,** the peace movement, and the "new education" later instituted at Harvard by Charles William Eliot—resulted in years of sharp opposition from many faculty members at Oberlin College. Mahan finally agreed to resign in 1850. In 1861, after a failed attempt to create a new university in Cleveland, Ohio, and serving as a pastor in Jackson and Adrian, Michigan, Mahan became the president of Adrian College—a newly founded school of the abolitionist Wesleyan Methodist Connection of America. During this period, he published several volumes on moral philosophy that exerted an influence on the development of American philosophy.

Mahan turned again to the theology of perfectionism, first addressed in his 1839 book *Scripture Doctrine of Christian Perfection.* His new work, *Baptism of the Holy Ghost* (1870), defined an explicit connection between the historic Pentecost event and the personal experience of entire sanctification. Its basic teaching paralleled the understanding of sanctification that was emerging in the Methodist Holiness revival of this period. More specifically, Mahan distinguished the cleansing work of the Spirit from the empowering work of the Spirit. Although he himself always held that these two aspects represented the "second blessing" of Wesleyan holiness theology, he had opened the door for a separation between the work of purification and that of empowerment. The book helped to set the stage for the later birth of the **Pentecostal** movement, which sprang out of the Holiness revival at the end of the century. In 1874 Mahan moved to England. There he became involved with Holiness evangelists **Robert Pearsall Smith** and **Hannah Whitall Smith** and Higher Life evangelist William Boardman in meetings for the promotion of Christian holiness (1874–1875). The founding of the Keswick Convention for the Promotion of Holiness in 1875, one of the most lasting results of those meetings, marked a turning point for Mahan's Oberlin perfectionism. Keswick, Higher Life, or the Victorious Life Movements now became the dominant expressions of Calvinist Holiness teaching and revivalism.

His 15 years of evangelism and writing in England, until his death at almost 90 years of age, were some of the most productive of Mahan's life. He was widely respected for the clarity and thoughtfulness of his **preaching** and writing. Seven of his 18 major works were published during this period. From 1877 until his death in 1889 he edited and published *Divine Life*, a journal promoting revivalism and his perfectionist theology. Mahan is buried in Eastbourne, England.

Further Reading: Madden, Edward H., and James E. Hamilton. *Freedom and Grace: The Life of Asa Mahan.* Metuchen, NJ, and London: Scarecrow Press, 1982; Mahan, Asa. *Autobiography: Intellectual, Moral, and Spiritual; The Natural and the Supernatural in the Christian Life and Experience.* London: Haughton, n.d.; Mahan, Asa. *Baptism of the Holy Ghost.* New York: Palmer, 1870.

Melvin E. Dieter

MASON, CHARLES HARRISON (1866–1961)

Charles Harrison Mason was a prominent **African American** figure in the **Holiness movement,** the founder of the **Church of God in Christ** (COGIC) denomination, and a leader among early

Pentecostals. He was born in 1866, one year following the freeing of slaves throughout the United States, on a farm just outside of Memphis, Tennessee. His parents, Jerry and Eliza Mason, were former slaves and members of a Missionary **Baptist** church. When he was 12 years old, a yellow fever epidemic forced his family to leave the Memphis area for Plumerville, Arkansas. There the family lived on a plantation as tenant farmers. Mason worked very hard to help his family and had little time to attend school. In 1879, when he was 13, Mason's father died, and Mason became ill with chills and fever. His mother Eliza **prayed** for him and gave him home remedies. Mason experienced **healing** on the first Sunday in September of 1880 and was baptized by his half brother Rev. I. S. Nelson.

Mason soon left home and became a lay **preacher,** regularly giving his testimony and calling others to salvation, especially during summer **camp meetings.** In 1891, Mason was licensed and ordained a Baptist minister in Preston, Arkansas. He married Alice Saxton, the daughter of his mother's closest friend, and yet Alice opposed his ministerial plans. They divorced after two years of marriage and she later remarried. Mason was determined at this point to get an education. During 1893–1894 he was enrolled in Arkansas Baptist College. In 1895 Mason met Charles Price Jones (1865–1949), who was a graduate of Arkansas Baptist College and was a Baptist pastor in Jackson, Mississippi. Mason and Jones were friends who shared similar views on the topic of holiness and had both undergone an experience of **sanctification.** By preaching sanctification and the "second work" of grace to those who were already converted, they caused a religious stir among black Baptists. Between 1896 and 1899, the Holiness conventions and revivals brought division among black Baptists. Moreover, many black Methodist congregations, including those in the **African Methodist Episcopal Church** and the **African Methodist Episcopal Zion Church,** were also breaking away to become "sanctified" or Holiness churches. The consequence for Mason was that he and Jones and their followers were expelled from the African American **National Baptist Convention.**

While walking the streets of Little Rock, Arkansas, in 1897, Mason prayed for a new denominational name for his group, and reported that he received the phrase "Church of God in Christ" (based on 1 Thessalonians 2:14 and 2 Thessalonians 1:1). Mason and Jones shared a common rural background and ethical standards. They established strict rules requiring that church members abstain from tobacco, intoxicating liquors, tea, coffee, dances, gambling, public ball games, circuses, short hair for **women,** long hair for **men,** immodest attire, and participation in secret societies. Mason and Jones did not appoint women as leaders of congregations—though certain other Holiness groups at this time, such as the Fire-Baptized Holiness Association, ordained women to ministry and had female elders. They advocated pacifism and rejected capital punishment. Some African Americans, however, were not happy with Mason's practices. In the early twentieth century, there were conflicts among black Baptists concerning the use of musical instruments such as guitars, prolonged revival meetings, and other new ideas and practices taken over from Holiness churches. Despite these points of contention, however, the Holiness movement gained control of many black denominational churches in the **South.**

Mason and Jones learned in 1906 of the **Azusa Street revival** in Los Angeles led by **William Seymour** (1870–1922). Mason and Jones agreed that one leader should travel with two witnesses to investigate. Accompanied by J. D. Young and J. A. Jeter, Mason traveled in 1907 to Los Angeles, where he learned about and experienced the **baptism in the Holy Spirit.** When the three men returned to Memphis, their church was already divided over the doctrine of the baptism in the Holy Spirit and had concerns about the integration of blacks with whites in the South. In August 1907, a general assembly of the Church of God in Christ met in Jackson, Mississippi, for three days and three nights to discuss the future of the church. In consequence, the "right hand of fellowship" was withdrawn from Mason and all who promulgated the Pentecostal doctrine of **speaking in tongues.** A majority of the ministers followed Jones, who opposed the new

Pentecostalism, and the remainder continued with Mason. For two years Mason and Jones were involved in a court battle over the name of the church and control of properties. A 1909 legal decision allowed Mason and his followers to keep their charter and the name Church of God in Christ (COGIC). The date of the church's founding was changed to September 1907, and the church's articles were emended to emphasize belief in the Holy Spirit.

The COGIC group elected C. H. Mason as general overseer and appointed D. J. Young as editor of the *Whole Truth* newspaper and Sunday school materials. In 1910, Jones and his followers became the Church of Christ (Holiness) USA and maintained a Holiness tradition with church governance by bishops. Because of the COGIC's legal incorporation, many whites and blacks in the Holiness

Charles H. Mason was cofounder and leader of the Church of God in Christ, which, during his long lifetime, became the largest Pentecostal denomination in the world. Courtesy of Flower Pentecostal Heritage Center, Springfield, MO.

revival and in the early Pentecostal movement obtained their ministerial credentials through the COGIC. Preachers with ministerial credentials could perform marriages, bury the dead, and qualify for reduced clergy rates on railroads. During the key years from 1909 to 1914—when the white Pentecostal denomination of the **Assemblies of God** took shape—Mason's church ordained many white ministers. By ordaining ministers of all races, Mason performed an important service to the early twentieth-century Pentecostal movement. From the very inception of the COGIC, women have played a central role in ministry. They have encouraged the youth, collected donations, conducted home visitations, cared for people in need, and led in prayer meetings and in **foreign missions.** In many cases, the establishment of new congregations has been due to women who would first drum up local interest and recruit new members, and then ask the COGIC headquarters to send a male pastor to serve as the leader.

In the early years of the Pentecostal movement, Mason and Seymour traveled together spreading the Holiness and Pentecostal message of sanctification and Spirit baptism, and telling everyone that the color line separating blacks from whites was "washed away in the blood [of Christ]." They traveled to Virginia; Washington, DC; Chicago; and other regions. Yet the color line soon reasserted itself. In December 1913, E. N. Bell and H. A. Goss convened a general council of "all white Pentecostal saints and Church of God in Christ followers." In April 1914, the General Council of the Assembly of God was formed in Hot Springs, Arkansas. Mason aroused opposition during this period both because of his rejection of segregation in the church and his pacifist stand during the First World War. In 1918, some of Mason's followers in Los Angeles, Texas, and some southern states were identified as Germans. Mason was jailed in Lexington, Mississippi, for preaching against the war, and he was repeatedly incarcerated for preaching alongside of white ministers—thus violating the official or unofficial Jim Crow policies of racial separation. His FBI file made reference to Mason's interracial religious activities and "seditious" statements, and to the clause in the

COGIC's 1917 creed in opposition to all bloodshed or participation in warfare.

By 1934, Mason's COGIC had 345 churches in 21 states, and a membership of more than 25,000. The church's continuing growth was phenomenal and its membership increased 10-fold during the next three decades. By 1958, the COGIC was the fourth-largest Protestant denomination in the world. After the death of Mason's first wife (from whom he had been divorced), he married Lelia Washington Mason in 1903—the mother of his eight children. After Lelia's death in 1936, he married Elsie Washington Mason in 1943. Elsie has described Mason as a quiet man who would hum spiritual and gospel songs. He was known for having an especially deep prayer life, and would read the Bible for hours while making groans, moans, and utterances to the Lord. He regularly practiced **fasting** and each day "wanted to greet God in his best," which led him habitually to dress with a bow tie, white shirt, and suit. He had a wide-ranging impact on black education and health, college attendance, family life, prayer ministries, prison ministries, and gospel music. Mason died in Detroit in 1961, and during his 95 years he had lived to see the COGIC become the largest Pentecostal denomination in the world.

Further Reading: Black History Review. "Charles Price Jones." http://www.blackhistoryreview.com/biography/CPJones.php; Daniels, David Douglas, III. "The Cultural Renewal of Slave Religion: Charles Price Jones and the Emergence of the Holiness Movement in Mississippi." PhD dissertation, Union Theological Seminary, New York City, 1992; DuPree, Sherry Sherrod. *African-American Holiness Pentecostal Movement: An Annotated Bibliography.* New York: Garland, 1996; DuPree, Sherry Sherrod. *Biographical Dictionary of African-American Holiness-Pentecostals, 1880–1990.* Washington, DC: Middle Atlantic Regional Press, 1989; Mason, Elise Washington. *The Man Charles Harrison Mason.* Memphis, TN: Church of God in Christ, 1991.

Sherry Sherrod DuPree

MATERIAL CULTURE OF REVIVALS

Scholars have long based their interpretations of religion on the analysis of doctrinal texts, ethical rules, rituals and ceremonies, and accounts of spiritual experience. It is only recently that most religion scholars have discovered what anthropologists have long known—namely, that one cannot study religion in depth without paying attention to the material objects that are a part of religious practice. At first glance, revivalist Christianity would seem to offer little in the way of a distinctive material culture. All one really needs for a revival service is a place for people to gather and a **preacher** to stand and deliver a message. Yet, on closer examination, material objects and physical settings play a distinctive and important role in the practice of revivalism.

Revival objects come from popular culture and from the needs of preachers and people. Originally the needs of these services are very simple and direct: a brush arbor for **camp meetings,** a tent or storefront church, a Bible, songbooks, chairs or benches, and lights. Revival objects contain simple messages easily understood by the people. Revivalist Christians often see nothing wrong with advertising Jesus Christ, just as one might advertise Coca-Cola or another commercial product. They present messages on signs, posters, trees, or sides of barns. These objects may be mass-produced or hand lettered. The interior organization of a tent or church used for revival services is usually simple—rows of wood or metal chairs facing in one direction, a podium or small table in front with a Bible on it, electric lights strung overhead, sawdust on the ground if there are summer rains, a piano or other source of music, a microphone for the preacher, a bench or chairs in front turned backward as a "mourners' bench" for the **altar call** where those "convicted of sin" may sit. The revivals around 1800 on the border of Tennessee and Kentucky at first involved both black and white worshippers with large sheets that separated the races. Later, the participants tore down the sheets in an enthusiastic demolishing of racial barriers—a fitting symbol of the revival's egalitarian spirit.

The objects associated with revivals are not usually revered, and yet the Bible is an exception. Not only does the Bible contain a sacred message, but as a physical object it is sacred too. In a traditional revival context, one would think twice before setting a Bible on the floor or doing anything that might be seen as disrespectful to "the Word of God." Family Bibles—containing records of births, deaths, and marriages, and passed down as heirlooms over generations—are hallowed objects. They might be reminders of a **praying** grandmother or the faith of other godly forbears. An individual's Bible can also be charged with sacred memories and associations. Someone may underline verses, write marginal comments, or insert calendar dates and place names to indicate the time and location that he or she "claimed" a particular promise in faith. In this way the various passages of the Bible become associated with an individual faith journey, and the copy of the Bible containing these notations will likely become a treasured possession. Revival preachers often convey a sense that the Bible is a sacred object or talisman. They may strut back and forth across the front of the sanctuary brandishing a large, leather-bound Bible, held open or closed and sometimes lifted into the air or even shaken in the air for emphasis during the sermon.

Other sacred objects used in religious revivals include **healing** oil (i.e., a small bottle of oil from the grocery store) or healing cloths (small patches of fabric) sent to believers who are too sick to come to the worship service. Some objects find occasional use, such as plastic or metal pails for foot washing, and towels used after creek baptism (or after foot washing). In revivalist Christianity there is usually no sense of sacredness associated with the physical objects used in celebrating the Lord's Supper. After cups for wine or grape juice and crackers have been used, they may be thrown into a trash can. This indifferent attitude is in contrast to **Roman Catholicism** and other traditional churches that attach sacred value to objects—chalice, flask, paten, altar cloth, and so on—associated with the celebration of the Eucharist.

Revivalist churches often feature pictures of Jesus and the apostles, foreign lands with missionaries, hands **praying** or healing, and little children going to church. Such images appear in cheap paper reprints or on black velvet paintings produced in Mexico or another foreign country. Church societies produce cards, photographs, bumper stickers, posters, and booklets. The most popular works on paper are signage: large or small, black and white or colored, crowding all available space, and dramatically presenting a preacher, movie, visiting missionary, or anything else to attract people to the services. The podium in the front of the church may have one or more metal license plates tacked onto it exhorting all to "Be saved!" "Meet me in church on Sunday!" "Praise the Lord!" or "Prepare to meet God!" Another common object is the paper fan stapled on a wooden stick with religious pictures—the Last Supper is a favorite—on one side and a mortuary advertisement and the church's name on the reverse. Originally the fans were of palm leaves, in reference to Jesus' triumphant entry into Jerusalem, when palms were waved over his head. Such fans are set out on the top of the chairs prior to a revival service.

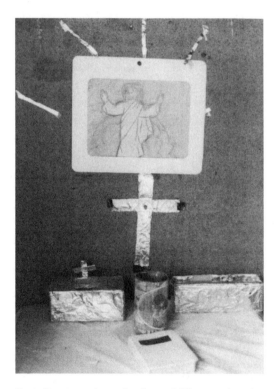

Revivalism in rural areas has fostered folk art, such as this homemade altar in West Virginia, featuring a picture of Jesus on the clouds of heaven, with strips of aluminum foil representing his glory, and a foil-covered cross and offering boxes below. Copyright by and courtesy of Eleanor Dickinson.

Along with the fans most chairs will have a paperback book of hymns and songs with titles such as *Victory Songs, Jubilant Voices, Revival Songs,* or *Songs of the Assembly.* Revival hymnals may be printed with shape-notes, a form of musical notation popularized by the singing masters in the 1700s and early 1800s. Within these hymnbooks one can find "Romish Lady," an 11-verse story of a girl who was caught reading the Bible and ends up being burned at the stake at the order of the Pope because she will not give up her Bible. Another favorite is the story of "Wicked Polly," who "liked to go to parties to dance and sing" and so "one Sabbath morning she fell sick, her tongue stuck out her nails turned black her wicked heart began to crack," and she died a sinner. One might recount U.S. history through popular hymns such as "The Royal Telephone," written when the phone was invented; "Life's a Railroad to Heaven," when the railroads were built; "The Bible Tells Me So," at the time of the Scopes trial; and "I Don't Want to Get Adjusted to This World," in the era of popular psychology.

The musical instruments used in revivals include those found in orchestral music, such as pianos, organs, trumpets, horns, flutes, drums, and cymbals. Other possible instruments include guitars, banjos, and Dobros—all of which may be electrified or acoustic. One also finds folk instruments such as "stomper-dolls," thumb-tubs, washboards, and spoons. Not all these instruments are likely to be used at once, though they may be played in unusual combinations. The most ubiquitous instrument may be the tambourine, and many worshippers come to a revival service carrying one along with their Bible. Occasionally a preacher will use props to enhance the sermon such as a ring and a robe when telling the story of the Prodigal Son.

Some revival services feature unusual artifacts, such as those associated with **serpent and fire handling** or the consumption of deadly poisons, which has been a regional tradition during the twentieth century in **Appalachia.** The poison used is usually strychnine, bought at the drugstore, mixed up in a small bottle and kept behind the podium. For fire handling, a blowtorch may be kept behind the podium and removed as needed in the service. Snakes are placed three or four to a "serpent box." These are definitely poisonous, and the most common varieties are rattlesnakes and Georgia diamondbacks. They are kept in worshippers' homes and brought to church. Though one hears stories that serpents are kept on ice before the meeting, or "milked" of poison to reduce the danger of handling them, these stories seem to be false. Most members of the serpent-handling churches would rather face bodily harm than not follow what they take to be God's command to pick up a poisonous snake (Mark 16:17–18) or to expose themselves to fire.

Healing services often have a material dimension. Oil is placed on the ill person's body, and especially the area of the body associated with the sickness. If there is a generalized illness that affects the entire body, then the forehead may be anointed with oil. Usually the preacher or worship leader will place his hands on the head (or other body part) of the afflicted person and all persons in the tent or church will stretch out their arms and hands (i.e., "the hand of healing") and point it toward the sick person as prayers for healing are offered. Sometimes prayers for healing are accompanied with words of exorcism, such as "Devil, I command you *out* of her!" The person may scream, begin **speaking in tongues,** fall to the ground, writhe on the floor, or fall unconscious for a period of time. Churches that witness such healing rituals may use a large cloth to cover the legs of an unconscious woman, for modesty's sake.

Other material objects are occasionally associated with revivals: bicycles and trucks decorated with religious signs, newspaper advertisements, 15-foot-high concrete crosses with words like "Prepare to Meet God," or "Get Right with God" carved in them and erected along the highways. Speaking in tongues in written form (or *glossographia*) has appeared in Tennessee and Washington, DC, and other forms of revivalist folk art exist. Unusual objects range from religious carvings inserted in glass bottles, sealed, and thrown into creeks and rivers to huge horizontal signs at the end of airport runways urging passengers as they take off to "Prepare to Meet Thy God." The range of human inventiveness is limitless when linked to an impassioned desire to testify to the power and love of God.

Further Reading: Dickinson, Eleanor. *Revival!* New York: Harper and Row, 1974; Dickinson, Eleanor. *Revival! A Catalogue from an Exhibition on Protestant Revivalism at the Tennessee State Museum, November 15, 1981–March 21, 1982.* Nashville: Tennessee State Museum, 1981; Dickinson, Eleanor. *That Old Time Religion: A Catalog from the Exhibit, That Old Time Religion, a Documentation of Protestant Revivalism.* Oakland, CA: Oakland Museum History Department, 1979; McDannell, Colleen. *Material Christianity: Religion and Popular Culture in America.* New Haven, CT: Yale University Press, 1995.

Eleanor Dickinson

MATHER, COTTON (1663–1728)

The most illustrious and controversial Puritan clergyman in **colonial** New England prior to the **Great Awakening,** Cotton Mather was in the third of four generations in a family dynasty of ministers that shaped the development of Puritan theology and pastoral practice for more than 150 years. As pastor of the Second Congregational Church of Boston, he ministered—with his father, Increase Mather, as teacher—to more than 2,000 parishioners. He was instrumental in deposing Governor Andros during the Glorious Revolution in England (1688–1689) and played a leading role in the Salem witchcraft debacle (1692–1693), which damaged his reputation immeasurably. At the forefront of the early Enlightenment debate, he popularized Newtonian science, disseminated information on medical innovations such as smallpox inoculation, and published more than 450 works on all aspects of contemporary learning. Yet his primary significance for later American revivals was as a staunch advocate of **Pietist** ecumenism, with a view to preparing all Protestants—and even Jews and Muslims—for the Second Coming of Christ.

Mather's innovative practices earn him a prominent place in the genetic line that leads down to the Great Awakening of the mid-eighteenth century, the **Second Great Awakening** of the early nineteenth century, and evangelical movements after the

Civil War. Yet to call Mather an early revivalist is a misnomer: he neither organized **camp meetings,** nor embraced Arminian theology and its stress on the human will, nor called contrite sinners to an **altar call.** He did not sponsor emotional subjectivism, anti-intellectualism, or lay **preaching** and witnessing. For Mather, revivals were not effected by ministerial activism or triggered by any human activity. Instead they were a visible expression of an invisible occurrence—namely, the miraculous outpouring of the Holy Spirit (Joel 2). Mather's awakening efforts might more safely be called *renewalism,* instead of *revivalism,* to demarcate his **Calvinist** theology from that of many nineteenth-century successors.

During the late 1600s and early 1700s, the old order of Puritanism in America was declining, both because of its rigorous preparationist views of salvation and the influence of Deism and Enlightenment philosophy. Mather was acutely aware of the spiritual paralysis accompanying those marooned in the stage of contrition or conviction, and consequently he strove to simplify the so-called *ordo salutis* or order of salvation (i.e., a series of experiential stages on the way to full salvation). While still insisting on repentance, grace, and **assurance of salvation** prior to receiving the Lord's Supper, he also warned against morbid introspection and despair by calling on the contrite to focus on God's mercy and the sufficiency of grace instead of their own unworthiness. He allowed that people baptized in infancy might undergo insensible **conversions,** that is, conversions that could not be fixed in terms of time and place. But if he comforted the wounded by construing their soul's anguish as a hopeful sign of grace, he wounded the comfortable by preaching on the pains of hell. Mather sought to insure that no carnal hypocrite would presume to approach the Communion table. He also virtually ruled out sudden conversion as something reminiscent of the enthusiasm that had appeared in New England during the Antinomian Crisis of 1636–1637.

Like many of his Puritan peers, Mather employed the jeremiad sermon to combat the spiritual lethargy that seemed to set in after the mid-1600s.

Yet jeremiads failed to awaken the drowsy or indifferent because they reinforced existing doctrines and ecclesiastical structures without addressing the underlying problems. Drawing on the pastoral wisdom of German Pietist colleagues such as Johann Arndt, Philipp Jakob Spener, and above all, August Hermann Francke (Mather's correspondent), Mather laid out a plan for individual, parish, and social renewal. On the individual level, he stressed meditation and **prayer,** family prayer, biblical instruction, **hymn** singing, and the strict observance of the Sabbath. On the parish level, the focus lay on church meetings, weekly lectures, catechizing, individual prayer, and written covenants for the contrite. Family visits by appointment and the dissemination of Christian literature constituted the bulk of his pastoral regimen. The virtual absence of lay witnessing—so characteristic of later revivalism—shows that Puritan ministers did not measure pastoral fruitfulness by the numbers of new converts but by their quality of godliness or **sanctification.** Souls came to God not by instant penitence but generally through a lengthy and even agonizing process. On the communal level, Mather instituted voluntary religious societies such as family meetings in private households, young **men's** religious associations, **African American** religious groups, and reforming societies for the suppression of moral disorders in Boston. Inspired by English and Continental precedents, Mather's religious and social activism foreshadowed the "benevolent empire" of nineteenth-century revivalists.

The significance of Mather's revivalist activism cannot be fully appreciated unless we understand his Pietist ecumenism and the driving force behind it—his millennialist **eschatology.** While Increase Mather was in London to negotiate the new Royal Charter for Massachusetts (1691), his son Cotton campaigned to merge New England's Presbyterians and Congregationalists (Independents) into one church, to be called the United Brethren. Based on the millennialist interpretations of Joseph Mede, Pierre Jurieu, and Thomas Beverley, Mather expected a "New Reformation" accompanied by a worldwide outpouring of the Spirit in 1697, when the 1,260 years of the Antichrist's reign might run out and Christ's 1,000-year reign begin. Yet the failure of the United Brethren and the delay of the Second Coming did not diminish his interest in ecumenism or in the need for large-scale revivals. If anything, his premillennialism (now focusing on 1716, later on 1736) and his ecumenical vision expanded to embrace all Protestant denominations, Jews, and Muslims the world over. Inspired by Francke's Pietist world missions to India and Asia, Mather promoted "Universal Religion" under the auspices of 14, and then 3, "Maxims of Piety." By distilling true religion into three creedal essentials, sectarian strife and division might yet be overcome and usher in a worldwide revival if not the millennium itself. He taught himself French and Spanish to engage **Roman Catholics** to the north and south of New England. He sent Latin translations of his ecumenical tracts to his European correspondents for distribution. He reached out to North American Indians with tracts in the Algonquian language, strove to convert Jews, and advocated liberty of conscience—all to promote worldwide union through spiritual renewal.

Cotton Mather was a major sponsor of evangelical awakenings in the American colonies even if he did not live long enough to see his labors come to fruition. The kindling for the Great Awakening was delivered—more than four decades earlier—by a handful of New England clergymen inspired by Cotton Mather and his Pietist evangelicalism.

Further Reading: Lovelace, Richard. *The American Pietism of Cotton Mather*. Grand Rapids, MI: Christian University Press, 1979; Middlekauff, Robert. *The Mathers: Three Generations of Puritan Intellectuals*. New York: Oxford University Press, 1971.

Reiner Smolinski

MCGAVRAN, DONALD A. (1897–1990)

Donald McGavran was a **foreign missionary,** educator, author, and father of the **Church Growth movement.** He was a minister in the Christian Church/Disciples of Christ and worked as a missionary under the United Christian Mission Society in India (1923–1957). He was the founding dean of Fuller Theological Seminary's School of World Mission in Pasadena, California (1965–1971), and senior professor of missions at Fuller (1971–1990). McGavran was born in Damoh, India, of missionary parents and grandparents. His family returned to the United States in 1900. After his upbringing in Michigan, Indiana, and Oklahoma, he experienced **conversion** at the age of 14 and was baptized at the First Christian Church in Tulsa, Oklahoma. The outbreak of World War I and his stint in the army (1918–1919) interrupted his college education. He graduated from Butler College (1920), received a BD cum laude from Yale Divinity School, married Mary Elizabeth Howard (1922), and set sail for India. From 1923 to 1931 he served in Harda, India, directing religious education in the mission schools, and served on the missions executive committee beginning in 1928. On his 1931–1932 furlough from the mission field, McGavran earned his PhD from Columbia University in education. He returned to Jubbulpore, India and from 1933 to 1936 was secretary-treasurer of the mission. From 1936 to 1954 he served in Takhatpur, India, as the manager of a leprosarium and an evangelist to various castes, including the Satnamis. From 1954 to 1960 he lectured at seminaries in the United States, Puerto Rico, Jamaica, the Philippines, Thailand, and Zaire in addition to teaching from 1957 to 1960 at the College of Missions in Indianapolis, Indiana. He directed Northwest Christian College in Eugene, Oregon, and both founded and led that school's Institute of Church Growth from 1961 to 1965.

McGavran's experience as a missionary in India was the beginning of the Church Growth movement. He led a mission in which missionaries aided farmers; constructed buildings; ran schools, orphanages, and leprosariums; did evangelism; and witnessed a few conversions. Yet for all their hard work, they had little to show in terms of growing churches. Spurred on by this problem McGavran began his research. From missionary leaders of the early 1800s, Henry Venn and Rufus Anderson, he developed a model of missions in which the church community itself was central, rather than missions personnel, evangelistic techniques, or social service activities. From Roland Allen's *The Spontaneous Expansion of the Church and the Causes Which Hinder It* (1927), McGavran learned of the apostle Paul's missionary methods in the New Testament and sought to discontinue modern methods that proved to be unfruitful. From J. Waskom Pickett's *Christian Mass Movements in India* (1933), McGavran discovered how whole clans and tribes in India had rapidly become Christian despite minimal contact with Western missionaries. These mass conversions or "people movements" shifted McGavran away from the traditional missionary method of disseminating the Christian gospel widely and hoping to reach a few individuals. He sought to understand how social connections within tribes, clans, and castes ("people groups") could be used to build the Christian church. Pickett and McGavran collaborated in *Church Growth and Group Conversion* (1936). They advocated careful statistical reporting that documented the evidence for people movements, and a practical approach that directed the majority of mission resources to groups that were the most receptive to the gospel message.

McGavran's watershed book, *The Bridges of God* (1955), created controversy and helped launch the Church Growth movement. His term *bridges* referred to the social and cultural glue that held people groups together. Rather than fighting against these realities, McGavran sought to utilize them for the benefit of the Christian church. If approached properly, an entire group of people might embrace the Christian message en masse. McGavran defined evangelism not as mere verbal proclamation but as a process of instructing people in the Christian faith until they become disciples who are active in churches. He wanted missionaries and missions leaders to be held accountable for the numerical or quantitative results of their efforts. It was not enough for missionaries to be "sowing seeds" or "doing good deeds." People groups, in McGavran's view, were "homogenous, endogamous units" that could make collective decisions to follow Christ. New believers were not to discard their distinctive ethnic identities. Only after winning as many new Christians as possible, and then integrating them into churches, was it time for the church to perfect them in doctrinal teachings and denominational practices.

Further Reading: Billy Graham Center Archives. "Papers of Donald Anderson and Mary Elizabeth (Howard) McGavran." http://www.wheaton.edu/bgc/archives/guides/178.htm#301; McGavran, Donald A. *Church Growth and Christian Missions.* New York: Harper & Row, 1965; McGavran, Donald A. *Crucial Issues in Missions Tomorrow.* Chicago: Moody Press, 1972; McGavran, Donald A. *How Churches Grow.* London: World Dominion Press, 1959; McGavran, Donald A. *Ten Steps for Church Growth.* San Francisco: Harper & Row, 1977; McGavran, Donald A. *Understanding Church Growth.* Grand Rapids, MI: Eerdmans, 1970; Rainer, Thom S. *The Book of Church Growth: History, Theology and Principles.* Nashville, TN: Broadman Press, 1993; Towns, Elmer ed. *Evangelism and Church Growth: A Practical Encyclopedia.* Ventura, CA: Regal Books, 1995.

Bayard Taylor

MCGREADY, JAMES (1760–1817)

James McGready (or M'Gready), a **Presbyterian** minister in North Carolina and Kentucky, was a major figure in early American **camp meetings** and the "Great Revival" on the western frontier of the United States in the decade after 1800. Contemporaries best knew him for his animated preaching style, for which he earned the nickname "Son of Thunder." Though a committed revivalist preacher, McGready was a traditional **Calvinist** in his **theology of revival,** and therefore he eventually found himself fully welcome in neither the revivalist nor the **anti-revivalist** camp. Despite being an ardent supporter of the frontier revivals, he did not join his revivalist compatriots in forming the breakaway **Cumberland Presbyterian Church.** Born in Pennsylvania to Scotch-Irish parents, McGready later moved as a child to North Carolina. He was educated in a series of schools and academies in North Carolina and Pennsylvania run by ministers trained and educated in the **Great Awakening** revivalist tradition of **William Tennent's** Log College. At these schools he learned to combine a fiery preaching style with orthodox American

Presbyterian Calvinism. He left—or rather fled—from his first pastorate in North Carolina in the 1790s after his zealous preaching angered some communicants to the point that they threatened his life and burned his pulpit. Relocating in 1797 in Logan County, Kentucky, McGready again commenced his revivalistic preaching. Over the next few summers, increasingly larger crowds gathered near his three churches in Logan County, and McGready publicly urged visitors to camp on the grounds near the meetinghouse. These gatherings drew from several denominational traditions and were among the earliest large-scale camp meetings in America. The camp meetings soon spread across Kentucky and the southeastern United States and led ultimately to both the **Cane Ridge revival** of 1801 and the wider evangelical revival in the **South** during the decades after 1800.

McGready continued to preach and work in southwestern Kentucky from 1800 to 1806. He was a founding member of the Cumberland Presbytery of the Transylvania Synod and supported the pro-revival majority of that presbytery. By 1805, many in the synod had become suspicious of the more animated forms of **bodily manifestations** associated with the Great Revival (e.g., jerking, falling, and barking) and the Cumberland Presbytery's licensing of minimally trained or educated "exhorters" to preach in remote frontier areas. The synod dispatched a commission to investigate the presbytery's licensing actions and eventually the commission demanded that the licensees be reexamined by the commission. The pro-revivalist segment of the presbytery refused to submit to the synod's authority and set in motion the creation of a new revivalistic denomination that embraced Arminian theology: the Cumberland Presbyterian Church. McGready chose to remain loyal to the synod, however, and did not join the secession movement. Following a vicious personal attack on his reputation by members of the Cumberland Presbytery, McGready moved by about 1807 from Logan County to Henderson, Kentucky, on the Ohio River, and remained in Henderson for the rest of his life. Although he undertook several missionary ventures over the next decade into Indiana and

Illinois under the auspices of the Transylvania Synod, he never regained the leadership position he had held prior to the Cumberland split. He died in 1817 of natural causes. An edition of McGready's writings, including more than 40 sermons, appeared in the 1830s.

Further Reading: M'Gready, James. *The Posthumous Works of the Reverend James M'Gready*. Ed. James Smith. Nashville, TN: J. Smith's Steam Press, 1837; Scott, John Thomas. "James McGready: Son of Thunder, Father of the Great Revival." *American Presbyterians* 72 (1994): 87–95.

John Thomas Scott

MCLOUGHLIN, WILLIAM G. (1922–1992)

William G. McLoughlin, a member of the faculty of Brown University from 1954 until his death in 1992, was his generation's—and perhaps the twentieth century's—most influential historian of American revivalism. His writings on revivalism included interpretive histories, scholarly articles, edited volumes, and popular essays. His classic study *Modern Revivalism* (1959) discussed American revivalism from 1825 to the 1950s and contained many of the themes that McLoughlin would further develop in his subsequent scholarship. Distinguishing between great awakenings and localized or annual revivals, he contended that the former reflected theological and ideological reorientation, ecclesiastical conflict combined with a sense of social crisis, and recognition within the wider American culture of the relevance of religion to the current situation. In so arguing, McLoughlin distanced himself from those who invoked supernatural agency, mass hysteria, or economic conflict as the singular cause of revivals. Instead, he insisted that such great awakenings represented a reexamination and redefinition of the nation's social and intellectual values in order to maintain a necessary balance between tradition and change.

In addition to his broad interpretive studies, McLoughlin produced works on particular revivalists as well. In *Billy Sunday Was His Real Name* (1955), he portrayed **Billy Sunday** as a Fundamentalist response to the powerful forces transforming America in the late nineteenth and early twentieth centuries. More than simply a colorful personality, Sunday at the peak of his influence—from 1896 to 1912—represented an attempt to reconcile the social and intellectual realities of the emerging twentieth century with the beliefs and traditions of the nineteenth. In *Billy Graham, Revivalist in a Secular Age* (1960), McLoughlin sought to put the rising star of revivalism into historical context. **Billy Graham** was neither a freelance itinerant **preacher** traveling in a battered car, nor a religious prophet articulating a new message. Instead McLoughlin depicted Graham as a professional evangelist who served at the invitation of local pastors. A product of the Fundamentalist culture of the interwar period, Graham was more indebted to **Charles G. Finney** and **Dwight L. Moody** than his predecessor, Billy Sunday. Writing at the midpoint of Graham's career, McLoughlin noted that there was no doubt about Graham's sincerity. Yet he questioned whether Graham's individualistic and moralistic answers were adequate to answer the complex questions facing Americans in the late twentieth century.

In his 1960 edition of Charles Grandison Finney's *Lectures on Revivals of Religion* (1835), McLoughlin presented Finney as an expression of his era, particularly in his emphasis on postmillennialism and free will as well as his advocacy of "new measures" to promote revivals. Finney was the religious counterpart to the Jacksonian common man, and his writings and career provided historians, McLoughlin insisted, with an entry into the intellectual, social, and ecclesiastical changes occurring in America. Taken together, McLoughlin's early writings provided a sophisticated discussion of American revivalism in terms of its social functions and historical contexts. Though individuals such as Sunday, Graham, and Finney were important, a national experience, such as a great awakening, was always more than the work of an individual. As McLoughlin noted, there were always skillful evangelists, but they were not all equally successful, and even the best were not consistently successful, but had careers that rose and fell.

In the essay "Pietism and the American Character" (1965), McLoughlin introduced this theme as offering important insights into the nature of the American experience. *Pietistic-perfectionism*, as he preferred to call it, was a dynamic quality in the American experience that produced the classic dilemma of personal responsibility for purity versus social responsibility for order. The upshot was that Americans evaluated issues in terms of a perceived higher moral law (drawn from religious resources), and in order to avoid complicity with evil, they felt compelled in the name of that law to confront evil wherever it was found. McLoughlin recognized the potential for self-justification and duplicity in this invocation of a higher law. Yet he insisted that throughout their history Americans had invoked a language of higher laws to justify their personal and corporate actions. Evangelicalism, using revivalism as its method, transformed America in the nineteenth century. Revivalism molded it—McLoughlin wrote in his introduction to *The American Evangelicals* (1968)—into a pietistic-perfectionist nation that was active in social reform, missionary endeavor, and imperialistic expansion.

In another essay, "Revivalism" (1974), McLoughlin identified some of the multiple functions that revivalism had performed in American religious experience. On the spiritual level, revivalism had functioned to spread the Christian gospel by means of fervent preaching and mass evangelism throughout the nation and the world. On the ecclesiastical level, revivalism extended and energized membership in religious institutions, and sometimes created new forms of church organization. On the social level, revivalism functioned dynamically to engender *conservative impulses* that placed moral, legal, and institutional restraints upon change (e.g., the **temperance** movement), and also *radical impulses* that sought to bring about social change and perfectionist transformations through the abolition of evil (e.g., **abolitionism**).

American revivalism, in McLoughlin's view, manifested five great periods (or awakenings) in 1600–1640, 1725–1760, 1795–1835, 1875–1915, and 1950–1980. These awakenings were both the symptoms and the catalysts of social change in American society. These periods of religious ferment precipitated cultural reorientations in each case, reexaminations and reformulations in which a widespread sense of crisis was eventually resolved by the body politic as a whole. Thus the awakening of 1795–1835 faced the question "What kind of nation is the United States to be now that it is free and able, under God, to govern itself?" The awakening of 1875–1915 confronted the question "How can a Christian people reconcile scripture and science to deal with urban-industrial society?" In this way, McLoughlin developed a functional model of revivalism and great awakenings to encompass the whole of American history.

McLoughlin's influential work *Revivals, Awakenings, and Reform* (1978) drew together many themes he had been exploring for decades. Differentiating *revivals* (which transform individuals) from *awakenings* (which alter nations and cultures), McLoughlin presented awakenings as periods of cultural revitalization and transformation that keep a culture alive and dynamic. Beginning in periods of cultural disjunction, and extending over a generation or so, awakenings produce a reorientation of beliefs and values within the culture as a whole. Beneath this pattern of recurring change, there was a common core of beliefs and ideals that provided continuity and shape to American culture. Influenced by Ralph Gabriel, McLoughlin focused on Americans' self-image as a chosen people who have a destiny to lead the world into a millennium or golden age, with institutions operating under higher laws that increase the general welfare by allowing each individual to fulfill his or her potential. This pietistic-perfectionist cultural core provided the continuity that sustained American culture through its times of transition. This cultural core was flexible in that each awakening redefined the specific meaning of the core beliefs within each new historical and cultural context.

McLoughlin's work met with three challenges. First, some argued that Christianity never suffered cycles of declension and revival, but instead was consistently expanding under divine blessings—perhaps with contraction in one area but with increase elsewhere. Second, there was the nominalist challenge, presented by Jon Butler, that the very idea of a great awakening was an interpretive fiction that homogenized the irreducible variety of American religious life with a facile generalization. Third, Leigh Eric Schmidt proposed abandoning questions of causation in favor of an analysis of the mental world and ritual actions of the participants in revivals. In a 1983 symposium, McLoughlin responded to these challenges. Reaffirming the historian's task of giving naturalistic explanations rather than invoking supernatural causes, McLoughlin argued that the historical record demonstrated a pattern of growth and declension in American revivals rather than an irresistible expansion. Second, he insisted that the historian must seek cohesive order out of the heterogeneity of historical data, and attempt to identify patterns when possible. Finally, he welcomed interdisciplinary investigations of revivals, but he noted that historical investigations that stretched over generations were necessary to make sense of the phenomena of revivalism. In the end, William McLoughlin's work offered a stimulating, multidimensional analysis of revivalism that situated it in the very heart of American religious life and cultural experience.

Further Reading: McLoughlin, William G., ed. *The American Evangelicals*. New York: Harper and Row, 1968; McLoughlin, William G. *Billy Graham, Revivalist in a Secular Age*. New York: Ronald Press, 1960; McLoughlin, William G. *Billy Sunday Was His Real Name*. Chicago: University of Chicago, 1955; McLoughlin, William G., ed. *Charles Grandison Finney: Lectures on Revivals of Religion*. Cambridge, MA: Harvard University Press, 1960; McLoughlin, William G. *Modern Revivalism: Charles Grandison Finney to Billy Graham*. New York: Ronald Press, 1959; McLoughlin, William G. "Pietism and the American Character." *American Quarterly* 17 (1965): 163–86; McLoughlin, William G. "Revivalism." In Edwin Scott Gaustad, ed., *The Rise of Adventism*, 119–53. New York: Harper and Row, 1974; McLoughlin, William G. *Revivals, Awakenings, and Reform*. Chicago: University of Chicago Press, 1978; Schmidt, Leigh Eric. *Holy Fairs*. Princeton, NJ: Princeton University Press, 1989; "Symposium on Religious Awakenings." *Sociological Analysis* 44 (1983): 81–122.

Walter H. Conser Jr.

MCPHERSON, AIMEE SEMPLE (1890–1944)

From small beginnings in Mt. Forest, Ontario, in 1915, Canadian American evangelist Aimee Semple McPherson rose to prominence on the sawdust trail. With sure entrepreneurial instincts and a winning smile, she built a constituency that rivaled that of **Billy Sunday,** her nearest competitor. In the 1920s, as his appeal waned, hers waxed. By the mid-1920s, critics and partisans agreed that she had **preached** to more Americans than had any other living evangelist. Among North American **women,** none had a greater impact as a revivalist than McPherson during her heyday in the 1920s.

McPherson was born Aimee Kennedy on October 12, 1890, in rural southern Ontario. Her father, James Kennedy, farmed a rectangular plot just west of Salford, a village near the larger town of Ingersoll where the railroad connected the region's farmers to the larger world. Her mother, Minnie Kennedy, an avid **Salvation Army** officer, reared their daughter in the colorful, emotion-packed world of early Canadian Salvationists. Evangeline Booth, daughter of the movement's founders, headed the Canadian ranks and marketed a mix of old-fashioned revivalism and social engagement with a creative flair that captured Aimee Kennedy's imagination. In 1907, Aimee Kennedy met Robert Semple, an Irish-born proponent of **Pentecostalism.** The Pentecostal movement had only recently emerged in Canada, where it had indigenous roots but also owed something to the influence of the famous **Azusa Street revival** in Los Angeles. In Pentecostal storefront missions, **speaking in tongues** was common and participants were expected to manifest the **charismatic gifts** as described in the New Testament (1 Corinthians 12–14). Devotees understood tongues-speaking as evidence of the **baptism in the Holy Spirit,** an **eschatological** or end-times enduement with spiritual power. Convinced that they lived in the last days, they coveted life in the Spirit for a dual purpose—to assure their own readiness for divine judgment, and to empower them to convert the world before the imminent end.

Robert Semple worked for the railroad by day and preached and evangelized by night. He came to Ingersoll, Ontario, from nearby Stratford, and Aimee Kennedy found herself attracted to both message and messenger. Early in 1908, she spoke in tongues. In August she married Robert Semple. After a few months in Stratford, the couple moved in 1909 to Chicago to assist William Durham in his Pentecostal mission on the city's north side. Early in February 1910, they embarked for China, sailing via Europe, where they spent several weeks with the Semple family. They arrived in Hong Kong in June, intending to invest their lives in the Christianization of mainland China. Six weeks later, Robert Semple died of dysentery. His pregnant wife lay on a hospital bed struggling for her life. Fellow missionaries accompanied Semple's remains to a humble grave. A few months later, Aimee Semple and her young daughter, Roberta, sailed for home.

In 1912 Semple married fellow minister Harold McPherson. The next year, they had a son, Rolf. But McPherson could not settle into the traditional role of wife and mother. She seemed obsessed by the idea that she had betrayed the calling to preaching and public ministry that she and Robert Semple had discerned as their life vocation. In 1915, after months of agony, she took her children and set out from her Providence, Rhode Island, home for the Kennedy farm in Salford, Ontario. She left the children with her parents and made her way to a

This photograph of Aimee Semple McPherson, wearing an unusual outfit with a cape, shows the theatrical side of the popular evangelist (London, ca. 1920s). Courtesy of the Library of Congress.

Canadian Pentecostal **camp meeting.** There she began again to use her gifts for public ministry. A few weeks later, she preached her first solo revival in a small mission hall in Mt. Forest, Ontario. Harold McPherson joined her and tried for the next three years to accommodate his life to hers.

From the outset, McPherson borrowed heavily from her Salvation Army childhood. If crowds failed to materialize, she calculated how to attract them. Slowly, and with enormous effort, she developed a circuit that took her up and down the East Coast—through the **South** and into Florida during the winter and north through New England in the summer. For a few years, she drove a gospel car—a black automobile plastered with Bible verses and provocative questions. She loaded it with religious literature and stopped along her way to converse with field laborers, housewives, and factory workers. Harold McPherson saw to shipping the tent that accommodated her growing crowds. McPherson preached in simple white dresses that she bought in the servants' section of department stores. She had a flair for public speaking, innate dramatic ability, and the tenacity to keep going despite obstacles. Slowly she built a following and a reputation. By the end of World War I, her meetings in places like Philadelphia and Baltimore attracted press commentary.

In 1918, Harold McPherson decided to go his own way, and McPherson took the children and her mother and headed west. That year she began publishing a monthly magazine, the *Bridal Call*, an organ that conserved and expanded her following. As she drove across the country in her Oldsmobile touring car, she stopped along the way to share literature, preach, and build relationships with ordinary people, black and white. She drove the back streets and discovered places most tourists never saw and most nationally known evangelists never visited. The family camped by the side of the road, worshipped at nondescript missions, and took the pulse of America. In the fall, the McPhersons

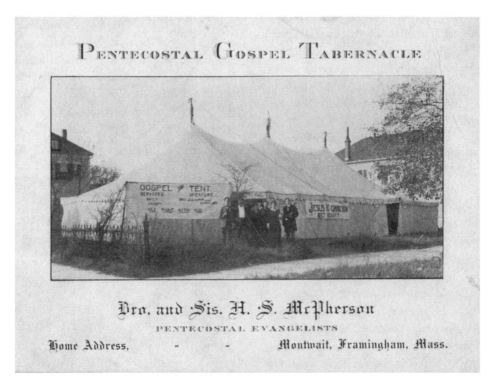

Invitation postcard for a tent crusade conducted by Harold and Aimee Semple McPherson. The slogan on the right reflects the apocalyptic mood of early Pentecostalism: "Jesus is Coming Soon. Get Ready!" (ca. 1916–1921). Courtesy of Dr. Kenneth O. Brown.

settled in Los Angeles. They already knew a handful of people—Pentecostals they had met in Chicago, Hong Kong, Ontario, or on the East Coast. McPherson settled her mother and children into a house provided by supporters and began pursuing preaching opportunities in Los Angeles and beyond.

Her message was simple and reassuring. It featured a homespun version of Bible Christianity, replete with insights into the prophetic significance of current events and assurances of a meaningful personal future even if earthly prospects seemed dim. She emphasized her solidarity with audiences. Like them, she had home responsibilities, children to rear, and bills to pay. She gushed sympathy and reassurance, and pointed to a reality that transcended life's hardships. She urged her audiences to recognize their sinfulness and trust in Christ as Savior. She believed that the Pentecostal movement signaled the return in the end-times of what she called the "full menu" of New Testament Christianity. Hebrews 13:8 became her theme verse: "Jesus Christ, the same, yesterday, today, and forever." Whatever he had once done, he could be trusted to do again now. She **prayed** for the sick, cared for the wayward, and developed a colloquial style that engaged her audiences. McPherson built many of her sermons around dramatic biblical narratives— the stories of Isaac and Rebekah, Ruth, or Joseph.

February 1919 found her in San Francisco, hosted by two intrepid Pentecostal advocates, Robert and Mary Craig. They convinced her to affiliate with the **Assemblies of God,** a relationship that lasted for three years. She conducted most of her meetings in the first half of 1919 under the auspices of Pentecostal congregations, large and small, moving from San Francisco to Tulsa to Chicago to Manhattan. In August she drove back to California for a camp meeting in the Los Angeles area. That fall, she branched out, holding meetings in the armory in Akron, Ohio, and the Lyric—Baltimore's finest theater. In Baltimore, McPherson moved decisively beyond the Pentecostal constituency that had nurtured her early efforts. She began presenting her message as generic "Bible Christianity" and favored the ordinary idiom of American Protestant

revivalism instead of fiery Pentecostal admonitions to "baptism with the Holy Ghost and fire" (Matthew 3:11). Her decision to distance herself from Pentecostals came as a considered response to the boisterous conduct of Pentecostals who attended her Baltimore meetings. She resisted noisy disorder and immediately gained support from local pastors and their congregations. She began 1920 with another series of meetings in Baltimore and then moved on to Washington, DC. This time her crowds gathered in a **United Brethren** Church and a **Methodist** Episcopal Church. From there, she went to Winnipeg for a series of meetings. In Winnipeg she initiated what became her custom of visiting the red light district and local dance clubs to bring the gospel to people where they were. In response, thousands crowded her meetings. A few weeks later, she returned to the East Coast for a series of meetings at McKendree Methodist Episcopal Church in the nation's capital.

In most places she went, responses exceeded expectations, and newspapers reported meetings "so tremendous that anything like a comprehensive record is impossible to ascertain" (Blumhofer, 153). By the end of 1920, she had developed a core of about 60 sermons, some of which she delivered with charts and illustrations. These were her stock-in-trade. She had also begun what became the most popular of all her presentations—a rendering of her own life. She recited it over and over, soon adding a farm-girl costume, until it became a means to understand the world, the church, and the supernatural. After spending the 1921 holiday season in California with her children, she set out in January 1921 for the first of a remarkable series of revival campaigns that filled the year. From early 1921, she elicited nearly reverential public response that both stimulated and mirrored her emergence as a star on the revival circuit. Wherever she went, reports were similar: "Never have such scenes been witnessed here" (Blumhofer, 156).

McPherson, by now known widely as "Sister," had secured San Diego's Dreamland Arena for her meetings. She arrived a day early, discovered that a boxing match had sold out the arena, and convinced the manager to introduce her to the crowd between rounds. She promised that the next night she would "go into the ring for Jesus" (Blumhofer, 158), and people promised to be there. For the next few weeks, she explained "the simple story of Jesus' love, and the outpoured Holy Spirit who has come to convict us of sin and draw us to the cross of Calvary, where, as we confess our sin, Jesus … cleanseth us from all unrighteousness" (Blumhofer, 159–60). Every room in the arena—including a walk-in refrigerator accommodating 20—was filled. Nearby churches hosted overflow crowds. Two weeks stretched to five, and still McPherson could not meet demands. Ministers of most Protestant denominations cooperated with her. In February, McPherson yielded to her mother's suggestion that she attempt an outdoor meeting featuring prayer for the **healing** of the sick. The Salvation Army band tuned up, San Diego police augmented by U.S. Marine and Army personnel took the crowds in hand, and a combined choir from local churches opened with "All Hail the Power of Jesus' Name." Police estimated that fully 30,000 people crammed into Balboa Park for the event. The sick streamed forward for hours, seeking Sister's prayers.

Her next triumph came in San Jose, California. She arrived as the guest of William Keeney Towner, pastor of the city's First **Baptist** Church. She preached morning and evening and her crowds confirmed the citywide interest in the meetings. The town ministerial association invited her back for a crusade in August. Meetings in St. Louis, Missouri, and Dallas, Texas, followed. Conservative estimates put her Dallas crowds at over 100,000. In June she arrived in Denver, Colorado, for a crusade that became a defining moment in her career. Hosted by Arthur C. Peck, a Methodist pastor, educator, and evangelist, she held weeks of meetings in the Denver Coliseum. The *Post* assigned a reporter to cover her visit, and the ill flocked in for prayers. The mayor welcomed her as "a wonderful woman doing good and great things" (Blumhofer, 172). Her audiences contributed $18,000 toward the church Sister planned to build in Los Angeles, provided $3,500 to cover expenses, and sent her on her way with a $3,600 love offering.

Her promised return to San Jose followed. By that August, crowds of the sick routinely arrived at her services. She resisted a focus on healing and insisted that her meetings were 99 percent salvation and 1 percent healing. Yet neither the press nor invalids believed her. In the next few weeks, she personally laid her hands on some 4,000 sick people and prayed for their healing. Meanwhile, over 7,000 professed conversion, and supporting congregations professed renewed fervor among their members.

The fall found McPherson in Canton, Ohio, and Rochester, New York. After a few weeks of recuperation over the holidays, Sister started off again in January 1922. During the summer, she held a two-week revival in Oakland during which she had a flash of inspiration that gave her message sharper focus and unity. From that summer on, she called her message the Foursquare Gospel, anchoring her message in four statements about Jesus: He was Savior, Baptizer, Healer, and Coming King. From Oakland, Sister sailed for Australia, where she found crowds eager for her "old message of the infinite love of Jesus Christ … with the old-time fervour and in the old-time way" (Blumhofer, 199).

She returned just in time for the flurry of activities that marked the fulfillment of one of her dreams—the dedication of her new Los Angeles church. It stood across the street from Echo Park, at the intersection of Sunset and Glendale Boulevards. The day began with a floral representation of this Angelus Temple that Sister entered in the Tournament of Roses. A musician sat inside, playing gospel songs on a pump organ, and 15 girls rode among the flowers singing. The float took a divisional prize. In the afternoon, attention shifted to the temple itself. Thousands filled surrounding sidewalks, streets, and the park, and ministers from many denominations joined Sister to mark the occasion. Angelus temple was intended as the hub of an evangelistic association. Sister was evangelist-in-residence. She did not give up traveling entirely, but she now poured most of her energies into Angelus Temple. It quickly became a tourist attraction. She soon expanded her physical plant to include a Bible school, LIFE (Lighthouse of

Foursquare Evangelism); a radio station; and a 24-hour prayer tower. Meanwhile, Sister's illustrated sermons gained fame as the best shows in show-crazed Los Angeles.

In the midst of this momentum, Sister's marriage to Harold McPherson ended quietly in divorce. Then in 1926, when Sister seemed unstoppable, she disappeared under mysterious circumstances from a beach in Santa Monica. Several people drowned searching for her body, and distraught thousands lined the coast to pray and peer into the ocean. An emotion-fraught memorial service at Angelus Temple attempted to bring closure. Six weeks after she had disappeared, she turned up in southern Arizona with a confused story of kidnapping and escape. On her return to Los Angeles, tens of thousands lined the streets to welcome her home. The police proved skeptical about the details of her kidnapping, and for the next six months, they conducted investigations and attempted to bring charges against the evangelist. She used her radio station to great effect, keeping her public on her side. By the end of 1926, charges were dropped, and the public spectacle finally ended. But the notoriety it had brought refused to go away.

McPherson resumed her schedule, but some now questioned her integrity. In 1929, she broke publicly and bitterly with her mother. Minnie Kennedy had managed her daughter's rise to fame, controlled the purse strings, and minded the children. The break was public and lasting. In the 1930s, she quarreled with her daughter, Roberta Semple. Roberta moved out to live with her grandmother and later chose to live out her life in New York as the wife of Jewish immigrant radio orchestra conductor Harry Salter, originator of "Name That Tune."

In 1933, ill and lonely, McPherson married David Hutton, a singer 11 years her junior. Her audience—diminished since the kidnapping, when some denominational pastors had quietly begun withdrawing support—now shrank again. Some had supported her despite her first divorce, but divorce and remarriage proved another matter. Before long, McPherson had second thoughts on the matter, too. She divorced Hutton and declared that remarriage after divorce was wrong. During the 1930s, she positioned herself more self-consciously as a Pentecostal evangelist. After the late 1920s, her followers, too, came largely from among those who self-identified with the Pentecostal movement.

During the 1930s, McPherson oversaw a widely acclaimed feeding program. Known as the Angelus Temple Commissary, it provided daily, no questions asked, for hundreds of victims of the depression. McPherson's health remained precarious, and she sought relief in foreign travel. In the fall of 1944, she planned to resume a more active itinerant evangelistic schedule. She began in Oakland, a place associated with her early successes. On September 26, a capacity crowd heard her opening sermon at the Oakland Auditorium. The next morning her son and associate, Rolf McPherson, found her unconscious in her bedroom. Two hours later McPherson died, having accidentally taken a lethal combination of prescription drugs. Her funeral took place on her 54th birthday, October 9, 1944, at Angelus Temple. During the two days before, some 50,000 people had filed past her coffin. Thousands followed the 600-car motorcade to her "private" committal service at Forest Lawn Memorial Garden in Glendale. She left behind a small but growing Pentecostal denomination, the **International Church of the Foursquare Gospel.** But that immediate legacy did not represent her broader participation in American Christianity. Her revival crusades had tapped into the persistent Protestant yearning for "old-time religion" by dressing it up in the most modern media available. Entrepreneurial and pragmatic to the core, McPherson gave big-time revivalism a woman's face.

Further Reading: Blumhofer, Edith L. *Aimee Semple McPherson: Everybody's Sister.* Grand Rapids, MI: Eerdmans, 1993; Epstein, Daniel Mark. *Sister Aimee: The Life of Aimee Semple McPherson.* New York: Harcourt, 1993; McPherson, Aimee Semple. *This Is That: Personal Experiences, Sermons and Writings of Aimee Semple McPherson, Evangelist.* Los Angeles: Bridal Call, 1921.

Edith Blumhofer

MEGACHURCH

Megachurch is a descriptive sociological term that today is commonly used to classify Christian churches with more than 2,000 in worship attendance. Though large churches have existed throughout Christian history, the sheer number of them in North America has dramatically increased since 1970, when there were only 10 megachurches. It is this recent development that has prompted religious analysts to coin the term *megachurch*. Though the megachurch is a local congregation, it can also be understood as an expansive structural and spiritual organization that acts as a collective social phenomenon.

Most research on megachurches considers only Protestant congregations, and the focus in this essay will be on non–**Roman Catholic** congregations. The majority of such megachurches in the United States are in southern Sunbelt states, with California, Texas, Georgia, and Florida having the highest concentrations. Virtually all are evangelical and conservative in theology. Furthermore, there are numerous megachurches in Korea, Brazil, and several African countries, though no actual count exists. In 2005, the largest church congregation in North America was Lakewood Church in Houston, Texas—under the leadership of Joel Osteen—averaging more than 30,000 per week in attendance. At least 10 megachurches in the United States currently have more than 15,000 weekly worshippers. Several megachurches in Korea claim as many as 250,000.

Recent research suggests that there are over 1,200 megachurches in the United States, with new congregations added to the list every week. (If Roman Catholic congregations were included, then the number in the United States could be as high as 2,500.) These 1,200 megachurches account for only 0.3 percent of all congregations in the United States, but include 4 million members, and possibly as many as 8–12 million attendees, prompting one researcher to suggest that the largest 10 percent of congregations in the United States now account for

Interior of Willow Creek Community Church (South Barrington, IL), which during the 1990s averaged more than 15,000 worshipers at its multiple services each week. Photograph by and courtesy of Paul R. Kilde.

half of all churchgoers. Currently there are no signs that this phenomenon is slowing down. Alan Wolfe observes that the dominant message within megachurches "tends to be more upbeat [than other churches], one of empowerment" (Axtman, 1). Many megachurches in their **preaching** and teaching offer some version of "positive thinking" or so-called **prosperity theology.**

The megachurch phenomenon is linked to the **Church Growth movement,** which has used social science to analyze systematically how churches grow numerically. American evangelicals embraced these principles intentionally to build large congregations on the principle of homogeneity—that is, the idea that growth will be greatest if one gathers people who are alike, or share in an affinity group of some kind. Research indicates that megachurches are generally located in suburban communities near large cities, and tend to attract highly mobile and well-educated middle-class families as members. Both evangelical and mainline Protestant denominations have featured megachurches as success stories to be emulated by pastors and church leaders. Yet critics have offered any number of arguments against megachurches: they have made largeness an end in itself that takes priority over other concerns; they focus on success, pleasure, and self-esteem rather than service, repentance, and self-denial; they are consumer oriented and market driven and so function as "McChurches"; they make worship services a happy time with no discordant notes of pain and loss; and they are usually built around an individual leader with singular gifts and charisma, and so function as a kind of personality cult.

Because of their large budgets, megachurches have the personnel and resources to function as full-service organizations and meet a wide range of human needs. For this reason they are increasingly replacing the older, denominational model of church and church mission. A new kind of denomination seems to be rising out of the megachurch movement, just as revivals in the past led to new church structures and patterns. One of the strongest features of the contemporary megachurch is its orientation toward Christian outreach to unchurched people. It has also provided a means

whereby a church congregation can conspicuously benefit a metropolitan community through numerous programs that offer spiritual, social, emotional, and financial support.

Further Reading: Axtman, Kris. "The Rise of the American Megachurch." *Christian Science Monitor,* December 30, 2003, 1; Gilbreath, Edward. "The Birth of a Megachurch." *Christianity Today,* July 18, 1994, 23; Hartford Institute for Religion Research Web site (with research and papers). http://www.hartsem.edu/; Miller, Donald E. *Reinventing Protestantism: Christianity in the New Millennium.* Berkley: University of California Press, 1997; Roof, Wade Clark. *A Generation of Seekers: The Spiritual Journeys of the Baby Boom Generation.* San Francisco: Harper, 1993; Thumma, Scott L. "The Kingdom, the Power, and the Glory: The Megachurch in Modern American Society." PhD dissertation, Emory University, 1996; Vaughan, John N. *Megachurches and America's Cities: How Churches Grow.* Grand Rapids, MI: Baker, 1993.

John Armstrong

MEN AND MASCULINITY IN REVIVALS

Revivals of religion within American Christianity historically have taken a variety of forms, and the roles played by men in revivals have been correspondingly diverse. Men have served as leaders of revivals and other public performances of religious piety more often than **women,** especially before the twentieth century, and they have generally discouraged women from assuming similar roles. The revivalist **Dwight L. Moody** in the 1870s fired Emma Willard from his revival tour just as her reputation was growing. Some revivalists, however, such as **Charles Grandison Finney** in the 1820s and 1830s, cut against the grain by encouraging women to take more visible public roles in revival. A few charismatic women, such as **Phoebe Palmer** and **Aimee Semple McPherson,** made inroads into male control of revival through theological innovation, emphasizing holiness or **sanctification, healing,** the **baptism in the Holy Spirit,** or other ideas.

Men **preached** religious revival and managed revivals through appeal to their formal training as ministers and to institutional protocol, through display of masculine personality traits, and by virtue of cultural patriarchy. Male charisma was an essential component of revival, although the nature of that charisma varied from place to place and over time. **George Whitefield,** the dramatically inclined Englishman whose itinerancy was at the popular center of the **Great Awakening,** modeled a style of preaching characterized by masculine boldness laced with feminine sensitivity. **Jonathan Edwards** at that same time succeeded in **Northampton** by exercising a charisma based on his forceful use of language and his logical argumentation—a feature of male revival style that has endured in some quarters from the eighteenth century up to the present. **Peter Cartwright** and **Lorenzo Dow,** known for their antebellum preaching to rural populations, were less formal and more audacious than either Whitefield or Edwards, while later revivalists such as Moody attracted auditors with a folksy, anecdotal, somewhat feminized style. In the twentieth century, nationally recognized male revivalists have been characterized by performances of weeping (**Jim Bakker, Jimmy Swaggart**), fiery provocation (**Billy Graham, Jerry Falwell**), and the blending of businesslike demeanor with professed tenderness and warmth (**Pat Robertson**).

Though there are exceptions to the rule—as noted below—women generally participate in religious services more often than men. In most periods of the national history, approximately two-thirds of attendees in religious services have been female. Religious revivals have unfolded for the most part in keeping with that pattern. Male reticence to join religious revivals follows from an assortment of cultural frameworks, not the least of which is the male suspicion that revivalist religion involves the renunciation of manliness. That concern has marked male religious life, especially in the **South,** since the mid-eighteenth century, when joining the "evangelical revolt" often meant risking one's hold on power in a male society grounded in the display of prowess in fighting (or dueling), gambling, drinking, and dancing. The path of personal reform that followed from **conversion** obliged males to behave less contentiously. Yet many males shrank from the prospect of public emotional expression, and particularly emotional rituals involving tears and moaning that in other public contexts denoted humiliation. Consequently, in cases where men have been unusually involved in revival movements—as in the Businessman's **Revival of 1857–1858,** the Men and Religion Forward movement of the early twentieth century, and movements such as **Promise Keepers** in the 1990s—these anxieties have been attenuated by various means. In the hugely popular nationwide revival of 1858, named after the businessmen who gathered for noon-hour **prayer** meetings before returning to their office desks, the religious proceedings in churches, chapels, and public halls were characterized by a blending of point-blank requests, offered to God in prayer, with a more limited display of emotion than revival ordinarily included. Male identity, and especially its correlation to enactments of ambition, pluck, and bold action, was satisfied through the conceptualization of revival as a series of formal occasions for aggressively pressing one's case to God for favor of some sort—whether that be a better job, a higher woodpile, or peace of mind. The rules governing the noon-hour meetings—which often included a limit of three minutes on prayer requests and one hour on the meeting itself—likewise lent a tone of masculinized, businesslike operation to the revival. At the same time, weeping was accepted as useful practice of piety, though it, too, was confined to dignified forms. The large number of male clerks, trading-house and bank employees, and retail workers who participated in the Businessman's Revival made it as much a men's event as a women's event. To a certain extent the revivals preached by Dwight L. Moody after the **Civil War** embodied some of the spirit of the 1858 revival, sometimes attracting men as a majority in the audience.

The Men and Religion Forward movement exemplified another style of revival and another way in which men participated in revival. In 1911–1912 an interdenominational initiative to bring 3 million men into the Protestant churches produced revivals in over a thousand towns. The revival took shape as an evangelical project to cultivate the spiritual renewal of men and boys through their acceptance of Jesus Christ as their personal savior, and as a program to promote religion as a practical means to worthwhile ends, such as business success, improved personal relations, and patriotic involvement. Undertaken specifically in response to the perception that men's participation in religious life was declining, the movement stressed the strength, practicality, and efficiency of male leadership in everyday life. It encouraged its participants to cultivate traits from an imagined nineteenth-century masculinity: logical thought, controlled demeanor, savvy, inventiveness, and results-producing work in the world. Accordingly, the movement deemphasized emotional expression and emotional sensitivity.

Though men have participated in popular revivals, such as those associated with **Billy Sunday** and Billy Graham, female participants have generally outnumbered males. In certain cases, however, men were present as a majority when revivalists targeted them directly. Dwight L. Moody's affiliation with the **Young Men's Christian Association** (YMCA) provided him virtually limitless opportunity to address the young men who had left their rural upbringings for city life, and by his own account, he was successful in evangelizing a great many of them. Men formed an audience for revivalists who ministered to the military services, and preachers made especially impressive progress in wartime. During the Civil War, there were widespread revivals in both the Union and Confederate armies.

Historically there has been one setting in which men have with some consistency turned out for revivals, and that is on **college** campuses. Protestant Christianity on nineteenth-century college campuses—at a time when almost all college students were male, excepting the women's colleges—made itself most visible in the revivals that periodically took place there. In the nineteenth century, campus revivals occurred with cyclical regularity, region by region, leading to hundreds of conversions in, for example, the Connecticut River valley and the Shenandoah region. These collegiate "seasons of refreshment" have continued into the twentieth century and beyond, attracting females as well as males since coeducation became the norm in higher education. Still, they have often been mounted with an eye to reaching men. Revival-minded groups such as the Fellowship of Christian Athletes, **Inter-Varsity Christian Fellowship, Campus Crusade for Christ,** and **Navigators** initially took shape on campuses as largely male organizations inflected with a Billy Sunday–like "muscular Christianity," and they continue to supply men and boys for revivals on campuses, alongside, in more recent years, female participants.

The Promise Keepers movement, founded in 1990, offered a model of manliness that synthesized both traditionally masculine and traditionally feminine elements. Imbued with the spirit of manly struggle enacted on the athletic field, the movement was organized by a former football coach, held gatherings in football stadiums, and featured athletes as guest speakers. Yet the Promise Keepers also presented feminized virtue as an ideal, and fostered an atmosphere in which men cried and held each other, publicly owned up about their shortcomings, and promised to serve their families and friends more generously and compassionately. Their large public gatherings—which initially were exclusively male—represent a style of revival that differs from the church or **camp and tent meetings** in highlighting social obligation rather than internal and individual transformation.

Further Reading: Bederman, Gail. "'The Women Have Had Charge of the Church Work Long Enough': The Men and Religion Forward Movement of 1911–1912 and the Masculinization of Middle-Class Protestantism." *American Quarterly* 41 (1989): 432–65; Bendroth, Margaret. "Why Women Loved Billy Sunday: Urban Revivalism and Popular Entertainment in Early Twentieth-Century American Culture." *Religion and American Culture* 14 (2004): 251–71; Corrigan, John. *Business of the Heart: Religion and Emotion in the Nineteenth Century.* Berkeley: University of California Press, 2002; Lindman, Janet Moore. "Acting the Manly Christian: White Evangelical Masculinity in Revolutionary Virginia." *William and Mary Quarterly* 57 (2000): 393–416; Lippy, Charles H. "Miles to Go: Promise Keepers in Historical and Cultural

Context." *Soundings: An Interdisciplinary Journal* 80 (1997): 289–304.

John Corrigan

METHODIST REVIVALS

Methodism emerged in the American colonies as a revivalistic movement, heir to the evangelistic, field-**preaching** style of the Anglicans **George Whitefield** and John Wesley. By 1784, when with John Wesley's blessing the Methodists acquired status as a separate church, the Methodist Episcopal Church was revivalistic in its *constitution, program, structure, style, theology,* and *rhetoric*. Moreover, its history and development contributed to the evolution of revivalism, at least through the nineteenth century.

Early American Methodists would have recognized instinctively that their movement was revivalistic in its *constitution*—though they might not have articulated this insight in terms of political theory. Most could or would have explained Methodism's revivalistic character by pointing to elements in their own personal experience—to the revival season or event in which their own **conversion** occurred, to the invitational doctrine they heard, to the evangelistic effectiveness of itinerant preaching, to the importance of exhorters as well as preachers and presiding elders, and to the evangelistic style and substance of their movement as a whole. The people called Methodists knew revival to be their business.

The Methodist Church's *Discipline*—its quasi *constitution*—was published in 1787 in a form "Arranged under proper HEADS, and METHODIZED in a more acceptable and easy MANNER." Before this statement said anything about the Bible, the sacraments, authority, or church government and polity, it addressed the topic of revival. Following Wesley's question-and-answer style, the church asked in its third query, "What may we reasonably believe to be God's design in raising up the Preachers called Methodists?" The answer to this question is still cited as a central definition of Methodist purpose. God's design, in the words of the *Discipline*, was "to reform the Continent, and spread scripture Holiness over these Lands. As a Proof hereof, we have seen in the Course of fifteen Years a great and glorious Work

of God, from New York through the Jersies, Pennsylvania, Delaware, Maryland, Virginia, North and South Carolina, even to Georgia." Thus the *Discipline* gathered the entire Methodist movement into divine providence and construed history in revivalistic, redemptive terms.

The *Discipline* laid out a revivalistic program for the new church as an organization and in its *program* at all levels. Indeed, the early versions of the *Discipline* were in effect a set of revival rules and regulations—a revival manual for an entire denomination. They included a sharp directive to preachers: "You have nothing to do but to save Souls.... Observe. It is not your Business to preach so many Times, and to take care of this or that Society. But to save as many souls as you can; to bring as many Sinners as you possibly can to Repentance, and with all your power to build them up in that holiness, without which they cannot see the Lord." Reinforcing this exhortation, the *Discipline* demanded results. To encourage preachers to pursue the business of saving souls, they were required each year to answer the question: "What numbers are there in the Society?" That numerical tally, along with various other statistics, was published in *The Minutes of the Methodist Conferences*. This regular auditing process let the whole church and the wider public know whether individual circuits and the entire movement were experiencing growth or decline.

Methodists expressed a revivalistic program in their preaching styles, **Pietist** or small-group practices, a moral code that marked out a way of salvation, and preeminently in their *structure*. American Methodists gradually transformed the British system of conference governance, centering on John Wesley himself, into an open, expansive system of church organization that welcomed new initiatives. Two key elements in this system were the appointments of preachers and the periodic ministerial gatherings or conferences. In one sense, appointments involved a centralized or monarchical style and to that extent might seem to have been unconducive to revivals or revivalism. Bishops appointed preachers to circuits and exercised authority over the entire system. Yet the bishops' authority generally enabled rather than frustrated evangelistic initiative. Circuits,

HARPER'S WEEKLY.
JOURNAL OF CIVILIZATION
Vol. XI.—No. 563.]   NEW YORK, SATURDAY, OCTOBER 12, 1867.   [PRICE TEN CENTS.

Methodist circuit rider traveling on horseback in a rainstorm. By the 1860s, the rugged, itinerant Methodist preacher was already becoming an iconic, larger-than-life figure. (Wood engraving Alfred Rudolph Waud, artist; *Harper's Weekly*, October 12, 1867, p. 641.) Courtesy of the Library of Congress.

Yet Methodism had an inward as well as an outward thrust. It combined aggressive, expansive energy with a social system that gathered in and gathered together. Methodists gathered "those fleeing the wrath to come" (i.e., its adherents) into classes weekly, for circuit preaching on a regular rhythm (at two-, four-, or six-week intervals), in meetings of the entire circuits quarterly, in conferences annually, and, after 1792, in general conferences quadrennially (i.e., every four years). All of these gatherings—including the annual and quadrennial meetings—had revivalistic potential, if for no other reason than that they brought together people who heard one soul-stirring sermon after another.

American Methodists, from 1780 onward, prescribed the quarterly meeting or quarterly conference as a two-day event, preferably held on a Saturday and Sunday. Almost immediately the quarterly meetings began to attract crowds. Some quarterly meetings on the Delmarva Peninsula brought together more than 10,000 persons at one time and so provided one essential of a revival—people to be revived. The presiding elder of the circuit, the two traveling preachers, all local preachers, exhorters, class leaders, and stewards gathered on Saturday to take care of circuit business. On Sunday during the quarterly meeting, "love feasts" (featuring testimonies, **hymn** singing, and a simple meal), the Lord's Supper, and multiple sermons engaged both the Methodist faithful and onlookers in a kind of evangelistic festival. Not every quarterly meeting produced revival but Methodists **prayed** for and expected just that. Faithful Methodists all contributed toward creating a climate and support system for revivals. One element of the preparation for revival was prayer on behalf of the unconverted in one's home or network. **Women,** who were predominant in early Methodism, as in most evangelical movements, played a special role in prayer. Though they could not be ordained, women were instrumental in generating revivalistic expectations for the quarterly meetings and for Methodist life generally. When revivals did occur, they typically emerged out of quarterly conferences. And when Methodists embraced **camp meetings,** they

particularly in frontier regions, incorporated territories that could be nearly as large as the later states. Once preachers were sent to a particular circuit, they made their own decisions regarding "preaching points" or locations for ministry. They were able to add new preaching points, or, occasionally, to subtract, as the ingathering of souls or the migration of people might dictate. Evangelistic expansion in terms of new members and new terrain resulted from the Methodist preachers' effectiveness in promoting conversion, their initiative in preaching in new locations, and their success in forming classes—the smallest membership unit. This system was well adapted to shifting populations and settlements. At the next conference, the bishop could divide an existing circuit and send out more laborers into the harvest.

combined them with their quarterly meetings. This allowed Methodists, as Bishop **Francis Asbury** (1745–1816) observed, to fish with a large net. This made the camp meeting a part of the Methodist machinery and helped to insure that Methodism would remain revivalistic.

Camp meetings became a Methodist signature or *style* through much of the nineteenth century but were never formally scripted in or prescribed by the *Discipline*, a point to which we will return below. Camp meetings proved, as Asbury proclaimed, an effective device for promoting revivals. Though non-Methodists held camp meetings, they were especially associated with Methodism. Indeed, they emerged out of efforts on the part of various denominations to assemble their dispersed adherents (or potential adherents) for essential religious services such as baptism, instruction, preaching, and the Lord's Supper. Public outdoor gatherings had been a staple of community life in the Chesapeake and upper **South**, where Methodism first prospered in the late 1700s. The quarterly meeting adopted this southern or Chesapeake custom. Under Asbury's guidance, Methodists transformed this Chesapeake custom into a national practice. The camp meeting erected a city in the wilderness whose spatial layout, order, and rules were all oriented toward conversion and revival. The chaos and disruption that came from assembling a mixed multitude were a part of the plan. The goal was to transform wilderness, disorder, mischief, and sin into Christian civility, order, morality, and piety. Camp meetings adapted Methodist structures to serve the aims of revivalism.

Itinerant ministry was another feature of Methodism's revivalistic ethos. *Traveling preacher* was both the popular Methodist designation for a minister and the official terminology used in the *Discipline*. All those under appointment—bishop, presiding elder, elders, deacons—were required to travel. The bishop's duties included traveling "through the connection at large." The first duty of the presiding elder was to "travel through his appointed district." The two lower orders carried the imperative in their name—*traveling elders* and *traveling deacons*. They traveled to preach, with the

bishops setting a pace and pattern. Asbury ruefully noted in his journal as "dumb" days when there had been no occasion for him to preach, and he seemed to regard such occasions as though they were mortal sins. As a traveling preacher, the Methodist minister had to come supplied with two gifts for ministry—strong lungs and a horse. He would find accommodations along his circuit, which was laid out in two, four, or six weeks' circumference. He needed only a saddlebag to hold his evangelistic tools—the Bible, *Discipline*, and *Hymnbook*. Thus equipped and deployed, he undertook revival as his calling. Moving almost constantly to preach, and specifically to preach for conversion, the itinerant took revival to be his business. Much of what traditionally had been the work of the parish priest fell to those Methodist leaders who did not itinerate, or only traveled locally—that is, the local preachers, exhorters, and class leaders. Their nurturing work was vital in preparing for and consolidating the effects of itinerant preaching. Yet their localized labors were not adequately documented. What we know instead is the image of the traveling Methodist circuit rider who became and remains to this day a Methodist icon.

Methodism was revivalistic because Wesley had animated it with an evangelistic gospel. Known officially as Arminian, this *theology* ultimately spread beyond the boundaries of Methodism and became a kind of American standard. How much it owed specifically to Wesley and the Methodists and how much it derived from the democratic-republican ethos of the new nation is difficult to determine. Unlike the **Calvinistic** revivalists of the **Great Awakening,** who respected the decrees of the Synod of Dort, presumed that God revived only the elect, and tended to discern election as respecting ethnic and confessional lines, Methodists preached "y'all come." Their preaching was an invitation, and they offered it to **African Americans,** to New Englanders, to Germans—indeed, to the multiethnic and polyglot peoples that would become the United States. In taking on the name Arminian—Wesley entitled his mouthpiece the *Arminian Magazine*—Wesley embraced the theological alternative to Calvinism associated with Jacobus Arminius (1560–1609) and repudiated what he took to be Calvinism's unevangelistic, fatalistic doctrines. Wesley was clear that, when conversions occurred, God was the primary actor and agent, and yet he was equally clear that human beings had the ability to respond to the divine initiative. American Methodists became, if anything, more vocal than their British counterparts in favoring a theology that preached welcome, demanded repentance, and respected individual decision and responsibility. They taught the Wesleyan doctrines of an atonement universal in its scope, of forgiveness of sin offered therefore to all, of all peoples as children of God, of the freedom of all to accept God's saving initiative, and of the human responsibility to grow into Christ's likeness or "perfection." The Methodists' deliberate, concerted efforts to evangelize Africans, both slave and free, and the early commitment to abolitionism, attest to the Methodists' radical, egalitarian gospel.

Methodism was revivalistic in its *rhetoric* as well as its structures, program, style, and practices. Preachers eagerly monitored their circuit for signs of revival, reported them in their journal, and reported such occurrences at conference meetings. Revivals attested to the effectiveness of their ministry. The *Minutes,* and later the *Christian Advocates* and early Methodist histories, were efforts to take the church's spiritual temperature. An early and eloquent expression of such diagnosis is the first history of the denomination, **Jesse Lee**'s *A Short History of the Methodists* (1810). As the primary Methodist evangelist to New England, Lee tells the story of Methodism from first to last as a series of revivals. Beginning his narrative with the revivals under **Devereux Jarratt** and Robert Williams, moving on to later awakenings, and highlighting those he had witnessed or led, Lee covers the essentials of Methodist organizational development. He construes Methodism as a whole as a series of revivals. Appropriately enough, Lee concludes his narrative by describing camp meetings, while noting that the Methodist Church had never formally authorized them or incorporated them into the conference system.

The evolution of the Methodist camp meeting tells much about the changes that occurred during the 1800s. After the **Civil War,** the camp meeting figured in one of Methodism's schisms. By then, urban and urbane parts of Methodism had gravitated toward more formal patterns of life and worship, symbolized by elegant Main Street churches led by stationed or nontraveling preachers, and sometimes financed by pew rents (i.e., money given in exchange for reserved seats during Sunday services). Other Methodists held that these new practices compromised Methodism's vital piety, its evangelistic style, and its core teaching on sanctification or perfection. They rallied in Camp Meetings for the Promotion of **Holiness.** Holiness advocates employed various means but their commitment to camp meeting revivalism most fittingly symbolized their endeavor to recover primitive Methodism. This desire to return to the ethos of early Methodism animated such Holiness denominations as the **Free Methodist Church,** the **Church of the Nazarene,** and the Wesleyan Church. The resulting schisms showed that the Methodist mainstream had moderated its revivalistic style. Though conversion still played a role, Methodists had replaced earlier revivalism with a more multivalent style of ministry.

The change had been gradual. The revivalistic circuit rider, preaching once every fortnight in a frontier locale, had, as it were, gradually dismounted to become the settled community's Methodist pastor preaching to the same congregation all the time. Congregations internalized the quarterly conference as a business meeting. The community's relation to the camp meeting shifted and would continue to shift. Members had once convened every summer in a different place as the circuit's camp meeting locale moved around. In the decades leading up to the Civil War, church members on the circuit purchased property that would be dedicated and consecrated as a permanent camp meeting site. Families staked out their place and erected a crude wooden "tent." After the Civil War, the summer camp became a ritual for families who made the occasion into a family reunion and a time of vacation. Their tents became more ornately

Victorian and more livable, their stays lengthened beyond the duration of the camp meetings, and scenic sites drew many campers. They rode to camp by train. They knew by the published advertisements whom to expect as preachers for the occasion.

By the end of the nineteenth century, **Chautauqua** in upstate New York offered Sunday school training and emerged as a kind of upscale sequel to the primitive camp meeting. In time Chautauqua became a full-scale cultural festival involving lectures, theater, musical performances, and a range of outdoor activities. Local gatherings in various parts of the United States modeled themselves after the New York Chautauqua. Mainstream Methodists by this point had recognized that personal transformation and cultural enrichment went together. The Sunday school supplanted the sawdust trail. Though primitive camp meetings continued, both within and without the Methodist Episcopal Church, much of Methodism expected revivalism to be a part, rather than the entirety, of the Christian life. Churches nodded to the camp meeting in their annual revival, with homecoming and dinner on the grounds. They might invite an evangelistic preacher and sing the usual repertoire of revival tunes. Such camp meeting residuals continued well into the twentieth century. Members grew up treasuring the memories of their youth assemblies or weeks at Junaluska or Seashore. Revival surrogates appeared, the greatest of which was the **temperance** crusade and temperance pledge. Revivals lived on in other denominational crusades as well. National or regional assemblies have often felt like camp meetings. On **campuses,** revivals took the form of the religious-emphasis week. On a congregational level, Methodists geared up for the annual financial pledge or membership drives. Their pursued their efforts to help the homeless with the gusto and enthusiastic resolve once reserved for revivals. Methodism's revivalistic theology and style remain stronger, to be sure, in its evangelical wing than in the center or on its progressive side. Today much of the Methodist denomination embodies the moderation of Anglicanism, rather than the fervor of revivalism—two aspects of the legacy of its founder, John Wesley.

Further Reading: Andrews, Dee E. *Religion and the Revolution: The Rise of the Methodists in the Greater Middle Atlantic, 1760–1800.* Princeton, NJ: Princeton University Press, 1999; Hatch, Nathan O. *The Democratization of American Christianity.* New Haven, CT, and London: Yale University Press, 1989; Heyrman, Christine Leigh. *Southern Cross: The Beginnings of the Bible Belt.* New York: Knopf, 1997; Lyerly, Cynthia Lynn. *Methodism and the Southern Mind, 1770–1810.* New York and Oxford: Oxford University Press, 1998; Richey, Russell E. *Early American Methodism.* Bloomington and Indianapolis: Indiana University Press, 1991; Wigger, John H. *Taking Heaven by Storm: Methodism and the Rise of Popular Christianity in America.* New York and Oxford: Oxford University Press, 1998.

Russell E. Richey

MILLENNIALISM AND MILLENNIUM

see Eschatology and Revivals; Jehovah's Witnesses; Miller, William; Seventh-day Adventists; White, Ellen Gould (Harmon)

MILLER, WILLIAM (1782–1849)

William Miller was an American **Baptist** layman whose prediction that the Second Coming of Jesus would occur about 1843–1844 gathered a large following in the early 1840s. Born in Pittsfield, Massachusetts, Miller grew up in Low Hampton, New York. After marrying Lucy Smith in 1803, he moved to Poultney, Vermont, and by 1806 had abandoned Baptist Christianity in favor of Deism. Having held several local offices, including sheriff, constable, and justice of the peace, in 1810 Miller organized a unit of the Vermont Militia, which elected him a lieutenant and two years later became part of the regular army. By 1815 Miller had risen to the rank of captain. After the War of 1812 ended, Miller moved to Low Hampton, where he began attending the local Baptist church. This town in New York State lay within a region later called the **Burned-Over District,** and known in the early 1800s for having numerous religious revivals and for spawning a number of

new religious movements. In 1816 Miller had a **conversion** experience, and thereafter his life was directed by spiritual concerns. For the next two years Miller examined the Bible verse by verse. Becoming interested in biblical **eschatology** and understanding that a prophetic day represented a year of actual time, he determined that the 2,300 days of Daniel 8:14 specified a period that began with Artaxerxes's decree in 457 B.C. to rebuild Jerusalem. Interpreting the phrase "and then shall the sanctuary be cleansed," which marked the end event of this time span, as referring to the premillennial Second Coming of Jesus, Miller in 1818 concluded that Christ would return about the year 1843.

Miller waited until 1823 before privately explaining his conclusions to acquaintances but made no public presentation until 1831. In 1832 he published a series of 16 articles in the *Vermont Telegraph*, which the following year he combined into a pamphlet entitled *Evidences from Scripture and History of the Second Coming of Christ about the Year A.D. 1843....* Receiving a **preaching** license from his local Baptist church in 1833, between 1834 and 1839 Miller gave about 800 lectures in upstate New York, Maine, and Vermont. After inviting Miller to speak at his church in Boston, Christian Connection pastor Joshua Vaughan Himes began publishing the *Signs of the Times* in March 1840, the first of several Millerite papers. He also encouraged Miller to speak in New York and Philadelphia and organized a general conference that took place in October. Through Himes's promotional efforts a movement emerged that, although based on Miller's ideas, was largely led by others, among them Josiah Litch, Charles Fitch, and Joseph Marsh. Over 125 Millerite **camp meetings** took place, beginning in 1842, and by 1844 it was estimated that some 50,000 people, largely in the Northeast, had adopted Miller's ideas. Meanwhile, Miller felt pressure to identify the date of Christ's return more precisely. After analyzing the Jewish calendar, in January 1843 he announced that Jesus would return between March 21, 1843, and March 21, 1844. Responding to growing opposition from the established churches, in July 1843 Fitch called on the movement to "Come Out of Babylon" in a sermon that was printed in several papers and fomented a separationist impulse that Miller did not favor.

When Christ had not come by March 21, 1844, some Millerites, using a different Jewish calendar, revised the date to April 18, an interpretation that again proved incorrect. In August 1844 Samuel Sheffield Snow took the now uncertain movement by storm when he argued that Jesus would come on the Jewish Day of Atonement, which he identified as October 22, 1844. Miller originally opposed the "seventh-month movement," as it was called, but on October 6 publicly accepted the new date. Miller expressed deep disappointment when October 22 passed uneventfully but maintained his belief in Jesus' imminent return. He attended a conference of mainstream Millerites that took place in Albany, New York, at the end of April 1845, where he strongly warned against the adoption of radical theories. Physical disability prevented Miller from taking an active role in the movement from 1846 until his death in 1849.

The movement Miller inspired spawned several new churches. Out of the mainstream represented in the Albany conference, the American Evangelical Adventist Conference, the Advent Christian Church, and the Church of God of the Abrahmic Faith eventually developed. From the radicals rejected at Albany, the **Seventh-day Adventist Church**—with **Ellen Gould (Harmon) White** among its early leaders—emerged as the largest of all groups with roots in the Millerite movement.

Further Reading: Dick, Everett N. *William Miller and the Advent Crisis, 1831–1844.* Berrien Springs, MI: Andrews University Press, 1994; Knight, George R. *Millennial Fever and the End of the World.* Boise, ID: Pacific Press Publishing Association, 1993; Numbers, Ronald L., and Jonathan M. Butler, eds. *The Disappointed: Millerism and Millenarianism in the Nineteenth Century.* Bloomington: Indiana University Press, 1987; White, L. Michael. "Apocalypse! Prophetic Belief in the United States: William Miller and the Second Great Awakening." *Frontline* Web site. http://www.pbs.org/wgbh/

pages/frontline/shows/apocalypse/explanation/amprophesy.html.

Gary Land

MILLS, BENJAMIN FAY (1857–1916)

Benjamin Fay Mills was a revivalist of the late nineteenth century who, in midlife, moved away from his earlier evangelical beliefs to embrace Unitarianism and the Social Gospel, and yet returned to evangelicalism near the end of his life. Mills attended four different colleges and had one failed business venture before graduating from Lake Forest University in 1880. Before he graduated, he was ordained in the Congregational church at Cannon Falls, Minnesota, in 1878. After graduating, Mills spent time as a missionary in the Black Hills, as a pastor for a church in Greenwich, New York, and as a pastor for another church in Rutland, Vermont. In Rutland, Mills oversaw a revival in 1886 that added 89 converts to a congregation of 214. At his request, the church reluctantly let Mills go so that he could become an itinerant evangelist.

Mills quickly graduated from conducting revivals in small towns like Middlebury, Vermont, to cities like Boston, Philadelphia, and New York. Mills made a name for himself by working in unity with different denominations, and by winning converts without emotionalism. An admirer stated, "Mr. Mills is an attractive … speaker, but rarely in what are termed, 'flights of eloquence,' except as the truth is eloquent" (Nelson, 31). In 1891, 46 churches sponsored his meeting in Cleveland, and over 5,000 individuals made decisions for Christ. The Cleveland revival firmly established him as a premier urban evangelist and the heir apparent to **Dwight L. Moody.**

In the early 1890s, Mills began to be influenced by the Social Gospel. He believed that the Christian principles of love and charity could and should be used to eradicate endemic social problems like poverty, disease, and poor working conditions that had been brought on by industrialization. In 1894, Mills joined with a group of other Social Gospel ministers in what came to be called the Kingdom movement. All of their teachings were directed toward establishing God's kingdom here on earth. Mills was an associate editor of their paper, the *Kingdom*, and he led seminars at the group's annual conference that focused on social justice. By 1898, frustrated that the larger church did not share his vision for social justice, Mills joined the Unitarian church. He moved to Oakland, California, to become pastor of the city's First Unitarian Church in 1899.

Since 1895, Mills had been studying religious texts other than the Bible. His readings of the Upanishads, the Bhagavad-Gita, and the works of Emerson and Whitman slowly led him to a frame of mind wherein even Unitarianism was too constrictive, and he left the Unitarian church in 1903. In 1905, Mills inaugurated a "free religion" society named simply "the Fellowship" in Los Angeles. The Fellowship was Mills's vision for a new world order, where everyone practiced "unselfishness" in order to establish a perfect community. By this point, Mills's theology had come to focus exclusively upon humanity and its innate capacity for perfection. Mills left in 1908 to promote the growth of the Fellowship elsewhere, but was not able to do so. The failure of the Fellowship to materialize as an ideal society was a bitter disappointment for Mills. His final attempts to establish Fellowships in Chicago and New York were both failures.

Mills's disappointment over the failure of the Fellowship led him back to evangelicalism in 1915. The horrors of World War I shattered any remaining illusions he might have had concerning the potential for perfect community here on earth. Mills stated that he "felt the need of a Spiritual Master." **J. Wilbur Chapman** and William E. Barton arranged meetings for Mills in New York and Chicago, where he was able to retract his former views before the clergy of those cities. Mills left the evangelical church because he was frustrated that the church was not addressing the social problems of the day. He came back to the church when the social problems of the world proved too strong and human nature seemed resistant to change. He went back to what he had done so well many years before—revival **preaching.** But the audiences that came to hear him were more interested in gawking at a prodigal son come home than hearing his message. Mills died on May 1, 1916, in the midst of a revival in Grand Rapids. The *Los Angeles Times* wrote a eulogy: "Then came the great disappointment. The message was not received as he had hoped. It is not unfair to say that he was no longer successful in the orthodox church. He died of a broken heart" (Nelson, 251).

Further Reading: Francis, John Junkin. *An Account of the Great Revival in Cincinnati and Covington, January 21st to March 6th, 1892, under the Leadership of the Distinguished Evangelist, Rev. B. Fay Mills, Assisted by the Eminent Gospel Singer, Mr. Lawrence B. Greenwood; and Also, for Part of the Time by Rev. J. Wilbur Chapman, D.D., and Mr. Geo. C. Stebbins.* Cincinnati: Standard, 1892; Nelson, Daniel Wilhelm. "B. Fay Mills: Revivalist, Social Reformer, and Advocate of Free Religion." PhD dissertation, Syracuse University, 1964; McLoughlin, William G., Jr. *Modern Revivalism: Charles Grandison Finney to Billy Graham.* New York: Ronald Press, 1959.

David Simpson

MONEY AND REVIVALS

The role of money in the history of revivalism has been a two-edged sword. On the one hand, revivalism's organizational and logistical realities have demanded a different approach to finances than the fiscal routines and structures required for normal congregational and denominational life. In this light, revivalists' penchant for organization combined with their ability to attract support from common folk and well-heeled backers has enabled them to flourish. Yet on the other hand, their special relationship with money has often been their undoing—undercutting the impact of the message while casting doubts on the motives and goals of the revivalists.

The earliest revivals associated with the evangelical awakenings in North America such as those reported in **Jonathan Edwards**'s *A Faithful Narrative of the Surprising Work of God* (1737) were generally set within a congregation or a group of churches under the guidance of local clergy. As the movement spread, however, the rise of traveling and itinerant evangelists like **George Whitefield** attracted crowds that were usually too large for any single church, propelling the revival meeting into the open air and other community venues beyond the scope and control of the churches. This new phenomenon of revivalism had financial repercussions. For his part, Whitefield nimbly adapted to his sudden success, capitalizing upon his newfound celebrity by supporting his ministry—including an orphanage in Georgia—through collections and the printing of his sermons and journals. To better concentrate on his **preaching** duties he used preaching assistants to conduct the great bulk of his correspondence and to pave the way for his tour as advance men.

Charles G. Finney gave revivalism and its practitioners a streamlined rationale, theology, and methodology in his famous *Lectures on Revivals of Religion* (1835). Finney's career likewise reflected the evolution of the economic realities surrounding the institution and its standard-bearers. Ordained and licensed as a Presbyterian in upstate New York, Finney's work as a revivalist largely steered clear of denominational barriers. Key to this independence was the financial support he received from pious benefactors. From his modest beginnings as an agent of western New York's Female Missionary Society, Finney was peppered with gifts of money, clothing, and hospitality by the rising business class of the Erie Canal district. As his career took him from small towns such as Utica, New York, to major urban centers like Philadelphia, Boston, and New York, and later to his long-term presidency of Oberlin College in Ohio, the pattern magnified. Finney attracted financial support from evangelical business magnates such as Arthur and Lewis Tappan, Anson Phelps, and Josiah Chapin.

Through the years Finney lived in relative modesty, thus dodging one of the main snares that moneyed support brought his way. Yet Finney's dependence upon a small group of benefactors opened the way for other problems. One of these was the potential influence that benefactors' political, social, and theological views had over the evangelist who relied on their donations. Another problem was the impact that volatile market cycles could have upon benefactors' fortunes, and hence on the ministry—a lesson he learned well in the wake of the Panic of 1837 and the ensuing national depression. This economic downturn threatened

Oberlin College and the stability of Finney's ministry until new supporters were able to step forward and pick up the slack.

No evangelist in the history of revivalism tapped more successfully into the deep pockets of wealthy backers than did Chicago's **Dwight L. Moody,** a "businessman's revivalist" in the decades following the **Civil War.** The tone was set in his early days as the young president of the Chicago **Young Men's Christian Association** (YMCA), where he attracted enormous support for his endeavors from wealthy businessmen such as Cyrus McCormick and George Armour. As Moody discovered his preaching gifts and began to move into full-time evangelistic work, these same men—and their contacts in other cities—provided him with the staff, equipment, and personal funds to pursue his mission.

It was Moody's 1873–1874 tour of Britain that catapulted him to **transatlantic** evangelical celebrity status. However, Moody found himself reaping not only souls but pounds (i.e., English money) from his British admirers. Such was the outpouring of money—offerings and outright gifts—that Moody came under a cloud of suspicion from the British press. As a result, Moody took the step of permanently eliminating nightly offerings at his public meetings. Still, the money rolled in. Despite turning down numerous gifts, by the time he left for America he had accumulated enough money to finish the building of his Chicago tabernacle and could purchase a large farm in Northfield, Massachusetts, as the site of a conference center.

Back in the United States Moody perfected the art of weaving together the support of wealthy businessmen to fund and equip his revival meetings. Meetings in urban centers like Philadelphia and New York City attracted the visible support of men like John Wanamaker and Cornelius Vanderbilt as well as contributions in the form of cash, materials, and labor from the business community. All the while, ongoing proceeds from the sales of his and song leader Ira Sankey's songbooks netted huge profits for the pair, even as large portions of the proceeds were funneled into various religious and charitable causes.

Building on the success of Moody, evangelical preachers in the late nineteenth century and the early decades of the twentieth century brought revivalism to an even greater level of influence in American society. During this period no evangelist advanced the "science" of revivalism—or reaped more of its rewards—than did the converted ex-baseball player **Billy Sunday.** As his reputation and crowds increased, Sunday, with the help of his wife and business manager, Nell, assembled a well-oiled revivalistic team that might have been the envy of any contemporary marketing firm or political campaign. A team of advance men handled publicity, relations with local church and civic leaders, and logistical support for the campaign, including the construction of a Sunday-approved wooden tabernacle in each city. Sunday's song leader, Homer Rodeheaver, supervised musical staff and industriously hawked sheet music and songbooks, from which he received the lion's share of his own compensation. Through it all Sunday became a rich man as well as a celebrity. Despite donating several major campaigns' collections to various causes, Sunday biographer Lyle Dorsett estimates that in one 12-year period the evangelist made well over a million dollars. Yet Sunday and his many imitators during this period came under increasing fire from critics like Sinclair Lewis—author of the anti-revivalist novel *Elmer Gantry* (1927)—for their fund-raising methods and all-too-cozy relationships with wealthy backers.

A new form of revivalism during the 1920s was **radio** preaching, which spawned the first generation of the "electronic church." Fundamentalist broadcasters—who were generally locked out of the public-service time doled out by large urban stations and the new radio networks to the liberal Federal Council of Churches—were forced to develop alternative strategies to get their message on the air. As a result, evangelists like Paul Rader of Chicago and Southern California's **Charles E. Fuller** appealed to their audiences for the financial wherewithal to purchase airtime on local stations and, in Fuller's case, to cobble together a home-grown network of stations. In time this method—supplemented by souvenirs, giveaways, and other increasingly sophisticated appeals—proved effective and led to the conservative Protestant domination of the airwaves. With the advent of **television** the same methods would be used by others, particularly **Pentecostal** revivalists like **Oral Roberts** and Rex Humbard, to create a conservative hegemony in the realm of religious television.

The meteoric rise of **Billy Graham** amid the prosperity of the postwar period took the economic complexities of revivalism to a whole new level. Under the auspices of the Billy Graham Evangelistic Association (BGEA; founded 1950), Graham and his savvy business manager, George Wilson, created an evangelistic megacorporation that not only organized and funded evangelistic "crusades," but oversaw a parachurch empire that would include associate evangelists, the *Hour of Decision* radio program and televised crusade meetings, *Decision* magazine, a record label, a full-fledged motion picture company (World Wide Pictures), schools to train laypeople and pastors in evangelism, and Grason, a for-profit company that reinvested profits—from books and trinkets like bumper stickers and buttons—back into the ministry. While Graham attracted and received donations for projects from wealthy backers like Sun Oil magnate J. Howard Pew, the principal source of his funding came through direct mail to grassroots supporters, followed up by dozens of staff members at BGEA headquarters in Minneapolis, who were equipped with the most up-to-date technology to process funds and keep track of donors.

Given the huge amounts of money coming into his organization, Graham was extremely sensitive to the Elmer Gantry–like stereotypes that plagued evangelists. Accordingly, he and his staff placed themselves on regular salaries and refused to take any of the customary "love offerings" that had traditionally played such an important part in financing revivalists' ministries. Although Graham and his family lived a comfortable life, he steered clear of the opulence that had marked the lifestyles of predecessors such as Billy Sunday and **Aimee Semple McPherson.** In 1979, Graham was a major player in the establishment of the Evangelical Council for Financial Accountability (ECFA), which hoped to open ministries' books and set fiscal standards for parachurch organizations. Untainted by scandal, Graham's organization was able to avoid the financial downturn that affected so many ministries in the wake of the 1980s televangelist scandals.

While Billy Graham was undoubtedly the preeminent American evangelist of the second half of the twentieth century, from the mid-1960s onward he was increasingly regarded as something of a unique and iconic figure in the minds of many Americans. In the vacuum left by his cultural apotheosis, it was the vibrant figure of the Pentecostal evangelist—particularly the growing array of Pentecostal and **Charismatic** televangelists—that came to define the public image of the revivalist. Far removed from the backwoods tent revivals and storefront churches of previous generations, new wave figures like **Jimmy Swaggart, Jim and Tammy Faye Bakker, Pat Robertson,** Robert Tilton, Joyce Meyer, and Paul and Jan Crouch had a penchant for going first class—from their equipment to their lifestyles. Though stunningly successful, their penchant for flashy clothes, grandiose projects, and protracted appeals for financial support fed into the Gantryesque stereotypes of the revivalist. Some televangelists lived in beautiful mansions and had expensive cars or airplanes that were legally owned by their nonprofit organizations. Technically speaking, they may have had only modest personal wealth, and yet they enjoyed a standard of living that would be characteristic of a high-paid corporate executive.

In the late 1980s a series of scandals—financial and sexual—struck the world of televangelism. Dubbed "Pearlygate" by the media, the financial portion of the scandal nexus ranged from **Oral Roberts's** questionable fund-raising strategy (his vision of an 800-foot tall Jesus telling him to raise money or he would soon die) to Jim Bakker's financially unsound multimillion-dollar time-share plan at his Heritage USA compound in Fort Mill, South Carolina. Taken together, the Pearlygate scandals not only ended or severely damaged a few televangelist ministries, but triggered a larger downturn in giving to parachurch organizations and tarnished the entire evangelical subculture. By the late 1990s, however, Pentecostal televangelism had revitalized itself—if not necessarily its public image—through a proliferation of dedicated cable and satellite channels and the rise of a new set of Word of Faith or **prosperity theology** preachers such as **Kenneth Hagin Sr., Kenneth Copeland, Benny Hinn,** Dwight Thompson, Creflo Dollar, and Joel Osteen.

The unique status of the revivalist has always required a different organizational and economic structure than that faced by local congregations, or even religious denominations. Through the years, revivalists have honed their methods and organizations to attract and utilize the funds necessary to carry out their increasingly sophisticated and diverse ministries. In the process, however, ties to wealthy benefactors with blatant or underlying social and political agendas—coupled with many revivalists' attraction to personal wealth—have given revivalism a collective black eye. Despite recent efforts to insure organizational transparency, greater fiscal accountability, and personal integrity, it is doubtful that the stereotype of the greedy, money-grubbing evangelist will be overcome anytime soon.

Further Reading: Dorsett, Lyle A. *Billy Sunday and the Redemption of Urban America.* Grand Rapids, MI: Eerdmans, 1991; Hambrick-Stowe, Charles E. "'Sanctified Business': Historical Perspectives on Financing Revivals of Religion." In Larry Eskridge and Mark Noll, eds., *More Money, More Ministry: Money and Evangelicals in Recent North American History,* 81–103. Grand Rapids, MI: Eerdmans, 2000; Martin, William. *A Prophet with Honor: The Billy Graham Story.* New York: William Morrow, 1991; McLoughlin, William G., Jr. *Modern Revivalism: Charles Grandison Finney to Billy Graham.* New York: Ronald Press, 1959; Stout, Harry S. *The Divine Dramatist: George Whitefield and the Rise of Modern Evangelicalism.* Grand Rapids, MI: Eerdmans, 1992; Voskuil, Dennis M. "The Power of the Air: Evangelicals and the Rise of Religious Broadcasting." In Quentin J. Schultze, ed., *American Evangelicals and the Mass Media,* 69–95. Grand Rapids, MI: Zondervan, 1990.

Larry Eskridge

MOODY, DWIGHT LYMAN (1837–1899)

On the afternoon of May 24, 1874, 5,000 souls packed into the Crystal Cathedral hours before the scheduled start of the final meeting in Glasgow led by Dwight Lyman Moody. Reports characterized many of them as "unusually unsettled" and anxious to hear the words of the famous evangelist who one year before had come to Britain a relative unknown. By the time Moody's carriage arrived, an estimated 30,000 had gathered, many eager for a look at the man whom the Scottish press was calling the greatest revivalist since **George Whitefield.** Unable to get into the meeting hall, the 37-year-old Massachusetts layman stood atop a coachman's box and began **preaching.** Those inside the church now hurried to come outside to hear what was happening. It was a spectacle never before seen in the city. "Currents mingled," contemporary accounts recorded, and "an ocean emerged." R. C. Morgan, veteran editor of the *Christian,* was moved to tears. Two thousand reportedly experienced **conversion** within an hour. The Scottish press likened what was happening to the **Great Awakening** of the 1740s. Moody's "inner vitality made men fresh," while "deeply stirring thousands." It had led to "a strange and solemn night" and a "citywide shaking" of unprecedented proportions. (*Christian,* May 28, 1874, 4–7; *Glasgow Daily Mail,* May 25, 1874, 2; *Glasgow Evening Star,* May 25, 1874, 3.)

There was little in Moody's early life that foreshadowed the public acclaim he later received. He was born as the sixth of nine children to Betsy and Edwin Moody, farmers in East Northfield, Massachusetts. His father died when Dwight was four, leaving the boy only four years of formal schooling before he went to work on neighboring farms. Dwight, however, was strong, stubborn, and particularly determined to make something of himself. His mother noted his self-reliance, and commented that Dwight "used to think himself a man when he was only a boy" (Daniels, 13). At 17, Moody went to work in his uncle's Boston shoe store. He was resigned to church attendance being a condition of that employment and generally slept through the sermons. Under the influence of a Sunday school teacher, Moody became a Christian but was initially denied membership in the Mount Vernon Congregational Church because of his inability to verbalize his personal faith in Christ. In

September 1856 he arrived in Chicago, hoping to make a fortune in the boot business.

Chicago was America's fastest-growing city on the eve of the **Civil War.** Moody sold shoes, lived frugally, and spent his evenings increasingly absorbed in the activities of the **Young Men's Christian Association** (YMCA). He began going along the cholera-infested Chicago River finding indigent and orphaned children that he could bring to Sunday school. The North Market Mission aided more than a thousand people and was visited by President-elect Abraham Lincoln. Moody soon abandoned his business pursuits, gave himself to full-time Christian work, and married co-laborer Emma Revell in 1862. He worked on the front lines of battle in the Civil War for the United States Christian Commission, which sought to address the spiritual needs of Union soldiers. In 1863 he organized and built a nondenominational church in Chicago and three years later became president of the Chicago chapter of the YMCA. Moody earned the epithet "Crazy Moody" for bursting into newspaper offices, urging editors to publicize efforts in Christian uplift in the city. The Great Chicago Fire in October 1871 forced him into **transatlantic** fund-raising and set the stage for his revival campaign in Great Britain between 1873 and 1875.

When Moody, accompanied by gospel singer Ira D. Sankey, arrived in Liverpool on June 17, 1873, the local press paid little attention. When he left the same city two years and two months later after preaching all over England, Scotland, and Ireland, he had established his reputation as the best-known revivalist in the English-speaking world. Starting slowly in York and Sunderland, Moody began rapidly to build alliances with nonconformist churches (i.e., congregations not within the state-supported Church of England), and he established an organizational and publicity apparatus that unified evangelical pastors in supporting him. Like **Charles G. Finney** before him, Moody believed that human efforts created the necessary conditions for God-given revivals. He based his revival campaigns on belief in the power of **prayer** and the efficacy of human agency in bringing about God's purposes. Encouraging people "to expect a blessing of unusual

magnitude," he told ministers in Carlisle to create "a spirit of excitement among the people" (*Carlisle Daily Journal*, November 18, 1873, 3). He defended his marketing strategy by saying, "It seems to me a good deal better to advertise and have a full house than preach to empty pews." He argued that the church could learn something about salesmanship from the world. "They advertise very extensively," he told his detractors. The modern church competed with the world for the attention of its people. That was why Moody did not "think it beneath a man's dignity to go out and ask people to come in" (*Christian*, October 23, 1873, 3; D. L. Moody, 33–34).

Contemporaries lauded Moody for his organizational abilities. Others observed how Moody's earnestness and sincerity bred conviction among his hearers. The *Daily Review* of Edinburgh noted that "a spirit of excitement and expectation has been built up in many" (November 24, 1873, 4). During the fall of 1873 Moody and Sankey were compelled to rotate between three of Edinburgh's largest churches and its Music Hall because of "a widening desire to see and hear him" (*British Evangelist*, December 8, 1873, 2). The "awakening" in Scotland was described as "a democratic movement" among "the backslidden, the intemperate, the skeptical, the rich and the poor, the educated and the uneducated, the wounded and the burdened." Moody was credited with uniting Scotland's churches in "a frontal assault against spiritual slothfulness" for "the revival of the spiritually dead" (*Christian*, December 11, 1873, 11; *Edinburgh Daily Review*, December 15, 1873). In January 1874, a week of prayer launched by 2,600 participating pastors had yet more dramatic results. More than a thousand reportedly believed in Christ at the Grassmarket slum in a single evening and several thousand more after weeks of meetings at Edinburgh's 6,000-seat Corn Exchange.

Members of the state-supported or Established Churches (i.e., Anglican or Presbyterian) joined in as Moody's campaign swept through working-class Glasgow, Ulster, and **Roman Catholic** Dublin. Between December 1874 and mid-March 1875, Moody's entourage, which now included a personal

Moody and Sankey counsel well-dressed women from New York City in postures of dignity and restraint. The caption reads: "The great revival conducted by the evangelists messrs. Moody and Sankey at the hippodrome, Madison and Fourth Avenues. Mr. Moody personally exhorting penitents in the room for the women's prayer meetings." (Frank Leslie's *Illustrated Newspaper*, March 4, 1876.) Courtesy of the Billy Graham Center Museum.

secretary to answer the letters he was receiving, put its organizational acumen to work in Manchester, Sheffield, Birmingham, and Liverpool as final preparations were made for his four-month campaign in the heart of London. The crowds came to hear Moody's message of God's grace and unremitting love told in "a wonderfully simple an straightforward style" (*Sheffield Post*, January 9, 1875, 4). Moody's Greater London campaign began on March 9, 1875, and ended 285 meetings later with 2,530,000 in attendance.

Beginning in Brooklyn in October 1875 and continuing through Philadelphia, New York, Chicago, and Boston in the two years that followed, Moody and Sankey staged a series of record-breaking evangelistic campaigns. Moody's revival machinery, though constructed overseas, was perfected in

his Gilded Age campaigns in urban America. Moody told his organizing committee that water ran downhill, and if they were successful in evangelizing the big cities of America, the whole country might be captured by revival. Brooklyn was the nation's third-largest city when Moody opened his campaign at the Brooklyn Rink on the night of October 24, 1875. After the auditorium's 4,300 seats were filled, police locked and blocked the doors, preventing an estimated 20,000 additional people from getting in to see the celebrity evangelist. More than 300 familiar faces of local politicians and municipal ministers filled the stage, along with Sankey's volunteer army of 250 choir members. Reporters described the broad-shouldered, round-faced, heavily bearded Moody as a man who "appeared to be a businessman coming to work" and "eager to get on with it" (*Brooklyn Daily Times*, October 25, 1875, 1).

In Philadelphia, Moody received strong support from John Wanamaker, the department store magnate, who had been a coworker with Moody in the YMCA movement. Wanamaker helped refurbish the Pennsylvania Railroad Depot for the meetings (see above), which began on the evening of November 21, 1875, before a capacity crowd of 13,000. The daily press chronicled nine weeks of Moody's sermons in verbatim front-page transcripts. Some Christian households kept these reports in scrapbooks as souvenirs of the spiritual extravaganza. Seventeen thousand anxious inquirers met with Moody and his workers after the meetings and 4,200 prayed to become Christians. Some criticized Moody's meetings as mere religious sensation. The *Evening Bulletin* differed: "Sure it's sensational. The American people like sensation!" (December 24, 1875, 5). Moody next preached in P. T. Barnum's New York Hippodrome in meetings that would attract more than 1.5 million between February and April of America's centennial year (*Harper's Weekly*, March 11, 1876, cover plate). Moody's positive message seemed the perfect antidote to a spreading financial panic that had created an atmosphere of uncertainty in one of the nation's most

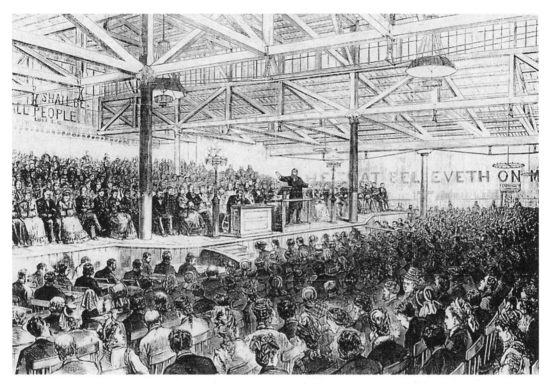

Moody's Philadelphia crusade began on November 21, 1875. Despite heavy rain, 13,000 people arrived for the opening service, which was held in a converted railroad freight station on Market Street. (Frank Leslie's *Illustrated Newspaper*, ca. 1875–1876.) Courtesy of the Billy Graham Center Museum.

secular cities. Eleven thousand tickets were nightly issued in the interest of crowd control. Even 150 New York policemen were unable to prevent one determined attendee from getting in through a skylight. Moody's meetings in Chicago between October 1876 and January 1877 and Boston between January and April 1877—referred to at the time as the "Great Western Revival" and "New England Revival" respectively—demonstrated the regional reach of Moody's municipal meetings. Evangelical teams fanned out across a several state area, capitalizing on the press coverage and mounting enthusiasm of Moody's missions.

Moody's preaching focused on the love of God, and included little or no reference to God's wrath or **Calvinistic** notions of original sin, the enslaved human will, or divine predestination. When once asked about his theology, Moody said that he was not aware that he had a theology. On another

occasion, Moody stated that his gospel consisted in the "three R's," namely, "Ruin by sin, Redemption by Christ, and Regeneration by the Holy Ghost" (McLoughlin, 246). While it might not be accurate to describe him as untheological, Moody showed little interest in the technicalities of Christian doctrine. His nondogmatic approach to Christianity allowed him to maintain good relationships with Protestant ministers who, during the 1870s through the 1890s, were holding increasingly divergent views. Some, under the influence of German biblical criticism and Darwin's theory of evolution, were to emerge in the years after 1900s as Modernists. Others, affirming the inerrancy of the Bible and rejecting the theory of evolution, were later to become known as Fundamentalists. Because of Moody's clear salvation message, his strong emphasis on the truthfulness of the Bible, and his premillennialist **eschatology** (teaching that the world will degenerate prior to Jesus' Second Coming), it was the later Fundamentalists rather than the Modernists who would lay claim to Moody as their forebear. Moody's revivalist successor, **Reuben A. Torrey,** was one of the architects of American Fundamentalism. Yet during his later life Moody maintained cordial relations with Protestants who held to a range of theological views.

Moody was essentially a pragmatist, concerned with attaining evangelistic results and willing to use various methods to win converts. He once said, "It doesn't matter how you get a man to God provided you get him there" (*Boston Daily Advertiser*, February 3, 1877, 4). Moody's sermons were designed to touch the hearts of his hearers. He told folksy stories of erring sons who later repented, and the long-suffering, prayerful mothers who waited expectantly for their sons' return. From his early experiences in the so-called Businessmen's Revival, or the **Revival of 1857–1858,** Moody understood the power of emotion and its capacity to stir people to action. His meetings were places where **men** could experience tender and sentimental emotions and yet not feel any shame at a loss of their masculinity. Moody, during his lifetime, was generally praised in the press, though political progressives and radicals had little use for him. The Earl of Shaftesbury in England lauded Moody for quelling the "ocean of unstable mind" among the urban masses, while the communist pioneer Friedrich Engels spoke of preachers "imported from American revivalism, Moody and Sankey and the like" as drugging the masses with the opiate of religion (McLoughlin, 179–80). It is noteworthy that a conservative aristocrat and a communist held similar views regarding Moody's social influence. Moody declared that he regarded the world as a "wrecked vessel," and had a mandate to rescue as many people out of the world as he could. Liberal Protestant critics, during the twentieth century, have blamed Moody's premillennialism for weakening his commitment to social reform programs aimed at improving the lot of the urban poor in the late 1800s.

During the final third of his life, Moody continued his evangelistic work in England in 1891, Palestine in 1892, and at the Great Columbian Exposition of Chicago from May to November 1893. Yet during his later years, Moody increasingly devoted himself to educational efforts designed to prepare young men and **women** for Christian service. He lived between campaigns in East Northfield with his wife and three children. There, he launched the Northfield Seminary for girls in 1879 and the Mount Hermon School for boys two years later. Revival meetings in New Haven, Baltimore, St. Louis, and San Francisco were followed by 19 months of evangelistic work in Britain that extended through June 1884. In 1886 he began a series of widely publicized annual conferences of college students at Mount Hermon and Northfield that stimulated the growth of the YMCA and the **Student Volunteer Movement,** which is credited with sending some 20,000 college students abroad as **foreign missionaries** over a 50-year period. Moody also played a key role in the distribution of Bibles and other Christian literature. Through the use of colporteurs (i.e., individuals who distributed Christian literature), Moody sent millions of gospel tracts and pamphlets to homes across America. Moreover, Moody's brother-in-law, Fleming Hewitt Revell, established a major Christian publishing house bearing Revell's name. In 1889, Moody established the Chicago Bible Institute. After his death, a decade later, it would be named the Moody Bible Institute in his honor. Moody, in addition to evangelistic work, made an impact in these three areas—foreign missions, Christian education, and the dissemination of Christian literature.

Moody last preached on the evening of November 16, 1899, on the marriage supper of the Lamb before a capacity crowd in a Kansas City convention center. He became ill, and was diagnosed with congestive heart failure. Returning by special train to Northfield, Moody received word that admirers and well-wishers from Booker T. Washington to William Jennings Bryan were praying that God's man for the

Gilded Age might be spared for a nation that still needed him. Moody had spoken to 100 million men and women across the century, **J. Wilbur Chapman** told readers, probably reducing the population of hell by more than 1 million for having done so. The *Chicago Tribune* shared in the sentiment. It could think of no man since John Wesley "who has exercised a more potent moral influence" or been "a greater power for good" (November 19, 1899, 36).

When he died on the eve of the twentieth century, Moody was widely eulogized as one of the most beloved men of his generation. The *New York Times* reported that "the death of no man now living could so greatly stir the hearts and minds of so great a multitude on both sides of the ocean" (December 24, 1899, 22).

In 1954, as Billy Graham was beginning to build his reputation by retracing Moody's steps in Britain, he admitted to "standing on the foundations that Moody had laid" that remained "everywhere apparent." Moody's work had "changed the entire religious structure of a nation," Graham observed, and with it the future of big-city evangelism (*Moody Monthly*, October 1954, 32–33). By the millennium's end, technology had so evolved that Graham could preach to the wired world via satellite from a single small studio. Moody, who only preached below a sounding board, would have greatly admired this outcome. In his day, urban revivalism had to be built brick by brick in planning, preparation, prayer, and publicity. Yet Moody's efforts became the basis of the modern, mass-mediated revivalism of the twentieth and twenty-first centuries.

Further Reading: Curtis, Richard K. *They Called Him Mister Moody.* Garden City, NJ: Doubleday, 1962; Daniels, W. H. *Moody: His Words, Work, and Workers.* New York: Nelson and Philips, 1877; Dorsett, Lyle W. *A Passion for Souls: The Life of D. L. Moody.* Chicago: Moody Press, 1997; Drummond, Henry. *Dwight L. Moody.* New York: McClure, Phillips, 1900; Evensen, Bruce J. *God's Man for the Gilded Age: D. L. Moody and the Rise of Modern Mass Evangelism.* New York: Oxford University, 2003; Findlay, James F., Jr. *Dwight L. Moody: American Evangelist, 1837–1899.* Chicago: University of Chicago Press, 1969; Gundry, Stanley. *Love Them In: The Proclamation Theology of D. L. Moody.* Chicago: Moody Press, 1976; Hall, John, and George H. Stuart. *The American Evangelists D. L. Moody and Ira Sankey in Great Britain and Ireland.* New York: Dodd and Mead, 1877; McLoughlin, William G. *Modern Revivalism: Charles Gradison Finney to Billy Graham.* New York: Ronald Press, 1959; Moody, D. L. *New Sermons, Addresses and Prayers.* St. Louis: N. D. Thompson, 1877; Moody, Paul D. *My Father: An Intimate Portrait of Dwight Moody.* Boston: Little, Brown, 1938; Sankey, Ira D. *My Life and the Story of the Gospel Hymns.* Philadelphia: Sunday School Times, 1906.

Bruce J. Evensen

MORAVIANS

The renewal of the Unity of the Brethren in Herrnhut, Germany, in 1727 was a key event in Protestant history. The Herrnhuters are best known for their extensive and innovative missions to tribal and enslaved peoples in North America, the Caribbean Basin, and sub-Saharan Africa, but they also were a distinct voice in the **transatlantic** eighteenth-century **Great Awakening.** Though few in number, the Moravians left "an indelible mark on the history of Protestantism" (Ward, 124).

In the late 1400s—decades before Martin Luther posted his Ninety-five Theses in Wittenberg—the Unity of the Brethren was established in Czech lands as a separate community of faith that rejected the idea of a state church. Like the later **Pietist** movement that swept through Germany in the late 1600s and early 1700s, the Unity emphasized lay ministries, a personal decision to follow Christ, and an active, service-oriented Christian life. The Unity was destroyed during the Thirty Years' War (1618–1648), but remnants survived in a few villages in Moravia and Poland. In 1708 a Pietist revival broke out in Silesia, near the traditional lands of the Unity. Johann Adam Steinmetz (1689–1762), pastor of the Jesus Church in Teschen, was the most effective **preacher** of the revival. One of the troubled young people who showed up in Teschen was a Czech émigré named

Christian David (1690–1751). After his **conversion** in 1719, David began to make secret forays to villages in Moravia where there were still memories of the Unity. He convinced some of them to flee Moravia so they could worship openly as Protestants in Germany.

Steinmetz advised David to make contact with a Saxon nobleman named Nikolaus Ludwig Graf von Zinzendorf (1700–1760), and in 1722 the Moravian refugees arrived on his estate where they established a village they named Herrnhut ("under the Lord's watch"). Their new protector was one of the most controversial and compelling figures of the Pietist movement. Educated at Halle and Wittenberg, he attempted to bridge the gap between the Pietists and the **Lutheran** Orthodox, but he was also closely connected to the more radical branches of the Pietist movement. Zinzendorf shared Jean Leade's vision of a *philadelphian* (brotherly love) church that could put aside disputes over doctrine and join together in genuine brotherly and sisterly love. He was also a creative proponent of the idea of a "theology of the heart" that gave priority to religious experience and active faith over intellectualism and doctrinal precision. Through **hymns,** liturgies, catechisms, and sermons, Zinzendorf sought to lead people into an intimate relationship with the Savior. Moravian hymns often emphasized Christ's suffering—his "blood and wounds." Zinzendorf and the Unity shared the conviction that Christianity is existential rather than theoretical.

As the village of Herrnhut grew to some 300 residents, Zinzendorf was forced to give greater attention to their social and religious life. About half of the residents were from Moravia and wanted to resurrect the Unity of their ancestors, which was illegal under the Treaty of Westphalia. Herrnhut had also attracted religious seekers from different theological backgrounds. The Saxon authorities were concerned that Herrnhut was becoming a nest of heretics, and the crown eventually exiled Zinzendorf because of his involvement in Herrnhut. For his part, Zinzendorf wanted to turn Herrnhut into an embodiment of the philadelphian ideal of true Christianity, and he called his followers the Brüdergemeine, or Community of the Brethren, which included the Moravians. But within a few years the community was on the verge of collapsing into a Babel of confusion and bitterness. The doctrinal disputes and conflict increased in 1726 after the arrival of an apocalyptic prophet who convinced Christian David and others that Christ's return was imminent. He proclaimed that Rothe and Zinzendorf were the False Prophet and the Beast from the book of Revelation.

Zinzendorf intervened by meeting with the heads of households, and with their assistance he drew up 42 statutes that the residents signed on May 12, 1727. This Brotherly Agreement was a key factor in a religious revival that began in 1727. The Herrnhuters agreed that doctrinal controversy was contrary to true Christianity. They resolved to live in love with one another and to seek to live according to the simple teachings of Christ. They also joyfully acknowledged that salvation is only through the grace of Christ, and therefore no one has cause for pride or self-righteousness. The agreement established clear guidelines for ordering social life and discipline in Herrnhut, and the Moravians agreed that their new Brotherly Agreement captured the spirit of their ancestors' church.

Pastor Rothe led a celebration of Holy Communion on August 13, 1727, that brought the entire community together in worship, song, and **prayer.** The presence of Christ's spirit was felt so strongly among the participants that they later compared it to biblical day of Pentecost (Acts 2). The gifts of the Spirit received on August 13, according to the participants, included forgiveness, joyfulness, and the ability to live in intimate community. This experience was followed two weeks later by an unexpected religious awakening among the children in Herrnhut. Christian David wrote, "It is truly a miracle of God that out of so many kinds of churches and sects as Catholic, Lutheran, Reformed, Separatist, Gichtelian, and the like, we could have been melted together into one" (Reichel, 35).

According to tradition, the Moravian love-feast ritual began with the meal that was shared during the daylong service on August 13.

The revival in Herrnhut led to the creation of more than two dozen Herrnhut-style communities in Europe and North America. The Moravians also carried out what they called "diaspora" work (1 Peter 1:1). Teachers and evangelists were sent throughout central and northern Europe to lead Pietist societies within the official state church. In 1735 they tried to establish a permanent base in North America, but their community in Savannah failed within a few years, in large part because of their refusal to bear arms. John Wesley—founder of the **Methodist** Church—had his first experience of Moravian Pietism on board a ship to Savannah, where he was going to be a pastor. The Moravians, especially Peter Böhler and August Spangenberg, played a role in the conversion of both John and Charles Wesley.

Zinzendorf was also attracted to Pennsylvania as a potential site for Moravian missions and place of refuge. Penn's "Holy Experiment" guaranteed freedom of religion for residents of his colony, which meant that it was the most religiously diverse American colony. True to the experience of the August 13 revival, Zinzendorf believed that religious revival included overcoming divisions. One of his goals during his visit to the New World in the early 1740s was to establish a synod of all German-speaking Protestants, which he called the Church of God in the Holy Spirit. This early ecumenical project faltered after only six meetings. One reason for its failure was the decided opposition of **Henry Melchior Muhlenberg**—a major Lutheran leader in colonial America.

Zinzendorf was a leading figure in German Pietism, but he was viewed with suspicion by many preachers in the Great Awakening, including **Gilbert Tennent** and **George Whitefield.** Some objected to the prominent role of woman in the church, while others accused the Moravians of antinomianism (i.e., rejecting moral rules) and Universalism (i.e., teaching that all will be saved).

Despite opposition, the Moravians established several permanent communities in Pennsylvania, most notably Bethlehem. In 1753 they purchased 100,000 acres of land in North Carolina to begin the Wachovia colony. Salem was the central town of Wachovia. In the 1850s the Moravians in America were granted independence from German administrative control, and two provinces (Northern and Southern) were established.

The Moravians sent their first missionaries to the New World in 1732, five years after the August 13 revival. Leonard Dober and David Nitschmann were the first Protestant missionaries sent specifically to bring the good news of salvation to enslaved African peoples. Their work in the Virgin Islands led to the conversion of a freed slave named Rebecca who married a Moravian missionary named Matthäus Freundlich. "Rebecca's revival" meant that more Moravians were **African American** than European American in the New World at the time of the American Revolution. Their success inspired the later Methodist and **Baptist** missionaries to the slaves. The Moravians' most notable evangelistic work in America was among Indians or native peoples. Their success was due to many factors. Foremost was the Moravian commitment to preaching in the language of the people and providing hymns, prayers, and the Bible in native languages. Also missionaries lived among the people and used "native helpers" as evangelists and church leaders. They preached the gospel in simple terms with a primary focus on the sacrifice of Christ for all people. In order solidify conversion, the Moravians established a number of separate native villages, such as Shekomeko in New York and Gnaddenhütten in Ohio, in the colonial period. In 1781 an American militia massacred all residents of the Gnaddenhütten community. In the 1830s Moravians were helpless to prevent their Cherokee brothers and sisters in Springplace, Georgia, from being forced to join the Trail of Tears to Oklahoma. Outsiders often objected to the Moravians' practice of treating natives and Africans as brothers and sisters, which included the kiss of peace.

The Moravian communities in America, like those in Europe, were highly regulated religious villages until the mid-nineteenth century. For 20 years (1741–1762), Bethlehem had a completely communal economy where residents were given what they needed in exchange for working as they were able. The other villages were communes that had centralized control while allowing private property and salaries. Secular life was part of the religious mission of the community and the elders assigned all jobs. Their communal society was an object of admiration and criticism from their neighbors, and they suffered because of their pacifism in times of war. Residents in the Moravian villages were grouped into "choirs" according to age, gender, and marital status, and each choir had assigned daily devotions. Marriages were carefully arranged by the elders in consultation with those to be married. Members had to confess their sins to their "choir helper" before being allowed to share in Holy Communion. Discipline was strict, but corporal punishment was discouraged. After the death of Zinzendorf in 1760, the Moravians in North America turned inward, and the communal villages gradually declined. After the American Revolution, the Moravians began to adopt the perspective of their American neighbors. Moravians in North Carolina, for instance, began owning slaves and even established a militia. Around 1850 the Moravians gave up the last vestiges of communal living, opened their villages to non-Moravian residents, and became largely indistinguishable from American Protestants in general. They did maintain a number of rituals and customs that still identify them, such as the communal meal or love feast.

There were periods of renewal and expansion in the nineteenth and twentieth centuries, however, especially among the growing immigrant population in the Midwest. John Fett, Andrew Iveson, and Neils Otto Tank were the most effective Moravian preachers and church organizers in this period. Immigrants with connections to Moravian work in Europe, they itinerated throughout the upper Midwest. Tank attempted to create a Herrnhut-style settlement in Green Bay, Wisconsin, but he was not successful. In North Carolina, religious revival and expansion was connected to the reconstruction following the **Civil War.** Bishop Edward Rondthaler encouraged Methodist-style revival services that resulted in a rapid increase in the size of the church. Accounts of the tearful Moravian prayer meetings and revivals in the nineteenth century, though, highlight the contrast between Pietist quietism and the effusive and dramatic revivals of the American Methodists and Baptists. Moravian evangelist John Greenfield published *Power from on High* (1927) to commemorate the bicentennial of the August 13 revival and encourage Moravians to become more revivalistic.

Since 1800, the Moravians have gradually assimilated to mainstream North American Protestantism—building homes for the elderly, establishing Moravian College and Salem College, and participating in ecumenism through the National Council of Churches and the World Council of Churches. By World War II almost all of the congregations in the United States and Canada had adopted English as the language of worship, and the contemporary Book of Worship exhibited the influences of Lutheran and Methodist models. There are over 50,000 Moravians in North America today, but almost 1 million in Africa and the Caribbean.

Further Reading: Atwood, Craig D. *Community of the Cross: Moravian Piety in Colonial Bethlehem.* University Park: Pennsylvania State University Press, 2004; Freeman, Arthur J. *An Ecumenical Theology of the Heart: The Theology of Count Nicholas Ludwig von Zinzendorf.* Bethlehem, PA: Moravian Church in America, 1998; Hamilton, J. Taylor, and Kenneth G. Hamilton. *History of the Moravian Church: The Renewed Unitas Fratrum, 1722–1957.* Bethlehem, PA: Moravian Church in America, 1967; Reichel, Gerhard. *The Story of the Thirteenth of August 1727: The Spiritual Birthday of the Renewed Moravian Church.* Trans. Douglas L. Rights. Winston-Salem, NC: Moravian Archives, 1994; Schattschneider, David A. "Moravians in the Midwest 1850–1900: A New Appreciation," *Transactions of the Moravian Historical Society* 23 (1984): 47–69; Sensbach, Jon. *Rebecca's Revival: Creating Black Christianity in the Atlantic World.* Cambridge, MA: Harvard University Press, 2005; Ward, W. R. *The*

Protestant Evangelical Awakening. Cambridge: Cambridge University Press, 1992.

Craig D. Atwood

MORMONS AND MORMONISM

Members of the Church of Jesus Christ of Latter-day Saints are commonly called Mormons, and their doctrines Mormonism, because of their acceptance of *The Book of Mormon* (1830) as scripture. Along with the Bible, it is one of the four canonical standard works of their faith. Founded by **Joseph Smith** in 1830, the church moved, under persecution, from New York to Ohio and Missouri, and then to Illinois, before being driven in the aftermath of Smith's 1844 assassination to what is today the state of Utah. From its headquarters in Salt Lake City, the movement has grown rapidly throughout the Western Hemisphere and beyond.

Mormonism's complex doctrines sharply separate it from mainstream Christendom, but, on one level, it can plausibly be viewed as originating in a reaction against revivalism. The young Joseph Smith was appalled at the religious strife that accompanied the revivals of his childhood. The initial success of the church he established may have been due to a quest for refuge from the plurality of revivalistic groups in the **Burned-Over District** of New York State. Smith reported having had a **vision** in which he was told not to join any of the existing Christian denominations. Many early Mormons seem to have been resistant to revival practices. Smith later recalled that during the period before his first vision he "wanted to get religion too, wanted to feel and shout like the rest, but could feel nothing" (M. V. Backman, Jr., *Joseph Smith's First Vision* [1980], 177). His younger cousin, George A. Smith, was "sealed up" to "eternal damnation" when he remained the last sinner still seated in the gallery at the conclusion of one **preacher**'s sermon. Brigham Young (1801–1877), Smith's successor as president of the church, disapproved of the revivalistic emotionalism he recalled from his youth in New York, which seemed to him to convey no useful information. He had declined to join any church, and when he heard of

Mormonism in 1830, he first "watched to see if good common sense was manifest" (*Journal of Discourses* 8:38). This emphasis on reasonableness is apparent in the style of Mormon meetings and homiletics. An influential treatise by a church leader bears the title *A Rational Theology* (1915).

Yet Mormonism is neither rationalistic nor anti-emotional. Monthly "testimony meetings" center on spontaneous personal witness and testimony from ordinary members, and the attainment of religious certainty through private individual revelation is a fundamental doctrine of the faith (see *The Book of Mormon*, Moroni 10:4–5). The 1836 dedication of the first Mormon temple, in Kirtland, Ohio, and attendant events might be compared to revivalistic phenomena. Many participants reported visions of angels, flames of spiritual fire, and the like. Yet, characteristically, they were conducted under the supervision of the church's centralized and hierarchical leadership, and culminated in a reinforcement of the status and authority of the Mormon priesthood and the establishment of the still flourishing, uniquely Latter-day Saint tradition of temple building, with its associated rituals. According to Joseph Smith and Oliver Cowdery, Jesus himself appeared to them, accepting the building. That theophany was followed by appearances of Moses, "Elias," and Elijah, who restored the "keys of the priesthood"—including the authority to lead the literal gathering of dispersed Israel and to perform the "sealing" ordinances for the living and the dead fundamental to Mormon temple doctrine. With its **primitivism**—that is, the impulse to reestablish the ethos and practice of early Christianity, and even Old Testament customs—early Mormonism had something in common with other contemporaneous groups, such as the adherents of **restorationism and the Stone-Campbell movement.**

The nearest analogue in the history of the Latter-day Saints to full-fledged revivalism is the Reformation of 1856–1857, during which church leaders, newly established in Salt Lake City, exhorted members to recommit to their faith. Initially punctuated by anxious and spontaneous **confessions,** the reformation soon become more measured, systematic, and orderly, under direction of church headquarters. In some cases, Latter-day Saints who declined to signify their recommitment through rebaptism were expunged from the membership rolls. John Taylor, successor to Brigham Young as third president of the church, undertook a program of reform and recommitment in 1882–1884, but it was cut short when the U.S. government launched a massive campaign of prosecution and disenfranchisement against the Mormons for their practice of polygamy (which ended in 1890). Further episodes of recommitment to specific principles, but lacking any of the characteristic elements of revivalism, can easily be discerned in Mormon history. The administration of the fifth president of the church, Lorenzo Snow (1898–1901), saw a renewed emphasis on the principle of tithing. Heber J. Grant (1918–1945) summoned Latter-day Saints to greater compliance with the church's dietary code, the "Word of Wisdom," entailing abstinence from tobacco, alcohol, tea, and coffee. Under the motto "Lengthen Your Stride," Spencer W. Kimball (1973–1985) encouraged greater missionary efforts. Ezra Taft Benson (1985–1994) refocused attention on *The Book of Mormon.*

Further Reading: Allen, James B., and Glen M. Leonard. *The Story of the Latter-day Saints.* 2nd rev. ed. Salt Lake City: Deseret Books, 1992; Arrington, Leonard J., and Davis Bitton. *The Mormon Experience: A History of the Latter-day Saints.* New York: Knopf, 1979; Church of Jesus Christ of Latter-day Saints Web site. http://www.lds.org/; Ludlow, Daniel H., ed. *Encyclopedia of Mormonism.* 5 vols. New York: Macmillan, 1992.

Daniel C. Peterson

MOTOR MISSIONS

Motor missions were a form of outreach by **Roman Catholics** who traveled by automobile to speak in communities that had had little contact with Catholicism. The motor mission was the American clerical offshoot of a movement launched in England by Vernon Redwood, founder of the Catholic Evidence Guild, an organization of lay street **preachers** who sought to lessen anti-Catholic bigotry by explaining the tenets of the Roman faith to anyone who would listen. Frank and Maisie Ward brought the Evidence Guild to the United States. An outgrowth of the Guild, motor missions began in the 1930s and lasted until the mid-1960s. While the **parish mission** sought to renew and revitalize the faith of nominal or practicing members of a Roman Catholic congregation, the motor mission centered primarily on non-Catholics and took place outside the boundaries of existing Catholic parishes, buildings, and institutions.

Motor missions received their impetus from a priest of the diocese of Tulsa–Oklahoma City, Father Stephen Leven, who had learned the street preacher's craft from the Evidence Guild while he was a student in Europe. Upon returning home, he was appalled by the anti-Catholic prejudice of rural folk and set about to counter it by traveling throughout the countryside explaining the Catholic faith in towns and villages. In the mid-1930s, the priests of the Congregation of the Mission (Vincentians), who studied street preaching under Leven, institutionalized the motor missions, so called because the missioners traveled about by car carrying their equipment with them. The apostolate quickly spread beyond the Vincentians to the Benedictines, Paulists, Redemptorists, Glenmarians, and even some diocesan missionary bands. Soon, missioners began towing trailer chapels complete with living quarters, an altar, and a fold-down platform on which to say Mass and preach. Because the missions were open-air events, priests typically conducted them only in the summer months. Motor missioners traveled alone or in pairs. They fanned out to rural towns throughout the **South,** Midwest, and Northwest. Missioners usually arrived in a town on Saturday and asked the mayor's permission to speak in a public place, preferably on the courthouse steps or lawn, at the park bandstand, or in the heart of the business district. They visited local shopkeepers to secure approval for placing placards in store windows advertising the mission.

The motor mission lasted a week, beginning on Monday and ending the following Saturday, with no services on Sundays out of deference to Protestant worship. The street preaching took place in the evenings after farm chores and supper. The missioners would deploy a collapsible pulpit and set up a

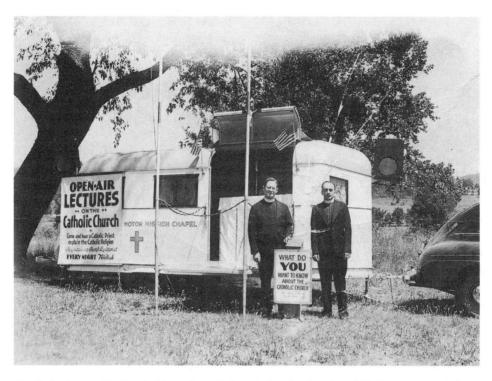

The St. Anthony trailer chapel with speaker's platform deployed and an altar visible. These motor missionaries traveled through rural Missouri and adjoining states in the Midwest from the 1930s through the 1950s. Courtesy of the DeAndreis-Rosati Memorial Archives.

loudspeaker system over which they played popular tunes for about a half an hour in order to gather a crowd. They began each evening with a short talk, followed by a 30-minute discourse on some aspect of the Catholic faith that was the subject of frequent misunderstanding, like the papacy, Catholic schools, the Virgin Mary, and the sacraments. The priests addressed the audience in plain and simple language, avoiding esoteric Catholic terminology. In citing scripture, missioners always used the King James Version of the Bible, with which their listeners were familiar. The highlight of the evening was the question-and-answer period, when missioners responded to written queries about the church, which the townspeople had deposited in a question box earlier in the day. In most instances, missioners were accorded a respectful hearing, though at times they were heckled or driven from town. On occasion they spoke to empty benches, and not uncommonly they had to put up with a competing Protestant revival meeting hastily organized after their arrival.

Motor missioners had several ways of determining the success of their efforts. The most tangible was the number of persons in attendance each evening. As repeat visits were made to the same town, another sign of effectiveness was the emergence of Catholic life as former church members long bereft of ministration took heart and established a parish. A third indicator came in the numerous requests from non-Catholics for more information about the Roman faith. By 1953, the Vincentians alone had received more than a million inquiries. Finally, although the purpose of the motor mission was the explanation of the tenets of Catholicism rather than proselytization, conversions were an expected by-product. While a massive influx of converts never materialized, conversions did occur.

As modernity reached the countryside and touched the Catholic church, motor missions became obsolete. With the spread of electricity to rural America, more and more farms had air conditioning and television, two appliances that kept inhabitants

This automobile carries an apocalyptic message for politicians in the nation's capital. The vehicle's side warns that the United States is "Mammon's 7th King" and that President Franklin Roosevelt is "soon to be destroyed." (Photographer John Vachon, July 1939.) Courtesy of the Library of Congress.

indoors on warm summer evenings. Street preaching could not compete with these conveniences. Moreover, Catholic theology underwent a seismic shift in the Second Vatican Council (1962–1965), one element of which was the church's openness to the ecumenical movement, and its declaration that Protestant Christians were "separated brethren." These changes in the Catholic Church's posture toward non-Roman Catholic Christians made motor missions seem anachronistic.

Further Reading: Marlett, Jeffrey D. *Saving the Heartland: Catholic Missionaries in Rural America, 1920–1960.* DeKalb: Northern Illinois University Press, 2002; Slawson, Douglas J. "Catholic Revivalism: The Vincentian Preaching Apostolate in the United States." In Michael J. McClymond, ed., *Embodying the Spirit: New Perspectives on North American Revivalism,* 211–52. Baltimore: Johns Hopkins University Press, 2004; Slawson, Douglas J. "Thirty Years of Street Preaching: Vincentian Motor Missions, 1934–1965." *Church History* 62 (1993): 60–81.

Douglas J. Slawson

MOURNERS' BENCH

see Altar Call

MUHLENBERG, HENRY MELCHIOR (1711–1787)

Henry Melchior Muhlenberg, founder of the **Lutheran** Church in America, was a product of the university at Halle, the Prussian center of Lutheran **Pietism** in Germany. He was born in Einbeck in Hannover, and began his studies in preparation for the Lutheran ministry at Göttingen before transferring to Halle. His initial plans to become a missionary to Jews in Palestine were interrupted by a call from Gotthilf August Francke to serve the United Congregations of Philadelphia, New Hanover, and Providence in Philadelphia. He arrived in Philadelphia in 1742, with little understanding of the frontier conditions he would encounter in the colony. Numerous German Lutherans had already settled there, who represented a scattered flock that was awaiting to be gathered into a parish life.

Entering this heady mix, Muhlenberg began itinerating, making visitations and proceeding to implement the rudiments of parish life. He found himself mediating between the needs of the frontier and the expectations of the mission society in Halle that had commissioned him. This interaction took several precarious turns. The Pennsylvania authorities were unreceptive to the introduction of ecclesiastical structures. Where congregations had been formed, laity were unaccustomed to pastoral oversight, particularly from one of Pietist bent, as in the case of Muhlenberg. The year of Muhlenberg's arrival was also the occasion of Count Nicholas Zinzendorf's abortive effort to organize the **Moravians** and all other Pennsylvania German sects into his projected Congregation of God in the Spirit. Muhlenberg mistrusted the motives of the count, and regarded his efforts as undermining the integrity of Lutheran congregations in the colony.

After shoring up the congregation in Philadelphia, which had been victimized by an irregular **preacher,** Valentine Kraft, Muhlenberg succeeded in garnering support from key Pennsylvania German families by marrying the daughter of the influential Indian agent Conrad Wieser in 1745. With this consensus, he took legal means to dismiss the Moravians who had occupied the pulpits of Lutheran congregations in Tulpehocken and Philadelphia. In 1748 he formed the Pennsylvania Ministerium to be the governing body of American Lutheranism. His Pietist sympathies led him to assert control over the anti-Pietist leader of the New York synod, Wilhelm Christoph Berkenmeyer (1686–1751), whose intent was to promote his link with the orthodox Amsterdam Consistory rather than with Halle.

The consequence of these actions was that Muhlenberg's style of churchmanship would become normative for colonial American Lutheranism. The constitution of the Pennsylvania Ministerium limited the autonomy of laity in relation to the clergy, and upheld the German Lutheran liturgy over against the excesses of revivalism. His journal discloses his pastoral focus and itinerating pattern of parish visitation. It presents a pastor-administrator who had a pragmatic style in adapting his Hallensian training to the frontier milieu. He could be confrontational when he believed the interest of the church was at stake. In addition to his actions against Zinzendorf, his journal contains a critical discussion of the effects of revivalistic ministry at Frederick, Maryland, and of the German **Reformed** Pietist leader **Philip William Otterbein**

(1726–1813). **Quakers** and the Ephrata Brethren came under particularly harsh criticism in his reports to his European sponsors, as when he declares that the former "do not need to trouble themselves with the written Word of God and the sacraments." Despite his criticism of what he regarded as revivalist and sectarian excesses, it is clear that he continued to reflect the Pietist outlook of Halle, as when he writes that "I must also lament over some in our own church" who "have the illusion that they are already converted if they have performed the *opus operatum* [i.e., outward work] of external worship … although on other occasions they curse enough and horrify heaven" (*Hallesche Nachrichten*, 1:520, trans. Theodore Tappert).

With regard to social issues, Muhlenberg supported the appeals of those who called for self-defense against acts of physical aggression, whether from Native Americans or from the British during the Revolutionary War, although he avoided publicly identifying with the colonial cause. In fact, two of his sons actively participated in the Continental cause, with their father's blessing.

Further Reading: Riforgiato, L. R. *Missionary of Moderation: Henry Melchior Muhlenberg and the Lutheran Church in English America.* 1980; Stoeffler, F. Ernest, ed. *Continental Pietism and Early American Christianity.* Grand Rapids, MI: Eerdmans, 1976.

J. Steven O'Malley

MUSIC

see Hymns, Hymnody, and Christian Music in Revivals

N

NATIONAL BAPTIST CONVENTION USA AND NATIONAL BAPTIST CONVENTION OF AMERICA

Today many **African Americans** belong to **Baptist** churches that stand in a tradition stretching back to the mid-1700s. Blacks founded their first Baptist congregation in what became the United States in 1758 in Lunenburg (now Mecklenburg, Virginia) on the plantation of William Byrd III. Because of the unstable conditions of slave life, the church organization was also unstable and soon collapsed. Yet four black **preachers**—the brothers Moses, Benjamin, and Thomas Gardiner, with another man, known only as Farrell—reconstituted the church in 1772. Baptist churches originated in 1776 in Virginia in the cities of Williamsburg and Petersburg.

George Liele (1752–1825) established the Silver Bluff Church in South Carolina in 1774 and a church in Savannah, Georgia, in 1777. In 1782, Liele, who was pastor of the First African Church of Savannah, hearing that the British pursued peace with the colonies, indentured himself to a British officer in order not to be reenslaved by his former master's heirs. He and his family moved to Kingston, Jamaica. After two years he paid back his indenture and was able to devote all his energy to preaching. Because of his sojourn in Jamaica, Liele was a pioneer missionary among black Baptists. With four other former American slaves, he formed the First African Baptist Church of Kingston in 1783. In 10 years the church grew to include more than 500 members. A slave in Savannah and possible pupil of Liele, Andrew Bryan (1737–1812) founded Bryan Baptist Church in 1788. The Silver Bluff congregation in South Carolina closed and moved further south because of the Revolutionary War, and some of its members joined Liele's congregation in Savannah. Others moved to Augusta, where, with Georgia Jesse Peter, they formed the Springfield Baptist Church. In the early 1800s, a prominent black Baptist leader was Lott Carey, who in 1821 established a mission in Sierra Leone, and authored *A History of Black Baptists*.

With the **Civil War**'s ending in 1865, black Baptists began to set up programs and agencies to aid the newly emancipated slaves. To do this more effectively, the churches in several states organized themselves into associations. In 1866, Baptists in North Carolina organized the first state convention. By 1870, every state in the **South** had formed a Baptist Convention and there were more than 500,000 Baptists. The growth of the state conventions paved the way for the formation of a national Baptist organization in Montgomery, Alabama. In 1880, a convocation representing various southern black Baptist churches, associations, and state conventions founded the Foreign Mission Baptist

Convention of the USA, with W. H. McAlpine as its first president. In 1893 W. Bishop Johnson in Washington, DC, established the National Baptist Educational Convention (NBEC) to give support for the education of ministers.

In 1895, more than 2,000 clergymen met in Atlanta, Georgia, including representatives from the Baptist Foreign Missionary Convention (BFMC), the American National Baptist Convention (ANBC), and the National Baptist Educational Convention (NBEC). These separate bodies merged to form the National Baptist Convention of the United States of America (NBC USA Inc.), which brought together northern and southern black Baptist churches, with Elias Camp Morris as the first president. In 1901, Nannie Burroughs formed the Woman's Auxiliary of the NBC USA. In 1915 at the Baptist convention in Chicago, internal problems arose. The issue was whether the National Baptist Publishing Board—the organization that printed nearly all of the Sunday school and Christian education materials—was a part of the convention or a separate entity and able to keep the monies received from its sales. The Publishing Board, under Richard H. Boyd, incorporated, and this caused a legal battle that brought the severance of the National Baptist Convention of America (NBCA) from the National Baptist Convention (NBC).

Thomas A. Dorsey (1899–1993), often called the father of gospel music, was a trained composer, songwriter, pianist, and baritone singer and a musical leader within the new denomination. He has had great influence in the development of **hymns** and Christian music. In 1933, the National Convention of Gospel Choirs and Choruses Inc. (NCGCC) was formed by Dorsey along with Sallie Martin (1896–1988), Magnolia Lewis Butts (ca. 1880–1949), Theodore R. Frye (1899–1963), and Beatrice Brown. The NCGCC convention took place in a different city each year, with new songs introduced, performed, and taught to local choirs at each gathering. "The Queen of Gospel," Mahalia Jackson (1911–1972), was associated with Dorsey and Theodore R. Frye, who founded the National Baptist Music Convention (NBMC) in 1948 for the training of

church musicians. Dorsey helped usher in a golden era of gospel music from 1945 to 1955.

The civil rights era brought new challenges and opportunities for black Baptists. In 1961 members of the NBC USA withdrew from the denomination based on civil rights issues. President Joseph Harrison Jackson of the NBC USA advocated a different approach than Martin Luther King Jr. King did not want a schism at the convention, yet King's supporters made him head of the Progressive National Baptist Convention (PNBC).

In Dallas in 1988, the National Missionary Baptist Convention of America (NMBCA) was formed to support churches in the southwest. The formation of the Full Gospel Baptist Fellowship in New Orleans by Bishop Paul Morton in 1993 created an organization for the **Holiness-Pentecostal** wing of the Baptist church. In January 2005, the four presidents of the NBC USA, PNBC, NMBCA, and NBCA met in Nashville, Tennessee. This historic summit of the four major African American Baptist conventions was intended to heal relationships and to work together for the good of African Americans.

Further Reading: DuPree, Sherry Sherrod, and Herbert C. DuPree. *African-American Good News (Gospel) Music.* Washington, DC: Middle Atlantic Regional Press, 1993; Fitts, Leroy. *A History of Black Baptists.* Nashville, TN: Broadman Press, 1985; Fitts, Leroy. *Lott Carey: First Black Missionary to Africa.* Valley Forge, PA: Judson Press, 1978; Jackson, Joseph. *A Story of Christian Activism: The History of the National Baptist Convention, U.S.A., Inc.* Nashville, TN: Townsend, 1980; Lincoln, C. Eric. *Race, Religion and the Continuing American Dilemma.* New York: Hill and Wang, 1984; Mays, Benjamin E., and Joseph W. Nicholson. *The Negro's Church.* New York: Arno Press, 1969; Washington, James Melvin. *Frustrated Fellowship: The Black Baptist Quest for Social Power.* Macon, GA: Mercer University Press, 1986.

Sherry Sherrod DuPree

THE NAVIGATORS

The Navigators are an evangelical parachurch ministry of Christian discipleship founded in 1933 by Dawson Trotman (1906–1956). Trotman, a lumberyard worker before his conversion in 1929, had been active in T. C. Horton's International Fisherman's Club in the early 1930s. While living in Southern California, Trotman organized an outreach to sailors originally known as the Servicemen's Bible Club but soon renamed the Navigators. Trotman emphasized Bible memorization and **prayer,** and a life of evangelism through one-on-one discipleship and spiritual multiplication (e.g., the belief that those discipled would evangelize and disciple others). By the end of World War II, the Navigators had begun ministries at 450 army bases and on 350 navy vessels. Trotman and his associate Lorne Sanny developed follow-up materials designed to help Navigators staff in their work of discipleship. One of the early tools was the *B Rations*, a package that introduced individuals to the concept of Bible memorization. Following the war, the ministry expanded its focus beyond the armed forces to colleges, churches, and the business world. In 1949, the Navigators inaugurated the ministry's international work by sending a representative to China.

Although Trotman's emphasis on one-on-one discipleship steered the organization away from holding its own mass evangelistic campaigns, the Navigators played a significant role in postwar revivalism. In the early 1950s, **Billy Graham** asked Trotman to develop counselor training and follow-up procedures for his crusades. Graham was increasingly worried about insufficient efforts by local churches to contact and nurture Christian converts. Trotman and his staff designed an *Introductory Bible Study* that instructed disciples in a "wheel" of prayer, fellowship, scripture, and witnessing (or personal evangelism). Trotman traveled to numerous Graham campaigns, met with volunteer counselors who would greet those who came forward at the close of Graham's sermons. Counselors received training in how to present a clear three-minute testimony to encourage uncertain individuals to make a decision to accept Jesus Christ as Lord and Savior. Churches sent representatives to Trotman for training so that they would be prepared to follow up the names they received on decision cards mailed by the Graham team.

Numerous evangelical churches and ministries in the 1940s and 1950s began using the Navigators' method of discipleship and materials. In the early years of the **Campus Crusade for Christ,** for example, Bill Bright regularly met with Trotman and exchanged ideas regarding evangelism and the follow-up of new converts. Trotman assisted Bright by loaning him a number of his own staff members to help with latter's fledgling ministry. Before the organization developed its own materials in the late 1950s, Crusade staff used the *B Rations* and the *Introductory Bible Study* to nurture collegiate converts. In 1953, the ministry moved its headquarters from Los Angeles to a ranch purchased in Colorado Springs, Colorado. While at a lake in the Adirondack Mountains, Trotman suffered a heart attack while rescuing a woman from drowning. Loren Sanny succeeded him as president and led the ministry until 1986. As of 2001, there were nearly 4,000 Navigators staff serving in over 100 countries. The ministry has maintained its initial emphasis on in-depth, one-on-one discipleship and training.

Further Reading: Navigators Web site. http://www.navigators.org/; Skinner, Betty Lee. *Daws: The Story of Dawson Trotman, Founder of the Navigators.* Grand Rapids, MI: Zondervan, 1974.

John Turner

NETTLETON, ASAHEL (1783–1844)

Asahel Nettleton was a widely traveled **preacher** who led quiet, orderly, and yet powerful revival services in the churches and colleges of the northeastern United States from the 1820s to the 1840s. He was a **Calvinistic** minister who opposed **Charles Finney's** "new measures" revivalism because of what he saw as its harsh, judgmental, and prideful spirit, its tendency to promote divisions in churches, its use of emotional manipulation and high-pressure tactics in revival services, and its tendency to produce false **conversions.** Nettleton was born in North Killingworth, Connecticut, in 1783. His parents, Samuel and Anne, were farmers and "halfway" covenant members of the Congregational church who had never professed an experience of conversion and so could not partake in Communion. As a child Nettleton was required to memorize the Westminster Catechism (1648), and this exercise shaped his lifelong theological convictions. During the "Great Revival" of 1800, which marked the beginning of what is known as the **Second Great Awakening,** Nettleton reportedly experienced what his parents apparently had missed, namely, rebirth through the Holy Spirit. His conversion resulted in an intense desire to serve God in **foreign missions.** Yet soon after his conversion his father died, and as the eldest son it became necessary for him to look after the family farm and finances. During this period, his desire to communicate the Christian message increased. However, it was not until 1805 that he was free to enter Yale College in preparation for the ministry, and he graduated in 1809. Nettleton did not distinguish himself as student at a Yale but did become known for his passion for saving souls. Following graduation he served briefly as college butler while also studying theology. He joined himself to Rev. Bezaleel Pinneo of Milford, Connecticut, for further theological training, and was licensed to preach in 1811 by the Western Association of New Haven County.

Nettleton commenced his evangelistic labors as an itinerant evangelist in an area of eastern Connecticut that had been disrupted by excesses, disorders, and divisions during the earlier **Great Awakening.** Nettleton's ministry brought spiritual healing to troubled congregations and lasting conversions to the faith. Though still desiring foreign mission service, the requests for his preaching in New England together with his own feeble physical health led him to delay foreign service until it was no longer an option. Nettleton was ordained as a Congregational evangelist by the Consociation of Litchfield County, Connecticut, in 1817 and continued in this role until his death. Except for a single year spent in ministry in England, Nettleton's labors were confined to New England, New York, and Virginia. Nettleton never served as a settled pastor, never married, never asked for payment for his services, and never sought fame or notoriety. He expected those converted under his ministry to remain faithful to their profession, and a large proportion did so. Nettleton's ministry led to a series of revivals in the Capital District area of New York State during 1819 and 1820. The entire region was spiritually moved but Union College in Schenectady was especially affected. Students and tutors at the college emerged as "revival men" whose influence was felt for years to come in divergent places.

Having observed the excesses of revivalism in the eastern part of the nation in the 1820s, Nettleton was opposed to what became known as the "new measures" evangelism. His **theology of revivals** was God centered, and he regarded Charles Finney's preaching and ministry as shallow and human centered. Nettleton sought to halt the spread of Finneyite revivalism, and yet a face-to-face meeting of its opponents and proponents in New Lebanon, New York, in 1827 failed to stem the tide. Before the New Lebanon meeting, the influential New England minister **Lyman Beecher** had declared his opposition to Finney's revival techniques and had coauthored with Nettleton a series of letters criticizing Finney. Yet after the meeting, Beecher shifted his position, began to favor Finney, and later invited Finney to speak from his own pulpit in Boston. Beecher's support for Finney did much to weaken Nettleton's position and that of other traditional Calvinists who were among Finney's sharpest critics. Before long the new theology of Finney and the new measures were entrenched in American religious culture and had largely supplanted the earlier theologies of conversion and revival taught by **Theodorus Jacobus Frelinghuysen, Jonathan Edwards,** and **Gilbert Tennent.**

Nettleton joined other like-minded individuals in the formation of the Theological Institute of Connecticut, which was later moved to Hartford and renamed the Hartford Theological Seminary. He was offered a professorship, which he declined, though he occasionally lectured there. Nettleton was largely a forgotten figure for a century after his death, but in recent decades there has been some renewal of interest in his life and ministry. Though Nettleton has largely been known as a critic of Charles Finney, he was a significant revivalist in his own right who may have been responsible for as many as 30,000 conversions during his preaching career.

Congregational revivalist Asahel Nettleton, portrayed with Bible in hand. The stiff collar is emblematic of a restrained, Calvinistic style that contrasted with the wildness and emotionalism of other revivalists during the early 1800s. Courtesy of the Connecticut Historical Society, Hartford, CT.

Further Reading: *Letters of the Rev. Dr. Beecher and the Rev. Mr. Nettleton, on the "New Measures" in Conducting Revivals of Religion.* New York: G. & C. Carvill, 1828; McAuley, Thomas. *A Narrative of the Revival of Religion within the Bounds of the Presbytery of Albany, in the Year 1820.* Schenectady, NY: Isaac Riggs, 1821; Nettleton, Asahel. *Village Hymns for Social Worship.* Ames, IA: International Outreach, 1977; Nichols, William C., ed. *Asahel Nettleton: Sermons from the Second Great Awakening.* Ames, IA: International Outreach, 1995; Thornbury, John F. *God Sent Revival: The Story of Asahel Nettleton and the Second Great Awakening.* Welwyn, UK: Evangelical Press, 1977; Tyler, Bennet. *Nettleton and His Labours: The Memoir of Dr. Asahel Nettleton.* Edinburgh: Banner of Truth Trust, 1975.

Richard Owen Roberts

NEVIN, JOHN WILLIAMSON (1803–1886)

John Williamson Nevin was an American theologian who opposed **Charles Grandison Finney** and his "new measures" revivalism, which involved **altar calls** (or calls to the "anxious bench"), prolonged meetings, and emotional appeals in evangelism. Of Scottish descent, Nevin was raised in Pennsylvania and nurtured in the **Presbyterian** Church. He studied at Union College, where he attended a revival under the leadership of the traveling evangelist **Asahel Nettleton.** Afterward Nevin experienced a **conversion** as he went to student-led religious meetings. In his retrospective work *My Own Life* (1870), Nevin commended Nettleton for practicing a churchly form of revivalism but castigated the student leaders at Union for devaluing the role of the regular ministry of the church in rearing children in the faith and demanding, instead, a crisis-oriented conversion. Nevin earned a degree from Princeton Seminary in 1826 and became a professor at Western Theological Seminary in 1830. In Pittsburgh Nevin got his first unfavorable taste of Finneyite revival techniques when James Gallaher promoted a revival there in 1835. Nevin began to read widely in German theology, gaining an appreciation for church history and the objective nature of the church. The German **Reformed** Church heard of Nevin's interest in German theology, and, needing a seminary professor, called him to join the faculty of Mercersburg Seminary in Pennsylvania in 1840.

Nevin was soon embroiled in a controversy over the orthodoxy and legitimacy of revivalism with John Winebrenner, a new measures promoter and a former minister in the German Reformed Church who had broken ties with the denomination to found the Church of God (one of several denominations with this name). In 1842 William Ramsey, a fellow student of Nevin's from Princeton, presented himself as a candidate for a pastoral position at the church in Mercersburg and at the end of his sermon made a high-pressure evangelistic appeal. Soon thereafter Nevin published a stringent and widely read critique of new measures revivalism, *The Anxious Bench* (1843). This tract drew both praise and censure, and Nevin responded to his critics and added a constructive section on godly nurture in a second edition in 1844.

Nevin's argument against new measures was theological. By its very nature the altar call—or what Nevin called the "system of the bench"—created a false issue for the conscience. The issue was no longer whether one was willing to repent of sin and believe the Christian message, but whether one was going to come forward to the anxious bench. Appeals to come to the bench aroused emotions and inner conflicts, engendering what Nevin

believed to be spurious rather than genuine conversions. The implied theology of the anxious bench was anti-**Calvinistic** and perhaps Pelagian. It presumed that sinners were not helpless but rather self-determining individuals with an inherent ability to choose God. Instead of nurturing parishioners through the ordinary means of grace—**preaching,** the sacraments, **prayer** meetings, catechetical instruction, and pastoral visitation—new measures revivalism placed undue emphasis on isolated emotional experiences.

In contrast to the anxious bench or altar call, Nevin proposed his own method of rearing godly souls, "the system of the catechism." Nevin's High Church, sacramental, liturgical theology—later developed in conjunction with his seminary colleague, Philip Schaff—is nascent in *The Anxious Bench.* Spiritual life, for Nevin, is gained and maintained through the regular ministries of the church. Revivals may come, but only because extraordinary grace is working through ordinary means. Revivalists were guilty of denying the objective efficacy of baptism and the Lord's Supper because of their focus on subjective, individual experience. Nevin's later works were directed against the theological assumptions of new measures revivalism. *The Mystical Presence* (1846) argued for Christ's objective presence in the Eucharist.

Further Reading: DiPuccio, William. *The Interior Sense of Scripture: The Sacred Hermeneutics of John W. Nevin.* Atlanta: Mercer University Press, 1998; Nichols, James Hastings. *Romanticism in American Theology: Nevin and Schaff at Mercersburg.* Chicago: University of Chicago Press, 1961; Wentz, Richard E. *John Williamson Nevin: American Theologian.* New York: Oxford University Press, 1998.

T. Chris Crain

NEW LIGHTS

see Anti-revivalism, History and Arguments of

NEW MEASURES

see Finney, Charles Grandison; Nettleton, Asahel; Nevin, John Williamson

NEW RELIGIOUS MOVEMENTS AND REVIVALS

New religious movements (NRMs) is a category coined by scholars to avoid the stigma attached to other terms that have often been applied to dissenting religious groups. The terms most frequently employed in the past for such communities, namely, *sect* and *cult*, have legitimate and useful etymological meanings linked respectively to Latin verbs for "follow" and for "cultivate." Unfortunately, those meanings have been clouded by the contemporary use of these words as terms of condemnation and opprobrium. Among the new categories employed for NRMs are *alternative religions, outsider groups, dissenting religious communities, marginal religious groups,* and *fringe communities.*

Through more than two centuries, the relationship between America's NRMs and evangelical revivalism has been both creative and complex. Evangelicalism has spawned NRMs that reflected certain evangelical values and practices at the same time that they criticized evangelical values and practices. Other NRMs have grown up in open opposition to the religious ideas and lifestyles of evangelicals and have employed that sense of animosity to create their own identities as new movements. Still other NRMs have patterned themselves after aspects of evangelicalism that they have found attractive, including such aspects as religious authority, leadership, theology, worship, lifestyle, and outreach. Sometimes they later went on to challenge those very patterns. Rarely have these dependencies been acknowledged publicly by either party to these relationships. For that reason, therefore, this essay seeks to identify these diverse relationships and to provide historical examples that illustrate the creativity and complexity that has been involved in the links between evangelicalism and NRMs.

The NRMs that illustrate the variety of these complex relationships include religious groups that emerged initially in the United States. Among the most prominent are the **Mormons,** or the Church of Jesus Christ of Latter-day Saints, founded by **Joseph Smith** (1805–1844); the **Seventh-day Adventists,** a community linked to the founding efforts of **Ellen Gould (Harmon) White** (1827–1915); the Christian Scientists, a church established by Mary Baker Eddy (1821–1910); the **Jehovah's Witnesses,** a religious body first known as the Watchtower Bible and Tract Society, organized by Charles Taze Russell (1852–1916); and the **Pentecostals,** a religious movement linked with several different figures at the beginning of the twentieth century, including **William Joseph Seymour** (1870–1922), who led the **Azusa Street revival** in Los Angeles. Among the most controversial NRMs to emerge in the United States are the **Oneida Community,** founded by John Humphrey Noyes (1811–1886); the Peace Mission Movement, founded by **Father Divine** (1877?–1965); the Nation of Islam, led by W. D. Fard (b., d. unknown) and Elijah Muhammad (1897–1975); the Peoples Temple, founded by Jim Jones (1931–1978); and the **Branch Davidians,** led in their last stage by David Koresh (1959–1993). Other prominent NRMs in the United States have been imported from abroad, including the **Quakers,** or the Religious Society of Friends, followers of George Fox (1624–1691); the **Shakers,** or the United Society of Believers in Christ's Second Appearing, followers of **Ann Lee** (1736–1784); and the members of the Unification Church, founded by the Reverend Sun Myung Moon (1920–).

The most striking example of a powerful NRM that arose from the immediate context of the evangelical movement is Pentecostalism, which has given birth to a large group of denominations that share with evangelicalism a primary commitment to the necessity of a **conversion** experience as the defining feature of the Christian life. Yet Pentecostals go further and declare that conversion is followed by the **baptism in the Holy Spirit,** an experience evidenced by supernatural or **charismatic gifts,** most notably the gift of **speaking in tongues,** as well as other gifts of the Spirit identified in the New Testament (see 1 Corinthians 12–14), including **healing.** This experiential dimension of the Christian life sets Pentecostals apart from evangelicals, a line of division that has remained clear even though both movements value highly the role of the minister or revivalist, and though both have shared in the growing **megachurch** movement—which includes non-Pentecostal congregations like **Willow Creek Community Church** as well as many Pentecostal or neo-**Charismatic** congregations. The public prominence of these contrasting movements was especially evident in the second half of the twentieth century in the contemporary and competitive careers of **Billy Graham** (1918–) and **Oral Roberts** (1918–). The two movements have never been completely comfortable with one another, and Pentecostalism represents a challenge to the theological sufficiency of evangelicalism.

Among the NRMs that emerged in open opposition to evangelical revivalism, the most successful has been the Church of Jesus Christ of Latter-day Saints. Crafted from Joseph Smith's own experience in western New York in what historians have called the **Burned-Over District,** a region dominated by evangelical religion in the nineteenth century, Mormonism rose as a rejection of those traditions. When Smith asked God which of the churches he should join, he was instructed, "None of them." His spiritual search led, in turn, to the discovery of what he reported as a buried text, which he translated and published as *The Book of Mormon* (1830), representing in his judgment another testimony concerning Jesus Christ. Smith assumed the role of prophet, and he was the recipient of new revelations that shaped a community that saw itself as the only true church, a restoration combining the ancient practices of Israel with the beliefs of the early church. The opposition engendered between Mormonism and the evangelical world was intense, triggered in part by claims regarding *The Book of Mormon,* by Smith's role as prophet, the system of plural marriage he inaugurated, and the willingness of the community to defend itself with arms. Smith's murder by a lynch mob is symbolic of the animosity directed against the Mormons during the nineteenth century. Later, in the 1860s the U.S. Army conducted raids in Utah looking for polygamists.

Evangelicals consider the Bible to be the ultimate religious authority. They regard the Bible as a divinely inspired text containing all that is needed for salvation and for the Christian life. Yet even with a shared commitment to the authority of the Bible, evangelicals often have debated the proper interpretation of the biblical text. Many of the NRMs mentioned above, including the Pentecostals, the Seventh-day Adventists, and the Jehovah's Witnesses, also regard the Bible as the primary source of religious authority. It would be impossible to overstate the significance of the Bible for them. Yet differences in scriptural interpretation separate these groups from one another and from the evangelicals. Both Adventists and Witnesses, for example, assign special importance to the apocalyptic or **eschatological** portions of the Bible. Members of both groups live with the expectation that they might see the end of the present order during their lifetimes. For neither group is that prospect a source of terror or fear. Rather, they regard that vision of the future as a potential vindication of their beliefs. Based on their interpretation of the Bible, Jehovah's Witnesses reject the doctrine of the Trinity, and assert that Jesus is not divine in the sense that God the Father is divine.

Based on yet another interpretation of the Bible, the Seventh-day Adventists depart from almost all other Christian groups by declaring that the seventh day of the week, or Saturday, is the divinely established day for worship. At least in their early history, Seventh-day Adventists declared that Sunday worship was worthless if not evil in God's sight. Other NRMs value the Bible highly, too, but some, like the Mormons, place alongside it other sacred texts of equal or greater importance. The Christian Scientists, for instance, regard *Science and Health with Key to the Scriptures* (1875), written by Mary Baker Eddy, as a text that unlocks the full meaning of the Bible. Therefore in some sense it is the more significant of the two documents. Members of the Unification Church (formally the Holy Spirit Association for the Unification of World Christianity) view Rev. Moon's *The Divine Principle* as a sacred text of primary importance alongside the Bible.

Religious leadership in evangelical communities rests largely in the hands of male ministers who function publicly as **preachers,** revivalists, and expositors of the Bible. The most successful leaders are gifted, charismatic individuals whose interpersonal skills increase their influence and dominance over their congregations and communities. The most telling measure of their leadership lies in their skill as revivalists. The long line of successful revivalists in the United States includes **Jonathan Edwards, George Whitefield, Charles Grandison Finney, Dwight L. Moody, Billy Sunday, Aimee Semple McPherson, Billy Graham,** and **Jerry Falwell.** Powerful preachers and charismatic leaders have also shaped many of the NRMs. Father Divine, Jim Jones, and Rev. Moon all achieved their leadership in considerable measure on the strength of their rhetorical abilities. These **men** were respected and admired by their followers because of their skills in the pulpit. The contrasting pattern of leadership with some of the other NRMs will be obvious on several grounds. The most apparent point of contrast for some of these groups is the presence of female leaders. Ann Lee, Ellen Gould (Harmon) White, Mary Baker Eddy—all of these **women** were powerful leaders who exercised influence in very different ways. Lee assumed a stern motherly role, White was a visionary, and Eddy was a mix of a grandmother and a near autocrat. None of the three was principally a preacher. They occupied very different physical circumstances during their lifetimes. At times they could be aggressive, but other times they carried out their roles of leaders in less conspicuous ways. But their power and influence were critical in shaping their respective traditions. Other contrasting patterns of leadership are evident in: Mormonism, which links the role of prophet with the presidency of the Latter-day Saint Church; in Shakerism, which empowers the members of the central ministry with the power to receive "gifts" for the community; in the Jehovah's Witness organization, which provides the ruling elders with control and supervision over all aspects of the community's activities; and in the Peoples Temple in Guyana, where Jim Jones used force, intimidation, and sexual coercion to accomplish what he pleased.

The center or heart of evangelical theology lies in the notion that salvation is obtained when an individual undergoes a personal religious experience. Called a rebirth or a conversion, this experience becomes the central fact in an evangelical Christian's life. This moment marks the start of a lifelong commitment to Christian activity, leaving behind sin and evil and pursuing godliness, charity, and proper moral causes. The conversion experience is an empowering moment for evangelicals. It enables them to rise above temptations and sinful pleasures. This rebirth is a constant point of reference for them during the remainder of their lives. Pentecostals share this same primary religious focus on conversion. Other NRMs, however, mark different moments of insight as the turning point in one's life. Friends, or Quakers, for example, describe the need for individuals to recognize that they have the Light of Christ within. That critical insight will then transform them. Following the Light, or listening to the Voice within, empowers one to live the simple Christian life and to avoid pride, vanity, sensuality, or violence. The salvific vision of the Mormons is more elaborate. Premised on the principle that the Mormon saints are "saved by grace, and exalted by works," Mormons believe in a doctrine of eternal progression through which humans may evolve to godhood by obeying the rules and ordinances revealed to the Mormon Church. The phrase "As man is, God once was; as God is, man may become," summarizes this vision of potential spiritual progress. Christian Science has a different, but also very positive, notion of human nature based on a judgment concerning reality itself. Eddy stated that only God and spiritual manifestations exist; therefore evil, sin, and even matter are illusions. Recognition of this true spiritual reality frees one from the grip of these misperceptions.

Evangelical worship services typically include **hymns** or music, **prayer,** Bible reading, preaching, testimonies, and an **altar call** presided over by the minister or revivalist. These meetings may be held in church buildings, auditoriums, or athletic facilities, or outside in fields or under tents. The historical precedents for these diverse settings are nineteenth-century **camp meetings** and "protracted meetings" (i.e., religious services lasting for many hours or for days). Hymns have always played a major role in evangelical meetings. With the passage of time, instrumental music has been incorporated into the meetings; more recently, popular musical forms have also been introduced into the services and revivals. The same is true in Pentecostal revivals where music, testimonies, and altar calls are present. The Mormons held their own camp meetings in the nineteenth century. In the twentieth and twenty-first centuries, the Jehovah's Witnesses have held huge rallies in athletic stadiums that have had the effect of reinforcing their religious identity and announcing their presence in a very public manner. Similar gatherings called by two **African American** leaders, Father Divine and Elijah Muhammad, had the effect of bringing their movements into the public eye. Rev. Moon adapted his large gatherings into mass weddings for his followers. In the nineteenth century, Shaker brothers sometimes attended evangelical revivals and worked the edges of the crowd, trying to gain converts for their movement from among the participants. They were often successful in that goal. Jim Jones and David Koresh presided over extended meetings of their followers at which they instructed, inspired, and cajoled them. An even more striking contrast to these worship patterns occurs among traditional Quakers, who gather in silence without clergy or a presiding minister until someone is moved to share his or her testimony. In the nineteenth century, when the Shakers gathered in their meetinghouses, they marched and danced as an expression of their communal beliefs. The Sunday meetings of contemporary Jehovah's Witnesses are learning sessions with lectures by presiding elders and scripted lessons from the *Watchtower* magazine.

The lifestyle of evangelical Christians underscores the importance of moral virtues, including honesty, hard work, temperance, chastity before marriage, faithfulness in marriage, family values—all in a context presided over by the father. That does not mean the role of the mother is unimportant, but it is clearly subordinate to that of the father and is focused in the home. Children are to be nurtured in the faith, taught at home and at church. Sunday school was one institution employed for that purpose. This pattern of ideal evangelical family life was

also reflected in Pentecostal and Adventist families. There were, however, striking contrasts to these lifestyles among the Mormons, the Shakers, and members of the Oneida Community. The nineteenth-century experiment of the Mormons with plural marriage or polygamy, and the system of "complex marriage" established by John Humphrey Noyes at Oneida, reinforced group identity by allowing forms of sexual activity that were generally not tolerated outside the group. The structured system of total celibacy that governed relations between the sexes in Shakerism, and the prohibition of marriage for all except Father Divine in his communal "heavens," were social arrangements that contrasted sharply with evangelical lifestyles as well as with those of most other NRMs. In more recent times, controversy has surrounded the sexual relations that Jim Jones had with both men and women in the Peoples Temple and the polygamous relations of David Koresh with Branch Davidian members in their compound in Waco, Texas.

Evangelicalism in America has been characterized from the very beginning by a vigorous program of outreach, seeking to win converts to the movement by individual contact as well as by carefully organized missionary efforts. Traveling revivalists, circuit riders, home and **foreign missionaries**—these were early expressions of this impulse. The nineteenth century witnessed the full utilization of the printing press as publishers printed books and journals, and societies distributed tracts and spread the word. Each new advance in the field of communications in the twentieth century—**radio, television,** cable networks, the **Internet**—has been utilized by evangelicals to spread the word. Evangelicals, however, are not alone in this process. In fact, they may have been surpassed in many ways by the successes of Pentecostals in the third world, especially in South America. The Mormons are spreading their faith throughout the world with their system of missionaries begun by Joseph Smith, an outreach effort now involving both young males and females. The Jehovah's Witnesses are perhaps unsurpassed in their capacity to spread printed materials around the world. These and other NRMs are making use of the new forms of communication, and in doing so they are competing vigorously for converts throughout the world. At the same time, many of these groups continue to use door-to-door techniques for spreading their respective gospels.

There is every reason to believe that NRMs for the foreseeable future will continue to mirror selectively the diverse aspects of evangelical revivalism. NRMs that are rooted in non-Christian religions—including Hinduism, Buddhism, Taoism, indigenous religions, Islam, and other traditions—are growing in North America, fueled in part by the 1965 changes in immigration law that facilitated a larger influx of Asian, African, and Middle Eastern immigrants to the United States. Therefore it seems likely that the latest NRMs will continue the patterns described above, some reflecting religious ideas and social configurations similar to those of evangelicalism as they form their own identity. At the same time, others may construct their own identity and attract adherents by standing in opposition to the evangelical movement in America.

Further Reading: Chryssides, George D. *Historical Dictionary of New Religious Movements.* Lanham, MD: Scarecrow Press, 2001; Conkin, Paul K. *American Originals: Homemade Varieties of Christianity.* Chapel Hill: University of North Carolina Press, 1997; Lewis, James R., ed. *Old Gods: New Religion and the Cult Controversy.* Amherst, NY: Prometheus Books, 2001; Melton, J. Gordon. *Encyclopedia of American Religions.* 6th ed. Detroit: Gale Research, 1999; Miller, Timothy, ed. *America's Alternative Religions.* Albany: State University of New York Press, 1995; Partridge, Christopher H. *New Religions: A Guide; New Religious Movements, Sects and Alternative Spiritualities.* New York: Oxford University Press, 2004; Stein, Stephen J. *Communities of Dissent: A History of Alternative Religions in America.* New York: Oxford University Press, 2003.

Stephen J. Stein

NORTHAMPTON REVIVAL OF 1734–1735

During the 1730s, a religious "stir" occurred in Northampton, Massachusetts, under the leadership of **Jonathan Edwards** (1703–1758), which he made famous in *A Faithful Narrative of the Surpris-*

ing Work of God (1737). Otherwise known as the Little Awakening, because it is viewed as a prelude to the so-called **Great Awakening** of the 1740s, the revival had its beginnings in late 1733, when Edwards, after consciously working to promote a revival since becoming full pastor of Northampton in 1729, noticed a "flexibleness, and yielding to advice in our young people" (Edwards, 147). Taking a cue from his predecessor and grandfather, **Solomon Stoddard,** who in the "harvests" he had overseen during his long tenure deliberately targeted young people, Edwards tailored his message to the younger generations, with apparent success. In April 1734, the death of a young person in the congregation set off a general religious concern among the youth. In the months that followed, Edwards saw "soul concerns" spread through the town. He believed that over 300 people were converted. Well over 200 were admitted into church membership in the two-year period—at one point as many as 100 in one day. Equally pleasing to Edwards was the atmosphere of harmony and Christian behavior that prevailed in notoriously contentious Northampton. Even more, he received reports from nearly 30 communities up and down the Connecticut River valley and beyond that the revival spirit had spread there.

For Edwards, the revival was every bit as much a testimony to the evangelical **Calvinist** "heart religion" that he **preached** as it was a broadside against the incursion of heterodoxy in the form of Arminianism. The term *Arminianism* was used broadly to malign anyone who advocated non-Calvinist doctrines or **theologies of revival** that included such ideas as meritorious works or the freedom of the will. Arminianism had reared its head in Hampshire County just prior to and during the revival. When the Reverend Robert Breck was chosen by the Springfield, Massachusetts, church as their new pastor, Edwards and the members of the Hampshire Association of ministers rose up to prevent his settlement because of charges that Breck was an Arminian. In the end, Breck was installed by a group of Boston ministers, despite the objections of the Hampshire clergy. In November 1734, Edwards delivered a series of two lectures on the doctrine of justification as a means of confuting Arminianism. These lectures were later published in 1738, in greatly expanded form, as *Justification by Faith Alone* along with four other sermons from the revival period. Edwards identified these lectures as a major spur to the growth of the breadth and intensity of the revival, which hit its height in the early months of 1735.

As reports of the awakening in Northampton spread, provincial leaders began to inquire into the truth and nature of the phenomena. Edwards expanded an initial abridged description of the revival into a London publication in 1737, and again for a Boston imprint the following year, followed by translations in German and Dutch. *A Faithful Narrative of the Surprising Work of God in the Conversion of Many Hundred Souls in Northampton* put Edwards and his church before the eyes of an international audience. Here Edwards provided a social and demographic profile of the town and a sophisticated portrait of the religious psychology that he observed among his parishioners. In particular, he made famous two of his converts, the dying Abigail Hutchinson and the four-year-old Phebe Bartlett, by providing an extended account of their religious experiences. *A Faithful Narrative* became nothing less than the model for future revivals, a manual for conducting and monitoring them. Even as he finished the very first account of the revival, however, an ominous event occurred. In June 1735, Edwards's uncle Joseph Hawley, despondent over the state of his soul, killed himself by slitting his throat. The tragedy cast a pall over the town, and the revival waned precipitously. Edwards watched as his congregation, including many of those he supposed converted, returned to their vicious habits and indifference to religion.

In retrospect, Edwards saw that he had made mistakes during the events of 1734–1735. His youth and inexperience, he realized, had led him to be too optimistic, too ready to accept persons' accounts as true. Through it all, however, he never doubted that the Northampton revival, nor the Great Awakening that followed a few years later, were true works of the Holy Spirit.

Further Reading: Crawford, Michael J. *Seasons of Grace: Colonial New England's Revival Tradition in Its British Context.* New York: Oxford University Press, 1991; Edwards, Jonathan. *The Great Awakening: The Works of Jonathan Edwards, Volume 4.* New Haven, CT: Yale University Press, 1972; Gaustad, Edwin G. *The Great Awakening in New England.* New York: Harper and Brothers, 1957; Lambert, Frank. *Inventing the Great Awakening.* Princeton, NJ: Princeton University Press, 1999; Marsden, George. *Jonathan Edwards: A Life.* New Haven, CT, and London: Yale University Press, 2003.

Kenneth Minkema

O

OLAZÁBAL, FRANCISCO (1886–1937)

Francisco Olazábal—a **Latino Pentecostal preacher** and **healer**—was among the greatest evangelists of the twentieth century and conducted revival services throughout the United States, Mexico, and Puerto Rico during the 1920s and 1930s. His life's journey took him from **Roman Catholicism** to **Methodism** to the **Assemblies of God,** and, finally, to creating an independent movement for Latino Pentecostals. He preached to an estimated 250,000 people, organized an estimated 130 churches, and created the first legally organized independent and indigenous Latino Protestant movement in the United States.

Olazábal was directly influenced by North American revivalism—and specifically the Methodist tradition—during his study at the Wesleyan School of Theology in San Luis Potosí, Mexico, from 1908 to 1910. During this time he conducted small-scale evangelistic and revival campaigns in the Mexican states of Durango, San Luis Potosí, Zacatecas, and across the U.S. border in Texas. While in Texas, Olazábal met an Anglo American Methodist woman who encouraged him to study at the Moody Bible Institute in Chicago. Following her advice, Olazábal enrolled in 1912. It was here that he developed his English skills and read Bible commentaries, church history, and the history of missions and evangelism. He was deeply influenced by the legacy of **Dwight L. Moody** and **Charles Finney's** *Lectures on Revivals of Religion* (1835). This book shaped Olazábal's future ministry and served as a bedside companion for the rest of his career. The Methodist Episcopal Church leaders claimed that he was doing "splendid" and "valuable" work in Southern California. Concerned for the spiritual well-being of his parishioners, he conducted fund-raising activities to build new churches. Soon Olazábal was transferred north, where he served in the Methodist tradition of circuit preacher for two Spanish Methodist churches in San Francisco and Sacramento, California. His evangelistic, revivalist, and fund-raising work caught the attention of the Anglo American Methodist bishops.

After moving to San Francisco, Olazábal ran into George and Carrie Montgomery. To Olazábal's surprise, they had attended the **Azusa Street revival** in Los Angeles and had become Pentecostals, a group that he had often criticized from the pulpit. After initially rejecting the Montgomerys' newfound message, Olazábal was persuaded that the **baptism of the Holy Spirit** was a second definite experience of grace (following **conversion**) and a necessary part of the Christian life. He also became convinced that divine healing was available for all who asked for it in faith. Olazábal's belief was put to the test when he, the Montgomerys, and a few others laid hands on and **prayed** for his ailing wife, Macrina. Olazábal claimed that she was healed as a result of their prayers. Yet his new beliefs in **speaking in tongues** and in divine healing placed him at odds with the Methodist Church. For this reason, he decided to leave the denomination in order to preach the "full gospel."

Soon after Olazábal left the Methodist Church, he joined the Assemblies of God and received ministerial credentials. In 1918, Olazábal traveled to Los Angeles, where he conducted an evangelistic and revival campaign for Alice E. Luce, a leader in the Spanish-speaking Assemblies of God. Subsequently he moved to El Paso, Texas, and opened a Mexican mission to reach immigrants streaming across the U.S.–Mexico border, and he succeeded in converting several hundred individuals. As Olazábal's popularity continued to grow, he ran into conflict with H. C. Ball and Alice Luce and in 1923 he organized the Interdenominational Mexican Council of Christian Churches (Pentecostal) in the state of Texas. By 1924 the new Latino denomination included about 30 churches in California, Texas, Arizona, New Mexico, Kansas, Illinois, Michigan, Ohio, and Indiana, and in Mexico. Olazábal's ministry began to take on national proportions as a result of the alleged healing of the 12-year-old deaf and dumb daughter of Guadalupe Gómez. Empowered by a new confidence in God's ability to heal, Olazábal crisscrossed the nation preaching before thousands of Mexicans in migrant farm labor camps, factories, and *barrios*. In Los Angeles, his campaigns caught the eye of another former Assemblies of God evangelist and Pentecostal revivalist, **Aimee Semple McPherson.** The glamorous McPherson was fascinated by the reports she heard about Olazábal. After witnessing the thousands of Latinos that attended his services in Watts, she dubbed him the "Mexican **Billy Sunday.**" Shortly after McPherson preached at his revival in Watts, she invited Olazábal and his Mexican congregants to her 5,000-seat Angelus Temple in Los Angeles. At a historic meeting in October

1886-1937

Revivalist, healer, and Latino Pentecostal pioneer Francisco Olazábal (ca. 1920s). Courtesy of Gastón Espinosa.

1927, McPherson and Olazábal went to the podium, where McPherson preached and Olazábal translated her sermon into Spanish. McPherson later asked him and the council to merge with her Foursquare Gospel denomination (now known as the **International Church of the Foursquare Gospel**). To her disappointment, they declined.

As word of Olazábal's healing campaigns spread across the United States, he was invited to speak at the Palace Opera House in Chicago. His evangelistic healing and revival campaigns attracted more than 3,000 a night for several weeks. Police were needed to control the crowds. He went on to conduct other evangelistic and revival services in many towns, including Chicago; Joliet, Illinois; Indiana Harbor, Indiana; Houston, Texas; Modesto, California; Laredo, Texas; and Mexico City. Word of Olazábal's evangelistic healing campaign in Chicago soon spread to New York City. At the invitation of a local minister, Olazábal traveled in 1931 to Spanish Harlem for what would become the most important chapter of his life and the birth of his transnational ministry. One periodical claimed that 100,000 persons had attended his meetings in New York City.

Olazábal's services blazed with power and emotion and regularly included an **altar call** and opportunity to seek divine healing. While Latinos traditionally had turned to a *curandera* or a spiritualist for healing, many now looked to El Azteca, or the mighty Aztec, as he was called. Olazábal and his followers claimed that hundreds were healed of blindness, tuberculosis, deformity, tumors, heart conditions, rheumatism, deafness, and other ailments in his 1931 Spanish Harlem campaign. As at the Azusa Street revival in Los Angeles, the "relics" of their former life—canes, crutches, amulets, and Catholic items such as rosaries—were thrown into a large pile on stage as symbols of God's power to transform their broken bodies. The overwhelming response led Olazábal to organize the mother church of his movement in New York City, Bethel Temple. This church had grown from a handful of members in August of 1931 to over 1,500 members by 1932, making it one of the largest churches in New York City. Most of his parishioners were former Roman Catholics, spiritists, or agnostic socialists, though some came from Protestant churches. **Women** who joined this movement had a chance to go into ministry. Influenced perhaps by his mother, Refugio Olazábal, and Carrie Judd Montgomery, **Maria Woodworth-Etter,** and Alice Luce, Olazábal allowed women to have an official public role in the church. Though he did not ordain women to pastoral service, he and the council granted them the right to preach from the pulpit and organize, pastor, and administer churches, and serve as evangelists and missionaries—though not to serve Communion, perform baptisms, or conduct weddings without a male elder or pastor present. Olazábal's movement produced such prominent female pastors and evangelists as **Leoncia Rosado Rousseau (Mama Leo),** María Jiménez, María Teresa Sapia, and Julie and Matilde Vargas.

Despite protests from critics and cynics, news of Olazábal's healing and revival crusades spread to Puerto Rico. Soon invitations began to pour in from the island. In 1934 he conducted the first

mass Pentecostal islandwide evangelistic healing and revival crusade in Puerto Rican history. *El Mundo,* the largest newspaper on the island, claimed that he converted 20,000 people throughout the island. In 1936, Olazábal stood at the height of his popularity. By that year, he had already sent or had plans to send missionaries and revivalists to Puerto Rico, Cuba, the Dominican Republic, Mexico, Chile, Argentina, Spain, Venezuela, and Ecuador. The Anglo American churches gave more attention to Olazábal than ever before. Energized by his recent crusade in El Paso, Olazábal attended the 1936 Annual Assembly of the **Church of God (Cleveland, Tennessee)** and conducted revival and healing meetings. The white audience from the **South** responded enthusiastically to Olazábal's revival message and healing ministry.

A year later his work came to a sudden end when he was killed in a car accident in Texas on June 12, 1937. Yet his brief, meteoric ministry as an evangelist and healer laid the foundation for the later expansion and consolidation of Latino Pentecostalism in the United States, Mexico, and Puerto Rico.

Further Reading: Espinosa, Gastón. "Francisco Olazábal and Latino Pentecostal Revivalism in the North American Borderlands." In Michael J. McClymond, ed., *Embodying the Spirit: New Perspectives on North American Revivalism,* 125–46. Baltimore: Johns Hopkins University Press, 2004.

Gastón Espinosa

OLD LIGHTS

see Anti-revivalism, History and Arguments of

ONEIDA COMMUNITY

Founded in 1848, the Oneida Community was a **new religious movement** that took its rise in the **Burned-Over District** of upstate New York, which spawned many innovative religious groups in the early 1800s. The Oneida Community took the logic of Christian perfectionism—that is, the idea that believers can become free of sin—in a novel direction. Perfection or total **sanctification,** for the members of the Oneida Community, meant overcoming the "jealousy of exclusiveness" and sharing spouses within the community. The group required its members to be married collectively—each man to all women, and each woman to all men—in a condition known as "complex marriage."

The group's founder, John Humphrey Noyes, studied at Yale Divinity School, and in 1833–1834 shocked his professors and his fellow students by claiming to have become free from all sin. After leaving the seminary, he suffered rejection by the woman he loved, and struggled to find his vocation. He was captivated by the idea of what he called "Bible communism"—a fellowship in which all selfish tendencies were overcome and no one claimed anything as belonging strictly and properly to himself or herself as an individual. While the New Testament describes the earliest Christians as pooling their money and sharing a common purse (Acts 4:32–35), Noyes took the concept yet further. God, he argued, wanted the powerful currents of erotic and sexual love to flow beyond the bounds of traditional marriage. Noyes's position was not that of the "free lover" or sexual libertine. Only a community of "perfect Christians," Noyes argued, would have the necessary discipline to pass beyond "idolatrous love" or "the marriage spirit."

Until the experiment in complex marriage came to an end in 1879, the Oneida Community drew several hundred adult members. After an early phase in which they practiced contraception and few pregnancies occurred, the group made decisions as to which men and women would propagate, and the children born from these unions were raised by the entire community rather than their parents alone. After some early years of financial struggle, the Oneidans began manufacturing steel animal traps, and the income from their sale gave the community a solid financial footing. The steel traps also laid the foundation for the silver plate and tableware manufacture that continues to this day under the Oneida name. Life in the Oneida Community offered women a greater measure of equality than was customary at the time. With short hair and pantaloons, the Oneida women were known for their lack of feminine adornment. Cultural life at Oneida was rich. Members put on musical concerts, plays, and dances.

The later 1860s and 1870s were an unhappy period for the Oneidans. Internal conflicts divided the community, and the issue of Noyes's successor as leader remained in doubt. Many turned to spiritualism in the quest for authoritative guidance while others drifted into agnosticism or atheism. The young people began to ignore the wishes of their elders and started to pair off with one another in quasi-marital relationships. As a last resort, Noyes argued that celibacy be considered as an alternative to marriage. Yet, when opposition mounted, Noyes consented to allow traditional marriage beginning in 1879. The Oneida Community refashioned itself as a business corporation. Noyes had argued that marriage and Bible communism could not be reconciled, and in the end marriage prevailed. While the **Shakers** opted for celibacy, and the **Mormons** promoted polygamy, the Oneidans with their complex marriage were perhaps attempting the hardest thing of all. In the name of Christian perfection, they had tried to eliminate exclusiveness from the marriage relationship and yet failed.

Further Reading: Edmonds, Walter. *The First Hundred Years, 1848–1948*. Oneida, NY: Oneida Community, 1880; Foster, Lawrence. *Religion and Sexuality: Three American Communal Experiments of the Nineteenth Century*. New York: Oxford University Press, 1981; Klaw, Spencer. *Without Sin: The Life and Death of the Oneida Community*. London: Penguin, 1993; Noyes, John Humphrey. *The Berean; Male Continence; Essay on Scientific Propagation*. New York: Arno Press, 1969; Noyes, John Humphrey. *Home-Talks*. New York: AMS, 1975.

Michael J. McClymond

ORR, JAMES EDWIN (1912–1987)

James Edwin Orr was an extensively published and popular author of the twentieth century on the topic of religious revivals, and himself a globetrotting revival **preacher.** Translated into more than a dozen languages, his books together sold more than 1 million copies. He was one of the most widely traveled preachers of his age, a leader in the post–World War II evangelical awakening, an influential figure during the **campus and collegiate revivals** in 1948–1950, and an intellectual mentor to **Billy Graham** and other evangelical notables. Though he did not pursue an academic career or write for an academic readership, he produced a dozen volumes that provide extensive documentation on spiritual awakenings in various regions of the world, emphasizing Great Britain and North America, but also including Africa, Asia, Latin America, and Oceania.

Born into a devout, working-class family in Belfast, Northern Ireland, in 1912, Orr was raised as a Baptist and professed conversion at age 9. By age 14 he had already written an historical novel set in Palestine, and he began to demonstrate skills as a researcher and writer. Yet his father's death from tuberculosis forced him to become the family breadwinner—working in a bakery—from ages 15 to 21. After his mother entered a sanatorium, he and his three siblings were forced to care for themselves. His sister suffered a nervous breakdown and a brother died during this period. In 1933 Orr experienced "full surrender" to God after breaking off a budding relationship with a woman. In later years he regarded this as his spiritual turning point. Soon thereafter Orr determined that God had called him to preach the Christian gospel throughout the world. Having turned down an offer of employment, he set off for England in 1933 with an old bicycle and the equivalent of 65 cents—a self-described "tramp preacher." This was all the money Orr needed, because he found people throughout England, and later throughout the world, who were ready to support his preaching expeditions. In time, he visited all 40 shires in England, 12 in Wales, and 30 on the Scottish mainland. In 1935–1936, he went to Canada, the United States, New Zealand, Australia, and South Africa, and was greeted by 4,000 well-wishers on his return to London. Eventually he visited all but two cities in North America with more than 100,000 inhabitants, 500 of the world's 600 largest cities, every state of India, almost all regions of Australia, and much of Africa, Asia, Oceania, and Latin America. He wrote travel books with a spiritual focus that sold by the hundreds of thousands.

Though Orr did not begin his higher education until he was 28, he quickly made up for lost time, and completed an MA in geography at Northwestern University and a BD and ThD from Northern Baptist Seminary within a period of only three years. By 1948 he completed a DPhil from Oxford University with a dissertation on the **Revival of 1857–1858.** He and his wife, Carol, made their home in Southern California following World War II, and there they participated in the postwar boom in evangelicalism. Orr was a leader in the Hollywood Christian Group for film and media stars during the 1950s. From 1966 to 1981, he taught at the School of World Mission at Fuller Theological Seminary in Pasadena, California.

Orr adhered to the so-called Keswick teaching that dated back to the **Holiness movement** of the nineteenth century. **Sanctification** or holiness of life began with a crisis experience (such as Orr had had in 1933) followed by a lifelong process of spiritual growth. He insisted that Christian believers needed to submit entirely to God's will in all matters and trust God in all aspects of daily life. When preaching, Orr expected the Holy Spirit to reveal the themes and doctrines that needed to be preached on any given occasion. Orr firmly believed and taught that extraordinary **prayer** was the key to spiritual awakening and that Christian believers who wished to see revival in the church should set aside their differences and engage in united prayer. Church divisions hindered revival, and revival in turn overcame divisions. **Confession of sins,** for Orr, was another major factor in promoting revival. Unconfessed sin drained Christians of spiritual vitality.

Orr criticized the work of **William G. McLoughlin**—the century's leading academic scholar on the subject of revivals—because of the latter's reliance on social-scientific theory and his neglect of the Revival of 1857–1858, which Orr regarded as the greatest spiritual event of the nineteenth century. In his earlier years, Orr used *revival* and *spiritual awakening* as synonyms, but he later preferred the latter term since it suggested something spontaneous rather than planned. He spoke of the "outpouring of the Holy Spirit" as "exclusively the work of God" (Orr, *Call for the Re-study of Revival,* 1). Orr thus seemed to reject all efforts in social-scientific analysis or naturalistic explanation in the study of revivals.

Because revival for Orr was "exclusively" a divine work, every revival was like every other revival—whether in India or Indiana. Differences of social, cultural, and historical context played no essential role in Orr's treatment of revivals. Another possible criticism of Orr's scholarship was his neglect of the **Pentecostal** and **Charismatic** movements. In discussing twentieth-century revivals, he said surprisingly little about world Pentecostalism and its burgeoning influence. Notwithstanding such weaknesses, Orr's books brought the history of Christian revivals in Britain and North America to a wide readership, and his book series on evangelical awakenings (published 1975–1978) is a wide-ranging survey of twentieth-century Christian revivals in Africa, Asia, Latin America, and Oceania.

Further Reading: Appasamy, A. J. *Write the Vision! Edwin Orr's Thirty Years of Adventurous Service.* Madras, India: Evangelical Literature Service, 1964; Munton, Douglas Wayne. "The Contributions of J. Edwin Orr to an Understanding of Spiritual Awakenings." PhD dissertation, Southwestern Baptist Theological Seminary, Fort Worth, TX, 1991; Orr, J. Edwin. *A Call for the Re-study of Revival and Revivalism.* Pasadena, CA: School of World Mission, 1971; Orr, J. Edwin. *Campus Aflame.* Glendale, CA: Regal Books, 1971; Orr, J. Edwin. *The Event of the Century: 1857–1858 Awakening.* Wheaton, IL: International Awakening Press, 1989; Orr, J. Edwin. *The Flaming Tongue: Evangelical Awakenings, 1900–.* 2nd ed. Chicago: Moody Press, 1975; Orr, J. Edwin. *The Second Evangelical Awakening in America.* London: Marshall, Morgan and Scott, 1952; Orr, J. Edwin. *The Second Evangelical Awakening in Britain.* London: Marshall, Morgan and Scott, 1949.

Michael J. McClymond

OTTERBEIN, PHILIP WILLIAM (1726–1813)

Philip William Otterbein was the leader of the **Pietist** wing of the German **Reformed** Church in colonial America and the cofounder of the Church of the **United Brethren in Christ**— among the earliest indigenous denominations formed in the United States. Born in Dillenburg, Nassau (Germany), the son of a pastor in the German Reformed Church, he was educated at the Herborn Academy,

Profile portrait of Philip Otterbein, 1858. (A. Krebs and Bros, Lithographers; Pittsburgh, Pennsylvania.) Courtesy of the Library of Congress.

center of Pietism in that church. Here he was influenced by the covenant theology of Friedrich Lampe. He and his brothers were avid expositors of the theology of the Heidelberg Catechism (1563), the chief confessional symbol of his church, though he later declared his disagreement with John Calvin on the doctrine of predestination.

After serving a parish at Ockersdorf, he was one of six Herborn graduates recruited for missionary service in the New World by Michael Schlatter, who superintended the pioneer work of that church in America. Serving under the auspices of the Amsterdam Synod of his church, Otterbein arrived in Philadelphia in 1752 and proceeded to serve five parishes in Maryland and Pennsylvania, including Lancaster (where he required interviews with parishioners before serving the Lord's Supper), Tulpehocken (where he instituted **prayer** meetings), Frederick (where he began his brief marriage to Susan LeRoy, which ended with her death), York, and, his longest tenure, Baltimore (1774–1813). Asked by **Methodist** Bishop **Francis Asbury** to describe when he was converted to saving faith, he replied, "by degrees … while at Lancaster"—a response that reflects the Reformed Pietist order of salvation, which proceeded stepwise from God's initial call to final **sanctification** in Christ. His lengthy homily, *The Salvation-Bringing Incarnation and Glorious Victory of Jesus Christ over the Devil and Death* (1760), set forth the tenets of his Reformed Pietist theology.

Although challenged by his orthodox opponents in the *coetus* (ruling church body) of the Reformed Church, Otterbein remained a pastor in good standing until his death in 1813. A turning point in his ministry was his encounter with the **converted** Mennonite **preacher,** Martin Boehm, whom he embraced at a "big meeting" at the Isaac Long barn (Pennsylvania) on Pentecost 1767, with the declaration *wir sind Brüder* ("we are brothers"). This is regarded as the inception of the revival movement he headed, which he continued to nurture during the years of his Baltimore pastorate. He was called to an evangelical wing of that parish, from which base he also pursued an itinerant ministry promoting the awakening movement among the German population. A personal mentor to Asbury, Otterbein was asked by his friend to participate with Thomas Coke in ordaining and consecrating him as the first bishop of the Methodist Episcopal Church in Baltimore (1784). Asbury referred to Otterbein as "one of the best scholars and greatest divines in America" (J. Manning Potts, *Journal and Letters of Francis Asbury* [1958], 3:478). His "church order" of 1785 outlined a Pietist program of renewal for his parish, and the confession of faith of the future denomination is traced to his authorship (1789).

In 1800 Otterbein met with Boehm and others to organize the United Brethren in Christ, whose protocol describes their focus as an "unpartisan" fellowship of diverse believers, reborn in Christ, whose intent was to effect a "higher unity" in Christ that would not displace their traditional church relationships. He and Boehm were elected as the first elders or bishops of this brotherhood. In actuality, a new denomination was being formed, rooted in the postmillennial theology of radical and Reformed Pietism. It would embrace a **Presbyterian** doctrine of ministry, but increasingly would be modeled by influences from Methodist polity and theology in the nineteenth century. Otterbein's relationship to the new movement waned in his declining years, although he accepted the invitation to ordain two of the brethren from "the West" (i.e., Ohio) shortly before his death, thereby inaugurating an ordained ministry for the brotherhood, which would not, however, call itself a church until 1889.

Further Reading: Core, Arthur. *Philip William Otterbein: Pastor, Ecumenist.* Dayton, OH: Evangelical United Brethren Church, 1968; Drury, A. W. *Philip William Otterbein.* Dayton, OH: Evangelical United Brethren Publishing House, 1884; O'Malley, J. Steven. *Early German-American Evangelicalism: Pietist Sources on Discipleship and Sanctification.* Lanham, MD: Scarecrow Press, 1995; O'Malley, J. Steven. *Pilgrimage of Faith: The Legacy of the Otterbeins.* Metuchen, NJ: Scarecrow, 1973.

J. Steven O'Malley

P

PALMER, PHOEBE WORRALL
(1807–1874)

Phoebe Palmer, **Methodist** author, lay theologian, revivalist, and defender of **women's** rights to public ministry, was born in New York City in 1807. Her four decades of pioneer **Holiness** promotion in the United States, Canada, and Great Britain shaped the rise and progress of the nineteenth-century Holiness movement of the nineteenth century so significantly that she is commonly acknowledged as the mother of the movement. Together with **Hannah Whitall Smith** (1832–1911) and her husband, **Robert Pearsall Smith** (1827–1898), she was one of the most celebrated Holiness teachers of the 1800s.

In 1827, Phoebe married Walter C. Palmer, a New York City physician. In 1835, she and her sister Sarah Lankford began to hold what became known as "Tuesday Meetings for the Promotion of Holiness" in the common parlor of the Manhattan home shared by their families. By 1839, the meetings, now led by Palmer, had become more denominationally diverse and open to both sexes. Supported by some of the most respected leaders of the Methodist Episcopal Church and a network of hundreds of other Tuesday Meetings that sprang up all across the northeastern and western (now

midwestern) United States and Canada, Palmer began a lifelong ministry involving her in more than 300 revival gatherings and **camp meetings.** Her reputation throughout evangelical Protestantism, both nationally and internationally, was greater than that of any other female evangelist of her day.

Palmer's blending of John Wesley's **sanctification** teaching with biblical interpretation and common-sense realism provided her hearers with a simplified path to the experience and practice of biblical perfection. At the heart of it was her "Altar Theology"—a simple syllogism that brought thousands of seekers after holiness to profess their entire devotion to God and to claim the "second blessing." Her teaching included the following points: (1) holiness of heart is the goal of God's plan of redemption, and God commands all believers to seek it and expect to experience it in this life; (2) God's commandments carry with them their promise of fulfillment, and, through the merits of Christ death and the infilling of the Holy Spirit in a second crisis of faith, God will cleanse believers from remaining sin and free the believer to enjoy an expanding life of love and service; (3) this promise will be fulfilled in seekers the moment that they, by faith, yield themselves fully to Christ at the Christian's altar; and (4) having met these conditions, believers are to claim God's promise and testify to an inward work of cleansing even in the absence of any objective witness of having received this grace and cleansing.

Some Methodists saw this "shorter way" as a radical departure from earlier Methodist teachings. Palmer, in turn, appealed to the Bible and to the teaching and practice of John Wesley and early American Methodism to defend herself. In her advocacy of receiving the reality of God's promises by "naked faith," some have seen intimations of the "name it; claim it," Word of Faith, or **prosperity theology** that appeared in twentieth-century **Pentecostalism.** Others have chided Palmer for failing to support the pre–**Civil War abolitionism** of the Wesleyan Methodists and the **Free Methodists**—both Methodist Holiness churches. Her supporters have responded that she was personally involved in prison ministries, maintained a lifelong involvement in homes for orphans and the homeless, and was secretary of the Female Assistance Society, which brought medical aid to New York's poor. She was also a leader in the establishment of the Five Points Mission, a pioneer complex of Christian relief agencies designed to address the poverty and degradation in New York City's worst slum.

From 1859 to 1863, the Palmers lived and ministered in England, often within the context of the Evangelical Alliance's union movement. She frequently turned to the imagery of the first Pentecost to describe her wonder at the unusual spiritual dynamics and nonsectarianism that marked her meetings. Her English evangelism resulted in more than 10,000 **conversions** and sanctifications and, in its course, Palmer's example encouraged Catherine Booth to exert her own right to **preach** and play a prominent role in the organization and advancement of the **Salvation Army,** just as it did Frances Willard in her **temperance** reform. Palmer never claimed to be a preacher, but only an exhorter. Yet her extended biblical and theological defense of her public ministry, *The Promise of the Father* (1859), was an early and influential argument in favor of women's public ministry.

Upon Palmer's return to the United States in 1863 she continued her itinerant Holiness promotion. After 1867, however, her leadership in the revival gave way to an association of Methodist pastors who utilized large national **camp meetings** and conventions to lead the movement into a new era of expansion. Palmer now gave more and more attention to her editing of the *Guide to Holiness*, the journal that had advanced the revival since its founding in 1839. Its circulation of 40,000 or more gave her a continuing voice in the Holiness movement until her death in 1874. Reprints of her most important works have perpetuated her influence in Holiness and Pentecostal churches where thousands of women were ordained as pastors and evangelists decades before pulpits in mainline churches were opened to them. At her death in 1874, Palmer received glowing tributes from various sectors of evangelical Protestantism, and an official journal of the Methodist Episcopal Church set her alongside the church's bishops as a major figure in American Methodism.

Further Reading: Dieter, Melvin E. *The Holiness Revival of the Nineteenth Century.* 2nd ed. New York and London: Scarecrow Press, 1996; Oden, Thomas C. *Phoebe Palmer: Selected Writings.* New York: Paulist, 1988; Raser, H. E. *Phoebe Palmer: Her Life and Thought.* New York: Edwin Mellen Press, 1987; White, C. E. *The Beauty of Holiness: Phoebe Palmer as Theologian, Revivalist, Feminist, and Humanitarian.* Grand Rapids, MI: Zondervan, 1986.

Melvin E. Dieter

PARHAM, CHARLES FOX (1873–1929)

Charles Fox Parham was the theological innovator behind the emergence of twentieth-century **Pentecostalism.** Though a number of his ideas were eventually discounted, he pioneered the emergence of the Pentecostal movement in the American Midwest from 1901 through 1906. Just as importantly, his teaching that **speaking in tongues** (or glossolalia) was the decisive sign or "Bible evidence" of receiving the **baptism in the Holy Spirit** became a hallmark of Pentecostalism. Known as the "initial evidence" doctrine, this teaching was formally included in the constitutions of numerous Pentecostal denominations, including the **Assemblies of God.** Yet with the emergence of the **Azusa Street revival,** beginning in Los Angeles in 1906, Parham's ministry and reputation went into decline. His overt opposition to the Azusa Street revival—even though it was led by his own former student, **William J. Seymour**—caused many in the twentieth-century Pentecostal movement to view him unfavorably.

Born in Muscatine, Iowa, in 1873, Parham suffered a host of childhood illnesses, including encephalitis and rheumatic fever. Frequent bouts of disease left him weak and yearning to experience a dramatic **healing.** In 1885, shortly after the death of his mother, Parham dedicated his life to Christ and became active in a local Congregational church. By 1890, he had entered Southwest Kansas College, where he planned a career in either medicine or the ministry. After more than a year of struggling with this career decision, Parham experienced healing and a new spiritual contentment, convinced that his recurring physical ailments came as a result of his inability to trust God fully for his healing. Parham viewed divine healing by faith as a neglected Christian doctrine that his ministerial career should emphasize. In 1893, he dropped out of Southwest Kansas College and accepted an appointment as supply pastor for the Eudora Methodist Church, located not far from Lawrence, Kansas. Not content to occupy a pastorate within a conventional denomination, and now an ardent proponent of **Holiness** doctrines that had become suspect within the Methodist hierarchy, Parham left the Methodists in 1895 for a life as a full-time independent healing evangelist within the Holiness movement.

Over the next five years, Parham enjoyed marginal success as an itinerant Holiness evangelist. Concentrating his efforts in Topeka, Kansas, by 1898 he founded the Beth-el Healing Home, an independent institution that concentrated on **prayer** and teaching for anyone interested in giving up traditional cures and medications in favor of total reliance on faith. In addition, the Beth-el Home turned its attention to ministering to Topeka's poor and downtrodden street residents, and Parham began issuing a monthly journal entitled the *Apostolic Faith*—activities that created some local respect for the young minister's efforts. Despite his success, Parham sought more. He was influenced

by an array of theological opinions, among them the British-Israel theory (i.e., that modern-day Britons derived from the lost tribes of ancient Israel), an emphasis on biblical **eschatology** and the premillennial return of Christ, and an expectation that new manifestations of the Holy Spirit would accompany a dramatic end-time revival. Parham traveled across the country during the summer of 1900, visiting a number of well-known Holiness worship centers. Influenced by Frank W. Sandford's Holy Ghost and Us Bible School in Shiloh, Maine, where he heard several students speaking in tongues during prayer sessions, he returned to Topeka late in 1900 determined to form his own Bible school and seek the fulfillment of the end-time "sign" of apostolic power. Giving up their interest in the healing home, Parham and his wife Sarah located their Bible school in an unusual rented mansion on the outskirts of Topeka—a large unfinished home known to locals as "Stone's Folly." There, with about 35 students, Parham entered the holiday season of 1900 convinced that God was about to bestow on his small band of believers a miraculous sign of end-time power.

That miraculous sign seemed assured when Agnes Ozman, one of the students, spoke in tongues after a New Year's Day service on the evening of January 1, 1901. Over the next few weeks, amid a flurry of newspaper coverage, Parham and a number of his band experienced speaking in tongues—a phenomenon they identified as actual foreign languages (technically *xenolalia*—a spiritually conferred ability to speak a foreign language). Given the preoccupation with an end-time sign and a coming revival, Parham interpreted the new gift as a missionary bonanza—an equipping of latter-day Christians, through the immediate influence of the Holy Spirit, with the capability of traveling to the far corners of the earth to **preach** and teach in languages they had never studied.

Over the next few months, the small band traveled to Kansas City and smaller towns in the Midwest in an effort to demonstrate their newfound authority. Discouraged by the lack of an enthusiastic reception—other than obvious curiosity seekers—and stung by the sudden death of Parham's young

Holiness-Pentecostal pioneer Charles Fox Parham. Courtesy of Flower Pentecostal Heritage Center, Springfield, MO.

son to disease, the Bible school disbanded in the spring of 1901 with Parham vowing to continue his work as an itinerant evangelist now preaching the power of "Holy Ghost baptism" along with the Holiness doctrines of entire **sanctification,** divine healing, and the premillennial Second Coming. During the ensuing years, Parham achieved some success across the Midwest from Kansas to Texas, first by concentrating on the mining region along the borders of Kansas, Missouri, and the Oklahoma territory and later because of a successful revival and healing campaign in Houston, Texas. By the spring of 1906, his movement included as many as 10,000 people organized loosely into assemblies, with Parham proclaiming himself the "Projector of the Apostolic Faith Movement."

Seemingly at the height of his career, Parham suffered a devastating series of setbacks. William Seymour, an **African American** associate from Texas, who had sat under Parham's teaching in Houston, began preaching in 1906 with marked success of his own in the **Azusa Street revival** in Los

Angeles. Seymour's deference to Parham ended when Parham insisted on complete control and authority over the Azusa revival and wanted Seymour and other blacks to follow Jim Crow rules of racial decorum and separation. Parham and his apologists later recalled that Seymour and his integrated, multiracial, and multiethnic band of followers suffered from "an unteachable spirit and spiritual pride" (Parham, 163). In the final weeks of 1906, Parham failed in a concerted effort to gain control of the beleaguered remains of Zion City, Illinois—a community that had emerged out of the healing ministry of **John Alexander Dowie.** Despite favorable press reports regarding Parham, Wilbur Glenn Voliva emerged as Zion's new leader, and Parham's following in that city—like his following in Los Angeles—remained marginal.

Contributing to Parham's decline were rumors that he engaged in bouts of immoral behavior. Some rumors dated back to the evangelist's days at Southwest Kansas College, and now, with controversy swirling over authority and leadership within the emerging Pentecostal movement, they resurfaced. In the summer of 1907, there were newspaper reports that Parham and a young **hymn** singer had been arraigned in San Antonio, Texas, on a charge of sodomy. Though the charges were dropped several days later, word traveled quickly through the burgeoning Pentecostal community, and Parham's authority as a spokesman and leader all but vanished. After the events of 1906–1907, Charles Parham was virtually ignored by the larger Pentecostal denominations that sprang up in the wake of the Azusa Street outpouring. Over the next two decades of his life, until his death of heart failure in 1929, Parham enjoyed a small but loyal following in the Midwest corridor centered on his Bible school and church in Baxter Springs, Kansas. Generations later, as Pentecostals sought to uncover their roots, he reemerged—a man of immense promise and tragic failure.

Further Reading: Callahan, Leslie D. "Fleshly Manifestations: Charles Fox Parham's Quest for the Sanctified Body." PhD dissertation, Princeton University, 2002; Goff, James R., Jr. *Fields White unto Harvest: Charles F. Parham and the Missionary Origins of Pentecostalism.* Fayetteville: University of Arkansas Press, 1988; Parham,

Sarah E. *The Life of Charles F. Parham*. Joplin, MO: Tri-State Printing, 1930.

James R. Goff Jr.

PARISH MISSIONS

In **Roman Catholic** congregations, the nearest equivalent of the Protestant revival meeting is the parish mission, an innovation of the seventeenth-century Catholic Reformation aimed at the revitalization of the faith and piety of local communities in the Catholic countries of Europe. Conducted by itinerant missionaries belonging to various religious orders, the mission was a systematic intervention in the life of a parish by outside priests who instructed the faithful in the basic doctrines of the Catholic church and rekindled the spirit of religion within them. This custom arrived in America in 1792, and through the 1840s maintained a missionary character in gathering pastorless Catholic immigrants, scattered throughout cities and countryside, into formal parishes to revive their spiritual lives.

By 1850, with the majority of Catholics situated in regular parishes, the parish mission began to undergo a process of formalization that brought it more and more into line with its European counterpart. Pastors contracted to have a mission conducted in their parishes every five years or so in order to win back wandering sheep and to deepen the piety of regular churchgoers. The typical mission lasted two to four weeks, and by the end of the century it was routine practice to divide a two-week event with the first dedicated to the **women** of the parish and the second to the **men,** the idea being that religiously renewed females would convince their menfolk to attend the later session. A four-week mission had the same intent, with married women attending the first week, single women the second, married men the third, and single men the fourth. By thus dividing the congregation, missioners could tailor sermons to the clientele of each week. Each day began with Mass at 5 A.M. followed by a 20–30-minute catechetical instruction. After breakfast there occurred a second Mass and the same instruction. The initial instructions of the week focused on how to make a good **confession of sins,** for the mission aimed at provoking repentance that took sacramental form in the rite of penance and the reception of Communion. The evening ceremony consisted of a brief instruction, the recitation of the rosary, and the mission sermon—the main event. The service concluded with benediction of the Blessed Sacrament.

The mission sermon was evangelical in style, calculated to elicit an emotional response from listeners, a response of the heart, rather than of the head, that resulted in the **conversion** of the sinner and an increased devotion among the already pious. The intent was to shock—even scare—congregants into repentance. Sermons followed a set pattern: the first was on salvation and sin; the second on the horror of an untimely death after a life of unrepented sinning; the third on the eternal terrors of hell to which a just God consigned the sinner; the fourth on divine mercy bestowed through the excruciating passion of Jesus, pleading from the cross for the conversion of the sinner; and the last on perseverance in the life of grace. After the first or second day, missioners began hearing confessions that began after the first Mass and lasted well into the night. So great were the number of penitents that priests from neighboring parishes had to be summoned to assist in the confessional. Indeed, the principal criterion of the success of a mission was the number of confessions heard. A second criterion was the number of lost sheep returned to the fold, though missioners lamented that the repentance of these souls was often short-lived before relapses occurred. During the second half of the nineteenth century, the parish mission remained a novelty. While it continued into the first half of the twentieth century, the newness had worn off. It had become a routine feature of Catholic life, as evidenced by the fact that missioners no longer tabulated the number of confessions or Communions, nor did their letters and diaries comment on the emotional reactions of parishioners or the return of hardened sinners. The mission had become a routine of American Catholic life.

The Second Vatican Council (1962–1965) dramatically altered the parish mission as Catholic theology shifted from a legalistic notion of sin to a more personal notion of opting for or against God. In other words, one serious sin or even a series of such sins might not constitute grounds for condemnation as long as a person was earnestly seeking to love God. With this new understanding of sin and salvation, the mission became less penitential and more hortatory in nature, deemphasizing the avoidance of sin and stressing the love of God and love of neighbor.

Further Reading: Dolan, Jay D. *Catholic Revivalism: The American Experience, 1830–1900.* Notre Dame, IN: University of Notre Dame Press, 1978; Slawson, Douglas J. "Catholic Revivalism: The Vincentian Preaching Apostolate in the United States." In Michael McClymond, ed., *Embodying the Spirit: New Perspectives on North American Revivalism,* 211–52. Baltimore: Johns Hopkins University Press, 2004; Slawson, Douglas J. "'To Bring Glad Tidings to the Poor': Vincentian Parish Missions in the United State." In John E. Rybolt, ed., *The American Vincentians: A Popular History of the Congregation of the Mission in the United States, 1815–1987.* 163–227. New York: New City Press, 1988.

Douglas J. Slawson

PENSACOLA (BROWNSVILLE) REVIVAL

The revival that began at Brownsville **Assembly of God** (BAOG) in Pensacola, Florida, on Father's Day 1995 (commonly referred to as the Pensacola Outpouring) had its roots in the **Toronto Blessing** (or Father's Blessing) at the Toronto Airport Christian Fellowship (TACF), beginning some 16 months earlier in 1994. Although streams of the same revival movement, Toronto and Pensacola are as different as the cities in which they were birthed. Cast in the classic Pentecostal mold of the **South**—rather than the more relaxed and informal style of the **Charismatic** and so-called Third Wave movements—Pensacola became the revival site of choice for many **Pentecostals,** and a site of convenience for conservative Christians located in the southeastern United States. The Pensacola revival and the Toronto Blessing are the two best-known and longest-running streams of the "Spirit-filled" (i.e., Pentecostal-Charismatic) revival that swept across the North American continent in the 1990s.

People stream across the street to attend revival services at Brownsville Assembly of God Church, Pensacola, Florida (January 4, 1997). Courtesy of photographer Cathy Wood.

On June 18, 1995, the Assemblies of God missionary and evangelist Steve Hill was invited to **preach** at the Brownsville Assembly of God, a church founded in 1948 and led by Pastor John Kilpatrick since 1982. Hill was Kilpatrick's friend and a longtime Assemblies of God colleague. Although John Kilpatrick had not visited the TACF, his wife, Brenda, had, and was reportedly changed by her experience there. Hill had also been indirectly affected by the Blessing through the Toronto-sparked revival at Holy Trinity Brompton, a Spirit-filled Anglican church in London, associated with the **Alpha Course.** Worship leader Lindell Cooley (who came to Pensacola shortly after the revival began) had visited Toronto before he joined the Pensacola team and acknowledged being left with a deeper desire for a "quiet intimacy with God" and a new vision for church music inspired by the Toronto Blessing. This trio of evangelist, pastor, and worship leader provided the original cast of leaders for the Pensacola revival. Dr. Michael Brown, a Messianic Jewish scholar who was hired to establish the Brownsville Revival School Ministry in 1997, later joined the original group of three.

Unlike the Toronto Blessing, which began with many "nameless and faceless" visiting speakers and musicians who ministered during the nightly gatherings, the entire Pensacola team was generally present for each revival service from Wednesday through Sunday nights. Whether on the home front at BAOG or with the traveling *Awake America!* crusades, the Pensacola revival was staffed by the permanent revival team of Hill, Kilpatrick, Cooley, and Brown, which established revival norms and a level of quality control for each service. The team began to unravel in 2000 when Michael Brown was fired from his position as president of the revival school for refusing to secure ministerial credentials with the Assemblies of God. In the same year Steve Hill began gradually to reestablish

Early "break-out" worship at Brownsville Assembly of God Church, Pensacola, Florida. The revival, which began on Father's Day 1995, is here celebrating its anniversary on Father's Day 1996 (June 18, 1996). Courtesy of photographer Cathy Wood.

his own revival ministry and eventually left BAOG. By 2003 John Kilpatrick had resigned from the church in which he had served as pastor for over 20 years, marking the end of the Pensacola revival and the beginning of a new chapter for BAOG.

In the early months of the Pensacola Outpouring, long lines formed outside the church building as early as 4 A.M. for evening services. The services captured the attention of pilgrims and the press alike. Many asserted that BAOG was the home of a "real revival," and not simply a source of "spiritual refreshing," such as that offered in the Toronto Blessing. Participants held that the Pensacola Outpouring brought widespread repentance from sin, introduced changes into secular society, and had **eschatological** meaning as a sign of the impending return of Jesus. In contrast to the holy **laughter** (and even animal sounds) that erupted in the more bubbly services at the TACF in Toronto, BAOG was noted for its hellfire preaching, **altar calls,** and testimonies filled with moaning and weeping. Its emotional style better served those who were eager for revival but preferred that it wear classic Pentecostal dress. Both revivals seemed to offer the same affective substance, but presented the emotional experiences in different ritual and symbolic packaging. Visitors to both centers of revival commonly experienced a range of the controversial **bodily manifestations** together with an unusual sense of God's presence that somehow changed their lives. Toronto appealed largely to independent Charismatics who were heirs to the mid-twentieth-century **Latter Rain** and **healing** movements that had been rejected by many established Pentecostals. The Pensacola revival, by contrast, attracted those who preferred a more traditional Pentecostal style.

The imagery and symbols evoked by the leaders and teachers of the Toronto Blessing was one of a loving God (or Father) playing with his children. The Pensacola revival employed the images and symbols of **Jonathan Edwards,** who spoke of "sinners in the hands of an angry God." Active repentance rather than passive restful play was the norm. At Pensacola, revival was defined as conviction of sin and "reaching the lost" rather than what was pejoratively described as "charismatic hoopla."

Rev. Steve Hill's impassioned preaching at Brownsville Assembly of God Church, Pensacola, Florida (ca. 1996–1997). Courtesy of photographer Cathy Wood.

At the altar call that formally closed each service and followed Steve Hill's sermon, Charity James could be heard plaintively singing "Mercy Seat," a haunting anthem that urged sinners to find refuge in Jesus. The symbols were about repentance and soul saving, but many testimonies suggested that the personal experiences of those at BAOG were not unlike those of Toronto pilgrims. Despite the playful tone of most services at TACF, most visitors reported an awareness of their own sin and underwent repentance, just as visitors to BAOG reported fresh experiences of divine love. The comment that Pastor John Kilpatrick made in the documentary video *The Brownsville Revival* could readily have been made about the Pensacola revival itself: "Steve Hill preaches hellfire, but he has love in his voice."

Despite the Pentecostal revival style and packaging of the Pensacola revival, the reception by BAOG's

Dr. Michael Brown speaks during the altar call at Brownsville Assembly of God Church, Pensacola Florida (ca. 1996–1997). Courtesy of photographer Cathy Wood.

Pentecostal parent denomination, the Assemblies of God (AG), was mixed. Although the AG had been a frequent critic of other historic waves of revival—including the Latter Rain movement, the 1950s healing movement, and the **Charismatic Revival** of the 1970s—the leadership was cautiously supportive of what had occurred in Pensacola. Evidence indicates, however, that most pastors were less receptive to the Pensacola Outpouring than the AG's denominational leadership. According to a survey taken during the height of the Pensacola revival, the vast majority of AG pastors had not visited BAOG or any of the other associated revival sites across America. Though nearly all pastors stated that they desired a revival, most limited themselves to reading reports of spiritual awakenings without involving themselves or their congregations in the revival fires that swept through local communities in North America.

Further Reading: *The Brownsville Revival: A Comprehensive Documentary.* Videocassette. Pensacola, Florida: Brownsville Assembly of God, 2000; Grady, J. Lee. "Suddenly, God Came." *Charisma*, June 1996, 46–50; Poloma, Margaret M. "The Spirit Movement in North America at the Millennium." *Journal of Pentecostal Theology* 12 (1998): 83–107; Poloma, Margaret M. *Main Street Mystics: The Toronto Blessing and Reviving Pentecostalism.* Walnut Creek, CA: AltaMira Press, 2003; Wood, Cathy. *The Visitation: The Brownsville Revival.* Cantonment, FK: River Books, 1997.

Margaret M. Poloma

PENTECOSTAL ASSEMBLIES OF THE WORLD

The Pentecostal Assemblies of the World Inc. (PAW) is the largest Oneness (Godhead, or "Jesus Only") and predominately **African American** church denomination in the **Holiness-Pentecostal** tradition. Based on interpretations of certain biblical passages (e.g., Acts 8:16, Acts 19:5, Isaiah 9:6), the PAW rejects the traditional Christian doctrine of the Trinity and teaches instead that Jesus is God

Dr. Michael Brown praying with attendees at Brownsville Assembly of God Church, Pensacola, Florida (ca. 1996–1997). Courtesy of photographer Cathy Wood.

Participants "overcome by the Spirit" or "resting in the Spirit" at Brownsville Assembly of God Church, Pensacola, Florida (ca. 1996–1997). Courtesy of photographer Cathy Wood.

the Father. The denomination's leader and founder was **Garfield Thomas Haywood** (1880–1931), who had visited the **Azusa Street revival** in Los Angeles in 1907. Haywood became pastor in 1909 of a small congregation—the Apostolic Faith Assembly—in Indianapolis, Indiana. From his early years as a pastor, he was active in producing Christian literature, and published the first *Voice in the Wilderness* magazine in 1910, the *Christian Outlook* (which appeared until 1939), and a hymnal called *The Bridegroom Cometh*. His congregation in Indianapolis joined the PAW and hosted its annual meeting. Haywood guided the denomination's major doctrinal change in 1915 in which the PAW accepted the new non-Trinitarian or Jesus Only theology. In 1918, Haywood was elected secretary-treasurer. Because the PAW began ordaining **women** as ministers and pastors (though not as bishops), one of the early leaders, Robert Clarence Lawson (1883–1961), left the PAW.

Until 1925 the PAW was an interracial fellowship with black and white leaders and members working together. In 1924, the white members left to organize the Pentecostal Ministerial Alliance that is now part of the **United Pentecostal Church.** Beginning in 1925, the PAW was under the direction of a board of bishops, and in 1928 several white bishops were added to the board. Between 1924 and 1937, there was a further exodus of white members and leaders from the PAW, and it then became primarily a black organization. During

these early years, the PAW expected its members to follow a strict code, requiring separation from so-called worldly activities. Haywood traveled to the Holy Land and recorded his experience on film. When he returned, he found that many PAW members were unwilling to watch any motion pictures, and this prevented Haywood from sharing his trip with many people.

After Haywood's death in 1931, Bishop Samuel Joshua Grimes (1884–1957), born in the West Indies, was appointed as presiding bishop of the PAW. Samuel N. Hancock (1883–1963), Karl L. Smith, and other black leaders left the PAW to join the white ministers who had created the Pentecostal Assemblies of Jesus Christ (PAJC). Rejecting the merger established by the PAJC, Grimes reorganized the PAW in 1932. Yet when Hancock and others found that white Pentecostals in the PAJC did not accept them as equals in the PAJC, they returned to the PAW. Hancock married G. T. Haywood's widow, and challenged Grimes for the office of presiding bishop, claiming that the late Haywood had wanted him to be the leader. The church voted and again chose Grimes as their leader. Hancock left the PAW a second time and formed a new organization in Detroit. Grimes encouraged the growth of the PAW in many cites in the United States, in Africa, and in the West Indies, traveled extensively, and founded the Samuel Grimes Maternity and Welfare Center in Liberia, West Africa. For 31 years he continued in leadership in the PAW. Following Grimes's death, the PAW has been led by white ministers (Ross Paddock and Lawrence Brisbin) and by black ministers (Francis L. Smith, James A. Johnson, Paul A. Bowers, and Walter Smith). The PAW is unique among Oneness Pentecostal denominations for maintaining both black and white leadership.

Charles William Watkins (1923–1988), a PAW bishop, received a gold album for his original gospel song "Heartaches," and is known for his songbook and his work in organizing church choirs. The PAW is headquartered in Indianapolis, Indiana, and has more than 1 million members worldwide, with over 2,100 churches and 1,000 missions. The organization supports Aenon Bible College and publishes the *Christian Outlook*, *Apostolic Light*, and the *International Foreign Missions Newsletter*.

Further Reading: Bodenhamer, David J., and Robert G. Barrows, eds. *The Encyclopedia of Indianapolis*. Indianapolis: Indiana University Press, 1994; DuPree, Sherry Sherrod. *African-American Holiness Pentecostal Movement: An Annotated Bibliography*. New York: Garland, 1996; DuPree, Sherry Sherrod. *Biographical Dictionary of African-American Holiness-Pentecostals, 1880–1990*. Washington, DC: Middle Atlantic Regional Press, 1989; Golder, Morris E. *The Bishops of the Pentecostal Assemblies of the World*. Indianapolis: Self-published, 1980; Golder, Morris E. *The Life and Works of Bishop Garfield Thomas Haywood*. Indianapolis: Self-published, 1977; Payne, Wardell J., ed. *Directory of African American Religious Bodies*. 2nd ed. Washington, DC: Howard University Press, 1995; Tyson, James L. *The Early Pentecostal Revival: History of Twentieth-Century Pentecostals and the Pentecostal Assemblies of the World, 1901–30*. Hazelwood, MO: Word Aflame Press, 1992; *We've Come This Far by Faith: Celebrating 50 Years of Service, 1953–2003*; *Pastor's Golden Anniversary Honoring Bishop Clarence E. Moore*. Bluefield, WV: Greater Mt. Zion Pentecostal Church, 2003.

Sherry Sherrod DuPree

PENTECOSTAL HOLINESS CHURCH

see International Pentecostal Holiness Church

PENTECOSTAL REVIVALS

Pentecostals have always seen their movement as one of the major revivals in Christian history. From the beginning of the twentieth century, Pentecostal leaders wrote of a threefold revival heritage that included the **Lutheran** Reformation of the sixteenth century (stressing justification by faith), the Wesleyan or **Methodist** evangelical revival of the eighteenth century (highlighting **sanctification**), and the Pentecostal revival of the twentieth century (centering on the **baptism in the Holy Spirit** as evidenced by **speaking in tongues**). Also cited as part of the Pentecostal heritage are three periods of revival in North America, including the **Great Awakening** (1739–45) as led by **George Whitefield** and **Jonathan Edwards** in New England and other maritime regions, the **Cane Ridge revival** in Kentucky (1800–1801) along with the larger **Second Great Awakening** of the early nineteenth century (ca. 1795–1830), and the **Revival of 1857–1858** that began in New York City and spread to cities and towns across the nation just before the **Civil War.** Each of these awakenings featured emotional demonstrations and **bodily manifestations** such as **shouting, dancing,** falling down, and loud cries of repentance. Many of these manifestations also characterized the revivals of John Wesley in eighteenth-century England. Pentecostals have viewed their own movement as connected with these earlier revivals even though there were only a few instances of speaking in tongues or other **charismatic gifts** reported in these eighteenth- and nineteenth-century revivals.

Pentecostals have also seen themselves as heirs of the revival tradition pioneered by **Charles G. Finney,** who popularized the so-called new measures to stir up religious fervor and mass conversions in churches, cities, and towns across the northeastern United States. Out of this tradition came the custom of seasonal revival services or "protracted meetings" in local churches, and the use of the "anxious bench" or **altar call** as a means of calling people to spiritual decision. Often called *revivals*, these annual or quarterly meetings might last for one or two weeks and might be the occasion of joint sponsorship by several local churches of different denominations. Since Pentecostalism arose in the context of the **Holiness movement** of the late nineteenth century, many of the revivalist practices of early Pentecostals were already well established before 1900. These included evangelistic meetings in local churches, in schoolhouses, or even in temporary outdoor "brush arbors" improvised for the occasion. The **camp and tent meeting** tradition, which by the late 1800s was especially associated with the Methodists, continued among Pentecostals into the twentieth century. Also from the Holiness tradition came the practice of holding **healing** crusades where the main attraction was **prayer** for the sick in meetings often held under tents.

The Pentecostal movement had its beginnings in a little Bible School in Topeka, Kansas, led by **Charles Fox Parham.** A former Methodist pastor turned evangelist and teacher, Parham made his living holding small Holiness revivals in Kansas before establishing the Bethel Bible School in Topeka in 1900. Here he taught his students that a tremendous revival would come at the turn of the century that would herald the second coming of Christ. On January 1, 1901, the first day of a new century, a student, Agnes Ozman, spoke in tongues, to the astonishment of Parham and the student body. This experience led to Parham's teaching that speaking in tongues was the "Bible evidence" of the Pentecostal baptism in the Holy Spirit. For four years, Parham and his students held revivals in towns and cities from Kansas to Texas where utterances in tongues drew multitudes of curious onlookers to his meetings. After establishing another Bible school in Houston, Texas, in 1905, he took his students on **preaching** tours featuring speaking in tongues and divine healing.

One of the students in Houston, **William J. Seymour,** an **African American,** took the Pentecostal message to Los Angeles in 1906, where a monumental revival broke out in an abandoned former **African Methodist Episcopal Church** (AME) building on **Azusa Street.** The worship services at this locale, which continued unabated for three and a half years, became one of the most

"Victory Through Christ" society—a Holiness or Pentecostal congregation in the agricultural community of Dos Palos, central California, during its Sunday service. Slivers of sunlight shine through gaps in the dilapidated building. A caption states: "He's such a wonderful savior. Glory to God. I'm so glad I came to home. Praise God. His love is so wonderful. He's coming soon. I want to praise the Lord for what he is to me. He saved me one time and filled me with the Holy Ghost. Hallalujah! [sic] He will fill your heart today with overflowing." (Photographer Dorothea Lange, for the Farm Security Administration, June 1938.) Courtesy of the Library of Congress.

famous and far-reaching revivals in Christian history. People came from all over the world to attend the services, which went on three times a day, seven days a week. Here it was said "the color line was washed away in the Blood [of Christ]" (Bartleman, 54), as blacks and whites worshipped in equality with one another under the leadership of the black pastor William Seymour. Spurred on by articles written by Frank Bartleman in the Holiness press, visitors came to Azusa Street, spoke in tongues, and went out as Pentecostal pilgrims throughout North America and to the far reaches of the world. The American pilgrims to Azusa Street included **Charles H. Mason,** Gaston B. Cashwell, and William H. Durham. Among those who took the Pentecostal message abroad were A. G. Garr (India), Mary Rumsey (Korea), Thomas Ball Barrett (Europe), Daniel Berg and Gunnar Vingren

(Brazil), Willis Hoover (Chile), Ivan Voronaev (Russia), and Luigi Francescon (Italy).

Under their pioneering ministries, Pentecostal revivals were ignited in many parts of the world. In time some of these developed into massive movements that gained tens of millions of converts during the twentieth century. Among the nations that saw the greatest growth were Chile, Brazil, Argentina, Korea, South Africa, and China. It is now generally accepted that the Azusa Street Mission served as the mother church and prototype for Pentecostal churches throughout the world. After the glory days at Azusa Street came to an end around 1909–1910, hundreds of Pentecostal churches were planted in the United States and carried on the Pentecostal revival tradition in the early decades of the twentieth century. In the face of persecution and opposition, the movement grew as local revival services drew curious crowds to witness such gifts as healing, **deliverance** from demons, and speaking in tongues. Often revivals scheduled for one or two weeks extended into months of services with large crowds. Itinerant evangelists commonly led the services and traveled from town to town holding revivals and planting churches.

Yet, even as Pentecostalism was expanding in its first generation, divisive tendencies appeared. A key issue was race and ethnicity. Charles Parham, who had been William Seymour's teacher, publicly opposed his former pupil and the Azusa Street revival, and used racial language to stigmatize Seymour and those associated with him. Sadly, the relationship between Parham and Seymour was permanently severed. Moreover, the original interracial, black and white leadership team at the Azusa Street Mission broke apart, and within a decade the mission became predominantly African American. The African American Holiness and Pentecostal leader Charles H. Mason founded and legally incorporated the **Church of God in Christ,** and this Pentecostal church body provided ministerial credentials for many early white Pentecostals. Yet, with the founding of the largely white **Assemblies of God** denomination in 1914, black and white Pentecostals moved apart from one another and racial separation in Pentecostal congregations and

denominations became the norm. The **Latino** Pentecostal healer and evangelist **Francisco Olazábal** had to contend with white church leaders who sought to take control of his movement. In 1923 he established the Interdenominational Mexican Council of Churches (Pentecostal) as an indigenous Latino Pentecostal denomination under Latino leadership.

Among the most sensational of the early Pentecostal revivalists was **Aimee Semple McPherson,** whose healing crusades packed the largest auditoriums in the United States from coast to coast in the 1920s and 1930s. In 1923 she settled in Los Angeles and built Angelus Temple, the nation's first **megachurch** with 25,000 members. She was first woman in the United States to obtain her own radio license, established one of the first Christian **radio** stations in North America, and in 1927 founded her own denomination, the **International Church of the Foursquare Gospel.** Following in her steps were a long line of healing evangelists that included **William Branham, Oral Roberts, Kathryn Kuhlman,** and **Jimmy Swaggart.** Of these, Roberts and Swaggart pioneered a new genre of media-based ministry known as televangelism.

In the late 1940s and early 1950s, a new wave of revival swept the Pentecostal movement from a local revival centered in a Canadian Bible School in Saskatchewan, Alberta. Known as the New Order of the **Latter Rain,** this movement represented a renewal of charismatic gifts such as **prophecy** and giving specific messages in tongues. In the end the Pentecostal denominations largely rejected the revival because of perceived excesses that included the bestowal of specific gifts by the laying on of hands and a teaching regarding "manifest sons"— thought to be individuals who will never die. The Latter Rain movement coincided with the beginnings of the healing revivals in 1948. In subsequent years, Oral Roberts, William Branham, T. L. Osborn, and Tommy Hicks led massive healing crusades in North America that spilled over and prompted comparable events overseas. The result was a massive growth of Pentecostal churches in many parts of the world. During this period some American congregations began to call themselves

This oddly designed mansion in Topeka, Kansas was called "Stone's Folly" after the name of its early owner. Charles Parham acquired the building for his Bible school in 1900, and here Agnes Ozman first spoke in tongues on January 1, 1901. Courtesy of Flower Pentecostal Heritage Center, Springfield, MO.

revival centers and conducted services six nights a week throughout the year.

By the 1950s laymen were joining in the revivalistic fervor that engulfed the Pentecostal movement. In 1951, Demos Shakarian, a millionaire dairyman from Los Angeles, started an organization called the **Full Gospel Business Men's Fellowship International** (FGBMFI). Laymen rather than clergymen directed the FGBMFI. Though **women** and preachers could attend and even speak at Shakarian's events, they could not be voting members of the organization. By the 1960s and 1970s over 4,000 chapters were operating all over the world, and at its height about 4 million persons attended FGBMFI events each month. This Pentecostal laymen's revival brought people from all denominations to hotels and restaurants for salvation and healing meetings. Referred to by Oral Roberts as "God's Ballroom Saints," the FGBMFI fueled the growth of world

Pentecostalism. A women's organization—known originally as the Full Gospel Women's Fellowship (FGWF), then called Women's Aglow, and finally renamed **Aglow International** (AI)—began in 1967 in Seattle, Washington, as a women's counterpart to the FGBMFI. In 2004, Aglow International reported 3,500 local groups in 155 nations, of which about 1,400 groups (or "lighthouses") are located in the United States. Both the **men**'s and women's organizations have encouraged the development of lay leadership in Pentecostal churches around the world.

Beginning in the 1950s, neo-Pentecostal revivals affected many of the historic denominations of African American Christians in North America. These revivals challenged and partially reversed a middle-class trend in the black church that had begun in the mid-1800s. Daniel Alexander Payne, who exemplified the trend, had de-emphasized

Despite Pentecostalism's early interracialism, many congregations and denominations were segregated on white-black lines by the 1920s. The 1994 "Memphis miracle" brought together white and black Pentecostals to confront racism and establish the interracial Pentecostal/Charismatic Churches of North America (PCCNA). Courtesy of Flower Pentecostal Heritage Center, Springfield, MO.

religious emotion and bodily manifestations. By the 1970s neo-Pentecostal ministers began to occupy pulpits in the **African Methodist Episcopal Church** (AMEC), and in some black **Baptist** congregations. St. Paul AMEC in Cambridge, Massachusetts, under the leadership of John Bryant, was a focal point of this emerging movement. By the 1980s, neo-Pentecostal AMEC congregations were among the largest in the denomination. In the **African Methodist Episcopal Zion Church** (AMEZ), the neo-Pentecostal movement during the 1980s and 1990s centered on John A. Cherry and his Full Gospel AMEZ Church in Temple Hills, Maryland. Among black Baptists, some of the key neo-Pentecostal congregations were Pilgrim Baptist Cathedral in Brooklyn, led by Roy Brown, and St. Stephen Full Gospel Baptist Church in New Orleans, under Paul Morton. In the 1980s, Brown organized a denomination (Pilgrim Assemblies), and Morton organized a neo-Pentecostal Baptist fellowship known as the Full Gospel Baptist

Fellowship. Alongside of these more recently "Pentecostalized" congregations and denominations, the **Church of God in Christ** (COGIC) and the **Pentecostal Assemblies of the World** (PAW)—a Oneness Pentecostal denomination—are among the most prominent Pentecostal denominations that are largely African American in membership (though the PAW has a strong tradition of interracial leadership). Perhaps the best-known black Pentecostal preacher as of 2005 is **T. D. Jakes,** pastor of the Potter's House, a Dallas **megachurch** with more than 20,000 members.

Before 1960, Pentecostal-style revivalism in white North American congregations was almost entirely confined to Pentecostal churches. Scorned by mainline Protestant churches, and often attacked by Holiness, Fundamentalist, and Evangelical churches, Pentecostalism long remained unpopular. The first neo-Pentecostal to make national news was the Episcopal minister Dennis Bennett of Van Nuys, California, who identified with Pentecostals when he publicly confessed to speaking in tongues in 1960. Over the next few years, Pentecostal revivalism entered most of the mainline Protestant churches. Some of its early leaders were Harald Bredesen and Larry Christenson (Lutheran), Gerald Derstine (Mennonite), Brick Bradford (**Presbyterian**), Howard Conatser and Pat Robertson (Baptist), and Tommy Tyson (Methodist). By 1965 these neo-Pentecostals adopted the label **Charismatic,** and by and large they achieved the approval of their ecclesiastical leaders and remained in their denominations. These newer Pentecostals did not adopt the revivalistic methods of their Pentecostal brothers and sisters. They spoke of their movements as a Charismatic Renewal within the church, and they were generally less ready than the Pentecostals to see the charismatic gifts as something that set them apart from noncharismatic Christians. The Charismatics had few local church revivals, in the classic sense, though they held conferences and rallies throughout the land that sometimes drew thousands or tens of thousands of participants. A 1977 Kansas City conference brought together some 45,000 Charismatics and may be regarded as the most public event of the 1970s Charismatic Renewal. During this period, many Charismatics attended services and revivals in Pentecostal congregations in addition to attending their own mainline Protestant churches.

In 1967 another wave of Pentecostal revival suddenly erupted in the **Roman Catholic** Church, to the surprise of nearly everyone, including the Pentecostals. Although there had always been Charismatics in the Catholic mystical tradition, few had expected that a Pentecostal spirituality would break out in the Roman Catholic Church. In calling the Vatican II Council in Rome, lasting from 1962 to 1965, Pope John XIII summoned every Catholic in the world to pray daily for the Lord to "renew your wonders in this our day as by a new Pentecost." Debates in the council recognized the presence of many "charisms" (i.e., spiritual gifts) in the church and called for spiritual renewal that would "open the windows of the church" for the fresh winds of the Spirit to blow through. Only two years after the close of the Vatican II Council, a Charismatic movement started in Duquesne University in Pittsburgh among theology students and professors, and emerged almost simultaneously in South America in the nation of Colombia. From Duquesne the movement traveled to Notre Dame University and the University of Michigan before spreading to the Catholic grassroots across America. Instead of adopting Pentecostal revival techniques, the Catholic Renewal made use of prayer meetings and "days of renewal" in local parishes. Soon the Catholic Charismatic Renewal was established in more than a hundred nations of the world. Large conferences at Notre Dame in 1972 and 1973 brought the movement to the attention of the Vatican. By 1976, Pope Paul VI gave official approval to the renewal and appointed Leon-Joseph Cardinal Suenens of Belgium to serve as his liaison to the burgeoning movement. The movement among Catholics grew fastest in Latin America and Asia. By the year 2000, more than 100 million Latin American Catholics were involved in the Charismatic movement.

As the twentieth century drew to a close, two major revivals broke out in local churches and had reverberations around the world. The first one originated in a Vineyard church in Toronto, Canada, in 1994. The Vineyard movement had begun in California under the leadership of **John Wimber,** a former **Quaker** minister, musician, and teacher at Fuller Theological Seminary from 1975 to 1985. In the Airport Vineyard Church in Toronto a local revival broke out that drew hundreds of thousands of visitors from all over the world over the course of several years. The pastor, John Arnott, saw his church explode in numbers as curious visitors came to worship services that continued six nights a week. Participants in what became known as the **Toronto Blessing** stressed the new awareness of God's love that they experienced, and they referred to their movement as "the Father's Blessing." In addition to such Pentecostal manifestations as speaking in tongues and **prophecy,** many people at Toronto experienced such unusual phenomena as **laughing** in the Spirit or even roaring like lions or barking like dogs during the services. John Wimber investigated the situation in Toronto, characterized what was happening there as "exotic manifestations," and excommunicated the congregation from the Vineyard fellowship in 1996. After this, Arnott formed his own denomination.

Another remarkable revival began in 1995 in the city of Brownsville, Florida, near the port city of **Pensacola.** This time the revival broke out in a local **Assemblies of God** church. As in Toronto, multitudes attended the services in Brownsville. Before the revival began to ebb, over 2 million persons had attended at least one service in the Brownsville church, and a Bible college with over 1,000 students was formed to train young ministers who were converted in the revival. Unlike the Toronto revival, the Assemblies of God denomination decided to oversee the meetings and to keep the church and the school within their denominational system. Both the Toronto and Brownsville revivals were highly publicized and triggered revivals in churches throughout the world, much as the earlier Azusa Street revival spread from Los Angeles to many other cities and nations.

At the end of the twentieth century, some of the largest Pentecostal revival crusades in history were taking place in Africa under the ministry of the German evangelist Reinhard Bonnke. Going to Lesotho, South Africa, as a conventional missionary in 1967, Bonnke soon became dissatisfied with the meager results of his ministry. Therefore, in 1975 he rented a large stadium in Botswana, where he began a spectacular evangelistic ministry. Traveling throughout Africa in a tent seating 34,000, Bonnke saw hundreds of thousands of conversions during his crusades. By 1990 he abandoned the tent and began to preach in the open air. He soon began to draw the largest crowds in the history of crusade evangelism, even surpassing the records set by Billy Graham. In Lagos, Nigeria, in the year 2000, it was reported that 1.6 million people attended one of Bonnke's services, with more than 1 million converted. In addition to Bonnke, the American Pentecostal evangelist **Benny Hinn** regularly drew crowds of more than 500,000 persons in India and Africa. This helped the Pentecostals to establish the world's largest Christian congregations or megachurches. The largest of these was the Full Gospel Church pastored by Yonggii Cho in Seoul, South Korea, which by 2000 claimed over 700,000 members in one congregation, the largest local church in Christian history.

Further Reading: Bartleman, Frank, and Vinson Synan. *Azusa Street: The Roots of Modern Pentecost.* South Plainfield, NJ: Bridge, 1980; Blumhofer, Edith W. *Aimee Semple McPherson: Everybody's Sister.* Grand Rapids, MI: Eerdmans, 1993; Burgess, Stanley M., and Eduard Van Der Maas, eds. *The New International Dictionary of Pentecostal and Charismatic Movements.* Grand Rapids, MI: Zondervan, 2002; Cox, Harvey. *Fire from Heaven: The Rise of Pentecostal Spirituality and the Reshaping of Christianity in the Twentieth Century.* Reading, MA: Addison-Wesley, 1995; Dayton, Donald. *The Theological Roots of Pentecostalism.* Metuchen, NJ: Scarecrow Press, 1987; Goff, James. *Fields White unto Harvest: Charles Fox Parham and the Missionary Origins of Pentecostalism.* Fayetteville: Arkansas University Press, 1988; Harrell, David Edwin, Jr. *All Things Are Possible: The Healing and Charismatic Revivals in Modern America.* Bloomington: Indiana University Press, 1975; Harrell, David Edwin, Jr. *Oral Roberts: An American Life.* Bloomington: Indiana University Press, 1985; Hollenweger, Walter. *The Pentecostals.* 1972. Reprint, Peabody, MA: Hendrickson, 1988; Jones, Charles Edwin. *A Guide to the Study of the Pentecostal Movement.* 2 vols. Metuchen, NJ: Scarecrow Press, 1983; McGee, Gary. *People of the Spirit: The Assemblies of God.* Springfield, MO: Gospel, 2004; Riss, Richard M. *A Survey of Twentieth-Century Revival Movements in North America.* Peabody, MA: Hendrickson, 1989; Synan, Vinson, ed. *The Century of the Holy Spirit: Pentecostal and Charismatic Movements in the Twentieth Century.* Nashville, TN: Thomas Nelson, 2001; Synan, Vinson. *The Holiness-Pentecostal Tradition.* Grand Rapids, MI: Eerdmans, 2001; Wacker, Grant. *Heaven Below: Early Pentecostals and American Culture.* Cambridge, MA: Harvard University Press, 2003.

Vinson Synan

PERFECTIONSIM

see Holiness Movement in the Nineteenth Century; Oneida Community; Sanctification and Revivals

PIETISM AND REVIVALS

Pietism originated as the renewal wing of post-Reformation German **Lutheranism.** Its chief precursor was John Arndt (1555–1621), author of the devotional classic *True Christianity* (1610), and the movement took definite shape through the labors of Philipp Jakob Spener (1635–1705), whose *Pia Desideria* (1675) has been the movement's manifesto. Pietism offered a program for church renewal based on the concept of the *collegia pietatis* ("fellowship of the godly") or *ecclesiola in ecclesiam* ("little churches within the larger church")—a system of small groups (or "conventicles") that Pietists tended to view as the heart of the Christian church. As originally proposed, these small groups were to be conducted under the auspices of the pastor, as a vehicle for realizing Martin Luther's ideal of a "priesthood of all believers." The preface to a new edition of Arndt's work in 1675 gave Spener an opportunity to promote these ideas. German Lutheran Pietism came to fruition in the work of August Hermann Francke (1663–1727), a professor at Halle University, whose educational and philanthropic work transformed a movement for inward spiritual renewal into a grand program of social reform and **foreign missions** around the world. His proactive revivalism deeply influenced the social fabric of Prussian society in ways that paralleled the influence of **Methodism** on eighteenth-century English society. The Prussian court adopted Pietism as its official ideology, while in much of Germany the situation was different. A Lutheran Orthodox party, based at Wittenberg and defended by the lower princes, entered into prolonged conflict with the Pietists. An underlying motif of the German Pietist writers was the necessity and centrality of **conversion** or the new birth (*der Wiedergeburt*) as the basis for genuine Christian identity. The Pietists rejected a formalized view of faith as assent to memorized doctrines imparted by catechesis or mechanical observance of the sacraments. The stress on conversion and rejection of religious formalism were at the core of the conflict between the Pietists and the Lutheran Orthodox party.

Similar viewpoints emerged in the **Reformed** states of Holland and the Holy Roman Empire, including late sixteenth-century Puritans and Dutch Precisianists—for example, William Ames (1576–1633) and Jodocus van Lodenstein (1620–1677)—who stressed the need for an experience of regeneration followed by an ordered life under the grace of God's law. The French émigré Jean de Labadie (1610–1674), whose work with conventicles predated and influenced Spener, shared the same general outlook. Reformed Pietism coalesced in the seventeenth century in the covenant theology of Johannes Cocceius and his Pietist adherents, such as the pastor-theologian of Bremen, Friedrich Adolph Lampe (1683–1729). The result was an ordered approach to the godly life that emphasized Christian perfection, a theme that would be brought into prominence in later Methodism.

Beginning in the eighteenth century, the renewal emphasis of earlier Pietism shifted into revivalism, beginning with the Reformed territories in the German Rhineland district, and extending from there to England and North America, and beyond. Beginning with radical Pietist itinerating **preachers** like Ernst Hochmann von Hochenau (1670–1721), the leading revival figure in eighteenth-century Germany was the ribbon maker Gerhard Tersteegen (1697–1769), who was drawn from the life of a reclusive ascetic to become a popular mass preacher of the deeper life in Christ. Tersteegen's travels ranged from northwest Germany into Holland. His legacy of **hymns** and tracts would influence an entire generation of revivalists, including John Wesley in the English Methodist movement. The **Moravian** leader Count Nicholas von Zinzendorf (1700–1760) can be counted as both a Pietist and revivalist, whose ministry took him and his Moravian colleagues on a **transatlantic** trajectory of preaching and community organization.

In the New World, Wesley's colleague **George Whitefield** preached in the **Great Awakening** (1739–1745) throughout the North American British colonies, which included preaching visits to Pennsylvania German and Dutch Reformed communities in the Middle Colonies. That mission bore fruit in the formation of the **United Brethren in Christ** (1800), which grew out of the revivalistic preaching of the German Reformed pastor **Philip William Otterbein** and the converted Mennonite bishop Martin Boehm, whose work is traced to a

Pentecost "big meeting" in 1767 in Pennsylvania. Although Methodists were slow to move into German-speaking areas in the colonial era, revivalism of a distinctively Methodist form took shape in the work of the Lutheran lay preacher Jacob Albright (1759–1808). Albright's followers ordained him as an evangelical minister and so helped launch a new German revivalist denomination, with Pietist roots, in 1816—the **Evangelical Association** (Evangelische Gemeinschaft). By 1850, their revival activity was extended to Germany, where a growing free church was organized among their converts in Württemberg in 1865. Pietist influences can also be traced in other revivalist denominations formed in nineteenth-century America, including the Brethren in Christ, the Winebrennarians, and the Swedish American denomination that became known as the **Evangelical Covenant Church**.

Further Reading: O'Malley, J. Steven. *Early German-American Evangelicalism*. Lanham, MD: Scarecrow Press, 1995; Stouffer, F. Ernest, ed. *Continental Pietism and Early American Christianity*. Grand Rapids, MI: Eerdmans, 1976.

J. Steven O'Malley

POSITIVE CONFESSION

see Prosperity Theology

PRAYER AND REVIVALS

Prayer and religious revivals have been inextricably linked throughout American history. From the first **Great Awakening** to **Billy Graham,** prayer has been widely practiced during spiritual awakenings and believed by participants to be an essential ingredient to a revival's success. While eighteenth-century evangelicals combined extensive use of prayer with ambivalence about prayer's ability to bring about revival, nineteenth-century revivalists and their modern descendants believed fervently in the efficacy of prayer and developed increasingly sophisticated methods of encouraging prayer for revival.

Seventeenth-century Puritans were known for their strict disciplines of prayer, but they typically directed their prayers toward personal moral reformation and social piety rather than spiritual revival. In the early eighteenth century, an apparent upsurge of interest in prayer and revival occurred in Anglo American culture, as church leaders urged prayers for a fresh outpouring of the Holy Spirit. Prayer manuals such as Isaac Watts's *Guide to Prayer* (1715) were enormously popular in both Britain and the American colonies. So-called prayer societies emerged in England and Scotland, in which Christians met regularly in small groups for fellowship, Bible study, and prayer for revival. These societies were usually led by laypersons, though ministers closely observed them and steered them away from controversial theological questions. Through the efforts of the New England pastor, theologian, and revivalist **Jonathan Edwards,** prayer societies spread to America. In 1734, Edwards organized youth and adult prayer societies in his **Northampton,** Massachusetts, congregation. When revival fervor swept through Northampton and other parts of New England, Edwards credited the establishment of prayer societies as an important predecessor to the awakening.

The **Moravians** in Germany anticipated the rest of the Protestant world, and exercised an influence out of proportion to their numbers, in their combined emphasis on constant prayer, unity among Christians, spiritual revival, and world evangelization. As a result of a 1727 spiritual awakening they experienced, the Moravians began "hourly intercessions" as a 24-hour, all-week, year-round practice. They were pioneers in Protestant missions work, established communities in Pennsylvania and North Carolina, and regularly offered prayers for their far-flung missionaries around the world. Though the hourly intercessions fell into neglect in the mid-1700s, they were revived in 1827 in anticipation of the centennial of the 1727 awakening, and then in the British province in 1872, and again in eastern Europe in the 1950s. In 1957, the Moravians at Herrnhut—now located in communist East Germany—were not allowed to send visitors or missionaries abroad, and they decided that their most effective contribution to the worldwide ministry of their church was to renew the hourly intercessions. The practice is now known as the Unity Prayer Watch, and the entire international Moravian Church is involved.

By the 1740s, days of united prayer were being employed in Scotland and New England to promote revivalism. Revivalists in Scotland established "concerts of prayer" in which Christian regularly united to pray for revival. In 1745, Edwards attempted to extend the concert of prayer to America. His 1747 book *A Humble Attempt to Promote an Explicit Agreement and Visible Union of God's People through the World, in Extraordinary Prayer, for the Revival of Religion*, stated explicitly his intention to usher in revival through the united prayers of believers. Encouraging the concert of prayer became a lifelong passion for Edwards even after he left Northampton and assumed the presidency of Princeton College.

Edwards believed that God preordained the concert of prayer as a foreshadowing of coming revival—a fact that reveals a somewhat awkward **theology of revivals** and prayer that typified this transitional generation between **Calvinism** and evangelicalism. The leaders of the Great Awakening believed that revivals were not accomplished by human means but solely through divine initiative. But they also believed that human prayers were important to a revival's success. The result was something of a dialectical understanding of the relationship between prayer and revival: The Holy Spirit caused a person to pray, but prayer brought an outpouring of the Holy Spirit. Prayer did not change God, but it did bring results. Subsequent revivalists would place greater weight on the power of prayer to move God to act.

The revivals generally associated with the **Second Great Awakening** of the early nineteenth century were also preceded by efforts in united prayer. In 1794, New England ministers meeting in Connecticut reread Edwards's *Humble Attempt* and were motivated to send a circular letter to churches throughout the nation urging them to organize prayer societies for revival. In the **South, Methodist** congregations, alarmed by seemingly negative cultural trends, formed prayer societies that combined repentance, **fasting,** and prayer. Presbyterian

Prayer meeting in a tent during a religious revival in Eastham, Massachusetts. (Wood engraving, from *Gleason's Pictorial*, vol. 3, 1852.) Courtesy of the Library of Congress.

minister **James McGready** had his Kentucky congregations adopt covenants to pray for a fresh outpouring of the Holy Spirit. When religious fervor broke out at **Cane Ridge,** Kentucky, and spread to other locations, ministers considered the events to be a direct result of their consistent, united prayers for revival. The Second Great Awakening inspired the establishment of American **foreign missionary** societies, many of which evolved out of concerts of prayer. To the earlier practice of monthly meetings for prayer and Bible reading were added missionary addresses and financial collections for missionaries. Signaling a new theological understanding of prayer and revival that was developing, the missionary societies emphasized a combination of prayer and "exertion": Christians should pray, but they should also partner with God in revival by working diligently to evangelize, raise money, and establish schools.

Charles Grandison Finney, America's best-known revivalist of the mid-nineteenth century, furthered the trend toward viewing prayer as a way to effect change. Finney's emphasis on "means" in revival solidified and extended changes that had been occurring within American evangelicalism.

Prayer during a revival meeting in a Pentecostal church, Cambria, Illinois. (Photographer Arthur Rothstein, January 1939.) Courtesy of the Library of Congress.

Thus, it comes as no surprise that Finney modified the earlier Calvinist understanding of the role of prayer in revival. For Finney, prayer was one of the means that God used to bring about revival. While Finney never went so far as to claim that prayer actually changed God's mind, he did believe that prayers initiated and orchestrated by humans could move God to bestow genuine spiritual revival, and, in his *Lectures on Revivals of Religion* (1835), offered a distinctive teaching regarding a "prayer of faith" that was especially efficacious. Finney's revivals were typically preceded and accompanied by public prayer meetings and lay prayer meetings in homes.

No stranger to controversy, Finney aroused opposition among fellow Christians for his innovations concerning revival prayer. Critics condemned what they considered to be Finney's excessive familiarity with God in prayer. ("I will not be denied!" Finney would sometimes exclaim to God in his public prayers.) Fellow revivalists such as **Lyman Beecher** and **Asahel Nettleton** attacked the practice of naming particular individuals as

especially needing conviction of sin in Finney's prayer meetings. Most importantly, Beecher and others condemned Finney's practice of allowing **women** to pray audibly in public prayer meetings—a common practice among Methodists but considered unscriptural by many of Finney's fellow Presbyterians. Meeting in New Lebanon, New York, in 1827, Finney and his critics reached a tenuous compromise over Finney's prayer methods: individuals could be named in small prayer groups, but not in public meetings. Similarly, women would be allowed to pray in small groups, but not in public prayer meetings where **men** were present. All parties agreed that "violent gestures" and "boisterous tones" in public prayer should be avoided.

The so-called Prayer Meeting **Revival of 1857–1858** applied and extended Finney's methods of prayer. The revival emerged out of noonday prayer meetings begun by Jeremiah Lanphier in 1857 at the Dutch **Reformed** Church on Fulton Street in New York City. At first sparsely attended, the meetings soon outgrew the Fulton Street church and spread to other churches. By early 1858, New Yorkers were packing Burton's Theater every day at noon for midday prayer. The prayer meetings spread to other cities in the United States and the British Isles. In Chicago, for example, over 2,000 people gathered daily for prayer in the Metropolitan Theater. The meetings followed a standard format. They began promptly at noon with a **hymn,** opening prayer, and brief reading of scripture, after which the meetings were opened up for participation from the audience. Prayers were limited to five minutes maximum, and like the eighteenth-century prayer societies, "controverted points" were to be avoided during the meetings.

The Prayer Meeting Revival reinforced the shift in emphasis in American revivalism from divine power to human activity. The events of 1857–1858 increased Christians' faith in prayer not only to bring about revivals but to transform the nation itself. Ironically, as Kathryn Long has argued, this expansion of faith in prayer was accompanied by a narrowing of Christians' social concern. The revival led Christians to believe that changes to the social order would be accomplished not by social activism, but that organized prayer would cause God directly to intervene in human affairs. Thus revivalists were led to pray for the oppressed slaves rather than to engage in **abolitionist** activity. During the prayer meetings, both the abolition of slavery and the public role of women in ministry were regarded as controverted points and thus were excluded from discussion. The Revival of 1857–1858 generally reinforced socially conservatism rather than social reform.

The Revival of 1857–1858 and its predecessors in American history occurred amid a cultural ethos that generally accepted prayer as a causative factor in the universe. With the rise of modern science in the second half of the nineteenth century, such views came under increasing scrutiny among intellectual and cultural elites in Britain and America. The British naturalist John Tyndall, for instance, mocked the traditional belief in prayer's efficacy and proposed a "prayer-gauge" by which to test prayer's effect on one's physical health. In 1872, Tyndall gave a speaking tour of America that generated widespread public interest as well as protests from Christians. In the wake of scientific attacks on prayer, late nineteenth-century revivalists employed written testimonies of answered prayer to assure the faithful and to combat skeptics. Samuel Irenaeus Prime, for example, the leading chronicler of the 1857–1858 revival, increasingly devoted his compiled accounts of answered prayer toward apologetic purposes. His three volumes of answered prayer testimonies served, he believed, to answer the skeptics' claims that prayer had no demonstrable effects on visible events.

If Prime's narratives placed revival prayer in a more modern key, so too did the revivals of the leading evangelist of the late nineteenth century, **Dwight L. Moody.** A former shoe salesman deeply affected by the Revival of 1857–1858, Moody applied systematic planning and modern organizational methods to revivalism. With respect to prayer, Moody applied the methods of earlier revivalists in a more thorough, systematic fashion. Weeks before Moody visited a city for evangelistic services, his team established "union" prayer meetings among Christians from a wide variety of denominations. Moody himself led noonday prayer meetings along the pattern established by the 1857–1858 revival. Meetings began promptly at noon and ended in an hour, and Moody did not hesitate to cut someone off who exceeded the five-minute maximum for prayer. Moody's evening evangelistic services were conducted on this base of daily, interdenominational, noonday prayer meetings.

A host of professional evangelists in the early twentieth century imitated (and often distorted) Moody's methods. **Billy Sunday,** the most important revivalist of this generation, mimicked many of Moody's rhetorical devices and organizational methods, but prayer meetings did not seem to play an integral role in his revivals. Elsewhere in the early twentieth-century religious landscape, prayer and revival acquired more dramatic characteristics. In 1901, the revivalist **Charles Parham** laid hands on Agnes Ozman and prayed that she would receive **the baptism of the Holy Spirit,** after which Ozman began **speaking in tongues.** By 1906 in

Los Angeles, California, the **African American** evangelist **William J. Seymour** began home prayer meetings that led to an outbreak of speaking in tongues and the birth of the modern **Pentecostal** movement. Ozman, Parham, and Seymour did not pray for revival as earlier Christians had done; they believed that they themselves *were* the revival. Their movement was a sign, they believed, that God's spirit was being poured out in anticipation of the return of Christ. Pentecostals did, however, pray for more intense, sustained, extensive "showers" of the so-called **latter rain.** In Pentecostal revivals, prayer often accompanied reports of supernatural phenomena such as speaking in tongues, miraculous **healing,** and **prophecy.** For some, prayer came to have almost magical qualities. The Pentecostal evangelist **Oral Roberts,** for example, mailed "anointed" prayer cloths to his supporters that, he claimed, would transmit God's healing power to those in need of physical cure.

The use of prayer by America's most prominent twentieth-century revivalist, Billy Graham, more closely resembled Dwight L. Moody's methods than those of Graham's more flamboyant contemporaries. Indeed, Graham's evangelistic campaigns demonstrated that, for modern mainstream revivalists, the theological understanding of prayer and revival did not differ substantially from that of their nineteenth-century counterparts. The use of organized prayer in revival, however, had undergone extensive development. Beginning his career as a staff evangelist for **Youth for Christ,** Graham perfected his revival technique in the late 1940s. In preparation for the 1949 Los Angeles campaign that made him a national figure, Graham sent veteran revivalists to Southern California nine months ahead of time to hold preliminary meetings. They formed nearly 800 small prayer groups that met regularly to pray for the campaign. Two weeks before Graham arrived, his assistant Grady Wilson organized all-night prayer meetings and around-the-clock prayer chains involving hundreds of people. A decade later, Graham's New York City campaign was accompanied by a massive worldwide prayer effort that surpassed anything that Moody's savvy organizers could have imagined. Ten thousand

prayer groups in at least 75 countries met daily to pray for the revival. Tribal Africans, Calcutta urbanites, and Japanese convicts joined over 150,000 New Yorkers in pledging to pray for the campaign. Reminiscent of nineteenth-century practices, a daily radio program was broadcast in New York City with the slogan "Noontime is prayer time."

During the 1980s and 1990s, North American evangelicals intensified their focus on intercessory prayer as a means of effecting social change (e.g., the pro-life or anti-abortion movement, pro-family legislation), inducing personal transformation (recovery from substance abuse, overcoming sexual compulsions, the healing of troubled marriages), and promoting evangelism and **foreign missions** work (the **conversion** of "unreached people groups" such as Muslims, Hindus, Buddhists, and others). During the 1980s, David Bryant sought to revive the "concerts of prayer" that Jonathan Edwards and a number of Scottish ministers had promoted in the 1740s. These were two-hour services in various localities that brought together Christians from various denominations to pray for spiritual renewal, church revival, and world evangelization. **C. Peter Wagner** and Charles Kraft—both professors at Fuller Theological Seminary in Pasadena, California—linked prayer with the idea of **spiritual warfare.** The teaching on warfare prayer implied that demonic forces were the hidden causes of human suffering and resistance to the Christian gospel, and that concerted prayer was the God-given means for overcoming these forces and releasing divine blessing. Frank Peretti's novel *This Present Darkness* (1986) struck a chord with evangelical readers in its fictional portrayal of a small band of praying Christians battling unseen forces in a midwestern college town. There was a new emphasis on **fasting** along with prayer, with growing numbers of people engaging in prolonged water-only fasts of up to a week, two weeks, or even 40 days (on the pattern of Jesus' 40-day fast in the desert; Matthew 4:2). A 24-7 initiative, especially strong among younger **Charismatics,** has sought to create centers where intercessory prayer will continue uninterrupted around the clock. One example is the International

House of Prayer, founded by the Kansas City pastor Mike Bickle (formerly associated with the **Kansas City prophets**), as a place for day-and-night prayer since the late 1990s. The 24-7 prayer movement is reminiscent of earlier efforts by the Moravians in the 1700s and 1800s.

Another major current trend is the globalization of evangelical and Charismatic prayer practices. Through the initiative of a Christian businessman from South Africa, Graham Power, an organized day of prayer in 2001 drew participants from cities and towns throughout southern Africa. By 2004 this annual event grew to include a reported 24 million participants throughout the continent of Africa. The first annual Global Day of Prayer took place on Pentecost Sunday, May 2005, and it involved more than 100 million Christians from about 150 nations in praying jointly for the "healing and blessing" of all nations. North American Christians, in partnership with African Christians, have played an instrumental role in planning and preparing for the Global Day of Prayer. In light of Billy Graham's methods and popularity, the prayer-and-fasting and 24-7 movements, and such recent initiatives as the Global Day of Prayer, one conclusion is clear: Many modern Americans share with earlier Christians the belief that genuine revival results from an outpouring of God's spirit, which is preceded, and perhaps even caused, by the prayers of God's people.

Further Reading: Bakke, Robert O. "Harvests, Missions, America's Pentecost and the Concert of Prayer." In *The Power of Extraordinary Prayer*, 63–116. Wheaton, IL: Crossway Books, 2000; Boles, John B. *The Great Revival: Beginnings of the Bible Belt.* Lexington: University Press of Kentucky, 1972; Dorsett, Lyle W. *Billy Sunday and the Redemption of Urban America.* Grand Rapids, MI: Eerdmans, 1991; Dorsett, Lyle W. *A Passion for Souls: The Life of D. L. Moody.* Chicago: Moody Press, 1997; Kidd, Thomas S. "The Very Vital Breath of Christianity: Prayer and Revival in Provincial New England." *Fides et Historia* 36 (2004): 19–33; Long, Kathryn. *The Revival of 1857–58: Interpreting an American Religious Awakening.* New York: Oxford Press, 1998; Lyrene, Edward Charles, Jr. "The Role of Prayer in American Revival Movements, 1740–1860." PhD dissertation, Southern Baptist Theological Seminary, 1985; Marsden, George M. *Jonathan Edwards: A Life.* New Haven, CT: Yale University Press, 2003; Martin, William M. *A Prophet with Honor: The Billy Graham Story.* New York: William Morrow, 1991; Ostrander, Rick. *The Life of Prayer in a World of Science: Protestants, Prayer, and American Culture, 1870–1930.* New York: Oxford Press, 2000.

Rick Ostrander

PREACHING AND REVIVALS

It is virtually impossible to consider revival or renewal movements in the Christian church without taking account of preaching. From the New Testament day of Pentecost (Acts 2) to the emergence of the Dominicans—the Order of Preachers—in the Middle Ages to today's new order of preachers who combine video images with spoken words, the renewal of the faith has involved preaching. With Martin Luther, the reformation of the church was at issue. With Martin Luther King Jr., the reformation of society was the concern. During the last 250 years, American revivalism formed a unique relationship with preaching. New sermonic forms emerged, and new phrases, such as "accepting Jesus Christ as your personal Savior," became part of the church's vocabulary. When a leading scholar of revivals, **William J. McLoughlin,** sought to define the term *revivalism* in his major work *Revivals, Awakenings, and Reform* (1978), he emphasized the role of the preacher in initiating spiritual awakenings in America: "Revivalism is the Protestant ritual … in which charismatic evangelists convey 'the Word' of God to large masses of people, who, under this influence, experience what Protestants call conversion, salvation, regeneration, or spiritual rebirth" (xiii). Although some revivals have begun without the instrumentality of a preacher or evangelist, this seems to be more the exception than the rule.

The relationship between preaching and revivals during the 1730s and 1740s might be viewed through the lives of **Jonathan Edwards** and **George Whitefield.** Edwards's ministry in **Northampton,** Massachusetts, brought a revival in 1734–1735. Edwards's preaching followed the methods of a **Calvinistic** and Puritan minister from the late sixteenth and early seventeenth centuries—William Perkins—who started with the reading of the biblical text, gave the sense of the passage by explaining the text from scripture itself, identified points of doctrine that could be extracted from the passage, and demonstrated how to apply the doctrine to human conduct. By this method, Edwards was able to emphasize the sovereignty of God and the authority of God's Word. The purpose of preaching, in Edwards's view, was to create the circumstances in which **conversion** might occur. Conversion was the first "degree" of salvation. It was the event in which an individual, through hearing the gospel message, might be brought to repentance and faith. Subsequent degrees of salvation would then include justification, sanctification, and glorification. To create the conditions that could effect a conversion, a preacher might demonstrate logically the connection between guilt and repentance. The role of the preacher was to provide a rationale; it was the will and the work of a sovereign God to convert the sinner. Neither the preacher nor the convert caused conversion, from Edwards's perspective. Within this homiletic approach, remarkable revivals occurred in Northampton. Edward's sermons appealed to reason, but the responses to his preaching were not merely rational. Emotional reactions were common.

George Whitefield—the best-known and most celebrated preacher of the **Great Awakening**—has been described by Harry Stout as a "divine dramatist." Whitefield's sermons were in effect a form of religious theater wherein the texts of the Bible were acted out before an audience. He himself exhibited holy emotions of love, awe, compassion, and fear, and was known for weeping as he preached and for eliciting emotions among his hearers that paralleled his own. Whitefield's style of preaching represented a break from Edwards's more formal approach to preparing and delivering sermons. Far from being a "manuscript preacher" who read a prepared message aloud, Whitefield often refused to decide in advance what he was going to say. Facing an audience of thousands, he would settle at the last moment on a text and a theme for his sermon, and then throw himself with passion into verbal improvisation. While such an approach might seem a sure route to homiletic mediocrity, in Whitefield's case the outcome was electrifying.

As North American revivalism moved into its next stage, two features emerged in revival preaching. One was the awareness that an emotional response to the proclaimed Word was not only acceptable but actually desirable. Thus sermons should be designed as well as delivered in an emotional manner and for an emotional outcome. A second development was a theological shift away from the concept that conversion is solely an act of divine sovereignty and toward the concept that, at some level, conversion is a result of human agency. Though **Nathaniel Taylor** and **Lyman Beecher** were influential in their theologies of conversion, it was **Charles G. Finney** who effectively brought together and popularized the new emphasis on religious emotion and a call for immediate decision. Beginning in the 1820s, Finney's preaching was based on the theological conviction that individuals had both the capacity and the responsibility to experience conversion, or to "make themselves a new heart," as he phrased it in one of his sermons. Finney believed that the evangelist's responsibility was to institute those devices or measures that would most effectively yield results, that is, conversions. Religious "excitements"—that is, emotions of hope, fear, sympathy, and so on—were a legitimate and even a necessary means whereby people were moved to decisions of faith. Finney devised a system of extended revival services over a period of days, usually scheduled during the middle of the week, as a way of reaching listeners' emotions and provoking their reactions. He instituted an "anxious bench" where prospective converts could be further prodded into responding from the front row. His sermons used blunt and direct language, and he called individuals by name when he preached. He believed that listeners should be made to *feel* their guilt. His sermonic technique included repetitions of words and the idioms of everyday speech. Thus Finney adapted, for a northern and a somewhat more urban audience, the techniques that had been developed for **camp meeting** preaching in the rural **South.** With their verbal images, dramatic pauses, rhythmic phrasing, and expressions of intense feeling, camp meeting sermons were devised with revival in mind.

Another feature of revival preaching in eighteenth- and nineteenth-century America was the presence of **women** exhorters and preachers. Each new wave of revival in American history—the Great Awakening, the **Second Great Awakening,** the **Revival of 1857–1858,** the **Holiness movement, Pentecostalism,** and the **Charismatic Renewal**—has brought in its wake a shift in attitudes toward women's public role in exhorting and speaking. Up to recently, women's public ministry during the 1700s and earlier 1800s was most often associated with **Quakers, Shakers,** and other religious groups that were outside the mainstream of American Protestantism. Catherine Brekus, in *Strangers and Pilgrims: Female Preaching in America, 1740–1845* (1998), demonstrated that American women often functioned as revival preachers in the era of the Great Awakening and Second Great Awakening, and offered a thoroughly orthodox message of sin, repentance, and faith in Jesus Christ. Though these women preached at camp meetings, counseled converts, and even presided at funerals, they generally did not seek to administer the sacraments or argue in favor of their own ordination to pastoral ministry. By the early 1800s, Protestant denominations that resisted having women as preachers or pastors in their local churches were often willing to authorize women as evangelists and church missionaries. **Phoebe Palmer,** for example, was not ordained and was not deemed to be acceptable as a preaching minister by the **Methodists.** Yet she preached at more camp meetings than nearly any ordained Methodist minister of the 1800s. **Hannah Whitall Smith** was among the best-known speakers and writers in the interdenominational Holiness movement, while the black Holiness preacher **Amanda Berry Smith**—an associate of Hannah Smith's—was able to circumvent the restriction against women preachers in the **African Methodist Episcopal Church** (AMEC) by leaving the United States to preach in England, India, and West Africa.

Another shift that occurred in revival preaching—paralleling the stress on human agency and

The energetic and even combative style of the revival preacher is apparent in this photograph of a Pentecostal preacher in Cambria, Illinois. (Photographer Arthur Rothstein, January 1939.) Courtesy of the Library of Congress.

human emotion—was an affirmation of the laity's role in assessing or discerning effectiveness in preaching. Among American revivalists—from **Theodore J. Frelinghuysen** in the 1720s to Jonathan Edwards and George Whitefield in the 1740s and Lyman Beecher in the earlier 1800s—preaching was considered as a ministry of the ordained to be evaluated by the ordained. Yet Finney was a self-taught lawyer who became a self-taught scholar of the Bible. Though he did not become a traveling revivalist until after the **Presbyterians** ordained him in 1824, he based his claim to authority not on ecclesiastical credentials but rather his successful techniques. In addition to the declining importance of ecclesiastical certification, there was a loss of emphasis on the sacramental and liturgical traditions of the church. Among Finney's leading critics was **John Williamson Nevin,** who derided the techniques of the anxious bench and bewailed the decline of the institutional church with its historic practices, creeds, and sacraments. Finney saw his work as constructive, and yet critics such as Nevin judged that Finney was destroying the very church he professed to be reviving.

Education for ministry, too, had been an expected credential in many circles. But on the frontier and in the camp meeting circles, blunt and direct speech was prized far more highly than literacy.

The standards were set by people like **Peter Cartwright,** who said that someone who felt called by God to preach should not look for a college or a Bible institute but instead should look for a good horse, begin traveling, and simply start preaching. Yet perhaps the preeminent sermonic form among non-seminary-trained preachers was and is the **African American** folk or "chanted" sermon, also known as "old-time country preaching." Though not based on formal education, the black folk sermon is a complex verbal art, governed by unwritten rules, and supported by black congregations that encourage the preacher's efforts. While the Bible provides the basic source of language, imagery, and plotline, the sermon's form arises from the preacher's improvisational skills, as described by Albert Raboteau: "The preacher begins calmly, speaking in conversational, if oratorical and occasionally grandiloquent prose; he then gradually begins to speak more rapidly, excitedly, and to chant his words in time to a regular beat; finally he reaches an emotional peak in which chanted speech becomes tonal and merges with the singing, clapping, and shouting of the congregation.... When necessary, he lengthens vowels or rushes together words in order to make a line match the meter.... The preacher's voice changes: the timbre becomes harsh, almost hoarse. His vocal cords are constricted; his breathing is labored. All the while he moves, gestures, dances, speaking with his body as well as voice" (143–44). Some black sermons are virtuoso performances in which scripture becomes *script*—a story reenacted and reexperienced during the course of the worship. This style of preaching is alive and well in today's black congregations, and the sermons of the contemporary Pentecostal preacher **T. D. Jakes** might be taken as illustrative.

These four trends, then, became integral to the relationship between preaching and revivalism—a theological shift toward the role of human agency and responsibility in conversion, a focus upon emotional response to the proclamation of the Word, a drift away from ecclesiastical credentialing and toward lay affirmation as a way to discern effectiveness in preaching, and a decline in the place of education in preparation for the preaching ministry.

Woman testifying from the pulpit at Langley Avenue All Nations Pentecostal Church in Chicago, Illinois. (Photographer Russell Lee, April 1941) Courtesy of the Library of Congress.

If there is a later American figure who best illustrates these trends, it was **Dwight L. Moody.** A shoe salesman who built upon Finney's measures, Moody was extremely successful as a revival preacher in major urban areas of the North. He added a music leader, Ira Sankey, to his revival techniques in preaching. He also conscripted American business and financial leaders for their support as he reached out to a largely middle-class audience. Moody's preaching did not involve many theological niceties, and he used to say that his gospel consisted of three Rs: ruin by sin, redemption by Christ, and regeneration by the Holy Spirit. Moody sought to touch his hearers' hearts with affecting stories that touched on such themes as wayward sons and the prayerful mothers who awaited their return. He also added to the tradition of revival preaching an American preoccupation with success, and so combined sentimentality with pragmatism.

In the twentieth century, Moody's style and legacy endured in the revival preaching of **Billy Sunday** and **Billy Graham.** There was an American patriotism in both figures that seemed inseparable from their preaching. Nonetheless, Sunday's combative, flamboyant pulpit style contrasted sharply with Graham's thoughtful, conciliatory approach. At the height of Prohibitionism, Sunday railed against everyone who drank alcohol as a "dirty low-down, whisky-soaked, beer-guzzling, bull-necked, foul-mouthed hypocrite" (Ahlstrom, 748). Such an outburst would be almost unthinkable for Graham, who in 60 years of public speaking has found good things to say about almost everyone he encounters. Yet, aside from stylistics, the gospel that Billy Sunday and Billy Graham preached did not differ significantly in its essential content from that proclaimed by Charles G. Finney and Dwight Moody in the nineteenth century. Their preaching sought to elicit a sense of guilt and a perceived need for repentance. It focused on individual transformation, and not on ecclesiastical rites or creeds or traditions. It emphasized the importance of an individual relationship with Jesus, initiated by a specific decision, at one particular time, to repent of sin and put one's trust in Christ.

During the twentieth century, Pentecostal and Charismatic preaching has generally maintained the core doctrinal teachings that are characteristic of evangelical preaching—sin, repentance, forgiveness, and faith in Christ. Yet most "Spirit-filled" preachers are less concerned with a formal analysis and application of the biblical text than with the performance and enactment of the message. White Pentecostal preachers are often closer in their sermonic style to black folk preachers than to white non-Pentecostal ministers. Moreover, Pentecostalism and the Charismatic Renewal have expanded the revival message so that it includes not only salvation for the soul, but health for the body, deliverance from addictions, restoration of broken relationships, and prosperity for all. The so-called **foursquare** gospel of **Aimee Semple McPherson**—adapted from the teaching of **A. B. Simpson** and others—presented Christ as Savior, Sanctifier or Baptizer (in the Holy Spirit), Healer, and Coming Lord. This "full gospel" message adds new emphases to the evangelical message of sin and salvation, and it represents the most recent phase in the development of American revival preaching.

Further Reading: Ahlstrom, Sydney. *A Religious History of the American People.* New Haven, CT: Yale University Press, 1972; Brekus, Catherine A. *Strangers and Pilgrims: Female Preaching in America, 1740–1845.* Chapel Hill: University of North Carolina Press, 1998; Coleman, Simon. "Words: From Narrative to Embodiment." In *The*

Globalisation of Charismatic Christianity: Spreading the Gospel of Prosperity, 117–42. Cambridge: Cambridge University Press, 2000; Dorsett, Lyle W. *Billy Sunday and the Redemption of Urban America.* Grand Rapids, MI: Eerdmans, 1991; Edwards, O. C. *A History of Preaching.* Nashville: Abingdon Press, 2004; George, Timothy, ed. *Mr. Moody and the Evangelical Tradition.* New York: T&T Clark International, 2004; Henry, Stuart C. "Revivalism." In Charles H. Lippy and Peter W. Williams, eds., *Encyclopedia of the American Religious Experience,* 2:799–812. New York: Charles Scribner's Sons, 1988; McLoughlin, William J. *Revivals, Awakenings, and Reform: An Essay on Religion and Social Change in America, 1607–1977.* Chicago: University of Chicago Press, 1978; Pope-Levison, Priscilla. *Turn the Pulpit Loose: Two Centuries of American Women Evangelists.* New York: Palgrave Macmillan, 2004; Raboteau, Albert J. "The Chanted Sermon." In *A Fire in the Bones: Reflections on African-American Religious History,* 141–51. Boston: Beacon Press, 1995.

William B. Lawrence

PREMILLENNIALISM

see Eschatology and Revivals; Jehovah's Witnesses; Miller, William; Seventh-day Adventists; White, Ellen Gould (Harmon)

PRESBYTERIANS AND PRESBYTERIAN CHURCHES

see Calvinistic, Presbyterian, and Reformed Revivals since 1730

PRIMITIVE (ANTIMISSION) BAPTISTS

The terms *Primitive Baptists* and *Antimission Baptists* refer to a collection of **Baptist** groups that reacted against the missionary structures of the Baptist Triennial Convention, which had organized in 1814. Concerned about the centralization of power and influence represented by missionary agencies, these frontier Baptists opposed the fundraising tours of Luther Rice and began a pamphlet war against the convention. At the heart of their opposition was a **primitivistic** reading of the Bible that did not provide for convention structures or missionary agencies. The only model for revival and evangelism they endorsed was church planting as sponsored by a local congregation.

John Taylor, one of the key leaders of this movement, penned his *Thoughts on Missions* (1820), in which he criticized the fund-raising efforts of Rice and other convention leaders as an attempt to coerce finances from frontier Christians for projects they could neither observe nor supervise. Taylor later wrote his *History of Ten Baptist Churches* (1823), which served as a positive example of how church planting, evangelism, **foreign missions,** and revival were to be conducted. Prevalent throughout Taylor's and other leaders' writings was a populist and localist revolt against centralized institutional structures. These men were not against evangelism and mission, but they opposed centralized control of evangelism and mission.

Eventually the Antimission movement transformed itself into a more rigidly anti-evangelism movement. Sometimes called Old School, these Primitive Baptists coalesced first in 1827 in the North Carolina Kehukee Association. Eventually, these Baptists separated themselves into their own loose organizations in order to maintain the purity of their **Calvinistic** doctrines and primitivistic understanding of the Bible. The Primitive Baptists continue to the present, generally meeting for worship once or twice a month in unadvertised meetings. Their ministers do not believe that they are called to tell people that it is their duty to believe the gospel message. Rather, extending the logic of divine predestination, they hold that God's elect will come to faith without any human prodding or manipulation. Furthermore, human preparation is unnecessary for ministerial labors. Their ministers do not receive seminary education and are typically bivocational. Finally, their associations continue to be generally informal, conducted by visitation of messengers and church correspondence. By sticking closely to their primitivist reading of the New Testament, Primitive Baptists consistently reject the organized revivalistic and evangelistic efforts of American Protestantism.

Further Reading: Crowley, John G. *Primitive Baptists of the Wiregrass South: 1815 to the Present.* Gainesville:

University Press of Florida, 1998; Mathis, James R. *The Making of the Primitive Baptists: A Cultural and Intellectual History of the Antimission Movement, 1800–1840.* New York: Routledge, 2004; Wyatt-Brown, Bertram. "The Antimission Movement in the Jacksonian South: A Study in Regional Folk Culture." *Journal of Southern History* 36 (1970): 501–29.

Sean Lucas

PRIMITIVE METHODISTS

Founded in England by Hugh Bourne (1772–1852) and William Clowes (1780–1851), the Primitive **Methodist** Church began when Bourne and Clowes decided that Wesleyan Methodism had abandoned the early practices—such as field **preaching** and contact with the poor—that had enabled it to flourish under the Wesleys. Bourne, a millwright, was converted by reading Methodist literature, joined a society, and became a local preacher. Using his own funds, he constructed a Methodist chapel at Harriseahead and became active in seeking to convert others. When business took him into the colliery district he was stirred to action by the conditions he saw there and began a revival that featured preaching in the open, fervent **prayer,** and **hymn** singing—a significant departure from Methodist practice at the time. Bourne became skilled as a revival preacher and was convinced a return to Methodist practice in the age of the Wesleys could renew the church. William Clowes was converted in a revival in 1805, joined a Methodist society, and soon began to preach in the countryside. Clowes, a potter by trade, was related on his mother's side to the famous Wedgewood family. In 1808, he was admitted into the Wesleyan conference as a local preacher. A more gifted speaker than Bourne, Clowes soon attracted a following of persons who came to be known as Clowesites.

About the same time Clowes joined the conference, the eccentric American evangelist **Lorenzo Dow** (1777–1834) was preaching in England. Dow had spoken often of the amazing outpouring of the Holy Spirit in **camp meetings** on the American frontier. Bourne had been reading about them and was interested in what Dow reported. As a result of the encounter, Bourne organized the first camp meeting ever held in England. It was an all-day affair held on Mow Cop, an outcrop above the plains of Cheshire and Staffordshire, on May 31, 1807. Both Dow and Clowes preached to a large crowd. The event was in violation of strict prohibitions passed the same year in the Wesleyan Conference that judged camp meetings to be improper. Heartened by the response, other revivals were conducted during the summer and fall in which Clowes and Bourne were also involved. A year later Bourne was dropped from membership in his society for his tendencies to set up "other than the ordinary worship" of the church, and in 1810 Clowes, who was preaching in a Methodist circuit, was left off the preaching plan by his superintendent and eventually lost his class ticket (i.e., a ticket for inclusion in the Methodist society) because of his participation in camp meetings and lay evangelization.

In 1811 Bourne's followers, known as Camp Meeting Methodists, united with the Clowesites and early in the following year took the name the Society of the Primitive Methodists. While the Wesleyans were accepting and promoting a higher degree of clerical control and formal organization, the Primitive Methodists moved in the opposite direction. They used no titles for either their preachers or the founders. Preachers were paid only a pittance, traveled on foot, and preached out of doors. Camp meetings provided the power of the movement. Sometimes designated "Ranters," Primitive Methodists were influenced by and were similar in their practice to **Quakers.** Most of the people who heard them were poor or ordinary working-class persons living in villages or small towns. From the beginning, Primitive Methodists allowed **women** to preach. The first of these, Sarah Kirkland, was recruited by Bourne and began serving as a paid evangelist in 1813. Missionary outreach was their highest priority, and, as a result, they grew rapidly. Circuits were organized in the midlands and north of England and in Scotland. Their first conference was held in 1820. Primitive Methodist preachers were often persecuted for their efforts, and sometimes detained or arrested. A few were actually imprisoned by county magistrates. But

they were not deterred in their mission, and by midcentury, 10 home districts were established, each of which had the power to station ministers, and the number of members had grown to more than 100,000, making the Primitive Methodists the second-largest Methodist body in England.

As the movement grew, it also began to expand overseas. The first missionaries sailed for New York and Canada in 1829. Bourne himself visited the United States in 1844. By 1900 Primitive Methodists in the United States had 100 congregations with about 7,000 members, mostly in Pennsylvania. During the 1840s, they also began work in Australasia. In 1902 they changed their name to the Primitive Methodist Church, and in 1932 they reunited with the Wesleyan Methodists to form the Methodist Church.

Further Reading: Kendall, H. B. *The Origin and History of the Primitive Methodist Church.* 2 vols. London: Edwin Dalton, 1906; Milburn, Geoffrey. *Primitive Methodism.* Peterborough, UK: Epworth Press, 2002; Werner, Julia Stewart. *The Primitive Methodist Connexion: Its Background and Early History.* Madison: University of Wisconsin Press, 1984.

James E. Kirby

PRIMITIVISM

Since the groundbreaking works of Borman, Hatch, and Hughes and Allen, scholars have pursued the theme of primitivism in American religious history. Groups as diverse as the Puritans, **restorationists, Mormons,** and **Pentecostals** all have been characterized as primitivist. Despite a scholarly interest in primitivism, no definitive history exploring the relationship between revivalism and primitivism exists. Stretching from the **Great Awakening** and **Second Great Awakening** through the **Holiness movement** and into modern Pentecostalism, a desire to restore the practices of the New Testament church was a powerful force within revivalism.

The primitivist impulse was driven by a desire to repeat or live in a pristine past where one could escape the chaos, error, and imperfection of profane history. Americans believed that in the New World they could leave behind the corruptions of the Old World and re-create a perfect Christianity modeled on the New Testament church. As various religious groups competed for adherents, different versions of restorationist Christianity emerged, each one claiming that it alone had faithfully replicated the perfect Christianity found in primitive times. Each group viewed all the others groups as corrupt, based on man-made traditions, and therefore false. The earliest American restorationists, the Puritans, constructed a rational version of restorationism that restrained emotion and the imagination. Later rational versions include the Stone-Campbell movement, which provided an anti-revivalist alternative on the frontier. In sharp contrast, revivalists offered a sacred drama filled with emotion, spirituality, piety, and divine power.

Many if not all revivalists believed that a true revival was a dramatic reenactment of the actions of the Holy Spirit found in the book of Acts in Christian scripture. True revival was a literal repeating of first times usually labeled *Pentecostal* or *apostolic*. For example, James Finley, a nineteenth-century **Methodist** circuit rider, described a Methodist revival as a "revival of Pentecostal times" where the Holy Spirit descended on participants and they "felt awful shocks of divine power" (Finley, 266). Samuel Rogers, a Stone-Campbell **preacher,** believed that revivalists were "the successors of the apostles" and would eventually "have all their functions and powers" (Rogers, 22–23). **Women** exhorters and preachers in the First and Second Great Awakenings believed that they were restoring the New Testament practice of women preachers. Nancy Towle argued that women as well as **men** were moved by the Holy Spirit to speak, "which amounts to none other, more or less, than the preaching of the gospel" (Casey, 9). After the **Civil War,** the Holiness movement embraced revivalism and used similar Pentecostal primitivist language as they sought the lost practices of spirituality and piety in holy living, perfectionism, and divine **healing.** At the turn of the century, with the emergence of the Pentecostal movement, they believed they were restoring the lost practice of **speaking in tongues** found in the primitive church. Later revival

movements during the twentieth century, such as the **Latter Rain movement** and the so-called Third Wave movement of neo-**Charismatics,** have also invoked the language of primitivism in describing themselves and their movements.

Further Reading: Blumhofer, Edith L. *Restoring the Faith: The Assemblies of God, Pentecostalism, and American Culture.* Urbana, IL: University of Chicago Press, 1993; Bormann, Ernest G. *The Force of Fantasy: Restoring the American Dream.* Carbondale: Southern Illinois Press, 1985; Casey, Michael. "The First Female Public Speaker in America (1630–1840): Searching for Egalitarian Christian Primitivism." *Journal of Communication and Religion* 23 (March 2000): 1–28; Dieter, Melvin E. *The Holiness Revival of the Nineteenth Century.* 2nd ed. Lanham, MD: Scarecrow Press, 1996; Finley, James B. *Autobiography.* Cincinnati: R. P. Thompson, 1854; Hatch, Nathan. *The Democratization of Christianity.* New Haven, CT: Yale University Press, 1988; Hughes, Richard T., and C. Leonard Allen. *Illusions of Innocence: Protestant Primitivism in America, 1630–1875.* Chicago: University of Chicago Press, 1988; Rogers, John I., ed. *Autobiography of Elder Samuel Rogers.* 4th ed. Cincinnati: Standard, 1909.

Michael W. Casey

PROMISE KEEPERS

Promise Keepers is a Christian **men's** parachurch organization begun in March 1990 for the purpose of teaching the basic principles of Christian discipleship. The ministry explains its name by saying that "God kept all the promises that he made to mankind and we rely upon God as the original Promise Keeper to keep our promises." Men are urged to express their commitment to Christ through keeping seven promises that stand at the core of the ministry. Bill McCartney, then the football coach for the University of Colorado, is the founder of Promise Keepers. McCartney had envisioned, for some time, a large group of **praying** and worshipping men gathered in the spirit of revival and taking a public stand for their marriages, families, churches, and communities. After several months of prayer, Bill with his friend Dave Wardell enlisted several others to form a men's accountability group. This group spent time **fasting** and praying for revival in the spring of 1990, and their number increased to more than 70 men by July, becoming the core of the nascent movement. A board of directors formally organized Promise Keepers in December 1990.

The organization held its first major men's conference at Folsom Field on the campus of the University of Colorado in July 1991. This event drew 4,200 to answer the question "Where Are the Men?" Each man was asked to bring 12 other men to a second event in July 1992, where 22,000 came seeking the renewal of their lives and families. The initial dream of 50,000 men at Folsom Field was realized in July 1993 as men sang, prayed, and exhorted one another to be good husbands and radically faithful Christians. Since that summer Promise Keepers has reached over 5 million men through similar events, through more than 150 stadium events and conferences. In addition, Promise Keepers has produced **radio and television** broadcasts, **Internet** ministries, and a considerable collection of CDs, printed materials, and related resources. Its vision statement is expressed in the words "Men Transformed Worldwide." This is carried out according to its original purpose by "igniting and uniting men to be passionate followers of Christ." There is no membership in Promise Keepers. Men are simply urged to participate in its ministries by individually living out their promises to follow Christ.

Among the most significant events Promise Keepers has conducted in its history were the Fan the Flame clergy conference in Atlanta in 1996 and the Stand in the Gap rally held on the National Mall in Washington, DC, in October 1997, attended by an estimated 1 million men. Both events highlighted repentance, prayer, and revival. Following the gathering on the Washington Mall, Promise Keepers was forced to lay off its entire staff because of a shortage of funding. Soon thereafter new funding allowed the ministry to rebuild a smaller staff and ministry that have been able to operate within their budget. Bill McCartney, who produced four books while leading Promise Keepers, resigned as president in 2003, and Dr. Thomas S. Fortson Jr. was named as the new president. It is

headquartered in Denver, Colorado. Though the large stadium events, attracting in excess of 50,000 men, are not part of the present ministry of Promise Keepers, it still conducts more than 15 arena events annually, drawing 10,000 to 20,000 men in most venues. Promise Keepers has worked to expand its reach outside of the United States, and it is committed both to revival and to interracial reconciliation with a staff that represents a widely divergent ethnicity. Speakers and musicians at Promise Keepers events represent this diversity.

Promise Keepers has not gone without criticism. Secular critics have linked it to far-right religious and political movements, though the organization has steadfastly defended itself against these charges. Opponents also raise the issue of **women's** subordination to men—a common motif in the teaching at Promise Keepers events. In response, Promise Keepers has argued that their purpose was never to oppose feminism except when it challenged Christian ethics on issues such as abortion. Perhaps the harshest criticism of the movement has come from within conservative Christian circles. These critics are repelled by the interdenominational and **Charismatic** nature of the meetings. When confronted by critics, Promise Keepers has shown a willingness to listen and to change.

Further Reading: Claussen, Dale. *The Promise Keepers: Essays on Masculinity and Christianity*. Jefferson, NC: McFarland, 2000; Promise Keepers Web site. http://www.promisekeepers.org/.

John Armstrong

PROPHECY, VISIONS, AND DREAMS

Most Protestants, since the time of the sixteenth-century Reformation, have understood *prophecy* in the postbiblical period as referring to biblical **preaching**, rather than a **charismatic gift** that goes beyond the written text of sacred scripture. Yet in the **Holiness movement** of the nineteenth century, prophetic inspiration was understood more broadly to involve spontaneous inspired speech and prophetic discernment. This discernment involved extraordinary communication from God through prophetic gifts such as visions and dreams. In such contexts, prophecy was used without tight institutional controls, leading to strong lay participation, including **women** as well as **men.** Key revivalists, such as **Charles Finney,** encouraged female participation in speaking forth the Word of God and guiding the church in discerning God's will in the latter days before Christ returns. Certain themes such as spiritual renewal, **eschatological** urgency, and **sanctification** or holiness tended to call into question institutional restrictions and traditions and to create greater inclusiveness in leadership and lay ministry.

Prophetic gifts of inspired speech, visions, and dreams implied a direct communication from God that might be accessible to ordinary Christians. As such, prophetic gifts seemed to diminish the separation between clergy and laity and to accent the possibility of charismatic empowerment among all members of the laity. Such was the case among the **Quakers,** who with their stress on God-inspired speech were among the first Christian groups to sanction women as public speakers and teachers. Another instance is **Pentecostalism.** Scholars have argued that the Pentecostal emphasis on charismatic gifts such as prophetic speech and discernment helped to fulfill the Protestant belief in the universal "priesthood of all believers" by inspiring broad lay participation in church ministry. Historically, mainline Protestant churches had tended to interpret the priesthood of all believers in the limited context of household **prayers** and devotions.

The connection between prophecy and direct communication from God through visions and dreams was forged for Pentecostals through texts such as Joel 2:28 and its fulfillment on the day of Pentecost in Acts 2:17. These texts state that in the last days the Spirit will be poured out so that sons and daughters "will prophecy," the young will "see visions," and the old will "dream dreams." This text inspired Pentecostal preacher **Aimee Semple McPherson** to view her ministry a continuation of the first-century Pentecost. She was convinced that she was ordained to preach under the anointing of the Spirit because the latter-day rain of the Spirit had overthrown the earlier restriction of the ministry to males. Recent studies suggest, however, that the institutionalization of Pentecostalism in its early decades brought restrictions of ministerial roles to males and limitations in female leadership.

Inspired speech, such as prophecy and **speaking in tongues,** and gifts of prophetic discernment, like visions and dreams, help the church to rediscover the neglected truth that one can have immediate experiences of the divine Spirit. Certain **Charismatic** theologians have embraced this neglected accent but have also warned that powerful immediate experiences of the Spirit in prophecy, visions, and dreams need to be practiced in the church within the contexts of biblical teaching, the sacraments, and pastoral guidance. Many regard this call to prophetic accountability as sound advice, especially in the light of certain tendencies in the direction of extreme or independent uses of prophetic gifts. Renewal movements termed Charismatic (among mainline Protestant and **Roman Catholic** churches) and Third Wave (among American Evangelicals open to extraordinary spiritual gifts), have sometimes made claims to inspired prophetic utterance. Written prophecies allegedly composed under direct inspiration by God have been circulated and treated as binding or authoritative revelation. This trend has drawn criticism. Opponents charge that such contemporary prophecies are not universally binding, like the biblical text, but are contextual and subordinate to scriptural teaching.

The establishment of schools for the training of prophets, who travel among Charismatic churches granting the "Word of the Lord" for the moment, is an attempt to restore to the church the office of the prophet allegedly implied in certain New Testament texts (e.g., Ephesians 2:20). This teaching is characteristic of the **Apostolic (or New Apostolic) movement.** Critics argue that such an office was not meant to endure, if indeed it ever existed in the form asserted by its contemporary proponents. It seems likely that new revelations and inspired utterances will remain a part of revival movements in the churches, while church leaders will continue to be concerned that prophetic messages are consistent with biblical teaching.

Further Reading: Gelpi, Donald. *Pentecostalism: A Theological Viewpoint.* New York: Paulist Press, 1971; Hardesty, Nancy. *Your Daughters Shall Prophesy.* New York: Carlson, 1991; Kelsey, Morton. *Tongue Speaking: An Experiment in Spiritual Experience.* New York: Doubleday, 1968; Lim, David. *Spiritual Gifts: A Fresh Look.* Springfield, MO: Gospel, 1998; Poloma, Margaret. *The Assemblies of God at the Crossroads: Charisma and Institutional Dilemmas.* Knoxville: University of Tennessee Press, 1989; Robeck, Cecil M., Jr. "Prophecy, Gift Of." In Stanley Burgess, ed., *The New International Dictionary of Pentecostal Charismatic Movements,* 999–1012. Grand Rapids, MI: Zondervan, 2002; Robeck, Cecil M., Jr. "Written Prophecies: A Question of Authority." *Pneuma* 2 (1980): 26–45; Wagner, Peter. *Apostles and Prophets: The Foundation of the Church.* Ventura, CA: Regal Books, 2000.

Frank Macchia

PROSPERITY THEOLOGY

Prosperity theology, or the prosperity gospel, is a Christian teaching that is strongest in certain **Pentecostal, Charismatic,** or so-called Third Wave churches in North America and abroad. It promises personal success, wealth, and material blessing to those who appropriately exercise faith, practice "positive confession" by speaking aloud the blessing they desire and expect to receive from God, and give generously to others out of their wealth as a sign of their confidence that God will give back to them even more than they have given out. The doctrine became prominent in the 1970s within the Charismatic Revival and Renewal and is variously termed the *word of faith, faith formula, health and wealth,* or *positive confession* teaching. Proponents assert that the prosperity message regarding faith and divine blessing is taught in the Bible in such passages as "The Lord … delights in the prosperity of his servant" (Psalms 35:27); "I pray that in all respects you may prosper and be in good health, just as your soul prospers (2 John 2); and "Let it be done to you as you have believed" (Matthew 8:13, New American Standard Version). Critics, by contrast, assert that the prosperity gospel contradicts mainstream Christian theology on the role of scripture, the nature of faith, the process of salvation, and the appropriate use of one's material goods. A popular neo-Charismatic version of the prosperity gospel may be traced back to Esseck William (E. W.) Kenyon (1867–1948), who had been exposed to the New Thought and metaphysical movements of his day. As a student at Emerson College of Oratory in Boston, Kenyon came to believe that prosperity was included in the atonement of Christ, was a divine right, and could be appropriated or created at will through positive confession. Though not a Pentecostal himself, he **preached** a message blending evangelicalism and metaphysical teachings that gained popularity primarily among Pentecostals.

As Kenyon is acknowledged as the father of the modern prosperity gospel movement, his most famous disciple, **Kenneth Hagin Sr.,** is credited with the popularization of the teaching in the second half of the twentieth century. Through extensive **radio** broadcasting, publishing, and education of ministers through his Rhema Bible Institute in Tulsa, Oklahoma, founded in the 1970s, a generation of pastors, evangelists, and teachers holding to a strong belief in the prosperity gospel has spread the teaching within and beyond the Charismatic movement. The result has been a vast promulgation of independent Charismatic churches pastored mostly by Hagin's disciples preaching prosperity theology as a key doctrine of the Word of Faith movement. In addition to Hagin, advocates of the prosperity gospel include a second tier of popular Charismatic television evangelists, pastors, and teachers. These preachers express their gratitude and allegiance to Hagin and Kenyon for pioneering the Word of Faith and prosperity gospel movement. The list includes **Kenneth Copeland,** Jerry Savelle, Charles Capps, Robert Tilton, Creflo Dollar, and Fredrick K. C. Price. Some others who hold a generally more conventional theology, but support certain aspects of the prosperity gospel, include Norman Vincent Peale (author of the widely read work *The Power of Positive Thinking*), the Christian broadcasting entrepreneurs Paul Crouch and **Jim Bakker,** Robert Schuller of the Crystal Cathedral in Southern California (who speaks of "possibility thinking"), and the Houston **megachurch** pastor

Joel Osteen, whose book *Your Best Life Now* (2004) was a number-one *New York Times* best seller in 2005.

Oral Roberts, healing evangelist and contemporary of Kenneth Hagin, became a separate and comparable influence in defining and promoting the prosperity gospel during the same time period through his highly popular teaching known as "seed faith." With a heritage grounded more in the **Methodist** and classical Pentecostal traditions of divine **healing,** Roberts contributed to the prosperity gospel by preaching his interpretation of Christ's parable of the sower (Matthew 13:1–23). He taught that individuals who give materially in support of gospel ministry should expect to receive a benefit in like kind. One application of the seed faith message appears in what is known as the "hundredfold return." This teaching asserts that according to the parable of the sower, certain material gifts may produce a hundredfold material return to the giver. The benefit of this teaching for fund-raising efforts is obvious and has made it controversial among its critics.

The prosperity gospel exists in two forms, one egocentric and the other cosmic. The egocentric version promises that the person who gives away resources will prosper. Individual prosperity will be the outcome of individual generosity. The cosmic version is more philosophical and presents universal principles of prosperity that yield a corporate or collective good for persons other than those who are giving their resources. These two teachings are sometimes intermingled. Prosperity teaching involves a cluster of related ideas that appear in various combinations, though few if any teachers include all of these ideas. Among them are the following: God wants his children to prosper; prosperity, like divine healing, is included within Christ's atonement for sin; a special faith based on "revelation knowledge" is needed to appropriate God's miraculous provision; positive confession is a key to the procurement of material abundance; seed faith giving is a practical strategy for producing material provision; the promises to Israel regarding material blessing apply to the church as well; Jesus and the apostles were not poor, as tradition holds, but were wealthy; and poverty is a manifestation of satanic and demonic powers, and is to be overcome by faith.

Further Reading: Farris, Charles, Jr. *From the Pinnacle of the Temple.* Plainfield, NJ: Logos, 1978; McConnell, Daniel R. *A Different Gospel.* Peabody, MA: Hendrickson, 1988.

Daniel Hedges

PSYCHOLOGY OF REVIVALS

see Conversion and Revivals; Ecstasy, Theories of

Q

QUAKERS (SOCIETY OF FRIENDS)

For many outside observers and students of religious history, the phrase *Quaker revival* seems paradoxical. Quakers, almost by definition, are quiet. They are also usually associated with liberal religion, in opposition to the evangelical Protestantism that usually underlay revivalism. This view, however, is flawed. Early Quakerism was characterized by practices that paralleled later revival practices. In the last third of the nineteenth century, moreover, a majority of American Quakers—more properly known as Friends—experienced a wave of revivalism that transformed their congregations and their way of life.

Quakerism rose in England in the late 1640s and early 1650s, under the leadership of George Fox (1624–1691) and an associated group of **preachers.** Fox, coming of age in the religious and social turmoil of the Puritan Revolution of the 1640s, found all of the churches around him wanting. On the basis of experiences in which he was convinced that God spoke directly to him, he called Christians to experience the Light of Christ within themselves—what later generations of Friends would label the "Inner Light." In Fox's view, this divine Light would show seekers their sinful state and their need of a savior, Jesus Christ. It could do so without any other intermediary, such

as priests or even the sacred scriptures. Associated with early Quakerism were other ideas and practices that were equally radical, such as an insistence on spiritual equality and preaching by **women.**

The very name *Quaker*, originally a nickname given to them by their opponents, is indicative of the emotionalism of early Quaker worship. An early Quaker critic, the Puritan minister Francis Higginson, wrote,

> Many of them, sometimes men, but more frequently women and children, fall into quaking fits....Those who are taken with these fits fall suddenly down, as it were in a swoon, as though they were surprised with an epilepsy or apoplexy, and lie groveling on the earth, and struggling as if it were for life....While the agony of the fit is upon them their lips quiver, their flesh and joints tremble, their bellies swell as though blown up with wind, they foam at the mouth, and sometimes purge as if they had taken physic. In this fit they continue sometimes an hour or two, sometimes longer, before they roar out horribly with a voice greater than the voice of a man....Greater sometimes than any bull can make. (Hugh Barbour and Arthur O. Roberts, eds., *Early Quaker Writings, 1650–1700* [1973], 73).

Higginson may have exaggerated, but many early Friends left similar accounts. The parallels with later revival scenes are striking.

The Friends began to proselytize in North America and the Caribbean in the 1650s. They became less aggressive after 1660, increasingly turning their energies inward to focus on organization and discipline. The major American Quaker center in colonial times was the Delaware Valley, around Philadelphia, which British Friends founded in 1682. After 1700, the Friends entered a period that historians have labeled *quietist.* The emphasis was on absolute subjection to the will of God and the leadings of the Holy Spirit, with a fear of any action not divinely inspired. Friends tightened their internal discipline, and hundreds of Quakers lost their membership for offenses ranging from drunkenness to bearing arms to marrying non-Quakers. Paradoxically, this turn inward coincided with a flowering of humanitarianism, as the Quakers became increasingly active in defending Native Americans and opposing slavery.

Another effect of quietism was suspicion of the practices of non-Quakers. The Friends were hostile toward ordained clergy, whom they dismissed as "hireling priests." They looked askance at the revivalism of **George Whitefield** and his heirs, regarding the excitement and manifestations of the **Great Awakening** and **Second Great Awakening** as delusional. Friends who were attracted to early revivals almost always left Quakerism for other denominations. At the same time, many were willing to work with other Christians in reform causes, such as education and **abolitionism.**

By the 1820s, a deep fissure had appeared within Quakerism. Friends in the British Isles, and a majority in North America, had increasingly come to express Quaker theology in terms of scriptural authority and the divinity of Christ in a way that paralleled non-Quaker evangelicalism. Central to this movement was the English Quaker minister Joseph John Gurney (1788–1847). These Friends became known as Orthodox. Opposed to them were Quakers, especially strong in New York, New Jersey, Pennsylvania, and Maryland, who saw the growing use of language and ideas taken from non-Quaker evangelicals as a mark of spiritual decline. They found their leader in the Long Island Quaker Elias Hicks (1748–1830) and became known as

Lithograph of William Penn's Old Meetinghouse at Chester, Pennsylvania. Penn landed in present-day Pennsylvania in 1682, renamed an existing settlement after the English town of Chester, and made it the first capital of the new colony. This building was used for Quaker services as early as 1675. (1815.) Courtesy of the Library of Congress.

Hicksites. The two groups formally separated in 1827–1828.

Between 1830 and 1870, most Orthodox Friends (or Gurneyites, as usually called) moved closer to the dominant evangelical culture of the United States. The most conservative Orthodox Quakers, known as Wilburites, separated from the others in the 1840s and 1850s. By the 1860s, many were calling for reform in Quakerism, including a greater openness to education and a relaxation of internal disciplines, such as the strictures against marrying non-Quakers. In the 1870s, the interdenominational **Holiness movement** in the United States had a profound impact on the Gurneyite Friends. Many young Quaker ministers became converts to the doctrine of instantaneous **sanctification.** They used this idea to transform Quaker worship.

Revivals were introduced, as were music and **hymn** singing. Traditional Quaker practices were denounced as "dead works." By the 1890s, the Gurneyite Friends (about 70 percent of all American Quakers) began introducing pastors into many of their congregations, even though the earlier Quaker movement had rejected the distinction between clergy and laity. The British Friends, however, did not follow suit.

Quakerism today spans the spectrum of world Christianity. The descendants of the Hicksite Friends still eschew a formal clergy and are usually liberal in theology. Gurneyite Quakerism, or what is now usually known as pastoral or programmed Quakerism, shows more diversity. Some pastoral Friends, much like mainline Protestants, regard revivalism as unenlightened. Others, especially in Evangelical Friends International, still hold revivals, like those of a century ago. Some employ all of the innovations provided by modern technology. Quakerism is growing fastest in Latin America and in Africa, especially Kenya, where pastoral missionaries established it during the twentieth century. There revival practices are common.

Further Reading: Hamm, Thomas D. *The Quakers in America.* New York: Columbia University Press, 2003; Hamm, Thomas D. *The Transformation of American Quakerism: Orthodox Friends, 1800–1907.* Bloomington: Indiana University Press, 1988.

Thomas D. Hamm

R

RADIO, TELEVISION, AND REVIVALS

The history of religious broadcasting in the United States can be traced back to January 2, 1921, when radio station KDKA provided live coverage of Sunday services at Pittsburgh's Calvary Episcopal Church. Over the next several years, dozens of religious organizations went on the air with their own, self-operated radio stations. By 1925, slightly more than 10 percent of the 600 existing stations were church owned. Virtually from the outset, religious broadcasting was marked by a territorial struggle between two powerful factions. The self-described liberals represented the mainline Protestant, **Roman Catholic,** and Jewish worship groups. Those referring to themselves as conservatives were comprised of Fundamentalists, evangelicals, **Pentecostals,** and **Charismatics**—all closely aligned with religious revivalism.

At first, many conservatives felt that radio, by the very nature of its popularity and universality, was immoral and sacrilegious. This consensus gave way to the realization that radio could reach a larger audience than all previous church revivals and traveling **camp and tent meetings** combined—and equally that the message of revivalism could be spread to those who could not attend live services due to illness or infirmity. Among the earliest radio evangelists were Pastor Paul Rader of the Moody Bible Institute and **Aimee Semple McPherson,** head of the **International Church of the Foursquare Gospel** in California. Both Rader and McPherson established their own very successful broadcast stations. Rader later became the first minister ever to speak over a national radio network hookup, while McPherson, taking full advantage of radio's value as an entertainment medium, staged her big weekly revival meeting in the manner of a spectacular Broadway musical revue. She also managed to incur the wrath of U.S. Secretary of Commerce Herbert Hoover by whimsically changing the dial frequency of her radio station whenever she chose.

As a means of preventing the fledgling broadcast industry from becoming the exclusive province of mavericks like McPherson, a governmental regulatory agency, the Federal Radio Commission (FRC), was set up in 1927. The FRC promptly established standards of technical expertise for local radio stations. Unable to meet the agency's new requirements, scores of conservative religious groups were forced off the air. During this same period, the Federal Council of Churches, an organization composed of 25 mainline Protestant, Catholic, and Jewish denominations, gained a foothold in radio by forging alliances with the two biggest networks, the National Broadcasting Company (NBC) and the

Columbia Broadcasting System (CBS). Honoring the FRC's insistence that they operate in the public interest, both NBC and CBS set aside portions of their broadcast schedules for public service programs, to be presented on a "sustained-time" basis— free of charge to the producers of those programs, with no commercial advertising. Agreeing to limit its members' broadcasts to these sustained-time slots, and promising to deliver strictly nondenominational and noncontroversial messages, the Federal Council of Churches was quickly assimilated into the network radio establishment. In so doing, the Federal Council had also effectively blocked conservative broadcasters from operating in the sustained-time hours. With few other options remaining, conservatives were obliged to offer their radio messages on a "paid-time" basis, purchasing air space on local broadcast stations.

While the NBC network and its affiliates refused to accept any paid-time religious programs, in its formative years CBS allowed conservatives to buy time on its nationwide hookup, thereby providing a forum for Dr. Walter A. Maier, a conservative Lutheran who launched his long-running series *The Lutheran Hour* in 1930. (As of 2005, *The Lutheran Hour* was broadcasting its messages through 821 stations in the United States.) The inflammatory sermons of Father Charles Coughlin prompted CBS to drop all of its paid-time religious shows in 1935, one year after the FRC had been reorganized as the Federal Communications Commission (FCC), imposing even more restrictions upon radio revivalists in the process. Fortunately for Dr. Maier and his colleagues, a new national network, the Mutual Broadcasting System, had no reservations about accepting paid-time programs. Among those benefiting from the formation of Mutual was Dr. **Charles E. Fuller,** head of the California-based Calvary Church, and one of the most outspoken disciples of evangelical broadcaster

The choir of the "Showers of Blessing" radio broadcast, which was produced by the Church of the Nazarene and broadcast over 700 stations between 1945 and 1990 (1940s–1950s). Nazarene Radio Commission Collection, Nazarene Archives.

Paul Rader. Beginning his broadcasting career in 1930, Fuller was the first radio revivalist to invite listeners to offer financial donations via telephone calls during his live broadcasts. In 1937, Fuller joined Mutual with his weekly *Old Fashioned Revival Hour.* By 1943, nearly 25 percent of Mutual's airtime was devoted to paid religious programming, largely as a result of Fuller's vast popularity.

Throughout the 1930s, pressure was brought to bear by the Federal Council of Churches upon both the FCC and the National Association of Broadcasters (NAB) to silence those whom liberal ministers regarded as the more extreme proponents of revivalism among conservative radio personalities. In 1939, the NAB established a policy whereby its member stations were prohibited from airing any form of "controversial" programming. Ostensibly designed to honor the United States' neutrality regarding the political turmoil in Europe, this policy also placed harsh limits upon religious broadcasters in conservative denominations and churches. Taking matters a step further, the FCC decreed that "private-interest" groups could neither recruit members nor solicit financial contributions over the airwaves, though some religious broadcasters were able to circumvent this last ruling by subtly suggesting that their listeners send in "free will" offerings. The FCC's Mayflower Decision of 1941, prompted by the questionable activities of a Boston radio station owned by Mayflower Broadcasting, imposed an all-out ban on "advocating" over the radio—yet another major setback for radio revivalists.

With the United States' entry into World War II, the rules against radio editorializing were relaxed, permitting religious conservatives to resume their evangelizing. Led by Charles E. Fuller, conservatives formed the National Association of Evangelicals in 1942, which gave rise to the National Religious Broadcasters (NRB) in 1944. The NRB's purpose was twofold: to form a united front against efforts by liberal broadcasters and government regulatory agencies to marginalize conservatives, and to maintain a high standard of ethics and quality within the revivalist

community, so that critics of conservative broadcasters would have less cause for complaint. In 1944, Dr. Fuller's home radio network Mutual decided to confine its paid religious broadcasts to 30 minutes per program, to be heard exclusively on Sundays. Reacting to these new limitations, Fuller began offering his *Old Fashioned Revival Hour* on a syndicated basis, whereby local radio stations could purchase recordings of Fuller's sermons and broadcast them at their convenience. Among the other major radio evangelists who followed the syndication route during the 1940s were A. A. Allen, R. W. Schambach, and Gordon Lindsay. While it would seem that an agreeable balance between liberal and conservative broadcasters had finally been established—liberals continuing to predominate on the networks, conservatives flourishing in syndication—it would not be long before the liberals had launched their own syndicated offerings, thus reigniting the battle for air space between the two factions.

A widespread revival movement in 1947, coupled with the postwar emergence of television as a major broadcast medium, created new friction between conservatives and liberals, whose principal organization had been renamed the National Council of Churches (NCC). Arguing that the members of the NRB lacked the financial and creative wherewithal to provide high-quality religious programming, the NCC was able to command the majority of network television's FCC-dictated public-interest time slots. Of the four major TV networks, only the American Broadcasting Company (ABC) was willing to provide airtime to such conservative televangelists as **Billy Graham,** and then only on a paid-time basis.

Although still generally confined to local and syndicated broadcasts, the NRB was able to counter the NCC's charges of substandard program quality with enormous technological advances that often outdistanced its liberal network competition. Oklahoma-based charismatic minister **Oral Roberts** pioneered the use of high-speed film, allowing his exuberant tent revival meetings to be seen on television almost exactly as originally conducted before a live audience. At the same time, Ohio revivalist Rex Humbard poured $3.5 million into building his Cathedral of Tomorrow, the first church specifically designed to accommodate television cameras and microphones.

Radio and television revivalism was given a major boost in 1960, when the FCC determined that the public-service obligations of broadcast stations could be satisfied by both paid- and sustained-time programs. The FCC further decreed that, unlike network news departments, who were obliged to honor the Fairness Doctrine, religious broadcasters were exempted from providing equal airtime to those with opposing viewpoints. In the wake of these regulatory decisions, conservative religious programming prospered as never before on both network and nonnetwork outlets during the next two decades, giving rise to such prominent televangelists as Garner Ted Armstrong, **Jerry Falwell, Jimmy Swaggart,** and **Kathryn Kuhlman.** Throughout this period, dozens of syndicated radio revivalists also enjoyed great success. Among these were C. M. Ward and Dan Betzer, the hosts of the popular *Revivaltime*, and **Kenneth Hagin Sr.,** creator of *The Faith Seminar of the Air.*

Although the FCC's 1960 decision opened new doors for revivalism, religious broadcasters were still prohibited from using their syndicated programs as 30-minute fund-raisers. The FCC did not, however, prohibit religious organizations from setting up radio stations that were listener supported, kept alive by financial contributions; nor were these organizations prevented from establishing viewer-supported television stations in the ultrahigh frequency (UHF) band, between channels 14 and 69. In 1961, charismatic evangelist **Pat Robertson** utilized a small UHF channel in Virginia as the launching pad for his Christian Broadcasting Network (CBN). Two years later, Robertson established *The 700 Club*, a daily inspirational talk show named in honor of the 700 viewers whose donations prevented CBN from going dark in its early years, as the service's flagship program. Along with such similar operations as the Trinity Broadcasting Network (TBN) and the Praise the Lord Network

(PTL), CBN took full advantage of the burgeoning cable television industry in the late 1970s, with satellite technology allowing these services to spread their message to a nationwide and ultimately a worldwide audience.

The decades-long battle between liberals and conservatives in the broadcast industry was ultimately resolved by the gradual demise of mainline religious programming on the major TV networks. The last of the weekly National Council of Churches programs, the CBS production *For Our Times*, was quietly canceled in 1988. Thereafter religious revivalism, as personified by conservative televangelists, reigned supreme on the airwaves. Even such challenges as 1964's Red Lion case, in which the FCC compelled a Pennsylvania radio station to provide free airtime to an author who wished to rebut a political attack leveled against him by the Reverend Billy James Hargis, and 1975's Lansman-Milam case, wherein the FCC was urged to block future sales of noncommercial TV and radio stations to religious organizations, were insufficient ammunition against the remarkable upsurge of conservative religious broadcasting in the 1970s and 1980s.

The year 1987 brought an onslaught of financial and sexual scandals involving such prominent broadcast personalities as PTL founders **Jim and Tammy Faye Bakker** and Pentecostal minister Jimmy Swaggart. Further casting televangelism in an unfavorable light was Oral Roberts's grim assertion that God would "call him back" (i.e., cause his death) unless Roberts's followers helped him raise millions of dollars to save his university and church. Although the evangelical establishment was for the most part able to survive these crises, by the early 1990s the number of religious programs had dropped significantly.

Foremost among the factors contributing to this decline was the FCC's new laissez-faire attitude toward half-hour infomercials, encouraging local broadcast stations to fill their early-morning time slots, traditionally reserved for religious shows, with 30-minute commercial programs. Struggling for survival in an ever-tightening market, many of the revivalists still active in broadcasting endeavored to broaden their viewer base by offering less prose-lytizing and more entertainment. Exemplifying this trend was Pat Robertson's CBN cable service, which, having emerged from a series of corporate takeovers as the ABC Family Channel in 2001, was thereafter devoted almost exclusively to entertainment programs. By the final decade of the twentieth century, such charismatics as **Kenneth Copeland,** Creflo A. Dollar, and Joyce Meyer had all but forsaken straight sermonizing in favor of the more universally popular Bible-study and motivational-lecture formats. Other televangelists, among them **Benny Hinn** and Marilyn Hickey, were using their programs primarily to promote their upcoming revival crusades, replete with flashy highlight segments.

Likewise anxious to appeal to a wider audience, several American religious radio stations had altered their formats, offering a menu of generic contemporary Christian music in lieu of sermons and evangelical talk shows. Similarly, a significant number of religious television channels had become full-time affiliates of the new, all-entertainment PAX network—named for the network's creator, home-shopping entrepreneur Lowell Paxson. As of the early twenty-first century, many of the traditional religious revivalists in the American broadcasting industry were concentrating their activities on low-power radio and television outlets in smaller cities, and on privately owned shortwave radio stations, a tradition established decades earlier by such missionary-radio pioneers as Clarence Jones and Reuben Larson.

Further Reading: Bruce, Steve. *Pray TV: Televangelism in America.* New York: Routledge, 1990; Burgess, Stanley M., and Eduard M. Van Der Maas, eds. *International Dictionary of Pentecostal and Charismatic Movements.* Rev. and expanded ed. Grand Rapids, MI: Zondervan, 2002; Dunning, John. *On the Air: The Encyclopedia of Old-Time Radio.* New York: Oxford University Press, 1998; Hayden, Jeffrey K., and Anson Shupe. *Televangelism: Power and Politics on God's Frontier.* New York: Henry Holt, 1988; Hoover, Stewart M. *Mass Media Religion: The Social Sources of the Electronic Church.* Newbury Park, CA: Sage, 1988.

Hal Erickson

REBIRTH

see Conversion and Revivals

REFORMED CHURCH

see Calvinistic, Presbyterian, and Reformed Revivals since 1730

RENEWAL

see Charismatic Revival and Renewal; Roman Catholic Revivals

RESTORATIONISM AND THE STONE-CAMPBELL MOVEMENT

North American religious groups that seek to recover the power, purity, and unity of the Christian apostolic era or New Testament church are often called restorationist (or **primitivist**). These groups are also linked with religious revivals. Indeed, the restoration of an ancient order and religious revival evolved as parallel quests in eighteenth- and nineteenth-century North America. Many Christians thought that "restoration" and "revival" were identical goals. Revival, they believed, would restore what Thomas Campbell (1763–1854) called "the unity, peace, and purity" of the church, and would speak to spiritually apathetic as well as spiritually zealous persons. Conversely, restoration of a pure gospel and unified church, founded on the Bible alone, shorn of all human affectations and compromises, would revive true religion, free from what **Barton Warren Stone** (1772–1844) called "the demon of partyism."

Yet while restorationist movements are rooted in Continental and American revivals of the **Second Great Awakening,** they cannot simply be seen as an expression of revivalistic religion on the frontier. Restorationists offended **Pietists** and revivalists not only with their Enlightenment worldview and commonsense epistemology but also with the very notion of restoration itself. Restorationists proposed that Christianity could be revived, purified, and united by dismissing all "human creeds," dogmatic platforms, and institutional superstructures, and relying on the New Testament alone. True religion, in the minds of many revivalists, consisted in adherence to human creeds and prescriptions for worship and life that restorationists could not find in scripture, while revival, in the minds of many restorationists, consisted in effusive enthusiasm and subjective emotion rather than a rational understanding of God's plan of salvation and lifelong commitment to it. Nonetheless, restorationism in America emerged in the context of religious revival and revivalism.

James O'Kelly (1735?–1826) had "by the kind illuminations of the invisible Holy Spirit" recognized his need for God and had come to God "with the Bible in my hand," vowing that "during life that sacred book should be my guide." Soon after his midlife conversion, in 1776, O'Kelly encountered **Methodist** preachers who brought with them sermons and pamphlets by John Wesley, whose "writings magnified the Bible and gave it preference and honor; he declared he regarded the authority of no writings but the inspired" (quoted in P. J. Kernodle, *Lives of Christian Ministers* [1909], 27–28). Wesley's commitment to the Bible persuaded O'Kelly to become a traveling evangelist in the Methodist cause, riding circuits in southern Virginia and North Carolina as the American Revolution raged. By the late 1780s O'Kelly's **preaching** had stirred a massive awakening in the Brunswick and Sussex circuits of southern Virginia, as O'Kelly and Philip Cox testified in letters to Wesley. As many as "a hundred in a day have professed to find peace with God," O'Kelly wrote, adding, "You will scarce believe what the Lord is doing, unless you had seen it with your own eyes" (O'Kelly, "Extract of a Letter," *Arminian Magazine* [September

Christian unity was an aspiration within nineteenth-century Restorationism. This symbolic picture shows nine men of different Christian denominations gathered around a Bible, with a lion and lamb in the foreground, and a Native American and African man in the background. (Thomas S. Sinclair, lithographer, 1845.) Courtesy of the Library of Congress.

1788], 488). In publishing the letters from Virginia in Wesley's *Arminian Magazine*, Thomas Coke remarked in 1788 that O'Kelly "has been tried and proved; is much owned by God, and of the most undaunted courage: fearing, neither men nor devils. He has for some time borne the boldest, and most public testimony against Negro-Slavery of any one in America" (Thomas Coke, "Extracts of Several Letters," *Arminian Magazine* [September 1788], 485).

Coke had already ordained O'Kelly a Methodist elder, on Wesley's behalf, during the famous Christmas Conference of 1784 in Baltimore. Yet Coke's appointment of **Francis Asbury** as superintendent of Methodist societies and evangelists in North America aroused O'Kelly's fierce opposition. According to O'Kelly, he and others forced Asbury to convene a General Conference in 1792, but failed to modify the powers of the superintendent. O'Kelly withdrew under protest, imploring the conference to "put away all other books and forms" and accept the New Testament as "the only criterion." O'Kelly's "Republican Methodists" soon claimed the Bible "as our only creed, and a sufficient rule of faith and practice," for a church that would have "the Lord Jesus Christ as the only Head." Rice Haggard (1769–1819), author of *An Address to the Different Religious Societies, on the Sacred Import of the Christian Name* (1804), convinced the former Methodists to take "the name Christian to the exclusion of all party and sectarian names" (Burnett, *Rev. James O'Kelly*, 12, 14–15).

Meanwhile, the "Great Revival" of 1801 at **Cane Ridge** in Bourbon County, Kentucky, brought together a coalition of revived but denominationally alienated **Presbyterian** ministers whose strict adherence to the Bible as the source for faith in a loving God, available to all who would seek salvation, estranged them from their Calvinist colleagues in the Washington Presbytery. Trying to remain Presbyterians, even without creed beyond the Bible, they hastily organized the Springfield Presbytery. Yet the experience of revival amid an interdenominational gathering of Protestants soon convinced them that the Presbytery itself evoked "a party spirit," and they dramatically dissolved it in a landmark document, *The Last Will and Testament of the*

Springfield Presbytery (1804). Of the six men who signed that will, Richard McNemar (1770–1839) and John Dunlavy (d. 1826) soon left Christian restorationism for the **Shaker** movement. McNemar in 1808 remembered the "Kentucky revival" as a preparation for the true gospel that the Shakers had revealed to him—"that kingdom of God in which all things are new." Robert Marshall (1760–1832) and John Thompson (1772–1859) returned to their Presbyterian roots. For them, McNemar was an "eccentric genius," and with Barton W. Stone they found irreconcilable differences "on some very important points" rooted in "the terms commonly used by Divines" (Levi Purviance, *The Biography of Elder David Purviance* [1940 reprint], 256–58). Stone and David Purviance (1766–1847) persevered on the path that the last will had prescribed, hoping to "sink into union with the Body of Christ at large," taking "the Bible as the only sure guide to heaven," and abandoning "partyism" (Stone, 23).

In tasting the "sweets of gospel liberty," Stone and his churches discovered and took to heart Haggard's admonition to abandon "all party and sectarian names," becoming "Christians only." Meanwhile, Stone's continuing quest for personal **conversion** led him from a search for religious certainty through anticipated demonstrations of divine grace to a simple assurance of God's love through Christ—and, as early as 1807, to **assurance of salvation** through baptismal immersion of the believer, even though his insight was not well received at the time in his own sphere of influence. Stone's spiritual journey toward immersion found a parallel in **Alexander Campbell** (1788–1866), who as a youth also searched for "a divine interposition of a peculiar character at a certain crisis," but eventually judged such demonstrations of divine favor as preacher-based, subjective, self-affirmations, and the "experience of a bad education" (Alexander Campbell, "Reply to the Above," *Christian Baptist* 4 [4 June 1827], 342; Campbell, "Conscience, No. 2," *Christian Baptist* [7 February 1826], 217–18). Although he had at first understood baptism symbolically, Campbell eventually found immersion to be an objective, biblical alternative to the revivalist's

altar call and the Pietist's penitential struggle. In contrast to August Hermann Francke's classic Pietist conversion narrative, Campbell described the early Christian experience as "ceasing to do evil, learning to do well. It was washing themselves, making themselves clean in the blood of the Lamb, and forsaking the evil of their doings. The first act of which, was their sensible, visible, memorable burial and resurrection with Jesus Christ in immersion for the remission of sins" (Campbell, "Remarks on the Conversion of Professor Francke," *Millennial Harbinger* 1 [1 November 1830], 497–98).

Thomas Campbell (1763–1854), father of Alexander, had already in 1809 penned a prophetic foundation document for restorationists, the *Declaration and Address of the Christian Association of Washington* (for Presbyterians in western Pennsylvania)—a document owing as much to the Second Great Awakening as *The Last Will and Testament*. Hiram Lester has argued that the *Declaration and Address* represents an **eschatological** plan to meet the spiritual needs of frontier America. By restoring to the church its original unity and purity, the Campbells hoped to create the peaceful conditions among Christians, to promote effective evangelism, and eventually to usher

in a millennial Zion. Thomas Campbell's "restoration of the ancient gospel and discipline" and his son's "restoration of the ancient order of things" were grounded in a perceived need to transcend ecclesiastical divisions so that Christian proclamation and fellowship could bloom without restraint. The revivals of the Second Great Awakening, with their universal appeal, and their interdenominational or ecumenical thrust, had created the conditions that gave birth to the converging movements of Stone and Campbell. The events in the churches indicated for Thomas Campbell an appointed season for gospel action. Walter Scott (1796–1861) imposed "order" on the "ancient gospel" in a series of clearly defined steps or "conditions of salvation"—belief in Jesus Christ as Son of God and Savior, public confession of that faith, repentance from sin, immersion in water for remission of sin, and reception of the indwelling Holy Spirit in baptism. These appointed steps prepared the believer to begin a faithful, eternal life. Scott applied this formula with great success in Ohio and Kentucky from 1827 to 1830, and a decade later wrote of *The Gospel Restored* (1840). By 1832 the groups now known as "Christians" (allied with Stone) and "Disciples" (aligned with the Campbells) had united in a common fellowship that would survive the trauma of the **Civil War.** After 1865, their union was intact but shaken. Internal tensions—social and cultural as well as theological—were already at work, and the original movement for unity fractured in the twentieth century into three distinct religious bodies: the Disciples of Christ, the Churches of Christ, and the independent Christian Churches and Churches of Christ. Today they have several million members and span the spectrum from mainline Protestantism to radical sectarianism.

Restoration theology offers a critical contrast to the revivalist tradition of the Second Great Awakening in which it developed. It is grounded in an objective understanding of salvation in baptism, a "sensible pledge" of the forgiveness of sins and incorporation in the community of believers. This rejection of the traditional conversion narrative, as understood in both Calvinist and Arminian **theologies of revival,** is the characteristic that distinguishes restoration theology from historical and

Barton W. Stone, leader in the nineteenth-century Restorationist movement. Courtesy of Dr. Keith J. Hardman.

contemporary evangelicalism. It is rooted biographically in the personal disillusionment of Barton W. Stone, Alexander Campbell, and others who could not find religious certainty through the drama of a conversion experience.

Campbell, while "fully convinced that there are real and genuine revivals of religion at different times and places, and that much good has resulted from them," remained skeptical of the many "mock revivals" that seemed to legitimate doctrinal and ecclesiastical distinctions but did little to overcome denominational differences. Revival, Campbell thought, ought not only to save sinners, but also to heal the devilish divisions of the revivalists (Campbell, "Revivals," *Christian Baptist* 5 [7 January 1828], 405). Stone could recall, "with a mournful pleasure," his participation in "the great revival of the West" 30 years earlier. That revival's fruits had justified all of its excesses and shortcomings: "The good so far exceeded the evil, the latter almost disappeared." Works worthy of repentance defined for Stone "a revival" and "the work of God." Opposition to that revival, Stone noted, had emerged among "philosophers, dogmatists, and formalists … measuring religion according to their own rule." Reports of eastern revivals had "Christians of all denominations lovingly united in worship, even in the breaking of bread at the Lord's table." Stone would "rejoice" in such a work, yet he feared "that the demon of partyism will check and destroy it" (Barton Stone, "Revivals of Religion," *Christian Messenger* 5 [July 1831], 164–67). Soon he saw that not only criticism and partisan jealousy would endanger revival. By 1833 it was clear to him that in "many things called revivals" the excitement was transient, cyclical, and "evanescent." Revival would "continue but a short time, and then disappear for years…. converts soon dwindle, sicken and die, and become more hardened against the fear of God, than they were before." Stone dared to hope for "revivals without ceasing," but he recognized that "few, if any, would be thus daring" (Stone, "Revivals," *Christian Messenger* 7 [July 1833], 210–12).

Surely the name *revival* faded among the heirs of Stone and Campbell. After the Civil War, the Disciples evangelized in "protracted meetings." By the end of the nineteenth century, as their unity movement divided, the Churches of Christ continued the earlier emphasis on evangelism, calling adherents of all "sects" to unity based on the Bible alone, while Disciples increasingly sought an end to "partyism" by merging the "parties," substituting ecumenical conversation for evangelistic conversion. Among Churches of Christ the protracted meetings, which might continue indefinitely, day and night, as long as they yielded converts, evolved into "gospel meetings" of diminishing duration as the twentieth century progressed. Such meetings conducted by the premillennial evangelist and editor Robert Henry Boll (1875–1956) or his ardent opponent Foy E. Wallace Jr. (1896–1979) would, in isolated instances, be called a revival, but such language was seen or heard rarely. Boll's ally Stanford Chambers (1876–1969) could in 1916 compose a brief guide to the reasons and makings of revival, concluding that "nothing revives like a revival" ("Revival: What, When, Why, and How," *Word and Work*, 198). Perhaps he was right, but few then and fewer now would follow his recipe.

Further Reading: Burnett, John Franklin. *Rev. James O'Kelly: A Champion of Religious Liberty*. Dayton, OH: Christian Publishing Association, 1921; Casey, Michael W., and Douglas A. Foster, eds. *The Stone-Campbell Movement: An International Religious Tradition*. Knoxville: University of Tennessee Press, 2002; Harrison, Richard L., Jr. "Barton Warren Stone and Cumberland Plateau Revivalism." *Lexington Theological Quarterly* 29 (1994): 77–87; Hicks, John Mark. "'God's Sensible Pledge': The Witness of the Spirit in the Early Baptismal Theology of Alexander Campbell." *Stone-Campbell Journal* 1 (1998): 5–26; MacClenny, W. E. *The Life of the Rev. James O'Kelly and the Early History of the Christian Church in the South*. Raleigh, NC: Edwards and Broughton, 1910; Olbricht, Thomas H., and Hans Rollmann, eds. *The Quest for Christian Unity, Peace, and Purity in Thomas Campbell's Declaration and Address: Text and Studies*. Lanham, MD: Scarecrow Press, 2000; Randall, Max Ward. *The Great Awakenings and the Restoration Movement*. Joplin, MO: College Press, 1983; Scott, Walter. *The Gospel Restored*. Cincinnati: Ormsby H. Donogh, 1836; Stone, Barton W. *Works of Elder B. W. Stone: To Which Is Added a Few Discourses and Sermons*. Cincinnati: Moore, Wilstach, Keys, 1859; Toulouse, Mark G., ed. *Walter Scott: A Nineteenth-Century*

Evangelical. St. Louis: Chalice Press, 1999; West, Earl Irvin. "1827—Annus Mirabilis—and Alexander Campbell." *Restoration Quarterly* 16 (1974): 250–59; Williams, D. Newell. *Barton Stone: A Spiritual Biography.* St. Louis: Chalice Press, 2000.

Hans Rollmann and Don Haymes

REVIVAL OF 1857–1858

The Revival of 1857–1858, known as the Great Revival of 1858, the Businessman's Revival, the Layman's Revival, the Union Prayer Meeting Revival, and the Third Great Awakening, among other descriptors, was a period of widespread religious fervor particularly evident in urban areas throughout the United States. It marked a transformational moment in the history of American revivals and could perhaps be described as the closest thing to a truly national revival in U.S. history. Instead of centering on single **preacher** or revivalist, the 1857–1858 revival revolved around **prayer** meetings, especially mass meetings in churches, auditoriums, or even theaters in the downtown business districts of urban areas. In line with nineteenth-century usage, these were called "union" prayer meetings, meaning "united" or "interdenominational." They often took place during the noon hour and attracted what to observers seemed a disproportionate number of businessmen. The meetings were organized down to the minute and featured prayer requests, brief prayers, religious testimony, and singing. "Come to Jesus" was the central message of the revival, and the invitational **hymn** "Just as I Am" was first popularized among Americans during the prayer meetings of 1858. Controversial subjects such as slavery were prohibited. Although ministers participated, the leaders often were nonclerics or laymen.

As a mass religious awakening, the events of 1857–1858 appeared most visibly in the North, where systems of communication and commerce were more highly developed than in the **South** and the population more densely concentrated in cities and towns. Revival prayer meetings did extend to the southern states, however, and were particularly significant for their influence on young men who

later encouraged revivals during the **Civil War** in the Confederate army. Churches in Canada, especially the provinces of Ontario (then Canada West) and the Maritimes, also reported revivals. The 1857–1858 revival began during the fall of 1857 and spread in North America for about a year, although it reached its most intense, publicized phase from February to April 1858. Major Protestant denominations in the United States gained more than 474,000 new members during a three-year period that included the revival, almost twice as many as during the previous three-year period. **Methodists** and **Baptists** experienced the greatest growth. The revival also brought membership growth and new energy to the **Young Men's Christian Association** (YMCA), floundering since its establishment in the United States in 1851. From about 1858 to 1862, revival spread to the British Isles, with particularly intense and dramatic religious fervor among Ulster (i.e., Northern Irish) Protestants during the summer of 1859.

One highly publicized locus of the revival and the most famous of the noon meetings was the Fulton Street Prayer Meeting, begun September 23, 1857, by city missionary Jeremiah Lanphier at the North Dutch Church, William and Fulton Streets, in New York City. Only a few people arrived at first, but attendance swelled in the wake of a financial panic that shook the United States from October 14 to December 14, 1857. The panic and subsequent recession served as a stimulus to the revival. Other factors, including the social stresses of immigration and rapid urbanization, the absence of major political campaigns, and family members' concern for one another's salvation also played a role. Participants themselves viewed the revival as an answer to prayer. By February 1858 several hundred people were crowding the Fulton Street church lecture hall to pray, many of them businessmen from the Manhattan commercial district surrounding the church. The YMCA, which had helped to publicize Lanphier's meetings, began two more noon gatherings in New York City and one in Philadelphia in response to the growing interest. By early March, the *New York Tribune* and the *New York*

INCREASE IN NET MEMBERSHIP FOR MAJOR U.S. DENOMINATIONS, 1853–1856 AND 1956–1959[a]

Denominational Group	Net membership increase, 1853-1956	Net membership increase, 1856-59
Methodist, North & South	111,098	250,365
Regular Baptist	88,711	122,984
Presbyterian, OS/NS	12,781	52,971
Episcopal	14,404	20,071
Total net increase	226,994	446,391
Congregational (1857-60)[b]		27,840
Total		474,231[c]

Source: From Table 12, Appendix B, in Kathryn Teresa Long, *The Revival of 1857–58* (1998). See tables 1–12, Appendix B, of Long's book for more detailed information. Used with permission.

[a] The year 1853 is used as a baseline for the three-year period ending in 1856; 1856 as a baseline for the three-year period ending 1859. Numbers for 1856 are only counted once.

[b] Reliable data available only for these years.

[c] Approximate net increase among major denominational groupings for the three-year period including the 1857–1858 Revival. Because of difficulties in securing full and accurate reports, figures should be viewed as representing the best count for the denominations included rather than as absolutely reliable totals.

Herald, two of the most prominent mass-circulation daily newspapers in the nation, began to cover "the Religious Awakening" and the unusual feature of businessmen at prayer. As the news spread, picked up by daily papers throughout the nation, so did the prayer meetings, organized throughout March and April in Boston, Louisville, Chicago, New Orleans, Cincinnati, Cleveland, Indianapolis, St. Louis, Nashville, Mobile, and Charleston, as well as other cities and towns. Publicity in the secular press, stories in weekly religious newspapers, and messages exchanged via telegraph were all key factors in helping participants feel part of a widespread, simultaneous religious awakening that was a national event. Together with several popular histories of the revival in book form published by the end of 1858, newspaper publicity helped to shape the public profile of the revival.

There also was a less publicized, grassroots side to the revival. Methodist **Holiness** teacher and revivalist **Phoebe Palmer** drew large crowds on the **camp meeting** circuit in southern Canada during late summer and early fall 1857. In mid-October, Palmer and her husband, Walter, held two weeks of meetings in Hamilton, Ontario, where Palmer encouraged ordinary churchgoers, both **men** and **women,** to become active in evangelism and to bring their friends to church. Many did, and some 500 people indicated conversion to Christianity during Palmer's visit. For Methodists this marked the first real sign of the spiritual awakening that would become the Revival of 1857–1858. Local church revivals in New England, the Midwest, and the upper South seemed to begin with New Year's Eve "watchnight" services. They extended and spread during January and February 1858, and were widely reported in the Methodist and Baptist religious press. **College campuses** throughout the United States also were affected, including Oberlin, Dartmouth, Brown, Yale, Rutgers, Princeton, the University of Michigan, Ohio Wesleyan, the University of Virginia, Davidson, the University of North Carolina, and others. The grassroots revivals involved young people, women, children, and men of the "middling sort"

"The Fulton Street Prayer Meeting," during the Revival of 1857–1858, excerpted from *Harper's Weekly*. Courtesy of the Billy Graham Center Museum.

(emerging middle class) of small-town and rural America. There were reports of unusual religious fervor among **African Americans** and among some immigrant religious groups, such as the Mennonites. Even in more urban areas, although businessmen got the attention, well-known Protestant figures such as **Charles and Elizabeth Finney,** Francis Wayland, **Horace Bushnell,** John A. Broadus, and Harriet Beecher Stowe helped tend the revival fires.

The Revival of 1857–1858 marked the emergence of an evangelical urban revivalism—particularly in the northern United States—that fused the decorum and respectability of earlier **Calvinist** revivals with the mass appeal of Methodist and Baptist revival practices. Prayer, publicity, and entrepreneurial lay initiative across denominations became standard practices characterizing subsequent urban revivals and northern evangelicalism more generally. Specific influences extended in many directions. Patterns of piety from the revival were institutionalized in the YMCA and its Civil War affiliate, the United States Christian Commission, as well as in the postwar urban revivals of

Dwight L. Moody. Nearly all the characteristic practices of the 1857–1858 revival became hallmarks of Moody's later urban mass evangelism, including revival services in downtown business districts, noon prayer meetings, newspaper publicity, support from prominent businessmen and the YMCA, and an emphasis on order. Other future Christian leaders influenced by the revival included Philadelphia businessman and evangelical activist John Wanamaker, inspirational author **Hannah Whitall Smith,** Mennonite publisher and bishop John Fretz Funk, missions promoter A. T. Pierson, and chaplain and Confederate apologist John William Jones. Gospel rescue mission pioneers Jerry McAuley and Charles Crittenton found their callings as lay Christian workers indirectly from the revival.

The emphasis on prayer meetings in the commercial centers of America's great cities celebrated a new sense of compatibility between the worlds of religion and commerce. Mass-circulation daily papers viewed the revival as entertainment and featured sensationalized religious news, along with more straightforward reports. Attention given to Orville Gardner, a notorious boxer who became the first "celebrity convert" in American evangelicalism, illustrated the new approach to revival news in the press. Packaging the story of a religious awakening for commercial consumption rather than for nonprofit religious edification had the long-term effect of pushing American revivalism toward a business-like frame of mind. Despite the reality of women's participation, the public face of the revival and its impact in shaping modern American evangelicalism emphasized the role of men and bore a masculine stamp. The minute-by-minute format and uniform instructions for the noontime meetings resembled an agenda as much as a liturgy. Prayer was considered a productive activity. Even emotion, historian John Corrigan has suggested, was commodified. The methods of business were used to further the revival, and the Christian businessman stepped into place alongside the praying mother as an icon of Protestant piety. The publicity and ongoing impact of the 1857–1858 revival point to its significance as the most important overtly masculine

Entrance to the consistory rooms of the Collegiate Reformed Protestant Dutch Church, where revival meetings began in 1857–1858. As the revival spread, distinguished citizens, like the man with top hat and cane, began coming to the noon-to-one-o'clock meetings. (From Talbot Chambers, *The Noon Prayer Meeting*, 1858.) Courtesy of Dr. Kathryn T. Long.

expression of popular Protestant piety in the United States prior to the Men and Religion Forward movement about half a century later. Throughout the twentieth century, American evangelical missions to the world bore the stamp of this businesslike Christianity with their entrepreneurial cast, orientation toward efficiency, and problem-solving mentality.

Although the ethos of the urban prayer meetings in 1858 emphasized male piety, women, too, shared in the legacy of the revival. In addition to her personal revival work, Phoebe Palmer wrote *The Promise of the Father* (1859), a book defending women's right to speak in religious assemblies and to share fully with men all other responsibilities of Christian lay work. *The Promise of the Father* presented a gender-inclusive vision of true revival piety. In November 1858, Caroline D. Roberts became the first "directress" of the Ladies' Christian Association, an organization that grew out of a women's union prayer meeting and that became a precursor of the **Young Women's Christian Association** (YWCA) in the United States. Other women employed strategies from the revival to help launch the first mass movement in American Protestantism after the Civil War, the Women's **Temperance** Crusade (WTC), a group that led to the formation of the Woman's Christian Temperance Union (WCTU). The women's missionary movement also gained impetus from the spiritual energy of the revival. Sarah Doremus, long a promoter of **foreign missions** and networker for benevolent causes among the Dutch **Reformed** churches of New York City, took advantage of the spirit of interdenominational cooperation engendered by the revival to found the Woman's Union Missionary Society (WUMS) in 1861.

Historians have differed in their assessments of the impact of the Revival of 1857–1858 on Protestant involvement in nineteenth-century social reform efforts. Timothy L. Smith in his classic *Revivalism and Social Reform* (1957) emphasized the connection between nineteenth-century revivals and humanitarian concern and placed the 1857–1858 revival within that context. Smith stressed the link between evangelism and ethical perfectionism in the Wesleyan revival tradition. Others, including the author of this entry, have suggested that the 1857–1858 revival had very little direct social impact. The noontime prayer meetings stressed personal religious transformation and prohibited any mention of controversial subjects, particularly the deep divisions of the day over slavery and **abolitionism.** From this perspective, the 1857–1858 revival marked a shift in the public role of revivals in American life. It signaled a rejection of the combination of religious conversion and community moral reform that had been a part of the New England Calvinist tradition since the colonial revivals. Instead, a more limited, pietistic image of revivals emerged, one focused on prayer and evangelism and in which *community* meant experiences of shared feeling among middle-class people. This shift of urban revivalism in a more inward direction reflected the changing nature of community in a rapidly industrializing society and promised northern evangelicals spiritual harmony in the midst of an increasingly complex society.

The Revival of 1857–1858 both summed up and altered the revival traditions that had gone before it. What emerged was a businesslike, consumer-sensitive approach that further blurred what was already a fuzzy line between revivals and mass evangelism. The urban revivalism subsequently associated with **Dwight Lyman Moody, Billy Sunday, Billy Graham,** and others had taken

Brethren are earnestly requested to adhere to the 5 minute rule.

PRAYERS & EXHORTATIONS Not to exceed 5 minutes, *in order to give all an opportunity.*

NOT MORE than *2 CONSECUTIVE* PRAYERS OR EXHORTATIONS.

NO CONTROVERTED POINTS — *DISCUSSED.* —

Rules for prayer during the meetings of the Revival of 1857–1858. Because "no converted points [were to be] discussed," the meetings forbade debates over slavery, and women were instructed not to speak or pray publicly. (From Talbot Chambers, *The Noon Prayer Meeting,* 1858.) Courtesy of Dr. Kathryn T. Long.

shape. With its dramatic conversions and stories of transforming grace, the 1857–1858 revival also became a beloved historical benchmark for Fundamentalists and evangelicals alike in the twentieth and twenty-first centuries. Historians might debate the revival's significance, but groups as distinct as the **Promise Keepers** and the Reformed Church in America claimed it as an exemplary historical moment, the model of a national awakening to the power of prayer.

Further Reading: Carwardine, Richard. *Transatlantic Revivalism: Popular Evangelicalism in Britain and America, 1790–1865.* Westport, CT: Greenwood Press, 1978; Chambers, Talbot W. "The Prayers of a Generation." Reformed Church in America, July 2004. http://www.rca.org/images/aboutus/archives/chambersfulton.pdf; Corrigan, John. *Business of the Heart: Religion and Emotion in the Nineteenth Century.* Berkeley: University of California Press, 2002; Hempton, David, and Myrtle Hill. *Evangelical Protestantism in Ulster Society, 1790–1890.* London: Routledge, 1992; Jeffrey, Kenneth S. *When the Lord Walked the Land: The 1858–62 Revival in the North East of Scotland.* Carlisle, UK: Paternoster Press, 2002; Long, Kathryn Teresa. *The Revival of 1857–58: Interpreting an American Religious Awakening.* New York: Oxford University Press, 1998; Orr, J. Edwin. *The Event of the Century: The 1857–1858 Awakening.* Ed. Richard Owen Roberts. Wheaton, IL: International Awakening Press, 1989; Smith, Timothy L. *Revivalism and Social Reform: American Protestantism on the Eve of the Civil War.* Baltimore: Johns Hopkins University Press, 1980.

Kathryn Teresa Long

REVIVALS AND REVIVALISM, DEFINITIONS AND THEORIES OF

Authors use the terms *revival* and *revivalism* in various ways. *Webster's Third New International Dictionary* defines the term *revival* as "a period of religious awakening: renewed interest in religion" with "meetings often characterized by emotional excitement." *Revivalism* is "the spirit or kind of religion or the methods characteristic of religious revivals." Yet these simple definitions conceal much complexity, arising from competing **theologies of revival** and a centuries-long debate over the appropriateness of human efforts to promote revivals.

Calvinists—who believe that God's purpose and power undergird all human decisions—understand revival as an unplanned event that reflects God's initiative, and revivalism as a humanly orchestrated effort to stir up religious interest. A Calvinist revival is like a sudden summer storm—powerful and unpredictable. By contrast, Arminians assert that revivals occur through divine-human cooperation, and such strenuous exertions as **prayer, fasting,** and the persuasion of potential converts. The Calvinist Iain Murray viewed eighteenth- and early-nineteenth-century Calvinistic revivals as shifting into late nineteenth- and twentieth-century Arminian revivalism, with **Charles G. Finney** as the key figure in this transition. It seems accurate to say that American revivalists since the 1830s or 1840s tended to place more emphasis on strategies to promote revivals. Yet it is hard to draw a clear line between revivals and revivalism. Calvinists, who wait on God to bring revival, also exert themselves to cause it to happen. Arminians, who exert themselves to cause revival, also have to wait on God. The two theologies of revival may be closer in practice than they are in theory.

Revivals are corporate, experiential events. To call a religious gathering a revival is to suggest that an *intensification* of experience has occurred. The fact that numbers or multitudes attend a religious service does not make it a revival as such. What distinguishes a revival from the ordinary course of affairs is a deepening of religious feeling and expression among a group of people. Because revivals are events, they have beginnings and endings, and it is possible to assign chronological dates to such awakenings as the **Northampton awakening of 1734–1735,** the **Great Awakening** of 1740–1741, **Cane Ridge revival** of 1801–1802, the **Revival of 1857–1858,** the **Azusa Street revival** of 1906–1909, and other lesser-known occurrences. The chief literary expression of a revival is a narrative or testimony describing the religious experiences of an individual or a community. **Jonathan Edwards's** *Faithful Narrative* (1737)—which did more than any other text to establish the genre of the revival narrative—spoke of an awareness of God's presence among the inhabitants of Northampton, Massachusetts in

1734–1735 that intensified until the entire city was "full of the presence of God" (Edwards, *Works,* 4:151). Edwards's account was especially influential because of the insight and intricacy of his descriptions of spiritual experience.

While revivals are corporate, experiential events, the religious experiences in revivals are intertwined with intellectual formulations of belief or doctrines. Indeed, the very word *revival* is shot through with explicit Christian associations. The literature of the North American revival tradition makes constant reference to the Christian doctrines of God, God's love, the Trinity, the divinity of Jesus, Jesus' atoning death, **eschatology** or Jesus' Second Coming, the Holy Spirit, faith, repentance, salvation holiness or **sanctification,** and so forth. There is no way to disentangle revival experiences from Christian ideas and teachings. Movements of reform and renewal occur in non-Christian religions, and sometimes in ways that parallel Christian revivals. Yet religious revivals of North America have commonly occurred within a larger context of Christian history, belief, and practice, and this context is needed properly to interpret revivals.

Revival accounts from different eras, geographical regions, and ethnic groups in American history have common themes. Participants in revivals speak of their vivid sense of spiritual things, great joy and faith, deep sorrow over sin, passionate desire to evangelize others, and heightened feelings of love for God and fellow humanity. In times of revival, people often crowd into available buildings for religious services, and fill them beyond capacity. The services may last from morning until midnight or later. News of a revival usually travels rapidly, and sometimes the reports of revival—in person, print, or broadcast media—touch off new revivals in distant localities. During a revival, clergy and other Christian workers may receive many requests for their services, and find themselves harried by inquirers. Sometimes people openly **confess their sins** in public settings. Another mark of revivals is generosity—individuals willing to give their time, money, or resources to support the work of the revival. Revivals are usually controversial, with opponents and proponents who vehemently criticize one another. **Anti-revivalism** typically arises in the wake of revivals. Often there are **bodily manifestations** in revivals, such as falling down, rolling on the ground, involuntary muscle movements, **laughing or shouting,** and spiritual **dancing.** Another common feature is an assertion of **signs and wonders,** such as the **healing** of the sick, **prophecies, visions** or **dreams** revealing secret knowledge, **deliverance** or exorcism from the power of Satan and the demonic, and **speaking in tongues.** Such paranormal manifestations have been common in twentieth-century **Pentecostal revivals** and the **Charismatic Revival and Renewal,** though many of these phenomena—with the possible exception of speaking in tongues—occurred with some regularity in revivals prior to 1900.

The twentieth century's leading scholar of revivals and revivalism, **William G. McLoughlin,** described revivals in a series of pioneering books. In an earlier work he described revivalism as "any series of spontaneous or organized meetings which produce religious conversions whether they occur in one church, a dozen churches, or in hundreds of churches under the leadership of a spectacular itinerant evangelist" (*Modern Revivalism,* 7). Some 20 years later, he wrote, "Revivalism is the Protestant ritual (at first spontaneous, but, since 1830, routinized) in which charismatic evangelists convey 'the Word' of God to large masses of people, who, under this influence, experience what Protestants call conversion, salvation, regeneration, or spiritual rebirth" (*Revivals, Awakenings, and Reform,* xiii). Common to both the earlier and later descriptions of revivals is a stress on the dominating personality of the revivalist and on **conversion** as the revivalist's goal.

Michael McClymond criticized McLoughlin for emphasizing the influence of revival **preachers** and neglecting the influence of laypersons in initiating and guiding revivals. He noted that the Revival of 1857–1858 was a widely diffused and powerful revival and yet not directly associated with any notable preacher or leader. McClymond argued that

Gipsy Smith revival, inside the 7th Regiment Armory building in Chicago. (Photographer George R. Lawrence, October 13, 1909) Courtesy of the Library of Congress.

revivals occur in **Roman Catholic** as well as Protestant contexts, and that **conversion** is only one possible aim in revival meetings. Early **Methodist revivals** and the later **Holiness movement** focused on **sanctification,** while Pentecostal and Charismatic revivals stress the **baptism of the Holy Spirit,** healing, deliverance, and speaking in tongues. McClymond objected to McLoughlin's separation of *revivals* from *awakenings,* claiming that this distinction between individual experience and large-scale cultural change was unhelpful. He argued that the individual and corporate aspects of revivals are intricately connected and cannot be interpreted in isolation from one another. On the other hand, revivalism has an inherently individualistic aspect in its call for individuals to make "a self-conscious decision" of faith (McClymond, 7–14).

Believers and scholars have generally interpreted revivals in differing ways. Participants in revivals have often asserted that revivals are God's work and that no natural causes can explain them. Genuine revivals are due to a supernatural "outpouring of the Holy Spirit," which, if due to any human factors at all, is a result of concerted prayer. The twentieth-century revival preacher and scholar of revivals **James Edwin Orr** made such claims. On the other hand, there are devout authors—including Jonathan Edwards—who invoked natural causes alongside of supernatural or divine factors as causes or reasons for revivals. In the aftermath of the Revival of 1857–1858, Christian writers noted that the financial panic of 1857 helped to set the stage for the revival among New York City businessmen, and so they invoked natural alongside of supernatural forms of explanation. Among scholars, there is no consensus as to why revivals occur. Some have noted that the causes of revivals are complex and cannot be reduced to a single causal factor, and that poverty or economic depression alone is not a cause for revivals. If poverty were a major causal factor, then the 1930s would have been a golden age for religious revival in America—which it was not. Eras of religious revival do not seem to correspond to periods of social strain or turmoil in American history.

Scholarly explanations for revivals move in multiple directions. McLoughlin's approach, as noted, highlights the personality and influence of the revivalist in causing revivals. Another viewpoint is based on an idea of communications and networking. According to this view, revivals "happen" when information and enthusiasm flow between otherwise isolated groups and they develop a sense of participation within a larger movement. The star preacher of the Great Awakening, **George Whitefield,** had a shrewd sense of how to connect evangelical believers scattered into different denominations, how to use the newspapers to gain publicity, and how to use even the opposition against him to advance his cause. Richard Lovelace stressed Whitefield's unifying influence among evangelicals, while Harry S. Stout identified Whitefield's theatricality and media skill as essential to his appeal. Both viewed networking as a key aspect of the Great Awakening. A different approach to explanation is based on so-called primitive psychology. In a 1905 book, Frederick Davenport viewed American revivals as an expression of nonrational instincts and emotions that needed to be put under rational control. Davenport implied that religious revivals were destined to disappear in the process of social evolution—an idea challenged by the stunning growth of twentieth-century Pentecostalism. He also aligned his theory of primitive psychology with indefensible racist and chauvinist notions of the superior rationality of white males. Yet Davenport's work highlighted an important theme that deserves fuller consideration, namely, the involuntary or nonrational aspects of revivals, such as "the jerks," falling down, and other bodily manifestations that occurred in the Great Awakening, the Cane Ridge revival, and Pentecostal revivals. Ann Taves has recently written on the "fits, trances, and visions" associated with revivals, and so addresses some of the questions posed by Davenport a century ago.

The theory of material or social deprivation—propounded by sociologist Charles Glock, and applied to Pentecostalism by historian Robert Mapes Anderson—holds that revivalist groups offer their members a superior religious status to compensate for their inferior social or economic status. While this theory helps to explain the spread of revivalist movements like Pentecostalism among

America's—and later the world's—impoverished masses, it fails to explain why some revivals (e.g., the Charismatic Revival and Renewal) influenced people of wealth and influence. The deprivation or compensation theory, argues Grant Wacker, does not account for the initiative, drive, and self-reliance of the leaders and laypersons participating in revivals. The theory portrays them as passive spectators to revival movements, and not as agents in their own individual and social transformation. Wacker, together with Alan Gilbert, Bernard Semmel, and John Corrigan, offers an interpretation of revivals that might be classified as functionalist. This perspective, indebted to Emil Durkheim, interprets revivalist religion in terms of its function in establishing personal identity and a sense of communal belonging. Wacker comments that early Pentecostalism was "less an effort to escape adversity than a creative resource for dealing with it" (Wacker, 10). Gilbert and Semmel viewed eighteenth-century evangelicalism in Britain as a response to the "anomie and social insecurity" that was caused by urban migration and separation from the life of traditional village communities. Early Methodism offered a "revolutionary message of liberty and equality" to masses of people alienated by the new industrial society (Alan D. Gilbert, *Religion and Society in Industrial England* [1976], 87–93; Bernard Semmel, *The Methodistic Revolution* [1973], 5–9, 198). The Revival of 1857–1858, for John Corrigan, provided American males an opportunity to show their emotion—even through public weeping—and thus established the display of emotion as a category of collective identity.

While it is not clear that any one of the proposed theories of revivals is superior to all the rest, the functionalist viewpoint—when combined with insights from the other viewpoints—may go furthest in explaining how those who have participated in religious revivals both responded to the influences of their culture and shaped their culture in intentional ways. Yet after all the explanations have been wagered and weighed, North American revivals recall the eighteenth-century words of Jonathan Edwards, who referred to them as a "surprising work."

Further Reading: Anderson, Robert Mapes. *Vision of the Disinherited: The Making of American Pentecostalism.* New York: Oxford University Press, 1979; Corrigan, John. *Business of the Heart: Religion and Emotion in the Nineteenth Century.* Berkeley: University of California Press, 2002; Davenport, Frederick M. *Primitive Traits in Religious Revivals: A Study in Mental and Social Evolution.* New York: Macmillan, 1905; Glock, Charles. "The Role of Deprivation in the Origin and Evolution of Religious Groups." In R. Lee and Martin Marty, eds., *Religion and Social Conflict,* 24–36. Oxford: Oxford University Press, 1964; Lovelace, Richard F. *Dynamics of Spiritual Life: An Evangelical Theology of Renewal.* Downers Grove, IL: InterVarsity Press, 1979; McClymond, Michael J. "Issues and Explanations in the Study of North American Revivalism." In Michael J. McClymond, ed., *Embodying the Spirit: New Perspectives on North American Revivalism,* 1–46. Baltimore: Johns Hopkins University Press, 2004; McLoughlin, William G. *Modern Revivalism: Charles Grandison Finney to Billy Graham.* New York: Ronald Press, 1959; McLoughlin, William G. *Revivals, Awakenings, and Reform: An Essay on Religion and Social Change in America, 1607–1977.* Chicago: University of Chicago Press, 1978; Murray, Iain H. *Revival and Revivalism: The Making and Marring of American Revivalism, 1750–1858.* Carlisle, PA: Banner of Truth Trust, 1994; Riss, Richard M. *A Survey of 20th-Century Revival Movements in North America.* Peabody, MA: Hendrickson, 1988; Stout, Harry S. *The Divine Dramatist: George Whitefield and the Rise of Modern Evangelicalism.* Grand Rapids, MI: Eerdmans, 1991; Synan, Vinson, ed. *The Century of the Holy Spirit: 100 Years of Pentecostal and Charismatic Renewal, 1901–2001.* Nashville, TN: Thomas Nelson, 2001; Taves, Ann. *Fits, Trances, and Visions: Experiencing Religion and Explaining Experience from Wesley to James.* Princeton, NJ: Princeton University Press, 1999; Wacker, Grant. *Heaven Below: Early Pentecostals and American Culture.* Cambridge, MA: Harvard University Press, 2001.

Michael J. McClymond

ROBERTS, BENJAMIN TITUS (1823–1893)

Benjamin Titus Roberts is known as the principle figure in the founding of the **Free Methodist Church** in 1860. A "converted" minister in the **Methodist** Episcopal Church, Roberts was a proponent of revival and became a strong enough force in the Genesee Conference of New York State that his enemies moved to censure and expel him, while his friends rallied around him to form a new sect. Roberts led a fledgling movement toward becoming a new denomination and served as bishop in the Free Methodist Church from its inception until the time of his death. Along with the Free Methodist Church, Roberts's legacy includes four books and 33 years as editor of a monthly magazine entitled the *Earnest Christian.* Throughout his ministry he promoted "experimental" or experiential piety and holiness of life through freedom from sin and zeal in service and evangelism. He saw this sort of religion as a direct continuation of the Wesleyan Revival that began with John and Charles Wesley in England and continued in America under **Francis Asbury** and Thomas Coke. In defense of pure Methodism Roberts found himself embroiled in a dispute fueled by the issue of **abolitionism** and the radicalism of the **Burned-Over District.**

In May 1857 Roberts penned and published a controversial article in the *Northern Independent* entitled "New School Methodism." It sought to clarify the theological and practical differences between the revivalistic factions in the Genesee conference and those opposing them. In his scathing critique, Roberts accused the group that he derisively called "the Buffalo Regency" of betraying both the theology and spirit of earlier Wesleyanism. He predicted that if the Methodist church did not return to its roots it would flounder and die. In response, the opposition pressed the Genesee Conference to censure him for unchristian conduct and ordered him silenced for a year. Although he challenged the irregular judicial procedures used against him and the gag order placed on him, he nonetheless lost both his case and an appeal. Supported by a large number of equally earnest laymen, Roberts continued to **preach** and to condemn the "new" Methodists for their lack of spirituality and theological error. As the controversy intensified he became the first of many Methodists to be expelled from the conference during the turbulent pre–**Civil War** years.

The new movement—consisting of laymen supporting Roberts and other rejected colleagues— organized itself around the concept of freedom and

named itself the Free Methodist Church. In 1860 Roberts was elected as its first general superintendent. Roberts sought to establish what he called "free churches." He insisted on the cessation of pew rentals—a system wherein donors claimed the right to occupy the best seats in the church building, leaving the poor in the back of the sanctuary, and preventing the use of the front pews for the evangelistic **altar call.** Roberts demanded freedom for **African American** slaves and promoted freedom of expression in worship. Above all, he proclaimed the possibility and responsibility for Christians to live a life free of sin. Though estranged from the Methodist mother church, Roberts maintained close ties with all who promoted **sanctification** and with the emerging **Holiness movement.** Well educated for a minister of his day, with a master's degree, Roberts combined the earnestness of revivalism with rigorous but practical academic pursuit. He established Chesborough Seminary in 1867, a school that exists today as Roberts Wesleyan University near Rochester, New York.

Roberts advocated revival because he believed it to be biblical, authentic, and effective. He promoted the ordination of **women** because it did not make sense to limit the ministry of over half the converted population and because the Bible states that in Christ "there is neither male nor female" (Galatians 3:28). His final book, *Ordaining Women* (1892), outlines the arguments that eventually led the Free Methodists to sanction the ordaining of women shortly before his death in 1893. Under Roberts's leadership, the Free Methodists embraced an expression of Christianity that some see as proto-**Pentecostal.** Roberts did not favor outlandish behavior in the name of God, yet he feared "quenching the Spirit" by imposing rules and regulations in Christian worship. He remained a firm believer in the necessity of a **conversion** experience followed by a second work of grace called "entire sanctification" that led to freedom from sin. He spoke out for **temperance,** favored the prohibition of alcohol, and opposed all manner of conduct that he regarded as immoral, ranging from tobacco usage to skating. He worked to start or support works like the Five Points Mission in New York City—an urban outreach supported by **Phoebe Palmer**. Roberts's personal papers are archived in the Library of Congress and copies of those as well as the vast corpus of secondary literature devoted to him can be found in the Marston Historical Center at the Free Methodist World Ministry Center in Indianapolis, Indiana.

Further Reading: Chesbrough, S.K.J. *Defense of Rev. B. T. Roberts.* Buffalo, NY: Clapp, Matthews, 1858; Kostlevy, William C. "Benjamin Titus Roberts and the Preferential Option for the Poor in the Early Free Methodist Church." In Anthony L. Dunnavant, ed., *Poverty and Ecclesiology: Nineteenth-Century Evangelicals in the Light of Liberation Theology.* 51–67. Collegeville, MN: Liturgical Press, 1992; McPeak, Rick H. "Earnest Christianity: The Practical Theology of Benjamin Titus Roberts." PhD dissertation, Saint Louis University, 2001; Reinhard, James A. "Personal and Sociological Factors in the Formation of the Free Methodist Church, 1852–1860." PhD dissertation, University of Iowa, 1971; Roberts, B. T. *Living Truths: Vital Selections from the Writings of B. T. Roberts.* Ed. E. D. Riggs. Winona Lake, IN: Light and Life Press, 1960; Roberts, B. D. *Ordaining Women.* 1892. Reprint, Indianapolis: Light and Life Press, 1992; Roberts, B. T. *Why Another Sect?* Rochester, NY: Earnest Christian, 1879; Zahniser, Clarence H. *Earnest Christian.* Circleville, OH: Advocate, 1957.

Rick H. McPeak

ROBERTS, ORAL (1918–)

Oral Roberts has been a revival **preacher, healer,** evangelist, and educator, with a large influence among both **Pentecostal** and non-Pentecostal Christians during the later twentieth century. A son of an Oklahoma Pentecostal preacher, his life direction was set early when he was healed of tuberculosis at the age of 17. He emerged from this crisis reporting that God had spoken to him: "You are to take My healing power to your generation. You are to build Me a university. Build it on My authority and on the Holy Spirit" (Oral Roberts, *Expect a Miracle* [1995], 158). After 10 years of service as a Pentecostal **Holiness** pastor (see **International Pentecostal Holiness Church**), Roberts developed a distinctive approach to ministry centered on the notion of **prosperity.** He was influenced by the biblical text 3 John 2 (Authorized Version): "Beloved, I wish above all things that thou mayest prosper and be in health, even as thy soul prospereth." By the 1940s, the spontaneity of early Pentecostalism had diminished and Roberts perceived a narrow and even oppressive religious subculture within the movement. He saw the Pentecostal acceptance of poverty as inconsistent with Jesus' promise of abundant life. Roberts emphasized God's goodness and purpose for his children to experience health and material provision. Locating in Tulsa, Oklahoma, in 1947, Roberts began holding healing crusades in large tents (see **Camp Meetings and Tent Revivals**), preaching and ministering to thousands throughout the United States and beyond. It was said that his audiences grew as rapidly as his tents.

After founding the monthly magazine, *Healing Waters*, and preaching regularly by **radio**, Roberts began his **television** ministry in 1954. Television

Oral Roberts speaks into the microphone as he lays his hand on a young boy for healing and a woman stands alongside praying with arm upraised. (Pensacola, Florida, 1957.) Courtesy of the Oral Roberts Evangelistic Association.

was in its infancy, and Roberts took a financial risk in broadcasting his healing crusades on weekly national TV. Yet the broadcasts brought new support for his ministry. In addition, millions of Americans began to view Pentecostalism in a new and positive light as a result of hearing Roberts's positive messages and seeing dramatic healings take place on the air. As the **Charismatic** movement burst onto the scene in the 1960s, Roberts formed a strategic alliance with this emerging group, which was mostly unfamiliar with earlier Pentecostalism, and held membership in mainline Protestant, **Roman Catholic,** and independent churches. Though Roberts embraced his Pentecostal roots, he discerned the momentum shifting toward the Charismatics, and so in his preaching and healing ministry he cooperated with a diversity of churches and pastors. Though many church services continued to be racially segregated at this time, Roberts insisted on integrated services. Wishing to establish a closer relationship with mainline Protestant Charismatics, he joined the United **Methodist** denomination in 1968. His series of prime-time TV specials, beginning in 1969 and enlisting popular celebrities, touched a cross section of the American public.

Appealing to a broad constituency of Charismatics and Christians of all persuasions served Roberts well in his second major endeavor, namely, to build a full-fledged, accredited university, distinctively charismatic in orientation. Oral Roberts University (ORU) was dedicated in 1967, with **Billy Graham** as the keynote speaker at the ceremonies. ORU had an enrollment of more than 5,000 students in the year 2004, and stresses both academic excellence and the spiritual and physical development of each student. Oral Roberts's son, Richard Roberts, succeeded him as president in 1993. To assess the historical legacy of a contemporary leader is difficult. Yet it seems likely that Oral Roberts will loom as one of the significant religious figures of twentieth-century America. He exceeded others in his ability to discern changes in the churches, to adapt creatively to new contexts, and to offer a new paradigm for spiritual life.

Further Reading: Harrell, David Edwin, Jr. *Oral Roberts: An American Life.* Bloomington: Indiana University

Press, 1985; McCoy, Michael R. "Oral Roberts." In Charles H. Lippy, ed., *Twentieth-Century Shapers of American Popular Religion*, 342–49. New York: Greenwood Press, 1989; Roberts, Oral. *Oral Roberts' Life Story as Told by Himself.* Tulsa, OK: n.p., 1952.

David Dorries

ROBERTSON, PAT (MARION GORDON) (1930–)

Pat Robertson is a renowned Christian **television** broadcaster and a onetime Republican candidate for the U.S. presidency. He was born in Lexington, Virginia, and raised in an environment of power, influence, and public service. His father, A. Willis Robertson, served in the U.S. House of Representatives and Senate for 34 years, and was a descendant of Benjamin Harrison (a signer of the Declaration of Independence) and William Henry Harrison and Benjamin Harrison (two presidents of the United States). Robertson's mother, Gladys Churchill Robertson, was related to Britain's wartime prime minister Winston Churchill.

After serving in the Marine Corps during the Korean War, Robertson studied law at Yale University, failed an attempt at the bar exam, and said that he felt "empty" as a "swinging" executive with a Manhattan-based electronics firm. Encouraged by his mother's admonition that he must be born again, Robertson's soul-searching led to a master of divinity degree from New York Theological Seminary in 1959. In November of that year, he left New York with his wife, Dede, and their three children, and drove to Tidewater, Virginia, where he bought a bankrupt television station. Christian Broadcasting Network (CBN) went on the air on October 1, 1961, with religious programming over WYAH-TV, whose call letters were taken from the Hebrew name of God, Yahweh. CBN grew into a television network with owned and operated stations in Portsmouth, Virginia; Atlanta, Georgia (acquired in 1971); Dallas, Texas (in 1973); and Boston, Massachusetts (in 1977).

In the fall of 1963, CBN held its first telethon, asking 700 viewers to join the "700 Club" by pledging $10 a month to meet the ministry's $7,000 in monthly expenses. The success of the strategy led in 1966 to the premier of *The 700 Club*, a daily broadcast of **prayer,** interviews, music, and stories presented in a Christian context. In 1975 the show premiered in Europe and in 1976 it was first broadcast in the Philippines. A year later the program debuted in Japan, Taiwan, and Puerto Rico. Daily broadcasts into Hong Kong began in 1978. In 1979 CBN began 28 hours of weekly programming in Israel, a place of particular interest to Robertson because of his belief that God's end-time or **eschatological** purpose was taking place through the establishment of the state of Israel and events in the Middle East. Four months later, **Billy Graham** dedicated CBN's International Communications Center "to the glory of God" on the site of its first satellite transmission from Israel. By that time, *The 700 Club* had evolved from religious talk to a daily 90-minute news-oriented format. Robertson's engagement with the major issues of the period, including the arms race, activist courts, the sexual revolution, and attacks on the integrity of the family, led to a politicization of his programming and his unsuccessful 1988 bid as a Republican candidate for the presidency of the United States.

Robertson's return to the network in the 1990s stimulated a period of expansion. CBN programming penetrated the former Soviet Union in 1990 with eastern-bloc countries joining the network in 1992 and 1993. During the 1990s, programming spread in Africa and the Caribbean. Beginning in 1995, the network launched WorldReach as an evangelistic outreach in Latin America, Africa, the Muslim world, Europe, India, Indonesia, Southeast Asia, the Philippines, and China. The sale of CBN's Family Entertainment subsidiary in 1997 to the Fox Corporation created $136.1 million in revenue for Robertson and his network, and facilitated new satellite programming in the Middle East and India. As of 2005, Robertson's network produced programming in more than 200 nations and was heard in more than 70 languages, including Russian, Arabic, Spanish, French, and Chinese. Operation Blessing, a companion undertaking, offered humanitarian relief valued at $750 million to 175 million individuals, 50 states, and 96 nations. Regent University, launched by Robertson in 1977, near the site of the network's first earth satellite station, offered training in a number of academic disciplines but gave emphasis to courses in mass communication.

Robertson aroused controversy following the September 11, 2001, terrorist attacks when he concurred on the air with a statement by Rev. **Jerry Falwell** on September 13, 2001, that blamed the attacks on "pagans," "abortionists," "feminists," "gays," the "ACLU" (American Civil Liberties Union), and other groups that had angered God by promoting secularism. Robertson issued a partial retraction the next day, and yet reaffirmed that antireligious groups had removed "the mantle of divine protection" from the United States.

Further Reading: Gerbner, George, Larry Gross, Stewart Hoover, and Nancy Signorielli. *Religion and Television.* Philadelphia: University of Pennsylvania, 1984; Hadden, Jeffrey, and Charles Swann. *Prime Time Preachers.* Reading, MA: Addison-Wesley, 1981; Harrell, David Edwin, Jr. *Pat Robertson: A Personal, Religious and Political Portrait.* San Francisco: Harper and Row, 1987; Linenthal, Edward Tabor. "Pat Robertson." In Charles H. Lippy, ed., *Twentieth-Century Shapers of American Popular Religion,* 349–56. New York: Greenwood Press, 1989; Robertson, Pat. *The End of the Age.* Dallas: Word, 1996; Robertson, Pat. *My Prayer for You.* Old Tappan, NJ: Fleming H. Revell, 1977; Robertson, Pat, and Jamie Buckingham. *Shout It from the Housetops.* Plainfield, NJ: Logos International, 1972; Robertson, Pat, and Bob Slosser. *The Secret Kingdom.* Nashville, TN: Thomas Nelson, 1982.

Bruce J. Evensen

ROMAN CATHOLIC AWAKENINGS IN FRENCH CANADA

The closest that **Roman Catholics** in French Canada have come to a spiritual awakening during their history is the Ultramontane revival of the 1840s. It began in Montreal under the leadership of Bishop Ignace Bourget (1799–1885) of Montreal and spread throughout his vast diocese for over a decade until it became institutionalized in schools, hospitals, charitable organizations, and, after 1850, in the *bleu* (i.e., blue) political party that eventually dominated the political life of

Canada East (i.e., Quebec Province after 1867). It was at its most enthusiastic when, under the influence of Father Charles Chiniquy (1809–1899), it joined itself to the **temperance** movement at the end of the decade.

Schooled in ultramontane thought by his predecessor Jacques Lartigue (1777–1840), the earnest and authoritarian Bourget made it clear soon after becoming bishop that he intended to renew Catholicism in French Canada. He organized a great mission throughout the diocese conducted by Bishop Charles-Auguste de Forbin-Janson (1785–1844), then one of France's most spectacular **preachers.** Between September 1840 and December 1841, Forbin-Janson traveled across Canada East, visiting some 60 villages and preaching rousing two-hour sermons to crowds usually estimated at 5,000–6,000 people. His message was dramatic—a theatrical denunciation of sin, a terror-filled description of hell, and a call for repentance and confession. The climax was a collective act of faith and a Mass followed by the erection of a memorial cross. The cross blessed at Saint-Hilaire before a crowd of 25,000 on October 16, 1841, was 100 feet high, 6 feet wide, and 4 feet deep, so that people could climb ladders to the top. While Forbin-Janson was still in Canada, Bourget left on the first of some five voyages to France and Rome, after each of which he came back with renewed energies for Catholic revival. He arranged for the return to Canada of the Jesuits and Oblates who, along with the Redemptorists, had lately initiated in France the dramatic preaching of eight-day **parish missions.** He brought over the Religious of Sacred Heart, and the Sisters of the Good Shepherd. He founded two Canadian religious congregations of his own, and he organized over the next dozen years a whole series of parish missions that were superbly managed to stir the emotions. He also multiplied great liturgical ceremonies, such as that of the crowning of a holy picture of Saint Anne at Varennes in 1842. There were 4,000 people at that event, 60 priests to hear confessions, and Bourget, in the full splendor of his office, to do the crowning. A salvo of musketry, interrupted by outbursts of cheering, preceded the lighting of huge bonfires.

By the mid-1840s the awakening's greatest preacher was undoubtedly "little Father Chiniquy"—the apostle of temperance. Though a short man, he was attractive and projected an impression of modesty, self-controlled shyness, and, to many, holiness. His gestures were delicate, and his voice, it was said, melted the hardest hearts. When he began to preach he quickly became feverish, stared at his audience, and alternated between tones that recalled angels or demons. His words, it was said, splashed out in an uncontrolled stream that both drowned his listeners in fear and then raised them up to hope and joy. His enthusiasm was Catholic and sacramental, and he insisted that repentance led to confession and Communion. His preaching reinforced the ultramontane ethic that taught submission to the clergy and passivity in political matters.

As parish priest at Beauport, near Quebec City, in March 1840, Chiniquy enrolled some 1,300 of his parishioners in a Temperance Society. He then began a progress across the province that lit a fire of enthusiasm wherever he went. Sometimes he enrolled as many as 17,000 in a single month. By 1849 he had given some 500 sermons in 120 parishes to over 200,000 people and listed some 370,000 **men** and **women** on the rolls of the society. This was almost the whole of the adult Catholic population of the province, the total population of Canada East in 1850 being estimated at 800,000. Not surprisingly, Chiniquy's popularity soon made him attractive to politicians. By 1846 he was being courted by offers hard to resist, especially by the moderate Reformers who would soon found the *bleu* party. They needed help from church authorities to defeat the growing appeal of radical republicans, the *rouge* party, whose anticlericalism troubled Bourget. Chiniquy began to preach against *rouge* anticlerical views and, in 1848, he took the short next step of appearing, then preaching, at political meetings. His voice helped bring the Reformers to power. Between 1848 and 1851 the government of the Reform leader, Sir Louis-Hippolyte LaFontaine, consolidated the alliance of priests and politicians. It gave legal recognition to the Catholic Church's schools, hospitals, and charitable institutions. It also assigned power over these institutions to the clergy.

The 1840s awakening was unprecedented. The only—and remote—parallel was the reaction to the great earthquake that struck Quebec City during the Carnival of 1663. At 5:53 P.M. on February 5 the earth shook with such force that it opened deep fissures in the ground, rocked houses, and diverted streams. The night before, a native woman distinctly heard a voice from beyond announcing terrible and marvelous events for the next day. Later that morning, another "excellent Christian" woman also heard a premonitory voice, deep in the forest this time, announcing strange events for later that day. The earthquake killed no one, but the superior of the Jesuits, Father Jerome Lalemant, saw it as a warning if not a punishment. He preached repentance with such vigor that carnival time became penitential. One priest heard 800 confessions, out of a total white population in New France at that time of about 2,500. These events in French Canada might be considered as religious revivals to the extent that they conveyed an enthusiastic and intense spirituality and strengthened many in the faith.

Further Reading: Monet, Jacques. *The Last Cannon Shot: A Study of French-Canadian Nationalism, 1837–1850.* Toronto: University of Toronto Press, 1969; Pouliot, Léon. *La Réaction Catholique de Montréal, 1840–1841.* Montreal: Le Messager, 1942; Trudel, Marcel. *Chiniquy.* Trois-Rivières, QC: Bien Public, 1955; Voisine, Nive, ed. *Histoire du Catholicisme Québécois.* Vol. 2. Montreal: Boréal, 1991.

Jacques Monet, S. J.

ROMAN CATHOLIC REVIVALS

Roman Catholicism, as Gabriel Garrone noted, "periodically needs an extraordinary thrust of Spring, an irruption of the word of God, a salutary jolt, a prophetic action" (Jean-Francois Motte, Médard Dourmap, *The New Parish Mission* [1962], 12). One form of Catholic revival has been the **parish mission,** developed in the sixteenth and seventeenth centuries in Europe. By the nineteenth century, **men's** religious orders were giving missions to various ethnic groups and to **African Americans** throughout the United States. The goal was to preserve the faith of immigrant Catholics, to reinvigorate piety, to move sinners to a heartfelt repentance, to bring people to the sacraments, and to a resolve to live a holy life and persevere therein. The **preacher** appealed to the heart, so sinners would recognize their waywardness, tremble with the fear of God through sermons on the "four last things" (i.e., death, judgment, heaven, and hell) and awaken to hope and God's love. The U.S. context—with its nonestablishment of religion, reliance upon persuasion, and anti-Catholic sentiment—was conducive to parish missions as a successful form of revival.

Parish missions rested on clergy initiative, a kind of revival from above. Yet by the twentieth century, a theology of the "Mystical Body" (stressing each individual's role in the church) gave rise to vigorous lay Catholic action that included lay street preaching. The Catholic Evidence Guild trained laity to speak publicly about Catholic teachings and to arouse interest in **conversion.** With the emergence of motor vehicles, the parish missions of the nineteenth century evolved into a new form in the twentieth century, known as **motor missions.** In the 1930s and 1940s, **women** from the Catholic Evidence Guild at Rosary College near Chicago held summer revivals outdoors in Oklahoma and other states of the **South.** The women preached from the back of a truck and used several methods associated with clerical street preachers. Some Catholics, critical of this method, compared the women to Protestant revivalists. In the nineteenth century, Isaac Hecker (1819–1888), founder of the Paulists, laid emphasis on the workings of the Holy Spirit as part of missions to non-Catholics. Archbishop John J. Keane (1839–1918) promoted the Confraternity of the Servants of the Holy Spirit as an antidote to materialism and a tool of lay spiritual formation, the fruits of which would influence America. A **Roman Catholic awakening in French Canada** took place through the impassioned oratory of Father Charles Chiniquy (1809–1899), who preached repentance from sin, abstinence from alcohol (or **temperance**), and obedience of laypersons to the clergy. A more pervasive interest in the power of the Holy Spirit came at the time of liturgical and scriptural renewal, which had been occurring since at least the 1920s and which bore fruit in the Second Vatican Council of the 1960s.

In 1967, two Duquesne University faculty members, who were studying the church in the New Testament, were especially impressed by the action of the Holy Spirit. They had read David Wilkerson's *The Cross and the Switchblade* (1964) and were exposed to the **baptism in the Spirit** and **speaking in tongues** in their contact with Protestant **Pentecostals.** In February, the small group that gathered for **prayer** and scripture reading first spoke in tongues and experienced other **charismatic gifts.** About the same time, some faculty and students at Notre Dame and in Ann Arbor also felt a powerful surge of the Holy Spirit. Ralph Martin, Steve Clark, and Kevin and Dorothy Ranaghan were among the early leaders in the Roman Catholic **Charismatic Renewal.** *Catholic Pentecostals* (1969) contained the Ranaghans' description of their experiences. Notre Dame and Ann Arbor became early centers for the formation of Charismatic groups, but the movement spread quickly throughout the United States. Father Edward O'Connor became the theologian of the group and the biblical scholar, Josephine Massyngberde Ford, pointed out a scriptural basis for Pentecostalism. While the movement has had strong lay leadership from the beginning, some critics noted a tendency to follow stereotypical gender roles. Some Charismatics began to live in covenant communities. True House, at Notre Dame, among the first of these, began in 1970. Annual international conferences on the Charismatic Renewal demonstrated the growing strength of Pentecostal phenomena among Catholics.

Catholic Charismatic prayer meetings, often lasting for one or more hours, typically involve praise and thanksgiving to Jesus, petitions for **healing** or other favors from God, scripture reading and reflection, music and **hymns,** prayer, speaking in tongues, and baptism in the Holy Spirit. Charismatic gifts of **prophecy** or wisdom, and testimonies of the Spirit's action in the lives of individuals, are shared in the group. In periods of silence the group listens to and discerns God's Spirit. Members also gather for Charismatic Masses that include charismatic healing, experiences of **deliverance,** and joyous praise. Charismatics are usually involved in various forms of outreach, ranging from spiritual direction to prison ministry. The intensity of Charismatic religious experience was disturbing to some Catholics and surprising to Protestants. In the late 1970s, the movement gained a measure of legitimacy through the advocacy of Leon-Joseph Cardinal Suenens and acceptance by recent Popes. Some Roman Catholic Dioceses have local Charismatic Renewal offices. National magazines, such as *New Covenant* (1971–) and *Catholic Charismatic* (1976–1980), allow for members to communicate their experiences more broadly.

Another revival group, arising in the ferment of Catholic Action, is the Cursillo de Cristianidad (a short course in Christianity), began in Spain in 1949 and was brought to the United States in 1957. Two airmen from Spain training at Lackland Air Force Base, together with Franciscan Father Gabriel Fernandez, gave a weekend Cursillo retreat in Waco, Texas, for **Latino** or Hispanic Catholics. Within a few years, the movement spread across the country and the group's magazine, *Ultreya* (Onward), began in 1959. Until 1961, all Cursillos were given in Spanish. The movement is organized in many dioceses with a national office in Corpus Christi, Texas. While Roman Catholic in origin, other denominations have used the Cursillo format. In the United States, there are about 500,000 *cursillistas*, some of whom have also become active in the Charismatic movement. Cursillo is a three-day, intensive, tightly woven experience of prayer, talks, liturgy, and activities, initiating people into a dynamic appropriation of Christianity. Priest leaders provide talks on the theology of Christian living and lay leaders speak and witness on how the gospel permeates their lives. Leaders work closely with each other as a team. The movement retains Spanish terms for key parts of the experience (*de colores, palanca,* etc.), regardless of what language is used throughout the weekend.

Thursday evening's talks center on knowing oneself, the need for forgiveness, and the "three glances of Christ." A purposeful disorientation of the participant lays the ground for a greater openness to God's grace. Music, including De Colores, accompanied by guitars and other instruments, punctuates the weekend. The theme Friday, considered the

Catholic revivals, in contrast to their Protestant counterparts, typically occur in the context of sacraments, saints' devotions, and church holidays. This photograph shows a feast day procession at San Estevan del Rey Mission in Acoma Pueblo, New Mexico. (Photographer Charles Fletcher Lummis, January 21, 1890.) Courtesy of the Library of Congress.

first day, is proclamation, and includes several *rollo* (small roundtable groups), including groups on the Holy Spirit and piety. The Saturday topics are transformation and becoming a fully responsive Christian. Participants receive *palanca*, expressions of prayer or sacrifice from friends and strangers on behalf of participants, sometimes in the form of personal notes written prior to the Cursillo weekend. The surprise in receiving these highlights the need for practical love and caring. Sunday's talks revolve around ways to live Christian life beyond the weekend, through active participation in the Christian community, identification of a daily spiritual plan, and effecting change in one's environment. The fourth-day talk assists the participant in bridging the weekend into the next days and weeks. Toward the end of the gathering, participants witness to their experience, just as the leaders had witnessed to them. An important follow-up for those

newly initiated is the *ultreya* gatherings or group reunions, which meet weekly or bimonthly, as a form of accountability and as encouragement to keep the spirit alive. The Cursillo has been a particularly effective experience of revival for Hispanic Catholics in the United States and has provided leadership training, a sharpened sensitivity to Hispanic culture, and increased Hispanic male participation in the sacraments and in church ministries.

The literature of Catholic revival groups is often heartfelt and enthusiastic. Each of the groups considered provides a specific way of living one's baptismal call in an intentional manner with a view to ministry in society. With the exception of parish missions, much of the leadership of the revival groups is in the hands of laity. Many groups have experienced a tension between individual spiritual experience and the claims of church authority. Most participants have chosen to remain in the Catholic community and not to separate from it. Yet some Roman Catholics have left the church because they did not find the same spiritual intensity in their parishes that they did in the Charismatic movement.

Other forms of revival occurred in parishes after the initial surge of renewal at the time of the Second Vatican Council. The proliferation of small faith communities, such as Cursillo and the Charismatics, is noted in other national programs beginning in the 1980s, including *Renew* and the North American Forum for Small Christian Communities. While perhaps not thought of as a revival, the reinstatement of the *Rites of Christian Initiation of Adults* (1972) introduced a formation process into Christian life, highlighting community involvement, intensity of religious experience, commitment to Christ, and participation in his mission. Cursillo and the Charismatic renewal carried similar dynamics, for those whose baptism was long ago. Revival among U.S. Roman Catholics has provided a sense of the immediacy of the Holy Spirit, reinsertion into the Catholic community, a new vision of Christian life, accountability for living it, and a desire for the evangelization of nonbelievers.

Further Reading: Dolan, Jay. *Catholic Revivalism: The American Experience, 1830–1900.* Notre Dame, IN:

University of Notre Dame Press, 1978; Mansfield, Patti Gallagher. *As by a New Pentecost: The Dramatic Beginning of the Catholic Charismatic Movement*. Steubenville, OH: Franciscan University Press, 1992; Marcoux, Marcene. *Cursillo: Anatomy of a Movement; The Experience of Spiritual Renewal*. New York: Lambeth Press, 1982: National Conference of Catholic Bishops. *A Pastoral Statement on the Catholic Charismatic Renewal*. Washington, DC: United States Catholic Conference, 1984; National Cursillo Center Web site. http://www.cursillo.org/.

Angelyn Dries, O.S.F.

ROSADO, LEONCIA ROUSSEAU (MAMA LEO)

Leoncia Rosado has been a pioneer Puerto Rican **Pentecostal** pastor in New York City and is the cofounder of the Damascus Christian Church. Born in 1912, in Toa Alta, Puerto Rico, Leoncia was converted during a Pentecostal crusade on the island in 1932. Under the tutelage of her pastor, Vicente Ortiz, she began evangelizing youth throughout the island. Prompted by a **vision** from God in 1935, she migrated to New York City, where she attended **Francisco Olazábal**'s church in Spanish Harlem. After Olazábal's death, the Latin American Council of Christian Churches split into a number of councils or denominations, which, among them, included the Damascus Christian Church founded by Victor and Leoncia Rosado in 1939. The Damascus Christian Church directs its ministry toward drug addicts, prostitutes, alcoholics, and others on the margins of society. The ministry expanded after 1957 when Rosado organized the Damascus Youth Crusade. Rosado's pioneer work among social outcasts in the *barrio* has earned her the nickname "Mama Leo." Her social work attracted the attention of political leaders such as former governor of New York State Nelson Rockefeller. Currently, at 85 years of age, she is still pastoring in New York City and is well known among Puerto Rican and other **Latino** Pentecostals.

Further Reading: Korrol, Virginia Sanchez. "In Search of Unconventional Women: Histories of Puerto Rican Women in Religious Vocations Before Mid-century," *Oral History Review* 16 (1988): 47–63; Villafañe, Eldin. *The Liberating Spirit: Toward an Hispanic American Pentecostal Social Ethic*. Grand Rapids, MI: Eerdmans, 1993.

Gastón Espinosa

S

SALVATION ARMY

The Salvation Army is the largest Protestant social agency in the world and also the largest of the Protestant churches that were organized out of the diverse groups included in the nineteenth-century **Holiness movement.** Its symbols of "blood and fire" express its commitment to a biblical theology centered on the person of Jesus Christ, and its call to radical Christian discipleship through the **sanctifying** and empowering work of the Holy Spirit. The organization's founders were William Booth (1829–1912) and his wife, Catherine Booth (1829–1890). Both had religious backgrounds in the British Wesleyan **Methodism** and the separatist Wesleyan bodies associated with it. After their marriage in 1855, their evangelistic ministry eventually led to them to withdraw from the Methodist New Connexion in 1861 and to serve in a mission in the slums of East London. By that time Catherine had become an active partner with William in public speaking as well as other aspects of the ministry. Encouraged by her spouse and the example of American Holiness evangelist **Phoebe Palmer,** Catherine was soon caught up in her own public ministry in London, having published a defense of **women**'s right to **preach** in 1862. She was especially effective in communicating the movement's vision and values to Britain's upper classes.

The Booths formed the independent Christian Mission in 1869. Because of its aggressive street evangelism, enthusiastic testimonies in worship, gospel songs set to barroom tunes, strong **temperance** stance, and nonsacramental theology, its workers met intense opposition and even persecution from critics in church and society. Nevertheless, the work of the mission expanded rapidly. By 1878, the mission's 57 stations in London and its environs reported thousands of **conversions** and **sanctifications** annually. In the same year, in response to a growing conviction of the Booths that they and their volunteers were engaged in **spiritual warfare** to recapture lost souls enslaved by Satan, they renamed their organization the Salvation Army. They brought every aspect of the mission's administrative structures, theological rhetoric, evangelistic strategies, and missionary vision under military imagery and nomenclature. The group's official paper, the *Christian Mission Magazine*, became the *War Cry* in 1880. Thereafter the organization experienced a period of rapid expansion. In 1880, William Booth, now General Booth, sent George Railton, his personal secretary, and seven women officers to establish a beachhead in the United States. Three years later their work had expanded into a dozen states. Posts were also established in Canada, Australia, France, Switzerland, India, Iceland, and South Africa.

William's book *In Darkest England and the Way Out* (1890) emphasized the increasing attention being given by the Salvationists to the social welfare of poorer urban areas where they served. Catherine Booth died in 1890 and William in 1912. By the time of their deaths, both had been highly honored by church and state leaders around the world.

At the beginning of the twenty-first century, the Salvation Army's worldwide constituency numbered about 2 million, with its international headquarters in London, England. Seventeen thousand officers directed the work of the Army in 109 countries. The Salvation Army has always been a vitalizing force within the Christian Holiness Partnership, a coordinating agency for most of the Wesleyan-Holiness churches and agencies around the world. Since 1927 its office of general has been an elective office. Two women have been elected to that office since then. The largest of the Army's national organizations is the U.S. sector, with a constituency of 450,000. They and hundreds of thousands of volunteer supporters from civic and faith organizations raise more than $1 billion annually in support of the movement's social programs in the United States. Its income exceeds that of any other of the country's nonprofit charitable organizations. Eighty-six percent of the Salvation Army's budget goes directly to the support of its social agencies.

Despite persistent tensions in the Army as it seeks to integrate its ecclesiastical, charitable, and

Street evangelism in San Francisco by a Salvation Army preacher, accompanied by men with an accordion, trumpet, and drum. Nearby stores sell "work clothes" for "union men." (Photographer Dorothea Lange, April 1939.) Courtesy of the Library of Congress.

evangelistic aims, the Army's ability to continue as a conservative Wesleyan-Holiness evangelical church and as a world leader in social services for the poor testifies to the commitment and adaptability of the movement's leadership and its supporting constituency.

Further Reading: Coutts, John. *The Salvationists.* Oxford: Mowbray, 1977; Dieter, Melvin E. *The Holiness Revival of the Nineteenth Century.* 2nd ed. Metuchen, NJ: Scarecrow Press, 1996; McKinley, Edward H. *Marching to Glory: History of the Salvation Army in the United States.* San Francisco: Harper and Row, 1980; Winston, Diane. *Red-Hot and Righteous: The Urban Religion of the Salvation Army.* Cambridge, MA: Harvard University Press, 1999.

Melvin E. Dieter

SANCTIFICATION AND REVIVALS

The theological doctrine of sanctification, sometimes referred to as holiness, Christian perfection, perfect love, the second blessing, or **baptism in the Holy Spirit,** provided a major stimulus to eighteenth- and nineteenth-century American religious revivals. At the same time, critics of revivals seized on a distinctive interpretation of the doctrine—one that highlighted gradual rather than sudden change—to argue against revivalistic activities. During the **transatlantic** revivals of the **Great Awakening,** John Wesley played a pivotal role in renewing interest in sanctification. Wesley taught that Christians could experience what he termed "entire sanctification" or "perfect love": an intense experience of God's love after which the Christian no longer committed intentionally sinful acts. The Holy Spirit testified or gave witness to the experience in part through the believer's emotions, causing the person to feel all love and no sin. Whereas justification liberated the sinner from the guilt of sin through the imputation of Christ's righteousness, sanctification freed the Christian from the pollution and power of sin through the agency of the Holy Spirit. Wesley taught that sanctification, like justification, was a gift from God, but that the Christian should also use the means of grace that God had provided for growth in holiness, including scripture reading, the Lord's Supper, and prayer. Although entire sanctification could take place instantaneously, growth in holiness occurred both before and after the experience, and Christians who ceased striving after holiness could lose their sanctification. Although Wesley himself never professed the attainment of entire sanctification, he began **preaching** the need to pursue perfect love in the 1750s, and he popularized the doctrine through his *Plain Account of Christian Perfection* (1767). British **Methodist** interest in sanctification was at its peak on the eve of Methodist expansion into the American colonies in the revivals of the 1770s–1780s, thereby ensuring the centrality of the doctrine to early American Methodist experience.

As the revivals of the **Second Great Awakening** swept across America, interest in sanctification again peaked, this time through the preaching of the itinerant Methodist revivalist **Phoebe Worrall Palmer.** Beginning in the 1830s, Palmer's Tuesday Meetings for the Promotion of Scriptural Holiness renewed interest in entire sanctification not only within Methodist circles but also in **Reformed** churches. Palmer placed greater emphasis on human effort and less emphasis on "the witness of the Holy Spirit" than did Wesley, teaching that any Christian could follow a definite progression of three steps to receive and keep the second blessing. The first step was the decision of entire consecration, which Palmer described as laying everything on the altar of sacrifice to God. The second step was what she termed naked faith in the Bible's promise that God will receive the consecrated Christian. The final step, without which the sanctified Christian risked losing the blessing, was public testimony of the experience to others. Palmer taught that any Christian could receive sanctification instantaneously without an experience of "the witness by the Spirit." In diminishing the importance of an emotional experience, which Palmer herself did not undergo, Palmer made sanctification more accessible to the rising middle classes of Methodist and Reformed churches, for whom the emotionalism traditionally associated with revivals was objectionable.

The best-known revivalist of the Second Great Awakening, the **Presbyterian** preacher **Charles**

Finney, did not in the early years of the revivals emphasize sanctification, but instead focused on the **conversion** experience. Once the revivals had produced a crop of new converts, Finney increasingly, between 1835 and 1840, began preaching the need for Christians to go on to perfection. Finney, with his colleague **Asa Mahan,** gathered a group around themselves at Oberlin College who, like Wesley and Palmer, promoted entire sanctification. The Oberlin perfectionists departed from Reformed theology in teaching that entire and permanent sanctification is attainable in this life as Christians exercise their will to abstain from sin. Yet, unlike the Wesleyans, who believed that Christians needed divine grace to obey God, Finney and Mahan taught that it was possible fully to obey the moral law through natural human ability. Another difference was that the Wesleyans taught that Christians could only avoid intentionally sinful acts, while Finney and Mahan seemed to assert that freedom even from unintentional sins could be attained.

By the 1850s, Palmer and the Oberlin perfectionists had all begun to link sanctification and baptism in the Holy Spirit, an experience that they viewed as enduing the Christian with power for ministry. The **Revival of 1857–1858** reflected this growing interest in the outpouring of the Holy Spirit in power for service, leading the Presbyterian William E. Boardman to publish his influential book *The Higher Christian Life* (1858). Boardman represented the Reformed view of sanctification that developed in the 1860s, a tradition also known as the Higher Life or the Keswick movement, the latter name referring to the English city that hosted annual, interdenominational conferences to promote sanctification beginning in 1875. Although sharing many concerns with the Wesleyan and Oberlin groups, the Higher Life movement, in keeping with Reformed theology, taught that humans' tendency to sin could be suppressed but not eradicated in this life. According to the Reformed view, no Christian had ever attained, nor could ever hope to achieve, entire sanctification. Higher Life advocates participated in revivals, **camp meetings and tent meetings,** and conferences like the Keswick conventions, cross-pollinating with

the conversion-centered preaching of revivalists like **Dwight Moody** and **Reuben A. Torrey.**

In the post–**Civil War** period, it was the Wesleyans, rather than the Higher Life advocates, who most clearly associated sanctification with revivalistic camp meetings. A group of Methodist ministers called for a national camp meeting at Vineland, New Jersey, in 1867 for the express purpose of promoting entire sanctification. The National Camp Meeting Association for the Promotion of Holiness was founded in 1869, marking the emergence of an interdenominational **Holiness movement.** The 1906 **Pentecostal revival** at **Azusa Street** in Los Angeles drew on the Holiness revival for theology and leadership, and like the earlier movement, it emphasized sanctification, now even more closely associated with the baptism in the Holy Spirit as evidenced by **speaking in tongues.** A sizable minority in the Holiness and Pentecostal movements argued that entire sanctification can cleanse the body of disease as well as sin, since Satan is the author of both, leading to renewed emphasis on divine **healing.** Over the course of the twentieth century, Pentecostals and neo-Pentecostal **Charismatics,** who experienced dramatic revivals in mainline Protestant and **Roman Catholic** churches in the 1960s–1970s, retained their emphasis on the baptism of the Holy Spirit and yet deemphasized the doctrine of sanctification.

Even as interest in sanctification has accompanied religious revivals, at least up through the nineteenth century, opponents of revivals have grounded their critiques in a distinctive view of sanctification. Reformed theologians in particular have envisioned sanctification as a gradual, lifelong work that should not be restricted to sporadic bursts of revival activity. Dependence on revivals, they argued, exhibited too low a view of the Holy Spirit's power to sanctify the ordinary times and spaces of everyday life. This gradualist theology of sanctification provided an alternative to revivals as engines of spiritual growth for such diverse nineteenth-century theologians as **Horace Bushnell,** Charles Hodge, and **John Williamson Nevin.** Whereas one implication of the Holiness-Pentecostal view of sanctification was belief in divine healing, the Reformed doctrine implied that Christians should patiently endure suffering because it was sent by God as a means of sanctification.

Further Reading: Alexander, Donald L., ed. *Christian Spirituality: Five Views of Sanctification; Reformed, Lutheran, Wesleyan, Pentecostal, Contemplative.* Downers Grove, IL: InterVarsity, 1988; Cooley, Steven D. "Possibilities of Grace: Poetic Discourse and Reflection in Methodist/Holiness Revivalism." PhD dissertation, University of Chicago, 1991; Dieter, Melvin E. *The Holiness Revival of the Nineteenth Century.* 2nd ed. Metuchen, NJ: Scarecrow Press, 1996; Dieter, Melvin E., Anthony A. Hoekema, J. Robertson McQuilkin, and John F. Walvoord. *Five Views on Sanctification: Wesleyan, Reformed, Pentecostal, Keswick, Augustinian-Dispensational.* Grand Rapids, MI: Zondervan, 1987; Peters, John Leland. *Christian Perfection and American Methodism.* New York: Zondervan, 1956; Synan, Vinson. *The Holiness-Pentecostal Movement in the United States.* Grand Rapids, MI: Eerdmans, 1971; Taves, Ann. *Fits, Trances, and Visions: Experiencing Religion and Explaining Experience from Wesley to James.* Princeton, NJ: Princeton University Press, 1999.

Candy Gunther Brown

SCANDINAVIAN AMERICAN REVIVALS

see Lutheran, German American, and Scandinavian American Revivals

SECOND COMING (OF JESUS)

see Eschatology and Revivals; Jehovah's Witnesses; Miller, William; Seventh-day Adventists; White, Ellen Gould (Harmon)

SECOND GREAT AWAKENING (ca. 1795–ca. 1835)

The term *Second Great Awakening* (SGA) is used to designate the nationwide Protestant evangelical revivals from the post-Revolutionary period to the 1840s. The SGA reconfigured the social and religious landscape so profoundly that it is often considered the most significant revival in the history of the United States. Due to perceived continuities with the **Great Awakening,** evangelical leaders

labeled the second wave of revivals the Second Great Awakening. Both were spiritual movements that brought **conversion** to the unchurched and reinvigoration to the spiritually apathetic in an atmosphere of radical piety, heightened emotion, and soul-searching **preaching.** Both periods of awakening were "great" in reaching thousands of people. Both resulted in efforts to transform the culture, and both resulted in controversy and schism. Yet there are noticeable differences. The SGA was far more geographically extensive, theologically diverse, and denominationally varied. Indeed, the most significant feature of the SGA was the populist upsurge of revivalist **Baptists** and **Methodists,** who turned the religious landscape topsy-turvy by displacing the once culturally and numerically dominant Congregationalists, **Presbyterians,** and Anglicans of the colonial era to become the two largest Protestant denominations in the United States by 1850.

Several broad developments created an environment conducive to the emergence of the SGA. First, the **transatlantic** evangelicalism of the Great Awakening in the colonies and the Evangelical Revival in Britain highlighted revivals as God's primary means for building the church and extending the church's influence. Devout Protestants **prayed** for and anticipated another "outpouring of the Spirit." In addition, local, episodic revivals traceable to the Great Awakening persisted through the American Revolution and merged into the SGA. Second, political events associated with the American Revolution accelerated the growth of revivalist religion. Challenges to authoritarian political structures gave way to individual liberty and popular sovereignty, and thus opened a wedge for populist, revival-oriented groups whose message of the new birth and individual interpretation of the Bible undercut traditional religious authorities and institutions. Third, disestablishment (i.e., the separation of the churches from government authorization and support) energized evangelicals to compete in a religious free market to win over potential converts by persuasion, often by means of revival. Fourth, a variety of social and political upheavals contributed to the appeal of the SGA. The new nation faced many challenges, such as the uncertainties of an emerging market economy, extensive geographical mobility, the isolation of people living in frontier regions, and a population explosion. Amid these difficulties, evangelical religion, most powerfully communicated through revivals, provided a sense of belonging, spiritual community, individual empowerment, and personal discipline for new converts. Fifth, several direct challenges to the Christian faith galvanized evangelicals to redouble their efforts to save the nation from "infidelity" or freethinking. Enlightenment rationalism, popularized by the writings of Thomas Paine and others, undermined confidence in the Bible and lambasted Christianity as superstition. The French Revolution, with its violence against the church, alarmed American Christians who were uncertain about the direction of their own post-Revolutionary nation. These threats, combined with a general indifference toward religion following the war, heightened clerical fears that evangelical religion and the nation itself were threatened by forces within and without. Evangelicals responded to these fears by praying, preaching, and organizing for revival.

The SGA was a multifaceted, complex phenomenon, characterized by denominational and regional variations and contrasting cultural contexts. The awakening cut a broad swath, affecting such groups as merchants and village farmers in established, stable communities in New England; laborers, artisans, and small shopkeepers in the growing cities of Baltimore, Providence, and Rochester; and plain folk on the western frontier. There was no overarching unity to the SGA, and yet the revival showed some common features.

First, the expansion of a transportation network of roads and canals, stimulated by the push into western territories and a rising market economy, enabled the news and momentum of revival to spread from one area to another. Second, a vast print enterprise, augmented by a rapidly growing postal system, spread the news of revival. Books, tracts, newspapers, pamphlets, and periodicals focused specifically on revivals with the explicit intention of defending, popularizing, and spreading revival to other areas. Third, emotionally stirring

hymns, hymnody, and song played an increasingly important role in revival meetings. Isaac Watts's *Hymns and Spiritual Songs* (1707), used during the Great Awakening to rousing effect, remained popular among many evangelical groups, but this classic hymnal was often supplemented or replaced with songs appropriate to the mood or theological convictions of the revival-minded. Methodist itinerants, for example, used the Wesleyan *A Pocket Hymn-Book*, while the Congregational itinerant **Asahel Nettleton** compiled the hugely popular *Village Hymns* (1824), and frontier church folk created their own spiritual choruses for **camp meetings.**

Fourth, a general aspect of the SGA that merits attention is the increased role of **women.** Female converts outnumbered males, often by a ratio of two to one. There are several reasons for this disparity. Religion offered women public opportunities of service and leadership that were available nowhere else in society. Moreover, traditional wifely submission in the marriage relationship had its theological analogue in the spiritual relationship in which individuals submitted to God. This made evangelical religion seem more culturally appropriate for women than for **men** in this era. The post-Revolutionary cultural environment also deemed women more virtuous than men. Ministers coveted women's prayers, exulted in their conversions, and encouraged their participation in lay religious activities. In some cases, however, the new religious loyalties of women could infuriate a husband, detract from their interest in family, and bring divisions into homes. Women also sensed the call of God to preach. During the first four decades of the nineteenth century, more than 100 women preachers or exhorters from dissenting sects gave voice to what they took as the Spirit's beckoning. Though theologically uneducated, they envisioned themselves as possessed of a gift of **prophecy,** and affirmed that God communicated with them through **dreams, visions,** and voices. Within established evangelical denominations, women played prominent but more conventional support roles as loyal supporters of religious meetings, as "prayer warriors," and as members of "female societies" created for the purpose of spreading the spiritual and organizational aspects of the SGA.

Fifth, the SGA not only resulted in the conversion of thousands of individuals, but expressed itself institutionally. The SGA provided the impetus for nationwide social and political reform, and displayed an activism and energy perhaps unparalleled in American history. Predominant among the **Reformed** denominations in New England and the mid-Atlantic region, a plethora of parachurch and voluntary organizations (missionary, tract, educational, etc.) harnessed the spiritual energy of the awakening into a massive effort to reform society, Christianize the nation, and extend the evangelical message around the world. Sixth, with its emphasis on personal rebirth, the validity of emotions and sentiment in religious life, and human agency in conversion, the SGA contributed significantly to the development of a generic Protestant evangelicalism.

As a regionally describable phenomenon, the SGA may be examined from the perspective of the western frontier, New England, or upstate New York. Admittedly these geographical regions do not neatly correlate with denominational traditions, since Methodist and Baptist expansion knew no geographical boundaries, New England Congregationalists supplied missionary evangelists to the Midwest, and Presbyterians conducted revivals throughout the Atlantic region. Still, the SGA showed distinct regional qualities. The beginnings of the revivals on the frontier date to the late 1780s. Although in some areas of the **South** the Great Awakening extended into the 1780s—making it indistinguishable from the SGA—several noticeable revivals took place in 1787, when more than 4,000 people were converted at a Methodist revival in southern Virginia and a **campus** awakening at Hampden-Sydney College (a Presbyterian school) in Virginia that spread as far west as Kentucky. Yet the **Cane Ridge revival** in Kentucky in August 1801—sometimes called the Great Revival—heralded the beginning of mass conversions and provides a useful marker for the inauguration of the SGA on the frontier.

The Great Revival owed its genesis to **James McGready,** a Presbyterian minister, whose evangelical educational pedigree can be traced back

Theodore Dwight Weld, age 41, in an engraving made from an 1844 daguerreotype. A disciple of Charles Finney, Weld was an abolitionist leader and coauthor of *American Slavery As It Is* (1839) with sisters Sarah and Angelina Grimké, the latter of whom became his wife. Courtesy of Dr. Keith J. Hardman.

several generations to **William Tennent'**s Log College, a breeding ground for New Side Presbyterian revivalists of the Great Awakening. McGready's stirring evangelical **Calvinist** preaching to Scotch-Irish and Scottish Presbyterian congregations resulted in revivals in North Carolina and Logan County, Kentucky. McGready played a role in popularizing the camp meeting—itself a revision of Presbyterian "sacramental occasions" or **holy fairs**—when he organized the successful Gasper River camp meeting revival in July 1800. The following August, **Barton Stone,** a fellow Presbyterian who attended the Gasper River meeting, followed McGready's lead and organized a camp meeting at Cane Ridge. An interdenominational affair of Presbyterians, Baptists, and Methodist—groups occasionally cooperating but increasingly competing with one another—the revival at Cane

Ridge was a defining moment in American Christianity. Attended by up to 25,000 people, the revival displayed raw emotion and physical energy never before witnessed on such a massive scale. People groaned, wept, sang, fell down, **shouted, laughed, danced,** jerked, barked, and generally exhibited a wide range of **bodily manifestations.** Whether judged as rampant fanaticism or as an authentic outpouring of the Holy Spirit, Cane Ridge defined the direction of southern evangelicalism. Presbyterians and Baptists repudiated the wild excesses of the revival, but the camp meeting became a primary recruiting device among Baptists and especially Methodists. In 1811 alone, Methodists held over 400 camp meetings. The Presbyterians continued to make institutional gains, but their growth was limited by internal conflicts that resulted in the separations of the **Cumberland Presbyterians** and the **restorationist or Stone-Campbell movement.** Also hampering the Presbyterians was an insistence upon an educated clergy, and an organizational structure that proved unwieldy in frontier settings.

Because of their zeal and organizational structure, the Methodists were best suited to extend revivalist religion into the continuously expanding frontier. Any discussion of the Methodist contribution to the SGA must begin with **Francis Asbury** (1745–1816), the father of American Methodism. Asbury arrived from England in 1771 and assumed leadership of a small movement in 1772. Like John Wesley, Asbury itinerated throughout his career, traveling 300,000 miles on horseback, crossing the Allegheny Mountains no less than 62 times. His disciplined, abstemious life epitomized the missionary zeal of early American Methodism. Under Asbury's direction, Methodism became America's most significant large-scale popular religious movement of the antebellum period. With fewer than 1,000 members in 1770, Methodists numbered over 250,000 in 1820; by 1850 they had captured 34 percent of the total church membership in the United States. Three major factors—meticulous organization, the camp meeting, and an Arminian theology that stressed the human will—account for Methodism's spectacular gains.

The genius of the Methodist system lay in its organization. Asbury gathered Methodists into circuits, assigning itinerants to frontier regions and ministers to more settled areas. By 1796 the country was divided into districts, each overseen by a presiding elder. The system was at once autocratic and flexible. Asbury, the superintendents, and other bishops could make on-the-spot decisions to assign personnel and other resources where most needed. A mobile band of uneducated, single, youthful males served 200-mile circuits as itinerant preachers. They preached a simple, often extemporaneous message of sin, salvation, and sanctification, with a "holy knock-'em down power."

Camp meetings, the great vehicle of Methodist expansion, were planned with meticulous care, from the choice of campsite to the layout of benches and tents to the choice of leaders (preachers, exhorters, testifiers, etc.) and activities (songs, love feasts, etc.). **Conversion** and church connection were the primary intention of the camp meeting, but for many frontier plain folk, the camp meeting also provided social opportunities, and perhaps more importantly, a sense of place and a feeling of control over one's life. Although the camp meeting was used extensively and effectively on the frontier, it became a Methodist trademark throughout the United States during the 1800s.

The Methodists' Arminian theology and emphasis on enthusiastic religion appealed to many. Emphasizing God's love, free grace, the ability to accept or reject the gift of salvation, and a life of **sanctification** (or perfection), Methodist preachers offered an egalitarian message that was widely popular among the masses. Early Methodists also affirmed emotional expression and contact with the supernatural. Shouting, fainting, dreams, and visions typified, but were not exclusive to, frontier religion, and were widely practiced among socially marginal people such as women and **African Americans.** These were interpreted as tangible evidence of the Spirit's work.

Among Baptists, the ripple effect of the Great Revival resulted in immediate growth, doubling their numbers in Kentucky to over 10,000 by 1803. A half century earlier, the enthusiastic piety of the

Great Awakening in New England had been transplanted in the southern backcountry of Virginia and the Carolinas by Separate Baptist missionaries from New England. When combined with the existing presence of the creedally rigorous and emotionally restrained Regular (i.e., Calvinistic or Reformed) Baptists, the result was a distinctive blend of revivalism and orthodox Calvinism among the Baptists in the region.

Like the Methodists, Baptists made extensive use of the camp meeting and lay preachers. The critical figure in the surge of Baptist growth on the frontier was the farmer-preacher. A man of humble origins and limited education, this hardscrabble farmer had typically been converted and baptized by an itinerant evangelist, and subsequently sensed a call to preach. Following the apostolic precedent of self-support, the unpaid Baptist preacher-farmer gathered a congregation in the local area, obtained a license to preach, and was ordained. This pattern was repeated, as other candidates sprang from these congregations, held revival meetings, and gathered new followers. Unlike Methodist episcopacy and Presbyterian polity, Baptist congregational autonomy offered freedom of movement on the ever-expanding frontier. With explosive growth in the west and continued gains back east, Baptists represented 20 percent of the total church membership in the United States by 1850.

The emotionally charged, experienced-based, and conversion-oriented faith of Methodists and Baptists took hold not only among whites but also among the slave population of the South. Baptists, with their emphasis on instant conversion, and Methodists, with their stress on the Holy Spirit, tapped into a deep spiritual reservoir among African Americans. The spiritual explosion of the SGA reverberated so completely throughout the African American community that by 1815 evangelical Christianity had become dominant. Yet blacks embraced Christianity on their own terms, fusing it with indigenous African practices and creating their own faith of survival and hope.

Precisely when and where the SGA began among New England Congregationalists is uncertain, but reports of scattered revivals surfaced in the early 1790s. In 1792, for example, Alvin Hyde in Lee, Massachusetts, reported "a marvelous work" at his church and in the surrounding area that continued for nearly 18 months. By the turn of the century, hundreds of revivals had spread throughout New England, most notably to northwestern Connecticut, western Massachusetts, and the sparsely settled regions of Vermont and New Hampshire. In addition to churches, **colleges** became hotbeds of revival. Beginning in 1802, under the ministrations of President **Timothy Dwight,** successive revivals visited Yale College over a period of decades. Other New England colleges such as Williams, Amherst, and Dartmouth experienced waves of revival up through the 1830s.

Led primarily by New Divinity or Edwardsean pastors—the self-designated heirs of **Jonathan Edwards**—the SGA in New England was largely the effort of settled ministers who organized extensive "concerts of prayer," led common or "circular" fasts, and joined in alliances with one another for prayer, mutual encouragement, regular pulpit exchanges, and team preaching or revival tours. Some ministers such as Edward Dorr Griffin, Timothy Dwight, **Lyman Beecher,** Asahel Nettleton (who saw as many as 30,000 conversions), and **Nathaniel Taylor** excelled in revivalist preaching, but all Edwardseans defended and promoted revivals and heartfelt, "affectionate," or "experimental" religious experience as a legitimate expression of the Holy Spirit. Theologically, the Edwardseans revised Reformed theology into a handmaiden of revival and missionary outreach by insisting on the necessity of the new birth, calling for immediate repentance, exhausting all "means of grace," and advocating the unlimited sufficiency of the atonement. Much of this revision centered in recalibrating the relationship between divine grace and human activity. Increasingly, though not without debilitating and dividing the Edwardsean movement, the theology of conversion among Edwardseans shifted toward a heightened emphasis on the human will and human initiative in salvation.

Charles Finney (1792–1875), the greatest revivalist of the SGA, was more a product than the creator of revival. Born in Connecticut and raised in the small towns of central New York, Finney apprenticed briefly for the legal profession in Adams, New York, when a dramatic conversion in 1821 changed the course of his life. Finney soon became a rising star within Presbyterian and Congregationalist circles. A gifted speaker with an intuitive knack for publicity, Finney toured the **Burned-Over District** of New York and the major cities on the East Coast from 1825 to 1835, reaching thousands with the message of the new birth. At the 1830–1831 revival in Rochester, Finney reached the height of his evangelistic career and gained international fame. An estimated 100,000 to 200,000 new members were added to church rosters in Rochester and outlying areas.

Although Finney formulated his theology in Edwardsean language, his controversial "new measures" and theological revisions challenged Reformed practices and orthodoxy. Impressed by Methodist successes, he made extensive use of "protracted meetings," called the convicted to the "mourners' bench" or "anxious bench" (related to the later **altar call**), and permitted women to testify in public meetings. Finney's aggressive evangelism also connected personal conversion, "disinterested benevolence" (a self-sacrificial commitment to the common good), and entire sanctification to social renovation, including support for **temperance** and **abolitionism.** Extending Edwardsean theological revisions even further, he rejected such traditional Calvinistic teachings as the imputation of Adam's sin to all humanity (i.e., the doctrine that all persons are born in the guilt of Adam's sin) and the doctrine of Christ's limited atonement (i.e., that Jesus died only for the elect or those predestined to salvation). While not denying the sinfulness of all persons, he highlighted free moral agency and insisted that Jesus died for all persons. Aided by the Holy Spirit, penitent sinners can "change their own hearts." Finney also argued that revival is "not a miracle," but essentially a human activity and the result of "the right use of the constituted means" (Finney, *Lectures* [1960], 13). His views of revival as a humanly calculated, predictable event repre-

sented a radical and controversial turn from the traditional understanding that God alone awakens sinners to new life. Finney left full-time evangelism in 1835 to become a professor and then president of Oberlin College, but he continued evangelistic tours into the 1840s and 1850s, cooperating with Methodists, **Free Will Baptists,** and other like-minded evangelical groups.

Further Reading: Boles, John B. *The Great Revival, 1787–1805: The Origins of the Southern Evangelical Mind.* Lexington: University Press of Kentucky, 1972; Brekus, Catherine A. *Strangers and Pilgrims: Female Preaching in America, 1740–1845.* Chapel Hill: University of North Carolina Press, 1998; Bruce, Dickson D., Jr. *And They All Sang Hallelujah: Plain-Folk Camp-Meeting Religion, 1800–1845.* Knoxville: University of Tennessee Press, 1974; Hambrick-Stowe, Charles E. *Charles G. Finney and the Spirit of American Evangelicalism.* Grand Rapids, MI: Eerdmans, 1996; Hatch, Nathan O. *The Democratization of American Christianity:* New Haven, CT: Yale University Press, 1989; Heyrman, Christine Leigh. *Southern Cross: The Beginnings of the Bible Belt.* New York: Knopf, 1997; Kling, David W. *A Field of Divine Wonders: The New Divinity and Village Revivals in Northwestern Connecticut, 1792–1822.* University Park: Pennsylvania State University Press, 1993. Wigger, John H. *Taking Heaven by Storm: Methodism and the Rise of Popular Christianity in America.* New York: Oxford University Press, 1998.

David W. Kling

SERPENT- AND FIRE-HANDLING BELIEVERS

The handling of poisonous serpents and fire—specifically the exposing of hands, feet, arms, and necks to the flames of alcohol- and kerosene-filled lamps, propane torches, and hot coals—occurs most often among certain **Holiness** and **Pentecostal** groups in Georgia, Alabama, Tennessee, Virginia, Kentucky, and West Virginia. Serpent handling and fire handling are two of the **signs** affirmed within these groups based on their literal interpretations of biblical passages such as Mark 16:17–18, Isaiah 43:2, Hebrews 11:33–34, 1 Peter 1:7, and Daniel 3:20–27. The handling of serpents and fire by Christians in North America is a relatively recent development when compared to similar practices that have existed for centuries among some Egyptian and Indian religious sects.

The origin of serpent and fire handling among the "sign followers" is unclear. The communities that practice it draw from the nineteenth-century Holiness movement and the earlier eighteenth-century **Methodist** doctrine of Christian perfection or entire **sanctification.** Yet the practice of serpent handling in the **South,** and specifically **Appalachia,** has been traced back no earlier than the first decade of the twentieth century. Whether this form of serpent and fire handling began with George Went Hensley in east Tennessee remains uncertain. Yet by the late 1800s, some of the foundational beliefs underlying this practice had been established in the South, namely, a literal approach to biblical interpretation and a strong devotion to tradition. Early serpent handlers were members of several Fundamentalist religious organizations, but later formed independent Pentecostal Holiness churches.

Individuals may be moved to handle serpents and fire through a deliberate faith decision, or through a more spontaneous spiritual "anointment." The anointing—in which God's Spirit descends on, enters, possesses, fills, and baptizes an individual—is manifested in behaviors that vary among individuals and in different church services. Some receive the "blessing" to handle serpents but not fire. Others receive the anointing to handle fire, drink strychnine, or to speak words of **prophecy.** One believer's spiritual experience may last only a few seconds, while another's may extend over a longer period of time. No two experiences are the same. The anointing can occur at any time during a church service and may be initiated by the Spirit in a number of ways, which may include the singing of a favorite gospel song, hearing or **preaching** a moving sermon, the laying of hands on the sick, or the administering of foot washing. Whatever the activity that precipitates the anointing and the spiritual behavior, serpent-handling believers always attribute their experiences to an unshakable faith in the initiative and activity of the Holy Spirit.

Dewey Chafin of Jesus' Church, Jolo, West Virginia, holds a serpent box containing rattlesnakes. The box bears paintings of snakes by Eleanor Dickinson (1981). Copyright by and courtesy of Eleanor Dickinson.

By the 1930s the handling of serpents during some church services had grown to such an extent that leaders in various communities began passing laws prohibiting the practice. In 1936, the city of Bartow, Florida, was the first to pass an ordinance that prevented individuals from handling poisonous reptiles. The Florida ordinance was enacted after a man named Alfred Weaver died of a serpent bite that he received during a revival service at a Pentecostal church. In 1940, Kentucky enacted a similar law, and Georgia, Virginia, Tennessee, North Carolina, and Alabama soon followed. West Virginia was unable to pass similar legislation and is the only state within the Appalachian region today that does not prosecute serpent handlers for their religious practice.

Some serpent- and fire-handling believers find their spiritual calling early in life, while others

Men handling rattlesnakes in a church service featuring a literal practice of the words of Mark 16:18: "They shall take up serpents" (1981). Copyright by and courtesy of Eleanor Dickinson.

discover it much later. Those who handle serpents and fire understand the dangers they face. Their religious practices are often passed from one generation to another through a continuous cycle in which children watch and imitate their parents' activities during the church services, eventually participating alongside them, although some may choose not to follow in their parents' footsteps.

Further Reading: Burton, Thomas. *Serpent-Handling Believers.* Knoxville: University of Tennessee Press, 1993; Covington, Dennis. *Salvation on Sand Mountain: Snake Handling and Redemption in Southern Appalachia.* Reading, MA: Addison-Wesley, 1995; Kimbrough, David. *Taking Up Serpents.* Chapel Hill: University of North Carolina Press, 1995; Schwartz, Scott W. *Faith, Serpents, and Fire: Images of Kentucky Holiness Believers.* Jackson: University Press of Mississippi, 1999.

Scott W. Schwartz

SEVENTH-DAY ADVENTISTS

The Seventh-day Adventists are a Protestant denomination with roots in the Millerite movement, based on the **eschatological** teachings of **William Miller.** The Millerite movement may be seen as an outgrowth of the **Second Great Awakening** of the early 1800s. The name "Adventist" reflects the expectation of a literal, premillennial Second Coming (or Advent) of Jesus Christ. "Seventh-day" refers to observance of the Sabbath on the seventh day of the week, or Saturday. Adventists are evangelical in holding that eternal life cannot be merited, but is received only as a free gift through faith in Christ. They rest from ordinary work on the Sabbath as an outward sign of the inward spiritual rest in Christ's gift of salvation (Hebrews 4:1–3, 9–10) and in obedience to the

Ten Commandments (Exodus 20:8–11). Both revivalism and **restorationism**—which sought a return to apostolic Christianity—influenced the development of Adventism. Of the three cofounders of the Seventh-day Adventists, Joseph Bates and James White had been nurtured in the restorationist Christian Connection, and **Ellen G. White** had been raised **Methodist** before accepting the message of William Miller.

Miller's influence and teaching was essentially revivalist. He never intended to start new denominations, but only to awaken spiritually sleeping Christians. His expectation of the Second Coming of Christ around the year 1843, later revised to 1844, was a dearly held conviction for him for revivalist reasons: he considered the returning Jesus to be his dearest friend and wanted others to have the same experience. After the Millerites' "Great Disappointment," when there was no visible sign of Jesus' return in 1843–1844, their restorationist convictions led them to further Bible study and to adopting New Testament practices not maintained by most Christians. These practices included baptism by immersion, foot washing as a religious ordinance, and observing Sabbath on Saturday. Despite these minority views, if the aim of revivalism is personal religious awakening, leading to changed life, then Adventists remain a revivalist-restorationist body.

An obsession with evangelistic success to the neglect of personal piety and genuine **conversion** led some Adventist evangelists in the 1860s and 1870s to adopt a confrontational, debating style. This method produced converts who were characterized more by self-reliant rule-keeping than by a deep, heart-changing love for Jesus Christ. By the 1880s, this emphasis had given the denomination a pervasive tendency toward legalism. Seeking to counteract this trend, Ellen White urged the need for authentic revival. In this effort she was joined by two young **preachers** and editors, E. J. Waggoner and A. T. Jones, who called on Adventists to repent of their self-righteousness and to rely on Christ alone for **holiness** and salvation. They still upheld the law of God, but gave supremacy to the cross of Christ. Despite initial opposition at a conference in

1888, the new emphasis on grace profoundly influenced later Adventist revivals.

Other aspects of Adventist revivalism include a stress on health and education. While many Christians view healthful living as a matter of personal preference, Adventists see it as a religious obligation based on the teaching of 1 Corinthians 6:19–20 that the Christian's body belongs to God and is "a temple of the Holy Spirit." This led to the development of a global network of 561 health-care institutions and 27 health-food manufacturing plants as of 2002. Concern for their young prompted the development of Adventist schools that in 2002 included more than a million students in 5,600 schools, ranging from the elementary to university levels.

Seventh-day Adventists in the twenty-first century still retain some of the practices of classic American revivalism, such as **camp meetings,** tent evangelism, **altar calls,** and a circuit-riding approach to pastoral ministry. The "amen" as a response of agreement and solidarity with the preacher is still widely used in North America, but with greater enthusiasm and variety of expression among **African American** and **Latino** Adventists than among predominantly Caucasian congregations. Moreover, because of the widespread use of satellite television in evangelism, the satellite dish has largely replaced the tent as the iconic symbol of Adventist evangelism. In 2003, Adventists numbered about 1 million in North America, and 13 million worldwide.

Further Reading: Knight, George R. *A Search for Identity: The Development of Seventh-day Adventist Beliefs.* Hagerstown, MD: Review and Herald, 2000; Schwarz, Richard W., and Floyd Greenleaf. *Light Bearers: A History of the Seventh-day Adventist Church.* Rev. ed. Nampa, ID: Pacific Press, 2000; *Seventh-day Adventist Encyclopedia.* 2 vols. Hagerstown, MD: Review and Herald, 1996; *Seventh-day Adventist Yearbook 2004.* Silver Spring, MD: General Conference of Seventh-day Adventists, 2004.

Jerry Moon

SEYMOUR, WILLIAM J. (1870–1922)

William J. Seymour was the key leader in the **Azusa Street revival** as well as the founder and pastor of the Apostolic Faith Mission in Los

Angeles, California, from 1906 to 1922. From the very beginning, services at the mission on Azusa Street blazed into dramatic revival, drawing visitors from around the world, and making the Azusa Street revival a primary catalyst for the early expansion of the **Pentecostal** movement—a global force in twentieth-century Christianity. William Seymour was born in 1870 in Centerville, Louisiana. He was the oldest among four children born to Simon and Phillis Seymour. Both parents had once been slaves. Seymour learned to read and write, although he was provided with little formal education. Information about Seymour's early years is scarce, but we know that he identified with the spirituality of his **African American** Christian heritage. He enjoyed the music and lyrics of the African American **spirituals,** experienced **visions** from God, and studied Bible prophecies related to **eschatology** and Jesus' Second Coming.

In 1895, Seymour moved to Indianapolis, Indiana, center of the prewar Underground Railroad system for helping fugitive slaves to freedom. He worked as a hotel waiter, and joined the **Methodist** Episcopal Church. More than other largely white denominations at the time, they sought an active outreach to blacks. Cincinnati, Ohio, became Seymour's home in 1900. He joined the Church of God Reformation Movement (Evening Light Saints), a progressive interracial church. While in Cincinnati, he contracted smallpox, which he interpreted as the result of his disobedience to accept the call to ministry. Smallpox left him with facial scarring and a loss of sight in his left eye. Through this ordeal, Seymour submitted to ministerial ordination with the Evening Light Saints, and became a traveling evangelist.

Seymour traveled to Houston, Texas, in 1903 in an effort to locate family members who had been separated during the era of slavery. While establishing his family connections, he made Houston his base of operations. In 1905, Seymour was introduced to **Charles F. Parham,** a **Holiness** evangelist and founder of the Apostolic Faith movement. Seymour gave Parham entrance into the black community, where they ministered together. In turn, Parham allowed Seymour to attend his short-term

Bible school in December 1905. Parham's complicity with local Jim Crow laws denied Seymour a seat in the classroom, but Seymour listened from outside the open door. Seymour found his mentor's teaching to be compatible with his own Wesleyan Holiness convictions, except for Parham's unconventional view of **baptism in the Holy Spirit.** Since 1901, Parham had taught that **speaking in tongues** was the evidential sign of Spirit baptism. Holiness teaching generally allowed for the experience of Spirit baptism, but no specific evidential sign was recognized. Parham's efforts to promote his doctrinal position had met with only limited success, although the Houston area looked like a promising mission field. Seymour's attraction to Parham's message seemed insignificant at the time, but would prove to have far-reaching consequences.

While Seymour's doctrinal convictions were taking shape in Houston, a group of Holiness believers in Los Angeles were in search of a pastor. Their home group had enlarged, leading them to establish a mission on Santa Fe Avenue. Their experience was but a microcosm of a broader phenomenon sweeping through the Holiness churches of the city. As a result of close Los Angeles connections with key leaders of the Welsh revival of 1904–1905, intense anticipation of revival preoccupied many Los Angeles Holiness believers. The group on Santa Fe Avenue shared this longing, but needed a pastor to lead them. Seymour's name surfaced through a personal recommendation, and he was recruited for the position. On February 22, 1906, Seymour arrived in Los Angeles, and reported for pastoral duties at the Santa Fe Avenue mission. Seymour **preached** daily, but met with immediate resistance from the group. His Spirit baptism and tongues emphasis, learned from Parham, did not gain acceptance from most his audience. Within four days, the mission doors had been padlocked and Seymour found himself without a job or place to stay. Edward Lee offered Seymour temporary residence in his home, and the rejected preacher began a season of **fasting** and **prayer** in search of future direction.

Not everyone had been resistant to Seymour's message. The Asberry family, living at 214 Bonnie Brae Street, invited Seymour to move into their

Rev. William J. Seymour, leader of the Azusa Street revival and pastor of the Azusa Street Apostolic Faith Mission of Los Angeles. Courtesy of Flower Pentecostal Heritage Center, Springfield, MO.

home and begin worship services there. Interest in the meetings began to grow. Within two months, Seymour went from rejection to respect. He had gained a reputation as a man of prayer, and his leadership potential began to be recognized. Attendance mounted at the home meetings. The need was apparent for a more adequate meeting place. A facility was secured at 312 Azusa Street. Used as a place for storage, the building earlier had served as a church building for an **African Methodist Episcopal Church** (AMEC) congregation. The meeting place was downstairs, as makeshift seating was arranged on the dirt floor. Upstairs, a prayer room was prepared, known as the "Pentecostal upper room." Seymour's living quarters were also upstairs.

The Apostolic Faith Mission, as the church congregation was named officially, was strategically located in light of the function that the congregation and its building were soon to serve. Situated in an industrial area in the original black district of Los Angeles, the mission building was an ideal setting for crowds to come and go freely at all hours, and for the sounds of exuberant worship to penetrate the vicinity without disturbing anyone. The facility's humble conditions ensured that no one would feel too lowly or poor to step inside. One's appearance did not matter at the mission.

After much cleaning and repair, services began at the mission starting on April 14, 1906, which was the day before Easter Sunday. More than a hundred people attended the first meeting. Interest escalated, and crowds soon began to flock to Azusa Street. A *Los Angeles Times* article, sensationalizing the events at the mission, appeared on April 18, 1906—the same day as the San Francisco earthquake in which more than 10,000 people perished. It seemed to some that the end-times had arrived, with the Pentecostal manifestations at Azusa Street as a sign of Jesus' Second Coming. Such speculations served to arouse curiosity and intensify interest in the revival. After only a month in operation, the mission was receiving a multitude of visitors from virtually every race, class, and nationality on earth. Services convened three times a day, and sometimes, especially on weekends, they merged into one continuous service, night and day. During peak periods, 800 people would often be jammed into the building, with another 500 waiting outside to get in. The revival intensity achieved at the Azusa Street meetings was not just a passing fancy. The high level of activity and attendance was sustained for three years, well into 1909. People converged on the mission desiring **conversion, sanctification,** and, especially, baptism in the Holy Spirit. No one wanted to miss their opportunity to receive the "new tongues." **Prophetic** messages were delivered at the meetings. Miracles of **healing** were commonly reported. The walls of the building were soon lined with discarded crutches, braces, and other medical paraphernalia, serving as proof to participants that a healing God was present in the meetings.

At the helm of this revival was William Seymour. His nondirective leadership style allowed the services to unfold spontaneously. No order of service was needed. Although decisive and capable of intervening when necessary, he was content to supervise the proceedings from behind the scenes, following what he took to be the guidance of the Holy Spirit. With no time constraints, the various components of the service would emerge unplanned. Singing might give way to testimonies or prophecies. Preaching might come forth from three or four speakers. Seymour often preached, but he was comfortable sharing his pulpit with others. Sometimes silence would fall upon the crowd. At other times the noise would be deafening, and **shouts** and cries would supercharge the atmosphere. On occasion Seymour placed himself in an empty wooden crate that served both as a makeshift pulpit and as a hiding place for prayer during the meetings. Seymour often worked his way through the crowd, laying on hands for people to receive the Spirit's manifestations. He moved amid the crowd, exhorting people to victory. He saw himself not as controlling the revival, but as serving it.

The revival at Azusa Street exhibited many spiritual manifestations, especially speaking in unknown tongues. Yet Seymour identified the key to revival in the experience of Jesus' love, producing unity, harmony, and unconditional acceptance among all of God's people. At Azusa Street, diverse races and classes of people freely worshipped together and ministered to one another. Seymour insisted upon an atmosphere of equality at Azusa Street, reminding the participants that God is no respecter of persons. In Seymour's view, "the blood of Jesus" (i.e., Jesus' atoning death on the cross) had abolished all divisions among people, whether of race, class, or gender. The spiritual manifestations at the Azusa Street Mission were a result of God's people coming together in unity. Charles Parham had taught that speaking in unknown tongues is the "Bible evidence" of legitimate Pentecostal experience. Seymour adopted Parham's teaching, but recognized that someone speaking in tongues while harboring pride and prejudice does not manifest God's presence and blessing. While Parham's

Pentecostalism tended toward a narrow dogmatism, Seymour's stressed a loving inclusiveness. During the 1910s and 1920s, Pentecostalism became denominationally institutionalized and changed in its ethos. Most white Pentecostals by the 1920s had adopted Parham's dogmatic style, though African American Pentecostals generally retained much of Seymour's original vision. Because of a failure to understand the Azusa Street revival and its inclusive spiritual community, many white Pentecostals did not see any inconsistency between the "initial evidence" of speaking in tongues and the practice of racial segregation. Moreover, most white Pentecostals—at least up to recent decades—regarded Charles Parham, and not William Seymour, as the father of the Pentecostal movement.

Seymour's and Parham's differences could not have been more poignantly illustrated than in Parham's visit to Azusa Street in October 1906. Seymour invited his Houston mentor to come to Los Angeles to seek his assistance in the possible expansion of the revival to other areas of the city. Seymour did not anticipate Parham's negative reaction upon arriving. The Azusa Street service was anything but a true revival for Parham. He was repulsed by the spontaneity and diversity of expression characterizing the Azusa worship, and was offended by the open intermingling of blacks and whites in the service. Without regard for Seymour's role and authority, Parham seized the pulpit and proceeded to denounce in scathing and racially disrespectful language the behavior that he was witnessing. Parham acted as if he were in charge of the mission, and he attempted to shut down the meeting. Seymour and his team went into action. The takeover attempt was rebuffed, and Parham was removed from the premises. Unwilling to exit gracefully where he was not wanted, Parham set up rival meetings nearby, thinking that he could destroy the revival by stealing the flock. After four months of unsuccessful subversion, Parham gave up and left Los Angeles, though he continued to criticize the revival. In contrast, Seymour refused to utter unkind words against his former mentor. After these events in Los Angeles, Parham's influence and reputation declined. Shortly after leaving Los Angeles, Parham was charged in a San Antonio, Texas court with committing sodomy (i.e., a homosexual act) with a young male hymn singer. Although the charge was later dropped, Parham's reputation was damaged and he never regained his former influence.

Meanwhile, during late 1906 and through 1907 and 1908, revival continued unabated at Azusa Street. The publicity engendered by the newspaper—the *Apostolic Faith*, published upstairs at the mission—encouraged high attendance at the meetings. Seymour and his staff wrote articles containing firsthand accounts of the revival, describing events they regarded as miracles. During the peak years, more than 50,000 copies of each monthly issue went out. Revival reports were of particular interest among leaders and members of the Holiness denominations. Readers took great interest in reports of spiritual manifestations, and many were motivated to travel great distances to witness for themselves the revival occurrences. Upon arriving, many white visitors reported that they had to overcome attitudes of pride and prejudice that blocked their way to receiving God's blessings. The Azusa Street "alumni" became missionaries of the revival, spreading good news to others, and giving shape to an emerging Pentecostal movement. The number who went out from Azusa Street as missionaries has never been tabulated, but Pentecostal missions took root in at least 50 countries as a direct result of the revival. In the United States, the revival spread rapidly within Holiness denominations, which generally found that they could not remain neutral toward the new Pentecostalism. Some Holiness organizations embraced the revival, altering their theology and restructuring their practices to become Pentecostal. Others resisted it, and had to stand against the Pentecostal revival to legitimate their own identity.

In 1909 Seymour married Jennie Evans Moore, who had been a part of the original Bonnie Brae Street group and had labored alongside Seymour in ministry. A capable minister in her own right, she effectively led the mission while her husband was traveling. After Seymour's death in 1922, Jennie pastored the church, continuing in that role until 1931. Yet Seymour's marriage in 1909 was not a happy occasion for everyone at the mission. Another charter member, Clara Lum, editor of the *Apostolic Faith* newspaper, strongly disapproved of the marriage. Possibly influenced by a romantic interest in Seymour, and disappointment over the loss of a marriage prospect, Lum abruptly decided to leave the mission after Seymour married Moore. Lum moved to Oregon, taking with her the national and international mailing lists of the newspaper without Seymour's permission. His repeated efforts to retrieve the mailing list proved unsuccessful, including legal action. As a consequence, the newspaper's readership lost touch with the events transpiring in Los Angeles. The attendance and intensity at the services began to decline after 1909. A rebound was underway until a failed takeover attempt by William Durham in 1911 forced a temporary closing of the mission. When the mission reopened, attendance remained low.

After 1911, Pentecostalism was expanding and forging its own identity apart from the Azusa legacy. Seymour stayed at the helm of the mission, seeking to restore interest and vitality, but he found himself increasingly disenfranchised from the movement he had helped to create. He was disheartened at Pentecostalism's emerging racial segregation. In an effort to prevent a white takeover of his largely black congregation, he reluctantly decided that only an African American was to be appointed as leader at the Azusa Street Mission. By 1922, Seymour was tired and worn. Only 20 persons regularly attended the mission's services. The leader of the Azusa Street revival would attend conventions, and sit among the congregation, and not be recognized from the platform. He suffered a heart attack and died in 1922, at age 52. Seymour's followers believed that he died of a broken heart.

Further Reading: Bartleman, Frank. *Azusa Street*. Plainfield, NJ: Logos International, 1980; Connelly, James T. "William J. Seymour." In Charles H. Lippy, ed., *Twentieth-Century Shapers of American Popular Religion*, 381–87. New York: Greenwood Press, 1989; Nelson, Douglas J. "For Such a Time as This." PhD dissertation, University of Birmingham, UK, 1981;

Robeck, Cevil M., Jr. *The Azusa Street Mission and Revival: The Birth of the Global Pentecostal Movement.* Nashville: Nelson Reference and Electronic, 2006. Robeck, C. M., Jr. "William J. Seymour and 'The Bible Evidence.'" In Gary B. McGee, ed., *Initial Evidence.* 72–95. Peabody, MA: Hendrickson, 1991; Robeck, C. M., Jr. "Seymour, William Joseph." In Stanley M. Burgess, ed., *The New International Dictionary of Pentecostal and Charismatic Movements.* 1053–58. Grand Rapids, MI: Zondervan, 2002.

David Dorries

SHAKERS

The Shakers—or the United Society of Believers in Christ's Second Appearing—are best known for their unique dancing during worship, their belief in celibacy, their emphasis on communal living, their belief in an androgynous (i.e., both male and female) God, and their insistence that Christ had already returned to earth in the form of a woman named **Ann Lee.** While the Shakers are most often described as a **new religious movement,** it is also clear that their history is intertwined with the history of revivalism on several levels. The Shakers trace their roots back to a small group of enthusiasts in Manchester, England, in the late eighteenth century. Their exuberant and emotional gatherings may have been influenced by the Camisard Prophets, the early **Quakers,** and, some suggest, **George Whitefield.** In any case, it is clear that the Shakers, even in the earliest years, emphasized the use of the body in worship and the power of supernatural forces to induce **bodily manifestations** such as those commonly seen in religious revivals. In both the English and American contexts, the Shakers were radically sectarian and boldly proclaimed an anticlerical and even antichurch agenda. The Shakers believed that a new age had dawned and that they were called to challenge the corruptions of traditional religion. In this respect Ann Lee had something in common with another female religious leader of the same era, **Jemima Wilkinson.**

Under Lee's stern and charismatic leadership a small band of Shakers left England and settled in Niskeyuna, New York, in 1774. Once in America, Lee and her followers expanded the movement by emphasizing communal living and enthusiastic worship. Within the tightly structured villages the **ecstatic** worship of the Shakers served to bind them closely together and promoted a profound sense of cohesion and communal identity. The number of Shaker converts increased through aggressive proselytizing, first throughout the Northeast and later as far west as Kentucky and Indiana. Much of this growth and expansion was tied to the revivalistic fervor that later came to be called the **Second Great Awakening.** As news of the grand **camp meetings** and enthusiastic conversions to Christianity spread through the Shaker villages, they seized the opportunity and made a practice of dispatching missionaries to work in the areas of the evangelical revivals. In these settings the Shakers appealed to the interest in new religious expression and physical engagement common among the religious seekers that frequented the revivals. The Shakers would sometimes use the opportunity to speak directly to those gathered at the revivals, tapping into the disaffection with traditional forms of religious expression that was evident among the congregants. At other times the Shakers simply took part in the energetic events without making any overt attempt to attract followers.

This proselytizing program yielded tremendous results for the Shakers, and served as the engine that pushed Shaker villages into the West in the first decades of the nineteenth century. Among other things, this success indicates the compatibility of the Shaker movement with the impulses that drove evangelical revivalism during this period, especially the desire to experience divine power in a physical and unmediated manner. Even after the expansion in the West ended and began to recede, the Shakers continued to show an interest in traditional evangelical revivals until the turn of the century. Shakers make mention of listening to such famous revivalists as **Henry Ward Beecher** and **Dwight L. Moody.** While often critical of the theology presented within evangelical revival settings, the Shakers appreciated the energetic challenge that revivalists posed to the staid demeanor of traditional Christian meetings.

SHAKERS near LEBANON state of N YORK.
their mode of Worship.

An engraving of the Shakers engaged in their distinctive dance during worship, with different steps for men and women. In dancing they "shook off sin" by renouncing sexual desire and embracing celibacy. Near Lebanon, New York (ca. 1830). Courtesy of the Library of Congress.

Many of the revivalist tendencies present in the earliest Shaker meetings were eventually domesticated and enshrined as elements in a less spontaneous and more orderly form of worship. Yet outbreaks of classic revivalism occurred out from time to time. The best example of this may be found in the so-called Era of Manifestations. Spanning the decade and a half between the late 1830s and the early 1850s, the Era of Manifestations consisted of a wave of **prophetic** activity characterized by the reception of **charismatic gifts** from disembodied spirits. These spirits, including Lee, other early Shaker leaders, some of America's founding fathers, and certain Native Americans, communicated through "instruments," or mediums, in each village. The gifts bestowed during the visions included drawings, songs, and spoken revelations dealing

with various aspects of Shaker village life. The Shakers perceived the Era of Manifestations as a sign of God's favor toward the group as well as the continuing concern held by "Mother Ann" even beyond the grave. Typical of revivalistic activities, this period resulted in tension between village leaders and the instruments of revelation in some of the communities. This challenge was eventually resolved when village leaders began to appoint as instruments individuals who would reinforce rather than undermine the village authority structure.

The waning of the Era of Manifestations ushered in a period of decline in which the number of Shakers fell rapidly and villages began closing at a brisk pace. During the twentieth century, the Shaker movement dwindled and became known more for the value of its distinctively quaint furniture than for its radical religious posture. Revivalistic elements also began to fade, but the mark left on the tradition's history is unmistakable.

Further Reading: Brewer, Priscilla J. *Shaker Communities, Shaker Lives.* Hanover, NH: University Press of New England, 1986; Garrett, Clarke. *Origins of the Shakers: From the Old to the New World.* Baltimore: Johns Hopkins University Press, 1987; Promey, Sally M. *Spiritual Spectacles: Vision and Image in Mid-Nineteenth-Century Shakerism.* Bloomington: Indiana University Press, 1993; Stein, Stephen J. *The Shaker Experience in America: A History of the United Society of Believers.* New Haven, CT: Yale University Press, 1992; Thurman, Suzanne R. *"O Sisters Ain't You Happy?" Gender, Family, and Community among the Harvard and Shirley Shakers, 1781–1918.* Syracuse, NY: Syracuse University Press, 2002.

Stephen C. Taysom

SHEPHERDING MOVEMENT

The Shepherding Movement, also known as the discipleship movement, was one phase of the **Charismatic Renewal** in the 1960s and 1970s that emphasized covenant relationships, accountability among believers, and submission to spiritual leaders. Under the leadership of charismatic Bible teachers—Bob Mumford, Don Basham, Derek Prince, Charles Simpson, and Ern Baxter—the movement became controversial among independent Charismatic churches in the 1970s. Some critics have called it the most significant heresy to emerge within the Charismatic Renewal. Others viewed it as a social and theological response to a highly individualistic and subjective spirituality among Charismatics who were leaving mainline churches during the Charismatic Renewal. The basic teaching of the movement was that every believer needed to become accountable to a "shepherd" or pastor who would provide spiritual mentoring and oversight. Controversy arose when problems and abuses within these relationships appeared on a major scale.

The movement grew out of an association formed in 1970 in Fort Lauderdale, Florida, by four popular charismatic Bible teachers: Don Basham (ordained by the Disciples of Christ), Derek Prince (**Pentecostal**), Bernard (Bob) Mumford (ordained

by the **Assemblies of God**), and Charles Simpson (a former Southern **Baptist** minister). W.J.E. (Ern) Baxter, a Canadian Pentecostal, became the fifth leader in 1974. These ministers submitted to one another in a covenant of mutual accountability as a model of their beliefs. They found a national audience for their teachings as they assumed leadership of *New Wine* magazine, which was becoming the most widely circulated Charismatic periodical. Through a series of conferences held from 1973 to 1975 in Leesburg, Florida; Montreat, North Carolina; and Kansas City, Missouri, the movement grew to include over 4,700 pastors and ministry leaders committed to the vision and values of the movement. In 1974 and 1975 a national network of churches and **prayer** groups supporting the shepherding cause was established. This network eventually included over 100,000 believers associated with the churches, groups, and network involved. Though rumors arose regarding the formation of a new Charismatic denomination, the leaders of the shepherding movement repeatedly stated this was never their intention.

The controversy over alleged abuses, heresies, and improprieties led to a crisis in 1975 when **Pat Robertson** condemned the shepherding movement on his nationally televised Christian Broadcast Network (CBN) for abusing its authority and controlling its followers. Soon thereafter he wrote an open letter to the leaders of the movement identifying their errors and calling them to repent. That same year several prominent charismatic leaders—including **Kathryn Kuhlman,** David Du Plessis, and Demos Shakarian of the **Full Gospel Business Men's Fellowship International**—denounced the movement publicly. An unsuccessful meeting was held in August 1975 to bring together shepherding movement leaders with their critics in the hope of reconciliation. Criticism continued through the subsequent decade, further weakening the morale and popularity of the movement. Personality clashes and disagreements among the five founders also led to a loss of solidarity. The group almost split up in 1980. Through the leadership of Charles Simpson, the cohort was able to reorganize, though only briefly. Derek Prince withdrew in 1983.

Charles Simpson became the dominant leader and established a new base for the movement at his congregation, Covenant Church, in Mobile, Alabama. As *New Wine* magazine halted publication in 1986, the formal relationship between Simpson and those who remained was dissolved, terminating the organization that supported the shepherding movement. During the following decade many churches and groups scattered into separate allegiances centering on the principal leaders, and others withdrew altogether. Out of the remnant loyal to him, Simpson organized the Fellowship of Covenant Ministers and Churches, which continues as the primary institutional extension of the movement. Basham died in 1989 and Baxter in 1993. Bob Mumford continues his teaching and writing ministry from Raleigh, North Carolina, and Derek Prince's ministry in based in Charlotte, North Carolina.

Further Reading: Moore, S. David. *The Shepherding Movement.* New York: Continuum International Publishing Group, 2003; Strang, Stephen. "The Shepherding Controversy Three Years Later." *Charisma Magazine,* September 1978, 14–15.

Daniel Hedges

SHOUTING

see Laughing and Shouting in Revivals

SIGNS AND WONDERS

Signs and wonders—as tangible demonstrations of God's power and presence—have often been associated with American revivals. What distinguished the revived from the sleeping church was not only an inner witness of the Holy Spirit but the visible signs and wonders of the Spirit's operation. Enthusiastic, spiritual life—like that depicted in the Acts of the Apostles and 1 Corinthians 12–14—rested on an experiential assurance of God rather than rational demonstration. After the nineteenth-century demise of the optimistic dream of a Christian America, a premillennial **eschatology** among American evangelicals emphasized the imminent return of Jesus and the coming of God's kingdom. This created an eschatological context for interpreting the signs and wonders of the Spirit.

The **Holiness movement** taught that a renewed "Pentecost" or "latter rain" of the Spirit would lead to the climax of the church age and the coming of Christ. In the late nineteenth century, Christian leaders proposed a radical strategy for evangelizing the world involving supernatural signs and wonders as a way of rapidly advancing the missionary cause. Among these signs and wonders was a spiritually conferred ability to **speak in tongues** and evangelize in the languages of the nations. The supernatural component of evangelism received unprecedented attention in the late 1800s. The slow progress of medical science and the cries of those suffering from illness caused radical evangelicals such as **A. B. Simpson, John Alexander Dowie,** A. J. Gordon, and Carrie Judd Montgomery to explore the possibilities of miraculous **healing** in their day.

The **Pentecostal** movement of the early twentieth century became a haven for this late nineteenth-century emphasis on signs and wonders. Pentecostals viewed miracles as intrinsic to the charismatic ministry of Jesus and his apostles, and necessary for an end-time revival of biblical evangelism. Signs and wonders, such as speaking in tongues and divine healing, were part of an extraordinary realm of the Spirit that was open to believers who received the **baptism in the Holy Spirit.** The **Charismatic Renewal** of the 1960s and 1970s in the mainline Protestant and **Roman Catholic** churches embraced the extraordinary gifts of the Spirit but showed less interest in signs and wonders. Generally they followed the advice of Vatican II that "extraordinary gifts," though acceptable today, are "not to be rashly desired" (*Lumen Gentium,* par. 12). Less restrained was the so-called Third Wave movement, consisting of evangelicals like **C. Peter Wagner, John Wimber,** and Charles Kraft, who intentionally advocated a signs and wonders movement. Wimber and Wagner cotaught a popular and controversial course on signs and wonders during the 1980s at Fuller Theological Seminary in Pasadena, California. To some, their teaching and the associated movement in the churches seemed rashly to seek after extraordinary spiritual gifts. Wimber's and Wagner's defenders viewed these critics as captive

Pentecostalism featured a number of child preachers during the 1940s and 1950s, such as Marjoe Gortner and "Little David" Davillo Walker, pictured here, who preached his first sermon at age 9 and at age 14 preached for two weeks in the Royal Albert Hall in London. Courtesy of Stanley M. Burgess.

to a post-Enlightenment rationalism. The supernaturalist spirituality embodied in the signs and wonders movement, they argued, is evident in the pages of the Bible and in most non-Western societies today.

Further Reading: Burgess, Stanley M., and Gary McGee. "Signs and Wonders." In Stanley M. Burgess, ed., *The New International Dictionary of Pentecostal and Charismatic Movements*, 1063–69. Grand Rapids, MI: Zondervan, 2002; Faupel, David William. *The Everlasting Gospel: The Significance of Eschatology in the Development of Pentecostal Thought.* Sheffield, UK: Sheffield Academic Press, 1996; Knox, Ronald A. *Enthusiasm: A Chapter in the History of Religion.* Reprint ed. South Bend, IN: University of Notre Dame Press, 1994; Pratt, Thomas. "The

Need to Dialogue: A Review of the Debate on the Controversy of Signs, Wonders, Miracles, and Spiritual Warfare Raised in the Literature of the Third Wave Movement." *Pneuma* 13 (1991): 7–32.

Frank Macchia

SIMPSON, ALBERT BENJAMIN (1843–1919)

Albert Benjamin Simpson—pastor, evangelist, and founder of the international mission society known as the **Christian and Missionary Alliance**—sparked an interest in **foreign missions** through his life's work. A. B. Simpson was born in Cavendish, Prince Edward Island, where he was baptized by a minister who became Canada's first missionary to the South Sea Islands. Raised in a strict Presbyterian home, Simpson experienced **conversion** at the age of 15 and became convinced he was called to **preach** the gospel. Simpson attended local schools and after graduating from high school accepted a teaching position to cover his expenses in attending Knox College in Toronto.

Simpson was interested in serving on the mission field, but after graduating from college in 1865 he accepted his first pastorate at Knox Church in Hamilton, Canada, where he was ordained and served with his wife, Margaret Henry. The couple formed a powerful team that served the Knox Church congregation until 1873. Simpson followed what he took to be God's calling, and he accepted the pulpit at Chestnut Street Presbyterian Church in Louisville, Kentucky, in 1874. Simpson was drawn to **healing** ministry, and his congregation in Kentucky provided the opportunity for him to pursue this. During this period, Simpson orchestrated citywide revivals that reconciled Christians to one another and ignited spiritual fervor among thousands. People were touched by these revivals and started attending local churches, or in some cases, establishing new congregations. The Louisville revivals, which attracted enormous crowds— 10,000 was not an uncommon attendance figure— stirred Simpson's worldwide vision for lost souls.

After five successful years in Louisville, Simpson moved the family to New York City, where he became the pastor at the 13th Street Presbyterian Church. This movement to New York marked a turning point in Simpson's life. Having suffered from a number of physical problems throughout his life, Simpson testified to the healing of a heart ailment at the Old Orchard Beach campground in Maine in 1881. Yet Simpson soon learned that his vision for the lost and his experience with divine healing put him at odds with the 13th Street Presbyterian Church. After two years of service, Simpson resigned his pastorate, and he directed his attention to New York City as a mission field. Simpson evangelized the downtrodden and the immigrant population and continued his strong interest in foreign missions.

Simpson held large independent revivals in New York City to spread the gospel. At this time he founded the Gospel Tabernacle and drew like-minded Christians who were devoted to world evangelism. Consistent with Simpson's missionary vision, he created two organizations, the Christian Alliance and the Evangelical Missionary Alliance. For 10 years the two organizations functioned separately, finally merging in 1897 to form the Christian and Missionary Alliance. Simpson then established a missionary training school in New York City, today known as Nyack College. His missionary vision and zeal brought him national repute. He remained active as a public speaker, published 70 books, and edited a weekly magazine. His career ended in 1919 when he slipped into a coma and died. His passing was mourned by many followers, but his legacy lives on in the missionary work of the Christian and Missionary Alliance.

Further Reading: Niklaus, Robert, John Sawin, and Samuel Stoesz. *All for Jesus: God at Work in the Christian and Missionary Alliance over One Hundred Years.* Camp Hill, PA: Christian Publications, 1996; Thompson, A. W. *A. B. Simpson: His Life and Work.* Camp Hill, PA: Christian Publications, 2001; Tozer, Alden. *Wingspread: Albert B. Simpson; A Study in Spiritual Attitude.* New York: Christian Publications, 1988.

Jeffrey Cook

SLAIN IN THE SPIRIT

see Bodily Manifestations in Revivals

SLAVES AND SLAVE REVIVALS

see African American Revivals

SMITH, AMANDA BERRY (1837–1915)

Smith—who called herself a "washerwoman evangelist"—was a celebrated female **African American** preacher in the **African Methodist Episcopal Church** (AMEC), a missionary to England, India, and West Africa, and the author of an engaging 500-page autobiography (1893). Her life was a constant struggle against unfavorable circumstances—birth into slavery, a lack of formal education, two unhappy marriages, the death in infancy of four of her five children, and lifelong opposition to her **preaching** from male ministers in her own denomination. After her marriage at age 18 to the first of her two husbands, she suffered severe complications from childbirth, and experienced a **vision** of herself preaching before crowds of people.

When Smith in 1871 went on a three-month preaching trip to an AMEC church in Salem, New Jersey, 156 people professed conversion. Soon Smith's preaching won her a following among white Christians who attended **camp meetings** connected with the **Holiness movement** during the 1870s. A tall, attractive, dignified woman in a simple, **Quaker**-like dress, she spoke movingly of her own life and often gave testimony to her experience of **sanctification.** Some blacks resented her popularity with whites, and the lack of support from black churches may have inclined her to align herself with the largely white **Methodist** Episcopal Church, which sent her to London in 1878—the beginning of her international preaching tours. Amanda Smith established new international connections in the 1870s through her association with another well-known female speaker named Smith, the white Holiness teacher **Hannah Whitall Smith.**

Before the formal organization of the AMEC, and as early as 1809, black **women** preached in the churches without official titles or positions. Jarena Lee, for example, was not ordained and yet received permission from AMEC founder **Richard Allen** to hold **prayer** meetings and exhort others. Allen arranged speaking engagements for Lee. Yet in the post–Civil War era, controversies erupted over female preachers. In 1868 the AMEC denomination established a "board of stewardesses" for each congregation, and yet it was only in 1900 that women deaconesses were formally recognized and in 1948 that women were fully ordained for ministry. During the late 1800s, women like Amanda Smith who preached were constrained to do so without denominational sanction. Smith's overseas journeys made her a pathfinder. No other African American woman had ever had such an international ministry. Crowds in cities like London and Calcutta were drawn to the spectacle of a foreign visitor who was female, African American, born as a slave, and eloquent in speech. Smith's overseas sojourns allowed her to circumvent the restrictions back in America regarding female preachers.

Smith returned to the United States in 1890 and suffered due to a lack of financial support and health problems—including backaches and rheumatism—incurred because of her arduous ministry and travel throughout the previous dozen years. She settled in Chicago, became involved in the Women's Christian **Temperance** Union (WCTU), and published her autobiography. Her growing concern for orphans led her to establish a school—the most important in Illinois—for black children. Unfortunately the school did not receive adequate financial support, and it perished through fire in 1918. While the school she founded did not long survive her, Smith's autobiography has been a monument to her fervent faith, indomitable spirit, and bold initiative as a revival preacher.

Further Reading: Andrews, William L., ed. *Sisters of the Spirit: Three Black Women's Autobiographies in the Nineteenth Century.* Bloomington: Indiana University Press, 1966; Smith, Amanda. *An Autobiography: The Story of the Lord's Dealings with Mrs. Amanda Smith the Colored Evangelist.* New York: Oxford University Press, 1988;

Amanda Smith (seated, second from left) accompanied by a number of Holiness leaders, including Rev. C. J. Fowler (seated, far right), a Methodist minister and president of the National Camp Meeting for the Promotion of Holiness (ca. 1890). American Camp Meeting Collection, Nazarene Archives.

Thomas-Collier, Bettye, ed. *Daughters of Thunder: Black Women Preachers and Their Sermons, 1850–1979*. New York: Jossey-Bass, 1998.

Michael J. McClymond

SMITH, HANNAH WHITALL (1832–1911) AND ROBERT PEARSALL (1827–1898)

Hannah Whitall Smith—evangelist, author, reformer, and social activist—remains well known for her book *The Christian's Secret of a Happy Life* (1875), the best-selling Christian devotional volume of the nineteenth century. She is less well known, as is her husband, Robert Pearsall Smith—businessman, revivalist, and author—for the couple's 1873–1875 evangelistic tour of England and the Continent in promotion of the **Holiness movement** or Higher Life teaching. Their renewal efforts left a lasting imprint upon existing evangelical constituencies in both the established and free churches and played a role in the birth of new Holiness and **Pentecostal** movements and churches. The Smiths both were born in Philadelphia, Pennsylvania, into birthright **Quaker** families. The Whitalls were well on the way to becoming wealthy glass manufacturers and the Smiths were socially well positioned through descent from James Logan, colonial secretary to William Penn. Hannah and Robert were married in 1851. Three of their six children lived to adulthood: Mary, married first to a barrister and member of the British parliament, Frank Costelloe, and then to celebrated art historian Bernard Berenson; Logan, professor at Oxford University and the first to introduce the trivia genre into English literature; and Alys Pearsall, the first wife of the renowned philosopher and religious skeptic Bertrand Russell.

The Smiths both confessed evangelical conversion in the **Revival of 1857–1858** and were baptized. The following year they resigned their membership in the Society of Friends. The couple associated briefly with the Plymouth Brethren. Yet with the rise of the post-**Civil War** Holiness revivals, the optimism of the entire **sanctification**

teachings from the **Methodist**-Holiness movement and New School **Calvinism's** Higher Life teaching captured them theologically and experientially. In a Methodist **camp meeting** in 1867, Robert testified to entire sanctification and an emotional **baptism of the Holy Spirit.** Hannah, too, testified to the experience, but only after concluding that its essence lay in an inner witness to God's cleansing and infilling of the Spirit and not in the outward manifestations that often accompanied it. Hannah and Robert quickly became widely sought after as lay speakers in renewal services in Philadelphia and surrounding areas.

During this period Hannah also was active in the founding of the Women's Christian **Temperance** Union (WCTU). She was the first president of the Pennsylvania chapter and was Frances Willard's chief supporter and advisor in Willard's successful campaign to take over the leadership of the union and to add **women's** suffrage to its activist agenda. Smith later became superintendent of the WCTU's evangelistic division, through which she promoted both her own and Willard's commitments to Holiness revivalism.

In 1873, through a series of fortuitous events, Robert, with associates William Boardman and **Asa Mahan,** found himself at the center of a dramatic series of Holiness meetings in England and Europe. Hannah's recently published *Frank: The Record of a Happy Life* (1873) enjoyed a wide circulation among English evangelicals both within and without the established churches. The work, regarding a young man who died while studying at Princeton, was a simple account of his life and witness to entire consecration and sanctification. Robert's revival journal, the *Christian's Pathway of Power,* also had paved the way for the Smith's ministry. In 1874, Robert's sponsoring committee invited Hannah to join in the work of the revival, but only after Hannah had agreed to mute, in her public teaching, a tendency toward Universalism (i.e., the doctrine that all persons will ultimately receive salvation). She became especially active in the summer Holiness meetings sponsored by Lord and Lady Mount Temple at their Broadlands estate in Hampshire, England. Intended mainly for university students who had responded to Robert's meetings in Oxford and Cambridge, these retreats attracted an eclectic group of speakers. Hannah and Robert, along with the **African American** Holiness evangelist **Amanda Smith,** whom Hannah had brought to England with her, shared the speaker's platform with George McDonald, Andrew Jukes, and other noted religious figures of the time.

The meetings in England, followed by Robert's whirlwind 1875 tour through Europe's established and free churches, culminated in the Brighton Convention for the Promotion of Christian Holiness in May of that year. There, among other revivalists on Brighton's agenda, audiences of 5,000 clergy, theologians, and laypersons from the established and free churches of England and Europe gathered to be taught at the feet of the "Angel of the Churches," as Hannah became known. Soon after the publication of glowing press reports of the Brighton meetings, rumors that cast doubt on Robert's moral and doctrinal integrity cast a shadow over the whole venture. Robert had been seen in the company of a younger woman, though it is not clear that anything inappropriate had ever happened between them. Nonetheless, the English sponsoring committee withdrew its support. Robert, who had responded promptly and openly to its queries, suffered a complete psychological collapse. Hannah went to a Paris hotel to rejoin her disconsolate husband, and they returned to America.

The Holiness–Higher Life movement in Britain and Europe had suffered a blow, but it did not collapse. The brief but dramatic three-year revival of the Smiths and their cohorts may have been one of the most exceptional episodes in nineteenth-century revivalism. Even a severe critic, Benjamin B. Warfield of Princeton Seminary, acknowledged the Smiths' wide influence. The outcome of the revival they led was a deep and lasting change in world evangelicalism. The Keswick Convention for the Promotion of Holiness was born out of the revival and created a coalition of evangelicals who spread "second blessing" Holiness teaching throughout Anglo-Saxon Protestantism. The overseas churches of the American Methodist denominations were more firmly established; the social outreach ministries of the German Inner Mission movement were regenerated; the **Pietist** impulses of the Fellowship movement within the established **Lutheran** and **Reformed** churches of Europe were renewed, and new indigenous Holiness movements sprang up, which in the first decades of the twentieth century became fertile ground for the rise of the European Pentecostal revival and churches. The revival came full circle when such leading American evangelicals as **Dwight L. Moody, Reuben A. Torrey,** and Arthur T. Pierson became advocates of the Keswick message. Through them and the subsequent Reformed Higher Life movements, the developing American Fundamentalist network was infused with Keswick Holiness teachings.

Most American and many European revival leaders had questioned the legitimacy of the charges against Robert, but after their return Hannah and Robert acknowledged that their revival ministries were ended. Robert took up a sales position with the Whitall Tatum Glass Company and Hannah attended to her family, her writing, and WCTU concerns. A book on parenting, Bible studies, and devotional guides, especially her *God of All Comfort* (1906) and her spiritual autobiography *The Unselfishness of God and How I Discovered It* (1903), continued to attract large numbers of readers. Most of her publications remain in print to the present.

In 1888, after the marriage of their daughter Mary to Irish barrister Frank Costelloe, the Smiths moved to London and spent the rest of their lives in England. Hannah, always active, in addition to writing and homemaking became a public advocate for many reform causes of the day, ranging from the prevention of cruelty to animals to the rights of women. She brought together her friends Frances Willard and Lady Somerset, leader of the British temperance movement, to form a world temperance union. She maintained her lifelong interest in higher education for women and women's suffrage. Not long before her death she asked her granddaughter to wheel her to the House of Parliament to rally support for pending women's suffrage legislation. Surrounded by a family circle in which the Smith children associated with and eventually intermarried with members of the Bloomsbury circle of rising young English Fabian socialists, intelligentsia, and artists, Hannah maintained a very simple biblical faith. Robert, on the other hand, except for his active support for some of the early efforts to standardize international copyright law, withdrew more and more into himself and his Buddhist meditations. Robert died in 1898. Hannah died at Iffly near Oxford in 1911.

Further Reading: Dieter, Melvin E., ed. *The Christian's Secret of a Holy Life: The Unpublished Personal Writings of Hannah Whitall Smith.* Grand Rapids, MI: Zondervan, 1994; Dieter, Melvin E. *The Holiness Revival of the Nineteenth Century.* 2nd ed. Metuchen, NJ: Scarecrow Press, 1996; Dieter, Melvin E. "The Smiths: A Biographical Sketch with Selected Items from the Collection." *Asbury Seminarian* 38 (1983): 6–42; Strachey, Barbara. *Remarkable Relations: The Story of the Pearsall Smith Family.* London: Victor Gollancz, 1981; Warfield, Benjamin Breckenridge. *Perfectionism.* 2 vols. New York: Oxford University Press, 1931.

Melvin E. Dieter

SMITH, JOSEPH (1804–1844)

Joseph Smith founded the **new religious movement** commonly known as the **Mormons** or Mormonism. His pivotal early religious experience is sometimes viewed as a reaction against the revivalism of the **Second Great Awakening** in western New York's **Burned-Over District**—a scene of intense revivalistic fervor during Smith's earlier years. Born in Vermont, Smith experienced his first **vision** near Palmyra, New York, in 1820. In 1830, he published *The Book of Mormon*, which he claimed to have translated, through divine power, from ancient inscribed metallic plates deposited in a nearby hill. Also in that year, he organized the Church of Jesus Christ of Latter-day Saints, which he understood to be the **restoration** of the ancient church founded by Jesus but lost in a general apostasy following the deaths of the apostles. Subsequent revelations were gathered into volumes entitled *Doctrine and Covenants* and *Pearl of Great Price*. Having already inflamed opposition to himself and his teachings in several states, Smith was assassinated by a mob in Carthage, Illinois, in 1844.

Smith's spiritual saga began amid what he later termed "an unusual excitement on the subject of religion" in the vicinity of Palmyra that commenced with the **Methodists** but soon became a competition for converts between Methodists, **Baptists,** and **Presbyterians.** His language about that event is strikingly negative. It was, he said, "a scene of great confusion and bad feeling," "a strife of words and a contest about opinions" compounded of "reason and sophistry." Only 14 years old at the time, he found himself both excited and confused, and he agonized over his inability to decide which denomination was correct. He experienced conviction of sinfulness and guilt, but not of the salvation that was promised to follow, and the competing claims appalled him. His own family appears to have become religiously divided, yet he himself "remained aloof": "In the midst of this war of words and tumult of opinions, I often said to myself: What is to be done? Who of all these parties are right; or, are they all wrong together? If any one of them be right, which is it, and how shall I know it?" (*Joseph Smith—History*, 1:5–6, 9–10). Then he came across a biblical promise that God will give wisdom to those who ask for it (James 1:5), and he determined to act upon it. While **praying** for guidance in a grove near his home, he later reported, God the Father and Jesus Christ appeared to him, granting him forgiveness but also commanding him to join none of the existing churches. Afterward, said Smith, "my soul was filled with love and for many days I could rejoice with great joy and the Lord was with me" (D. C. Jessee, ed., *The Papers of Joseph Smith* [1989] 1:7). But that joy was soon tempered by hostile responses from neighbors and clergy to his claimed vision.

Subsequently Smith recounted being led by an angel to the plates of *The Book of Mormon*. That text tells a complex story, concluding in the early fifth century, of pre-Columbian migrations from the Near East to the New World and of the rise and fall of civilizations, but also includes narratives of personal **conversion,** letters, sermons, and, most significantly, a visit of the resurrected Jesus to the Americas. Some have interpreted the notable sermon delivered by the Nephite king Benjamin (see Mosiah 2–5) as a nineteenth-century revival meeting in disguise, but the parallels are weak. On the other hand, believers in the book's antiquity see in Benjamin's address striking elements of an ancient Israelite covenant-renewal ceremony associated with the Feast of Tabernacles and the Day of Atonement.

Another experience that distanced Smith from surrounding revivalism was his claim, in company with Oliver Cowdery, to have been ordained to the Aaronic priesthood, under the hands of the resurrected John the Baptist, and, later, to have received the so-called higher or Melchizedek priesthood from the ancient apostles Peter, James, and John. Authority and status in the church were to be bestowed not through personal charismatic experience, but through formal, visible ordination. Accordingly, Joseph Smith struggled at first to establish his own unique authority as God's prophet and spokesman while not discouraging the enjoyment of **charismatic gifts** and revelations among his followers. His ultimate success in that effort gave to the Church of Jesus Christ of Latter-day Saints the hierarchical structure and the strong emphasis on priesthood authority as well as personal revelation that characterize it today.

Further Reading: Backman, Milton V., Jr. *Joseph Smith's First Vision: Confirming Evidences and Contemporary Accounts.* 2nd ed. Salt Lake City: Bookcraft, 1980; Bushman, Richard L. *Joseph Smith and the Beginnings of Mormonism.* Urbana: University of Illinois Press, 1984; Welch, John W., and Stephen D. Ricks, eds. *King Benjamin's Speech: "That Ye May Learn Wisdom."* Provo, UT: Foundation for Ancient Research and Mormon Studies, 1998.

Daniel C. Peterson

SNAKE HANDLERS

see Serpent- and Fire-Handling Believers

SOCIETY OF FRIENDS

see Quakers

SOJOURNER TRUTH

see Truth, Sojourner (Isabella Bomefree)

SOUTH, REVIVALS IN THE

While the phenomenon of revivals in America did not originate in the South, they appeared quite early in the region's history and have been more characteristic of popular religion there than elsewhere in the nation. Like revivals everywhere they began as spontaneous expressions of Christian piety, and in time began to follow a certain routine and pattern, though retaining an authentic spiritedness. The term *revival* suggests the enlivening of something lifeless or dormant. Revivals have often stirred Christian believers to deeper commitment, greater awareness, and more passion in their practice. Yet they have also been the mechanism by which the unchurched, the unbelieving, or lost souls in need of salvation have been brought to **confession** of their sinfulness, repentance, and **conversion.** Thus revivals in the southern United States have been a primary means of evangelism.

The earliest expressions of this form of ardent Protestant Christianity date from the late colonial period. In Hanover County, Virginia, **Presbyterian** churches developed it between 1735 and 1750. After its grassroots beginnings, this movement took shape and achieved success under the influence of **Samuel Davies,** who was inspired and trained in this way of converting the unchurched population in **William Tennent's** Log College near Philadelphia. Effective as this early start was, revivals did not fit the Calvinist heritage very well, with the result that the movement was to enjoy more currency among the **Baptists** and **Methodists.** There was one notable exception, namely, "sacramental meetings," derived from the Scottish **Calvinist** tradition of **holy fairs,** which were influential farther to the west and in the decades just before and after 1800.

The itinerant evangelical Anglican clergyman **George Whitefield,** from his base in New England, roamed the colonies' seaboard towns from 1738 up through the 1750s, making notable visits to Charleston, South Carolina, and Savannah, Georgia. Yet it was Baptist Christians—and specifically the nonconformist band that immigrated southward from Connecticut—who guaranteed that revivalism would become a permanent feature of southern church life. "Separate Baptists" settled in central North Carolina, south of present-day Greensboro, founding the Sandy Creek Church in 1755. From that beginning the movement caught on, spreading north into south-side Virginia, south into northeast Georgia, and then springing up in many locations throughout the South. Other, more traditionally English Baptists from Maine had planted that faith in low-country South Carolina in the 1690s. Yet the future, in numerical terms, lay with the upstart newcomers who had helped generate an American form of revivals.

"Methodists"—there was no such organized group in North America in the mid-1700s—were not far behind the Baptists in their embrace of revivalistic religion. Those groups that were later to emerge as a Methodist Church in 1784 were, at this time, spirited Anglicans who stirred many in Maryland and Virginia to a more fervent faith. They touched both the unchurched populace in these regions and others who were only nominal in their Christian profession. Once Methodism took form, it became the principal revivalist branch of Protestantism in America, a situation that prevailed until the later nineteenth century. Of great importance is the fact that Methodism from its earliest years was transregional. This gave Methodist revivalism a foothold in many parts of what was to become the United States. Presbyterian revivalism largely died out in the course of the 1800s, while Baptist revivalism flourished principally in southern regions. It was only later, during the twentieth century, that newer **Pentecostal, African American,** and evangelical groups embraced the revivalist program and spread it throughout the nation.

The "Great Revival" of 1800–1810 broke out west of the mountains, notably in southern Kentucky and in that state's Bluegrass section. Baptists and Presbyterians led the way. The famed **Cane Ridge revival** employed the old Scottish sacramental meeting concept, that is, it followed a plan of worship services stretching over several days and consisting of more than **preaching** and an **altar call.** The Cane Ridge gathering was among the first large-scale **camp meetings,** and helped to enshrine

a new tradition in which worshippers came with food and other provisions and anticipated several days of outdoor services. The Presbyterian holy fair, which had climaxed in the celebration of the Lord's Supper, was giving way to a camp meeting tradition characterized by intense emotionalism and a lack of interest in the Lord's Supper or other sacraments. From the Presbyterian perspective, a notable outcome of the Great Revival was the departure from the Presbyterian fold of **Barton W. Stone** and like-minded believers to form what they called "the Christian Church," later to take formal shape as the **restorationist or Stone-Campbell movement** that gave rise to the Disciples of Christ, the Churches of Christ, the Christian Church, and other related bodies. A segment of Presbyterians—known as the **Cumberland Presbyterians**—separated and perpetuated the ministry of revivals with a revised theology that excluded some elements of traditional Calvinism.

The Baptists employed revivals as their major way of winning converts, so much so that they became standard fare in almost all congregations. That device has maintained its power and role for that denomination up into the twenty-first century. The administration of revivals was relatively easy for that body because it primarily relied on bivocational **men**—devout souls who farmed six days a week and then preached on the seventh. That tradition did not establish high standards for the education and training of its ordained leaders—unlike the Presbyterians and Episcopalians. Having the "call" to preach was sufficient, apart from any training in theology. Later on, of course, the Southern Baptists provided and encouraged seminary education for their ministers.

The Methodist approach to revivalism centered on the camp meeting. Before many neighborhood Methodist churches had been founded, those who were already converted, and those who aspired to a salvation experience, gathered over weekends or longer periods for around-the-clock preaching, testimonies, **hymn** singing, and fellowshipping at a designated place, bringing along the whole family and provisions for eating and sleeping. The camp meeting was a remarkable adaptation of the revivalist impulse to the scattered nature of the frontier population, and it exercised great socializing power. That movement gathered strength in the decades before the **Civil War,** continued with the late nineteenth-century **Holiness movement,** and extended into the twentieth century. Even after towns were formed and churches were established, the camp meetings did not die out. Southern Christians continued to gather periodically at camps and summer resorts, where canvas tents or wooden cabins replaced the original practice of open-air camping.

Throughout the South, African Americans in slave days and after Emancipation were deeply affected by revivalism. Revivals were a principal avenue for the slaves to hear the Christian good news, leading many to conversion. While they were not permitted to sit with their white masters or socialize freely with whites or even among themselves, the slaves were invited and sometimes required to attend special revival meetings. Yet the real influence of revivalism in both white and black churches came through the growing practice of preachers who conducted even their regular Sunday services in the revivalist mode. Most of the sermons were evangelistic, the services became increasingly a means of fostering the conversion experience, and worship as such played a diminished role in the services. Once black people formed their own congregations, within months of the close of the Civil War, the revival form became standard within black churches. Yet African American churches conducted revivalist services with a special twist. The goal of these services was to inspire all who were present, with little distinction between those who had experienced conversion and those who had not. That is to say, all were already God's children, despite failures in performance and a recurrent need for forgiveness. Much like their Old Testament forebears, with whom they so closely identified, African Americans viewed themselves and one another as latter-day Israelites, chosen by God, and pilgrims on an arduous journey to a promised land of freedom.

Emergence of population centers and better means of transportation opened the South to "modern revivalism," an organizational technique already in existence in New England and the Midwest, and made popular by **Charles G. Finney** from the 1830s onward. This version tended to make the conversion less a "surprising work of God," and more a perfectly natural occurrence. Thus **Sam P. Jones** of Georgia, beginning in the 1880s, organized special events in cities and in towns of size, drawing big crowds and providing opportunities for conversion, revitalization, enthusiastic singing, new friendships, and more. **Dwight L. Moody** of Chicago, the most famous evangelist of the late nineteenth century, made a few forays into the South, as did **Billy Sunday** a generation later. So-called modern revivalism, featuring fervent preaching, contagious hymn singing and special music, effective organization, widespread advertising, and classes for the new converts, became increasingly influential in the South during the twentieth century. Yet regional denominations provided their own leadership, and southern revivalism did not depend solely or even primarily on visiting evangelists. The revival as a local church phenomenon entrenched itself more and more deeply, for town congregations as much as the rural ones. The two forms were rarely if ever in competition, since the citywide or general revival meetings served local churches that scheduled their own meetings at different times of the year. **Holiness** churches from the late 1800s, and Pentecostal churches from the early 1900s, adopted revivalism and made appropriate adaptations to it as essential aspects of their ministry. Especially in its early stages, Pentecostals interpreted their calling to include the restoration of the age of Christ's apostles or the New Testament church.

Billy Graham was converted at a general revival in Charlotte, North Carolina, led by a Louisville-based **radio** evangelist named Mordecai F. Ham, himself an example of a regional public evangelist. Graham's role in southern and general American revivalism is unique not only for its incomparable effectiveness—on a global scale—but also for his being from the South but not of it. That is to say, his message, form of organization, and community of support drew on northern resources more than southern. In the early years his context was northern Fundamentalism, though by the 1960s it had shifted to what might be called classic evangelicalism. The South has always taken pride in Graham, without a doubt, and responded to him, but his roots lie deepest and his connections spread most broadly in northern (i.e., upper midwestern) evangelicalism.

All the data, taken together, indicate that revivalism is simply a basic feature of the southern religious scene, in the setting of its most populous Protestant denominational families, that is, Baptist and Pentecostal, including both white and black denominations and congregations. The revivalist approach to church life, and especially to converting lost souls, has found little favor among Presbyterians, Lutherans, Episcopalians, and even among twentieth-century Methodists. Those traditions have developed their own ways of reviving Christians and congregations, and yet rarely engage in direct evangelistic activities to "win souls" or set the stage for a conversion experience. The most populous churches in the South have participated in national revivalist activities and developed and carried out their own. In this form of church life, along with so many others, southern religion has been distinctive.

Further Reading: Blumhofer, Edith W., and Randall L. Balmer, eds. *Modern Christian Revivals*. Urbana: University of Illinois Press, 1993; Bruce, Dickson D., Jr. *And They All Sang Hallelujah*. Knoxville: University of Tennessee Press, 1974; Conkin, Paul. *Cane Ridge: America's Pentecost*. Madison: University of Wisconsin Press, 1990; Mathews, Donald G. "The Second Great Awakening as an Organizing Process, 1780–1830." *American Quarterly* 21 (1969): 23–43; McLoughlin, William G. *Modern Revivalism*. New York: Ronald Press, 1959; McLoughlin, William G. *Revivals, Awakenings, and Reform*. Chicago: University of Chicago Press, 1978; Raboteau, Albert J. *Slave Religion*. New York: Oxford University Press, 1978.

Samuel S. Hill

SPEAKING IN TONGUES (GLOSSOLALIA)

Speaking in tongues can be defined as a phonologically structured human utterance that is not spoken in any language that the speaker has heard or studied, and yet bears some resemblance to a real language. The practice is especially associated with the twentieth-century **Pentecostal** and **Charismatic** revivals, and indeed, has been used as a way of distinguishing Pentecostal and Charismatic Christians from all other Christian groups. Persons who speak in tongues often believe that the practice results from a spiritually conferred ability to speak a real human language that they have never heard or studied before. On a subjective level, those who speak in tongues typically describe the practice as one that brings joy, inward peace, or a sense of spiritual release. Many scholars who have studied the phenomenon judge that glossolalia bears no systematic resemblance to any natural language, living or dead. While some evidence suggests that the phenomenon occurred in the context of prophecy in ancient Israel, no explicit mention of it is made in the Old Testament or Hebrew scriptures. Speaking in tongues appears to have played a part in the folk religion of ancient Mesopotamia and Egypt. In the New Testament, glossolalia is noted in the Acts of the Apostles and the Epistles of Paul. The author of Acts seems to have understood the utterances of Jesus' disciples on the day of Pentecost as known languages that were actually spoken in some part of the world. The early church accepted tongues-speaking as a sign that God was extending the mission of Jesus to the Gentile world (Acts 11:15–18).

The apostle Paul seems to have assumed that normally the tongues phenomenon is an actual language, though he allowed for ecstatic utterances as the "language of angels" (1 Corinthians 13:1). Yet Paul's First Letter to the Corinthians shows that the members of the Corinthian church could not interpret these utterances as they might interpret what is spoken in ordinary human languages. Thus Paul instructed that while such utterances might be a gift of the Spirit, they must be interpreted for the benefit of the congregation by a person possessing a "gift of interpretation" whenever they were uttered in a public meeting. Following the closing of the New Testament canon of scripture, around the end of the first century of this era, data on glossolalia is scarce. Speaking in tongues, when it happened, was not differentiated from the gift of prophecy. Often it occurred among radical groups that were labeled heretical within mainstream Christianity. Little is known about the significance that such groups may have assigned to speaking in tongues.

Modern tongues-speaking may be traced back to Scotland in the early 1800s, and a series of events that led to the establishment of the **Catholic Apostolic Church** in 1835. In this setting, the practice was related to **eschatology** or the expectation of Jesus' Second Coming. Interpretation of the spoken messages suggested that Christ was coming soon and the world was entering a period of tribulation. The Catholic Apostolic Church was established in the conviction that through it a worldwide revival would occur. This revival, among other things, would restore the **charismatic gifts** or gifts of the Spirit to the church. Though the influence of the Catholic Apostolic Church declined in the later 1800s, many of its themes were appropriated by such emerging groups of the nineteenth century as the Plymouth Brethren, the followers of **William Miller, Seventh-day Adventists,** the **restorationists and Stone-Campbell movement** (including the Churches of Christ and Christian Church), the **Church of God (Anderson, Indiana),** the **Church of God (Cleveland, Tennesee),** the Prophecy Conference movement, the Wesleyan-**Holiness movement,** and the Keswick or Higher Life movement. All of these groups believed that the charismatic gifts would be restored to the church preceding Christ's impending and speedy return. Glossolalia, in particular, was anticipated as the means to carry the end-time message to the various nations of the world.

Sporadic expressions of the phenomenon did occur in most of these groups toward the end of the century. It was the emergence of the Pentecostal movement, however, at the turn of the twentieth century that brought the phenomenon into the church on a sustained basis. Beginning with the Welsh revival of 1904–1905, many in the emerging Pentecostal movement believed that they were experiencing the beginning of a long-anticipated, worldwide, end-time revival. Glossolalia, they

contended, distinguished this movement from all other revivals in the history of the church, and signified that a second Pentecostal outpouring (or "latter rain") of the Holy Sprit had occurred. For adherents, speaking in tongues served three functions—as the eschatological sign that the church age had come to a close, as the means by which the nations would be warned in their own languages that Christ was coming, and as a seal that marked individual believers as part of Christ's church.

Rejection by mainstream Christendom, doubts that tongues-speaking consisted of real human languages, and the delay of Jesus' expected Second Coming led Pentecostals gradually to abandon their affirmation that glossolalia was an end-time or eschatological sign. They continued to insist, however, that it was a necessary, outward evidence of the inward reception of the **baptism in the Holy Spirit**—an experience subsequent to **conversion** that empowered the believer for Christian service. This doctrine, known as the "initial evidence" teaching, is upheld by classical Pentecostal denominations such as the **Assemblies of God,** Church of God (Cleveland, Tennessee), and others. As a result of the Charismatic Revival of the 1960s and 1970s, the phenomenon of speaking in tongues has penetrated mainstream Christendom, including the **Roman Catholic** Church and mainline Protestant churches such as the **Lutherans,** Anglicans, **Presbyterians, Methodists,** and **Baptists.** The so-called Third Wave or neo-Charismatic movement during the 1980s and 1990s brought a variety of charismatic gifts, including speaking in tongues, into many mainline and evangelical Protestant congregations. Charismatic and Third Wave Christians, even if they themselves speak in tongues, generally do not affirm the initial evidence doctrine that makes speaking in tongues a necessary evidence of Spirit baptism. Thus Christian tongues-speakers do not all interpret their experiences in the same way. Today nearly all Christian traditions or denominations have at least some members who occasionally or regularly speak in tongues. Tongues-speaking is commonplace in almost all the indigenous Christian churches of the developing world. It has been estimated that over 500 million Christians have spoken in tongues during the course of the twentieth century.

Further Reading: Carledge, Mark J. *Charismatic Glossolalia: An Empirical-Theological Study.* Aldershot, UK: Ashgate, 2002; Samarian, William J. *Tongues of Men and Angels: The Religious Language of Pentecostalism.* New York: Macmillan, 1972; Williams, Cyril G. *Tongues of the Spirit: A Study of Pentecostal Glossolalia and Related Phenomenon.* Cardiff: University of Wales Press, 1981.

D. William Faupel

SPIRIT, HOLY

see Theology of Revivals

SPIRITUAL WARFARE

Spiritual warfare involves the belief that demonic spirits are involved in human affairs to oppose God's will and must, therefore, be combated and neutralized if Christian ministry is effectively to progress. The rise of divine **healing** practices and apocalyptic **eschatology** in nineteenth-century revival movements in the United States inspired a new consideration for otherworldly causes of human suffering and evil. The demonic emerged in the "apocalyptic imagination" as the chief force that resists the accomplishment of God's will to heal and to redeem in the world. **Pentecostal** and **Charismatic** churches are especially known to have advocated spiritual warfare, as well as so-called Third Wave churches, that is, churches that advocate **charismatic gifts** or gifts of the Holy Spirit without identifying with the Pentecostal or Charismatic movements. The struggle against demons can occur on an individual, personal level, or else on a larger social and cultural level. Individuals who are oppressed and afflicted by evil spirits may receive **deliverance ministry**—a term used mostly in Pentecostal and Charismatic contexts to refer to exorcism, the casting out of demons, or the overcoming of demonic influences through the power of Jesus Christ. Another line of thought and practice pertains to demonic influences in society at large. The writings of recent authors such as Charles Kraft and **C. Peter Wagner** suggest that Christian believers can change the spiritual atmosphere of whole cities or regions through concerted **prayer.** Wagner has been president of the World Prayer Center in Colorado Springs that governs an elaborate network of prayer groups throughout North America, the major purpose of which is to discern and incapacitate demonic activities in various locations. Praying Christians identify territorial demons by name and then "bind" them—through invoking the name of Jesus and relevant texts of scripture—so that they cannot thwart the work of God within specific locations around the United States. Novelist Frank E. Perretti has promoted the idea of spiritual warfare through novels that depict an invisible battle between praying Christians and invading spirits. These works include *The Present Darkness* (1986) and its sequel, *Piercing the Darkness* (1988).

The idea of spiritual warfare derives from the New Testament. Texts such as Ephesians 6:10–18 offer a military metaphor of the Christian life and so provide a context for understanding spiritual warfare. This *textus classicus* for spiritual warfare from the New Testament notes that we wrestle not against flesh and blood but against "principalities and powers" in high places. Those who support the idea of spiritual warfare also typically point to a primordial battle between angelic and wayward angels in heaven (Jude 6; Revelation 12:7–9) and to the fact that Jesus himself claimed to have "bound the strong man" (i.e., Satan or the devil) to spoil his works (Matthew 12:29). Also noted is Jesus' commissioning his disciples to "bind" and "loose," so that the "gates of hell" would not prevail against them, references that seem to involve the continuation of thwarting and binding evil powers as well as setting people free from their influence (Matthew 16:18–19). So, it is further noted, the early Christian proclamation of the gospel involved the defeat of the devil (Acts 10:38; Hebrews 2:14–15), a proclamation that forms the basis of what Gustaf Aulen has termed the classical doctrine of Christ's atoning work. Prayer, scripture, and charismatic gifts of the Holy Spirit are thus seen as the fundamental means to combat and bind the dark forces that oppose the work of God in people's lives.

Critics of spiritual warfare, even those who accept the literal reality of the demonic, note that it tends to overplay the element of combat in the life of the church. Even Ephesians 6:10–18 does not encourage combat or aggressive action as such but merely gives an imperative to "stand firm" in Christ's victory (Ephesians 6:14). Another text urges believers to "resist the devil" (James 4:7) as they submit to God and God's purposes. There is also a danger of becoming preoccupied with the demonic realm in one's understanding of human problems, to the neglect of meaningful analysis and action. This can inspire a kind of spiritual paranoia or conspiratorial worldview that sees demonic dangers lurking at every turn. Nonetheless, recent authors support the idea of spiritual warfare in a variety of ways. Walter Wink sees a spiritual dynamic in institutional and corporate life that makes it meaningful to speak of combating the demonic in the contemporary world. Wink thus endorses a cautious form of spiritual warfare against "principalities and powers," that is, institutional forces of evil that oppress or destroy.

Further Reading: Aulen, Gustaf. *Christus Victor: A Historical Study of the Three Main Types of the Idea of the Atonement.* New York: Macmillan, 1969; Edwards-Raudonat, Riley. "At the World Prayer Center: Spiritual Warfare." *Christian Century* 116 (1999), 926–27; Guelich, Robert A. "Spiritual Warfare: James, Paul, and Peretti." *Pneuma* 13 (1996): 37–64; Kraft, Charles. *Defeating Dark Angels: Breaking Demonic Oppression in the Believer's Life.* Ventura, CA: Vine Books, 1992; Macchia, Frank D. "God's Victory over Satan and Demons." In Stanley Horton, ed., *Systematic Theology: A Pentecostal Perspective,* 198–213. Springfield, MO: Logion Press, 1994; Wagner, C. Peter. *Engaging the Enemy: How to Fight and Defeat Territorial Spirits.* Ventura, CA: Regal Books, 1991; Wink, Walter. *The Powers That Be: Theology for a New Millennium.* New York: Doubleday, 1998.

Frank Macchia

SPIRITUALS

African American spirituals have been a powerful and pervasive influence in North American church music during the nineteenth, twentieth, and twenty-first centuries. Spirituals brought a new genre of music to the world, which has influenced gospel, big bands, jazz, blues, rock and roll, hip-hop, and soul music. Between 1609 and 1870 over 12 million African slaves were captured and more than 400,000 were brought to the American **South**. The slaves worked under harsh conditions on plantations for white slave masters. Stripped of their African identities, family ties, and religious rituals, the slave masters allowed them to sing work songs. Slave masters set a rhythm to do hard tasks. The songs allowed the work to be done at a faster pace, saving the slave master money and forcing the slaves to do more work in a shorter span of time. At the same time, these work songs contained messages of liberation and freedom that gave encouragement and mental stability to the oppressed slaves. Perhaps half these songs contained cryptic references that the slaves could understand and slave masters could not. Many songs also included **prayer** and praise that represented an Africanized version of Christianity. Singers would witness in song, speaking of illness and life's pains and disappointments. The songs and singers exhorted hearers to continue in the "sun," "rain," or "storm." African American spirituals were a musical form that integrated sound with rhythm and bodily movements. The arms, feet, and bodies of the singers synchronized with their words. This tradition of chants and dancing has continued in **Holiness** and **Pentecostal** churches to this day and is sometimes known as the "holy dance."

The poetry and musicality of the spirituals are different from other forms of music. The songs have no identifiable authors. All of the spirituals originated in the South and reflect rural roots—a southern, oral tradition. Often the spirituals were spontaneously put together in the fields as slaves worked. They were songs about the work, the fields, and the hot sun beating down on them. Most were sung a cappella or with a handmade instrument such as a bottle to blow sounds or an object to give the beat of the music. The slave masters had banned drum playing since it was thought to be a means of secret communication among the slaves. The repetitiousness of these songs—as in West African music—is a memory device to help singers recall the words and tunes. Some of the songs allude to traveling or migration, and many are testimonies bearing witness to God's presence and work in individual lives. An example of a spiritual work song is the "Gandy Dancers" from Birmingham, Alabama—a name derived from the Gandy Manufacturing Company, which made railroad tools, equipment, and accessories. The term *dancers* applied to the dancelike movement of black workers who were laying and readjusting the tracks. The men laid railroad tracks by whistles, chants, and work songs. They lifted, hammered and moved rails to the rhythm. Often they would breathe, groan, and moan at the end of each line. Another song is entitled "Toiling to See King Jesus":

I am toiling to see the Master, King Jesus
[breathe with groans and moans]
I am toiling to see my family and friends
[breathe with groans and moans]
I am toiling to see some kindness and rest
[breathe with groans and moans]
I am toiling to see the River, Over Jordan.
[breathe with groans and moans].

These spiritual work songs allowed a pause for the slaves to breathe while toiling in hard physical labor.

The musical beats and rhythms not only set a pace for the work but allowed the slaves to express deep emotions arising from their stress and life experience. Since neither the adult slaves nor the children could read, the oral tradition of the spirituals offered counsel and guidance in daily life. For example, the lyrics to "Don't Drink Water That Is Standing Still" taught the children in the fields how to avoid sickness and infection. Even so basic a gesture as raising one's hands had special significance among slaves. This sign was used in the slave era to obtain permission from an overseer to come or go from place to place.

Before the birth of the spirituals in the late 1700s and the early 1800s, the first Christian songs among African Americans were the **hymns** of John and Charles Wesley and Isaac Watts as sung by Negro house slaves. These hymns came to America with the **Methodist** movement, beginning in 1766. Slaves blended these hymns with their own work songs, descriptions of experience, and interpretations of Christianity to produce what became known as Negro spirituals. Slave masters understood the song "'Tis the Old Ship of Zion, Get on Board" as a spiritual parable about one's journey through life. Yet, to the slaves, this song expressed a desire to ride a boat or train back to freedom. Though the slave ships that brought them to America were evil, there would be no danger in God's waters as they traveled back to their homeland in Africa. **Richard Allen** (1760–1831), who organized the **African Methodist Episcopal Church** (AMEC), compiled the first African American hymnal in 1801. It was a mixture of old English hymns and Negro spirituals. "Steal Away to Jesus" and "Swin' Low Sweet Chariot" were spirituals used by Harriet Tubman (ca. 1821–1913) in the movement known as the Underground Railroad, in which slaves escaped from southern states to freedom in the North.

After the **Civil War** many African traditions surfaced, particularly in the Deep South. In 1871, the Fisk Jubilee Singers, from Fisk University, Nashville, Tennessee, sang Negro spirituals adapted for a white audience. They even traveled to England to sing for Queen Victoria. The Fisk Singers gave birth to the Jubilee style of unaccompanied singing, and introduced Jubilee quartets that represented a more polished musical style that still included the moans and groans of the older slave songs. Educated African Americans often felt that the spiritual songs gave dignity to their era in slavery. On the other hand, many blacks believed that "swinging spirituals" contradicted their religious beliefs and demeaned their African American heritage. In the 1920s, Thomas A. Dorsey (1899–1993)—generally regarded as the father of gospel music—left behind his career as an outstanding blues composer and performer (who played with Ma Rainey) to devote himself exclusively to sacred music. In his later years he sought to preserve the spirituals and gospel songs from being co-opted by secular dance bands. Alto Peeples of Florida appealed to Louis Armstrong (1901–1971) to stop rearranging spirituals and gospel music, such as "When the Saints Go Marching In," for the entertainment of jitterbug dancers. When the gospel singer Rosetta Tharpe (1915–1973) and others became commercially successful, they were told that they had taken the spirituals and offered them as a sacrifice to a new god—money. Church singers and Holiness or "sanctified" evangelists, such as Rev. Utah Smith with the song "Two Wings," marketed spiritual music on black street corners and neighborhood churches to preserve the tradition of sacred music among African Americans. Yet music companies marketed "race records" to black consumers regardless of religion, following their commercial interests rather than spiritual considerations. Market pressures became increasingly influential in the dissemination of all forms of African American music, whether secular or sacred.

During the late 1930s record sales increased with the growth of radio broadcasting. Entertainment and sheet music companies also increased their sales of Negro spirituals. The golden era of gospel music from 1945 to 1955 made spirituals and the gospel genre a highly prized item, with live performances at ball fields, tents, auditoriums, and large churches. African American male harmony quartet groups were billboard hits. These quartet groups harmonized songs and introduced guitars into worship services. **Women's** groups became well known, such as the Clara Ward Singers and the Angelic Gospel Singers. As a result of the civil rights movement of the 1950s and 1960s, both black and white audiences were able to listen to the spirituals in a new political context and purchase a wider range of gospel music on the commercial market. African American artists such as Mahalia Jackson (1911–1972), the "Queen of Gospel Music," demonstrated that talented musicians did not have to leave the church to be successful. The Impressions—a black soul music group—recorded Curtis Mayfield's song "People Get Ready," and it made the *Billboard* charts in March 1965. As a successful gospel song, it is laced with spiritual and biblical language, reflecting Mayfield's religious upbringing in Chicago. Among the artists who later recorded Mayfield's anthem are the Blind Boys of Alabama, Al Green, Aretha Franklin, Bob Dylan, and the Staple Singers. The train image that dominates the song finds its roots in Negro spirituals from the black Baptist, Methodist, and Pentecostal movements, such as "Gospel Train":

The Gospel train's comin'
I hear it just at hand
I hear the car wheel rumblin'
And rollin' thro' the land

Get on board little children
Get on board little children
Get on board little children
There's room for many more

The fare is cheap and all can go
The rich and poor are there
No second class aboard this train
No difference in the fare

Contemporary gospel music continues the tradition of the spirituals. The song "Oh Happy Day," performed by the Edwin Hawkins Singers in California in 1968, helped to usher in contemporary gospel music with its musical styles and mass choirs. The spirituals find a place in the repertoire of such contemporary black performers as Shirley Caesar, Kirk Franklin, Fred Hammond, and Cece Winans. These traditional songs have influenced blues, ragtime, jazz, soul, rhythm and blues, do-wop, rock 'n roll, rap, hip hop, and alternative rock, and have inspired interracial choirs, musical recitals, modern dance, motion pictures, and television programming.

The spirituals are a major musical style today, and continue to appear in new recordings. The joys, sorrows, struggles, attainments, and aspirations of the slave are all encapsulated in these sacred songs. From the field to the small towns to the cities, and to other parts of the globe, the message of the Bible and the longing for freedom find expression in these songs. The spirituals have universal appeal, and are appropriate for any situation—war, peace, grief, commemoration, joy, love, or celebration. Above all, they express an attitude of hope in God. Spiritual musical is uplifting, and it is physical because one's body moves to the beat of the music with moans and groans that revive the soul.

Further Reading: *African American Heritage Hymnal.* Chicago: GIA, 2001; DuPree, Sherry Sherrod. *African-American Holiness Pentecostal Movement: An Annotated Bibliography.* New York: Garland, 1996; DuPree, Sherry Sherrod, and Herbert C. DuPree. *African-American*

Good News (Gospel) Music. Washington, DC: Middle Atlantic Regional Press, 1993; Jackson, Jerma A. *Singing in My Soul: Black Gospel Music in a Secular Age.* Chapel Hill: University of North Carolina Press, 2004; *Songs and Spirituals of Negro Composition for Revivals and Congregational Singing: The Largest Manufacturing Enterprise in the United States Owned and Operated Exclusively by Colored People.* Chicago: Overton-Hygienic, n.d.; Walker, Wyatt Tee. *Spirits That Dwell in Deep Woods: The Prayer and Praise Hymns of the Black Religious Experience.* Chicago: GIA, 1991.

Sherry Sherrod DuPree

STEARNS, SHUBAL (1706–1771)

Baptist evangelist and revivalist Shubal Stearns was born in Boston, Massachusetts, and was deeply affected by **George Whitefield**'s 1744–1745 evangelistic tour of New England. He joined with the pro-revival or New Light Congregationalists and soon began **preaching.** Sometime around 1751, he became convinced that only believers should be baptized. He joined the Baptists in Connecticut, was rebaptized by immersion, and was ordained to the ministry. Three years later, Stearns migrated toward the **South,** joining his brother-in-law, Daniel Marshall, in Virginia. The two Baptists preached there with limited success, and so decided to move with eight families to modern-day Randolph County, North Carolina. Arriving at Sandy Creek in late 1755, they formed the Sandy Creek Separate Baptist Church with 16 members and with Stearns as their main preacher.

The result of Stearns's preaching was immediate and impressive. Stressing the vital importance of the "new birth," the Sandy Creek Church exploded in numbers. Within three years, there were three churches with a membership of over 900. Seventeen years later, there were 42 churches and 125 ministers, all owing their existence to the revival at Sandy Creek. Combining **Calvinist** theology with evangelistic zeal, Stearns was both the driving force and the organizing genius in the Sandy Creek Baptist Church. In 1758, he led in organizing the Sandy Creek Baptist Association, which 12 years later subsequently divided into the General Association of Virginia, the Sandy Creek Association in North

Carolina, and the Congaree Association in South Carolina.

In many ways, Stearns was the father of the Baptists in the mid-Atlantic South. When the Separate and the Regular Baptists made peace in Virginia in 1787, the new situation allowed Stearns's followers to exercise a major influence within Virginia Baptist circles. Likewise, in South Carolina, the revivalist impulse of the Sandy Creek followers combined with the more formal elements of the Charleston Baptist Association to forge a style that became typical of nineteenth-century Baptists. Even in recent times, **Primitive Baptists,** who hearken back to the 1787 concord between Separates and Regulars, have staked claims to Stearns's influence and leadership in their movement.

Further Reading: Powell, Joshua W. "Shubal Stearns and the Separate Baptist Tradition." *Founders Journal* 44 (Spring 2001): 16–31; Sparks, John. *The Roots of Appalachian Christianity: The Life and Legacy of Elder Shubal Stearns.* Lexington: University Press of Kentucky, 2001.

Sean Lucas

STODDARD, SOLOMON (1643–1728/9)

Solomon Stoddard, scion of a prominent New England family, graduated from Harvard College in 1670. After a brief service as librarian at his alma mater, he assumed the pulpit of the late Eleazar Mather (whose widow he also married) in the frontier town of **Northampton,** Massachusetts. So commanding was his personality and **preaching,** and so large his sphere of influence, that in the Connecticut River valley he earned the nickname "Pope Stoddard." Stoddard's five "harvests" in 1679, 1683, 1690, 1712, and 1718, though more modest in size and temper, are considered precursors of the **Great Awakening** revivals of the 1730s and 1740s that were instigated and defended by his grandson, **Jonathan Edwards.** Each of these events in Stoddard's ministry brought a surge in professions of **conversion** and in new members for the Northampton congregation. Earlier awakenings in Scotland, such as those under David Dickson from 1625 to 1630, provided a precedent for Stoddard's harvests.

Stoddard's own **theology of revival** begins with the conversion experience, which became New England's unique and most enduring contribution to Protestant religion. Stoddard and most of the clergy in the region agreed on the necessity of a conversion experience in order to confirm true regeneration. Conversion in New England, at this time, went beyond mere faith in the Christian message or even holy living. It was a deeply personal, almost mystical, experience of God's grace. Stoddard held that conversion—the outward aspect of inward rebirth or regeneration through the Holy Spirit—was necessary for **assurance of salvation** and that believers could have certain knowledge of the time when their conversion occurred. Though conversion was a sovereign and gracious work of God, God did not work apart from the "means of grace," such as church attendance, listening to sermons, and private **prayer** and reflection. This deeply psychologized and introspective account of religious experience led Stoddard to speculate on the role of the preacher in bringing about conversions.

Stoddard prescribed both the correct method for promoting conversions and the essential order of a true conversion experience. Two crucial preparatory steps always preceded authentic conversion—awakening and humiliation. Awakening, or conviction, consisted in the awareness of one's own moral depravity and humiliation in the face of the paltriness of one's good works. Stoddard explained that awakening is brought about by the preaching of the law and of the terrors of eternal damnation. The preacher had to exhort sinners regarding their moral duty, not that they might rely on their good works, but that they might realize the impossibility of keeping the law. The preacher's style was also important because people had to be made "sensible" of their danger of eternal punishment. Stoddard advocated a plain rather than elaborate rhetoric of preaching, urged that notes be left out of the pulpit, and wanted preachers to aim at conviction and decision. Conviction of sin, however, was only a first step, and the gracious influences of God came subsequent to it. The first truly gracious act was divine illumination, the "letting of spiritual light into the soul," which moved the intellect and then

the will. The culmination of this movement was conversion.

Stoddard recognized the value of group meetings as an aid to conversion, and believed that social conditions could alternately favor or hinder individual conversion. While one could know the exact moment of one's own conversion, Stoddard perceived the difficulty—or rather impossibility—of knowing certainly whether others were converted. This led him to his distinctive approach to the sacraments, often referred to as Stoddardeanism. At this time in New England the accepted practice of the congregational churches was to admit converted church members to the Lord's Supper but not those church members who simply professed the faith and lived moral and decent lives. Stoddard rejected this practice because he believed that God's ways in conversion were ultimately inscrutable. His congregation in Northampton, as a result, practiced a more open form of Communion, allowing all church members to the Supper without any concern as to whether they had had a conversion experience.

Though he allowed both the converted and the unconverted to the table, Stoddard did not dissociate the Lord's Supper from conversion. Rather, he argued, in a novel way for his era, that the Supper is a "converting ordinance." The proper purpose of the Supper is to awaken as well as to confirm true faith. Thus Stoddard's sacramental theology and his revival theology were of one piece. Stoddard inveighed against Increase Mather and his son, **Cotton Mather,** for being too rigorous with the Lord's Supper and excluding moral and orthodox yet unconverted Christians from participating. Stoddard also rejected New England's institution of the "halfway covenant" whereby those church members who professed faith, lived morally, and "owned the covenant," but remained unconverted could present their children for baptism. Instead Stoddard kept only one church membership roll, which included both those who had reported a conversion experience and those who had not. Fundamentally, Stoddard's view of the church differed from that of the Mathers. Whereas the Mathers conceived of the church as exclusively consisting of converted members, Stoddard thought of the church as a "covenanted" community in which all who outwardly professed the faith were to be fully accepted as members and pastors were not obliged to determine who was or was not truly converted.

Historians debate Stoddard's legacy. Jonathan Edwards's theology of revival reflects many of his grandfather's concerns, such as the importance of conversion experience as a sign of God's grace and the organic connection between the intellect and the will in conversion. Edwards, however, disliked Stoddard's rigid programming of the conversion experience and his denial that God's grace was active in the earlier stages of humiliation, conviction of sin, and preparation for conversion. After Edwards, the sacramental piety so precious to both Stoddard and to the Mathers was largely lost in the subjective, individualistic emphasis of the emerging revival tradition. The idea that the Lord's Supper is a "means of grace" all but disappeared from many revivalist groups during the 1800s. On the other hand, the conversion experience—even to the present day—remains a hallmark of evangelical Protestantism in its many expressions. It may be anachronistic to call Stoddard a revivalist, but he was one of the earliest and most important transitional figures in the development from Puritanism to revivalism.

Further Reading: Hardman, Keith J. *The Spiritual Awakeners: American Revivalists from Solomon Stoddard to D. L. Moody.* Chicago: Moody Press, 1983; Miller, Perry. "Solomon Stoddard, 1643–1729." *Harvard Theological Review* 34 (1941): 277–320; Schafer, Thomas A. "Solomon Stoddard and the Theology of Revival." In Stuart C. Henry, ed., *A Miscellany of American Christianity: Essays in Honor of H. Shelton Smith*, 328–61. Durham, NC: Duke University Press, 1963.

John Halsey Wood Jr.

STONE, BARTON WARREN (1772–1844)

Barton Warren Stone was an organizer of the "Great Revival" in Kentucky in the decade after 1800, a pivotal figure in the nineteenth-century **restorationist (or Stone-Campbell) movement,** and a founder of what became known as the "Christian Church" in the western states. Reared as an Anglican in southern Maryland and western Virginia, Stone underwent a **conversion** experience in a **Presbyterian** context while studying at the North Carolina classical academy directed by Presbyterian revivalist David Caldwell. In August 1801, Stone was the Presbyterian host to a six-day interdenominational camp meeting at **Cane Ridge,** Kentucky, that has been called America's Pentecost. Reports spread of thousands in attendance and of hundreds of persons falling to the ground and exhibiting other unusual **bodily manifestations** under the influence of the Holy Spirit.

Two years later, while the revival still continued, Stone and four other Presbyterian revivalists separated from the Presbyterian Synod of Kentucky over their refusal to **preach** the Presbyterian doctrine of predestination. According to this doctrine, God has elected or chosen specific individuals to hear the gospel, believe in Christ as their savior, and receive salvation, while electing other individuals (who may also hear the gospel) to be damned. Stone and his colleagues rejected this teaching. They believed that it contradicted the gospel, which they understood to be the good news that God loves all sinners and desires that all shall be saved. Stone also rejected the view that the Holy Spirit must prepare the sinner's heart to accept Christ by some spiritual power other than the preaching of the gospel. He argued instead that the Holy Spirit prepares the sinner's heart to accept Christ as Savior *through* the preaching of the gospel—the message of God's love for sinners.

Calling themselves the Springfield Presbytery (after a town in southern Ohio where one of them was pastor), Stone and his revivalist colleagues continued to promote revival. Yet by June 1804 they became convinced that their new presbytery was standing in the way of Christian unity. Like other Presbyterians, they believed that Christian unity would be a mark of the dawning of the millennium—the thousand-year earthly reign of Christ foretold in biblical **eschatology** and anticipated by many nineteenth-century American Protestants. Encouraged to believe that the millennium was at hand because of the Christian unity they had experienced in the Great Revival, and because of the manumissions (i.e., emancipations of individual slaves) that had accompanied the revival, they dissolved their presbytery and issued a bold call for Christian unity. They published their action and appeal for Christian unity in a pamphlet entitled *Last Will and Testament of Springfield Presbytery* (1804). At the same time, they eschewed all names but "Christian," thus becoming known as the Christian Church in the West.

Following the dissolution of the Springfield Presbytery, Stone advanced interpretations of the significance of Christ's death and of Christ's divinity that challenged the traditional theology of most of his former Presbyterian colleagues. In 1805, two members of the former Springfield Presbytery joined the **Shakers,** who taught that the millennium had begun for all who would renounce their sins and adopt celibacy. Stone, who was happily married to a woman whom he believed had supported and encouraged his ministry, vigorously opposed the Shakers, whom he charged with separating husbands and wives in order to get their land. A tireless advocate of Christian unity, Stone led many of the Christians in the West to unite in 1832 with the followers of **Alexander Campbell,** known as Reformers or Disciples of Christ. By 1860 the Stone-Campbell movement, variously known in the nineteenth century as the Christian Churches, Disciples of Christ, and Churches of Christ (and sometime called restorationism or the Stone-Campbell movement), was the fifth-largest religious group in America, with a membership of nearly 200,000.

Prior to the Great Revival, Stone had emancipated two slaves he inherited from his mother. He later supported the colonization scheme for ending slavery in America. Ultimately he endorsed the call for immediate abolition issued by the **abolitionists** of the 1830s. In order to allow for the liberation of slaves willed to his wife and their children, Stone moved his family from Kentucky to Illinois in 1834. In the 1840s, his continuing millennial hope and concern with eschatology, coupled with his growing disillusionment with the social and spiritual effects of the American political system, led him to

recommend that Christians withdraw from civil government and military service and live as if Christ's reign had already begun.

Further Reading: Conkin, Paul. *Cane Ridge: America's Pentecost.* Madison: University of Wisconsin Press, 1990; Williams, D. Newell. *Barton Stone: A Spiritual Biography.* St. Louis: Chalice Press, 2000.

D. Newell Williams

STONE-CAMPBELL MOVEMENT

see Restorationism and the Stone-Campbell Movement

STUDENT VOLUNTEER MOVEMENT

The Student Volunteer Movement (SVM) was a student-led initiative in **foreign missions** and world evangelization during the late 1800s and early 1900s. It began in 1886, spread rapidly through the **colleges and campuses** of North America and western Europe, and, within four to five decades, was directly responsible for the greatest increase in the number of Christian missionaries in the history of Christianity. Prior to the SVM, the churches of the United States had sent out 2,000 cross-cultural missionaries to other nations. Yet more than 100,000 students joined the SVM, and over 20,000 of them went overseas as full-time long-term missionaries.

The **Presbyterian** missionary Royal Wilder had served in India through the Brethren Society (see **Haystack Prayer Meeting**) for 30 years before he was forced to return home because of illness in 1877. The family settled in Princeton, New Jersey, where his son Robert attended Princeton College and his daughter Grace attended Mt. Holyoke College. At Princeton Robert and his friends studied the Bible and **prayed** for missionaries. In his junior year he attended a conference of the Inter-Seminary Alliance and was inspired to challenge his fellow students to pray for revival and missions. That fall Wilder and his friends established the Princeton Foreign Mission Society and Grace began a similar group with 34 young **women** at Mt. Holyoke. In his senior year, Robert and Grace met regularly and prayed for a widespread missionary movement in the colleges and universities of America that would send out 1,000 new missionaries. In the summer of 1886, **Dwight L. Moody** in conjunction with the **Young Men's Christian Association** organized a four-week Bible conference for college students at the Mt. Hermon School in Northfield, Massachusetts. Before Robert left for the conference, Grace predicted that there would be 100 student volunteers for foreign missions enlisted at the conference.

The conference drew together 251 students from 86 universities, and Wilder immediately took the initiative to create a place for foreign missions by persuading Moody to have a world missions night. The evening was declared "The Meeting of the Ten Nations," with representatives from Japan, Persia, Native America, Siam, Germany, Armenia, Denmark, Norway, China, and India. Throughout the following days of the conference, 100 students made a pledge to serve the cause of foreign missions, and these student volunteers came to be called the "Mt. Hermon Hundred." Wilder then enlisted his Princeton college friend John Forman to join him in promoting the SVM across the country. During their first year, 162 campuses received a visit and 2,106 volunteers were secured, including Samuel Zwemer (a later missionary among Muslims), Samuel Moffett (a missionary to Korea), and Robert Speer (a statesman of the missions movement). The students not only pledged themselves to missionary service but also exhorted the American churches to embrace the cause of foreign missions. Many congregations came to believe that they had sinned in neglecting missions, resolved to change their priorities, and came together in what became known as the "forward movement" of the churches.

The SVM held its first conference from February 26 to March 1, 1891, in Cleveland, Ohio, where 151 colleges were represented, including 580 student delegates, 31 returned foreign missionaries, and 32 representatives of missionary societies. Wilder was 27 years old when this first conference took place, and by that time 320 SVM missionaries had already left for services on the mission field. Their motto was "The Evangelization of the World in this Generation"—a bold proclamation that became the distinguishing mark of the SVM. The SVM conferences were highly successful and held every 4 years for 76 years. Following the first conference Wilder traveled through England visiting campuses in Cambridge, Oxford, and London to create an international SVM movement. After 18 months in England he felt the need to fulfill his own promise of missions service, and he departed for India, the nation of his birth. After Royal Wilder's death, Robert's sister Grace and their mother also returned to India.

The second SVM conference in 1894 in Detroit drew 1,082 attendees. Renowned missionaries such as J. Hudson Taylor of the Chinese Inland Mission delivered addresses. At the 1898 conference 1,598 student delegates, visiting missionaries, and other delegates arrived, for a total of 2,221 participants. Wilder then spent two additional years visiting campuses in the United States and in Norway, Denmark, Sweden, and Finland. After two years of campus work, he again returned again to India. He continued, however, to make periodic trips to Europe to meet with student groups and organize conferences. Due to poor health, he at last left India for Europe while leaving the work in India to hundreds of missionary volunteers whom he himself had recruited. Robert Wilder died in 1938 at the age of 75.

The SVM reached its zenith in the years just before and after World War I. Beginning at the Des Moines Conference in December 1919 and January 1920, some participants in the movement began to question the traditional concepts of sin and salvation. The SVM began to focus its work on health, education, and social amelioration in foreign nations, and gave less attention to evangelism as such. With the theological changes brought by the Modernist movement in theology, there were a diminishing number of new missionary recruits in the 1920s and 1930s. While the SVM had a vestigial existence until the 1960s, it exerted its strongest influence from about 1890 through the 1920s.

Further Reading: Barnes, M. Craig. "John R. Mott." In Charles H. Lippy, ed., *Twentieth-Century Shapers of American Popular Religion*, 301–10. New York: Greenwood

Press, 1989; Howard, David. *Student Power in World Evangelism.* Downers Grove, IL: InterVarsity Press, 1979; Showalter, Nathan. "The End of a Crusade: The Student Volunteer Movement for Foreign Missions and the Great War." ThD dissertation, Harvard University, 1990; Tatlow, Tissington. *Student Christian Movement.* London: Student Movement Press, 1933; Wilder, Robert. *Christ and the Student World.* New York: Revell, 1935.

Mark W. Cannister

SUNDAY, WILLIAM ASHLEY (BILLY) (1862–1935)

From humble beginnings on an Iowa farm, Billy Sunday became one of the most sensational **preachers** in American revivalist history. At a time of dizzying technological and social change at the beginning of the twentieth century, Sunday stood for bedrock social values and political conservatism. At the same time, his extraordinary organizing acumen and personal magnetism anticipated **Billy Graham**'s mass evangelistic crusades in post–World War II America. He was born in 1862 in Ames, Iowa, the son of William and Mary Jane (Cory) Sunday and the younger brother of Albert and Howard Edwin (Ed). William, a Union soldier in the Civil War, died of illness at Camp Patterson, Missouri, without seeing his third son. In 1872, his mother, unable to cope financially with the demands of raising three children on the small farm, sent Billy and Ed to an orphanage in Glenwood, Iowa. After returning home for a time and then living with his grandfather, Sunday left the family to find work. He held several jobs as a fireman and janitor in rural Iowa towns. Later, with the help of a prominent local politician in Nevada, Iowa, on whose farm Sunday worked, he managed to attend high school.

Baseball rescued Sunday from poverty and obscurity and made him nationally famous. When Adrian "Cap" Anson, the celebrated manager of the Chicago White Stockings, discovered Sunday playing in a sandlot game in Marshalltown, Iowa, he quickly signed him to a major-league contract. Playing center field, Sunday was the fastest player in the major leagues, so fast that the White

Stockings sometimes arranged match races for him with track stars. But he could not hit with consistency. At a time when batting averages sometimes reached .400, his lifetime mark was .254. A few years into his baseball career in 1886, Sunday wandered into the Pacific Garden Mission in Chicago after a long night with fellow ballplayers in a seedy section of the city. Profoundly moved by the revival service, he underwent a **conversion** experience.

In 1888, Sunday married Helen Thompson, whom he had met at the Jefferson Park **Presbyterian** Church shortly after his conversion. Through the years, her husband and other friends called her "Nell" while the public knew her as "Ma Sunday." They had four children—Helen, George, William Jr., and Paul. In 1891, Sunday gave up baseball and joined the **Young Men's Christian Association** (YMCA) as an assistant secretary. In the course of his work with the YMCA, Sunday honed his remarkable natural speaking abilities. In 1894, he joined the nationally recognized evangelist **J. Wilbur Chapman** as an assistant. From Chapman, he learned the rudiments of the revival business. Sunday set out on his own as an itinerant evangelist in January 1896, beginning his ministry at a small gospel meetinghouse in Garner, Iowa. The Chicago Presbytery ordained him to ministry in 1903.

At an astonishing pace, his revivals in churches and tents in small towns became formidable mass meetings in larger and larger cities. His organization built temporary wooden tabernacles to hold masses of people who flocked to his campaigns. Sawdust covered the tabernacle floors and those listeners who responded to Sunday's call for converts marched up the aisles to shake his hand. Within a decade of the beginning of his revival work, the former center fielder had become the most exciting national evangelist since the great **Dwight L. Moody.** Moody, whose work dominated the revival movement from 1875 until his death in 1899, had pioneered large evangelistic revivals, drawing massive audiences to crusades in the United States and abroad and setting a pattern for extensive organization that included large numbers of recruits and big budgets. Sunday would expand

Postcard of Billy Sunday, containing the exhortation "It's up to you" (1908). Courtesy of the Billy Graham Center Archives, Wheaton, IL.

the scope of Moody's methods to a new level of big-time American evangelism.

By 1912, Sunday had become a national religious phenomenon. His simple message of sin and repentance and his acrobatic stage mannerisms rocketed him to fame. He was a commanding presence, leaping about the stage, slapping his hands, crashing his fists on chairs. He would pretend to shadowbox the devil, to pick up giant boulders and hurl them into the crowd, and to slide like a ballplayer crossing home plate. He used humorous rhymes, homilies, slang, and storytelling replete with mimicry. His performances were strikingly unconventional, even in the world of revival excitement. He drew huge crowds and extraordinary newspaper coverage. But the success of Sunday was attributable to far more than showmanship. He contributed substantially to the business of revivalism, especially in his methods of using a large team to carry out religious

crusades. He and his growing organization drew thousands of people together to carry off meetings in the larger cities. Melding superb organization with talented musicians, concentrated advanced planning, and attention to individual groups such as students, business groups, and **women,** Sunday approached revivalism with the big-business methods of emerging American capitalism. Systematic, thorough, and dedicated, the Sunday team forged a powerful force to gain converts. Ma Sunday stayed by his side during most of the crusades, handling finances and speaking at meetings for women and other events. Sunday's team inspired loyalty. Trombonist Homer Rodeheaver and businesswoman Virginia Asher, for example, stayed with the revival group for many years.

Sunday launched his career at a time of increasing labor tensions and growing crime, a time of massive immigration and the problems of cities beginning to choke in poverty, and a time of attacks against capitalism, religion, and tradition. Sunday's voice hearkened back to simpler times, back to traditional moral values and Fundamentalist theology. Sunday's morality was like a scoreboard—things to do and sins to avoid. **Prayer** was a manly duty; faith was mountain moving. The tough guys were on the side of God. He venerated hard work, godly living, and the **holiness** of motherhood; he condemned sin, vanity, scientists, liberals and radicals, alcohol, novel reading, theaters, and many other amusements. The message was not dainty piety but hard-muscled religion.

A battler for politically conservative causes throughout his life, Sunday opposed liquor, communism, evolution, and modernism—anything he associated with Satan. Never a theologian in any sense, Sunday's simplistic Christianity suited millions of Americans. To the thousands packed into the tabernacles, he was a prophet, a teacher, and an inspiration. His message was not grounded in sophisticated theological equation or subtle argument; it was simple, uncomplicated fundamentalist belief, the time-worn biblical stories told powerfully and coarsely in the language of the street and field. Billy had many enemies, from some church groups and religious figures who decried what they

A dense crowd surrounding the exit to the Pennsylvania Railroad Station in New York City, awaiting the arrival of revivalist Billy Sunday. (George Grantham Bain Photographic Collection, 1917.) Courtesy of the Library of Congress.

saw as his hard-sell, commercial religion to left-wing radicals who were convinced that Sunday's crusades were a serious menace to the rights of workingmen and that his message of conversion and moral uplift meant only to induce passivity. Championed by the Chambers of Commerce, the Rotary Clubs, and other business and fraternal groups, Sunday was telling workers to be loyal, thankful for those few blessings they had. Sunday lamented the decline of corporal punishment in schools and the laxity of parents in controlling their children. He vigorously opposed birth control, something he equated with abortion. At the time, disseminating contraceptive information was against the law, and Sunday believed that teaching birth control was morally evil. But the principal vice he fought was liquor.

By 1916 he was a central figure in **temperance** and the Prohibition movement, traveling the country giving his so-called booze-sermon. For Sunday liquor was anti-God and anti-American. His Detroit revival, held only two months before a statewide vote on Prohibition, was a huge success, and he took credit for the state going dry. Sunday's popularity grew to such proportions that some newspaper columnists suggested that he might be considered as a possible candidate for president of the United States. A national poll ranked him as one of the most popular individuals in the United States. Although he never seriously considered mounting a presidential run, he had become a powerful political voice. And his eagerness to interject his religious crusades in fights for political causes anticipated the later careers of such figures as **Jerry Falwell** and **Pat Robertson.** At the beginning of World War I Billy was an especially fervent prowar spokesman, using his revival platforms as a forum. With his evangelism taking on even more of a strident, patriotic sound, he began a vicious, anti-German assault and was as enthusiastic as anyone in America in promoting the sales of war bonds. He made speech after speech attacking the German menace.

In April 1917, Sunday arrived in New York City and began a revival that would eclipse all his earlier attempts to evangelize America. For over 10 weeks, Sunday preached to more than 1 million people, claimed nearly 100,000 converts, and raised $120,000 for various charities related to President Wilson's war effort. The New York campaign was the high-water mark for Sunday's career, demonstrating his mass appeal even in the country's largest metropolitan area with its diverse ethnic and political character. In filling his New York tabernacle night after night, Sunday put to rest the warnings from critics and friends alike that embarrassment and scorn awaited him. His New York success demonstrated the high degree of impact he had on both religious evangelism and social-political activism. In another remarkable demonstration of his national political influence, Sunday delivered a patriotic speech in the U.S. House of Representatives in Washington, DC, in January 1918. Not only lashing out at the German menace but also at radicals he felt were parading around the country tearing down its fundamental ideals, its religious heritage, and its values, he roused the Congress to its feet with his fervor and intensity.

Following the end of the war, it became clear that Sunday's evangelistic career was in eclipse. As he got older, the uniqueness and power of his revivals declined. The early 1930s ushered in **radio** evangelism, something that Sunday, at his advancing age, never mastered. As his revival crowds became smaller, he drastically reduced the size of the revival team and stopped building the large wooden tabernacles for his meetings. The great days of huge revivals gave way to stops in Mount Holly, New Jersey; Erie, Pennsylvania; and other smaller towns, especially in the **South.** Nevertheless, he refused to quit. His later years were personally wrenching. The well-publicized personal and financial difficulties of his sons George and William, and the deaths of his daughter Helen in 1932 and of George in 1933, apparently of suicide, took an enormous toll on both Sunday and Nell. Nevertheless, despite those trials and his increasing debilitation due to heart disease, he preached almost to the day he died in Chicago in 1935. He did not live to see further

tragedy in his family. In 1938 William was killed in an automobile accident and in 1944 the last surviving Sunday child, Paul, died in an airplane crash. Nell buried her husband and all four of her children.

Sunday remains a towering figure in the history of American revivalism. Within 15 years of his death, the great crusades of Billy Graham became like echoes of the Sunday crusades—the advance workers and massive publicity, the cooperation of local churches and civic organizations, the big choirs, and the call for converts. Evangelists such as **Oral Roberts** paid tribute to Sunday's extraordinary influence in showing how to run big-city revivals and in helping to meld Fundamentalist religion into a conservative political agenda. Through his uncompromising commitment, energy, and style, through his sound business strategies, and through his innovative revival methods, Sunday paved the way for a new generation of evangelists.

Further Reading: Billy Sunday Home and Visitors Center Web site, Winona Lake, Indiana. http://members. tripod.com/~kclocke/sunday.html; Bruns, Roger. *Preacher: Billy Sunday and Big-Time American Evangelism.* New York: Norton, 1992; Dorsett, Lyle. *Billy Sunday and the Redemption of Urban America.* Grand Rapids, MI: Eerdmans, 1991; Gullen, Karen. *Billy Sunday Speaks.* New York: Chelsea House, 1970; Martin, Robert F. *Hero of the Heartland: Billy Sunday and the Transformation of American Society, 1862–1935.* Bloomington: Indiana University Press, 2002; McLoughlin, William. *Billy Sunday Was His Real Name.* Chicago: University of Chicago Press, 1955; Billy Graham Center Archives. "What Does the BGC Archives Have about Billy Sunday?" http:// www.wheaton.edu/bgc/archives/faq/5.htm.

Roger A. Bruns

SWAGGART, JIMMY LEE (1935–)

Jimmy Lee Swaggart is a **Pentecostal** evangelist, **radio and television** broadcaster, pastor, and gospel singer. He became one of the world's most successful and popular television **preachers** of the 1970s and 1980s. In 1988 the **Assemblies of God**—the denomination that had ordained him to ministry—defrocked him for sexual misconduct, and then he commenced a less successful ministry as an independent evangelist. Born in Ferriday, Louisiana, Swaggart grew up in an Assembly of God church and began preaching and **hymn** singing in church and on street corners as a youth in Manghum, Louisiana. At age 17 he married Frances Anderson. By age 22 he had begun itinerant evangelistic ministry and soon became famous in part because of his association with his cousin, the rock-and-roll performer Jerry Lee Lewis. His evangelistic "crusade" work continued to grow through the 1960s and 1970s even though the popularity of **camp and tent meetings** was declining during this period.

After ordination by the Assemblies of God, Swaggart served a short time with his father as a pastor of a small church, but soon his passion for crusade work led him back into evangelism. In 1969 he began broadcasting his fiery brand of preaching and gospel music on radio, and soon he had gained a national audience. By 1973 he had switched to citywide crusades and began focusing on developing his television ministry. He gradually replaced most of his radio broadcasts with an increasingly popular television program and continued to build his crusade work through the 1970s and 1980s. In an attempt to communicate beyond southern Pentecostalism and reach out to mainstream America, Swaggart in 1981 softened his media image to become less hostile and emotional and more acceptable to the general public. His new approach soon produced one of the most successful religious broadcasts and evangelistic organizations in the country.

Swaggart's message was rooted in Fundamentalism. While the core of his supporters was Pentecostal he also had a following among mainline Protestants and **Roman Catholics.** As his audience grew, he founded a Baton Rouge congregation named the Family Worship Center and a Bible college, and he published a national monthly magazine, the *Evangelist.* Swaggart's success and popularity continued to grow in the 1980s as his fiery preaching, homey image, and extraordinary platform speaking and musical talent captivated audiences throughout the United States and in numerous **foreign missionary** crusades. At a time when many crusade ministries were floundering

and observers said their time had passed, Swaggart proved that he was still able to draw crowds and build a following. His sermons included open criticism by name of other evangelists and leaders, with reference to their alleged theological errors, character deficiencies, and financial improprieties. Swaggart was vehemently opposed to Roman Catholicism, even though, as noted, he had a Roman Catholic audience. He was also quite critical of independent **Charismatics** and the **prosperity gospel** or Word of Faith movements that taught believers to lay claim to health and wealth from God. This proved to be part of his later downfall, as many of those he criticized spoke out against him when he was in trouble.

While on the verge of starting his own Pentecostal fellowship, which might have threatened the Assemblies of God, Swaggart suffered a major setback when evidence surfaced regarding Swaggart's sexual misconduct with New Orleans prostitutes. The ensuing scandal led to a loss of credibility and severe financial problems for Swaggart's organization. Although Swaggart confessed that the charges were true and claimed to have repented, he refused to accept rehabilitative discipline from his denomination. In April 1988, when Swaggart failed to withdraw from ministry for a period of time, according to the terms of suspension imposed by his church superiors, the Assemblies of God removed him from ministry. Swaggart drew criticism from religious and secular leaders for failing to submit to the disciplinary process imposed by his denomination.

In Swaggart's struggle to survive he reestablished his ministry as independent organization. He appointed his son, Donnie, and wife, Francis, as leaders over the church and evangelistic ministry for a brief interim. Within months after his public confession of sin he declared himself to be spiritually restored and he returned to ministry. Though he attempted to maintain the former level of operations, the television ministry and Bible college suffered a devastating decline in donations. The church dwindled to less than 500 members. By 1990 it appeared that Swaggart's ministry was soon to end. During the next several years, rumors circulated regarding further sexual and financial misconduct on Swaggart's part, some of it related to a questionable real estate investment scheme that was enabling him to stay afloat financially. By 1998 he appeared to have weathered the crisis, and was able to maintain a modest television ministry. Though his influence has diminished from its peak in the 1980s, he has been able to maintain a core of loyal supporters and began to see modest growth in the period from 1999 to 2004.

Further Reading: Camp, J. "Rich in Disgrace: Salvation of an Empire." Interview transcript, CNN/Time Impact, May 3, 1989; Guiliano, Michael J. *Thrice Born: The Rhetorical Comeback of Jimmy Swaggart.* Macon, GA: Mercer University Press, 1999; Jimmy Swaggart Ministries Web site. http://www.jimmyswaggart.com/; Lundy, Hunter. *Let Us Prey: The Public Trial of Jimmy Swaggart.* Columbus, MS: Genesis Non Fiction, 1999.

Daniel Hedges

SWEDISH AMERICAN REVIVALS

see Lutheran, German American, and Scandinavian American Revivals

T

TATE, MARY MAGDALENA "LENA" STREET LEWIS (1871–1930)

Mary Tate was the **African American** female founder of a **Holiness-Pentecostal** denomination, Church of the Living God, the Pillar and Ground of the Truth. Born in Dickson County, Tennessee, to Belfield and Nancy Hall Street, she learned to read and was taught the rudiments of religion by her mother. While still in her youth, her knowledge of the Bible and her persuasive ability drew large crowds. She married David Lewis, a furnace worker, in 1888, by whom she had two sons. In the late 1890s Tate established the Latter Day Church of the Foundation of True Holiness and Sanctification based on the teaching that the pursuit of holiness or **sanctification** must direct one's entire life. From 1895 to 1902, her religious work was known as "the Do Rights," and Tate became known as "Little Miss Do Right." In 1903 she gave her church a name that she said had been divinely revealed to her—the Church of the Living God, the Pillar and Ground of the Truth without Controversy. The governing board of trustees and bishops ordained her as a bishop and she served as general overseer of the church from 1903 until her death in 1930. In 1908, Tate experienced **healing** from sickness and received "the baptism of the Holy Ghost and fire" in Greenville, Alabama. Some became afraid of her at this time because she was acting strangely, leaping, **shouting,** and **speaking in tongues.**

In the decade after Tate's **baptism in the Holy Spirit** her church grew rapidly. She was married a second time, to Robert Tate, around 1914. While in Philadelphia in 1930 she sustained frostbite in her foot, underwent surgery, suffered gangrene and sugar diabetes, and died at the Philadelphia General Hospital. She was buried in Dickson, Tennessee, and her body was moved in 1964 to Greenwood Cemetery in Nashville. The church organization was subdivided into three "dominions" in 1933, with separate governance, incorporating 16 states. Female as well as male bishops and **preachers** have continued to be a part of the church's tradition. For the centennial celebration of the church organization in 2003, the three dominions met together in Nashville, Tennessee.

Tate's church members include the father of gospel sacred steel guitar music, Rev. Willie Eason (1922–), who resides in St. Petersburg, Florida. Eason began by singing and playing gospel music to passersby on street corners in Chicago, New York, and Philadelphia. Each dominion within Tate's church has its own distinctive musical style and delivery, often including shouts, marches, and the use of steel guitars. The Keith dominion is the largest of the three dominions, with approximately 30,000 members in the United States,

Canada, England, Africa, and the Caribbean Islands.

Further Reading: DuPree, Sherry Sherrod. *African-American Holiness Pentecostal Movement: An Annotated Bibliography.* New York: Garland, 1996; DuPree, Sherry Sherrod. *Biographical Dictionary of African-American Holiness-Pentecostals, 1880–1990.* Washington, DC: Middle Atlantic Regional Press, 1989; Elliot, James C. Bishop. *Centennial Celebration 100 Years, 1903–2003, House of God, Which Is the Church of the Living God the Pillar and Ground of Truth, without Controversy, Inc. Keith Dominion.* September 18–21, 2003, n.p.; Lewis, Meharry H. *Mary Lena Lewis Tate: A Street Called Straight (Acts 9:11).* Nashville, TN: New and Living Way, 2002; Manning, Geraldine. "World Within, World Without: A Liberating View." D.Min. thesis, Wesley Theological Seminary, 1996; Payne, Wardell J., ed. *Directory of African American Religious Bodies.* 2nd ed. Washington, DC: Howard University Press. 1995.

Sherry Sherrod DuPree

TAYLOR, NATHANIEL WILLIAM (1786–1858)

Nathaniel Taylor was a Congregationalist theologian, pastor, and educator whose writings advanced a **theology of revivals** that modified traditional **Calvinist** teachings and stressed the role of human initiative and choice in the process of **conversion.** Born in New Milford, Connecticut, he entered Yale in 1800, but a condition affecting his eyes prevented his graduation until 1807. After graduation he studied with President **Timothy Dwight** and became his amanuensis. Ordained in 1812, he was called as pastor of First Church, New Haven. Handsome, eloquent, and dignified, he became one of the most powerful **preachers** of his day. In 1822 Yale formed its Divinity School, and he became a professor of theology, where he remained until his death.

In the eighteenth century, the creedal faith of the American Congregational and **Presbyterian** churches, as well as other groups, was the theology of John Calvin, adapted by **Jonathan Edwards.** To guard against the notion that humans can be saved by any merit of their own, Calvinism taught that people have only a limited freedom of choice.

In his classic *Freedom of the Will* (1754), Edwards wrestled with this problem, stating that humans have an ability to repent (or "natural ability") but are constrained by their fallen, depraved nature ("moral inability"). The human will follows the strongest motive, which, for unconverted sinners, leads them away from God and not toward God. This Edwardsean system, modified by Edwards's disciples—Samuel Hopkins, Joseph Bellamy, and Timothy Dwight—was the orthodox belief of most New England churches in 1822, and was widely influential in the **South** and the states of the West.

When Taylor began teaching at Yale, being an original thinker, he disagreed with this system, having for his motto "follow truth if it carries you over Niagara." He wished to be in accord with the emerging democratic ethos of Jacksonian America, and the **Second Great Awakening** (1795–1835), which had a strong appeal to the masses. For decades, churchgoers in New England had been taught to await patiently the Holy Spirit's movements—often for long periods—before they could expect salvation, and yet this teaching was an impediment to the mass evangelism of the early-1800s revivals. Believing that Edwardseanism did not accord with the demands of the times, Taylor's intention was to formulate a revival theology that would show how people could respond immediately to an evangelist's invitation. Insisting on the reality of free choice, he taught that the will is not another name for the strongest motive, but is an independent power to choose between motives. Modifying—if not denying—the doctrines of original sin and total depravity, Taylor said that no one became depraved but by his or her own acts, because sinfulness does not pertain to human nature as such. Rather than being born depraved, humans have sinful inclinations that invariably lead them into sin. "Sin is in the sinning," and therefore it is "original" only in being universal. Humans always have "power to the contrary" to avoid sin. Despite these new theological ideas, Taylor wished in a rather traditional way to facilitate revivals and conversions. He held that his teaching arose from a correlation of biblical truths with the facts of human consciousness. For successful evangelism, Taylor taught that appeals should be made to the natural desire for happiness in humans, that they must choose the highest good and reject evil ways. This desire for happiness he called "self-love," saying that it will lead one to choose Christ. In a regenerated person this will eventually become an unselfish love for God.

After **Charles G. Finney's** conversion in 1821, and his explosive career as a revivalist, he developed ideas almost identical to Taylor's. They taught that preachers must confront sinners with their lost state, and demand an immediate, on-the-spot response to the gospel message. Taylor regarded humans as free and rational, and therefore fully responsible for everything they did. No longer could they defer salvation by blaming Adam, or claiming that the Holy Spirit had not yet worked in their hearts. Taylor's and Finney's innovations were a far-reaching step in the move to modify Calvinism, interpreted by many as making concessions to Arminianism in teaching human ability and choice. This aroused a storm of controversy throughout the nation. In 1828 Taylor presented the "New Divinity" in his *Concio ad Clerum* address to the Congregational clergy of Connecticut, and open conflict broke out, dividing the churches into "Taylorites" and "Tylerites," the latter following Bennet Tyler. The controversy became so heated that a more orthodox seminary—the Hartford Seminary, in Hartford, Connecticut—was formed in 1834 with Tyler as president. The debate went far beyond New England, due largely to Finney's writings, and became the chief theological reason for the schism in the Presbyterian Church in 1838.

Further Reading: Bainton, Roland. *Yale and the Ministry: A History of Education for the Christian Ministry at Yale from the Founding in 1701.* New York: Scribners, 1957; Mead, Sidney E. *Nathaniel William Taylor, 1786–1858: A Connecticut Liberal.* New Haven, CT: Yale University Press, 1967; Sweeney, Douglas A. *Nathaniel Taylor, New Haven Theology, and the Legacy of Jonathan Edwards.* New York: Oxford University Press, 2003; Wayland, John T. *The Theological Department in Yale College, 1822–1858.* New Haven, CT: Yale University Press, 1933.

Keith J. Hardman

TELEVISION

see Radio, Television, and Revivals

TEMPERANCE MOVEMENT AND REVIVALS

Temperance (i.e., moderation) in the use of alcoholic beverages was the watchword of an important movement of social reform in U.S. history, and one in which **women** played a decisive role. The Women's Christian Temperance Union (WCTU), founded in 1874, not only served the crusade for temperance but furthered the cause of women's suffrage and other legal reforms on behalf of women. Religious leaders, as early as the **colonial** era, expressed their concern over the deleterious effects of alcohol abuse. Increase Mather **preached** two famous sermons in 1673 against the sin of drunkenness, expressing the common view that "drink is in itself a creation of God, and to be received with thankfulness" but that drunkenness is a sin. His son, **Cotton Mather,** inveighed against upper-class intemperance and published a 1726 address to those who frequently visit taverns. The early **Methodists,** including John Wesley and **George Whitefield,** opposed distilled spirits and yet were harsher in their view of tea drinking than they were regarding wine or beer consumption. Physician Benjamin Rush, a signer of the Declaration of Independence and physician for the Colonial Army during the American Revolution, prepared a pamphlet on the medical effects of alcohol in 1789 that influenced military policy and his own **Presbyterian** Church. In the same year, the General Assembly of the Presbyterian Church passed its first sobriety resolution. The need for temperance reform became imperative as the consumption of distilled spirits in the United States rose toward an average of about four gallons per capita per year by 1830.

The religious revivals of the **Second Great Awakening** (1795–1830) and the temperance movement of the same period overlapped in their leadership, in their emphasis on personal holiness, and in their methods. Ironically, the movement for temperance during the 1800s moved toward an increasingly radical or intemperate position insisting on a complete prohibition of alcohol consumption in society and an individual commitment to total abstinence from alcohol, or teetotalism. Historians have suggested two main ideas or motivations guiding temperance leaders. First, they held an optimistic viewpoint concerning human nature and its ability to refrain from sin—a mind-set encouraged by radical revivalists who affirmed God's ability to induce **sanctification** and eradicate all sin from human life. Second, from a sociological standpoint, temperance leaders were typically members of the elite class who wished to exert social control over the unruly conduct—fueled by alcohol consumption—they saw in the working classes.

Temperance and revival meetings shared a common structure and drama during the era of the Second Great Awakening. Taking lessons from Methodist itinerancy, Congregationalist and

This picture reproduces the printed pledge used for joining a temperance society. Two men stand at a table, with one holding out a feather pen to another with wife and child, stressing the family benefits of his promise to stop drinking. (Thomas S. Sinclair, lithographer, 1840s.) Courtesy of the Library of Congress.

Presbyterian ministers interested in various social causes (e.g., temperance, dueling, gambling) began organizing voluntary associations spread by itinerants and involving laypeople. **Lyman Beecher,** a prominent Congregationalist revivalist minister, took up the temperance cause and in 1810 began to develop an organized movement. The Presbyterians, in 1811, began serious inquiries into how intemperance might be countered. A year later, the Methodist Episcopal Church resolved that its ministers would participate in the temperance movement and advocated prohibition on the sale and use of various sorts of intoxicants. By 1818, 40 local temperance societies had begun in Massachusetts alone. The focus began to shift from opposing the use of distilled spirits to opposing all intoxicants apart from medicinal or sacramental use. This approach of "ultraism" can be traced directly to New School **Calvinism**'s emphasis on moral principles that were universally binding. There could be no legitimate uses for something so destructive in its effects as alcohol. A new line of biblical interpretation—the "two wine theory" endorsed by Eliphalet Nott in 1837–1838, which mistakenly held that the "wine" drunk in biblical times contained no alcohol—paved the way for the removal of fermented wine even from sacramental use in the Lord's Supper. In the United States today, **Baptist, Holiness, Pentecostal,** and nondenominational churches generally use unfermented grape juice rather than wine in their services of Communion— a long-term legacy of the nineteenth-century temperance movement.

The American Temperance Society (ATS), formed in 1826, marked the transition from regional societies to a national movement. Lyman Beecher's six-sermon series of 1826 was foundational to the movement. The ATS sent out itinerant agents and 10 years later had created about 8,000 auxiliaries with about 1.5 million members. The society also held awakening meetings, patterned after revival meetings, consisting of adapted **hymns,** public **prayers,** theatrical preaching, and testimonies from reformed drunkards, and culminating in the signing of a temperance pledge. This pattern of awakening, conviction, and decision—reminiscent of the **altar** call used to promote Christian faith decisions—showed the parallels between revival and temperance meetings. The eventual prominence of revival ministers such as **Charles Finney,** who preached a perfectionist message, illustrates the importance of human decision making and commitment to personal change common to both temperance meetings and revivals. Finney's famous career in the **Burned-Over District** of New York began at the invitation of a temperance leader in 1830. Finney's rhetoric included "demon rum" as a major hindrance to revival, and he portrayed the earthly life of a drunkard as a metaphor for the state of the condemned in hell. Finney brought an egalitarian emphasis to what had previously been an elite cause.

During the 1840s, a **Roman Catholic awakening in French Canada** centered on the theme of temperance. The awakening's greatest preacher was Father Charles Chiniquy (1809–1899), known as the apostle of temperance. As parish priest at Beauport, near Quebec City, in March 1840 Chiniquy recruited about 1,300 of his parishioners for membership in a Temperance Society. He began preaching throughout French Canada and sometimes enrolled as many as 17,000 in a single month. By 1849 he had given some 500 sermons in 120 parishes to over 200,000 people and he listed some 370,000 **men** and women on the rolls of the Temperance Society—almost the whole of the adult **Roman Catholic** population of the province. Chiniquy's influence with the masses made him an attractive figure to politicians, and by the late 1840s he had aligned himself with a moderate reformist or *bleu* party that worked for changes in Quebec and yet was favorable toward the Catholic Church. In the United States, Roman Catholic revival meetings and **parish missions** in the later nineteenth century often included a temperance pledge. Father Theobald Mathew, of Ireland, invigorated the Catholic temperance cause with his visit to America in 1849. The Catholic revival movement incorporated temperance reform, and "the drunken sinner" became a common cautionary feature of the revival sermon. Though German communities tended to eschew ultraism in favor of abstinence from distilled spirits, the Paulists zealously promoted the

total abstinence pledge. Parish temperance societies were a common feature of the movement, and temperance was linked with economic prosperity for Canadian Catholics.

The "Women's Crusade" of 1873–1874 was a religious movement in the United States that sought to reform American society through overtly opposing the buying and selling of alcoholic beverages. Carrie Nation was among the most vocal of the leaders, and she entered saloons to pray for the salvation of both owners and patrons. From its beginning in a small group of women who met in December 1873 in a Presbyterian church in Hillsboro, Ohio, the movement grew rapidly, and by the summer of 1874 the temperance crusaders had visited more than 900 towns and cities. The local branches of the movement were generally organized within churches and drew on preexisting networks of denominational and missionary societies. The Women's Christian Temperance Union (WCTU) was founded in 1874 as a direct outcome of the Women's Crusade. It was largely white, Protestant, and middle class in its constituency. By 1900, it was the largest women's organization in the United States, and it had expanded its set of causes to include issues other than temperance. The decision to exclude men from leadership in the organization made it an important outlet for the emerging women's movement, and a seedbed for female leaders of national stature, such as Frances Willard. The WCTU at first sought to achieve its aims through moral suasion, but later, when this failed, it advocated legislation to prohibit the consumption of alcohol.

America's best-known revivalist of the early twentieth century, **Billy Sunday,** was a vehement temperance preacher who denounced the use of alcohol in colorful language. After 1900, the temperance movement shifted from an emphasis on personal transformation toward legislative approaches to temperance, and the process culminated in the passage of the 18th Amendment to the U.S. Constitution in 1919, prohibiting "the manufacture, sale, or transportation of intoxicating beverages." One effect of the temperance movement was to secularize the revival pattern of spiritual and personal conversion. Antialcohol policies and attitudes continue today among certain groups of Fundamentalist, Holiness, and Pentecostal Christians in the United States, though Roman Catholics, mainline Protestants, and most evangelical groups generally allow a moderate use of alcohol.

Further Reading: Benowitz, June Melby. "Temperance Movement." In *Encyclopedia of American Women and Religion*, 345–47. Santa Barbara, CA: ABC-CLIO, 1998; Dolan, Jay P. *Catholic Revivalism: The American Experience, 1830–1900*. Notre Dame, IN: University of Notre Dame, 1978; Hirrel, Leo P. *Children of Wrath: New School Calvinism and Antebellum Reform*. Lexington: University Press of Kentucky, 1998; Rorabaugh, W. J. *The Alcoholic Republic: An American Tradition*. New York: Oxford University Press, 1979; Smith, Timothy L. *Revivalism and Social Reform*. New York: Abingdon Press, 1957.

Jonathan Barlow

TENNENT, GILBERT (1703–1764)

The **Presbyterian** clergyman Gilbert Tennent was a celebrated revival **preacher** during the **Great Awakening** of the 1740s, and stirred controversy when he suggested in a 1740 sermon that many of his fellow ministers were unconverted. He was born in County Armagh, Ireland, the first of four sons of William Tennent Sr. and Catherine (Kennedy) Tennent. The other sons were William Jr., born in 1705; John, in 1706; and Charles, in 1711; and they also had a daughter, Eleanor, in 1708. All four sons were educated by their father and entered the ministry. When Gilbert was 15 years old, in 1718, the family immigrated to America. He experienced religious turmoil during his teen years, and studied medicine for a year before undergoing **conversion** and deciding to enter the ministry. From his father he then received a classical education in Greek, Hebrew, and theology. He attended Yale College in the fall of 1724, and received an MA in 1725. Gilbert presented himself before the Philadelphia Presbytery in May 1725, passed his ordination examinations, and was licensed. In December he was called to a church in New Castle, Delaware, but remained only a short time and left abruptly. For this, the synod administered a rebuke in 1726. Apparently he then assisted his father for a time in training young **men** for the ministry. In the fall of 1726 he accepted a call to the church in New Brunswick, New Jersey, and was ordained there.

The people of this area, especially the Dutch, had been challenged for several years by the evangelistic labors of the Dutch **Reformed** pastor **Theodore J. Frelinghuysen,** who had become a storm center in that denomination since his arrival in 1720. Without a doubt he was the initiator of an awakening in New Jersey, but recent studies have cast doubt on the extent of his influence. A friendship grew Tennent and Frelinghuysen, and Frelinghuysen's **Pietism** encouraged Tennent's Puritanism. Tennent studied Frelinghuysen's methods—pointed application of sermons to hearers, seeking conviction of sins and conversion, and a pastoral style bringing the minister into close contact with new converts. Frelinghuysen's influence pertained to pastoral practice. In theological matters, Frelinghuysen added nothing new to Tennent's stance.

With this encouragement, Tennent's zeal increased, and his preaching became much more urgent. Soon a large number were aroused to spiritual concern, both in the New Brunswick region and on Staten Island, where Tennent also labored. In 1735, his father, William Tennent Sr., built the Log College in nearby Pennsylvania—the precursor of later Princeton University—and his determination to spread revival inspired students who studied there. At the same time, the publication of **Jonathan Edwards**'s *Faithful Narrative of the Surprising Work of God* (1737), describing his 1734–1735 **Northampton,** Massachusetts, revival, was arousing great interest on both sides of the Atlantic, going through three editions and 20 printings between 1737 and 1739. These initial thrusts of the Great Awakening were furthered by the arrival from England of Anglican **George Whitefield** on November 2, 1739. His successes in mass evangelism in the south of England had been widely heralded in the press, and expectations were high. William Tennent Sr. visited him, and the two agreed to cooperate. Whitefield visited

New Brunswick on November 13, 1739; preached for Gilbert Tennent; and stated in his journal, "He and his associates are now the burning and shining lights in this part of America." Gilbert Tennent accompanied Whitefield to New York, and Whitefield, hearing him preach there, declared on November 14, "never before heard [I] such a searching sermon.... He is a son of thunder, and does not fear the faces of men" (George Whitefield, *Journals* [1960], 347–48).

For years the anti-revival Old Lights in the Presbyterian synod had opposed William Tennent Sr.'s Log College and his training of New Light pro-revival pastors. In 1738 the synod passed a resolution requiring ministerial candidates to attend a New England or European college, and the Tennents regarded this as a direct attack on their students and school, which indeed it was. Each annual synod meeting was filled with wrangling between the two groups, and an explosive point was reached on March 8, 1740, when

Presbyterian revivalist Gilbert Tennent. Courtesy of the Billy Graham Center Museum, Wheaton, IL.

Gilbert Tennent preached one of the most famous sermons of that century, "The Danger of an Unconverted Ministry," in Nottingham, Pennsylvania. This intemperate sermon, widely reprinted, portrayed the Old Lights as unsaved and as religious hypocrites, and it did much to precipitate the schism of 1741. When Whitefield completed his preaching tour of New England in November 1740, he carried a request from some ministers for Tennent to come to New England and continue the work that Whitefield had begun there. Tennent arrived in Boston in December, and the effect of his preaching to great crowds was even greater than that of Whitefield. Before returning to the Middle Colonies in May 1741, Tennent preached in more than 20 towns, resulting in many conversions.

In 1743 Tennent moved to Philadelphia to take the pulpit of a newly organized New Light Presbyterian church, filled with Whitefield converts. As Tennent grew older he began to work toward the reunion of the church. When the College of New Jersey was established, he became one of its trustees, and in 1753 he went to England to solicit funds for the school. Tennent's first wife died in 1739, and in 1741 he married Cornelia Clarkson. She died in 1753, and he married Sarah Spofford. Three of his children survived him. He is buried in the churchyard at Abingdon, Pennsylvania. Gilbert Tennent may be ranked along with Whitefield, Edwards, and his father, William Tennent Sr., as a leading figure of the Great Awakening.

Further Reading: Fishburn, Janet F. "Gilbert Tennent: Established Dissenter." *Church History* 63 (1994): 31–49; Harper, Miles D. "Gilbert Tennent, Theologian of the New Light." PhD dissertation, Duke University, 1958; Maxson, Charles H. *The Great Awakening in the Middle Colonies*. Chicago: University of Chicago Press, 1920; Old, Hughes Oliphint. "Gilbert Tennent and the Preaching of Piety in Colonial America: Newly Discovered Tennent Manuscripts in the Speer Library." *Princeton Seminary Bulletin* 10 (1989): 132–37; Webster, Richard. *A History of the Presbyterian Church in America*. Philadelphia: Presbyterian Board of Publication, 1857.

Keith J. Hardman

TENNENT, WILLIAM, SR.

see Tennent, Gilbert

TENT MEETINGS

see Camp Meetings and Tent Meetings

THEOLOGY OF REVIVALS

Religious revivals and their supporting theology have occupied a central place in North American Protestant life since the middle of the eighteenth century. At that time, thanks to evangelists such as **George Whitefield** and pastors such as **Jonathan Edwards,** a surge of interest in religion led to what later generations called the **Great Awakening.** This awakening did not represent the first revival to mark American life, nor did it signal the last. Earlier Puritan pastors in **colonial** New England had from time to time noted sparks of increased interest in religion, times of "harvest" when new people came under the church's care. Often those earlier harvest times came after **preachers** offered jeremiads—sermons bemoaning an apparent decline of commitment to God and warning of horrible consequences that would follow from disobeying God's commands.

The concept of a religious upswing following a time of declension is inherent in the word *revival.* It implies that life is being breathed back into something that was once vibrant but is not so any more. The very idea of revival raises theological issues. For if the presence of God had previously manifested itself, one would not expect it to disappear unless God had chosen to withdraw his divine favor. At stake was the character of God. It would seem inconsistent for God to bestow blessings and then remove them. It might be better then to construe revivals in terms of what cultural anthropologists call revitalization movements. A revitalization movement need not follow an actual declension of piety, though some may perceive it as such. Instead revitalization involves a renewal or heightening of commitment among those who are already faithful as well as those who are coming to a new resolution. Revitalization also helps to explain why sociologists

often find that those who experience **conversion** in revivals are persons who are already church members or already religious in some sense, although they may have undergone a deepening of their commitment as a result of some new intensive experience. At the same time, the stated aim of much revivalism is to proclaim the Christian message to those who remain outside the churches and spur them to make a commitment to the Christian way. To this extent, revivalism's goal is conversion, and not just a rekindling of dedication on the part of those already familiar with Christian teaching. Membership gains and increased attendance at worship following revivals have historically been modest and temporary, unless part of a larger demographic movement where new congregations were being formed to accommodate an expanding population.

For New England Puritans, perceptions of decline were consistent with their interpretation of the Bible, particularly of the Hebrew scriptures or Old Testament. In the saga of ancient Israel, Puritans found precedents for their own experience of a cyclical pattern of heightening and declining spiritual life in their communities. God had entered into a covenant with the Hebrew people at Sinai, promising blessing so long as the people remained faithful. So, too, God entered into a covenant with Puritan Christians, likewise promising blessing so long as the people remained faithful to their commitments to God and their covenant with God. Following an Old Testament pattern (see Joshua 24), seventeenth-century Puritan communities periodically renewed their pledge to follow God and God's ways—something like a repetition of vows by a long-married couple. This was sometimes referred to as "owning the covenant," and it suggested a corporate rather than individualistic model of how God related to Christian people.

What complicated the theology of revival for the Puritans, however, was their grounding in the thought of John Calvin, especially as mediated through the writings of **Calvinist** theologians such as William Perkins and William Ames. The most difficult issue for Calvinists was to reconcile human decision making, responsibility, and covenant keeping with the notion of divine predestination. In Puritan understanding, predestination or election meant that God alone determined before all time who would be chosen for salvation and who would be numbered among the rejected or reprobate. Since all depended on God's eternal will, human choices seemed not to matter. Divine determinations were not contingent on the human will. Even the withdrawal of divine blessing might be construed as part of God's providential design for creation rather than a response to a change or decline in human faithfulness. For Calvinistic revival preachers, all persons were trapped by sin and therefore did not deserve to be chosen for salvation. Sin was inherent in human nature as a result of the Fall—the lapse of Adam and Even, the first human pair. Because of sin and depravity all merely human efforts to secure salvation were doomed. Furthermore, predestination logically seemed to require that Christ's death served to atone for the sin only of those whom God had elected for salvation. Strict Calvinists—maintaining the famous "five points" formulated at the Synod of Dort in the Netherlands in 1618–1619—used the term "limited atonement" to imply that the beneficial and salvific effects of Christ's death applied only to the elect. Such a Calvinistic theology of revival was characteristic not only of seventeenth-century Puritans, such as John Cotton, Richard Hooker, **Solomon Stoddard,** and Increase and **Cotton Mather,** but also of eighteenth-century preachers and teachers, such as George Whitefield, Jonathan Edwards, **Jonathan Dickinson, Gilbert Tennent, Samuel Davies, Samuel Blair,** the Anglican **Devereux Jarratt,** and the Baptist **Isaac Backus,** as well as nineteenth-century revivalists such as **James McGready, Asahel Nettleton,** and Bennet Tyler.

Another implication of Calvinistic predestination was that humans did not choose to accept the message of salvation purely as a result of their own volition. Why then would preachers like Edwards, Whitefield, and Nettleton urge their listeners to seek conversion? In actuality, what they urged was not so much a transformation of life in choosing salvation as a looking inward for signs that God

had already bestowed salvation. Through introspection, one could discern the incipient signs of salvation. On the other hand, the Calvinistic theology of salvation held that unconverted persons could dispose or prepare themselves for divine grace through use of the so-called means of grace, that is, attendance at worship, listening to sermons, personal **prayer,** Bible reading, and the keeping of a spiritual journal. One could speak of conversion if one was certain that inward signs provided assurance that one was among the elect.

The revival theology of American Calvinism involved a tension between individuals and the community. On the one hand, the individual had to experience the work of the Holy Spirit and testify to the signs of grace. Thus the individual, interpreting his or her own private and individual experience, was already starting to become an arbiter in matters of faith. This raised the question as to how pastors might determine whether or not an individual had received salvation. Jonathan Edwards, in his *Treatise on the Religious Affections* (1747), conceded that a genuine work of grace would most often manifest itself in behavior that others could observe. The elect were unlikely to live conspicuously immoral lives. On the other hand, a corporate dimension balanced out individual experiences during religious revivals. The church community had to distinguish those who were converted, and thus eligible for church membership, from those who were still unconverted and hence ineligible. Those judged to be converted could enter into the church covenant—a communal arrangement.

At the beginning of the nineteenth century, revivals again revitalized American religious life. They came first in the camp meetings that erupted in southern frontier regions of Kentucky and Tennessee and then in the urban revivals that swept through the emerging factory towns of upstate New York. So powerful were the latter that the some called the area the **Burned-Over District** to recall the revival fires that burned throughout the region. Theologically, these revivals signaled a shift away from the thinking that undergirded the eighteenth-century revivals. By the time this **Second Great Awakening** ebbed, most evangelical

Protestants based their summons to conversion on Arminian notions of free will and attached less importance to Calvinist ideas of predestination. That Arminian approach was especially associated with the **Methodists** and with many—though not all—of the **Baptists** who reaped a harvest of members in these revivals of the early 1800s.

The Calvinist and Arminian theologies of revival reflect different understandings of the nature of God and the role of humanity in the process of salvation. For Arminian Methodists, who traced their roots to John Wesley, humans were indeed mired in sin just as Calvinists believed. Yet if humans freely chose to disobey God's will, they must freely choose to accept the salvation offered to them. This offer came not to some, but to all persons through the atoning death of Christ for all people. When Arminians spoke of divine predestination, they described it not as unconditional—as Calvinists did—but as conditional. That is, God chose for salvation those persons whom God foreknew would freely choose to accept the Christian gospel. According to this conditional concept of predestination, God's choice is contingent on human choice, rather than vice versa. **Charles G. Finney,** who adapted frontier **camp meeting** techniques for his urban revivals, admitted to being ignorant of Calvinistic doctrine as taught in the Westminster Confession (1648), even though he had been ordained to serve as a **Presbyterian** minister in New York State. Finney prayed by name for sinners to respond to the gospel call and urged those who were uncertain about their spiritual state to come forward in an **altar call** to the "anxious bench," and there to wrestle spiritually until they came to **assurance of salvation.** Finney thus foreshadowed the late nineteenth- and early twentieth-century revivalist **Billy Sunday**'s invitation to hit the "sawdust trail" of his makeshift tabernacles and come forward to shake his hand as a sign of repentance. He also anticipated the master twentieth-century evangelist **Billy Graham**'s invitation to come forward to signal having made a decision for Christ.

Finney, Sunday, and Graham thus assigned greater importance to individuals and individual decisions than was the case in the earlier Calvinist

theology of revival. The work of God, on this view, was to stir humans to make a decision and accept the gift of grace that is offered in Christ's universal atoning work. The decline of Calvinism and the ascendancy of Arminianism resulted in part from the congruence of Arminian individualism with the spirit of American democracy. The political ideology of the new republic elevated the ordinary people and assigned to them the power to govern through elected representatives. Analogously, the emerging theology of revivals empowered individuals to search their souls, to cast aside sin, and freely to accept the gift of grace. Humanity thus became the theological master of its own destiny. Calvinism had had a pessimistic understanding of human nature according to which no one can extricate himself or herself from the state of sin. God must initiate the process of salvation, according to Calvinists. By contrast, Arminianism was more optimistic because it held that humans could choose to leave behind their sinful condition through a free choice to repent of sin, believe the gospel, and accept salvation.

From the eighteenth century onward, revivals often took on a highly emotional character. They frequently involved spiritual **ecstasy,** a moment when individuals surrendered control of themselves to the Holy Spirit. Not only powerful inward emotions, but various sorts of **bodily manifestations** have been common occurrences in American revivals. Some who heard George Whitefield preach fell to the ground, Jonathan Edwards's preaching on one occasion provoked **shouting** and shrieking from his hearers, and Methodist camp meeting revivalist **Peter Cartwright** described those who were seized by the jerking and barking exercises in the **Cane Ridge revival** of 1801. In the **Pentecostal** revivals of twentieth century, that ecstasy has commonly taken the form of **speaking in tongues (glossolalia).** Some Pentecostals claim to have practiced or experienced other New Testament **charismatic gifts,** such as the gift of **healing.** In the half century after World War II, **Oral Roberts** became one of America's best-known practitioners of divine healing. Yet even the participants in revival movements cautioned against equating every emotional outburst with genuine spiritual ecstasy. The Holy Spirit could continue to move quietly, as in the past, through meditation, prayer, and study of scripture, and not only in spectacular emotional and bodily manifestations.

Religious revivals have raised further theological issues. One concerns whether humans themselves can generate a genuine revival. If revivals are the work of God, it would seem that God must determine when and where they occur. But if spiritual revitalization may be stimulated by the proper use of means given by God, then revivals may occur as humans employ those means. Finney argued in his influential and controversial *Lectures on Revivals of Religion* (1835) that revivals occur through human initiative when the God-given means to promote them are properly used. He provocatively asserted in his first lecture that a revival is "not a miracle." Finney's Calvinist critics sometimes compared genuine revivals to a summer rainstorm that arrives unpredictably. A farmer might plant seed and prepare the soil, but he had to wait for rain to fall. Without the rain, there would be no crop to harvest. An adjective commonly invoked in Calvinist revivals was "surprising," as in the title of Jonathan Edwards's *Faithful Narrative of the Surprising Work of God* (1737)—an account of the 1734–1735 revival in Edwards's **Northampton,** Massachusetts congregation. In Finney's theology of revivals, by contrast, the spiritual outcome was less surprising, more predictable, and more a matter of human planning and control.

Another issue in revival theology relates to conversion and its effects. In the middle of the nineteenth century, many who had experienced conversion as a vital religious experience became spiritually impatient when the intensity of that experience faded. Indeed, a characteristic of any ecstatic experience is its transitory quality. The Methodist laywoman **Phoebe Palmer** and others began to seek a "second blessing" or an experience of **sanctification** or holiness that was as fruitful as the experience of conversion. This second transition signified a spiritual growth in which one's own will became conjoined with God's will and God's holiness infused all of one's life. Similar concerns

undergirded the **Revival of 1857–1858,** and the phenomenon of the second blessing would recur in revivals associated with the Victorious Life movement and the growing **Holiness movement** in the decades after the **Civil War.** The link here to revival as revitalization is obvious. The pursuit of holiness in no way suggested declension, but a deepening commitment, a time of nurture and growth that followed some initial experience of the Holy Spirit. Building on the theology of the Holiness movement, twentieth-century **Pentecostalism** offered a two-stage (and sometimes three-stage) conception of the Christian life. Conversion brought individuals into a state of salvation and justification before God. Following conversion, **the baptism in the Holy Spirit** as presented in Pentecostalism marked a further state of spiritual development, outwardly marked by speaking in tongues, and sometimes associated with the release of new charismatic gifts (such as healing or **prophecy**) intended for the benefit of Christians and non-Christians alike. Some Pentecostals of Wesleyan or Methodist background taught that sanctification comes as an intermediate step between conversion and Spirit baptism. Thus this subgroup of Holiness Pentecostals holds to three stages in the Christian experience: conversion, sanctification, and baptism in the Holy Spirit.

Another question for revivalism is the relationship between spiritual nurture—especially during childhood—and the conversion experiences that occur in the midst of revivals. The Connecticut Congregationalist pastor **Horace Bushnell** penned a classic critique of revivalism, entitled *Christian Nurture* (1847, revised 1860). Bothered by his inability to stimulate revivals in his congregation, Bushnell argued that if Christian parents and the church nurtured young children in the faith, they would grow up never thinking of themselves as anything other than devout Christians. A cataclysmic conversion experience would be unnecessary. In many respects Bushnell anticipated the work of psychologist and philosopher William James, who in his *Varieties of Religious Experience* (1902) identified two types of religious personalities. The twice-born type was the one who underwent a classic conversion, such as that proffered in revivals, and adopted a religious worldview. The once-born type was one for whom such an experience was superfluous. The once-born, from childhood onward, evidenced a religious belief system that gave life meaning, and so benefited from consistent Christian nurture in early life rather than a sudden, spasmodic conversion experience.

When James was conducting his studies, Protestant revivalism was experiencing yet another theological shift, one that focused on the understanding of scripture. In the later decades of the nineteenth century, revivalist **Dwight L. Moody** was drawn to the premillennial and dispensationalist **eschatology** of British Bible teacher John Nelson Darby. This approach presumed that history was divided into epochs or dispensations in which God offered humanity a way to salvation, followed in each instance by human failure and divine judgment. Darby claimed that the present era, or "church age," was the sixth of the seven dispensations to occur before the end of the world. Especially important to his thought were the apocalyptic prophecies of the Bible that Darby saw as keys to unlocking the meaning of contemporary events. A sense of urgency followed from Darby's teachings, for time was short to bring souls to salvation. This premillennial and dispensationalist approach to scripture buttressed revivalism's fervent calls for conversion, particularly after the 1909 Scofield reference edition of the King James Bible disseminated Darby's views widely and they became central to twentieth-century American Fundamentalism. The continuing influence of dispensationalism in evangelical and revivalist Christianity may be seen in Hal Lindsey's *The Late Great Planet Earth* (1970) and Tim LaHaye's *Left Behind* (1996–) fiction series, which by 2004 had sold more than 60 million copies.

From the eighteenth century to the present, revivalism has represented ongoing efforts to revitalize and renew religious life as well as to extend the outreach of Protestant churches. Its dominant theological base shifted from Calvinism to Arminianism, from the idea that God alone determined who would be saved to the notion that

individuals were responsible for their own destinies in accepting or rejecting the gift of salvation, although there remain committed Calvinists even today who support revivalism. Concomitantly, the general understanding of Jesus Christ among revivalists has shifted from one that regarded Christ's life and death as effective only for the elect into one that regarded Christ's work as universally accessible. At the same time, there continue to be theological debates over whether all persons need to have a conversion experience or rather may be nurtured into a genuine faith without undergoing conversion. Lively discussion also continues over whether conversion marks the end of the religious quest or a prelude to further intense experiences of sanctification or the reception of charismatic gifts. One cannot take the pulse of American Protestantism in the past or present without appreciating the role of revivals and the theologies sustaining them.

Further Reading: Evensen, Bruce J. *God's Man for the Gilded Age: D. L. Moody and the Rise of Mass Evangelism.* New York: Oxford University Press, 2003; Frank, Douglas W. *Less than Conquerors: How Evangelicals Entered the Twentieth Century.* Grand Rapids, MI: Eerdmans, 1986; Harrell, David E., Jr. *All Things Are Possible: The Healing and Charismatic Revivals in Modern America.* Bloomington: Indiana University Press, 1977; Lambert, Frank. *Inventing the "Great Awakening."* Princeton, NJ: Princeton University Press, 1999; Long, Kathryn Teresa. *The Revival of 1857–58: Interpreting an American Religious Awakening.* New York: Oxford University Press, 1998; Martin, William. *A Prophet with Honor: The Billy Graham Story.* New York: William Morrow, 1993; McLoughlin, William G. *Revivals, Awakenings, and Reform: An Essay on Religion and Social Change in America, 1607–1977.* Chicago: University of Chicago Press, 1978; Murray, Iain H. *Revival and Revivalism: The Making and Marring of American Evangelicalism, 1750–1858.* Edinburgh: Banner of Truth Trust, 1994.

Charles H. Lippy

TOMLINSON, AMBROSE JESSUP (1865–1943)

Ambrose Jessup Tomlinson was the cofounder and patriarch of one of the largest denominations in North American **Pentecostalism**—the **Church** of God (Cleveland, Tennessee). At the turn of the twenty-first century, this church together with its offshoots claimed over 1 million followers in North America and additional millions worldwide. Tomlinson was born in 1865 to nonpracticing **Quaker** parents in Westfield, Indiana. Following his marriage in 1889, Tomlinson joined a local branch of the Society of Friends frequented by **Holiness** ministers like Seth Rees, Charles Stalker, and William F. Manley. In 1893, after a brief foray into politics (he ran for county auditor as a Populist), Tomlinson experienced entire **sanctification** and gravitated toward the ministry. Under the tutelage of J. B. Mitchell, a Methodist colporteur (i.e., distributor of religious literature), he undertook short-term trips to **Appalachia** and in 1899 moved to Culberson, North Carolina, to establish a missionary orphanage and industrial school. By that time he had fallen under the sway of the Holiness prophet figure Frank Sandford, and Tomlinson's mission sought to apply the Christian communalism practiced at Sandford's Bible school in Shiloh, Maine. The Culberson mission foundered, but in 1903 Tomlinson joined the Holiness Church at Camp Creek (HCCC), a small holiness sect organized by Richard G. Spurling, William F. Bryant, and Frank Porter, local ministers with **Baptist** and **Methodist** roots. Bryant and Porter had ties to evangelist Benjamin Hardin Irwin's Fire-Baptized Holiness Association. Tomlinson, the best educated and most ambitious of the group, quickly assumed leadership and shepherded the young denomination through two decades of rapid expansion.

In January 1907 the sect changed its name to the Church of God (COG), and by 1909 it had been swept into the Pentecostal movement through the influence of evangelist Gaston Barnabus Cashwell—who received the **baptism of the Holy Spirit** at the **Azusa Street revival** before returning to **preach** the Pentecostal message in North Carolina and other southeastern states. Under Tomlinson's direction the COG combined growing professionalism and institutional discipline with freewheeling, improvisational worship. Emphasis on the **signs and wonders** mentioned in Mark 16 led to occasional **serpent handling,** which Tomlinson acknowledged but did not encourage. Like most Pentecostals in the **South,** the COG largely avoided the disruptions caused by the "Oneness" and "Finished Work" controversies that ruptured Pentecostalism between 1910 and 1920. With respect to the first, Tomlinson held steadfastly to the traditional Trinitarian position rather than the Oneness or "modalistic" teaching that Jesus himself is God the Father. With respect to the second, Tomlinson continued to teach entire sanctification as a second work of grace, preparatory to **baptism in the Holy Spirit,** and thus his theology of revivals involved three distinct stages (conversion, sanctification, and Spirit baptism), rather than two stages (conversion and Spirit baptism) as taught by the Finished Work Pentecostals.

The COG was distinguished from other Pentecostal movements because of its ecclesiology or doctrine concerning the church. Drawing on Landmark Baptist and Sandfordian precedents, Tomlinson insisted that the COG was the literal, visible restoration of the one true church of apostolic times, and he joined this **primitivist** or **restorationist** teaching to a High Church ecclesiology that exalted the role of a ruling bishop who was known as the General Overseer. By the early 1920s Tomlinson had been appointed General Overseer for life and had taken direct or indirect control over most aspects of COG polity. Paradoxically, Tomlinson's rising authority coincided with a loss of legitimacy, as resentment over his dominance and arbitrary allocation of church resources mushroomed into a denominational crisis. The struggle pitted a more corporate-oriented Council of Elders against Tomlinson and his loyalists. The final breach came in 1923, after which there were two rival branches of the COG, with Tomlinson and his followers as the smaller group. Tomlinson guided his followers—later known as the **Church of God of Prophecy** (COGOP)—through 20 years of steady if unspectacular growth, introducing several distinctive emphases along the way. Virtually alone among Pentecostal denominations, the COGOP cultivated notions of sacred space and time through agencies like the Church of Prophecy Marker

Association—which placed markers at the sites of pivotal events in sacred history—and an elaborate Fields of the Wood memorial park, built where Tomlinson had **prayed** before joining the HCCC. He also broke doctrinal ground by insisting that the church should be interracial (appealing to the "speckled bird" of Jeremiah 12:9) and he pressed to make that vision a reality despite opposition to interracialism in the Jim Crow South. Tomlinson died in 1943, two weeks after suffering a debilitating stroke. His youngest son, Milton A. Tomlinson (1906–1995), succeeded him and led the COGOP until his retirement in 1990.

Further Reading: Conn, Charles. *Like a Mighty Army Moves the Church of God, 1886–1955.* Rev. ed. Cleveland, TN: Pathway Press, 1977; Hunter, Harold. "Tomlinson, Ambrose Jessup." In Stanley Burgess and Eduard Van der Maas, eds., *The New International Dictionary of Pentecostal and Charismatic Movements.* 1143–45. Grand Rapids, MI: Zondervan, 2002; Robins, Roger. *A. J. Tomlinson: Plainfolk Modernist.* New York: Oxford University Press, 2004.

Roger Robins

TORONTO BLESSING

The **Toronto Blessing** is the longest-lasting revival in a network of revivals that swept through the global "Spirit-filled" movement—**Pentecostal, Charismatic,** and so-called Third Wave—during the mid-1990s. Regular meetings and conferences were still being held as of 2005. The Blessing quickly spread from the Toronto Airport Vineyard (renamed the Toronto Airport Christian Fellowship) in early 1994 throughout Canada, to England, from coast to coast in the United States, and to scores of other countries on six continents. Visitors—accurately estimated at more than 2 million—came to the Toronto church, observed and experienced paranormal "fits, trances, and visions" (a term used by scholar Ann Taves), and often carried what they believed to be a fresh influence of the Holy Spirit back to their home congregations in their respective homelands.

John Arnott, founding pastor of the Toronto Airport Christian Fellowship (TACF), and his wife, Carol, had persistently sought and **prayed** for revival after they experienced the **signs and wonders** of the Third Wave in the 1980s—following the waves of the Spirit that gave birth to Pentecostalism in the early twentieth century and to the Charismatic Renewal of the 1960s and 1970s. The Third Wave was most clearly represented by **John Wimber** and his Association of Vineyard Churches. The Arnotts reportedly longed for and prayed for even more Spirit empowerment than had been seen during the 1980s. After learning about large-scale revivals in Argentina, the Arnotts traveled to South America to witness the spiritual events in that country. During a crusade with revivalist Carlos Annacondia, another Argentine pastor, Claudio Freidzon, prayed with John and Carol. Carol reportedly was overwhelmed by the Spirit's power as she **laughed,** rolled, and was unable to walk in a straight line. John was left with an "impartation of faith for more of God and for miracles." They returned to Toronto in November 1993 with a heightened expectation of revival for their own small congregation that they had recently established in Toronto. The catalyst for the revival came within two months after the Arnotts' visit to Argentina. Vineyard pastor Randy Clark—then from St. Louis, Missouri—accepted Arnott's invitation to lead four days of revival services in the Vineyard church that met in an industrial district alongside of Toronto's bustling Lester B. Pearson International Airport. The revival fire fell on January 20, 1994.

Prior to his 1994 arrival in Toronto, Randy Clark had had an unusual and intense experience when he attended a revival meeting led by a South African evangelist who called himself a "Holy Ghost bartender." Beginning in 1991, crowds began to pack the services of Rodney Howard-Browne, who would walk the church aisles, call people out from the audience, point at them, and send them to the floor convulsing with laughter. Although Clark was reluctant at first to visit a Howard-Browne revival meeting, this self-described burned-out minister put aside his objections to attend a meeting in Tulsa, Oklahoma, in August 1993. Clark's skepticism and heaviness lifted when he found himself on the floor laughing. He soon saw the same laughter phenomenon sweep over his congregation when he returned to his own church in St. Louis, news of which prompted Arnott's invitation for Clark to come to Toronto. What began with some 200 persons at the Toronto Airport Vineyard intensified and spread like wildfire, drawing thousands of visitors—and ultimately hundreds of thousands—after Clark left Toronto in mid-March to return to St. Louis, Missouri.

Though often called the "laughing revival," the services at the TACF have always been about more than laughing. A variety of **bodily manifestations** were abundant during the earliest years of the revival, including **speaking in tongues (glossolalia), dancing,** spiritual drunkenness, deep weeping, uncontrolled jerking and shaking, and resting in the spirit (colloquially called "carpet time"). Seeing bodies fall limp to the ground was an even more common experience than holy laughter. Participants interpreted these manifestations as signs—that is, as indicators that God's power and presence were touching people in a most intense way. The Toronto Blessing (a name given by the British press) was reframed by Pastor John Arnott as the Father's Blessing, through which people were said to experience fresh encounters of the Father's love. Surveys conducted in 1995 and again in 1997 by Margaret Poloma supported Arnott's interpretation of the revival, with more than 90 percent of respondents indicating that they had "come to know the Father's love in a new way" through their experiences at the Toronto congregation.

Revival waves have periodically swept through the Pentecostal-Charismatic movement ever since its inception in the first decade of the twentieth century. Each revival could also be described as creating smaller waves within a century-long big wave, and the Toronto Blessing is no exception. A revival in Toronto was predicted in advance by some Pentecostal-Charismatic **prophets**—words seemingly fulfilled in 1994 by the Blessing. Led not by recognized leaders but largely by "nameless and faceless" believers, it was a movement that quickly spread around the globe with its unusual physical manifestations and reports of transformed lives. By 1996 the Blessing entered a phase described by British scholar David Hilborn as "decline and transmutation."

One notable change could be seen in the emergence of named leaders whose faces were recognized as they itinerated around the globe ministering revival in countless cities, towns, and villages. Another was the development of networks and organizational structures to promote varying programs and work of revival. Partners in Harvest was founded as a interdenominational network for revival pastors and churches, and the School of Ministry was established to train believers for revival ministry. During this time of transition new visitors continued to come into the experience of the Toronto Blessing, but many observers noted that the wave of revival had crested.

One noteworthy event that seemed to dampen the revival's initial momentum occurred when the Toronto Airport Vineyard was forced to leave the Association of Vineyard Churches by its founder, John Wimber, in December of 1995. During 1996 and 1997, some supporters of the Blessing withdrew, others expected a "new wave," and new organizational matrices developed for followers. Some predicted an impending "harvest of souls" as the revival broke out of Charismatic confines and still others suggested that this revival was heralding the **eschatological** era and Second Coming of Jesus. The establishment of new prophetic and apostolic ministries attracted many who wanted to see something new and unprecedented take place through the revival. As the millennium came to a close the revival entered what British scholar Martyn Percy called "adventure and atrophy." A smaller but steady stream of returning visitors and new visitors—approximately one-third of attendees at special conferences are coming for the first time—continue to attend TACF. Many continue to report being spiritually changed and refreshed by God's presence. The Blessing once again made front-page news in the late 1990s when the "laughing revival" became the "golden revival." Visitors reported that gold dental work miraculously appeared inside their mouths and others saw "flakes of gold" fall during meetings at Toronto and other affiliated renewal sites. This new phenomenon was interpreted, like the earlier physical manifestations, as a sign of God's presence and power.

On January 20, 2004, some 2,000 people came from around the globe to celebrate 10 years of the Toronto Blessing. Randy Clark was present to speak about how the revival in Toronto had opened doors for him to minister around the world with God's signs and wonders. Pilgrims came anticipating a fresh experience of the Holy Spirit—an experience affirmed in participants' descriptions of God's presence at the gathering. The theme that persists in this ongoing revival is that of God's loving and manifest presence. Even though revival waves may ebb and flow, those involved in the Toronto Blessing insist that an experience of God's love is available to all. This experience does not require trips to the TACF, as suggested by the church Web site's promotion of "soaking prayer" that can be practiced in one's own living room. Followers believe that signs and wonders, including prophecy and **healing,** are gifts for those who visit the TACF or one of the TACF-sponsored crusades around the world. The TACF remains a place of pilgrimage where those seeking a fresh experience of God still seem to find it.

Further Reading: Arnott, John, ed. *Experience the Blessing: Testimonies from Toronto.* Ventura, CA: Renew / Gospel Light, 2000; Dempster, Murray W., Byron D. Klaus, and Douglas Petersen, eds. *The Globalization of Pentecostalism: A Religion Made to Travel.* Irvine, CA: Regnum Books, 1999; Hilborn, David. *"Toronto" in Perspective: Papers on the Charismatic Wave of the Mid-1990s.* Waynesboro, Georgia: Acute / Paternoster, 2001; Hunt, Stephen, Malcolm Hamilton, and Tony Walter, eds. *Charismatic Christianity. Sociological Perspectives.* New York: St. Martin's Press, 1997; Poloma, Margaret M. *Main Street Mystics: The Toronto Blessing and Reviving Pentecostalism.* Walnut Creek, CA: AltaMira Press, 2003; Taves, Ann. *Fits, Trances and Visions: Experiencing Religion and Explaining Experience from Wesley to James.* Princeton, NJ: Princeton University Press, 1999.

Margaret M. Poloma

TORREY, REUBEN ARCHER (1856–1928)

The editor of the last two volumes of *The Fundamentals*, Reuben Archer Torrey is known as one of the chief architects of American Fundamentalism.

Yet Torrey also achieved recognition for his work as a pastor, educator, and revivalist. In his role as a revivalist Torrey provided an early twentieth-century link to the major nineteenth-century revivals of **Dwight L. Moody.** Born to upper-middle-class parents in Hoboken, New Jersey, Torrey was the third of five children. After finishing at the Walnut Hill School in Geneva, New York, Torrey matriculated at Yale in 1871 at the age of 15. He completed an AB in 1875 and also a BD at Yale Divinity School in 1878. From 1882 to 1883, Torrey studied at the Universities of Leipzig and Erlangen in Germany. Torrey's pastorates included Moody Church in Chicago from 1894 to 1906, and the Church of the Open Door in Los Angeles from 1915 to 1924. During both the Spanish-American War and World War I, he served as a **Young Men's Christian Association** (YMCA) chaplain at military bases in the United States. Torrey served as president of the Moody Bible Institute from 1889 to 1908, and dean of the Bible Institute of Los Angeles (BIOLA) from 1912 to 1924. In addition to his work with *The Fundamentals,* Torrey authored more than 40 books on topics such as **prayer,** the Holy Spirit, soul winning or personal evangelism, and revivalism.

Torrey's career as a revivalist was shaped by and in many ways paralleled the career of his mentor, Dwight Moody. Torrey learned the craft of mass revivals by observing and working in a number of Moody's crusades. When Moody died in 1899, Torrey seemed to be his logical successor. By 1901, Torrey increasingly felt drawn to the work of evangelism, and this led him to undertake an ambitious worldwide speaking tour from 1902 to 1905. During this campaign Torrey spoke to more than 15 million people in Hawaii, New Zealand, Japan, China, India, and Great Britain. The campaign culminated in London, where over a five-month period Torrey's **preaching** led to an estimated 17,000 **conversions.** Upon returning to North America, Torrey continued his evangelistic preaching, crisscrossing the continent. From 1906 until 1912, Torrey led crusades in Toronto, Philadelphia, Atlanta, Ottawa, Nashville, Omaha, Cleveland, Buffalo, Montreal, Chicago, Detroit, Denver,

Los Angeles, and numerous other smaller cities. The end of these crusades singled a change in focus for Torrey. For most of the next decade he concentrated on writing and education. Toward the end of his life, Torrey returned to evangelistic campaigns. Between 1919 and 1921, he made two trips to East Asia. His last years were devoted to itinerant evangelism and Bible teaching throughout North America. Yet these final campaigns never achieved the successes of the early years.

In his revival services Torrey avoided emotional appeals. Moody too had avoided excessive emotionalism, and yet was known for telling sentimental and affecting stories. Torrey's sermons, by contrast, were described as precise, reasoned, or dispassionate. His physical appearance reinforced the same impression. He wore a coat, starched shirt, and a bow tie on the platform and always comported himself as a Victorian gentlemen. Torrey followed Moody's lead by incorporating musicians and by keeping his meetings interdenominational. When queried about his church affiliation, Torrey described himself as "Episcopresbygationalaptist!" At the height of Torrey's career, singer Charles M. Alexander accompanied him. Despite their early successes, their relationship was often strained, partly a result of their divergent personalities. The pair finally parted in 1906 after debates about Alexander's attempt to profit off sales of his hymnbook. Shortly thereafter Alexander joined another evangelist, **J. Wilbur Chapman.** Torrey's general approach to revival preaching was in stark contrast with the freewheeling, flamboyant style of his more famous contemporaries **Billy Sunday** and **Aimee Semple McPherson.** Some of Torrey's declining popularity after World War I may be explained by the emergence of these more colorful revivalists.

Further Reading: Harkness, R. *Reuben Archer Torrey, the Man, His Message.* Chicago: Bible Institute Colportage Association, 1929; Marsden, George M. *Fundamentalism*

Postcard image from evangelist R. A. Torrey's and singer C. M. Alexander's revival campaign at Massey Hall in Toronto, Canada. The dignified Torrey and the ebullient Alexander differed in temperament and style, and they ended their collaboration in 1906 (ca. 1906.) Courtesy of the Billy Graham Center Archives, Wheaton, IL.

and American Culture: The Shaping of Twentieth-Century Evangelicalism, 1870–1925. New York: Oxford University Press, 1980; Martin, R. Apostle of Certainty. Murfreesboro, TN: Sword of the Lord, 1976; McLoughlin, William G. Modern Revivalism: Charles Grandison Finney to Billy Graham. New York: Ronald Press, 1959; Staggers, Kermit L. "Reuben A. Torrey: American Fundamentalist, 1856–1928." PhD dissertation, Claremont Graduate School, 1986.

Gregg Quiggle

TRANSATLANTIC DIMENSIONS OF NORTH AMERICAN REVIVALS

Revivalism is an Anglo American approach to religion, to Christian living, and to evangelism, developed in the context of the **Great Awakening** of the 1740s and the **Second Great Awakening** of the early 1800s. The fervent **preaching** of the English minister **George Whitefield** triggered revivals during a visit to the American colonies that began in 1739. Called "the divine dramatist" by historian Harry Stout, Whitefield brought a theatrical and emotive element to revival preaching that had earlier been absent. Whitefield's example encouraged other ministers (such as **Gilbert Tennent**) to become itinerants themselves, and preach outside their assigned parishes. Whitefield was innovative in making extensive use of the print media to promote himself and his preaching. He also promoted collaboration among Protestants belonging to different denominations. All of these elements—dramatic preaching, itinerancy, media savvy, and interdenominational cooperation—were to become characteristic in Anglo American evangelicalism during the 1800s and 1900s.

While the Great Awakening brought the Englishman George Whitefield to America, the Second Great Awakening reversed the direction of influence. American revivals featured **camp meetings** that melded the **Calvinistic** or Scotch-Irish tradition of the **holy fair** into new synthesis with **African American** and **Methodist** elements. In 1799 representatives of this new perspective began to influence Europe, first in Ireland and Great Britain and eventually the entire European continent.

The **theology of revivals** in American revivalism after 1800 was generally Arminian rather than Calvinist, insisting on the freedom of the will in **conversion.** During the early 1800s, revivals were usually coupled with an optimistic social agenda that included **abolitionism, temperance,** the rights of **women,** and rights for workers. Essential to revivalism beginning in the early 1800s was the issue of "means," that is, structural elements or tools of evangelism used to facilitate the gathering of people and conversions. In addition to outdoor and camp meetings, revival leaders employed protracted meetings (lasting for many hours or for days), extended **prayer** services, and the **altar call** as a way of demonstrating public commitment to Christ. Credit for developing the concept and practice of revivalism is often given to **Charles Grandison Finney.** Yet he learned his craft from David Marks, one of many revivalists in the **Burned-Over District** of western New York State, and Marks was for a time the assistant of **Lorenzo Dow** (1777–1834), who helped to define what would become the practice of revivalism on both sides of the Atlantic.

Dow had wished to be accepted as a Methodist evangelist and served briefly as a Methodist pastor. He was refused ordination, though tens of thousands had been converted under his ministry on both side of the Atlantic. He insisted that true spirituality was not restricted to a denomination, and even more radically that class, gender, and race did not matter. He preached regularly in **African American** churches and was a friend of the **African Methodist Episcopal Church** (AMEC) founder **Richard Allen.** He promoted women's writing, contributing introductions and subventions for many women's publications. He accepted **bodily manifestations** such as falling down and "the jerks" as a legitimate part of revivals. From 1799–1801, Dow unintentionally emerged as the first North American–born transatlantic revivalist to go from the United States to Europe. The reason for this initial journey was to improve his health, but upon arrival in Dublin he commenced to preach outdoors and was briefly imprisoned for his efforts. He was shocked at the moral and social state of Britain, and became convinced that British Methodists had generally abandoned Wesley's vision of **sanctification** or holiness in their preaching and their practice. The Wesleyan Methodist establishment censured Dow not only for his religious activism, but also because of his radical republican political viewpoints and his antislavery pronouncements. From December 1805 to April 1807, Dow and his wife, Peggy, traveled throughout Britain on a second evangelistic tour and on this occasion introduced the American frontier camp meeting and American revival songs to the British Isles. Dow's *Collection of Spiritual Songs Used at the Camp Meetings in the Great Revival in the United States of America* (1806) went through several printings and became the basis of the gospel-songs

genre in Britain. His encouragement of Hugh Bourne and like-minded radical Methodists resulted in the founding of the **Primitive Methodist Church** in 1811. He undertook a third excursion from early 1818 to 1819.

During the 1830s and 1840s, a number of evangelical "new measures" Calvinists visited England, including Nathaniel Sidney Smith and Edward Norris Kirk. Unlike Dow, they did not see themselves as provocateurs of change in English Christianity. Another figure who was more influential through his writing than his speaking was the western New York New School **Presbyterian** Calvin Colton, who sought to raise funds for

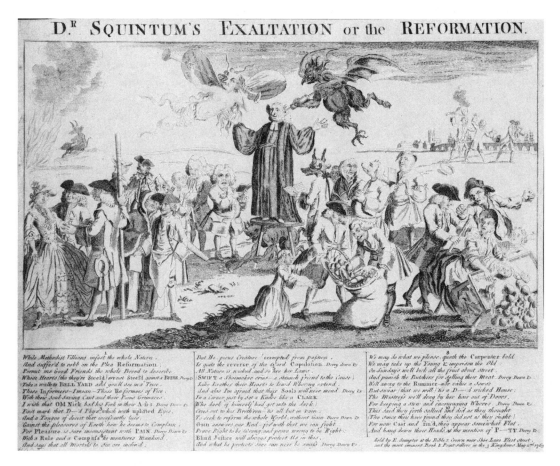

George Whitefield had critics on both sides of the Atlantic. This British engraving portrays him preaching while an imp pours inspiration through a clyster-pipe into his ear, a grotesque image of Fame listens to him with an ear-trumpet and repeats it into an ordinary trumpet, and the devil clutches gold from under his stool. "Dr. Squintum" was a satirical label given by opponents who mocked his cross-eyed gaze. (British Museum Print, Div. 1, v. 4, no. 4005; London, 1763.) Courtesy of the Library of Congress.

evangelism among **Roman Catholics** in the Mississippi Valley. His book *History and Character of American Revivals* (1832) defined and promoted American-style revivalism. Transatlantic revivalism also influenced Calvinism in Wales, as mediated by John Elias among the Calvinistic Methodists and Edward Williams and John Roberts among the Congregationalists. In Scotland, various American influences were felt, but especially important was the returning Scotsman David Nasmith. On a trip to the United States to found urban missions he discovered American revivalism, and when he returned to Scotland in late 1831, he organized successful revival meetings on the American model.

After Dow, an influential transatlantic revivalist was James Caughey (1810–1891). This Irish-born American Methodist preacher made four trips to England (1841–1847, 1857–1859, 1861–1862, and 1865–1866), where he led revival campaigns among the Methodists in central and northern England and became known as "the King of Preachers." The British Wesleyan Methodist leadership banned Caughey, as they had Dow, from the Methodist churches. Yet he drew large audiences and was responsible for thousands of converts and sanctification experiences at his "altars of prayer." He popularized the doctrine of **Holiness** throughout England, and influenced William Booth, the later founder of the **Salvation Army.** Later evangelists generally received invitations to speak in Britain after they became known through their publications. Such was the case of Charles Grandison Finney (1792–1875) and Elizabeth Finney (1799–1863). They made two voyages to England (1849–1851 and 1858–1860), and there promoted abolitionism, perfectionism, temperance, and the ministry of women. Toward the end of the first trip, Elizabeth Finney began holding meetings for women, a practice she continued more openly during the second visit. Finney did not have large numbers of converts, but his influence extended widely in the English churches.

American Methodist Holiness writer, editor, and speaker **Phoebe Palmer** and her physician husband, Walter Palmer, traveled to Britain after receiving numerous invitations. Phoebe spent 1859–1863 ministering in England, Scotland, and Wales, and reported her travels in *Four Years in the Old World* (1865). The couple had a significant influence on all of the British Methodist denominations. Among those influenced by the Palmers were William and Catherine Booth, who were forced from the Methodist New Connexion in 1861. Palmer promoted abolition, temperance, and women's right to preach, as had Dow and Finney.

The next wave of transatlantic revivalists came at the invitation of William Pennefather (1816–1873) of the Mildmay Mission in Mildmay Park, Islington, London, who promoted his work through the periodical *Servant of the King*. Active in ecumenical efforts, including the international Evangelical Alliance, Pennefather invited to London **Asa Mahan** (first president of Oberlin College); William Boardman, author of *The Higher Christian Life* (1858); Holiness teachers and leaders **Robert Pearsall Smith** and **Hannah Whitall Smith;** and **Dwight L. Moody** and song leader Ira Sankey. Moody was for a short time joined by William Taylor (1875–1876), maverick Methodist Episcopal missionary, who aroused opposition when he organized congregations for his lower-class converts in the slums of London. All of these revivalists, and many lesser figures, received support from Richard Cope Morgan and his influential periodical, originally the *Revival* and later the *Christian*. Holiness conferences convened at Broadlands (Oxford), Brighton, Keswick, Southport, and other sites, several of which still continue to host annual meetings. Boardman and Mahan, with collaboration from Charles Cullis, **John A. Dowie, Albert B. Simpson,** Frank Sanford, and others, organized international meetings to promote divine **healing** in London during the 1870s. From this period of ferment came also the **Salvation Army.** The biblical **eschatology** of dispensationalism originated in the writings of the British author John N. Darby. Though it began in Britain, Darbyite dispensationalism has had its greatest influence during the twentieth century in North America, as witnessed by Tim LaHaye's apocalyptic *Left Behind* novels, which sold more than 60 million copies between 1996 and 2004.

Evangelical Alliance colleagues in Europe—including Theodore Monod—invited Robert Pearsall Smith to lead revival campaigns in Germany, France, Switzerland, and the Netherlands. Among the converts in the Netherlands was Abraham Kuyper, who later was involved in publishing a short-lived Holiness periodical *De weg ter Godzaligheid*. In Germany the campaign resulted in the founding of the *Gemeinschaftsbewegung* (literally "community movement")—a renewal group within German Protestantism. Two theologians of this movement who remained within the State Lutheran Church were Theodor Jellinghaus and Jonathan A. B. Paul—the latter a founder of German **Pentecostalism.** Paul edited numerous periodicals. William Boardman undertook revival preaching in Sweden in 1878 and from his work there emerged the Holiness Movement Church of Sweden. Smith's translator in Germany, Dr. F. W. Baedeker (1823–1906), joined with William Waldegrave and Lord Radstock (1833–1913) in evangelizing first in Sweden and then in Russia, where their followers became known as Pashkovites because of the leadership of Vasil Alexandrovich Pashkov (1813–1902). Pashkov published periodicals entitled *Ruskii rabochii* (1883–1886) and *Beseda Vladikavkaz* (1891–1897) to promoted Holiness revivalism.

Many of the transatlantic revivalists from the United States to Britain or Europe were immigrants who experienced conversion in camp meetings or revivalist congregations in the United States and later returned across the Atlantic. Such was the case with the Evangelical Brethren (or **United Brethren**) and **Evangelical Association** missionaries in Germany, and in Norway among the Methodists. The Free Methodist Sivert V. Ulness became a missionary to Norway and founded a congregation, but just as importantly published the periodical *Ild-tungen* (1892–1900), later retitled *Sandhed og Frihed*, which introduced Holiness revivalist authors to Norway and throughout Scandinavia. Another influential immigrant was John Ongman, who became pastor of First Swedish Baptist Church in Chicago and then transferred to St. Paul, Minnesota. A disciple of Albert B. Simpson, he promoted Holiness teaching and revivalism among

the General Conference of Baptists before returning to Sweden to pastor a church in Örebro. Excluded from the Baptist Union, he established the Holiness Baptist Örebro Mission and published periodicals promoting his perspective. He organized mission bands to travel throughout Scandinavia on the model of the Pentecost Bands. He and his movement became Pentecostal in 1907. His school, the Örebro Missionsskola, has educated generations of revivalists, who have had an influence throughout the world.

The spread of Pentecostalism in Europe was due in large part to the influence of immigrants or visitors to the United States who later returned to Europe. Thomas B. Barratt, a Norwegian Methodist of British descent, was in the United States during much of 1905–1906, and did as much as any one person to promote Pentecostalism throughout the Continent. Barratt published periodicals in Norwegian, Danish, Swedish, Finnish, German, and Spanish. The Italian Pentecostal movement traces its roots to Italian Free Methodist and Pentecostal congregations in Chicago. The British pastor and writer Donald Gee was regarded as a leading Pentecostal thinker in the mid-twentieth century. Transatlantic developments fueled the growth of the **Seventh-day Adventists** and the **Jehovah's Witnesses.** Such exchanges operated in a more subtle fashion in major European state churches, and among the **Pietist** and *Réveil* groups of Europe, especially in France, Switzerland, Denmark, the Netherlands, Bulgaria, Romania, and Belgium.

Transatlantic revivalism has continued into the twentieth century through the work of such revivalists as the British preachers Rodney (Gipsy) Smith and Smith Wigglesworth, and the Americans **Reuben A. Torrey** and **Billy Graham.** During much of the twentieth century, when Europeans came to preach in the United States they tended to reinforce the existing American structures. Revivalism has long been a well-established American tradition. Yet since the 1950s, revivalists through the use of mass media such as **radio and television** and through international travel have become more accessible throughout the world. For example, the German Pentecostal preacher Reinhard Bonnke has conducted some of the largest Christian evangelistic crusades in history. Throughout Africa he regularly has drawn audiences of between 1 and 2 million people, and in 2002 he drew a record-breaking 6 million people to his preaching services in Lagos, Nigeria. Through personal appearances and use of mass media, he has become an influential figure in North America. One of the best-known television preachers in the United States since the 1980s, **Benny Hinn,** grew up in Lebanon. John Arnott—a leader in the **Toronto Blessing** revival—attributed his spiritual revitalization to the prayers of Claudio Freidzon, a revival preacher whom Arnott had gone to visit in Argentina. The North American **Church Growth** thinker **C. Peter Wagner** received new insight into prayer ministry and **spiritual warfare** from a visit to revivals in Argentina conducted by Carlos Annacondia. **John Wimber,** who founded the Vineyard Church, also reported that his interaction with international Christians highlighted the role of **signs and wonders** in evangelism. Wagner and Wimber went on to become influential figures in European Pentecostal and **Charismatic** churches.

Revivalist interactions between Africa and the Americas have taken place at least as far back as William Taylor's mission to South Africa in 1866. With the increased ease of transportation, revivalists have become a major means of cultural exchange between Africa and both North and South America, primarily, though not exclusively, within the Holiness, Pentecostal, and Charismatic communities. These interactions are part of increasingly complex patterns of revivalist connections. Consider, for example, the following sequence of events. The South African neo-Charismatic preacher Rodney Howard-Browne preached at revival meetings in various U.S. cities, and laid hands on and prayed over Randy Clark—a Vineyard minister from St. Louis, Missouri—whose preaching spawned the **Toronto Blessing** in Canada, which, in turn, spread to the Holy Trinity (Anglican) Church in central London, the site from which the **Alpha** evangelistic program has recently spread to nations throughout the world, including South Africa, where Howard-Browne began. This sort of global flow makes it difficult to say where any spiritual movement begins or ends. What began as trans–North Atlantic Christian revivalism has, in the twenty-first century, become a transoceanic, transcontinental, and fully international network.

Further Reading: Berggrav, Eivind. *Helliggjørelse.* Oslo: Grøndahl and Søns Forlag, 1934; Bundy, David. "Between the Réveil and Pentecostalism: The American Wesleyan-Holiness Traditions in Belgium and the Netherlands." *Asbury Theological Journal* 51 (1996): 106–13; Bundy, David. "Keswick and the Experience of Evangelical Piety." In Edith L. Blumhofer and Randall Balmer, eds., *Modern Christian Revivals,* 118–44. Urbana: University of Illinois Press, 1993; Carwardine, Richard. *Trans-Atlantic Revivalism: Popular Evangelicalism in Britain and America, 1790–1865.* Westport, CT: Greenwood, 1978; Dieter, Melvin E. *The Holiness Revivals of the Nineteenth Century.* Metuchen, NJ: Scarecrow Press, 1980; Dow, Lorenzo. *The Dealings of God, Man, and the Devil.* New York: Cornish, Lamport, 1852; Kent, John. *Holding the Fort: Studies in Victorian Revivalism.* London: Epworth Press, 1978; Klibanov, A. L. *Istoriya religioznogo sektantstva v Rossii.* Moscow: Nauka, 1965; Lange, Dieter. *Eine Bewegung bricht sich Bahn. Die deutschen Gemeinschaften im ausgehenden 19. und beginninden 20. Jahrhundert.* Giessen, Germany: Brunnen Verlag; Dillenburg, Germany: Gnadauer Verlag, 1979; Olesen, Elith. *Det frigjorte og trællefolket. Amerikansk-Engelsk indflydelse på dansk kirkeliv omkring år 1900.* Frederiksberg, Denmark: Anis, 1995; Werner, Julia Stewart. *The Primitive Methodist Connexion. Its Background and Early History.* Madison: University of Wisconsin Press, 1984; Westin, Gunnar. *Svenska Baptistsamfundet 1887–1914; Den baptistiska organisationsdualismens uppkomst.* N.p.: Westerbergs, 1965; Weyer, Michel. *Heiligungsbewegung und Methodismus in deutschen Sprachraum.* Stuttgart, Germany: Christliches Verlagshaus, 1991.

David Bundy

TRUTH, SOJOURNER (ISABELLA BOMEFREE) (1797–1883)

Sojourner Truth (born Isabella Bomefree) was an **African American** preacher, **abolitionist** lecturer, and advocate for the rights of **women** whose life was deeply shaped by the revivalism of the **Second Great Awakening.** A tall and dignified woman, six feet in height, she was the daughter of

James and Elizabeth Bomefree, slaves in Ulster County, New York. After almost 30 years in bondage, Isabella in 1828 escaped slavery with her teenage son, Peter, but lost touch with other members of her family, including her daughter, Diana. With Peter she moved to New York City, lived on Canal Street, and worked for a wealthy white family in Manhattan. Her first speaking and **preaching** was done in New York City in connection with a revival among unchurched people. She joined an **African Methodist Episcopal Zion Church** congregation, just under half of whose members had been African Americans in the John Street congregation in which they had limited membership rights. They had been told to wait until whites were finished before approaching the altar for Holy Communion, and were forbidden from holding positions in the church. In 1796, William Miller and Peter Williams withdrew along with several others and founded the African Chapel in a shop owned by Miller. The African Chapel later joined with the African Methodist Episcopal Zion Church to form the congregation in which Isabella was later a member.

In 1830, Isabella learned of the **Burned-Over District** in upstate New York, where people seemed to be ablaze with the Holy Spirit. She went there to receive **the baptism of the Holy Spirit.** A Christian preacher of Jewish descent named Prophet Matthias visited the home where Isabella was working, and Isabella felt that God had sent him to establish the kingdom of God on earth. After following his ministry and teaching, she later told the prophet that God had work for her elsewhere—particularly in New England. In June 1843, she left New York as a follower of **William Miller** and a Millerite. After the death of Isabella's son, she felt a need to adopt a new name for herself that suited her **vision** for serving God. She became known as Sojourner Truth, a preacher of God's word and antislavery in the northeastern states.

Truth was an extemporaneous preacher who never prepared in advance but simply followed what she took to be God's prompting whenever she spoke. She could not read, but children read to her

and so she listened to and memorized sections of the Bible. She fought for freedom for slaves and equality under the banner of Jesus' Golden Rule to do for others what you would have them do for you (Matthew 7:12). Truth was also an activist for women's rights. She viewed the various evils she opposed as parts of one and the same problem, namely, that some of God's creatures believed that God favored them over others. Truth's illiteracy and broken English caused some to consider her as intellectually inferior. In 1851, at the Women's Rights Convention in Akron, Ohio, she delivered the famous speech—"Ar'n't I a Woman?"—to confront those who opposed women's rights: "Ar'n't I a Woman? … Look at me! Look at my arm! I have plowed, and planted, and gathered into barns, and

I Sell the Shadow to Support the Substance.
SOJOURNER TRUTH.

Sojourner Truth, seated at table with knitting, with the caption below: "I sell the shadow to support the substance." (Photographic print, 1864.) Courtesy of the Library of Congress.

no man could lead me—and ar'n't I a woman? I could work as much and eat as much as a man (when I could get it), and bear de lash as well—and ar'n't I a woman? I have born thirteen children and 'em mos' all sold off into slavery, and when I cried out with a mother's grief, none but Jesus heard—and ar'n't I a woman?" (Mrs. F. D. Gage, "Sojourner Truth," *Herald of Progress* [New York], May 16, 1863, 3).

Truth traveled over 40 years speaking out against slavery and injustice. A biography written by abolitionist Oliver Gilbert enhanced her reputation. She petitioned Congress to give land in Kansas and other western states to former slaves. Yet Congress never acted. She herself bought property in Michigan in 1856 while continuing to serve as a traveling lecturer. In 1864, Truth met with President Abraham Lincoln at the White House. She served as a counselor for the National Freedman's Relief Association, and retired in 1875 to Battle Creek, Michigan—a town associated with the **Adventist** movement. Her former home in Battle Creek now commemorates the freed slave who fought for emancipation and for women's rights in lecture tours and in the law courts.

Further Reading: Gilbert, Olive, and Sojourner Truth. *Narrative of Sojourner Truth, a Bondswoman of Olden Time: With a History of Her Labors and Correspondence Drawn from Her "Book of Life."* New York: Oxford University Press, 1991; Thomas-Collier, Bettye, ed. *Daughters of Thunder: Black Women Preachers and Their Sermons, 1850–1979.* New York: Jossey-Bass, 1998.

Sherry Sherrod DuPree

U

UNITED BRETHREN IN CHRIST

The United Brethren in Christ was a **German American** revivalist denomination that has been identified as among the first indigenous religious denominations to be formed in the United States. It grew to rank among the 10 largest religious bodies in North America by the end of the nineteenth century. Its roots are traced to the meeting of the German **Reformed** missionary pastor **Philip William Otterbein** (1726–1813) and the converted Mennonite **preacher** Martin Boehm (1725–1812) at a "big meeting" on Pentecost Sunday 1767, in Lancaster County, Pennsylvania. This unlikely union of a magisterial and radical reformer, joined by the **Pietist** doctrine of the new birth and holiness of heart as the mark of Christian identity, led to an emerging fellowship of persons from a diversity of religious and nonreligious backgrounds. They experienced a "higher unity" in Christ that transcended their previous confessional differences, and this came to be represented in a church order, based on Otterbein's Church Order for his Reformed congregation in Baltimore, and a confession of faith (1789) that intermingled Reformed, Anabaptist and Pietist motifs. Concurrent with their organization in 1800, the United Brethren selected Otterbein and Boehm as their first "elders" or bishops, and soon their followers extended the mission to German Americans in the Midwest and the Shenandoah Valley of Virginia. Francis Scott Key, author of the national anthem, was a song leader in the Baltimore church during the War of 1812. Near the end of Otterbein's life, Otterbein ordained Christian Newcomer, who served as the missionary bishop to the West.

By 1821 the United Brethren had formally taken an **abolitionist** stance and adopted a rule prohibiting slavery among members. They were also involved in mission work among free blacks in the **South.** They commissioned **women** home missionaries at an early date, and sent their first mission team to the British territory of Oregon before the **Civil War.** Overseas missions began in the 1850s, with the newly formed missionary society sending a team that eventually included an **African American** couple to Sierra Leone, where they reached the homeland tribes beyond the borders of the British colony in Freetown. They became the largest American church body working in that land, and their members played a crucial role in achieving the independence of the nation of Sierra Leone after 1960. Other early United Brethren missions were directed to China, Japan, and Europe, with later missions to Central and South America, as well as home missions established among Hispanic-**Latino** populations in New Mexico and Florida. A distinctive feature of their mission work was their goal of forming indigenous, united churches in overseas fields that would not reflect the polity and worship patterns of the American sending church. Women played a prominent role in their overseas fields, and women began to be ordained in the North American conferences of the church by the end of the nineteenth century. The United Brethren in Ohio established Otterbein University in 1847 as one of the earliest coeducational colleges in America. Other colleges were founded in Pennsylvania, Indiana, and Virginia, as well as a theological seminary in the headquarters city of Dayton, Ohio, and many Bible schools in overseas territories.

The United Brethren experienced an internal division in 1889, with the secession of a conservative wing, led by the father of the Wright brothers (pioneers in the field of aviation), which opposed a new constitution and confession of faith that, among other points, changed the prohibition against participation in secret societies. By 1946 they had grown to more than 400,000 members and joined with their sister denomination, the Evangelical Church, to form the Evangelical United Brethren Church, at Johnstown, Pennsylvania. This united church continued its ministry until its union with the **Methodist** Episcopal Church in 1968 to form the United Methodist Church.

Further Reading: Drury, Augustus W. *History of the Church of the United Brethren in Christ.* Dayton, OH: Otterbein Press, 1924; Behney, J. Bruce, Paul Himmel Eller, and Kenneth W. Krueger. *The History of the Evangelical United Brethren Church.* Nashville, TN: Abingdon, 1979; O'Malley, J. Steven. *Pilgrimage of Faith: The Legacy of the Otterbeins.* Metuchen, NJ: Scarecrow, 1973.

J. Steven O'Malley

UNITED HOUSE OF PRAYER FOR ALL PEOPLE

see Grace, Sweet Daddy (Charles Emmanuel)

UNITED PENTECOSTAL CHURCH, INTERNATIONAL

The United Pentecostal Church, International (UPCI), the largest of North American Oneness Pentecostal denominations, formed in 1945 through the merger of two largely white Oneness groups, the Pentecostal Church, Incorporated (PCI), and the Pentecostal Assemblies of Jesus Christ (PAJC). The UPC and its Oneness antecedents descend from the early twentieth-century **Pentecostal revival.** In common with other **Holiness** and Pentecostal Christians, Oneness Pentecostals exhibit a **primitivist** or **restorationist** impulse to recover the zeal and the practices of New Testament Christianity. Even the distinctive Oneness doctrine of God and the rejection of the Christian doctrine of the Trinity reflect this primitivist-restorationist impulse to break free from the errors of the rest of Christendom and to be fully obedient to God's revelation in the Bible.

The early Oneness groups, in common with other Pentecostal groups, emphasized the "full gospel" of Christ as Savior, Sanctifier, Healer, Spirit Baptizer (with Spirit baptism signified by **speaking in tongues**), and soon-coming or **eschatological** King, and they sought to spread the full gospel worldwide, heralding and hastening the return of Jesus Christ through the power and **charismatic gifts** of the Holy Spirit. Yet Oneness Pentecostalism emerged as a distinct movement in 1913 when some began publicly to teach that water baptism must be administered in the name of Jesus only, following examples in Acts 2:38, 8:16, 10:48, and 19:5, and not in the threefold or triune name of "Father, Son, and Holy Spirit" as indicated in Matthew 28:19 and as practiced throughout Christian history. The apostles, as the argument goes, baptized "in the name of Jesus" because they understood that "Lord-Jesus-Christ" was the name to which the titles "Father-Son-Holy Ghost" corresponded. For many Oneness believers, the only baptism that remits sins is that done in Jesus' name only, and thus proper baptism (i.e., a Oneness baptism) is necessary for salvation. Baptism in Jesus' name—which many claimed to be a specific revelation from God to the early Pentecostal movement—was soon joined by three further discoveries or revelations: (1) that Jesus is the New Testament saving Name of God, corresponding to Jehovah (or Yahweh) in the Old Testament, and that this name alone has saving significance; (2) that Jesus is the one Person and the fullness of the Godhead, so that the titles of Father, Son, and Holy Ghost distinguish mere offices, functions, or manifestations of God, and not eternal personal distinctions within God (as in the Christian doctrine of the Trinity); and (3) that the new birth occurs through the acts specified in the double imperative of Acts 2:38—"repent, and be baptized … in the name of Jesus Christ"—resulting in the reception of the Holy Spirit.

These beliefs, along with the practice of rebaptizing believers who had previously received a Trinitarian baptism, constituted the "new issue" that precipitated the expulsion of one-fourth of the ministers from the fledgling **Assemblies of God** (AG) in 1916. The Oneness believers who were removed from the AG organized themselves with varying degrees of success. The **Pentecostal Assemblies of the World** (PAW) was the first Oneness denominational home to many, but racial tensions between **southern** white members and blacks led to schism in 1924 and the forming of an all-white church body in 1925 that later adopted the name Pentecostal Church, Incorporated (PCI). The predominantly white Pentecostal Assemblies of Jesus Christ (PAJC) formed in 1931. These two groups merged to form the UPCI in 1945 after they agreed to allow members to hold divergent theological views of the new birth. Some held that the new birth was equivalent to the water baptism and Spirit baptism mentioned in Acts 2:38; others maintained that the new birth was distinct from these.

Today the UPCI is headquartered in Hazelwood, Missouri (in the St. Louis region), and includes some 4,000 churches, over 8,000 ministers, and some 600,000 constituents in North America, with a greater international membership. It evangelizes aggressively and regards Trinitarian Christians as prospects for conversion as much as non-Christians. The UPCI publishes extensively, and maintains seven North American Bible colleges and a recently opened Urshan Graduate School of Theology. It forbids **women** to cut their hair (1 Corinthians 11:6, 15) or wear pants (Deuteronomy 22:5), and bans clergy from owning a television. The UPCI does not pursue ecumenical relations with Christians outside of Oneness circles, since the denomination regards them as unsaved. Nevertheless, the UPCI maintains that it teaches a doctrine of salvation by grace through faith in Christ, and not by works. Oneness and Trinitarian Pentecostals, including UPCI participants, have engaged in academic dialogue in the Society for Pentecostal Studies for several years, and some UPCI leaders and ministers participate in certain activities of **Promise Keepers** and **Aglow International,** though membership in most such groups requires belief in the doctrine of the Trinity.

Further Reading: Hall, J. L. "United Pentecostal Church, International." In Stanley Burgess and Eduard M. van der Maas, eds., *The New International Dictionary of Pentecostal and Charismatic Movements,* 1160–65. Grand Rapids, MI: Zondervan, 2002.

Mark E. Roberts

UNITED SOCIETY OF BELIEVERS IN CHRIST'S SECOND COMING

see Shakers

V

VALDEZ, ADOLFO C. (1896–1988)

Adolfo C. Valdez (1896–1988) was a **Pentecostal** revival **preacher** whose ministry took him through Southern California and as far as the South Pacific. He was a fifth-generation Mexican American and **Latino,** born and raised in Los Angeles, who traced his ancestry back to the founding of California by Junipero Serra. When he was 10, his mother, Susie Villa Valdez, began attending the famous **Azusa Street revival** in Los Angeles. After she converted to Pentecostalism, she brought her **Roman Catholic** husband and family to the Apostolic Faith Mission on 312 Azusa Street—site of the Azusa Street revival—where they too converted and joined the Pentecostal movement. Susie Villa Valdez was among the first Latina Pentecostal evangelists in North America and one of the first to work with the poor and prostitutes in the red light district of Los Angeles. As a traveling evangelist, she conducted evangelistic services in migrant farm-labor camps in Los Angeles, San Bernardino, and Riverside, California. Though less active in the lay ministry than his wife, José Valdez was healed at the Azusa Street revival. After his ordination in 1916, A. C. Valdez went on to become an important, though neglected, Mexican American Pentecostal evangelist. He preached throughout the United States to Anglo American, Mexican, and Native American audiences, especially in southwestern states. He also went on evangelistic tours to Australia and New Zealand, where he claims to have been one of the founders of the Pentecostal movement in those countries.

Further Reading: Espinosa, Gastón. "Borderland Religion: Los Angeles and the Origins of the Latino Pentecostal Movement in the U.S., Mexico, and Puerto Rico, 1900–1945." PhD dissertation, University of California–Santa Barbara, 1999; Valdez, A. C., Sr., with James F. Scheer. *Fire on Azusa Street.* Costa Mesa, CA: Gift Publications, 1980.

Gastón Espinosa

VISIONS

see Prophecy, Visions, and Dreams

W

WAGNER, C. PETER (1930-)

C. Peter Wagner is a former missionary, missions and **Church Growth** strategist, educator, and author of more than 60 books. He was a missionary to Bolivia for 16 years, the head of Fuller Theological Seminary's Department of Church Growth in the School of World Mission from 1971 until 1999, the founding president of Global Harvest Ministries, cofounder with Ted Haggard of the World Prayer Center in Colorado Springs in 1992, international coordinator of the Spiritual Warfare Network, chancellor of the Wagner Leadership Institute (since 1999), and presiding apostle of the International Coalition of Apostles (since 1999).

Wagner grew up on a dairy farm in upstate New York. He earned a BS from Rutgers University (summa cum laude, 1952), and an MDiv from Fuller Theological Seminary (1955). From 1956 to 1971 he and his wife, Doris, were missionaries to Bolivia engaged in evangelism, church planting, seminary teaching, and missions administration with what is now the Andean field of SIM International. He received his ThM from Princeton Theological Seminary (1962). On a furlough in 1967–1968 he studied under Donald McGavran at Fuller Seminary. McGavran invited him to come to Fuller but previous commitments intervened. Three years later Wagner moved from the mission field to Pasadena, California, and started teaching at Fuller full-time—turning the attention of the School of World Mission to North American church growth—as well as directing the Fuller Evangelistic Association. In 1972 Wagner and McGavran helped establish the Institute for American Church Growth with one of Wagner's students, Win Arn, as the founder. From 1974–1989 Wagner played a leading role in the ecumenical Lausanne Congress on World Evangelization (in Switzerland) and the consultations that followed Lausanne. Wagner earned a PhD from the University of Southern California in social ethics (1977). In 1993 Fuller Seminary appointed Wagner to the Donald McGavran Chair of Church Growth.

Wagner's commitment to Church Growth led him to realize that—though his own theological training had been anti-**Pentecostal**—it was the Pentecostal churches worldwide that were enjoying the most conspicuous growth. His book *Look Out! The Pentecostals Are Coming!* (1973) discussed the need to overcome this bias. In 1975 Wagner cotaught with **John Wimber** (founder of the Association of Vineyard Churches) the now famous Signs, Wonders, and Church Growth course for Fuller's doctor of ministry program, a class in which students were encouraged to **pray** for each other and expect miracles or **signs and wonders** to occur, just as in New Testament times. This class advanced a neo-**Charismatic,** neo-Pentecostal, or so-called Third Wave understanding of the church. *Your Spiritual Gifts Can Help Your Church Grow* (1979) drew attention to an aspect of church life that until then had seemed a monopoly of Pentecostals and Charismatics. Since the 1980s Wagner has linked his work on Church Growth with new understandings of **spiritual warfare** as well as **deliverance and deliverance ministry.** He authored a series of seven books on spiritual warfare called *The Prayer Warrior Series* (1992–1997). To advance strategic prayer against demonic entities, Wagner became the executive director of the AD2000 United Prayer Track (1992). In the same year—with Ted Haggard, Chuck Pierce, and George Otis of the Sentinel Group—Wagner founded Global Harvest Ministries to encourage and connect Christian prayer networks that are currently arising throughout the world.

Before 1980 Wagner primarily specialized in the technical aspects of Church Growth, and since then he has concentrated on its spiritual aspects. His books *The Rising Revival* (1998) and *Out of Africa* (2004) recount the recent Argentine and Nigerian spiritual awakenings and their implications for the wider church. Wagner is intimately linked with pastors in many of the world's largest congregations, including those in the **Apostolic movement,** which he has promoted in his books *The New Apostolic Churches* (1998), *Churchquake!* (1999), *Apostles and Prophets* (2000), and *Changing Church* (2004). Although the varied movements that Wagner has helped to establish—Church Growth, Signs and Wonders, Warfare Prayer, and the Apostolic movement—have all aroused controversy, Wagner's ideas have had wide influence in late-twentieth-century Christianity.

Further Reading: Wagner, C. Peter. *Apostles and Prophets: The Foundation of the Church.* Ventura, CA: Regal Books, 2000; Wagner, C. Peter. *Breaking Strongholds in Your City: How to Use Spiritual Mapping to Make Your Prayers More Strategic, Effective and Targeted.* Ventura, CA: Regal Books, 1993; Wagner, C. Peter. *How to Have a Healing Ministry without Making Your Church Sick!* Ventura, CA: Regal Books, 1988; Wagner, C. Peter.

Revival! It Can Transform Your City! Colorado Springs, CO: Wagner Institute for Practical Ministry, 1999; Wagner, C. Peter. *The Third Wave of the Holy Spirit: Encountering the Power of Signs and Wonders Today.* Ann Arbor, MI: Servant Publications, 1988.

Bayard Taylor

WESLEY, CHARLES

see Hymns, Hymnody, and Christian Music in Revivals

WESLEY, JOHN

see Free Methodist Church; Holiness Movement of the Nineteenth Century; Methodist Revivals; Primitive Methodist Church; Sanctification and Revivals

WHITE, ALMA BRIDWELL (1862–1946)

Alma Bridwell White may be the first female bishop known to have been ordained in a Christian church. Her career illustrates the development of both the **Holiness** and **Methodist** movements, as well as the struggle for the rights of **women** in the nineteenth and twentieth centuries. Born in Kentucky to a **Methodist** mother and a **Baptist** father, White and her family affiliated with the Methodist Episcopal church shortly after the **Civil War.** At 16 White experienced **conversion** during a revival and planned to begin **preaching** herself. Her denomination's stance against women in the pulpit, as well as arguments for becoming a minister's wife instead, initially dissuaded White from her goal. Gifted in school, she became a certified teacher and left Kentucky to work in Montana. There she met Kent White while he was studying to become a Methodist Episcopal minister. They wed in 1887. White bore two sons despite ill health and a rocky marriage. Her sons, too, were sickly, and the youngest survived pneumonia, White believed, after she promised God that she would preach regardless of others' objections.

Before speaking publicly for the first time, White sought the gift of **sanctification,** a second work of grace promoted by John Wesley and later popularized through the teaching of **Phoebe Palmer.** Following their writings, White believed that in addition to the forgiveness of sins experienced through justification in conversion, her sinful nature had been eradicated through sanctification. After experiencing a "deep soul rest and the consciousness that my heart was pure," she began preaching, crediting the Holy Spirit with curing her shyness and giving her enough stamina to preach despite illness (White, *The Story of My Life and the Pillar of Fire,* 2:206). She engaged in public exhortation first at the invitation of her husband in his Lamar, Colorado, pulpit that fall. Together they preached at revivals on his circuit, with White bringing in the campaign's first converts. The couple helped start the Colorado Holiness Association, organizing its first summer **camp meeting** in 1894. The growth of this organization paralleled that of the Wesleyan Holiness movement nationwide and was one of many regional groups formed to promote Holiness doctrine.

For their work in subsequent camp meeting revivals, the Whites received national attention in the 1895 *Guide to Holiness.* Yet many pastors in the movement frowned on independent evangelistic activities, and especially preaching by women. These **men**—including, at times, White's husband—promoted Victorian images of the home as women's sphere. Following Phoebe Palmer's message to sacrifice everything, including family, on the altar of Christ, White justified her long absences from home and her relatives' care of her sons by contending that duty to God superseded her maternal obligations. White also defended her preaching with arguments based on narrower interpretations of scriptural prohibitions against woman's speech and the widest possible readings of women's freedoms in the New Testament.

White's notoriety soon surpassed her husband's, who both envied his wife's talent and used it to his own advantage as a Methodist evangelist. Yet he followed her as she left Methodism and the Wesleyan Holiness movement in 1902 and started her own Denver-based Pentecostal Union Church as an ordained minister. White was consecrated as its bishop in 1918 and, despite the term *Pentecostal* in the title, this church body did not embrace the newly emerging teachings of Pentecostalism. White's move is illustrative of those who left the Wesleyan Holiness movement between 1893 and 1907 to start their own revivalist groups. Pentecostal Union branches soon formed in Colorado, Montana, Nebraska, and Utah while their missionaries began Bible schools in California. The church conducted revivals in Great Britain (1904–1905), published the *Pillar of Fire* magazine (for which the church later became named), and moved its headquarters to New Jersey (1907–1908). It became a self-supporting commune in which members wore uniforms (like their **Salvation Army** counterparts), shared possessions, and obeyed White's strict moral rules. In contrast to other communal experiments (such as the **Oneida Community** and the **Shakers**), the group avoided the opposing extremes of promiscuity and celibacy by advocating sexual relations only for married couples wanting children. Like **Seventh-day Adventists,** members practiced vegetarianism and avoided involvement with the world. They also distinguished themselves from and criticized the emerging **Pentecostals.** This was in part because White's husband accepted Pentecostalism and **speaking in tongues** in 1909 and subsequently left both the church and their marriage. Despite attempts to reconcile and accommodate each other's beliefs, the couple finally divorced in 1920 after White's husband attempted to take over and lead her church.

White criticized **Roman Catholicism** in the magazine *Good Citizen.* Her stance gained her notice by the Ku Klux Klan, with which she soon collaborated to fight Catholics, modernist theology, and immorality. Yet White never herself joined the KKK, and she held Jewish people, one of the Klan's targets, in high regard as harbingers of the millennium. Her premillennial views on **eschatology** led her to preach against the German persecution of Jews during the 1930s. Her journal, *Woman's Chains,* treated other social issues such as suffrage for women. In her later years, White's sons and granddaughter helped lead the Pillar of Fire, managing its many schools (including

Alma White College), where members separated themselves from worldly influences. White made use of **radio** technology to broadcast her message through the church's own East Coast and West Coast stations. By her death she had published almost 40 books and articles, including an 11-volume autobiography, four volumes of **hymns,** two sermon collections, anti-Pentecostal works, a vegetarian guidebook, and a biography of notable Christian women.

Further Reading: Stanley, Susie Cunningham. *Feminist Pillar of Fire: The Life of Alma White.* Cleveland: Pilgrim Press, 1993; White, Alma Bridwell, *The Story of My Life and the Pillar of Fire.* 11 vols. Zaraphath, NJ: Pillar of Fire, 1919–1943.

Kaley Carpenter

WHITE, ELLEN GOULD (HARMON) (1827–1915)

Ellen Gould (Harmon) White was a revivalist, writer, and cofounder of the **Seventh-day Adventists,** who consider her to have exercised the spiritual gift of **prophecy.** During her lifetime, White authored more than 5,000 periodical pieces and 40 books, and, with the possible exception of mystery writer Agatha Christie, White may be the most extensively translated female author in history. Born to **Methodist** parents near Portland, Maine, her personal **conversion** process began at age nine when she was struck by a rock thrown in her face and a broken nose led to life-threatening complications. Near death after an extended coma, she **confessed** her sins to God and reported having had an experience of God's forgiveness. Yet not until six years later did she resolve her fear of hell, and find God as a loving Father, through the doctrines of soul sleep (i.e., the loss of consciousness at death) and the second death (i.e., the annihilation rather than destruction of the wicked). On finding **assurance of salvation,** she immediately became known in Portland as a successful evangelist of other young people. Nonetheless, her childhood injury left her in a weakened condition, and she was unable to return to school and complete her formal education.

In 1843, and again in 1844, the followers of **William Miller** expected Jesus' Second Coming to occur based on their interpretation of biblical **eschatology.** In December 1844, during this time of disappointment, White had a **vision** assuring her that despite some human errors, the essence of the Millerite revival had been an authentic work of God. White reported that, while experiencing her visions, she was surrounded by light and brought into the presence of Christ and the angels. Her first vision showed her the Adventists following Jesus to the heavenly city. One of the first—of some 2,000 during her lifetime—to accept the visions as a genuine gift of prophecy was James White, a minister of the **restorationist** Christian Connection in Maine. Ellen and James were married in 1846 and had four sons.

The Millerites had expected that the Second Advent of Christ would occur on October 22, 1844, after which the door of salvation would be shut to all who had not had a conversion experience to Jesus Christ. They did not deny the salvation of those who had never heard the Millerite message, but those who had heard and yet rejected the message they regarded as lacking in true conversion. From 1847 to 1850, White's visions, further biblical study, and new converts to the Adventist movement led the Adventists to a reinterpretation of the "shut-door doctrine" and to the active evangelizing of persons who were not previously Adventists. Another distinctive teaching of Ellen White was her insistence on the seventh day of the week, or Saturday, as the biblical Sabbath to be kept holy by resting from ordinary labor and from secular entertainment. White also believed and taught that healthful living was conducive to spirituality. She recommended, but did not require, vegetarianism. She promoted abstinence from tobacco, alcoholic beverages, and caffeine. For more than half a century, White spent several months each year in revivalist traveling and **preaching,** especially at Adventist **camp meetings.** These typically lasted about a week, with the leading speakers attending one camp meeting after another for 8 or 12 weeks at a stretch. In addition to meetings of her own denomination, she often spoke in other churches. She was a popular lecturer on temperance, addressing conferences of the Women's Christian Temperance Union and other temperance societies. She also did similar work in Europe (1885–1887) and Australia (1891–1900). When James and Ellen White conducted revivals together, he would usually preach first, on doctrinal themes. She would follow, emphasizing heart religion and practical spirituality, which to her denoted not so much the practice of spiritual disciplines as ethical **holiness.** She both practiced and promoted personal Bible study, **prayer,** meditation, and other spiritual disciplines, but always with a strong ethical emphasis. She considered that revival (a change of heart) was not complete until it bore fruit in reformation (a change of behavior). She criticized some revivals for their emphasis on emotional excitement, to the neglect of the Bible and God's law.

Revivalist convictions and presuppositions are pervasive in White's writings. Her five-volume *Conflict of the Ages* series traces the struggle between good and evil from Creation to the end of the world, and points readers to the Bible as a guide for daily life. Her nine-volume *Testimonies for the Church* (1855–1909) is a collection of letters and manuscripts that apply the Christian message to the lives and conduct of individuals, churches, and denominations. Though White believed she received special guidance from the Holy Spirit, she never attributed to her own writings the authority of sacred scripture. She consistently upheld "the Bible, and the Bible only as the standard of all doctrines and the basis of all reforms" (E. White, 595). Concerning the relationship between scripture and the gift of prophecy, she wrote, "The Spirit was not given—nor can it ever be bestowed—to supersede the Bible; for the Scriptures explicitly state that the word of God is the standard by which all teaching and experience must be tested" (viii). At the age of 81, attending her last General Conference session (1909), she preached to the ministers from John 3:7, "Ye Must Be Born Again." Some were surprised that she would choose such an elementary text for a world gathering of ministers. Yet her choice of topic shows clearly her revivalist motivations. While her ministry had many facets, she always saw herself primarily as a Christian evangelist.

Further Reading: Douglass, Herbert E. *Messenger of the Lord: The Prophetic Ministry of Ellen G. White.* Nampa, ID: Pacific Press, 1998; Fortin, Denis, and Jerry Moon, eds. *Ellen G. White Encyclopedia.* Hagerstown, MD: Review and Herald, forthcoming; White, Arthur L. *Ellen G. White.* 6 vols. Hagerstown, MD: Review and Herald, 1981–1986; White, Ellen G. 1911. *The Great Controversy between Christ and Satan.* 1911. Reprint, Mountain View, CA: Pacific Press, 1950.

Jerry Moon

WHITEFIELD, GEORGE (1714–1770)

George Whitefield was an ordained minister of the Church of England whose career as an itinerant **preacher** encompassed the eighteenth-century **transatlantic** English-speaking world and contributed more than any figure of his day to the emergence of a distinctly modern evangelicalism. His dramatic outdoor preaching brought him vast audiences that often numbered in the thousands, and made him a key figure in the emergence of the **Great Awakening** (1739–1745) in the American colonies. While Whitefield played a role in John Wesley's decision in the 1730s to engage in outdoor or field preaching, and so indirectly helped to shape the emerging **Methodist** movement centered on Wesley, Whitefield's **theology of revivals** was **Calvinistic,** and this distinguished him from the Arminian theology of John Wesley.

Whitefield was born in Gloucester in 1714, the seventh child of a respectable innkeeper. His father, Thomas, died during Whitefield's second year, leaving his mother, Elizabeth, to coax and prod her son through grammar school in preparation for university and a clerical career. Despite the lad's indifferent scholastic performance, his family's small fortune, and a preference for reading plays and acting rather than study, Whitefield managed to complete his schooling and gain entrance to Oxford's Pembroke College as a "servitor" at the age of 17. Life as a servitor in eighteenth-century Oxford meant that Whitefield had to squeeze his studies into a schedule jammed with menial duties performed in lieu of tuition for gentlemen students and the college master. Though he never excelled,

Whitefield not only persevered but also managed to participate with John and Charles Wesley in a group of pious undergraduates known as the Holy Club. There he experienced an evangelical **conversion** and embraced the spiritual practices of private **prayer, fasting,** Bible study, and regular meetings that earned group members the name *Methodists.*

Whitefield's conversion infused fresh purpose into his study of divinity, and he wasted little time in employing his natural talent for moving oratory to proclaim the message of conversion or what he termed "the New Birth." Even before graduating from Oxford in 1736, the fervent young convert was bearing public testimony to his deliverance from the snares of his sinful past and the joys of experiencing a "saving change wrought in the heart" by Jesus. Within months of his ordination in the summer of that same year, Whitefield's dramatic preaching style was drawing large audiences to hear him in London. Reports in London newspapers stirred up curiosity and excitement to hear this "boy preacher," spreading his fame throughout the countryside and generating crowds wherever he went.

From the outset, Whitefield demonstrated an intuitive ability to adapt his message to the rapid growth of an eighteenth-century transatlantic marketplace of goods and information. His early sermons represented an adaptation of a long-established form: the charity sermon preached by a visiting Church of England clergyman to sponsor some benevolent cause. Whitefield preached his charity sermons in support of his planned voyage to America's fledgling colony of Georgia—then less than five years old—as a missionary of the Anglican Society for the Propagation of the Gospel. Yet none in his audience had ever attended charity sermons like Whitefield's, promoted as they were by shrewdly placed newspaper advertisements and delivered by an energetic young man with a flair for drama and a voice that Sarah Edwards compared to a bell and that others often likened to the "roar of a lion" (Stout, 42). Printed texts of his sermons became instant best sellers, generating more curiosity and larger crowds. The charity sermons afforded him access to pulpits across England, which, when coupled with the effective use of new marketing techniques, gave

Whitefield the means to launch an innovative ministry of itinerant gospel preaching.

Whitefield's mission to Georgia in 1738 provided opportunity to expand his budding itinerant ministry to a fledgling province of an expanding British Atlantic world. He sailed to a difficult frontier assignment from which his Methodist associates John and Charles Wesley had recently departed in disillusion after clashing with colonial authorities and enduring an embarrassing scandal over John's abortive romance with a local woman. Whitefield, however, enjoyed better success. In just three months, his talent for preaching and practical care for needy colonists won the approbation of Georgia officials. By the end of the summer, when his missionary support ran out, he had gained the Georgia trustees' endorsement of a philanthropic plan for an orphan house that would provide care, religious instruction, training in trades, and a start in life for orphans from the colonies and England alike. Whitefield returned to London that autumn determined to preach a new round of charity sermons to promote the endeavor.

The Georgia Orphan House provided the occasion for Whitefield's first great evangelistic tour of England and Wales. The charity sermons he preached in support of this benevolent cause extended far beyond the conventional scope of such discourses to urge on his audiences the "necessity of the New Birth." Listeners responded by the tens of thousands. During this tour he began taking his message outside church walls into fields and commons, where hostile ministers could not deny him a platform and where much larger crowds could gather to hear him preach. At places like Kennington Common and Moorfields in London, the spectacle of a black-robed clergyman taking his stand to preach near popular attractions such as juggling and bear baiting drew thousands of curious onlookers. The size of Whitefield's audiences grew exponentially, aided by word of mouth, paid newspaper advertising, and growing attention in the popular press. Whitefield became big news. Even the opposition of clergy in the established Church of England generated greater curiosity to hear this brash young itinerant speak.

George Whitefield, in a half-length portrait with hands raised. Elisha Gallaudet, engraver (New York, 1774). Courtesy of the Library of Congress.

Whitefield's eloquent appeals produced a flood of converts as well as donations, and by the fall of 1739 he was ready to return to America on an unprecedented wave of transatlantic popularity. Supporters declared that the English response to his itinerant revival preaching signaled a new work of God's Spirit unheard of since New Testament days. Colonial printers lifted English accounts of Whitefield's revivals and reprinted them in American papers, firing colonists with anticipation to hear this "Grand Itinerant" in person. The evangelist obliged, conducting a nine-month preaching tour to spread his message of New Birth through the colonies and to supplement English donations to the Orphan House with appeals for American funds.

George Whitefield's tour of British North America from December 1739 through October 1740 served as the most significant catalyst for the Great Awakening of the following decade. His emphasis on conversion resonated with a variety of local English, Scottish, and Continental revival traditions in calling on individual listeners to a personal, heartfelt experience of repentance from sin and faith in Jesus. Yet his itinerancy and his innovative exploitation of the long-distance capabilities of print communication stood in sharp contrast to the local, corporate character of earlier revivals, especially those in Congregationalist New England. Whitefield's revivals relied on a "stranger preacher" rather than the local minister. He invited converts not merely to full membership in a local congregation, but to participation in a movement that cut across boundaries of space and confession. "All places are equal to me—in America as in England," he declared, being "so many little parts of [God's] great family." He called on members of this great family to unite across barriers that had long divided them: "Don't tell me you are a Baptist, and Independant [sic], a Presbyterian, a Dissenter; tell me you are a Christian, that is all I want" (Hall, 33–34). His own itinerant preaching linked revivals in each region together into a perceptibly single phenomenon, a feature reinforced by a constant stream of newspaper reports and personal correspondence among evangelical ministers.

Whitefield understood the power of print to strengthen long-distance ties that had begun to emerge among his followers, and he used it effectively to complement his itinerant ministry. At the very beginning of his American tour he contracted with the Philadelphia printer Benjamin Franklin to print his sermons and a portion of a journal that he had been keeping on his voyage across the Atlantic. He continued publishing sermons and subsequent installments of his journal as he toured along the American coastline, whetting interest to see the author in person. Brisk sales convinced Franklin and other colonial printers of Whitefield's marketing appeal, and they cooperated by publishing accounts of the evangelist's latest preaching events and his upcoming itinerary. Whitefield even welcomed the controversy that soon began to rage in newspapers and pamphlets over his itinerant ministry, knowing that it would arouse greater curiosity and draw larger crowds.

Whitefield also observed how news of revival in one locale could spark revival in a second, and he generated volumes of correspondence to encourage its spread. Printers such as Franklin were among his correspondents, and they along with other friends ensured that the evangelist's letters appeared in newspapers and pamphlets alongside similar correspondence from enthusiastic followers. Within a few months after Whitefield's American tour, the London printer John Lewis began collecting such transatlantic revival correspondence into a weekly newsmagazine, the *Weekly History*, a project Whitefield supported and soon began managing himself. This, along with similar periodicals published in Scotland and America, strengthened the sense of readers throughout the British Atlantic that they had become participants in a single great "Work of the Spirit of God."

Whitefield returned to London late in 1740 and began preparing for a tour of Scotland to take place during in the spring and summer of 1741. The emphasis on "free grace" in his preaching had strengthened in America, and this increased his appeal among evangelical **Presbyterian** ministers in Scotland. News of the evangelist's success in England and America stirred anticipation among Scottish audiences, and Lewis's *Weekly History* gave Whitefield a ready tool for spreading advance word of his visit. His first tour of Scotland kindled revival fires that burned across the lowlands for months after his departure, blowing up during the spring and summer of 1742 into the Cambuslang Wark, a major revival near Glasgow. Appeals from the leaders of this revival brought Whitefield back for a second tour to fan the flames even further.

By the close of his second tour of Scotland in 1742, George Whitefield had come to embody a new form of revivalism. People across the British Isles and America had begun to think of revival in terms largely set by him: mass meetings drawing audiences across confessional boundaries to hear a charismatic preacher, often promoted in the press, through word of mouth, or by circular letters giving advance notice of meetings. Boisterous audience participation often accompanied the meetings as converts found themselves gripped with various bodily manifestations such as uncontrollable weeping, **shouting,** and fainting. In America, scores of clergy and hundreds of lay exhorters took up itinerant extemporaneous preaching in emulation of the evangelist, delivering fiery sermons in "the old Whitefield style." His message cut across lines of race and class as well as denomination in America, enticing converts of African descent into the fold of evangelical Christianity and creating opportunities for many of them to take up a call to preach as well. A number of **African American** slaves used itinerancy to escape their bonds, preaching their way to freedom.

While Whitefield refused to countenance all of the activities pursued in his name, he continued to pursue his itinerant calling throughout his life. He toured England regularly, delivering up to 20 sermons a week. He made 14 different trips to Scotland, 3 to Ireland, and voyaged to America 7 times. On each subsequent preaching tour he honed to an art the methods of publicity he had pioneered during his early years. By the time of his last visit to America in 1770, the Grand Itinerant had become an institution there, welcomed even by ministers who had opposed him during the 1740s. He died in Newburyport, Massachusetts, in 1770, only hours after preaching his last sermon atop a hogshead in a field near neighboring Portsmouth.

Whitefield's legacy extended far beyond the many volumes of sermons and correspondence he left behind. Indeed, the printed sermons do not convey the power of his presence in the pulpit or atop a wooden crate in an open field. Their text served Whitefield, in the words of biographer Harry S. Stout, as "scaffolding over which the body climbed, cavorted, and kneeled, all in an attempt—as much intuitive as contrived—to startle and completely overtake his listeners" (Stout, 40). Actor David Garrick, Whitefield's contemporary, famously declared that he "would give a hundred guineas if I could say 'Oh!' like Mr. Whitefield" (Stout, 237). The evangelist's voice also possessed exceptional quality and volume. Benjamin Franklin, who "had the Curiosity to learn how far he could be heard" (Franklin, 105), once walked a perimeter during one of the evangelist's sermons and calculated that, allowing two square feet per person, an audience of more than 30,000 could hear him clearly. Whitefield also left behind a set of institutional legacies that included a strain of Calvinistic Methodism to counter the Wesleys' Arminian stamp on the movement. Indeed, for a period during the 1740s, the erstwhile associates were engaged in a bitter feud over the availability of salvation, Whitefield insisting on the doctrine of divine election against the Wesleys' defense of the premise that the human will could freely accept or reject God's offer of grace. Though the two parties achieved partial reconciliation in later years, they continued to operate in different circles, with Whitefield joining the Countess of Huntingdon's Connexion.

Whitefield opened several Connexion chapels during the 1750s and 1760s and participated in the founding of the Connexion-sponsored theological college at Trevecca in 1768. He also assisted in sponsoring other Connexion projects in America, including Dartmouth College and Princeton College as well as providing ongoing support for the Georgia Orphan House. Critics often charged him with misappropriating the funds collected for such projects, lampooning him in print and satirical cartoons as a cross-eyed, money-grubbing hypocrite with a Bible in one hand and a bulging sack of coins in the other. Historical examination of his charitable accounts, however, has confirmed Benjamin Franklin's conviction that Whitefield "was in all his Conduct, a perfectly honest Man" (Franklin, 104).

These accomplishments constituted only a by-product of Whitefield's enormous influence over subsequent British and American Christianity. His intuitive grasp of how to take advantage of eighteenth-century developments in communication and transportation enabled him to adapt his message of the New Birth to a distinctly modern setting, one shaped by the methods and structures of a burgeoning transatlantic market economy. His dramatic itinerant ministry shattered old ecclesiastical and confessional structures, clearing the way for the emergence of new, mobile, often raucous ministers who competed for converts in an open marketplace of ideas. New movements of Separate Congregationalists, **Baptists,** and Methodists sprang into being and grew exponentially in succeeding decades by adapting his itinerant methods and style of extemporaneous preaching. It was Whitefield's brand of Christianity that began taking hold among African American communities in the later eighteenth century because of its openness to lay initiative and its adaptability to the spiritual needs of an oppressed people. Evangelicalism, in all its diverse, colorful, and sometimes outrageous forms, remains indebted to George Whitefield for the innovative, entrepreneurial character that has made it one of the most dynamic, expansive expressions of Christianity in the modern world.

Further Reading: Dallimore, Arnold. *George Whitefield: The Life and Times of the Great Evangelist of the Eighteenth-Century Revival.* 2 vols. Westchester, IL: Cornerstone Books, 1979; Franklin, Benjamin. *The Autobiography.* New York: Vintage Books/The Library of America, 1990; Hall, Timothy D. *Contested Boundaries: Itinerancy and the Reshaping of the Colonial American Religious World.* Durham, NC: Duke University Press, 1994; Lambert, Frank. *Pedlar in Divinity: George Whitefield and the Transatlantic Revivals, 1737–1770.* Princeton, NJ: Princeton University Press, 1994; Stout, Harry S. *The Divine Dramatist: George Whitefield and the Rise of Modern Evangelicalism.* Grand Rapids, MI: Eerdmans, 1991; Whitefield, George. *George Whitefield's Journals.* Edinburgh: Banner of Truth Trust, 1960; Whitefield, George. *George Whitefield's Letters: A Facsimile of Whitefield's Works, Volume One, 1771, with Supplements 1734 to 1742.* Edinburgh: Banner of Truth Trust, 1976.

Timothy D. Hall

WILKINSON, JEMIMA (1752–1819)

Jemima Wilkinson was the first woman in North America to found a religious group, the Society of Universal Friends. Born into a Rhode Island **Quaker** family governed by traditional values, in her teenage years she came under the influence of the enthusiastic **preaching** of the itinerant revivalist **George Whitefield.** Her ensuing zeal led the Smithfield Friends (i.e., Quakers) to read her out of their meeting. For a time she associated with the New Light **Baptists,** but found little in their fellowship to satisfy her spiritual longings. While still in her twenties, Wilkinson was to found a **new religious movement.**

An epidemic of typhus struck Rhode Island in 1776, and Jemima Wilkinson caught the fever. In the opinion of her family, friends and physician, her recovery was swift. Yet the young woman herself declared that she had died, and in her body there now resided a newly born spirit called "the Publick Universal Friend." She described a **vision** in which God had revealed that he had lifted up his hand, as she said, "a second time," and chosen to extend his promise of salvation through her person. For the next 33 years Jemima Wilkinson never deviated from this conviction, and those whose lives she touched referred to her not by her given name but affectionately and reverently as "the Friend."

Unlike her contemporary **Ann Lee,** the founder of the **Shakers,** Jemima Wilkinson did not require celibacy of her followers, though she herself never married. Neither did she, like Ann Lee, explicitly proclaim her own divinity. While Mother Ann identified herself as "Ann the Word," the Publick Universal Friend's invitation to "Worship God and His Holy One" left her estimate of her own identity in some doubt. The power of her personality enhanced her commonplace evangelical Christian message. The only printed work attributed to her, an eight-page pamphlet entitled *The Universal Friend's Advice*, was published in 1784. Although she founded several congregations in eastern New England, she traveled constantly, ordinarily finding a warm welcome both among farmers and trades people and in the homes of a society whose members had entertained Franklin and Washington. Even so, a certain sensationalism often preceded her coming, in that she regularly dressed in male clerical attire and, sometimes vehemently, declared herself to be neither male nor female. Her first visit to Philadelphia, in 1782, incited a minor riot, but the presence of the gentle and persuasive Friend herself usually calmed, if it did not fully convince, her audiences. A second visit to the city several years later passed without incident.

By the mid-1780s, the Friend's society had grown large enough to be listed among other denomina-tions in the census of 1789. Soon thereafter, how-ever, for reasons that are not altogether clear, she resolved to withdraw, with as many disciples as would accompany her, to the distant reaches of the New York frontier. On the shore of Keuka Lake, in Yates County, she founded the town she called Jerusalem, a community of perhaps 300 people at its most numerous, and in fact for some years the larg-est settlement in the Genesee region. She endeav-ored to rule Jerusalem as its matriarch and prophet until her death in 1819, but the strength and impact of her personality declined as she grew older and the vitality of her society gradually eroded. Rich land to the West seduced some of her former followers. Others sought claims in Jerusalem itself, and years after the Friend's death litigation still dragged on in local courts. The Public Universal Friend had desig-nated no successor and made no provisions for the future. Several persons tried without success to establish themselves as legitimate leaders, and while for a few years a handful of disciples remained loyal to the Friend's memory and message, the Society of Universal Friends may be said to have terminated with its founder's death.

Further Reading: Henretta, James. "Unruly Women: Jemima Wilkinson and Deborah Sampson Gannett." Archiving Early America. http://earlyamerica.com/review/fall96/biography.html; Wisbey, Herbert A. *Pioneer Prophetess: Jemima Wilkinson, the Publick Universal Friend.* Ithaca, NY: Cornell University Press, 1964.

Joel Tibbetts

WILLOW CREEK COMMUNITY CHURCH

Willow Creek Community Church is an interna-tionally known evangelical **megachurch** located in South Barrington, Illinois (suburban Chicago), begun in 1975 by 23-year-old Bill Hybels, then a student at Trinity College in Deerfield, Illinois. The congregation initially met in a rented theater, with an unpaid staff, borrowed equipment, and a vision for reaching the unchurched. The well-known **Church Growth** advocate Lyle Schaller has called it "the most influential church in North America" (quoted in David Leucke, "Is Willow Creek the Way of the Future?" *Christian Century*, May 14,

1997, 479). Hybels was previously a youth minister in an evangelical Congregational church in Park Ridge, Illinois, when a student-led revival took place in the Son City youth events. Stressful relationships with the leaders of South Park Community Church influenced the decision to plant a new church in the suburbs. With the encouragement of Wheaton College professor Gilbert Bilezikian, Hybels developed a vision for reaching the unchurched by dropping the traditional aspects of worship—creeds, **hymnals,** or references to older expressions of Christian faith. After conducting an informal neighborhood survey to discover the "unnecessary barriers" that kept people from attending church, Willow Creek's founders created an innovative weekend "seeker service" that utilized drama, contemporary music, and messages that answered the questions unchurched people were asking. These services have very little congregational participation and resemble entertainment more than liturgy. Willow Creek regularly answers questions about their numerical success by saying that they have simply stuck to their evangelistic purpose, expressed simply as "turning irreligious people into fully devoted followers of Christ."

Today Willow Creek is located on a 145-acre campus and attracts well over 20,000 people to its three weekend services on Saturday evening and Sunday morning. Its facilities look much more like a mall than a typical church building. There are no crosses, steeples, or stained glass windows. In the church's own literature the "seeker services" are described as providing a context where people can begin a journey that leads them to Christ, while believers can also grow toward full devotion to Christ. When critics suggest that this type of service is not worship, leaders regularly explain that it is not intended to be a worship service. Hybels has regularly suggested that he follows the pattern of the apostle Paul, who explained his own mission by saying, "I have become all things to all people, that I might by all means save some" (1 Corinthians 9:22). In 1992, as a result of numerous requests from other churches and leaders who were searching for ways to reach out to spiritual seekers, the Willow Creek Association began. More than 9,500 churches

around the world are part of the association. Members of the association are urged to attend major events. One of the biggest events is the annual August Leadership Summit, which features Christian and non-Christian leadership experts who offer motivational and instructional talks to thousands of people in scattered locations via satellite. The goal is to provide inspiration, motivation, and practical instruction on topics related to leadership, including self-management, team building, and managing change.

Willow Creek has a statement of faith that stresses orthodox Christian beliefs, a clearly written statement of purpose, and a clear membership policy that requires profession of faith and the expression of a personal desire to follow Christ as a disciple. Since the seeker services are designed for those making inquiry into Christianity, and the midweek services are designed for those who already profess faith, the membership size of Willow Creek remains considerably smaller than its attendance numbers. In addition to the large seeker services, the church runs thousands of small group meetings and includes specialized groups for eating disorders, parents of junior high students, hairdressers, young mothers, singles, and so on. Evangelical critic G. A. Pritchard argues that the church fails to understand and use social-science theory properly and does not embody the biblical tension between God's transcendent holiness and his immanent love. Pritchard comments, "A serious critique of American culture from a Christian perspective is generally absent at Willow Creek ... [because] Creekers do not think critically with the categories and content of Christian theology" (Pritchard, 272). This criticism could be applied to many revival movements in American history. Moreover, many observers and analysts believe that Willow Creek's major contribution lies in its focus on evangelizing the unchurched.

Further Reading: Bilezikian, Gilbert. *Christianity 101.* Grand Rapids, MI: Zondervan, 1993; Maudlin, Michael G., Edward Galbreath, and Kevin A. Miller. "Selling Out the House of God? Bill Hybels Answers the Critics of the Seeker-Church Movement." *Christianity Today,* July 18, 1994, 20–25; Olson, David L. *Church Leaders*

Willow Creek Community Church emerged from the ministry of Rev. Bill Hybels (above left) who led the Son City youth revival movement during 1972–1975 at South Park Church, Park Ridge, Illinois. (Early 1970s.) Courtesy of Dr. Fred W. Beuttler.

Handbook. South Barrington, IL: Willow Creek Community Church, 1993; Pritchard, G. A. *Willow Creek Seeker Services*. Grand Rapids, MI: Baker, 1996; Willow Creek Church Web site. http://www.willowcreek.org/.

John Armstrong

WIMBER, JOHN (1934–1997)

John Wimber was a pastor, teacher, author, musician, and founder and leader of the worldwide movement of churches known as the Vineyard Christian Ministries International. He became a leading advocate of the **signs and wonders** movement and key renewal leader in the neo-**Charismatic** or Third Wave revival movement during the 1980s and 1990s. Born in Kirksville, Missouri, John Wimber organized, and played keyboard in, the Righteous Brothers band in 1962. In 1963 he experienced **conversion** to Christian faith and later graduated from Azusa Pacific University in Southern California. He was ordained by the California

Yearly Meeting of Friends (**Quakers**) in 1970 and served as co-pastor of the Yorba Linda Friends Church for five years. In 1974 Wimber began a ministry with **C. Peter Wagner** that led to the formation of the Charles E. Fuller Institute of Evangelism and **Church Growth** in California. In this consulting capacity Wimber traveled to scores of churches, analyzing their growth patterns. Through this relationship he began to seriously consider the role of signs and wonders in evangelism and Church Growth. By 1977, when a portion of the Yorba Linda Friends Church had become charismatic, Wimber was asked to leave. Approximately 60 people left with him and affiliated with the well-known **Calvary Chapel** in Costa Mesa, California, under the leadership of one the most prominent leaders of the **Jesus People movement,** Chuck Smith.

After dramatic reports of **deliverance** and **healing,** and a large influx of conversions numbering in the thousands, Wimber left Calvary Chapel in 1982 to form a new church in Anaheim, California.

Shortly after Wimber had begun this new work he entered into a friendship with Kenn Gullicksen, another Calvary Chapel pastor who had left to begin a church called the Vineyard. Wimber and Gullicksen merged their respective congregations and began the Anaheim Vineyard Fellowship, which quickly grew to include more than 5,000 people. Over the next few years another 30 Calvary Chapels joined this new movement. A considerable number of Vineyard churches were "adopted" from previous denominations as the movement grew. Under John Wimber's leadership an aggressive church-planting effort was also begun. Today the Vineyard association is a well-defined denomination with an orthodox statement of faith including basic Christian doctrines such as the Trinity, the deity of Christ, salvation by grace through faith alone, and the divine inspiration of the Bible. Wimber never adopted the traditional **Pentecostal** teaching that made **speaking in tongues** the "initial evidence" of **baptism in the Holy Spirit.** Instead he emphasized healing, deliverance from demonic affliction, and **prophecy,** while encouraging speaking in tongues.

One of Wimber's lasting contributions may be his influence on the worship style of many evangelicals—both noncharismatic and charismatic—at the end of the twentieth century. A service under Wimber's guidance typically had three parts: (1) lively, upbeat, and mellow music; (2) teaching that was relational and included personal testimony; and (3) a more overt expression of **charismatic gifts** in the concluding "ministry time." Here individuals were invited to come forward for **prayer** and to experience the work of the Holy Spirit. Wimber wrote a number of songs and revolutionized the entire field of worship music. This led to the birth of Maranatha Music (see **Hymns, Hymnody, and Christian Music in Revivals**), a multimillion-dollar company that introduced new worship styles throughout the English-speaking evangelical world.

Wimber was an engaging and insightful leader, always willing to pioneer in new ventures. He was an initiator or participant in a series of spiritual movements stretching from the 1970s to the 1990s. In 1988 he became interested in a group called the **Kansas City prophets** and forged a link to their

prophetic movement, which prompted critics to challenge him, and led some Vineyard congregations to leave his association. Eventually Wimber withdrew his approval of the Kansas City prophets and worked instead with a team of pastoral coordinators or regional associates. Another controversial expression of revival, called holy **laughter,** touched the Vineyard through the now famous **Toronto Blessing** that broke out in the Toronto Airport Vineyard in 1994. By late 1995 Wimber concluded that the Airport Vineyard was "going over the edge" by encouraging unusual behavior—including "animal sounds" among worshippers—as normative. He recommended that the Vineyard remove the Toronto fellowship from formal recognition. Wimber stressed throughout his ministry that spiritual renewal was not simply about individuals but about the alteration of the forms and practices of the church. His impact upon larger movements of revival at the end of the twentieth century was much greater than his influence upon the Vineyard alone. He suffered from heart problems for some years and died of a massive brain hemorrhage in Santa Ana, California in 1997.

Further Reading: Armstrong, John H. "In Search of Spiritual Power." In Michael Horton, ed., *Power Religion.* 61–88. Chicago: Moody Press, 1992; Jackson, Bill. *The Quest for the Radical Middle: A History of the Vineyard.* Anaheim, CA: Vineyard International Ministries, 1999; Larsen, Timothy, ed. *Biographical Dictionary of Evangelicals.* Downers Grove, IL: InterVarsity, 2003; Springer, Kevin, ed. *Power Encounters.* Harper and Row, 1988; Wimber, John, and Kevin Springer. *Power Evangelism.* San Francisco: Harper and Row, 1986; Wimber, John, and Kevin Springer. *Power Healing.* San Francisco: Harper and Row, 1991.

John Armstrong

WOMEN AND REVIVALS

Women have been intimately involved in every aspect of North American revivals and revivalism. In addition to being the majority of those revived in virtually every recorded revival, women have initiated and instigated many revivals. They have supported and facilitated the work of male revivalists. Many women have been revival **preachers** themselves.

Revival movements in American history frequently provided women with opportunities for leadership and ministry that were not available in the formal structures of established churches, denominations, and theological seminaries. Throughout the nineteenth and twentieth centuries, women were activists in reform movements that began in, or were encouraged by, religious revivals—such as **abolitionism** and the **temperance movement.** The **foreign missions** movement in American Protestant denominations received much of its impetus from women missionaries and other women who remained in the United States but provided funding, **prayer,** and administrative support on behalf of foreign missionaries. Women led in the successful campaign to provide suffrage or voting rights for women, and many who led in the suffrage struggle had previously participated in the abolitionist, foreign missions, or temperance movements, including such organizations as the Women's Christian Temperance Movement (WCTU).

White women—such as **Phoebe Worrall Palmer** and **Hannah Whitall Smith**—and such **African Americans** as **Amanda Berry Smith**—were instrumental in the **Holiness movement of the nineteenth century,** and one might say that this entire movement was primarily female led. Another female leader in the American Holiness movement, **Alma Bridwell White,** may be the first woman to be consecrated as a bishop in a Christian church—the Denver-based Pentecostal Union Church. "Mother Mary Tate," or **Mary Magdalena "Lena" Street Lewis Tate,** was the African American female founder of a Holiness-**Pentecostal** denomination Church of the Living God, the Pillar and Ground of the Truth. Women founded many of the prominent **new religious movements** in U.S. history. While some of these women had virtually no relationship with religious revivalism (e.g., Mary Baker Eddy and Madame Blavatsky) there were some others (e.g., **Ann Lee** and **Jemima Wilkinson**) who led religious groups that bore at least some relationship to revivals. The twentieth-century **Pentecostal** movement featured a number of outstanding female leaders and preachers, including the first American woman with a **radio** license, **Aimee Semple McPherson**—the only woman commonly mentioned alongside of **Charles G. Finney, Dwight L. Moody,** and **Billy Graham** as an American revivalist of the first rank.

Charles Grandison Finney might never have become a revivalist had the women of the Female Missionary Society of the Western District of New York not hired him as their missionary to Jefferson County. These independent women raised the money to pay him and decided where to assign him. In his later *Lectures on Revivals of Religion* (1835) he acknowledges that it was often women who invited him to hold a revival in their communities. He speaks specifically of one woman who tried repeatedly to get her minister to host a revival meeting, and when that failed, she hired a carpenter to make rough benches for her own living room and invited a revivalist to preach there. Women also spread the word about the meetings, inviting family members, relatives, and friends. They further publicized the revival's progress and results through letters to friends and family near and far.

In the early years of American revivalism, there were no hotels. Traveling ministers were dependent on the hospitality of women willing to house them, feed them, and do their laundry for weeks at a time. Women prayed individually for revival to come and held corporate prayer meetings to that end. Once revival began, it was women who hosted and attended prayer meetings morning, noon, and night in support of the work. Women attended the meetings and made sure that the **men** in their families also attended. Sophie Clarke, a member of that New York Female Missionary Society, lured her recalcitrant nephew Theodore Dwight Weld into one of Finney's meetings in Utica. She and her female friends then blocked any exit from the pew until Weld responded to Finney's message. In early American revivals, in which **Calvinism** was the prevailing **theology of revivals,** women were concerned that those most dear to them—husbands and children—might be exposed to fervent expositions of the gospel. Given the high mortality rates of the era and the inherent uncertainty of divine predestination, women were especially grieved and racked with concern for the eternal destinies of loved ones who had not made some outward sign of commitment to Christ.

Women also prayed for and with those who came to the "anxious bench," seeking salvation in response to an **altar call.** South Carolina Holiness and **healing** evangelist Mattie E. Perry (1868–1957) began her career doing "altar work" with converts at local **camp meetings.** Beginning with Finney's revivals, personal testimonies from laypeople became an important aspect of revivals. Those converted were expected and encouraged to give their testimony as a spiritual incentive to others. To the consternation of his rivals, Finney encouraged women to speak about their faith in public settings. Phoebe Palmer (1807–1874), with her sister Sarah Lankford (1806–1896), founded the Tuesday Meeting for the Promotion of Holiness as a place where women (and later men as well) could be instructed in the way of holiness (or **sanctification**), pray for it, and then give testimony to their experience of it. Hundreds of similar meetings were founded worldwide as part of the Holiness movement. Many were converted through the testimonies given in these meetings as well as through

testimonies collected in such books as *Forty Witnesses*, edited by Olin S. Garrison, and published in the *Guide to Holiness* and other religious periodicals.

Other women provided what might be termed auxiliary services to revivals. Dwight L. Moody asked the **Methodist** Frances Willard (1839–1898) to address afternoon meetings on temperance during his three-month Boston crusade in 1877. There Willard met her secretary and lifelong companion Anna Gordon (1853–1931), a talented musician on Moody's team. Gordon also held morning children's services—a frequent feature of late nineteenth-century revivals and usually conducted by women. African American Holiness evangelist Amanda Smith (1837–1915) was often asked to sing at revivals and camp meetings, which gave her an opening to share her testimony and to preach. Beginning in the 1870s, Amanda Smith's connection with fellow Holiness teacher Hannah Whitall Smith afforded her the opportunity to speak in England, and Amanda Smith later traveled and preached also in India and West

Members of Langley Avenue All Nations Pentecostal Church in Chicago, Illinois fervently praying. Women's prayer meetings have often been instrumental in spiritual awakening. (Photographer Russell Lee, April 1941.) Courtesy of the Library of Congress.

Africa, and emerged as the first African American woman to have an international Christian ministry.

Some women, such as Frances Willard, when they were denied or discouraged from gospel ministry, applied the techniques of revivalism to social reform activities. Theodore Weld and Henry Stanton, as well as many female Finney students, such as Lucy Stone (1818–1893) and Sallie Holley (1818–1893), applied their considerable persuasive skills to abolitionism and women's rights. Willard herself confessed in *Woman and Temperance* that "The deepest thought and desire of my life would have been met, if my dear old Mother Church had permitted me to be a minister. The wandering life of an evangelist or a reformer comes nearest to, but cannot fill the ideal which I early cherished" (Willard, *Woman and Temperance* [1883], 30).

Many women, however, found ways to be revival preachers or evangelists down through the centuries. Women in the American Society of Friends, or **Quakers,** were among the first female speakers in America. Persecution by male Puritan ministers resulted in the execution of Quaker preacher **Mary Dyer** in Boston Common in 1660, who died during this period along with other Quaker martyr-preachers. Encouraged by their reading of early biographies of John Wesley's women preachers, a variety of American women, Methodist and otherwise, set out to convert souls in the 1700s and early 1800s. Young **Free Will Baptist** women preached revival in the eighteenth-century in New Hampshire and Vermont. Jarena Lee (1783–?) first sought to preach in the **African Methodist Episcopal Church** in 1809, but was not allowed to do so. After her husband died in 1818, she became an itinerant evangelist. Zilphia Elaw (1790–1845), a free black woman from Pennsylvania, also set out to preach after her husband's death in 1823. She preached from New England to the mid-Atlantic states, even risking her own freedom to preach to slaves in Maryland and Virginia. Sarah Righter Major (1808–1884) was converted under the ministry of John Greenleaf Whittier's "Pilgrim Stranger," Harriet Livermore. Major was denied a preaching license by the Church of the Brethren in 1834 but kept on spreading the gospel anyway. By the mid-nineteenth century women preachers flourished. In 1851 Lydia Sexton was the first woman licensed by the United Brethren Church. She evangelized from Ohio to Kansas. Space does not permit discussion of the thousands of American women who became evangelists on foreign mission fields. The name of Lottie Moon (1840–1912), legendary Southern **Baptist** teacher and evangelist in China, must suffice as representative.

After the **Civil War** a number of women evangelists were active in the Holiness movement, speaking and doing altar work at camp meetings across the nation. In the South, Mary Lee Cagle (1864–1955) evangelized on behalf of the Nazarenes from north Alabama to Texas. Fannie McDowell Hunter's *Women Preachers* (1905) tells the stories of the women who were active in Cagle's circle. In the Midwest Mary Cole (1853–?) preached either on her own, accompanied by one of her brothers or sisters, or with **Church of God (Anderson, Indiana)** founder D. S. Warner's revival team. Maye McReynolds (1874–1932) was a railroad agent when she joined the **Church of the Nazarene** and felt a call to preach to the many **Latinos** and Latinas in and around Los Angeles. Among her converts was Santos Elizondo (1867–1941). She returned to her hometown of El Paso, Texas, and planted churches in Juárez, Mexico, and along both sides of the border.

Many Holiness women preachers such as Mattie Perry eventually became Pentecostal. Most famous was **Maria Woodworth-Etter** (1844–1924), who had toured as a tent and tabernacle healing evangelist for many years before becoming Pentecostal. Later in life, after she settled down in her own church in Indianapolis, she was visited by a star of the next generation, Aimee Semple McPherson (1890–1944). Worldwide the most famous Pentecostal evangelist may have been Daisy Washburn Osborn (1924–1995), late wife of T. L. Osburn (1923–). Together they preached around the world, a calling still being carried on by their daughter LaDonna. Active in ministry among Latinos in the early and mid-twentieth century were the Pentecostal Latina preachers Nellie Bazán, Julia and Matilda Vargas, and "Mama Leo" or **Leoncia Rousseau Rosado.**

Rev. Mary Cagle preaching in a tent revival, probably in Texas. Cagle established the Church of the Nazarene's West Texas district and served her denomination from 1894 to 1950. (ca. 1900.) Mary Lee Cagle Collection, Nazarene Archives.

On **television** during the 1970s and 1980s, viewers responded to the emotional gospel message of **Tammy Faye Bakker,** who appeared alongside her husband, **Jim Bakker.** The husband-wife ministry team has often appeared in American revivals, stretching back to the era of the Holiness movement that featured Hannah Whitall Smith and **Robert Pearsall Smith.** During the last 10–15 years, viewers have tuned in to the forceful televised presentations of Joyce Meyer, Marilyn Hickey, and the African American preacher Juanita Bynum—all representatives of a Pentecostal wing of American revivalism that seems to be generally more open to female preachers than non-Pentecostal evangelicalism. While evangelist Billy Graham has officially passed the mantle of leadership to his son Franklin, by all accounts the more talented preacher in the family is daughter Anne Graham Lotz (1948–), who has founded her own evangelistic organization, AnGeL Ministries, to conduct crusades in major cit-

ies. Women have contributed substantially not only to the practice of revivals but also to the theology of revival. Most notably, Phoebe Palmer's *The Way of Holiness* and Hannah Whitall Smith's *A Christian's Secret of a Happy Life* were the pivotal theological expositions of Wesleyan Holiness and Keswick Holiness teaching, respectively. Together they legitimated a whole new wave of revivalism that encouraged those who had already experienced conversion or salvation to seek the "second blessing," to go on to perfection, to seek holiness of heart and life, to be entirely sanctified. Their teaching paved the way for the later Pentecostal and **Charismatic** revivals.

Further Reading: Andrews, William L., ed. *Sisters of the Spirit: Three Black Women's Autobiographies in the Nineteenth Century.* Bloomington: Indiana University Press, 1966; Blumhofer, Edith L. *Aimee Semple McPherson: Everybody's Sister.* Grand Rapids, MI: Eerdmans, 1993; Hardesty, Nancy A. *Faith Cure: Divine Healing in the Holiness and Pentecostal Movements.* Peabody, MA: Hendrickson, 2003; Hardesty, Nancy. *Women Called to Witness: Evangelical Feminism in the Nineteenth Century.* Knoxville: University of Tennessee Press, 1999; Laird, Rebecca. *Ordained Women in the Church of the Nazarene.* Kansas City, MO: Nazarene, 1993; Robert, Dana L. *American Women in Mission.* Macon, GA: Mercer University Press, 1996; Stanley, Susie. *Holy Boldness: Woman Preachers' Autobiographies and the Sanctified Self.* Knoxville: University of Tennessee Press, 2002.

Nancy Hardesty

WOMEN'S AGLOW

see Aglow International

WOODWORTH-ETTER, MARIA BEULAH (1844–1924)

A **camp and tent meeting** revivalist during the **Holiness movement of the nineteenth century,** and credited as the grandmother of the twentieth-century **Pentecostal revivals,** Maria Beulah Woodworth-Etter **preached** salvation and divine **healing** to crowds numbering as many as 25,000 in churches, theaters, and tents across the United States. After marrying P. H. Woodworth, Maria became the mother of six children, five of whom died in infancy. Charging her husband with immorality, she sought a divorce and later married Samuel Etter. "Sister Etter," as she was called, began her itinerant evangelism in 1880 at the age of 35, claiming inspiration from a God-given **vision.** Sponsored by the **United Brethren, Methodists,** and **Churches of God,** Woodworth-Etter was one of the few major leaders in the Holiness movement who also exercised leadership in the Pentecostal revivals. She founded 12 congregations and built the Woodworth-Etter Tabernacle in 1918, which she pastored until her death.

Woodworth-Etter was dubbed "the Trance Evangelist" because both she and several hundred auditors at a time fell into deep trances of perhaps several hours' duration in the middle of her preaching. She reputedly preached without notes, claiming to have received a text from the Holy Spirit at the last moment. Her meetings were famous, even in the secular press, for the phenomena of congregants' being "slain in the spirit" (falling to the ground), **speaking in tongues,** uttering **prophecies,** seeing visions, and exhibiting other **bodily manifestations.** Woodworth-Etter believed that Satan was the source of sickness, and she **prayed**—with the laying on of hands—for people to experience **deliverance** from demons as well as healing. She was known for her brusque tactics, imitated by later healing revivalists, including physically hitting diseased body parts to combat the demon spirits behind afflictions. Woodworth-Etter claimed that people were healed of all manner of diseases during her meetings, sometimes without specific prayers being offered, and that on particular occasions the dead had been brought back to life.

Woodworth-Etter publicized her ministry through books, most of which were autobiographical, including *Life and Experience of Maria B. Woodworth* (1885), *Revival Songs* (1888), *Acts of the Holy Ghost, or The Life, Work, and Experience of Mrs. M. B. Woodworth-Etter, Evangelist* (1912), *Signs and Wonders: God Wrought in the Ministry of Forty Years* (1916), *Holy Ghost Sermons* (1918), and *Marvels and Miracles: God Wrought in the Ministry of Mrs. M. B. Woodworth Etter for Forty Five Years* (1922). Preaching until the end, she died at age 80.

Poster advertising a 1922 revival meeting in Ottumwa, Iowa, led by Maria Woodworth-Etter, who proclaimed "salvation for [the] soul" and "healing for [the] body." Healings, visions, and tongues-speaking occurred in her meetings as early as the 1880s, and public controversy erupted during her 1890 visit to St. Louis. Courtesy of Flower Pentecostal Heritage Center, Springfield, MO.

Further Reading: Chappell, Paul Gale. "The Divine Healing Movement in America." PhD dissertation, Drew University, 1983; Warner, Wayne E. *The Woman Evangelist.* Metuchen, NJ: Scarecrow Press, 1986; Taves, Ann. *Fits, Trances, and Visions: Experiencing Religion and Explaining Experience from Wesley to James.* Princeton, NJ: Princeton University Press, 1999.

Candy Gunther Brown

WORD OF FAITH

see Prosperity Theology

Y

YOUNG LIFE

Young Life is an evangelistic organization aimed at high school students that was founded in 1940 by Jim Rayburn, a student at Dallas Theological Seminary. Between 1940 and 1943 Rayburn conducted youth rallies in various cities in Texas. These early efforts resembled other high school and **college revival** meetings taking place all over the country at the time. But Rayburn longed to evangelize young people who would not come to church or to a **tent meeting,** so he soon dropped revival meetings in favor of what he came to call an "incarnational" approach to youth ministry. He and a group of fellow seminarians began to visit high school events like football games and build friendships with the students they met. Rayburn called this process "winning the right to be heard." After establishing trust, leaders invited teenagers to the Young Life Club that was held weekly in the home of a local Christian family.

At club meetings, leaders provided lots of singing and games, and concluded with a personal testimony or gospel presentation. One of Rayburn's early slogans was "It's a sin to bore a kid with the gospel," so he made sure to include lots of stories, humor, and personal examples in his gospel presentations. This way of speaking came to be called a "conversational" style to distinguish it from the high-pressure appeals and even **shouting** that was more familiar in revival **preaching.** With the help of Chicago businessman Herbert J. Taylor, Young Life bought its first camp, Star Ranch, in 1945. Instead of subjecting non-Christian campers to hours of preaching or other revival techniques, Young Life camps relied on the personal relationships between counselors and campers to encourage **conversions.**

In the 1960s and 1970s Young Life challenged some of its constituents to relinquish legalistic approaches to scripture and to recognize an ethical responsibility to society. It promoted interdenominational and ecumenical communication between conservative Protestants, liberal Protestants, and **Roman Catholics.** Because of the growing emphasis on urban ministry, some leaders were concerned about alienating their predominantly suburban, middle-class, white constituency. The picture of a young black male on the cover of Young Life's magazine *Focus on Youth* in 1968 proved to be controversial. Over the years, Young Life camps established a reputation as evangelistic resorts that featured the best in recreational activities. By 2003, Young Life ran 20 different camps serving over 43,000 campers. A full-time staff numbering 3,232 gave the organization a presence in 4,073 schools or other locations worldwide, with a weekly U.S. club attendance of 109,291 and an estimated yearly attendance of 900,000. Young Life departed significantly from the traditions of revivalism by eliminating revival meetings and urgent calls for conversion and replacing them with an informal, fun, and relational approach to evangelism.

Further Reading: Meredith, Char. *It's a Sin to Bore a Kid: The Story of Young Life.* Waco, TX: Word Books, 1978; Pahl, Jon. *Youth Ministry in Modern America.* Peabody, MA: Hendrickson, 2000; Senter, Mark. *The Coming Revolution in Youth Ministry.* Wheaton, IL: Victor Books, 1992.

Thomas E. Bergler and Michael Pasquier

YOUNG MEN'S CHRISTIAN ASSOCIATION AND YOUNG WOMEN'S CHRISTIAN ASSOCIATION

The Young Men's Christian Association (YMCA) began in London, England in 1844, founded by George Williams and a small group of **men** who gathered in a room above a shop in St. Paul's churchyard in response to what they saw as the unhealthy spiritual and social conditions in the city. By the 1840s London was reeling from the impact of the Industrial Revolution. The growth and centralization of commerce and industry in Britain, along with the development of the railroads, had attracted many young men to the cities, and it was in this context that George Williams conceived the idea of an organization where young men could come together for Christian fellowship. The YMCA became a safe haven for young men who had moved to the city to find work, and it helped them to maintain their faith commitments after relocating to urban neighborhoods that afforded temptations to drunkenness, sexual immorality, and other vices. The YMCA provided a place to live, Bible studies, training for Sunday school teachers, weekly **prayer** meetings, public lectures, reading rooms, and refreshment areas that gave members the opportunity to make friends and settle into urban life. The spiritual background to the YMCA was the larger **transatlantic** movement of the **Second Great Awakening** from the 1790s to the 1830s. This

series of spiritual revivals had affected North America and Britain alike, and had spawned such social reforms as **abolitionism,** the **temperance movement,** and the **women's** suffrage movement. The YMCA carried many of the ideas, values, and practices of the Second Great Awakening into an urban context.

The American YMCA movement began through the initiative of Tom Sullivan in Boston's Old South Church in 1851. In less than five months, more than 1,200 young men had joined the YMCA in Boston and the first prayer meetings were established on Monday evenings. By December 1852 the Boston YMCA had distributed over 12,000 copies of its constitution and bylaws to clergymen across the country. Soon dozens of YMCA chapters were established across the country, including the New York City YMCA in the Fulton Street Dutch **Reformed** Church.

The **Revival of 1857–1858** and the YMCA were closely intertwined. This nationally and historically influential revival movement grew out of prayer meetings that began among the young men of the New York City YMCA, and were held at the Fulton Street Dutch Reformed Church in 1856. While the YMCA was growing, the churches of New York City were failing to maintain their congregations, and many of them chose to relocate from the urban center to more tranquil, outlying locations. The Fulton Street Church, however, resolved to reach out to the many businessmen in New York City who had fallen into hardship as a result of the financial panic of 1857. Consequently, the church hired 49-year-old Jeremiah Lanphier as a lay missionary to the city. Lanphier began his work on July 1, 1857, and he took the leadership of the Fulton Street noon-hour prayer meetings in September 1857. The prayer meetings were sparsely attended during his first few months, but by the middle of January 1858 attendance had increased to overflowing. Numerous noon prayer meetings were launched across the city and throughout the country as word spread through the YMCA network of associations. In addition to the approximately 500,000 converts that were added to the faith during the Revival of 1857–1858, the

American Protestant churches also gained a better understanding of the importance and effectiveness of organized lay ministry. An empowered laity had infused new energy and life into a church that formerly relied on pastors to do the work of ministry. Another result of the noon prayer meetings was the promotion of interdenominational fellowship. This revival did much to help members of different Protestant denominations view one another favorably, and not with distrust and suspicion.

In the late 1800s, through the influence of nationally known evangelist **Dwight L. Moody** and the **Student Volunteer Movement** leader, John R. Mott, the American YMCAs sent thousands of new workers overseas. They went out as **foreign missionaries** or as missionary-like YMCA secretaries in various localities. Later, during the First World War, the YMCAs sent out "war workers" to engage in Christian ministry among military personnel. The first foreign work secretaries, as they were called, reflected the missionary outreach by Christian churches at the turn of the century. Instead of planting new churches, however, they organized YMCAs that eventually were placed under local control. In this way the YMCAs encouraged lay initiative and lay leadership in various foreign nations, just as they had in North America and Britain. Both Moody and Mott served for lengthy periods as paid professional staff members of the YMCA movement, and both maintained lifelong connections with it.

Another outcome of the 1857–1858 revival was the establishment of the Young Women's Christian Association in America. The revival emphasized laymen's and laywomen's prayer groups, interdenominational unity, and women's role in the church and in Christian organizations. One prayer meeting during the 1857–1858 revival in New York City was held in the Church of the Puritans on Union Square and led by Mrs. Marshall Roberts. Reflecting on the remarkable prayer meetings in the Dutch Reformed Church on Fulton Street and the **Methodist** Episcopal Church on St. John Street that the YMCA had maintained, the ladies of the Church of the Puritans prayer meeting desired to establish a

similar organization for women. On November 24, 1858, a meeting was held in the chapel of New York University where the Ladies Christian Association was formed and Mrs. Roberts was elected as the "directress." This first association focused on social virtues, character, intellectual excellence, and the spread of evangelical religion. To become a member a young woman was required to be a member in good standing of an evangelical church. Associate membership was open to those nonbelievers who desired to participate in the association.

In 1859 Lucretia Boyd felt the need for an association in Boston that would care for the young women who were constantly coming to the city to earn a living. Without an agency to offer resources, protection, and advice, these women were often neglected when they became ill and helpless when they could not find work. Boyd's plans were dashed when the clergy and other lay Christian leaders in the city declared such an undertaking too risky for the women attempting it. Seven years later a missionary woman became concerned over orphaned, homeless, and other helpless young women in Boston. Organizing on the format of the YMCA, Mrs. Henry Durant opened the Boston Young Women's Christian Association (YWCA) in her home on Mt. Vernon Street in March 1866. The focus of the Boston YWCA was to care for the moral and religious welfare of young women and assist them in finding suitable housing and employment. Soon Durant secured two rooms in the Congregational building on Chauncey Street, and provided for a reading room, Bible classes, prayer meetings, and a variety of skills classes there.

In June 1867 another association was established on behalf of the working women of Hartford, Connecticut, by Mrs. Charles Smith, and was named the Women's Christian Association. Smith's husband's niece was Mrs. Marshall Roberts, who—along with Mrs. Durant of Boston and the newly formed Hartford YMCA—came alongside the ladies of the Hartford prayer group to develop the new association. Numerous women's associations sprang up across the country under a variety of names. Eventually most of the women's associations adopted either the name Women's Christian Association or Young Women's Christian Association. In 1906, these two associations merged their combined 186,000 members under the name Young Women's Christian Association. Grace Dodge, the founder of Columbia Teacher's College, became the first president, while Mable Cratty served as the first executive director of the newly merged association. In 1908 the YWCA conducted it first year-long training school at the estate of Grace Dodge. In 1912 the association expanded and built its own training center on Lexington Avenue in New York City. The building was a gift from six YWCA leaders and it housed the national offices until 1980.

Further Reading: Beardsley, Frank. *A History of American Revivals.* New York: American Tract Society, 1912; Doggett, L. L. *History of the Boston Young Men's Christian Association.* Boston: Young Men's Christian Association, 1901; Gladish, Kenneth. *YMCA: 150th Anniversary.* New York: Newcomen Society of the United States, 2001; Hopkins, Charles Howard. *History of the YMCA in North America.* New York: Associated Press, 1951; Mjagkijm, Nina, and Margaret Spratt, eds. *Men and Women Adrift: The YMCA and the YWCA in the City.* New York: New York University Press, 1997; Pahl, Jon. *Youth Ministry in Modern America.* Peabody, MA: Hendrickson, 2000; Wilson, Elizabeth. *Fifty Years of Association Work among Young Women.* New York: National Board of the Young Women's Christian Associations, 1916.

Mark W. Cannister

YOUTH FOR CHRIST

Youth for Christ (YFC) is an evangelistic organization aimed at teenagers that began as a youth revival movement in the early 1940s. At that time, a number of young evangelical **preachers** began holding weekly evangelistic youth rallies in urban centers. A combination of factors contributed to the success of Christian youth organizations at midcentury: the establishment of the National Association of Evangelicals, a religious upsurge in response to World War II, and a civic concern about juvenile delinquency. In 1944, a group of Protestant evangelists organized the Chicagoland Youth for Christ on the coattails of other youth

groups and **radio** shows receiving national attention. By the end of World War II, Jack Wyrtzen regularly drew 20,000 young people to Madison Square Garden and Torrey Johnson packed Soldier Field in Chicago with 70,000. Youth for Christ International was officially founded in 1944 with Chicago pastor and Wheaton College alumnus Torrey Johnson (1909–2002) as its first president and **Billy Graham** as its first vice president. Graham's friend Charles Templeton was another influential early figure in YFC.

The national press closely followed the movement in its early days. Leaders believed that they were on the cusp of an international revival that would begin among young people. American servicemen established branches of the movement all over the world. By 1946, the Saturday-night rallies of YFC quickly spread to an estimated 300,000 young people throughout the United States and into the ranks of the American military in Europe and the Pacific. Such overseas experiences led several of these **men** to found **foreign missions** and international relief organizations during the 1950s. Revival seemed imminent, as the number of cities holding weekly youth revival meetings mushroomed to 1,450 by 1949. Leaders adopted the old **Student Volunteer Movement** watchword "the evangelization of the world in this generation." They adapted the traditional methods of revivalism to the new tastes of youth, using the slogan "geared to the times, but anchored to the Rock." They broadcast their rallies live on the radio and employed musicians that sounded much like the popular big bands, girl trios, and male crooners of the era. Testimonies from celebrities like war heroes and star athletes drew young people to the rallies. Preachers offered brief, captivating messages tied to current events, and always ended with an **altar call.** They promised teenagers that converting to Jesus would be fun and would make them popular. Critics accused the movement of being superficial and of abandoning the traditional **hymns and hymnody** of revival, but leaders insisted that their rallies were not church services, so they could be more entertaining and could use more upbeat musical styles.

Around 1950, YFC president Bob Cook tried to refocus the organization toward the goal of sparking a youth revival. Motivating Cook and fellow YFC leaders at this time was their understanding of biblical **eschatology** and the end-times. Believing that the Second Coming of Christ and end of the world were imminent, they felt justified in calling for an all-out, innovative revivalism that was aimed at youth. The organization grew during the 1950s, benefiting from the revival of religion noted by many observers at the time. Student-led high school Bible clubs provided a place to preach the gospel to students and invite them to the weekly rally. The number of clubs peaked at around 3,000 in the 1960s. National talent contests, preaching contests, and Bible Quiz competitions drew students to rallies at the local level, with finals held at the annual YFC convention at Winona Lake campground. During the 1960s, leaders realized that weekly evangelistic rallies were no longer drawing youth. So they replaced rallies with what they called the Campus Life strategy, which used weekly club meetings and one-on-one relationships as the main evangelistic tools. During the 1970s, attendance boomed at these clubs, benefiting from the general upsurge in evangelical religion. The 1980s and 1990s saw the development of national training conferences designed to help teenagers evangelize their friends. Over the years, YFC created specialized ministries to juvenile delinquents, junior high students, and teen mothers. The YFC organization served as a training ground for major leaders in the evangelical movement. Just as importantly, YFC was the pioneer in a synthesis of youth and entertainment culture with the techniques of mass evangelism. Such an approach has been widely imitated among those seeking to evangelize both youth and adults. The best-known leader of the contemporary **megachurch** movement in North America, Bill Hybels, began his ministry with youth rather than adults, and later adapted many methods used by YFC in establishing the **Willow Creek Community Church.**

Today YFC boasts a presence in more than 100 countries worldwide and in over 200 cities in the United States. As of 2003, the organization reported 2,000 full-time staff in service, resulting in 100,000 conversions of young people annually. The organization, headquartered in Denver, Colorado, enjoys the volunteer efforts of over 16,000 adults who serve alongside the staff members. In addition to encouraging membership in churches, local Campus Life meetings among high school and junior high students have remained an important outlet for Christian fellowship. National conferences in Los Angeles and Washington, DC, which attract tens of thousands of young people every year, reinforce a positive message about Jesus' role as both friend and savior.

Further Reading: Pahl, Jon. *Youth Ministry in Modern America*. Peabody, MA: Hendrickson, 2000; Senter, Mark. *The Coming Revolution in Youth Ministry*. Wheaton, IL: Victor Books, 1992.

Thomas E. Bergler and Michael Pasquier

YOUTH WITH A MISSION

Youth with a Mission is a nondenominational, parachurch, **foreign missions** organization founded for the purpose of mobilizing youth to serve in cross-cultural evangelism and in benevolent relief work. Organized by an **Assemblies of God** minister, Loren Cunningham (1935–), Youth with a Mission, known colloquially as YWAM (pronounced *why-wham*), became one of the most successful and far-reaching ministries of its kind in the last quarter of the twentieth century. Beginning as an Assemblies of God–sponsored youth agency, YWAM was independently incorporated in 1964 when its founder, Cunningham, could not reach an agreement with the denomination's leadership regarding the future of the organization. Developing as an independent nondenominational ministry, YWAM drew primary support from the growing momentum of the **Charismatic Renewal** of the 1960s and 1970s and the spread of independent neo-Charismatic churches. The organization eventually attracted the support of many Protestant denominational churches and gained increasing recognition as a mainstream evangelical missions and relief agency.

YWAM's mission is based on Cunningham's life-changing dream received in Nassau in the Bahamas in 1956. On the ceiling of his bedroom he envisioned a global movement of youth missionaries covering the world like waves crashing against the shores of every continent. The organization he formed became a highly focused cross-cultural evangelistic and benevolent relief agency. Cunningham's theology for the organization was a simple application of Jesus' commandments to love God and love one's neighbor (Matthew 22:34–40). Cunningham's compelling vision and practical theology proved a powerful combination in building an effective mission enterprise. The organization grew to become one of the largest evangelical organizations in existence, with over 15,000 staff members and bases in over 130 countries, 30,000 active volunteers, and over 200,000 volunteers in short-term projects.

In 1972 YWAM missionaries gained international attention following a tragedy at the Olympics in Munich where several Israeli athletes were taken hostage and killed. The news media featured the image of several hundred YWAM workers reaching out to anxious and endangered persons in the Olympic community. They provided a calm presence in a volatile situation. This event and the worldwide exposure of the media opened new doors with religious and government groups for years to come, advancing YWAM's identity as an agency in international affairs.

Additional initiatives undertaken by YWAM include the development of "mercy ships" or floating medical relief services, and a network of educational institutions. Converting commercial ocean liners into mobile clinics, YWAM successfully launched the *Anastasis* and the *Good Samaritan*, and other similarly equipped vessels, to reach remote locations in critical need of medical and food intervention. During the 1980s, YWAM established the University of the Nations in Kona, Hawaii. Extension training centers were soon established in Holland, Australia, Germany, and several other nations. The purpose of these educational institutions was primarily to educate and train YWAM workers. A network of educational programs has been developed in more than 100 locations worldwide.

Further Reading: Cunningham, Loren. *Is It Really You God?* Seattle: YWAM, 1984; Hocken, Peter. "Youth with a Mission." *Pneuma* 16 (1994): 265–70; Pahl, Jon. *Youth Ministry in Modern America*. Peabody, MA: Hendrickson, 2000; Youth with a Mission Web site. http://www.ywam.org/.

Daniel Hedges

Z

ZINZENDORF, NIKOLAUS LUDWIG GRAF VON

see Moravians

List of Contributors and Contributions

Professor Philip J. Anderson
North Park Theological Seminary
Chicago, Illinois
"Evangelical Covenant Church"

Dr. John Armstrong
Reformation and Revival Ministries
Carol Stream, Illinois
"Assurance of Salvation," "Awana," "Falwell, Jerry,"
  "Megachurch," "Promise Keepers,"
  "Willow Creek Community Church," "Wimber, John"

Dr. Craig D. Atwood
Divinity School
Wake Forest University
Winston-Salem, North Carolina
"Moravians"

Professor Randall Balmer
Ann Whitney Olin Professor of American Religion
Barnard College
Columbia University
New York, New York
"Graham, William Franklin, Jr. [Billy]"

Mr. Jonathan Barlow
PhD Student
Department of Theological Studies
Saint Louis University
St. Louis, Missouri
"Temperance Movement and Revivals"

Dr. Douglas Beacham
Executive Director, Church Education Ministries
International Pentecostal Holiness Church
Oklahoma City, Oklahoma
"International Pentecostal Holiness Church"

Dr. Joel R. Beeke
Pastor, Heritage Netherlands Reformed
  Congregation
President and Professor, Puritan Reformed
  Theological Seminary
Grand Rapids, Michigan
"Frelinghuysen, Theodorus Jacobus"

Professor Timothy K. Beougher
Southern Baptist Theological Seminary
Louisville, Kentucky
"Campus and College Revivals"

Professor Thomas E. Bergler
Department of Educational Ministries
Huntington College
Huntington, Indiana
"Young Life" (coauthor), "Youth for Christ" (coauthor)

Professor Gerald Bergman
Instructor of Science
Department of Arts and Sciences
Northwest State Community College
Archbold, Ohio
"Jehovah's Witnesses"

List of Contributors and Contributions

Professor James Beverley
Tyndale University College and Seminary
Toronto, Ontario, Canada
"Kansas City Prophets"

Professor Edith Blumhofer
Department of History and
Director, Institute for the Study of American
Evangelicals
Wheaton College
Wheaton, Illinois
"McPherson, Aimee Semple"

Dr. Henry Bowden
Professor Emeritus of Religion
Rutgers University
New Brunswick, New Jersey
"Beecher, Lyman and Henry Ward," "Eliot, John"

Professor Candy Gunther Brown
Department of Religious Studies
Indiana University
Bloomington, Indiana
"Branham, William," "Dowie, John Alexander,"
"Healing and Revivals," "Kuhlman, Kathryn,"
"MacNutt, Francis," "Sanctification and Revivals,"
"Woodworth-Etter, Maria Beulah"

Dr. Kenneth O. Brown
United Methodist Minister (retired)
Hazleton, Pennsylvania
"Camp Meetings and Tent Meetings"

Dr. Roger A. Bruns
Deputy Executive Director (retired)
National Historical Publications and Records
Commission
National Archives
Washington, DC
"Sunday, William Ashley [Billy]"

Dr. David Bundy
Associate Provost for Library Services
Fuller Theological Seminary
Pasadena, California
"Transatlantic Dimensions of North American
Revivals"

Professor Stanley M. Burgess
Distinguished Professor of Christian History
Director of the PhD Program
School of Divinity
Regent University
Virginia Beach, Virginia
"Charismatic Revival and Renewal," "Church of God
of Prophecy," "Hagin, Kenneth, Sr."

Professor Mark W. Cannister
Department of Youth Ministries
Gordon College
Wenham, Massachusetts
"Haystack Prayer Meeting," "Student Volunteer
Movement," "Young Men's Christian Association
and Young Women's Christian Association"

Ms. Kaley Carpenter
PhD Student
Princeton Theological Seminary
Princeton, New Jersey
"Blair, Samuel," "White, Alma Bridwell"

Professor Michael W. Casey
Carl P. Miller Chair of Communication
Communication Department
Pepperdine University
Malibu, California
"Primitivism"

Professor Walter H. Conser Jr.
History Department
University of North Carolina at Wilmington
Wilmington, North Carolina
"McLoughlin, William G."

Professor Jeffrey Cook
North Greenville College
Tigerville, South Carolina
"Christian and Missionary Alliance," "Simpson, Albert
Benjamin"

Professor John Corrigan
Edwin Scott Gaustad Professor of Religion,
Professor of History, and Director of Graduate
Studies
Religion Department
Florida State University
Tallahassee, Florida
"Men and Revivals"

Dr. T. Chris Crain
Headmaster
Providence Christian School
St. Louis, Missouri
"Nevin, John Williamson"

Professor Terry L. Cross
Dean, School of Religion
Professor of Theology
Lee University
Cleveland, Tennessee
"Church of God (Cleveland, Tennessee)"

Professor David D. Daniels III
Professor of Church History
McCormick Theological Seminary
Chicago, Illinois
"African American Revivals"

Mr. David Di Sabatino
Independent Scholar and Author
Lake Forest, California
"Jesus People Movement"

Dr. Eleanor Dickinson
Artist and Professor Emerita
California College of the Arts
San Francisco, California
"Material Culture of Revivals"

Dr. Melvin E. Dieter
Professor, Provost, and Vice President Emeritus
Asbury Theological Seminary
Wilmore, Kentucky
"Holiness Movement of the Nineteenth Century,"
    "Mahan, Asa," "Palmer, Phoebe Worrall,"
    "Salvation Army," "Smith, Hannah Whitall and
    Robert Pearsall"

Professor David Dorries
Associate Professor of Church History and
Theological Librarian
Oral Roberts University
Tulsa, Oklahoma
"Azusa Street Revival," "Catholic Apostolic Church,"
    "Roberts, Oral," "Seymour, William J."

Professor Angelyn Dries, OSF
Danforth Endowed Professor
Department of Theological Studies
Saint Louis University
St. Louis, Missouri
"Roman Catholic Revivals"

Ms. Sherry Sherrod DuPree
DuPree Holiness Pentecostal Collection
Schomburg Center for Research in
    Black Culture
New York Public Library, New York
"African Methodist Episcopal Church," "African
    Methodist Episcopal Zion Church," "Allen,
    Richard," "Amen Corner," "Church of God in
    Christ," "Father Divine, Major Jealous (George
    Baker)," "Grace, Sweet Daddy (Charles Emman-
    uel)," "Jakes, Thomas Dexter, Sr.," "Mason,
    Charles Harrison," "National Baptist
    Convention USA and National Baptist
    Convention of America," "Pentecostal
    Assemblies of the World," "Spirituals," "Tate,
    Mary Magdalena 'Lena' Street Lewis," "Truth,
    Sojourner (Isabella Bomefree)"

Dr. Daniel J. Earheart-Brown
President and Professor
Memphis Theological Seminary
Memphis, Tennessee
"Cumberland Presbyterian Church"

Mr. Hal Erickson
Independent Scholar, Author, and Editor
Milwaukee, Wisconsin
"Radio, Television, and Revivals"

Professor Larry Eskridge
Institute for the Study of American Evangelicals
Wheaton College
Wheaton, Illinois
"Money and Revivals"

Professor Ellen Eslinger
History Department
DePaul University
Chicago, Illinois
"Cane Ridge Revival"

Professor Gastón Espinosa
Department of Philosophy and Religion
Claremont McKenna College
Claremont, California
"Blaisdell, Francisca D.," "Fierro, Roberto Felix,"
    "Kramar, Marilynn, and Charisma in Missions,"
    "Latino(a) Protestant and Pentecostal Revivals,"
    "Olazábal, Francisco," "Rosado, Leoncia
    Rousseau (Mama Leo)," "Valdez, Adolfo C."

List of Contributors and Contributions

Professor Bruce J. Evensen
Department of Communication
DePaul University
Chicago, Illinois
"Moody, Dwight Lyman," "Robertson, Pat (Marion
Gordon)"

Mr. Michael A. Farley
PhD Student
Department of Theological Studies
Saint Louis University
St. Louis, Missouri
"Christian Nurture Debate"

Dr. D. William Faupel
Professor of Theological Research
Wesley Theological Seminary
Washington, District of Columbia
"Assemblies of God, General Council of the,"
"Speaking in Tongues (Glossolalia)"

Professor James R. Goff Jr.
History Department
Appalachian State University
Boone, North Carolina
"Parham, Charles Fox"

Professor Philip Goff
Director, Center for the Study of Religion and
American Culture
Indiana University–Purdue University, Indianapolis
Indianapolis, Indiana
"Fuller, Charles Edward"

Professor John Grigg
History Department
Hampden-Sydney College
Hampden-Sydney, Virginia
"Brainerd, David"

Professor Allen Guelzo
Henry R. Luce Professor of the Civil War Era and
Professor of History
Gettysburg College
Gettysburg, Pennsylvania
"Great Awakening"

Professor Timothy D. Hall
Chair, Department of History
Central Michigan University
Mount Pleasant, Michigan
"Whitefield, George"

Professor Thomas D. Hamm
Professor of History and
College Archivist
Earlham College
Richmond, Indiana
"Dyer, Mary Barrett," "Quakers (Society
of Friends)"

Professor Paul Garnett Hammond
Dean, Warren M. Angell College of Fine Arts
Oklahoma Baptist University
Shawnee, Oklahoma
"Hymns and Hymnody in Revivals"

Professor Nancy Hardesty
Department of Philosophy and Religion
Clemson University
Clemson, South Carolina
"Women and Revivals"

Dr. Keith J. Hardman
Professor Emeritus of Philosophy and Religion
Ursinus College
Collegeville, Pennsylvania
"Anti-revivalism, History and Arguments of"
(coauthor), "Burned-Over District," "Dickinson,
Jonathan," "Finney, Charles Grandison," "Taylor,
Nathaniel William," "Tennent, Gilbert"

Professor Phil Harrold
Winebrenner Theological Seminary
Findlay University
Findlay, Ohio
"Deconversion and Revivals"

Dr. Darryl G. Hart
Director of Honors Programs and Faculty
Development
Intercollegiate Studies Institute
Wilmington, Delaware
Adjunct Professor of Church History
Westminster Theological Seminary
Escondido, California
"Calvinistic, Presbyterian, and Reformed Revivals
since 1730"

Professor Larry D. Hart
School of Theology and Missions
Oral Roberts University
Tulsa, Oklahoma
"Baptism in (of) the Holy Spirit"

Mr. Don Haymes
Librarian
Christian Theological Seminary
Indianapolis, Indiana
"Restorationism and the Stone-Campbell
    Movement" (coauthor)

Dr. Daniel Hedges
National Training Director, Foursquare Gospel
    Church
Adjunct Professor of Practical Theology
Oral Roberts University
Tulsa, Oklahoma
"International Church of the Foursquare
    Gospel," "Prosperity Theology," "Shepherding
    Movement," "Swaggart, Jimmy Lee," "Youth
    with a Mission"

Professor Kevin Hester
Department of Biblical and Ministry Studies
Free Will Baptist Bible College
Nashville, Tennessee
"Free Will Baptists"

Dr. Samuel S. Hill
Professor Emeritus of Religion
University of Florida
Gainesville, Florida
"South, Revivals in the"

Professor Ralph W. Hood Jr.
Department of Psychology
University of Tennessee at Chattanooga
Chattanooga, Tennessee
"Ecstasy, Theories of"

Mr. Todd Hunter
National Director
Alpha USA
New York, New York
"Alpha Course"

Dr. Stan Ingersol
Archives Director
Nazarene Archives
Kansas City, Missouri
"Church of the Nazarene"

Professor Paul L. King
School of Theology and Missions
Oral Roberts University
Tulsa, Oklahoma
"Charismatic Gifts"

Professor James E. Kirby
Perkins School of Theology
Southern Methodist University
Dallas Texas
"Asbury, Francis," "Cartwright, Peter," "Dow, Lorenzo,"
    "Garrettson, Freeborn," "Lee, Jesse," "Primitive
    Methodist Church"

Dr. Martin I. Klauber
Visiting Professor of Church History
Trinity Evangelical Divinity School
Deerfield, Illinois
"Evangelical Free Church in America"

Professor David W. Kling
Department of Religious Studies
University of Miami
Coral Gables, Florida
"Second Great Awakening"

Professor William Kostlevy
Department of History
Tabor College
Hillsboro, Kansas
"Abolitionism and Revivals"

Professor Gary Land
Department of History and Political Science
Andrews University
Berrien Springs, Michigan
"Miller, William"

Professor William B. Lawrence
Dean and Professor of American Church History
Perkins School of Theology
Southern Methodist University
Dallas, Texas
"Preaching and Revivals"

Professor Charles H. Lippy
LeRoy A. Martin Distinguished Professor of
    Religious Studies
Department of Philosophy and Religion
University of Tennessee at Chattanooga
Chattanooga, Tennessee
"Theology of Revivals"

Professor Kathryn Teresa Long
Chair, Department of History
Wheaton College
Wheaton, Illinois
"Revival of 1857–1858"

List of Contributors and Contributions

Professor Sean Lucas
Covenant Theological Seminary
St. Louis, Missouri
"Chapman, John Wilbur," "Primitive (Antimission)
Baptists," "Stearns, Shubal"

Professor Frank Macchia
Associate Professor of Christian Theology and
Director, Graduate Program in Religion
Vanguard University
Costa Mesa, California
"Deliverance and Deliverance Ministry," "Prophecy,
Visions, and Dreams," "Signs and Wonders,"
"Spiritual Warfare"

Professor Michael J. McClymond
Clarence Louis and Helen Irene Steber Professor
Department of Theological Studies
Saint Louis University
St. Louis, Missouri
"Altar Call," "Anti-revivalism, History and
Arguments of" (coauthor), "Internet and
Revivals," "Oneida Community," "Orr, James
Edwin," "Revivals and Revivalism, Definitions
and Theories of," "Smith, Amanda Berry"

Professor Rick H. McPeak
Department of Philosophy and Religion
Greenville College
Greenville, Illinois
"Roberts, Benjamin Titus"

Dr. Kenneth Minkema
Executive Editor
The Works of Jonathan Edwards
Yale Divinity School
New Haven, Connecticut
"Edwards, Jonathan," "Northampton Revival of
1734–1735"

Father Jacques Monet, SJ
Canadian Jesuit Archives
Toronto, Canada
"Roman Catholic Awakenings in French Canada"

Professor Jerry Moon
Chair, Department of Church History
Seventh-day Adventist Theological Seminary
Andrews University
Berrien Springs, Michigan
"Seventh-day Adventists," "White, Ellen Gould
(Harmon)"

Professor Robert Bruce Mullin
Sub-Dean for Academic Affairs
SPRL Professor of History and World Mission
General Theological Seminary
New York, New York
"Bushnell, Horace"

Professor Louis Nelson
School of Architecture
University of Virginia
Charlottesville, Virginia
"Architecture and Revivals"

Professor Thomas J. Nettles
Southern Baptist Theological Seminary
Louisville, Kentucky
"Backus, Isaac," "Baptist Revivals"

Professor Stephen J. Nichols
Lancaster Bible College and Graduate School
Narvon, Pennsylvania
"Davies, Samuel"

Professor J. Steven O'Malley
Asbury Theological Seminary
Wilmore, Kentucky
"Amana Community," "Evangelical Association,"
"Lutheran, German American, and Scandinavian
American Revivals," "Muhlenberg, Henry
Melchior," "Otterbein, Philip William," "Pietism
and Revivals," "United Brethren in Christ"

Dr. Rick Ostrander
Dean of Undergraduate Studies
John Brown University
Siloam Springs, Arkansas
"Prayer and Revivals"

Professor Daniel C. Palm
Department of Political Science
Azusa Pacific University
Azusa, California
"Free Methodist Church"

Professor Raymond F. Paloutzian
Department of Psychology
Westmont College
Santa Barbara, California
"Conversion and Revivals"

Mr. Michael Pasquier
PhD Student
Religious Studies Department
Florida State University
Tallahassee, Florida
"Young Life" (coauthor), "Youth for Christ" (coauthor)

Professor Daniel C. Peterson
Asian and Near Eastern Languages
Foundation for Ancient Research and Mormon
Studies
Brigham Young University
Provo, Utah
"Mormons and Mormonism," "Smith, Joseph"

Dr. Margaret M. Poloma
Professor Emeritus of Sociology
University of Akron
Akron, Ohio
"Pensacola (Brownsville) Revival," "Toronto
Blessing"

Professor Gregg Quiggle
Moody Bible Institute
Chicago, Illinois
"Torrey, Reuben Archer"

Professor Russell E. Richey
Dean, Candler School of Theology
Emory University
Atlanta, Georgia
"Methodist Revivals"

Professor Andrew C. Rieser
Assistant Professor of History
State University of New York–Dutchess
Poughkeepsie, New York
"Chautauqua"

Professor Richard M. Riss
Somerset Christian College
Zarephath, New Jersey
"Bakker, Jim and Tammy Faye," "Branch Davidians,"
"Calvary Chapel," "Confession of Sins in Revivals,"
"Copeland, Kenneth," "Full Gospel Business
Men's Fellowship International," "Hanegraaff,
Hendrik (Hank)," "Hinn, Benny," "Latter Rain
Movement"

Professor Dana L. Robert
Truman Collins Professor of World Mission
Boston University School of Theology
Boston, Massachusetts
"Foreign Missions and Revivals"

Dr. Mark E. Roberts
Director, Holy Spirit Research Center
Oral Roberts University
Tulsa, Oklahoma
"Aglow International (Women's Aglow)," "United
Pentecostal Church, International"

Mr. Richard Owen Roberts
International Awakening Ministries
Wheaton, Illinois
"Nettleton, Asahel"

Professor Roger Robins
Marymount College
Rancho Palos Verdes, California
"Tomlinson, Ambrose Jessup"

Professor Hans Rollmann
Department of Religious Studies
Memorial University of Newfoundland
St. John's, Newfoundland and Labrador, Canada
"Restorationism and the Stone-Campbell Movement"
(coauthor)

Dr. Scott W. Schwartz
Archivist for Music and Fine Arts and
Associate Professor of Library Administration
Sousa Archives and Center for American Music
University of Illinois
Champaign, Illinois
"Appalachian Revivals," "Serpent- and Fire-Handling
Believers"

Professor John Thomas Scott
History Department
Mercer University
Macon, Georgia
"McGready, James"

Mr. David Simpson
Research Assistant
Encyclopedia of Religious Revivals in America
St. Louis, Missouri
"Burchard, Jedidiah," "Jones, Samuel Porter," "Knapp,
Jacob," "Mills, Benjamin Fay"

Dr. Douglas J. Slawson
Vice President for Student Services
National University
La Jolla, California
"Motor Missions," "Parish Missions"

List of Contributors and Contributions

Dr. Lisa Herb Smith
Independent Scholar
Newark, Delaware
"Davenport, James"

Professor Reiner Smolinski
Department of English
Georgia State University
Atlanta, Georgia
"Mather, Cotton"

Professor Stephen J. Stein
Chancellors' Professor Emeritus
Department of Religious Studies
Indiana University
Bloomington, Indiana
"New Religious Movements and Revivals"

Professor Gordon T. Stewart
History Department
Michigan State University
East Lansing, Michigan
"Alline, Henry"

Dr. Daniel W. Stowell
Director and Editor
The Papers of Abraham Lincoln
Springfield, Illinois
"Civil War Revivals"

Professor Merle Strege
Chair, Department of Religious Studies
Anderson University
Anderson, Indiana
"Church of God (Anderson, Indiana)"

Professor Vinson Synan
Dean, School of Divinity
Regent University
Virginia Beach, Virginia
"Pentecostal Revivals"

Mr. Bayard Taylor
Editor, Gospel Light Publications
Ventura, California
"Apostolic Movement (New Apostolic Movement),"
"Church Growth Movement," "McGavran, Donald
A.," "Wagner, C. Peter"

Mr. Stephen C. Taysom
PhD Student and Associate Instructor
Department of Religious Studies
Indiana University
Bloomington, Indiana
"Lee, Ann," "Shakers"

Professor Arthur Dicken Thomas Jr.
Ecumenical Institute of Theology
St. Mary's Seminary and University
Baltimore, Maryland
Wesley Theological Seminary
Washington, DC
"Dwight, Timothy," "Jarratt, Devereux"

Professor Joel Tibbetts
Religious Studies and English Departments
Rockford College
Rockford, Illinois
"Wilkinson, Jemima"

Mr. John Turner
PhD Student
History Department
Notre Dame University
South Bend, Indiana
"Campus Crusade for Christ," "InterVarsity Christian
Fellowship," "Navigators"

Mr. Benjamin Wagner
Department of Theological Studies
Saint Louis University
St. Louis, Missouri
"Bodily Manifestations in Revivals," "Dancing in
Revivals," "Fasting and Revivals," "Haywood,
Garfield Thomas," "Laughing and Shouting in
Revivals"

Professor Timothy P. Weber
President, Memphis Theological Seminary
Memphis, Tennessee
"Eschatology and Revivals"

Professor D. Newell Williams
President and Professor of Modern and American
Church History
Brite Divinity School
Texas Christian University
Fort Worth, Texas
"Campbell, Alexander," "Stone, Barton Warren"

Mr. Joseph Williams
PhD Student
Religious Studies Department
Florida State University
Tallahassee, Florida
"Chauncy, Charles"

Professor Douglas Winiarski
  Department of Religion
  University of Richmond
  Richmond, Virginia
  "Colonial Awakenings prior
    to 1730"

Mr. John Halsey Wood Jr.
  PhD Student
  Department of Theological Studies
  Saint Louis University
  St. Louis, Missouri
  "Holy Fairs," "Stoddard, Solomon"

Index

Note: Volume numbers are in **bold** type. Page numbers for articles are in *italic* type.

About the Editor

Michael McClymond currently holds the Clarence Louis and Helen Irene Steber Chair in Theological Studies at Saint Louis University. He was educated at Northwestern University (B.A. in chemistry), Yale University (M.Div.), and the University of Chicago (M.A. in religion, Ph.D. in theology). Previously he held teaching or research appointments at Wheaton College (IL), Westmont College, University of California–San Diego, and Emory University. Following college, he worked briefly for Hercules, Inc. Research in Wilmington Delaware as a research chemist.

McClymond's first book, *Encounters with God: An Approach to the Theology of Jonathan Edwards* (Oxford University Press, 1998), received the 1999 Brewer Prize from the American Society of Church History as the best first book in the history of Christianity. He was coeditor of (with David Noel Freedman of University of California–San Diego) and contributor to *The Rivers of Paradise: Moses, Buddha, Confucius, Jesus, and Muhammad as Religious Founders* (Eerdmans, 2001), editor of *Embodying the Spirit: New Perspectives on North American Revivalism* (Johns Hopkins University Press, 2004), and author of *Familiar Stranger: An Introduction to Jesus of Nazareth* (Eerdmans, 2004; winner of the Award of Merit in 2005 from *Christianity Today* magazine). With Lamin Sanneh of Yale University, he is currently coediting the *Blackwell Companion to World Christianity* (Basil Blackwell, 2008). In 2003 he was featured in an hour-long National Public Radio program in Chicago on Pentecostalism, and he contributed a 25,000-word essay on Christianity for the *Worldmark Encyclopedia of Religious Practices* (Thomson/Gale, 2005).

Dr. McClymond is a frequent speaker in Protestant and Roman Catholic parishes and conferences. In 2005 and 2006 he was the Program Coordinator for Global Day of Prayer–St. Louis, which attracted an interracial and interdenominational gathering of some 3,000 Christians to Busch Stadium. He is founder and president of the Institute for World Christianity (www.worldchristianity.org), a nonprofit organization (501c3) that brings together emerging Christian leaders from around the world to explore new forms of collaboration. He is also a guitarist, singer, and songwriter for The Pneumatics—a blues-and-rock trio that opened for rock and roll legend Chuck Berry. He is the single father of a daughter, Sarah, who is now a high school senior, and, like her dad, plays the electric guitar.